THE NEVADA CORPORATION HANDBOOK

Eighth Edition

By Derek G. Rowley

STRATEGIC PRESS

Published by STRATEGIC PRESS, INC.

1460 Pittman Avenue • Sparks, Nevada 89431, U.S.A. • 775-331-7047 • www.strategicpress.com

Published by Strategic Press, Inc.
The Nevada Corporation Handbook
Eighth Edition
Copyright 1992-2000 by Strategic Press, Inc.

ISBN 1-886683-03-4

Printed in the United States of America

Please contact Strategic Press, Inc. with any comments or suggestions regarding this book, or any of our other products.

Strategic Press, Inc.
1460 Pittman Avenue
Sparks, Nevada 89431, U.S.A.
Telephone: 775-331-7047
Fax: 775-358-9675
Internet: www.strategicpress.com
Email: info@strategicpress.com

This publication is designed to provide accurate and authoritative information in regard to the subject matter covered. It is sold with the understanding that the publisher is not engaged in rendering legal, accounting or other professional service. If legal advice or other expert assistance is required, the services of a competent professional person should be sought.
— *From a Declaration of Principles jointly adopted by a Committee of the American Bar Association and a Committee of Publishers and Associations.*

TABLE OF CONTENTS

INTRODUCTION

When one thinks of a corporation, the mental image that frequently comes to mind is of the Fortune 500. These huge, multinational companies are often associated with either Wall Street or Madison Avenue or both. They have an enormous impact on our national and local economies, and as a result are frequently blamed by politicians for many of society's ills. However, the corporation is also the vehicle through which most significant and positive advances and discoveries are made that benefit each of us. The presence of a corporation allows people to do a lot of good that might otherwise go undone.

The media loves to paint a picture that would have us believe that for-profit corporations and people associated with them are inherently evil monoliths that are motivated solely by avarice and greed. Politicians and special interest groups sometimes imply that corporations serve only to abuse employees and raid the world of its natural resources.

The fact is, the typical corporation is a small company, often owned by family and friends turned business partners. Business studies have shown that the owners of these closely held companies often labor tirelessly at great personal sacrifice in hopes of establishing a viable, and hopefully profitable business enterprise. The overwhelming majority of corporations are privately held. In fact, of the millions of corporations functioning in the United States, an incredibly small percentage is involved in any type of public trading of shares.

The process of incorporating is deceptively simple, yet can be incredibly complex. Many small corporations are formed without the aid of an attorney, accountant or other professional. Most of the time, lack of professional assistance is of little consequence. However, there are thousands of horror stories that relay the stark reality that lack of proper legal guidance can be catastrophic.

This book is not intended to replace the guidance of competent professionals, but instead attempts to help fill the void between hopeful entrepreneurs and outside planning professionals. The contents of this book are based upon the real world experiences of the author, who is not an attorney, but has worked with thousands of closely held corporations as a consultant and advisor through his own incorporation company, Corporate Service Center, Inc. located in Reno, Nevada.

This book is specifically not intended to serve as promotional literature for any incorporating company. Instead, it is hoped that the reader will find the information contained in this book to be helpful in preparing for meetings with planning professionals. When their meter is running, it is important to be as prepared as possible in order to get the most mileage out of the time spent with your planning advisor.

Because a corporation is governed by statutes that vary from state to state it is important to verify the viability with your planning professional of any corporate strategy contained in this book or elsewhere before they are put into place. While much of the content of this book has application in any state, the reader will quickly discover that the author has definite opinions regarding certain jurisdictions in the United States that provide specific advantages in their corporate statutes. Those opinions come from hard-earned experience, working with thousands of closely held corporations from many different states. These corporate tax havens will be discussed in detail.

Before going into business, a number of important decisions must be made about what form of business to use. And increasingly, it has become important to make planning considerations that take into account the differences in state tax and liability laws. It is hoped that the information in this book helps you make the best decisions, save money, accomplish your goals and bury the competition.

Chapter

1

INCORPORATION

Creation of a Legal Person

> *"A corporation is an artificial being, invisible, intangible and existing only in contemplation of law . . . it possesses only those properties which the charter of its creation confers upon it . . . . among the most important are immortality, and . . . individuality; properties, by which a perpetual succession of many persons are considered as the same, and may act as a single individual. They enable a corporation to manage its own affairs, and to hold property without the perplexing intricacies, the hazardous and endless necessity, of perpetual conveyances for the purpose of transmitting it from hand to hand. . . By these means, a perpetual succession of individuals are capable of acting for the promotion of the particular object, like one immortal being."* John Marshall, Trustees of Dartmouth College v. Woodward.

BACKGROUND

IN THE UNITED STATES, THE POWER TO CREATE THE CORPORATION RESIDES IN THE **LEGISLATIVE BRANCH,** AND CANNOT BE DELEGATED.

A corporation is a form of business created according to the laws of a specific state or country. Individuals cannot create a corporation simply by agreement as they can a partnership. They can only do so with the authority of the government. The corporation is composed of other human or artificial entities, but is recognized separately from the entities that comprise it. Under the law, it is frequently treated as if it were a human.

An example of a corporation's individual treatment is shown when a corporation enjoys the Constitutional protection against unreasonable search and seizures. It may also invoke the attorney-client privilege of confidentiality or may sue for defamation of its good name. But it can also be punished if it violates the law.

> *"Only a sovereign authority can create a corporation."* - In re Lloyds of Texas, 43 F. [2d] 383.

Congress generally does not have the power to create a corporation, except in three instances. First as the legislature of the District of Columbia, it may create corporations within the district. Second, Congress may create corporations within US territories, although it usually confers the power upon the legislatures of the territories. Third, it "may create corporations as appropriate means of executing the powers of government; as, for instance, a bank for the purpose of carrying on the fiscal operations of the United States, or a railroad corporation for the purpose of promoting commerce among the States." (Luxton v. North River Bridge Co., 153 US 525, 38 L. Ed. 808.)

State legislatures have unlimited powers to create corporations. There have been many attempts to standardize the corporate laws of the various states. At different times committees of attorneys have drafted sample provisions of corporate laws and introduced them to the world as models for all to follow. The Uniform Business Corporation Act and the Model Business Corporation Act are two examples.

Nevertheless the world of corporate law finds great variety as states adopt only the portion of the uniform law in which they are interested, or engage in a series of partial revisions of corporation law over time without undergoing a total statutory transplant. Naturally, this creates differences between the various states' laws. Where some see differences, others see opportunities.

The owners of a corporation are the owners of the shares of that corporation. Ownership of shares may be readily transferred from one investor to another without the need to reorganize the corporation under the law, while a change of ownership often makes reorganization necessary with the sole proprietorship and partnership.

LIABILITY PROTECTION: THE CORPORATE VEIL

The corporation is traditionally the first line of defense in any asset protection strategy because of the long record of statutory and case law that supports the goal of achieving limited liability. This liability protection is only available because of the way the law separates the corporation from any associated individual.

AN ASSOCIATION, INSURANCE COMPANY, TRUST OR PARTNERSHIP MAY BE TREATED AS A CORPORATION FOR TAX PURPOSES IF IT OPERATES OR FUNCTIONS TOO MUCH AS A CORPORATION. [IRC SEC. 7701 (A)(3); REG. SEC. 301.7701-2]

Because of the presence of the *corporate veil*, the corporation is often recommended as the entity of choice whenever a business has employees. This is because employees bring certain risks that demand liability protection for the ownership of the company. Also, because corporations find general acceptance in the business world, it is a convenient entity to use.

But to maintain the corporate veil, certain formalities must be followed. Because these

THE "CORPORATE VEIL," REFERS TO THE SEPARATION BETWEEN THE INDIVIDUAL AND THE COMPANY. IT IS THE MOST VALUABLE QUALITY THAT THE CORPORATION OFFERS. CARE MUST BE TAKEN TO PRESERVE THE CORPORATE VEIL, BECAUSE IF IT IS "PIERCED," THE CORPORATION MAY HAVE NO ASSET PROTECTION VALUE WHATSOEVER.

> *"INCORPORATION, n. The act of uniting several persons into one fiction called a corporation, in order that they may be no longer responsible for their actions. A, B, and C are a corporation. A robs, B steals and C (it is necessary that there be on gentleman in the concern) cheats. It is a plundering, thieving, swindling corporation. But A, B and C, who have jointly determined and severally executed every crime of the corporation, are blameless. It is wrong to mention them by name when censuring their acts as a corporation, but right when praising. Incorporation is somewhat like the ring of Gyges: it bestows the blessing of invisibility -- comfortable to knaves. The scoundrel who invented incorporation is dead -- he has disincorporated." - Ambrose Bierce, The Enlarged Devil's Dictionary.*

formalities are not always attended to properly, the corporation can be imperfect, depending widely upon state law, in its ability to protect you from lawsuits. Nevertheless, it is usually much more effective in protecting the owners and managers from liability than using a general partnership or proprietorship.

LEGAL PERSON

The corporation is often described as having a juristic or legal personality. This means that it is viewed in the eyes of the law as a separate person from its owners, directors or officers. This is the element that provides the liability protections that people often look for when incorporating. The courts generally uphold the legal separateness of the corporation, although this will be discussed in greater detail later.

The corporation, as its own legal person, survives all changes in ownership. It can live on indefinitely. Because it is recognized as a completely separate "legal person," distinctively different from any other individual, the corporation's assets are kept separate from the assets of any of the stockholders, officers or directors. That means that the corporation is not responsible for the debts of the individual, and visa versa.

> *"A corporation . . . seems to us to be a person, though an artificial one, inhabiting and belonging to that state [of incorporation], and therefore entitled, for the purpose of suing and being sued, to be deemed a citizen of that state." James M. Wayne, Louisville, Cincinnati & Charleston R.R. v. Letson.*

The importance of keeping personal and corporate debts separate cannot be overstated, and is demonstrated in the following case: In 1984, a man who owns a small family farm in Northern California hired a laborer to use a utility truck (otherwise known as a "cherry-picker") to treat selected trees on his property infected with some exotic tree fungus. Unknown to the property owner, the laborer apparently began experimenting with the vehicle during his lunch break, and managed to electrocute himself on power lines that ran across the back of his property.

Clearly this was a tragedy in which the victim was partially responsible, and could have been avoided with a little common sense. Still, the victim's family filed a large lawsuit against the property owner, holding him liable for the accident that took place on his property. The property owner's attorney negotiated a settlement, because they did not want to risk losing the case before a jury. Insurance covered part of the settlement, but not all. When it was over, there were thousands of dollars in legal bills and judgments.

The real tragedy here is that the property owner's nephew had been pleading with him for years to incorporate the business, just in case something like this ever happened. Now, all of the family assets -- the home, the furniture, the cars, and the life savings -- can and may be attached to settle the claim.

PROCRASTINATION CAN BE EXPENSIVE. SIMPLY KNOWING THE VALUE OF INCORPORATING IS NOT ENOUGH.

Had this man followed the nephew's advice, he would have incorporated the family farm and his personal assets could have been saved. But now, a significant part of his life's works, including his personal possessions, savings, and investments are in serious but completely unnecessary jeopardy.

The corporation's primary role is as part of a strategy to reduce personal liability. Since the corporation is granted by law the powers and rights necessary to conduct its business, the corporation can choose to engage itself in activities that, while not illegal, may subject the corporation to potential risk.

It makes sense, then, for any individual involved in any business or personal activity that has any potential for liability to incorporate those activities into a separate "legal person." That way the risk is absorbed, and limited, by assets of the corporation.

Shareholders exchange assets (property, cash, or even services in some states) for stock in the corporation. The amount the shareholder invests in a corporation is the maximum amount that he can lose if things go sour.

Creditors to the corporation have no claim on shareholders personal assets, and in a few states have difficulty even finding out whom the shareholders are. This degree of liability protection and privacy is perhaps the single most important reason for choosing a corporation as the type of entity for starting a new business

Depending upon the jurisdiction, the shareholders, officers, or directors of a corporation are not individually liable for the obligations of the corporation. The protection of the "corporate veil" assumes normal corporate procedures have been followed in managing the corporation's affairs, and shareholders have not perpetrated fraud for their own benefit.

Limits of Corporate Liability Protection

SECTION 6672 OF THE INTERNAL REVENUE CODE CLEARLY STATES THAT THE LIABILITY ASSOCIATED WITH PAYROLL TAXES MAY BE ASSESSED AGAINST CORPORATE OFFICERS OR EMPLOYEES FOUND TO BE RESPONSIBLE FOR THEIR COLLECTION AND PAYMENT. IN THIS INSTANCE, THE PERSONAL LIABILITY OF THE RESPONSIBLE OFFICER OR EMPLOYEE IS NOT LIMITED TO THE AMOUNT OF THE CAPITAL INVESTMENT OF THAT PERSON. THERE CAN BE STATE LIABILITIES AS WELL AS FEDERAL CIVIL AND CRIMINAL PENALTIES IN THIS AREA.

If the corporation is used to evade the law, wrongfully escape payment of a just obligation, or perpetrate fraud, the limited liability is lost. If the court decides that it would be unfair to allow the corporation to shield the individuals behind it from liability, the courts may ignore the corporation completely and look directly to the officers, directors or shareholders as the responsible party. This piercing of the corporate veil is not as common as it once was, and will be discussed in greater detail later.

> *"It is. . . clearly established that mistakes or errors in the exercise of honest business judgment do not subject the officers and directors to liability for negligence in the discharge of their appointed duties."* - Harry E. Kalodner, Otis & Co. v. Pennsylvania.

Even when there are no legal problems as those described above, the corporation is not always a complete shield. Most states have established case law that allows the court to pierce the corporate shield under certain circumstances. A doctor, for example, is not able to avoid malpractice liability through incorporation. Further, if personal services are involved, the person who performed the service may be personally liable, even if the service is performed under the corporate name.

The most significant potential liability for corporate officers and directors pertains to the responsibility of collecting, accounting for, and paying payroll taxes withheld from the wages and salaries of corporate employees.

As Peter W. Huber explains in the following quote from his excellent book on the transformation of modern tort law, entitled Liability: The Legal Revolution and Its Consequences, the threat of a lawsuit is driving US business to its knees:

"Who would be building and fixing, developing and doing, treating, immunizing, and curing, while the lawyers were busy assessing the fines and keeping the jail? The answer, with growing frequency, (is) no one at all . . . When it comes to liability problems, the bold innovators are the most fleet-footed of potential defendants. More often than not, they adjusted to the threat of liability by doing less. Not innovating is a remarkably easy thing to do."

Strategies to reduce personal liability are perfectly legal. More important, there may also be a strict moral obligation of the "doers" of the world. Without these types of strategies, technological innovation is kept in a stranglehold by the current legal and insurance systems that dominate our society and keep us in disarray over liability lawsuits.

By using a corporation as part of an overall plan to reduce personal liability, it may still be possible for the innovators of the world to perform their necessary magic on our economy. Never before has the need for liability protection been greater in the world of business. While the corporation is not the "cure-all" to the current liability crisis, it is a piece of the puzzle that can provide tremendous relief from the liability burden.

One businessperson learned the value of this and restructured his multimillion-dollar real estate management company into more than twenty separate corporations, each with a separate role. Each real estate project now has several corporations involved in ownership, management, marketing, etc. One corporation owns all of the equipment and office furniture, which it leases to the other companies. Another corporation leases employees to the businesses. Still another corporation functions as an advertising agency that makes all of the media buys and conducts all the necessary marketing.

A taxicab company in one US city maintains a separate corporation for every three taxis. Then, in case of an accident, the potential for loss is limited to the value of three heavily worn automobiles. A major ski resort has incorporated each individual ski run separately for the same purpose.

Another individual uses two corporations for a similar purpose. One corporation runs a lumber store, and the other is used to manufacture and sell trusses for commercial and residential construction. Since the truss manufacturing business has extremely high potential for liability, the lumber store is set up completely separately. Then, if a structural failure in one of the trusses creates liability, only the assets of the manufacturing company are involved and the lumber store is protected separately.

SOME BUSINESSES, WHETHER THEY ARE CURRENTLY INCORPORATED OR NOT, MIGHT BE BETTER SERVED BY USING MULTIPLE CORPORATIONS TO SEPARATE THE DIFFERENT BUSINESS ACTIVITIES, ASSETS, TAXES, AND LIABILITIES. THEN, IF SOMETHING GOES WRONG, THE LIABILITY OF THE COMPANY WOULD BE CONFINED TO THE ASSETS OF ONLY THE ELEMENT OF BUSINESS THAT CREATED THE LIABILITY.

WHEN TO INCORPORATE

There are many good reasons for placing business activity under the umbrella of a corporation. While the tax laws change occasionally, the value of the corporation remains constant. The bottom line is this: People who incorporate are interested in liability protection, financial privacy, lower taxes, and flexibility in the management and control of the business.

So the first question many people ask about incorporating is, "When should I incorporate?" While many accountants and attorneys tend to give their clients the same, standard advice when asked this question, there are usually factors that reach beyond any "pat" answer. The fact is, the laws that govern our society are far too complex for any pat answer to this question to be correct in all circumstances.

The right time for you to incorporate depends on what you or your business has done in the past, what you are doing now, and what you are trying to accomplish in the future. Often, the "right" time for someone to incorporate was months or years before they ever get around to asking the question.

Recently, a nationally renowned radio talk show host who deals with a variety of personal and business related issues was asked about the best time to incorporate a business. The reply he gave was surprisingly shortsighted, but very demonstrative of the misinformation distributed by business professionals across the country on this important question. The talk show host gave an answer based on the amount of revenue that the business was generating.

I do not remember the exact figure he gave now, but it is typical for many business advisors to recommend that incorporation is not worthwhile until the business is generating a specified number of dollars in annual revenues. There can be no question that there are costs associated with incorporating, and from that perspective perhaps it makes sense to determine what the "break-even" point is for the corporation to make up those costs. Nevertheless, this perspective is too narrow an outlook of the value of the corporation.

Those who are concerned with financial privacy should probably incorporate before the fact if it is at all possible. The only way to preserve your privacy is to stay out of the paper trail in the first place. Let your corporation do that. That way, the history of facts related to the transaction never leads directly to you, but only to the corporation.

What value do you place on the protection that a properly maintained corporation offers? The fact that a certain asset or activity exists under the corporate umbrella may save the owners millions of dollars in liability and judgments over time.

Even from the cost/benefit perspective, there are other reasons to consider incorporation besides simply revenue figures. Remember that it is income used to determine your tax liability. Losses are used as deductions against your income, and the less income you have, the lower your tax liability. That is one reason it is common to hear of the huge, multinational companies reporting gargantuan losses from time to time that seem so incredible. They are simply lowering their tax bill.

Almost all new companies are expected to go through a period of financial struggles or loss. This period may last weeks, months, or years. Why shouldn't your corporation be allowed to take advantage of the tax losses that are being accumulated during this initial period? Quite simply, it should, and the tax laws provide for that through what is called a "loss carry-forward."

A new corporation can immediately begin spending money in many areas that you would otherwise be spending personal funds. The corporation's startup expenses may include automobile leases, maintenance, insurance, taxes, airline travel, meals, entertainment (still partially deductible), retirement plans, equipment purchase, and miscellaneous expenses. Many of these deductions have a greater value to the corporation than to the individual because of the limits on individual deductions.

As you can see, many expenses of the entrepreneurial individual can be spent by the corporation. As you build up your loss, you create a situation where you can reduce or eliminate future taxes by using a tax loss carry-forward or income averaging against future profits.

When you seek guidance on the right time for you to incorporate, make sure your advisors have their eyes open to all of the factors involved. Do not let them set an arbitrary income "incorporation line." If they insist, maybe you need to talk to someone with a broader sense of the business world.

WHERE TO INCORPORATE

Each state allows for the creation of the corporation entity through a set of laws that govern and control their formation and use. Those laws are commonly called the Corporation Code of that state.

As stated earlier, not all state's corporation laws are alike. Because each state has adopted its own version of the Corporation Code, there are tremendous differences between how corporations are handled, what powers they are given, and how they can conduct their internal operations. A corporation is a citizen of the state that formed it, and is subject to the Corporation Code as adopted in that state.

One of the most significant differences between the various states can effect your pocketbook directly. That is, taxes. Only a couple of states impose no taxes at all on corporate income. State corporate income tax rates can be as high as 12 percent. Obviously, with the proper planning, there can be tremendous tax savings where the income is earned in a tax-free state.

Therefore, it is important that you become familiar with the Corporation Code of the state in which you are planning to incorporate. You might also be advised regarding the differences between corporations formed in other key states known to be corporate havens, such as Nevada, Delaware, or Wyoming.

When differences exist between the laws of different states, it will create either an advantage or a disadvantage for you and your incorporated business. Once a corporation has been formed, the Code of that state directs the basic rights and duties of its shareholders, directors, and officers.

Other provisions may make the corporate management more restrictive and difficult. For instance, some states require three different individuals to act as the corporate officers, while others require only one. Some states regulate and limit the type of stock that can be issued by the corporation, while other states allow the corporation to make that decision. Some states require extensive public disclosure of corporate ownership, a few states allow degrees of confidentiality regarding ownership issues. The ways in which these differences effect your corporation are virtually limitless.

IINCORPORATING IN YOUR HOME STATE

Using a corporation formed in a tax haven like Nevada or Delaware requires an understanding of many interstate issues. Many of those issues are discussed later in this book. For now, suffice it to say that some businesses will gain no advantage to using an out-of-state corporation as their primary business entity.

A small business that depends wholly upon a local, intrastate market and has no intention toward establishing interstate operations is a prime candidate for local incorporation. It makes no sense for that business to maintain a corporation in another state and jump through the required hoops just to qualify to transact business in its home state. In effect, it would often cost more than maintaining two different domestic corporations.

Most local retailers, for example, have a public presence in a local mall or other commercial property, advertise extensively throughout the local area, and have one or more employees. The customers come to the store to make the purchase or engage the service. Under these circumstances it makes sense to deal with only one set of state laws, preferably the laws your accountant and attorney are most comfortable with on a daily basis. To use a corporation formed in another state will only bring unnecessary complications and costs.

When the time comes that the state corporate tax burden of the business is an issue, it may be appropriate to use a foreign corporation in a system that will reduce or eliminate them, providing you with a legal and competitive advantage over your competition. The discussion of the "dual corporation strategy, which is often used to accomplish those purposes, will be discussed in a later chapter and will provide additional insight on this fascinating topic.

PRE-INCORPORATION CONSIDERATIONS

During the pre-incorporation process, there are several things that should be thought out and addressed by the individuals participating in the incorporation process. How you resolve these issues might be addressed in either the bylaws or articles of incorporation, or as a separate written policy adopted by the board of directors. These items include:

- **Financing**. Who provides the funds and the other assets to the corporation? What considerations do those people receive in return?

- **Share Structure**. What will be the authorized number of shares that will be written into the articles of incorporation?

- **Securities Regulation.** Will the corporation have to comply with state and federal securities regulations?

- **Tax Election.** Will the corporation function as a C corporation or an S corporation? Will you take advantage of Internal Revenue Code (IRC) 1244 stock treatment or IRC 351 treatment for non-cash assets? Are there any potential tax problems, such as debt/equity ratios, personal holding company status, personal service corporation status, or imputed interest problems?

- **Management and Control**. What rules do you need to govern the stockholders meetings and voting rights? What latitude will the board of directors be given in decisions over daily operations?

- **Agreements**. Do you need stock restrictions, buy/sell agreements, employment or independent contractor agreements, or stock subscription agreements?

- **Benefits and Pension Plans.** What do the shareholder/employees expect in terms of benefits? What is the best way to provide it?

- **Estate Planning and Liquidity**. If shareholders are investing significant portions of their estate, how are they assured of liquidity at death? How will their ownership interests transfer to their heirs?

The reason that these issues are pre-incorporation considerations is that many approaches to these areas of concern can only be effective if they are put in place prior to the corporation papers being filed. For example, the articles of incorporation may contain any one of a number of provisions that will resolve these issues to the satisfaction of the parties involved, but that presumes that thought was given far enough in advance for the provisions to be drafted.

STOCK SUBSCRIPTION

Occasionally, there exists a need to raise capital for the operation of prospective corporate business before the actual incorporation. Although this is not generally necessary, there are situations in which the incorporators do not want to go to the trouble and expense of incorporating unless they know they can raise enough money to ensure the success of the business.

One method to accomplish this is with a stock subscription, which can be used either before incorporation, or after. A pre-incorporation stock subscription allows the incorporators to receive commitments from investors to purchase stock in the as-yet-unformed corporation. It is much like a letter of intent.

The subscriber cannot revoke any commitment made through a stock subscription for at least six months, unless the agreement specifically states otherwise, or unless there is unanimous shareholder consent to the revocation.

The subscription offer should be formalized in writing. It should firmly establish each specific offer in detail, including the number of shares offered and the price to be paid.

IF A STOCK SUBSCRIPTION CAN HELP YOU IN ACCOMPLISHING YOUR GOALS, BE SURE TO OBTAIN LEGAL COUNSEL, AS SECURITIES LAWS MAY APPLY. FRANKLY, MOST SMALLER CORPORATIONS DECIDE THAT THIS PROCESS IS UNNECESSARY DUE TO THE RELATIVELY HIGH COSTS ASSOCIATED WITH THE LEGAL COUNSEL THAT IS USUALLY REQUIRED.

PRE-INCORPORATION AGREEMENTS

A pre-incorporation agreement can be used by the organizers to map out a practical game plan for the company as well as to establish the relationships, responsibilities and expectations of the various parties. They may agree as to who will serve as the incorporator; who will serve on the Board of Directors; who will draft the organizational documents, etc.

It is generally better to wait until the corporation is formed before you enter into third party agreements, rather than enter into those agreements yourself. Why obligate yourself when your corporation can do it instead?

The agreement may also include provisions effecting third parties on behalf of the corporation. For instance, the agreement may deal with leasing arrangements for office space or primary business equipment.

Be careful about obligations to third parties. If a third party contracts with an unformed entity, there can be some sticky issues arise in the event the corporation is not formed, or if the corporation does not subsequently fulfill the contract. With whom did the third party contract? Certainly not with the unformed corporation. A case can be made that the party contracted with the organizers, who are individuals. The organizers may be found personally liable for fulfillment of the contract.

HOW TO INCORPORATE

Incorporation is a relatively simple process. Boiled down, it amounts to filing a piece of paper with the State that states a few facts about the company. The piece of paper is called the **Articles of Incorporation**.

The Articles of Incorporation must state the business purpose of the corporation. The Model Business Corporation Act allows for a corporation to engage in any legal business activity except for banking or insurance. Some attorneys draft Articles that are extremely specific and restrictive. Others prefer to use broader language that provides for any lawful business activity.

If the Articles restrict the business activity to "real estate investment and management," the corporation would need to amend its Articles of Incorporation if the directors decided to open an Italian restaurant or speculate in the stock market. Sometimes, when a corporation is applying for a loan, the lender may require that the corporation have restrictive language to prevent the company from using the loan proceeds for any other purpose than it has represented.

CORPORATE NAME

Another important issue is the corporate name. The name of the corporation should include the words "corporation," "company," "incorporated," "limited" or an abbreviation of one of them. These words or abbreviations provide notice that individuals dealing with the company are not dealing with an individual. They are dealing with an entity for which no individual may be held personally liable for company debts.

The name should accurately represent the nature of the business, and cannot resemble too closely the name of another corporation that does business in the same state, although each state has their own definition of what constitutes a resemblance to another company. The best way to get pre-incorporation approval for a company name is to pay a small fee to reserve the use of the corporate name for a period of time.

It can be wise to reserve a corporate name if there are no plans to use it immediately. This is particularly true in jurisdictions that have a lot of corporate activity. Good corporate names can be hard to find.

When the corporate name is reserved, only the individual who signed the official request can use it. Don't lose the reservation, or you will not be able to file the corporation under the reserved name until after the protection has expired.

Once the corporation has been filed, you may want to take additional steps to **protect the corporate name** against others. If the name is used to identify products or services, it should be registered as a trademark with the local Secretary of State, as well as the United States Patent and Trademark Office.

Federal registration and protection of a corporate name costs around $200 and can be obtained under either of two circumstances:

1. The company has used the name in interstate commerce in marketing goods or services; or

2. The corporation intends to use the name in interstate commerce.

If the trademark application is based on the second ground, the corporation must file an affidavit within six months that states that the name has been used. However, it costs an additional $100 to file the affidavit.

PROCESSING ARTICLES OF INCORPORATION

The Articles of Incorporation typically require the notarized signature of the incorporator or initial director. The original, along with two copies of "duplicate originals" is submitted to the State along with the appropriate filing fee. The State keeps one copy of the Articles of Incorporation, and returns the other two copies to the incorporator. Usually, one copy is kept in the corporate record book, and the Agent for Service of Process retains the other.

Within a couple of weeks, the incorporator will receive the processed Articles, with the official stamp of the State, and a file number that is used to reference the company by the

State. The corporation also receives a fancy Certificate of Incorporation, which is just for show. It is the file number that creates the corporation. When the file number is issued, the corporation exists.

Formalities necessary to properly establish a Nevada corporation are listed below as "Organizational Formalities." They are not meant to be an exhaustive list of all organizational corporate formalities and operations, but merely an overview of basic formalities and minimum requirements that are important for your corporation to follow in order to maintain the corporate veil.

ORGANIZATIONAL FORMALITIES OUTLINE FOR A NEVADA CORPORATION

- Draft proper Articles of Incorporation. Be sure to include a clause taking advantage of Nevada law that limits the liability of Officers and Directors.

- Notarize the signature of the Incorporator on the Articles.

- Appoint a Resident Agent.

- File Articles with Secretary of State.

- File Certificate of Acceptance of Resident Agent with Secretary of State.

- File certified copies of Articles and Acceptance of Resident Agent with County Clerk (in some counties).

- Draft Bylaws.

- Hold organizational meetings.

- Appoint additional directors, if desired.

- Adopt bylaws.

- Issue stock.

- Issue stock certificates.

- Record stock issuance in record book.

- Elect Officers.

- Officers sign acceptance of their appointment.

- Record minutes of organizational meetings.

- Secretary certifies minutes of meeting and bylaws.

- Draft proper resolutions (or minutes) for all acts of directors.

- File a copy of certified bylaws with Resident Agent.

- Send statement disclosing name and address of custodian of stock ledger to Resident Agent.

- File "Initial List of Officers, Directors and Agent" with Secretary of State by the first day of the second month following the date of incorporation.

- Secure a Federal Tax ID number from the IRS, Form SS-4.

- If Subchapter S election is desired, file US Treasury Department Form 2553 with the IRS.

- Open a corporate bank account.

- Obtain state and local business licenses as necessary.

- If you have been previously operating as a business, notify all clients and suppliers that the business is now a corporation.

SUMMARY

The corporation generally provides greater flexibility than other types of business entities in key areas by providing for better financial privacy, favorable tax treatment, including significantly increased business deductions and retirement options, and much greater adaptability when it comes to ownership and management. The corporation remains the most important form of business units in use today. Although other forms may outnumber it, the corporation transacts most significant business. That is a strong reason for considering the corporation as your business entity of choice. The power and influence of the nation's entire business community, including high-powered lobbyists at every level of government, are on your side of important issues.

ADVANTAGES OF INCORPORATING

- Shareholders have liability limited to their investment in the corporation.

- Lower Federal Income Tax rates in many instances.

- Centralized management, ease of doing business.

- More tax deductions available to the corporation than to other forms of business entities.

- Full fringe benefits available.

- Stability and permanence of business.

- Easy transfer of assets and ownership.

- Established case law.

- Flexibility in raising capital.

- Distinctly separate legal existence.

DISADVANTAGES OF INCORPORATING

- Can be complicated to form properly.

- Can be expensive to form and maintain.

- Possibility for double-taxation.

- Requires maintenance of certain corporate records and formalities.

- Activities limited by the corporate charter and various laws.

- May be subject to extensive governmental regulations and required local, state, and federal reports.

Chapter

2

UNINCORPORATED OPTIONS

When going into business you have many options.
Unfortunately, some of them are lousy.

T his chapter discusses the primary entities commonly used to conduct business throughout the United States. Although this book is about corporations, nothing else in this book will make any sense at all without a basis of understanding of the alternatives that are available.

Each method of doing business described in this chapter has its own strengths and

> *"Of course there's a different law for the rich and the poor; otherwise, who would go into business?"* - E. Ralph Stewart

weaknesses. It is important to recognize that no single type of business entity, *including the corporation*, is the "best" solution to every business problem. There is no such thing. In fact, it is sound advice to avoid spending money with any promoter who insists that "their" business product or program is the "only" way to achieving business stability, security or success.

Nevertheless, when used properly and the circumstances are right, a corporation is an excellent tool for reducing your taxes, protecting your personal assets and maintaining your financial privacy. This is particularly true when the corporation is formed in a state with favorable corporation laws and tax structures, such as Nevada or Wyoming.

THE WORLD IS FULL OF SHILLS AND SEMINAR "EXPERTS" WHO ARE HAPPY TO SELL YOU THEIR FOOLPROOF "PLANS". BUYER BEWARE.

The key here is in identifying those proper circumstances where the corporation is the right tool for the job. Ultimately, you can learn all you can about these issues, but most people still are best advised to seek the opinion of someone who knows more than they do about these things. Yes, believe it or not, there might yet be a place in this world for a few good attorneys.

There are many good reasons to take a long, hard look at the legal structure of your business. The complicated, challenging nature of conducting a successful business enterprise in today's environment makes your choice of business structure very important. For instance, federal and state tax laws change like the ebb and flow of the tides, sometimes favoring one type of entity over another. Some entities provide greater flexibility in raising working capital, as well.

Liability exposure is always a concern in the business world. Different forms of business handle this risk differently. The most common forms of business frequently provide no liability protection for the individual. Other entities contain this exposure in different ways. Unless you know the relative advantages and disadvantages of each type of entity in these situations, you might be rolling the dice when you make your decision.

So, in the business world, your first decision, whether by intent or default, must be what type of entity to use. It will determine your tax status and tax rate, the type of benefits available to you, retirement options, personal liability for business activity, and the amount of time it will take to administer the "paper shuffle" of the business.

> *"The most enlightened judicial policy is to let people manage their own business in their own way." - Oliver Wendall Holmes, in Dr. Miles Medical Co. v. Park & Sons*

SOLE PROPRIETORSHIP

A sole proprietorship is the most common form for conducting business activity. This is a disturbing fact because it is almost universally not the best choice. A wise man once told me that "we gravitate to the level of our own laziness." Because the proprietorship is the default business entity for the individual who makes no effort to organize or plan his affairs, I believe that the large number of sole proprietorships functioning in the business world is testament to that statement.

The sole proprietorship is, by definition, the business of a single individual. It is the least expensive form of business to establish, in terms of the cost of legal, accounting and other startup fees. However, other factors may make it the most expensive entity of all to use over the long run.

As a sole proprietor, there is absolutely no difference between you, the person, and your business. Business liabilities are your personal liabilities. Its bills are your bills. If it is sued successfully, you may get the judgment against your personal assets. And, the proprietorship cannot survive you. Your ownership interest ends when you die.

On the other hand, since the proprietor is the boss, he or she gets to do as they please with the business. For some people, that is the great attraction to the proprietorship. I suppose there can be great value in not having to answer to anyone. In the proprietorship, there are no formalities to maintain, no meetings to hold, and no organizational documents to draft and file. Although there are no legal hoops to jump through to setup the proprietorship, its business activity must still fall within federal, state, and local guidelines.

Since, as a sole proprietor, the individual is the business, it is easy to take profits out of the sole proprietorship. There are no difficult accounting procedures to maintain. And, there are no double-taxation problems that can be associated with the regular corporation distributing profits. In a proprietorship, you simply write yourself a check.

For tax purposes, you do not even have to file a separate business tax return. Instead, simply attach a Schedule C to your IRS 1040 where you report your business income. When you add it all up, you pay taxes at whatever personal income tax applies to you. Any gain or loss from the business is simply combined with your other taxable items.

> **TAXPAYERS WHO FILE S SCHEDULE C ARE MUCH HIGHER AUDIT RISKS, ACCORDING TO IRS FIGURES.**

Because of the great disparity in the current personal income tax rates, this can result in wide variations between what different individuals will pay in taxes on the same amount of income. As the chart shows, based on the 2000 federal income tax rates, the federal income taxes on $100,000 of net taxable income to a sole proprietor can vary, depending upon the filing status of the individual.

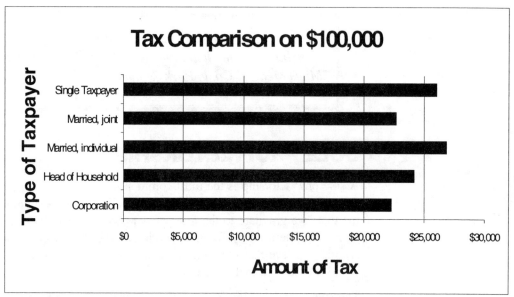

Compare these various personal tax rates with the corporate tax on the same amount. For federal income tax purposes, the proprietor is often at a disadvantage.

The proprietor is not required to withhold federal income tax on his or her own business income (as opposed to salary income). However, if the proprietorship has any employees, there is a responsibility for withholding taxes from their paychecks. The individual proprietor will likely be required to make quarterly estimated tax payments, and will definitely be subject to a 15.3% "self-employment tax" on business income, to offset what the government views as the proprietor's ability to save in social security and Medicare taxes.

Each asset in the sole proprietorship is treated separately for tax purposes, rather than part of one complete ownership interest. For example, a sole proprietor selling an entire business as a going concern, figures gain or loss separately on each asset, not on the value of the entire business as a whole.

Since there is no difference between business and personal assets, the sole proprietor risks everything he or she has on every business day. If a judgment is placed against the business, every personal asset of the owner can be used to satisfy that judgment. This can include homes, property, automobiles, furniture, checking and savings accounts, investments, and personal effects. Additionally, a proprietorship can find it difficult to raise capital resources, since it can only be accomplished if the individual can qualify for a personal loan.

Most local cities and counties require that sole proprietors file a fictitious firm name, sometimes known as a business alias or "DBA" (doing business as) in order to conduct business. This is generally done with the county and/or city clerk. The fictitious firm name allows a sole proprietor to function publicly as a business enterprise under a name other than that of the individual, (i.e., as Joe's Garage instead of as Joe Brown). Although a bank will likely require a fictitious firm name statement from the city or county to open a checking account in the name of Joe's Garage, it is important to remember that, as far as the legal world is concerned, Joe Brown and Joe's Garage are the same.

> *Do not mistake the existence of a **fictitious firm name** as if it represents any sort of legal separation between the individual and the business. The fictitious firm name does not provide any liability protection for the individual.*

A sole proprietor has been historically limited in his or her ability to participate in such things as federally qualified pension plans and medical reimbursement plans that are available to other entities. (Although federal legislation is pending as of this writing that will change this situation.) It may not be fair, but a proprietor can only deduct 25 percent of the cost of medical insurance for himself and his dependents. And, he or she may have more trouble getting full deductions for other business expenses. The IRS has a tendency to disallow some expenses if there can be any question whether a certain expenditure was for business or personal use. Where there is no legal separation between the person and the business, this line gets a little vague at times, which can favor the IRS position for denying the deduction.

The sole proprietor has several basic planning considerations to deal with that are particular to proprietorship status. If the proprietor intends to pass the business on to his or her heirs, there are a number of estate planning and taxation issues that must be overcome. And, from a practical perspective, there is no one else to rely on in case of disability or financial hardship.

Considering all these factors, a proprietorship is certainly not a long-term business solution. It would be difficult to imagine a situation in which a proprietorship is an appropriate entity for serious business use.

SUMMARY

Business activity should not be conducted as a sole proprietorship. Virtually every type of business has associated risk and liability exposure. Proprietors usually don't recognize this (if they did, they wouldn't be using a proprietorship), and as a result, face potential loss that they cannot possibly comprehend. The existence of a sole proprietorship is often the result of a general lack of planning and foresight. If you are currently a proprietor, you are not only gambling that you will not incur business liability, but you are also throwing away a whole host of potential tax benefits that you cannot get by yourself.

ADVANTAGES OF SOLE PROPRIETORSHIP

- The simplest form of doing business. Requires less formality and fewer legal restrictions. Needs no governmental approval.

- Usually less expensive than a partnership or corporation to form.

- Sole ownership of profits. Simple to take profits out.

- Requires no effort or expense to form or maintain.

- Pay taxes at only one level – your individual rate.

- Control and management is vested in one owner.

DISADVANTAGES

- Proprietor has full and unlimited liability for all business activities. This may include debts that exceed the proprietor's total investment. Potential liability extends to all of the proprietor's personal assets.

- Unstable business life, due to risks associated with death or disability of the owner, which could force the business to close.

- No differentiation between business and personal assets.

- Business income is taxed at personal tax rates, which is often much higher than corporate tax rates at certain income levels.

- Additional self-employment taxes.

- Certain business expenses are only partially tax deductible.

- Limitations on available benefits.

- Difficult to raise additional capital, depending upon credit worthiness of the individual.

"Two heads are better than one because the two heads often represent a richer set of experiences and because they can bring to bear on the problem a greater variety of insights." -Warren H. Schmidt.

GENERAL PARTNERSHIPS

A general partnership is just as easy to form as a sole proprietorship. The difference, of course, is that a partnership must have at least two involved parties or partners. If two people agree to start some new enterprise, but make no effort to set up a specific business entity, by default they are general partners.

The general partners are co-owners of the business and its assets. They are basically proprietors in partnership. Their ownership interests may not be identical, but each general partner usually has the same legal powers in relation to the business. Once you form a general partnership, it has its own identity for most purposes and can own property, make contracts, and conduct business in the name the partners have adopted for the general partnership (its fictitious firm name).

A PARTNERSHIP IS NOT A TAXABLE ENTITY, PER SE. HOWEVER IT MUST FIGURE OUT ITS PROFIT AND LOSS AND FILE AN INFORMATIONAL TAX RETURN (FORM 1065) WITHIN 3½ MONTHS OF ITS YEAR END. THIS INFORMATIONAL RETURN ESSENTIALLY REPORTS TO THE IRS THE INCOME TAX OBLIGATION OF EACH PARTNER.

The Internal Revenue Service considers a partnership to be any ordinary partnership, syndicate, group, pool, joint venture, or other unincorporated organization that is carrying on a business and that may not be classified as a trust or estate.

A general partnership is different from a limited partnership (which is discussed below) in the following ways:

1. Each general partner can legally bind the partnership by his or her actions.

2. Each general partner is fully liable for all the business activities of the partnership.

3. Each general partner must have the unanimous consent of all other partners before being admitted into the partnership.

4. If any general partner dies or withdraws from the partnership, the partnership is dissolved (unless a prior written agreement provides otherwise).

Although a general partnership is often formed by default, not all joint business activities are automatically classified as a general partnership. For instance, if two business people agree to share such business expenses as a reception area or a photocopier, that does not create a general partnership. But, if they then charge customers or clients to use the copy machine, the general partnership does exist.

Most states have adopted a version of the Uniform Partnership Act, a statute that provides some basic rules for deciding the rights of general partners and persons who have transactions with a general partnership. While this law provides general rules for determining the rights, powers and responsibilities of each individual partner in relation to the partnership and/or its other partners, the internal rules that govern the partnership specifically can be changed by a formal, written partnership agreement.

Although a general partnership can exist without a formal agreement, it is advised that the partners get together and draft a written partnership agreement to govern and control the partnership relationship. The agreement should cover at least the following points:

1. The name of the partnership;

2. The state of the partnership domicile;

3. The amount of cash or property to be contributed to the

general partnership by each partner, along with a schedule for making the contributions;

4. The duties of each partner in conducting the business, and the scope of authority of each partner to make decisions and incur obligations for the partnership, (which may be useful in settling legal disputes between the partners, but will not necessarily protect any one of the partners from liability exposure to others because of partnership activity);

5. Internal procedures for handling separate debts, including tax obligations;

6. Methods for changing the partnership agreement;

7. Operating procedures, such as maintenance of books and accounting, employee management, etc.;

8. The percentages by which the profits and losses of the general partnership will be shared among the partners; and

9. The events that would cause the partnership to be dissolved, with procedures for winding-down the business, discharging all debts, and distributing the available assets among the partners.

In some ways, the partners in a general partnership have responsibilities to each other that can be compared to those found in civil marriage. Though the partners may have assigned themselves to specific roles and responsibilities in their relationship, perhaps even by written agreement, they are nevertheless jointly and severally liable to the rest of the world for the activities of the business as a whole. The actions of one partner in the name of the business are binding upon all of the partners.

GENERAL PARTNERSHIPS ARE SUBJECT TO THE **SAME LIMITATIONS AS SOLE PROPRIETORS** CONCERNING THEIR ABILITY TO PARTICIPATE IN CERTAIN PENSION PLANS AND MEDICAL REIMBURSEMENT PLANS. CERTAIN BUSINESS EXPENSES ARE NOT ALWAYS FULLY DEDUCTIBLE, AND PARTNERS ARE SUBJECT TO THE 15.3% SELF-EMPLOYMENT TAX (12.4% SOCIAL SECURITY, PLUS 2.9% MEDICARE).

The effect of this reality cannot be understated. A general partner must realize that every personal asset may be attached to fulfill a legal obligation created by another general partner. In other words, all of the assets of all of the partners are in constant jeopardy.

It would be possible for one general partner, without the knowledge of the others, to get a multimillion dollar business loan in the name of the partnership, and then fly to some remote Caribbean island with the funds to live a life of luxury. That would leave the other partners fully liable for the debt, possibly forcing the sale of the remaining partner's personal assets to repay the loan to the bank.

Each of the individual partners include the income or loss from a general partnership on their own tax return. In that way, the general partnership passes its income or loss directly to the individual partners. This avoids the problem with "double taxation" issues associated with drawing profit out of other forms of business. The way the IRS looks at it, it's your money to do with as you please, as long as you report it and pay taxes on it on time.

General partnerships are usually not filed with the Secretary of State because there are no uniform standards for limiting the liability of any of the partners involved. It is not unheard of for general partnerships to be formed as oral agreements. As stated above, the law usually deals with informal or oral business ventures, such as joint ventures, as if they are a general partnership.

As with a sole proprietorship, a general partnership must file a fictitious firm name with the city or county clerk to conduct business by any name other than the given names of the individual partners. So, too, the acquisition of a fictitious firm name does not create any legal distinction between the partners and the business itself.

SUMMARY

A general partnership relies heavily on elements of trust between partners. I have learned, when it comes to business, trust alone is ultimately never sufficient. History is full of examples of partners whose talents allowed them to get a successful business off the ground, but whose talents were not sufficient to manage the enterprise over the long term. The changes that must be made in these situations are painful under the best of conditions. The general partnership provides a recipe for the worst of conditions. In addition to all of the problems that were previously associated with the sole proprietorship, evolutionary changes in the management of a general partnership commonly result in the forced dissolution of the enterprise when the partners do not agree.

ADVANTAGES OF GENERAL PARTNERSHIPS

- Simplest form of conducting business activity for more than one person.

- Does not necessarily require any effort or expense to form or maintain.

- Only one rate of taxation -- partners pay on their individual returns.

- Partners are motivated by direct rewards resulting from their efforts.

- No "double taxation" when taking profits out of the business.

DISADVANTAGES OF GENERAL PARTNERSHIPS

- Partners are fully liable for debts or judgments against the business.

- The acts of one partner can be binding on all other partners.

- Difficulty in disposing of partnership interest.

- No differentiation between business and personal assets.

- Additional self-employment taxes.

- Certain business expenses are only partially tax deductible.

- Limitations on available owner/employee benefits.

- Difficult to raise capital, depending on credit worthiness of partners.

> *"What makes a partnership work? First, a confidence in the integrity and competence of one's partners; secondly, a clear allocation of responsibility for office administration; and thirdly, good communications and a readiness to talk out problems before they become crisis." - Wolfe D. Goodman*

LIMITED PARTNERSHIPS

Limited partnerships have the same basic features as a general partnership, with one important exception: Limited partnerships have limited partners, who generally have neither liability for business activities nor management responsibilities; and general partners who have the same rights, responsibilities and status as a partner in a general partnership. The limited partnership is based on a principle that attempts to preserve the interests of the public good by requiring the existence of at least one general partner. That way, someone has responsibility and liability for the activities of the partnership.

However, the liability of the limited partner is limited to the amount they have invested in the partnership. Because their role in the partnership is viewed as passive, they are not held accountable for partnership activity. All they can do is lose their partnership investment.

NOTE: ALL LIMITED PARTNERSHIPS ARE NOT CREATED EQUAL. THEY ARE AS DIFFERENT AS THE DOCUMENTS THAT CREATE THEM.

Limited partnerships are only created by filing a Certificate of Limited Partnership with the State and establishing a formalized partnership agreement following State law. The partnership agreement is a legal document that specifically details the powers and responsibilities of the partners, and other factors that will decide how the partnership will function and react in specific situations.

Because of the complexity of the partnership agreement, it is important to recognize that all limited partnerships are not created equal. The effectiveness that a limited partnership will have in accomplishing your specific goals depends a great deal on the skill and knowledge of the person drafting the agreement. The wording of the agreement can greatly affect all aspects of the partnership, including the tax consequences of different partnership activities.

For example, a common use of a limited partnership is to protect assets from judgments or creditors. But the value of the partnership in accomplishing that goal is dependent upon the partnership agreement addressing any possible eventuality that a judgment creditor can create.

The most common and basic problem that I have seen with limited partnerships used for asset protection purposes is using an individual as the general partner. I wish I had a nickel for every time I saw a qualified attorney, purportedly an expert in the field of asset protection, set up a limited partnership that resulted in exposing the very client he is supposedly protecting to the unlimited liability associated with being the general partner. (I can only conclude that there are morons in every occupation.)

Unfortunately, not all partnership agreements are written with asset protection as a primary goal, and even those that do focus on asset protection are drafted by attorneys whose background, experience, and skills can vary widely. The result is that there are bad partnership agreements out there, and the average person, including many lawyers, couldn't tell the difference until it is too late.

As I said earlier, the limited partnership must be formed according to state law. Every state has adopted a version of either the Uniform Limited Partnership Act (ULPA) or the Revised Limited Partnership Act (RLPA). It is not necessary to detail the distinctions between these two acts here, especially since individual states have adopted different forms of these acts. But, the person drafting the agreement should be familiar with the version of the law being used.

Most states require that the partnership agreement, or a condensed version that contains the key points, be filed with the Secretary of State's office. This is required to allow individuals who may be dealing with the partnership to have access to information that will allow them to communicate with the partnership and to determine, among other things, the potential liability of the respective parties. This requirement also eliminates potential conflicts between the general and limited partners regarding their individual powers and limitations.

As you can see, it is far more complicated and expensive to form an effective limited partnership than it is to form a general partnership due to the wide range of attorneys' fees and state filing fees that will apply. And, as with other business entities, there are annual maintenance requirements that add to the cost.

Besides their limited liability, the limited partners have the advantage of dealing with a single level of taxation. Income into the partnership flows directly to the partners according to their individual interest, and is included on their personal tax returns.

There is no double taxation to worry about when taking profits, but the general partners are subject to the 15.3% self-employment tax on their income from the partnership.

Although the partnership itself is not taxable, it still must file an annual federal tax return on Form 1065 and provide K-1 schedules to each partner. The K-1 lists each partner's share of income, deductions and credits. Some states also require state income tax filings.

A limited partnership can hold virtually any asset, except some retirement plans, stock in professional corporations and shares of S corporations. Retirement plan contributions for limited partnership are based on "net employment income," (which is: Gross income, minus deductions, including the deduction for retirement plan contributions). Under this formula, you can contribute and deduct as much as 20% of the partnership's profits per year to an approved pension plan.

Limited partnerships are particularly effective in asset protection strategies, especially where the primary assets are real property. The technical explanation for this is beyond the scope of this book, but generally is because neither the limited partnership interest nor the partnership assets are attachable by a creditor. This protection is often called a "charging order limitation," which limits a judgment creditor to what is essentially a lien against partnership income.

Obviously, that makes it attractive to own and manage real estate through a limited partnership in some situations. Some individuals attempt to go so far as to transfer their primary residence into a partnership, however they lose the advantage of deducting the mortgage interest on their personal income tax. Careful thought and planning are required when making these decisions.

The proper uses of a limited partnership are found in three major situations:

1. As an asset protection tool against lawsuits or other judgments,

2. As a tool to spread income among the family and achieve a lower overall family income tax rate, and

3. As a tool in estate planning to lower estate taxes.

There is a lot of discussion these days about an entity called the Family Limited Partnership, which is touted as a suitable device for dealing with a variety of family and estate matters. For the most part, the Family Limited Partnership performs as advertised. But the entity is still a limited partnership, and subject to limited partnership law.

Regarding the asset protection use, a limited partnership provides the following generally accepted advantages, provided the document is drafted properly:

1. A creditor that has a personal judgment against you merely gets a "charging order" against your limited partnership interest, so (in 49 states) he cannot seize any partnership asset unless he is a creditor to the partnership itself. The charging order only gives the creditor a right to the income portion of a limited partner's interest in the partnership, and is usually the only means by which a creditor can reach a limited partner's interest. Charging orders give a creditor no voting rights, no annual income distribution rights (if the provision is included as part of the partnership agreement) and can be the most worthless asset a creditor could ever hold.

2. Creditors cannot remove the general partner of a limited partnership, so you can continue to control all partnership activities and assets by controlling the general partner.

3. Since the personal creditor has no vote, accounting or inspection rights in the partnership, he is treated as an assignee instead of a substituted limited partner. So, he is very much at the mercy of the other partners. He cannot force the sale of partnership assets to satisfy personal judgments.

There can be several drawbacks to using limited partnerships. For instance, a limited partner must be careful not to take an active role in management, or exercise too much control over his or her investment, or the partner's legal status can be elevated to that of general partner. The undesired result would be that the limited partners suddenly find themselves exposed to all the personal risk that has been described earlier. Also, if the partnership has not been filed appropriately, the limited status of the partnership may be jeopardized, possibly resulting in full liability exposure to all of the partners.

A LIMITED PARTNERSHIP IS NOT AN ABSOLUTE BARRIER AGAINST JUDGMENT AND CLAIMS.

The First District Court of Appeals for the State of California recently held in Centurion Corporation v. Crocker National Bank and other cases that a limited partnership interest may be sold on foreclosure of a charging order lien at the request of a judgment creditor. The court determined that the state law gave them implied power of equitable distribution to order the foreclosure sale of a partnership interest to satisfy a judgment creditor's judgment. This could have been avoided if the partnership agreement had been written differently, but the incident sets a disturbing precedent.

Unfortunately, this risk is likely to apply to all states as they update their individual partnership laws to conform with new drafts of uniform statutes on this subject. Recently the National Conference of Commissioners on Uniform State Laws released a draft of the latest revision to the Revised Uniform Partnership Act that provides for this power of foreclosure.

> *In section 504(b) of the Revised Uniform Partnership Act it states that "the court may order a foreclosure of the charging order at any time and under such conditions as it considers appropriate. The purchaser of the foreclosure sale has the rights of an assignee."*

There are ways to effectively reduce the impact of attacks on the limited partnership, but the partnership agreement must contain the appropriate provisions before this becomes a problem. Most drafters of limited partnership agreements simply do not know how to deal with this eventuality.

Additionally, any transfer of assets into a limited partnership must not be for delaying or defrauding creditors, or it is not considered a legitimate transaction. The individuals must be financially solvent both before and after the transaction, and must not be facing any claims. If a claim already exists against you, it may do no good to transfer assets into a limited partnership, since it probably will not pass muster in court. (This is true of all forms of business that offer a degree of insulation from liability.) Seek the professional advice of an attorney who has experience in these situations before you take action.

SUMMARY

The limited partnership is a terrific tool when in the right hands. Used improperly, it is dangerous as dynamite. Dangerous, because many people who think their partnership protects them from liability will be sadly disappointed when they find out that their partnership documents are full of holes. The attorney who specializes in asset preservation concerns, who monitors developments in case law and constantly revises his documents to reflect what he has learned is a good bet to establish a limited partnership properly. I wouldn't let the average attorney draft a limited partnership for me anymore than I would let my family doctor perform brain surgery.

ADVANTAGES

- Limited partners have limited liability.

- Partnership has one level of taxation.

- Effective tool for estate planning, asset protection, and tax planning under certain circumstances.

- Limited partnership interests are generally not attachable by a creditor.

- Mechanism for adjusting the tax basis of real property.

- Personal creditors are precluded from seizing or forcing sale of partnership assets.

- No double taxation for partners when taking profits.

DISADVANTAGES

- Complicated and expensive to form and maintain, not for the do-it-yourself crowd.

- Effectiveness of the partnership depends upon the provisions included in the partnership agreement.

- General partners have unlimited liability for partnership activities.

- Limitations on available fringe benefits.

- General partner may be subject to self-employment tax.

- Possibility of limited partners losing liability limitations in certain circumstances.

- Not an absolute guarantee against claims.

LIMITED LIABILITY COMPANIES

> *"Until the day when our institutions can be trusted to serve us as fiduciaries and when we can be educated to understand the limitations of the world we have constructed, litigation will remain the hallmark of a free and just society." - Jethro K. Lieberman, The Litigious Society*

An LLC is an **effective hybrid** between the single level of taxation provided by the limited partnership and the liability protection offered by a corporation.

The limited liability company (LLC) is a relatively new development in business law. Based on European tradition, it is the latest attempt to create a business entity that provides liability protection to its owners and managers, while preserving the pass-through tax status associated with a partnership or S corporation.

The partnership classification can be either good or bad, depending upon the circumstances. Sure it avoids double taxation, but you might find yourself paying tax on company income at a ridiculously high personal income tax rate, instead of at a lower corporate rate.

An LLC is an entity that is legally separate and distinct from its owners, just as a corporation is its own legal person. For tax purposes, the LLC is treated as a partnership. The LLC merely files an informational tax return that details the gain and loss of the individual members. The tax liability flows through to the owners. This tax treatment avoids double taxation problems that exist when profits are distributed to corporate shareholders. When this happens, the dollar is taxed at both the corporate and individual tax rates.

The states that have adopted a Limited Liability Company Code have been careful to comply with the IRS decisions that create the distinction between the LLC and other entities. This brings us to a very important, and often misunderstood point: A limited liability company is not a corporation. If it were a corporation, it would be taxed at corporate tax rates.

If these distinctions are not followed carefully, the LLC may be considered a corporation for federal income tax purposes, which can result in immediate, and sometimes retroactive double taxation. To be considered as an LLC, an entity may have no more than two of the following characteristics of a corporation:

- Continuity of Life Beyond that of Individual Members

- Centralization of Management

- Limited Liability

- Free Transferability of Interests

Because the LLC provides limited liability to all members and managers, as well as centralization of management, the remaining two characteristics of free transferability of interests, and continuity of life are not available. The LLC can not exist beyond the life of its individual members. When a member dies, the LLC is automatically dissolved. It must be reorganized, or it reverts to corporate tax status.

State statute frequently limits the life span of an LLC to less than thirty years. If an LLC is maintained beyond that, the IRS may consider it to be a corporation.

Free transferability of LLC interests is not available because the voting rights of ownership cannot be transferred. Only the original members of the LLC have the power to make decisions regarding the operation and administration of the company. If an ownership interest is transferred or sold to another party, it only carries a right to income.

As of this writing, all fifty states have now approved this new form of entity. Hawaii and Vermont were the final two holdouts. The dates each state approved LLC legislation are as follows:

Alaska (effective July 1995)	Hawaii (Apr. 1, 1997)
Alabama (May 20, 1993)	Idaho (Mar 26, 1993)
Arizona (Jun. 2, 1992)	Illinois (Sep. 11, 1992)
Arkansas (Apr. 13, 1993)	Indiana (May 13, 1993)
California (Sept 1994)	Iowa (Apr. 27, 1992)
Colorado (Sept. 13, 1990)	Kansas (1990)
Connecticut (Jun. 23, 1993)	Kentucky (March 29, 1994)
Delaware (Jul. 22, 1992)	Louisiana (Jul. 7, 1992)
District of Columbia (Jul. 23, 1994)	Maine (January 1, 1995)
Florida (1982)	Maryland (May 26, 1992)
Georgia (Apr. 5, 1993)	Massachusetts (1995)

Michigan (Apr. 14, 1993)

Minnesota (Apr. 29, 1992)

Mississippi (July 1, 1994)

Missouri (Jul. 2, 1993)

Montana (Mar 18, 1993)

Nebraska (Jun. 2, 1993)

Nevada (1991)

New Hampshire (Jun. 23, 1993)

New Jersey (Jul. 30, 1993)

New Mexico (Apr. 7, 1993)

New York (Oct 24, 1994)

North Carolina (Jun. 1993)

North Dakota (Apr. 12, 1993)

Ohio (July 1, 1994)

Oklahoma (May 1, 1992)

Oregon (Jun. 24, 1993)

Pennsylvania (effective Feb 5, 1995)

Rhode Island (Jul. 21, 1992)

South Carolina (June 16, 1994)

South Dakota (Mar 22, 1993)

Tennessee (June 22, 1994)

Texas (1991)

Utah (1991, amended 1992)

Virginia (1991)

Vermont (July 1, 1996)

Washington (Oct 1, 1994)

West Virginia (Mar 27, 1992)

Wisconsin (January 1, 1994)

Wyoming (Jun. 30, 1977)

The LLC was allowed in the U.S. in 1977 when Wyoming passed the first Limited Liability Company Act. In 1988, the IRS issued a formal opinion on Wyoming's Limited Liability Company Act (Rev. Rule 88-76, 1088 2 C.B. 360), with the conclusion that a LLC formed under that Act should classify for federal income tax purposes as a partnership, even though none of the members or managers are personally liable for the debts of the company. Since then, there have been 14 additional Revenue Rulings that support the original.

Personal creditors of a limited-liability company member may charge the member's interest with payment of the unsatisfied debt, but this only provides the creditor with the rights of an assignee of the member's interest. This functions very similar to the way a "charging order" limitation functions in a limited partnership.

One key advantage to the LLC is in the lack of restrictions regarding the type and number of stockholders. As will be explained further in the next chapter, the S corporation, which is the other entity that provides corporate liability protection and flow-though tax status, has severe limitations on the shareholders. But the LLC is not subject to restrictions on ownership that apply to an S corporation. Most trusts, estates, corporations, partnerships, and other LLCs are prohibited from owning stock in an S corporation.

The popular use of the LLC has been slow to develop. For example, Nevada has allowed for the creation of the LLC since October of 1991. Instead of the expected rush to form this type of company, the public response was initially cool. During the first eight months of availability in Nevada, fewer than fifty LLCs were formed. Since then the number has increased dramatically as attorneys and accountants have had opportunities to attend continuing education seminars that promote the LLC as a business entity and increase their ability to offer the LLC as an income producing product.

The owners are called **"members"** of the company, and are indemnified by statute for any judgment, debt or obligation of the company, including decrees of the court. The members may exercise direct control over the company, according to their individual percentage of ownership, or may appoint one or more managers. If managers are used, they perform functions commonly associated with corporate officers and directors.

In most states, the LLC is formed by filing articles of organization with the Secretary of State. This document must typically give the name of the company, the names of all of the members, including their capital contribution schedule, the period of its duration, the purpose for organizing the company, the address of its principal office in the state, and other provisions outlining the rights of the members and the management.

While the LLC has a lot to offer, and may become the entity of the future -- eventually replacing the S corporation -- there are still many questions that must be addressed. Originally, the problem with the LLC was that only a few states recognized them as a legal entity. This presented many questions about conducting interstate business. For instance, does a state without a LLC statute determine a foreign LLC to be a corporation or a partnership for state tax purposes? Further, will the LLC liability protection be recognized in other jurisdictions?

These problems are beginning to solve themselves as more states get on the LLC bandwagon. The question now is, how will the courts view the LLC in the broad spectrum of business law?

Will the courts allow for a judgment creditor to foreclose upon a member's interest in a limited liability company, as has been accomplished in some states with a limited partnership interest?

If that happens to one member, will the LLC be forced into the IRS definition of a corporation? Is so, all members will suffer serious negative tax consequences.

Unfortunately, these are complex legal issues, for which there simply is not enough case law for anyone to accurately predict what will happen. And, the fact that there is no uniform legal standard (although the experts say it is coming) among the various states does not help. These issues will be resolved in time. Just don't be a test case.

Another potential drawback to the LLC is in the lack of financial privacy it provides for its members. Since the members are frequently listed in the articles of organization, which are filed with the Secretary of State, they may be public record. Also, the resident or registered agent is required to keep an updated list of the names and addresses of all members and managers on file, along with tax returns and financial statements for the last three years. All of that information would be available to the person who could serve your resident agent with a subpoena for the company's records.

Nevertheless, you may want to wait for the idea to mature before getting on the bandwagon without reservation. For now, I believe the LLC is not always appropriate for general use. Certain types of business are a natural fit for the LLC, including research and development, oil and gas exploration, and real estate development. The reason this type of activity is such a good fit for the LLC is because of the inherent limited lifespan of the business. For example, in the oil business, you locate the well, drill it, pump it, and hope to walk away. The LLC allows that to happen.

The chief financial officer of a large manufacturing company in Nevada shared his thoughts about the LLC. He said that the real excitement in industrial circles about the LLC has to do with speculative development and research. In his words, "it's the closest thing there is to a collapsible company."

The LLC may replace the S corporation as a flow-through tax entity, making it obsolete. It may also replace the limited partnership in some instances, but not entirely. The LLC will not replace the C corporation, now or in the future. Besides the double taxation issue, there will likely always be income tax advantages for some people to using lower corporate tax rates. And, the free transferability of ownership interests of a corporation will always be a necessity in many circumstances.

SUMMARY

The limited liability company is destined for greatness in the business world, especially as it becomes widely available. As the legal systems of the individual states establish the appropriate case law to lay a solid foundation for the LLC concept, it will become a business standard.

ADVANTAGES

- Good liability protection for members, management and employees, when used in states that recognize this type of entity.

- No limitation on number or type of owners.

- No limitation on classes of membership interests.

- No limitation on ownership of other corporations.

- No citizenship requirements for members or managers.

- Is simple to take profits out, although the double-taxation issue may be unsettled in individual states.

- Personal creditors treated like assignees, and cannot force the sale or dissolution of the company.

DISADVANTAGES

- Has been limited in national use.

- Taxation issues may not be resolved at the state level.

- There is still a question about the flow-through tax status of a "one-man" LLC in those states that provide for such an entity.

- Lack of case law creates an unsettled legal atmosphere for the foreseeable future.

- Lifetime limited by state statute.

LIMITED LIABILITY PARTNERSHIP

The Limited Liability Partnership (LLP) is allowed in eighteen states for the purpose of enabling existing professional partnerships, such as accounting firms, to be transformed into a LLP without forcing the dissolution of the existing partnership.

Without the LLP designation and the liability protection that it provides, the professional partnership leaves the partners open to personal liability. The LLP protects the individual partners to different degrees, depending upon the jurisdiction. Some states insulate the partners from contractual obligations of the partnership, while others do not.

The LLP is taxed as a partnership, and even retains the original Taxpayer Identification Number of the existing professional partnership. The LLP is not the same as a Limited Liability Company. Most states do not allow a LLC to be established for the purpose of providing professional services.

The states that have enacted Limited Liability Partnership laws include:

• Arizona	• Maryland
• Connecticut	• Minnesota
• Delaware	• New York
• District of Columbia	• North Carolina
• Illinois	• Ohio
• Iowa	• South Carolina
• Kansas	• Texas
• Kentucky	• Utah
• Louisiana	• Virginia

> IT IS COMMON TO SEE MAJOR ACCOUNTING FIRMS, SUCH AS THE "BIG EIGHT," ORGANIZED AS A LLP.

BUSINESS TRUSTS

The Nevada Legislature approved the formation and use of business trusts under Nevada law in 1999 in a bill written and introduced by the Nevada Bar Association. The text of the Nevada law regarding business trusts is found in the appendices of this volume.

The term "business trust" generally refers to an unincorporated association which is created by a trust instrument under which property is held, managed and controlled by a trustee. There are many names by which promoters have marketed the business trust. Among these include: common law trusts; pure trusts, Massachussets business trusts; freedom trusts; and many other names. What the promoter calls it is not important.

Few business entities have been promoted with the accompanying hype and inflated promises as those surrounding business trusts. While there are properly constructed business trusts in use, the business trust may have been irreparably tainted by the questionable claims made by con artists and promoters of fraudulent tax schemes based on the use of the business trust.

Among the false promises made by trust promoters are the claims that the Trustor (the person who transfers assets into the trust) can be provided with free housing, free automobiles, free medical care, and elimination of income, gift and estate taxes. Naturally, the promoters promise total asset protection. These claims are frequently made within the "Patriot" movement by unsuspecting taxpayers who are unaware of the depth of case law that refute these ridiculous claims.

In 1975, the IRS began to attack defective business trusts by issuing Revenue Ruling 75-257 through 75-260. In these rulings, the IRS defined fraudulent business trusts as those that:

THE BUSINESS TRUST IS PROMOTED UNDER A VARIETY OF NAMES, SUCH AS: "THE PURE TRUST," "THE EQUITY TRUST," "THE LIBERTY TRUST," "THE BUSINESS TRUST ORGANIZATION (BTO)", "UNINCORPORATED BUSINESS ORGANIZATIONS," "MASSACHUSETTS BUSINESS TRUST," AND OTHERS. MOST TRUST PROMOTERS ARE USING DOCUMENTS THAT HAVE EVOLUTIONARY TIES TO DISBARRED ILLINOIS ATTORNEY HARRY MORGAN PHIPPS.

1. Involved an assignment of income;

2. Were "Grantor" trusts by definition of the Internal Revenue Code;

3. Were "associations taxable as corporations" as defined by the Internal Revenue Code.

The IRS ruled that the assets of the trust would be included in the grantor's gross estate for estate tax purposes. In addition, the faulty trusts provide no protection against the claims of personal creditors.

That said, it is true that many of the super wealthy, such as the Rockefeller and Kennedy families have used sophisticated trusts to achieve significant tax savings and asset protection. Unfortunately, those trusts were put in place under a different set of laws in much simpler times.

Remember that nobody has seen the trust documents they used. When Nelson A. Rockefeller sat before the Senate Judiciary Committee in 1974, attempts were made in vain to view family trust and foundation documents. If Congress could not access them, why would anyone believe that some disbarred attorney (a thinly-veled reference to trust promoters) knew their contents?

SUMMARY

Trusts can be properly used for business purposes only under very restrictive circumstances. Adoption of business trust legislation by states such as Nevada, Delaware and others does not necessarily validate the promises made be the promoters. It does indicate, however, that states are recognizing the need to codify and standardize business trust definitions and rules. If the business trust is "tax-neutral" (meaning that the trust provides no income tax benefits), it can utilized with only very limited asset protection benefits.

JOINT VENTURES

A joint venture is similar to a general partnership. Two or more parties agree to enter into a business venture, and split the responsibilities, risks and rewards according their internal agreements. The difference between a general partnership and a joint venture is that a general partnership is usually a venture between to individuals, while the joint venture is between two business entities.

Joint ventures are usually not done on an informal basis, as are many general partnerships. Most joint ventures involve detailed joint venture agreements that closely outlines every conceivable aspect of the joint venture operation.

The joint venture is taxed as if it were a partnership. If one party in a joint venture is a corporation, and another is a limited liability company, and yet a third is a limited partnership, the income of the joint venture will be distributed between the parties according to their agreement, and each entity will likewise pay or report tax obligations accordingly.

Chapter

3

CORPORATE HAVENS

*Some states grow better apples, some are proud of potatoes,
but these states specialize in corporations.*

W hat is a corporate haven? A corporate haven is a jurisdiction that provides a favorable climate for forming corporations. It is a pro-business state that provides flexibility in the management and structure of the company, and usually provides a measure of tax-favored treatment. A corporate haven is attractive to individuals located outside that specific jurisdiction, who live in places that don't provide the same advantages.

It is easy to spot a corporate haven. A corporate haven will form an unusually large number of corporations in comparison to the population of that state. That is a sure sign that the jurisdiction is attracting corporations from a much wider base.

There is an economic incentive for states to establish themselves as a corporate haven. The more corporations a state files, the more revenue it brings in through initial filing fees and the annual renewal fees necessary to maintain corporate status. Further, a state with favorable corporate laws attracts economic development and growth, in other words, it brings in new jobs.

MOST PEOPLE WHO INCORPORATE DO SO FOR ONE OR MORE OF THE FOLLOWING REASONS: 1) PROTECTION FROM PERSONAL LIABILITY, 2) TAX ADVANTAGES, 3) FINANCIAL PRIVACY, AND 4) FLEXIBILITY IN MANAGEMENT AND CONTROL. ALL CORPORATIONS PROVIDE ADVANTAGES IN THESE AREAS TO A DEGREE, BUT SOME STATES DO IT BETTER THAN OTHERS.

DELAWARE

In years past, Delaware stood head and shoulders above any other state in offering protection in these vital areas. Delaware aggressively protected its stature as the incorporating capital of the United States. As a result, many of the Fortune 500 companies in the United States are incorporated in Delaware. They went to Delaware to protect the interests of their stockholders, directors, officers, and the corporation itself. More than 230,000 companies are incorporated in Delaware, which leads the nation as a major corporate domicile for American and international corporations. Each day, over 130 new companies file incorporation papers in Delaware.

The reasons why Delaware has established such a reputation as a corporate haven are many:

> *Delaware has found itself in a difficult position regarding closely held companies. It's laws have been systematically designed to protect the rights of the minority shareholder in a large, public company. However, this is at the expense of protecting the corporate officers and directors from liability, and of disclosure requirements.*

- The Delaware General Corporation Law is one of the most advanced statutes of its kind in the nation, especially on issues relative to public corporations.

- Delaware touts its non-jury Court of Chancery, which is unique in America and has exclusive Delaware jurisdiction with business matters relating to corporate government and operations. This court has over 200 years of legal precedents.

- The Delaware legislature works to continually update and modify the statutes to reflect changing business conditions.

- Delaware does not tax corporate activity that takes place outside Delaware.

Delaware's corporation law is written to protect the rights of shareholders of the public corporations that are the standard-bearers in the Delaware corporation system. The emphasis is placed on shareholder protections to attract the large, public companies that trade shares in the various exchanges across the country. It's laws regarding corporate takeovers are the most sophisticated in the entire world. There is established legal precedent for any conceivable corporate situation. It is a stable legal environment for many public companies to use as their base.

Although Delaware remains a favorite for public corporations, in recent years Delaware has become less aggressive in protecting the rights of small corporations. In many areas, they have taken a step backward. Nevada has been one of the first states to step in and fill the void. Now, there are several states who are pursuing the incorporation market, focusing their efforts on the needs of the closely held company.

Closely held corporations, where the shareholders often take a managerial role as an officer or director, are not concerned with protecting their shareholder rights. What they need is protection as an officer or director from outside liability.

Nevada and Wyoming, on the other hand, are attractive to a completely different market. They have written their corporation laws to protect the rights and privacy of the small, privately held corporation. Nevada and Wyoming statute is concerned with strong management protection for the closely held company. These concerns are inherently in conflict with the Delaware school of thought.

OFFICERS AND DIRECTORS LIABILITY

Delaware has adopted a statute that allows the corporation to limit the liability of a director for monetary damages, however it is far less broad than similar statutes adopted by Nevada. For example, the following are acts for which officers and directors would be protected under Nevada law, but exposed under Delaware statutes:

1. Breach of a director's duty of loyalty.

2. Acts or omissions not in good faith.

3. Transactions involving undisclosed personal benefit to the officer or director.

4. Acts or omissions that occurred prior to the date that the statute which provides for indemnification of directors was passed and approved.

5. Acts by officers are not exempt from monetary damages under Delaware law.

STANDARD OF CARE

Delaware follows the Model Business Corporation Act with regard to how it defines the standard of care that is expected of corporate officers. That is, Delaware requires that an officer act with at least some objective standard of care. This standard is usually expressed as the care of an ordinarily prudent person under similar circumstances.

In other words Delaware requires that officers reasonably believe that he or she is performing his or her duties in a manner that is in the best interests of the corporation. Nevada, on the other hand does not have this requirement, which will prevent judicial review of the actions of corporate officers and directors in all cases except where the directors act in bad faith or in a manner that they actually believe to be opposed to the best interest of the corporation.

Delaware also has developed a substantial body of case law that sets the standard of care required of directors. This standard is generally defined as "gross negligence," which means "reckless indifference to or a deliberate disregard of the whole body of stockholders."

> *Microsoft Corporation recently moved its corporation domicile out of Delaware and into its home state of Washington to get away from the bureaucracy and corporate taxes.*

DELAWARE'S FRANCHISE TAX

A primary difference between corporate havens is in the establishment of Delaware's administrative procedures that govern and regulate corporate dealings. Unfortunately, once a bureaucracy is established, history has proven that it must continually grow to justify its existence to the taxpaying public.

All corporations incorporated in the State of Delaware that have not filed a dissolution or merger with the State of Delaware in the current calendar year are required to file an Annual Franchise Tax Report and pay the Franchise Tax. A minimum $30.00 filing fee is required for the annual report.

The Franchise Tax in Delaware may be calculated one of two ways:

- **Authorized Shares Method**. Corporations that have shares with no par value must use this method. If the corporation has less than three thousand shares, the tax is $30.00, which is the minimum. Where there are between three thousand and five thousand authorized shares, the tax is $50.00. Then, the tax for up to ten thousand authorized shares is $90.00, with an additional $50.00 for each additional ten thousand shares or portion thereof. For example, a corporation with 25,000 shares of No Par Value will pay $190 in franchise taxes every year.

DELAWARE OFFERS LITTLE, IF ANY FAVORABLE TAX TREATMENT. THE CORPORATION IS FORCED TO CHOOSE BETWEEN PAYING DELAWARE'S 8.7% TAX, OR THE TAX APPLICABLE IN ANOTHER JURISDICTION WHERE IT IS ACTUALLY CONDUCTING BUSINESS.

- **Assumed Par Value Capital Method.** To use this method, the corporation must provide detailed figures for all issued shares, including treasury stock, as well as the total gross assets of the company as reported on IRS Form 1120, Schedule L. This information becomes public record with the Delaware Secretary of State. The tax rate under this method is $200.00 per million or portion of a million dollars of the corporations gross value. The maximum tax is $150,000.00. For example, if a corporation has 1,000,000 authorized shares (500,000 are issued) at $1 par value, and a total gross asset value of $1,000,000, the franchise tax would be $400 per year.

In addition, Delaware has a corporate income tax of 8.7% on revenues earned inside the state. While Delaware touts this tax treatment as an advantage, it actually causes a lot of problems for individuals from other states that incorporate in Delaware. The reason is simple. If the income is not earned in Delaware, it must be earned somewhere else, where it will most certainly be taxed.

Nevada

Nevada has spent more than a decade developing the infrastructure to support its claim as the incorporating capital of the West. Instead of resting on its laurels, Nevada has become much more determined to establish itself as a leader in incorporation, as evidenced by the complete revision of Nevada's Corporation Code in 1987, and again in 1991 that makes the entire incorporation process quicker and more efficient, with greater liability protection than ever before.

In 1996, Nevada made it's first appearance in the Top Ten List of states with the highest number of incorporations. That's not bad, considering there are 36 states with larger a larger population than Nevada. Approximately 1,500 corporations are formed every month in Nevada, which is three times higher than in 1985.

Because of Nevada's pro-business attitude, **Inc. Magazine** and **Money Magazine** have rated Nevada #1 among all States in recent years for favorable business climates. In the last decade, Nevada has clearly established itself as the "Corporation Capital of the West," and has shown significant annual growth in the number of new businesses that incorporate there each year. And, Nevada's legal system, while not as experienced as Delaware's, has naturally grown to accommodate the need for establishing legal precedents that support the state law.

Nevada offers many advantages as a corporate haven:

1. Nevada has **no state corporate taxes**.

2. Nevada has **no franchise tax**.

3. Nevada has **no tax on corporate shares**.

4. Nevada has **no personal income tax**.

5. Nevada provides **total privacy** of shareholders.

6. Nevada is the **only state** without a formal information-sharing agreement with the IRS.

7. Nevada is the only state that allows for the issuance of **"bearer shares."**

8. Nevada has minimal reporting and disclosure requirements.

9. Nevada has nominal annual fees.

10. Nevada allows for a **one-man** corporation.

11. Nevada has established case law that **prevents easy piercing of the corporate veil**.

12. Corporate officers and directors can be **protected from any personal liability** for their lawful acts on behalf of the corporation.

13. Stockholders, directors and officers need not live or hold meetings in Nevada, or even be U.S. citizens.

14. Only the names and addresses of the officers and directors are on public records. No other information, listings, or minutes of meetings are filed with the State.

15. There is no minimum initial capital requirement to incorporate.

16. Nevada corporations may issue stock for capital, services, personal property, or real estate. The directors alone may determine the value of any such transactions, and their decision is final.

Nevada's Corporation Code has been criticized by some as too pro-management, offering far too much flexibility in maintaining the corporation's affairs. Critics have said that the law in Nevada is not concerned enough about the rights of stockholders or employees. However, since the 1991 version of the Corporation Code was adopted, Nevada has experienced a 35% increase in the number of corporations filed in the state.

Most of these corporations are being formed by small companies, where the stockholders and the management are the same. These people are concerned very little with protecting their rights as a stockholder, since they also manage the company and receive all of the benefits of Nevada's liberal Code.

From the Reno Gazette-Journal, Monday, April 29, 1991:

INCORPORATING BECOMES BIG BUSINESS FOR NEVADA

"They come from all over: the busy streets of New York, the snowy slopes of Colorado, the oil fields of the Yukon, and they all want the same thing: the painless, cheap and anonymous security of Nevada's business world.

"Scores of companies fill out a few documents, list a few officers, pay a nominal fee and presto) a new corporation is born. For instance:

"A New York City cab company has established 50 Nevada corporations -- one for every two vehicles in its 100-taxi fleet. If the company gets sued, its liability is limited to the value of individual properties, just two cabs, unless the plaintiff wants to file lawsuits against 50 different companies.

"Some ski resorts have followed the same principle, setting up corporations for each ski lift, lodge and snack bar. A major petroleum company set up Nevada corporations for each

of its 100 Alaska Oil wells. 'It's really the idea of making a new basket, every time you have an egg you want to insulate,' said one Nevada incorporation expert.

"Several entertainers have also started their own corporations. Rock stars Madonna, Prince, Michael Jackson and Paul Simon all reportedly have Nevada corporations, as do Chevy Chase and Rodney Dangerfield. Some have their big-money salaries paid to accounts in Nevada, where there is no income tax or corporate tax, and the entertainers draw a salary from the corporation. "They buy boats, cars and take trips to Europe and everything," said Nevada businessman Brian Foote, who helps out-of-staters set up Nevada corporations. "They have the corporation buy for them."

"All of this is made possible because Nevada lawmakers drafted its liberal corporation laws over the past several decades, said Cyndy Woodgate, state deputy secretary for corporations.

"Officials didn't want to be hard-nosed about business coming to Nevada, Woodgate said. "And not being restricted here, they're able to come here and do business. We like that fact."

"There are several benefits of having a Nevada corporation. These include low filing fees, minimal information requirements, and no standard corporate tax. Most other states, including California, have a tax.

"To make matters even better, Nevada is the only state without a reciprocal agreement with the IRS to exchange tax returns. This is especially attractive to some corporations or individuals who want to legally protect their privacy.

"With all these advantages, it's sometimes feasible for a single person or company to set up several Nevada corporations. The same thing would be a paperwork nightmare in California, where basic individual filing fees are us to $800 or more.

"The liberal laws have spawned their own growth industry: businesses that specialize in helping other businesses set up corporations. And business is booming, in part because it's getting more complicated and costly to do business in other states.

"At least for now, Nevada remains the second most popular state for incorporating on a per capita basis. The leader is Delaware, but local corporation makers aren't impressed: Nevada, they say, has several benefits Delaware doesn't have, like privacy, no franchise taxes and other benefits."

> *"The number of lawyers confounds all belief in the land of the fee and the home of the brief." - Leon Frielich*

LIABILITY PROTECTION

There is a national trend developing where people are steadfastly refusing to serve on the board of directors of corporations because of their exposure to stockholders and the public. Gone are the days in which someone tries to embellish their resume by listing all of the corporations for which they serve as a director or vice-president. People are slowly realizing the liability exposure that they have in those situations.

In 1987, the Nevada Legislature passed a revolutionary law that allows corporations to place provisions in their articles of incorporation that eliminates the personal liability of officers and directors to the stockholders of Nevada corporations. Delaware and a few other states soon adopted lesser versions of Nevada's law, but Nevada's remains among the most thorough and comprehensive in the country.

Contained in the Nevada Revised Statutes (78.037), the law in part reads as follows:

"The articles of incorporation may also contain:

1. A provision eliminating or limiting the personal liability of a director or officer to the corporation or its stockholders for damages for breach of fiduciary duty as a director or officer, but such provision must not eliminate or limit the liability of a director or officer for:

> *(a) Acts or omissions which involve intentional misconduct, fraud or a knowing violation of law"*

Additionally, Nevada's Corporation Code allows for the indemnification of all officers, directors, employees, stockholders, or agents of a corporation for all actions that they take on behalf of the corporation that they had reasonable cause to believe was legal. This indemnification can include any civil, criminal and administrative action. (See NRS 78.751.) These two laws can provide comprehensive protection for the officers and directors of Nevada corporations as long as they act prudently in their roles.

Additionally, Nevada law allows a corporation to make "financial arrangements" to provide a buffer against any possible liability that an officer or director may incur. These "financial arrangements" are described under the statute as" (1) the creation of a trust fund; (2) the establishment of a program of self-insurance; (3) securing the obligation by granting a lien on corporate assets; or (4) the establishment of a letter of credit, guaranty, or other surety.

Tort Reform

Nevada has joined a group of states that have enacted tort reform legislation in response to the increased cost of doing business resulting from potential liability. The goal of tort reform is to reduce the exposure of businesses and their insurers. The key features of Nevada's legislation are provisions which limit exemplary damages and abolish joint and several liability except in certain cases.

Before the tort reform legislation, it was common for courts to award exemplary damages three to five times greater than the compensatory damages. Nevada statute now limits exemplary damages to an amount no greater than $300,000 when the amount of compensatory damages is less than $100,000. These limitations do not apply to situations involving insurer bad faith, the release of toxic substances, or product liability.

IN NEVADA, THE OFFICERS AND DIRECTORS OF THE CORPORATION ARE THE ONLY PEOPLE LISTED ON PUBLIC RECORDS, SO THEY HAVE THE ONLY REAL EXPOSURE TO THE OUTSIDE WORLD. STOCKHOLDERS CAN BE INDEMNIFIED AS WELL, ALTHOUGH THAT IS SECONDARY PROTECTION TO THE FACT THAT NO ONE CAN FIND YOU ON PUBLIC RECORDS IN THE FIRST PLACE. HOW CAN SOMEBODY SUE YOU - OR AT LEAST COLLECT AGAINST YOU - IF THEY CAN'T FIND YOU?

IN PRODUCT LIABILITY CASES, THE DAMAGES ARE CATEGORIZED AS ONE OF TWO TYPES. THE FIRST TYPE IS REFERRED TO AS "COMPENSATORY," WHICH ARE INTENDED TO COMPENSATE THE INJURED FOR SOME LOSS, WHICH CAN INCLUDE ECONOMIC (SUCH AS LOST INCOME, MEDICAL BILLS, ETC.) OR NONECONOMIC (FOR EXAMPLE, PAIN AND SUFFERING).THE SECOND TYPE OF DAMAGES ARE CALLED "EXEMPLARY," ALSO KNOWN AS "PUNITIVE." EXEMPLARY DAMAGES ARE IMPOSED TO PUNISH THE WRONGDOER FOR CONDUCT WHICH BY CLEAR AND CONVINCING PROOF IS SHOWN TO INVOLVE OPPRESSION, FRAUD, OR MALICE, EITHER EXPRESS OR IMPLIED. THESE DAMAGES ARE DESIGNED AS A DETERRENCE TO OTHERS.

The other significant change in Nevada law is the abolishment of joint and several liability. Joint and several liability means that if a judgment is entered against several defendants, they are each equally liable for the full amount of the judgment, without regard to their relative fault in causing the damages. Nevada now requires the court to assign a percentage of fault to each defendant, from zero to one hundred with the total equal to 100 percent. Each defendant found liable is required to pay a share of the total judgment no greater than his/her percentage of fault.

TAXES

All US corporations are subject to federal income tax liability. Although there are many strategies involving the corporation that may reduce the federal tax liability, the state of incorporation is not a direct factor in reducing federal taxes. However, some strategies that will reduce federal income taxes for corporations may require the use of a corporation from a specific jurisdiction, such as Nevada, due to several factors that are inherent in Nevada corporations.

State Corporate Income Tax

The difference in tax liability becomes immediately apparent when looking at state corporate tax rates. The rate of tax among the forty-five states that have state corporate income tax, ranges from 1 percent (Arkansas' corporate tax on the first $3,000 of income) to 12.25 percent (Pennsylvania's corporate tax). Many states have additional surtaxes, and allow local governments to assess their own corporate taxes on top of that.

Nevada has been fiscally conservative throughout its history. Nevadans have never had high regard for taxes. So much so, that several years ago the Nevada legislature approved a measure that made a **state personal income tax unconstitutional.**

Nevada is one of only four states with no corporate income tax. Additionally, Nevada has

> *"Anyone may arrange his affairs that his taxes shall be as low as possible; he is not bound to choose that pattern which will best pay the Treasury; there is not even a patriotic duty to increase one's taxes."* - Learned Hand, in Helvering v. Gregory.

no franchise tax, no taxes on corporate shares, and no succession tax. This type of tax structure is made possible in Nevada by a state economy centered in three major industries, namely; (1) gaming, (2) tourism, and (3) mining.

The revenue generated by these industries has historically paid for a substantial portion of Nevada's budget needs. Any visitor to the Las Vegas Strip can testify that Nevada's entertainment industry has poured billions of dollars into protecting it's title as the entertainment capital of the world. Besides the gaming taxes generated on the casino floor, the millions of visitors add substantially to state coffers each year in sales revenue from purchases made during their visit.

So, by incorporating in Nevada instead of California and with careful structuring that distinctly separates the Nevada source income from the California source income, you can create an entity that has it's tax domicile in Nevada. This could save the business $9,300 in state corporate income taxes on every $100,000 of taxable income. What's more, your corporate structure would be in complete compliance, and legally justified.

Remember, there is a difference between "tax avoidance," which is perfectly legal, and "tax evasion," which is very illegal. Tax avoidance is avoiding situations which are taxed, while tax evasion is failing to pay taxes that are due.

The best example I know that demonstrates the difference between tax avoidance and tax evasion is in consideration of a toll bridge. Crossing the toll bridge without paying the toll would be evasion, while choosing another route, even if it adds a few miles to the trip, is simply avoidance. There is nothing illegal or immoral about it.

Nevada's Business License Tax

The one business-related tax that you should be aware of may not even apply to your Nevada corporation. Effective July 1, 1991, the tax is often called the Nevada Business License Tax, which is based on the average number of employees the company has on the payroll during each quarter of the year. The tax is paid quarterly by every person, corporation, partnership, or proprietorship that conducts an activity for profit in Nevada. The only exempt companies are nonprofit organizations and government entities.

Only businesses that have employees working in Nevada are subject to the tax. If you don't have employees, the tax does not apply. Independent contractors are not considered employees of the company, and are liable for their own tax under the law.

The procedure for administrating and collecting the tax is as follows: an application is mailed to all new businesses by the Nevada Department of Taxation within weeks of incorporating or securing local business licenses. The original application must be accompanied by a $25.00 filing fee, and a current list of corporate officers and directors. All new businesses must return the application, if for no other reason than to say that the company had no employees.

The tax amounts to $100 per employee per year. To dissuade the critics of this tax, who properly complain that it produces a negative reward for hiring new employees, the tax is now based on the number of hours worked by employees, instead of the number of employees hired. The total hours worked are then divided by the number of hours the state thinks a full-time employee should work each quarter, and the result is the number of employee-equivalents that the business has.

CALIFORNIA HAS A STATE CORPORATE TAX RATE OF **9.3%,** WITH A MINIMUM TAX OF $800 PER YEAR. **ARIZONA** HAS A TAX OF **9.3%** ON ALL TAXABLE INCOME OVER $6,000. **NEW YORK'S** TAX RATE IS **9%,** (10% ON UNRELATED INCOME) WITH A MINIMUM REQUIRED TAX OF $800 PER YEAR, IN ADDITION TO TAXES LEVIED BY LOCAL JURISDICTIONS (NEW YORK CITY IMPOSES AN 8.85% CORPORATE TAX). EVEN **DELAWARE** HAS A CORPORATE TAX OF **8.7%** AND A MINIMUM $40 PER YEAR FRANCHISE TAX.

> *"The makers of our Constitution undertook to secure conditions favorable to the pursuit of happiness. They recognized the significance of man's spiritual nature, of his feelings and of his intellect. They knew that only a part of the pain, pleasure and satisfactions of life are to be found in material things. They sought to protect Americans in their beliefs, their thoughts, their emotions and their sensations. They conferred, as against the Government, the right to be let alone - the most comprehensive of rights and the right most valued by civilized man." - Louis Brandeis, in Olmstead v. United States.*

PRIVACY

For many people, privacy is the primary issue in their financial life. It seems that in our society, so bent as it is upon litigation and lawsuit, the less people know about your assets, the better off you are. It is no coincidence that people without significant assets do not get sued nearly as often as those who are perceived as having "deep pockets." Individuals with any assets at all should anticipate the possibility of being sued during their lifetime. This is the very reason many people incorporate their business activities.

From the Reno Gazette Journal, Monday, April 29, 1991:

SILVER STATE'S REGULATIONS ALLOW FOR 'HIDDEN' FIRMS

"Taking advantage of a new Nevada law, some Silver State corporations now are able to withhold from the public the location of their principal offices.

"But a top official in Nevada's Secretary of State's office said she believes the new law isn't causing problems, although the number of hidden corporate sites is unknown.

"Under the previous regulation, corporate papers available to the public were required to list the location of a corporation's principal office. That's not required under the new rule, which mandates only that a corporation list the address of its Nevada resident agent.

"The updated law requires that the resident agent keep a record of the corporation's principal office address. But there's no requirement that a resident agent reveal a corporate office site, except under court order.

"However, corporate directors must list their names and addresses - information that sometimes can be used as a clue to the area a principal office is located, said Cyndy Woodgate, deputy secretary of state.

"Nevada's corporation law remains liberal, and finding a corporation "is no easier than it was before," she said. That's partly because a Nevada corporation doesn't necessarily have to conduct business, and its address can be listed as a post office box.

"The rule changes were approved by the 1991 Legislature."

FRIVOLOUS LAWSUITS
ARE EXPECTED AND
PLANNED FOR BY COMPANIES
ACROSS THE COUNTRY.
BECAUSE IT IS WIDELY
RECOGNIZED THAT
INSURANCE COMPANIES
REGULARLY SETTLE CLAIMS -
EVEN FRIVOLOUS AND
UNSUBSTANTIATED CLAIMS -
RATHER THAN DEAL WITH
THE EXPENSE OF, OR RISK
THE DECISION OF THE
COURT, WE HAVE BECOME A
SUIT-HAPPY SOCIETY.

To protect your assets from the disturbing trend toward frivolous lawsuits, you need a specific plan of action that isolates your assets from yourself. If someone has no reason to believe that you have access to a million dollars, it is not likely that someone would pursue a million-dollar judgment against you. If you keep your assets private, you will greatly reduce your chances of being sued. Certainly no attorney would work on a contingency against you unless they see some way of getting paid. Suing poor people has never made an attorney rich.

The Nevada corporation offers many ways to protect your privacy as a stockholder. To appreciate how this is possible, it is necessary to understand that there are essentially five ways to identify the stockholders of a corporation:

1. Call the Secretary of State's office (or it's equivalent) where the corporation was formed. In some states, the Secretary of State requires that a list of stockholders, including their capital contribution and the value of their stock be on file. Often, this information is available over the telephone.

2. Obtain a copy of the corporation's tax return in that state. Every state that has a corporate income tax or franchise tax requires that the return be filed on a state-approved form. It is common for the state income tax return to require a list of stockholders, (particularly when that state also has a personal income tax.) This is difficult to get over the phone, but can be accessed, depending upon the state's policy, either through the mail to any individual who asks, or to anyone who has a subpoena for the record.

3. The corporation's resident agent in that state is required to have information on file regarding the ownership of stock. Usually, this means that the corporation is required to provide the resident agent with a copy of the stock ledger for file. This is not available to just anyone, but a subpoena will have immediate access to it.

4. The corporation itself maintains the original of the stock ledger. This ledger contains all the information regarding the amount, type and value of stock owned by each stockholder. A subpoena can get to any corporate record.

5. The corporate officers or directors can be deposed under oath about their direct knowledge of the ownership of the corporation.

It can be difficult or impossible to find out who the stockholders are of a Nevada corporation using any of the methods described above. Let's discuss each of these avenues individually.

First, the only filing required of a Nevada corporation to the Secretary of State is an annual list of officers and directors. This list represents the only information that the Secretary of State will have regarding the ownership and management of the corporation. This list is due on the 1st day of the 2nd month after incorporation, and annually after that.

Although there is room on this list for many names, only five lines need to be filled out. The required offices that the Secretary of State must have on file include the president, the secretary, the treasurer, at least one director, and resident agent. The most significant thing about that is the fact that one person may serve in all of those capacities, and is not required to be a stockholder.

If someone calls the Secretary of State in Nevada and requests information on a corporation, they will learn several things. They will learn whether or not the corporation is in good standing with the state. They will learn the names of the president, secretary, treasurer, and director (as well as any additional officers which may have been reported, such as vice-president and/or additional directors). They may learn that all of those positions are filled by the same individual, which usually suggests a one-man corporation, or by several different individuals. They may discover that the officers and directors appear to have residency in the US, or that conversely, they appear to be citizens of a foreign country. They have also discovered who the resident agent is, but we'll get to that later.

What they could not learn is significant:

- The Secretary of State could not reveal information regarding whom the stockholders are, or even how many exist, or how much stock is issued;

- The Secretary of State could not tell what assets the corporation owned, how much capitalization exists, or what their value was, and;

- The Secretary of State could not say if the officers and directors had changed since the last list was filed, since filing the list is only required once a year.

The corporation could conceivably call another meeting the following September and put the original officers and directors back into office in time for the next annual filing. So, you have no guarantee that the names you found have any relevance to the current situation.

Because Nevada has no corporate income tax, or the inherent bureaucracy that such a tax creates, there are no state corporate tax returns to look at. The only document the Department of Taxation has, is a filing form for the Nevada Business License Tax, which is not immediately available as a public record, and if it were it would only disclose the number of hours worked by employees of the company.

Let's assume the resident agent for the corporate records has been subpoenaed for the records it has in its possession relating to this particular corporation. The Nevada resident agent is not required to have a copy of the actual stock ledger on file as is required in most states, instead it is merely required to have a statement that provides the name and address of the person who has the stock ledger in their possession. The actual stock ledger could be in Sri Lanka, Swaziland, or Senegal.

The law does not require the stock ledger to be in Nevada at any time. If the corporation so desired, it could force a potential litigant to spend a lot of time and money to pursue that information. As a creditor, you would have to be asking yourself how much trouble this is all worth.

The corporate secretary is another potential source of stockholder information. This person has no legal obligation to you to reveal any information at all about the stockholders of the corporation. In fact, the corporate secretary is not required, or even allowed, to provide that information even to another shareholder of the company unless the shareholder controls enough voting power to force the issue.

NRS 78.257 provides that any stockholder who owns at least 15% of the issued shares of a corporation has a right to inspect all books and records, but must bear the costs of such an inspection. Minority shareholders with less than 15% ownership do not enjoy this right.

IF THE LIST OF OFFICERS AND DIRECTORS WAS FILED, FOR INSTANCE, ON OCTOBER 1ST, IT ONLY REPRESENTS THE OFFICERS AND DIRECTORS OF THE CORPORATION ON THAT DATE. IT IS THEORETICALLY POSSIBLE THAT THE CORPORATION HAD A MEETING ON OCTOBER 2ND, WHERE NEW OFFICERS AND DIRECTORS WERE ELECTED. THE NEW OFFICERS AND DIRECTORS WOULD NOT BE ON PUBLIC RECORD FOR A YEAR, IF THEN.

THE RIGHT FOR JUDGMENT CREDITORS TO ACCESS A CORPORATION'S STOCK LEDGER WAS REMOVED BY THE NEVADA LEGISLATURE IN 1993.

In essence, a potential judgment creditor does not seem to have the ability to access corporate records or documents to suit his interest, unless he is a stockholder, or a criminal investigation warrants it. If a potential creditor attempts to obtain and use these corporate records for any interest other than a shareholder's, he could face civil penalties.

Beyond those limitations, ultimately the stock of the Nevada corporation may have been issued as bearer shares. This means that they may be issued and recorded on the stock ledger as having been written to the "bearer" of the certificate. Perhaps the shares were first issued to the trustee of a voting trust, or care of an attorney, who exercises attorney/client privilege. In any event, the corporate secretary may have no direct knowledge regarding who currently possesses those shares.

BEARER SHARES

Nevada is the only state that allows corporations to issue stock to the "bearer," which is very much like writing a check to "cash." The person who controls the bearer certificates, or has the shares in their possession, technically has the power to redeem those shares as the beneficial owner. As a negotiable instrument, it may be difficult to determine how many times the stock has changed hands since it was first issued.

The use of "bearer shares" to own and control a Nevada corporation has been touted in seminars, newspaper advertising, and promotional brochures of many Nevada-based incorporating companies. Bearer shares are generally considered to be an attractive solution for individuals who desire to own or control assets or business activities, while maintaining a high degree of financial privacy. It is true that privacy can be accomplished through bearer share ownership, however there are many issues which are broadly misunderstood regarding the use of bearer shares.

How Bearer Shares Are Allowed

Most states base their corporate law extensively on the Revised Model Business Corporation Act as developed by the Committee on Corporate Laws of the American Bar Association. It should surprise no one, then, that there are amazing similarities in the Corporation Codes of the various states. However, because the Model Act has been refined and modified over time, and because of the stubborn independence of the various states not to conform entirely to the Model Act, each state has developed its own eccentricities that set it apart from the others.

In Nevada's case, one area in which it separates its Corporation Code from the Model Act is in the information required on the stock certificate of a corporation. Under the Model Act, for instance, a stock certificate is required to contain: 1) the name of the issuing corporation and the state under which it is organized; 2) the name of the person to whom the stock is issued; and 3) the number and class of shares and the designation of the series, if any, the certificate represents.

THE MODEL CORPORATION ACT DOES NOT CONTEMPLATE OR ALLOW THE USE OF SHARES ISSUED TO BEARER.

The Nevada Revised Statutes (NRS) reads differently, and by omission of the language of the Model Act, creates an opportunity to issue shares of a Nevada corporation to "The Bearer". NRS 78.235 (1) reads in part as follows: *"every stockholder is entitled to have a certificate, signed by officers or agents designated by the corporation for the purpose, certifying the number of shares owned by him in the corporation."*

In other words Nevada law specifically only requires two things: 1) the name of the corporation, and; 2) the number of shares represented by the certificate. According to an attorney with the Nevada Attorney General's office assigned to the Nevada Secretary of

State's office, Nevada is the only state with this language. Since the name of the shareholder is not specifically required on the certificate, there has been broad use and acceptance of bearer shares in the State of Nevada for many years.

Even so, officials with Nevada agencies such as the Attorney General's office, the Securities Division and Corporation Division of the Secretary of State's office are reluctant to take an official position one way or the other on bearer shares. There are no Attorney General's Opinions on this issue, and surprisingly, there is absolutely no case law on the subject. The most positive affirmation I have received on the viability of bearer shares came from Mr. John Cunningham, an attorney with the Securities Division who confirmed that bearer shares could be used as long as the corporation was not required to qualify for a public offering.

Why Bearer Shares Are Used

There are two clear reasons why a corporation would issue bearer shares: First, as a tool to achieve total privacy in corporate ownership due to the fact that true ownership is extremely difficult to determine, and; Second, as a vehicle to provide for convenient transfer of ownership interests. Let's discuss these individually.

PRIVACY

There are only two tangible sources of information on ownership of a Nevada corporation: the stock certificate, and; the stock ledger. The stock ledger has its own legal requirements under Nevada law. The ledger must contain, in alphabetical order, the names of the stockholders, their residence address, and the number of shares owned by each. This list must be revised annually, and would be a significant document for a legal adversary to obtain.

However, Nevada law provides a statutory barrier to getting and using information on the stock ledger that includes its own penalties. As discussed above, NRS 78.257 provides that any stockholder who owns at least 15% of the issued shares of a corporation has a right to inspect all books and records upon five days notice, but must bear the costs of such an inspection. But subsection 3 of that statute states that:

> *"Any stockholder **or other person** exercising (these rights) who uses or attempts to use information, documents, records or other data obtained from the corporation, for any **purpose not related to the stockholder's interest in the corporation as a stockholder, is guilty of a gross misdemeanor."** (Emphasis added.)*

In other words, the penalty for using corporate information for any other purpose than to have a stockholder defend or demonstrate his or her interest in the corporation is up to one year in the county jail and up to a $2,000.00 fine. Clearly, a non-shareholder in a Nevada corporation has no legal right or authority whatsoever to view the stock ledger. (However, the burden of proof, in the cases of Roney v. Buckland, 4 Nev 557 (1868) and Wayman v. Torreyson, 4 Nev 619 (1868), falls on the corporation to prove improper motivation for such a request.

With those protections in place, the only other tangible source of ownership information is found on the stock certificate itself. A bearer certificate, even if obtained, could only be considered circumstantial.

Individuals who attempt to use bearer shares should exercise extreme caution to avoid the potential for civil or criminal liability. When in the discovery phase of litigation, there is no guarantee that the court will not require full disclosure of stock ownership. In a criminal case, a grand jury may do likewise, although materials submitted to a grand jury are confidential unless presented in support of a criminal indictment.

Examples of individuals who might use bearer shares include:

- Persons contractually obliged not to compete in a particular business. Such persons may establish a Nevada corporation issuing bearer shares to enter into that market, recognizing the possibility of civil litigation if their employer or former employer learns of their indirect involvement.

- Persons engaged in contested divorce or family support proceedings. Once a court of proper jurisdiction establishes alimony or child support requirements, the person making such payments might wish to establish a Nevada corporation issuing bearer shares to avoid addition support appeals from future income.

- Persons who wish to maintain a low profile in their business dealings. Many wealthy and prominent people want to avoid having their names associated with high-profile investments. Bearer shares are an ideal form of ownership for such individuals

- Persons who wish (or may need) to remain anonymous to close a business deal. When personal relationships could otherwise jeopardize profitable business dealings, it may be possible to use a corporation with bearer ownership to close the deal. I know of a wealthy dentist who wanted to buy a condominium complex he was living in. Unfortunately, he had developed a poor relationship with several of the other owners in the complex, and disliked him so much they refused to sell. Along came a Nevada corporation, which made an offer slightly less than the dentist's and the deal closed quickly. The more the dentist complained about the "low-ball" offer, the more the others wanted to sell.

TRANSFER OF OWNERSHIP

Most of the confusion surrounding bearer shares has to deal with the issue of transfer of ownership. A bearer instrument is negotiated differently than an instrument made payable to order. If an instrument is made payable to the order of John Doe, it is negotiated by delivery with any necessary endorsement. If an instrument is made payable to bearer, it is negotiated by delivery. It is commonly believed that bearer shares allow you to transfer ownership of a Nevada corporation in complete privacy, without any adverse impact. Three important facts must be established on this topic:

> **1. A stock certificate is not stock itself.** The stockholder may own the stock with or without the stock certificate. The Nevada Attorney General has published a formal opinion on this subject (AGO38). The certificate is merely

a piece of paper that indicates ownership. Because Nevada does not require corporations to issue certificates at all, it would be foolish to assume that possession of the certificate equals ownership of the shares.

2. The Nevada Revised Statutes (78.240) specifically state that shares of stock are personal property. So, all rules, regulations, and applicable taxes that would otherwise apply to transfers of personal property will also apply to transfers of bearer shares. Bearer share certificates, like personal property, may be stolen, borrowed, obtained under false pretenses, lost, copied, sold, inherited, bought, willed, etc. My car is personal property also. On occasion I have lent my car to a friend. Simply because he was in possession of my car during that time did not mean he was the owner.

3. Nevada case law requires a transfer of stock to be registered upon the corporation's books before the transfer is valid against the corporation. This is done to protect corporate officers in determining ownership of and the right to vote corporate shares. (61 Nev. 431, 132 P.2d 605. (1942))

So, can bearer shares be used to transfer ownership of a Nevada corporation? Absolutely. But the new owner must register his ownership with the corporation before the corporation can grant ownership rights, including dividends. And, the transfer may trigger other things, like federal gift and estate or capital gains taxes.

This issue is widely misunderstood. I recall attending a seminar on corporate strategies in Carson City several years ago where the founder of a large incorporating company suggested that he could legally avoid disclosing his ownership of corporate stock, even if he were called to testify in court under oath. His solution was to have the stock issued to bearer, and give the stock certificate to someone seated next to him immediately prior to being called to the stand. Then, he said, he could testify that he did not legally own the stock, and upon returning to his seat receive the certificate back.

Over one hundred people were in attendance at that seminar, and heard an "expert" in the field describe how to perjure oneself. Perhaps he did not know the three important rules outlined above. I should not be surprised, because none of the real experts contacted by my office in preparation for this article could offer anything more than a personal opinion on how bearer shares are handled.

> THE FACT THAT THERE IS SO LITTLE PUBLISHED OR KNOWN ON THE ISSUE OF BEARER SHARES COULD BE INTERPRETED AS UNSETTLING EVIDENCE THAT WE ARE WANDERING IN THE "GREAT UNKNOWN". BUT KEEP IN MIND THAT THERE IS NO STATUTE THAT DISALLOWS ITS USE, AND NO CASE LAW THAT INVALIDATES IT.

Recently, I called six prominent Nevada attorneys, including the head of the business law section of the Nevada State Bar, with specialties ranging from business law and contracts, to litigation and bankruptcy, and asked them what they could tell me about bearer shares. No one admitted any knowledge of bearer shares, besides the confirmation that they were used. Three attorneys in the Nevada Attorney General's office claimed only a passing acquaintance with bearer shares. The head of the Securities Division and three other administrators in the Secretary of State's office could offer us nothing.

How to Issue Bearer Shares

If a corporation chooses to issue bear shares, I believe the following formula can be effective:

Step One. Hire a reputable attorney who understands the need for strategic planning. If the attorney can form the corporation in Nevada directly, let him do it. If an incorporating company/resident agency must be used, let the attorney make all necessary arrangements and communications.

Step Two. Have the attorney hire nominee officers and directors who have no personal contact with the shareholders, but receive all instructions through the attorney. This way the testimony of officers and directors relative to their personal knowledge of corporate ownership is limited.

Step Three. In the organizational meeting of the corporation, the nominee officers and directors issue stock certificates to "bearer" in increments provided in instructions from the attorney. In the stock ledger, the transaction is recorded with the stock being issued "in care of" the attorney.

Step Four. The stock certificates and stock ledger are forwarded to the office of the attorney. The certificates are held in file in the attorney's office. The stock ledger may also be held in the attorney's office, or may be transferred to any location in the world. The attorney provides the corporation's Resident Agent with the name and mailing address of the individual who holds and maintains the stock ledger.

Step Five. All instructions from the shareholders to the corporate officers and directors are communicated by the attorney. All communications between the shareholders and the attorney represent privileged information.

As a defense against revealing corporate ownership in civil litigation, this can be a very effective strategy. Nevertheless, it may not be absolutely bullet-proof. When a civil case is in the discovery phase there is no guarantee that the court will not require the attorney to provide information over his objections. It is not as likely that this information would be allowed in the trial itself, but you may be defeated in your attempt to preserve absolute privacy.

On the other hand, I asked a partner in a prominent Southern California law firm that frequently utilizes the strategy outlined above concerning their experience in handling information requests for corporate ownership. "Some lawyers don't know what they are doing and simply comply with every request," I was told, "but we simply object on basis of privileged information and attorney/client work product, and we've never been forced to produce anything."

INFORMATION SHARING - THE IRS

From the Reno Gazette-Journal, April 29, 1991:

MILLER CLOSES RECORDS TO IRS

"Hands off: Governor says federal agency can't use state computers to find tax cheats.

"Carson City Gov. Bob Miller isn't going to let the IRS use state computers to track tax-delinquent Nevadans.

"Miller said Tuesday that he refused to open up employment, motor vehicle and other records to the IRS because there is too great a potential for abuse of peoples right to privacy.

AS YOU CAN SEE, IF IT IS TOTAL FINANCIAL PRIVACY YOU ARE AFTER, NEVADA IS THE ONLY STATE TO CONSIDER FOR INCORPORATING. IF YOU KNOW WHAT THE LAW ALLOWS YOU TO DO, AND HOW TO STRUCTURE YOUR AFFAIRS, IT CAN BE VIRTUALLY IMPOSSIBLE TO UNCOVER THE OWNERSHIP IN A NEVADA CORPORATION.

"He gave examples of IRS undercover operations into Las Vegas bookmaking and a Reno-area crackdown on reporting casino dealers tip earnings.

"'The IRS, to date, hasn't treated us the same way its treated residents of other states,' Miller said.

"Millers announcement during a Las Vegas news conference came a week after the IRS proposal surfaced. Since then, Millers Carson office has received about 70 phone calls from irate people.

"'None of them was in favor of agreeing with the IRS,' said spokesman Mike Campbell.

"In Washington D.C., Sen. Harry Reid, D-Nev., was pleased. 'Gov. Millers decision was the right one,' Reid said, 'It puts the people of the state first, rather than the IRS.'

"Reid and Sen. Richard Bryan and Rep. James Bilbray, both D-Nev., still await word on a meeting they've requested this week with the IRS commissioner on IRS activities in Nevada.

"Millers order directed Perry Comeaux, director of the state Department of Taxation, to notify the IRS office in southern Nevada that state records will not be shared.

"'I told them we weren't going to do anything to expand any cooperative effort with the Internal Revenue Service at this time,' Comeaux said.

Nevada has repeatedly denied the access of the Internal Revenue Service to these records, and is the only state that does not comply with IRS requests for information. As recently as July of 1991, Nevada's Governor ordered the directors of the state Department of Taxation and other agencies to seal state records from the Internal Revenue Service.

We live in the age of the electronic superhighway. Information about each of us is bought and sold every day by list brokers, advertising agencies, demographers, and statisticians. Computer links between government agencies make entire databases available for convenient cross-checking of vital data. This is an alarming trend. Those who value their privacy should know of the following aspects of Nevada corporations.

Every state in the United States, with the singular exception of Nevada, has an information sharing agreement with the Internal Revenue Service. California residents, for instance, who file either individual or corporate state income tax returns, will have their financial information checked against their federal return without their knowledge. States have agreed to this, for the most part, because the sharing agreements allow the states to have access to IRS records to verify state personal and business tax returns.

INFORMATION SHARING - SERVICE BUREAUS

There are a large number of companies, such as Dun & Bradstreet, which maintain computer links with the various governmental offices across the country in order to access and sell commercially information on companies contained in each state's database. All of the information that each Secretary of State collects is readily accessible through this channel, including the officers, directors, and stockholders, if the state records provide it - complete with mailing addresses.

Also available in some instances is detailed information on company revenues and net worth. The interest these companies have in this information is, of course, to provide targeted mailing lists to anyone who is willing to pay for it.

Nevada offers a computer link as well, but the only information it can provide is that which the Secretary of State already collects - and we have already discussed how limited that is. The names of stockholders are not available from the Secretary of State of Nevada, because the office does not collect that information. Neither do they collect financial information on Nevada corporations.

MANAGEMENT & CONTROL ISSUES

Nevada allows corporations a great deal of flexibility in organizing its ownership interests to fit the needs of that particular business. The Nevada corporation may issue different classes of capital stock, and assign different series within each class. The owners of any one of the classes or series of stock may be assigned different rights and privileges.

There may be several classes of common stock and several classes of preferred stock, each with specific rights described in the articles of incorporation. The preferred stock is differentiated from common stock by the fact that it has the first right to receive a distribution upon the liquidation of the corporation. When several classes of preferred stock are present, they may be ranked in order of preference.

If the articles of incorporation permit, the board of directors may divide a class of preferred stock, without the approval of the stockholders, into a series with it's own assigned rights. The effect of this is that the board of directors can tailor series of shares to be issued in a special circumstance without the costs and delays of conducting a special meeting of the stockholders to authorize a new class of stock. The more stockholders a corporation has, the more this convenience is appreciated.

Minimum Capital Requirement.

Nevada Corporation Code does not place any requirement that any minimum amount be invested in a corporation. If, however, the corporation loans out a disproportionate amount of its funds, the IRS may reclassify the loans as stock purchases by determining that the corporation is undercapitalized.

Shareholder Rights to Privacy.

Concerning the rights of a minority shareholder to inspect financial books and records, the Nevada Revised Statutes [78.257] provides that any shareholder who owns at least 15% of the issued stock of a corporation has a right to inspect all books and records, but must bear the costs of such an inspection. The following points are made:

1. If a stockholder holding less than 15% of the issued stock is denied the right of inspection, then certainly third parties can be denied inspection of corporate records, unless the courts grant access to the records under subpoena.

2. Clearly the statutory intent of this access is for the interest of the shareholders, not for any third party. Anyone who obtains information from the corporation books and records for "any purpose not related to the stockholder's interest" commits a crime. That is rather good protection.

Approval required on sale of assets.

Nevada Corporation Code requires that the shareholders approve the sale of all of the assets of the corporation. Approval takes a majority of the vote of shareholders that have voting rights, unless the articles of incorporation require a larger portion of the outstanding shares. In the dissolution of the corporation, any proceeds not required to pay existing debt is distributed to shareholders, and their shares are then canceled.

THE NEVADA SECRETARY OF STATE'S OFFICE

This section will describe the process of incorporating in Nevada, as well as providing you with a general background on the variety of services and associated fees for the other services provided by the Corporation Division of the Secretary of State's office.

Name Availability & Reservation

The first step in forming a corporation is in selecting a name for the corporation. The name you choose should be an asset to the company, since most of your advertising and public relations will likely revolve around it. It should tell people what the company does, should be consistent with the image you want to convey, and should be easy to remember and pronounce.

The Secretary of State's office can tell you whether or not the name you have selected is available for use. Nevada's Corporation Code requires that the name of a corporation cannot be "deceptively similar" to the name of any other corporation or limited partnership authorized to conduct business in the state.

> *To reserve a corporate name, log into the Secretary of State's web site, where you can do a preliminary name search and reserve the corporate name online. The web address is: http://sos.state.nv.us/comm_rec/index.htm*

YOU COULDN'T INCORPORATE A RESTAURANT AS MCDONNALS HAMBURGERS, INC., SINCE THAT WOULD BE UNFAIR TO THE ORIGINAL MCDONALDS. THIS RESTRICTION IS INTENDED TO PROTECT THE RIGHTS TO CORPORATE NAMES, PROTECT THE PUBLIC FROM FRAUD AND DECEPTION, AND PREVENT UNNECESSARY LITIGATION.

Under Nevada law, the similarity of the corporate names "Peoples Furniture Exchange, Inc." and "Peoples Furniture Company, Inc." is not enough for the Secretary of State to refuse to file the second corporation (Nevada Attorney General's Opinion A-52, 2-15-1940). The two corporations must be given names that distinguish them from any other company. If a name is determined to be too similar to that of another corporation, the Secretary of State will only agree to file that corporation if a written consent to the use of that name by the other company accompanies the articles of incorporation. The Secretary of State has complete discretion in deciding whether such a similarity exists, and his/her decision may only be reviewed in court.

Corporations cannot gain the right to exclusive use of geographical words in corporate names, unless the words themselves have acquired a meaning in the mind of the public associated with the business of the corporation. (Attorney General's Opinion 50, 4-26-1951) So, Nevaco Trading Corporation would be considered a valid name, even though

Nevada Trading Corporation already exists, but Trading Corporation and Trading Corporation of Nevada are deceptively similar.

In order to show that the company is a corporation, a number of designations may be included in the name; e.g., Corporation, Corp., Incorporated, Inc., Limited, Ltd., etc. These designations are not required to be part of the name of the corporation unless without the designation the name would sound like the name of a natural person. For example, a corporation cannot be called simply "John Doe," but can be called "John Doe, Inc."

The use of the specified designations should be strongly encouraged. In fairness to others who may conduct business with the corporation, when a designation is used by the company, the public is aware of the limitation on the liability of the individuals who may represent the corporation.

There are also words that must have prior clearance from other state agencies before they can be used to name your corporation. Among these words are:

- Accident,
- Appraisers,
- Assurance,
- Banco,
- Banking,
- Bonding,
- Casualty,
- College,
- Engineer,
- Engineering,
- Fire,
- Gaming,
- Guarantee,
- Guaranty,
- Indemnity,
- Insurance,
- Investor,
- Liability,
- Life,
- Loan,
- Mutual,
- Protection,
- Purchasing Group,
- Realtor,
- Reassurance,
- Reinsurance,
- Risk,
- Risk Retention Group,
- Savings,
- Surety,
- Trust,
- Underwriter,
- University,
- Variable,
- Warranty,

While it doesn't cost anything to check with the Secretary of State to see if a name is available for use, for a $20 fee, they will reserve the rights to any specific corporate name that they determine to be available for your use and your use alone. This reservation is good for ninety days, and may be renewed if necessary.

If you're in business now, or are planning to go into business soon, you should either reserve the name you want to use to prevent another company form using your name on that state's records, or incorporate under that name now. If you plan to do business in a number of states, the chances are greater that one of the states will have a conflict with the name you would like to use. Only by checking and rechecking can you insure that your chosen name is available for use. Many states may allow you to register the name of your foreign corporations without qualifying it to do business in that state, so remember to ask if that service is available.

Status

A corporation must be maintained by filing the annual list and officers and directors, and paying the annual $85 fee. If the corporation does not follow this procedure and is between sixty and two-hundred seventy days late, it lapses into "delinquent status." A delinquent corporation may be brought current any time during this period by paying an additional $15 fee. The Secretary of State will only notify the resident agent in writing of a delinquency or revocation of corporate charter, not the directors, officers, or shareholders.

If the corporation has not been brought current within nine months, the corporate charter will be revoked by the state. A corporation that has been revoked may be reinstated any time within five years, by paying all of the fees that would have applied during the period of revocation and an additional $50 penalty.

The catch is, that once your corporation has been revoked, your corporate name is no longer reserved by the Secretary of State, and someone else can incorporate under your name. Also, any action taken during the period of revocation is outside the protection of the corporate veil.

Certificate of Good Standing

Upon request, the Secretary of State will issue a "Certificate of Good Standing" to any corporation that is current in its filings and fees with the state. This certificate costs $15, and validates that the corporation was in good standing as of the date the certificate is issued.

Anytime that you qualify a Nevada corporation to do business in another state, you are required to provide to that state a Certificate of Good Standing from the Secretary of State's office. Banks also will require a Certificate of Good Standing in many instances, especially when applying for corporate credit or loans.

Customer Service

The Nevada Secretary of State's office has been traditionally extremely responsive to the needs of Nevada corporations. The number of corporations filed with the State in recent years has forced some limits on their ability to respond to some requests. Frankly, in many respects the Secretary of State's office has become bureaucratic to a degree you might expect of a larger state.

Even so, they continually make changes to improve. In the 1991 Nevada Legislature, the Secretary of State petitioned for several new changes that continue to put the office in the forefront of existing customer service technology.

The Secretary of State now allows for a 24-hour rush for any filing of corporate status. The 24-hour rush includes filing articles of incorporation, amendments or mergers, corporate searches, or reinstatements. If you need to use this service, be aware that the Secretary of State's office reserves the right to use all 24 hours of the window they provide.

Small Corporate Offering Registration (SCOR)

Nevada has recently adopted the Small Corporate Offering Registration Form, (SCOR Form U-7) which allows a business to reach capital through a public offering of up to $1 million every twelve months. The SCOR program was developed by the North American Securities Administrators Association (NASAA) in cooperation with the Securities and Exchange Commission and the American Bar Association, and contemplates an exemption from federal registration by virtue of Rule 504 of Regulation D of the federal securities code.

This type of registration has been made available in 34 states across the country. The program allows easier access to public capital at a lower cost. The principal innovation of this program is the creation of the simplified form with a question-and-answer format that permits an officer of a corporation to fill in the blanks, file it with a state securities administration, and, upon approval, use it as a disclosure document in a public offering. One of the notable features of this program is the requirement that shares be sold at a minimum of $5 per share to avoid the common pitfalls of a penny stock offering. A SCOR offering is far less expensive than a regular initial private offering (IPO), and you don't need a high-paid underwriter.

A SCOR filing may be easier than a fully registered stock offering, but it is not necessarily a breeze to accomplish. It can still be a challenging process involving the preparation of necessary forms and documents, getting state approval for the offering, selling the stock, and dealing with the administrative tasks of having additional investors. As a rule of thumb, a SCOR offering should take at least three to six months to complete.

The U-7 application is designed in a question and answer format, and asks for information on the company's history, directors and officers, risk factors, assets, capitalization, use of proceeds and plans for distribution. There are about 250 questions in all. In addition, the application requires that the articles of incorporation, bylaws, and audited financial statement be submitted. Even then, expect to resubmit the application several times until it's format is approved.

Several methods can be used to sell the shares, including direct mail, telemarketing, commercial advertisement, networking, and sales presentations. As an alternative, the corporation could engage an underwriter or bank, which usually charge a 10 to 15 percent fee.

WYOMING

Following Nevada's successful example, the Wyoming Legislature passed a new set of corporate statutes in 1989 that revolutionized their corporation laws. While the total number of corporations formed in Wyoming is small in comparison to other corporate havens, Wyoming is experience tremendous growth as more people learn of Wyoming's benefits.

In an effort to promote economic growth and diversification, Wyoming is making its business climate as attractive and user-friendly as possible. The law, called the Wyoming Business Corporation Act, is unique in many key areas and creates corporate possibilities that are simply not available elsewhere. Wyoming offers the following advantages as a corporate haven:

1. Wyoming has **no state corporate income tax**.

2. Wyoming has **no tax on corporate shares**.

3. Wyoming has **no franchise tax**.

4. The annual fees are based on the value of corporate assets that are **physically located in Wyoming**, not on assets located elsewhere.

5. **One person** may be all required corporate officers and directors.

6. Stockholders are **not revealed** to the State.

7. No annual report is required until the anniversary of the incorporation date.

8. The articles of incorporation may provide for **unlimited stock** without a requirement for stating par value.

9. Wyoming statute has provisions for **"bearer scrip"** which can be used when stockholders capitalize the corporation in increments less than the par value of the stock.

10. Wyoming allows for **nominee shareholders**.

11. Share certificates are not required.

12. There is no minimum capital requirement.

13. Meetings may be held anywhere in the world.

14. Corporate officers, directors, employees and agents are statutorily indemnified from personal liability associated with their corporate activity.

15. Additional indemnification is allowed even after suit is filed by a potential judgment creditor.

16. Wyoming has a continuance procedure, which allows a corporation formed in another state to change it's domicile to Wyoming while maintaining its corporate history.

The result of these advantages is a corporation product that demands strong consideration from those looking for a legitimate, low-key U.S. corporate haven. Wyoming joins Nevada as one of the premier incorporation centers in the United States, easily surpassing Delaware in the race to provide ease of use, liability protection, financial privacy and tax savings.

UNLIMITED AUTHORIZED SHARES

Many states base the amount of the fee required to file articles of incorporation on the dollar value of the shares the corporation is authorized to issue. Accordingly, a corporation with any combination of a large number of authorized shares or with a high par value is likely to pay a much higher fee to incorporate. Additionally, the annual maintenance fee is often based on the same figure, resulting in expensive annual maintenance costs.

> A LAW FIRM LOCATED IN NEW YORK USES WYOMING CORPORATIONS FOR CLIENTS THAT ARE ANTICIPATING A FULL-SCALE PUBLIC OFFERING IN COMING YEARS. THIS ALLOWS THE CORPORATION TO PROVIDE FOR THE NUMBER OF SHARES NECESSARY FOR A PUBLIC OFFERING, AT AN APPROPRIATE PAR VALUE, WITHOUT PAYING EXORBITANT STATE FEES THAT ARE BASED ON TOTAL CAPITALIZATION FOR THE PRIVILEGE.

For example, a Nevada corporation with 20,000,000 shares of No Par Value stock would have to pay $8,975 to file the Articles of Incorporation. The filing fee for a Nevada corporation with 10,000,000 shares of $.50 par value will be $2,225.

A Wyoming corporation, on the other hand, may state in its Articles of Incorporation that it is authorized to issued an unlimited number of shares at either a specific par value or no par value. Yet, there are no additional fees from the State to provide for this.

CONTINUANCE: IMPORTING CORPORATIONS

If a foreign corporation decides to domesticate, it either creates a new corporate entity in that state or it adds additional domiciles. Continuance, however, is the process by which Wyoming creates the legal fiction that the corporation has always maintained its domicile in Wyoming. A new corporation is not created, it simply acts as if it had always been a Wyoming company.

> *Wyoming is one of only two states that provides for true continuance in its corporate laws. Many states provide for "domestication," but that is not quite the same thing.*

Corporations can find the continuance very useful in several circumstances:

- To take advantage of Wyoming's favorable tax and business environment;

- To change the geographical location of the corporate domicile to meet the needs of a changing business climate;

- To avoid hostile government action by another state, such as confiscation and expropriation;

- To permit the management to take advantage of Wyoming's statutory regulations on issues such as takeovers, buy-outs, mergers, or hostile shareholder actions; or,

- To obtain favorable consideration on Wyoming public works contracts, where resident corporation receive preferential treatment.

PIERCING THE CORPORATE VEIL

Wyoming has well established criteria concerning the piercing of the corporate veil. In Miles v. CEC Homes, Inc. (753 P.2d 1021, 1023-1024), the courts determined that the following factors must be considered when determining if the corporate veil is to be pierced:

- Commingling of funds and other assets, or the failure to segregate funds of separate entities, and the unauthorized diversion of corporate assets.

- Treatment by an individual of the assets of a corporation as his own.

- Failure to obtain authority to issue or subscribe to shares.

- The holding out by an individual that he is personally liable for the corporate debts.

- Failure to maintain minutes or adequate corporate records.

- Failure to adequately capitalize the corporation.

- Absence of corporate assets.

- The disregard of legal formalities and the failure to maintain arms-length transactions among related entities.

- Contracting with another party with the intent to avoid performance by use of a corporation as subterfuge for illegal transactions.

> **WHERE FRAUD IS NOT PRESENT, A WYOMING CORPORATION THAT DOES NOT COMMINGLE FUNDS AND MAINTAINS SOME FORM OF CORPORATE FORMALITIES, INCLUDING HOLDING MEETINGS OF SHAREHOLDERS AND DIRECTORS, WILL NOT BE PIERCED.**

PRIVACY

Shareholders of Wyoming corporations are not disclosed on any public documents. This assures a strong measure of shareholder privacy. Nevertheless, "bearer shares" are not provided for under the Wyoming Corporation Act.

There are, however, provisions of the Wyoming Act that allows for shares held by nominee shareholders, or by voting trusts. If a nominee shareholder is used, the name of the nominee must appear in the stock ledger of the corporation, but the beneficial owner of the corporation is not revealed.

Bearer Scrip: Anonymous Ownership

While "bearer shares" are not allowed under Wyoming law, the statute does provide for another type of bearer instrument, of which very little is known by even the most sophisticated in the legal community. That instrument is called "bearer scrip, and is provided for in the revised Model Business Corporation Act of 1984, as well as Section 17-16-604 of the Wyoming Business Corporation Act, which reads:

> *"A corporation may issue scrip in registered or bearer form entitling the holder to receive a full share upon surrendering enough scrip to equal a full share." Section 17-16-604 of the Wyoming Business Corporation Act.*

Scrip was originally intended as a means of dealing with fractional shares that can be created when a corporation splits its stock. It is intended, as the Wyoming law suggests, that the scrip be exchanged for full shares when there is enough scrip available to do so. However, there is no requirement that the scrip be exchanged. That can only be done by the scrip holder through the process of redemption of the scrip.

WYOMING EVEN ALLOWS THE BEARER SCRIP HOLDER THE RIGHT TO VOTE, TO RECEIVE DIVIDENDS, AND TO PARTICIPATE IN THE ASSETS OF THE CORPORATION UPON LIQUIDATION, IF THE SCRIP SPECIFICALLY PROVIDES FOR IT. IN OTHER WORDS, SCRIP HOLDERS ARE TREATED AS STOCK HOLDERS UNDER WYOMING STATUTES.

If the Board of Directors of a Wyoming corporation established a par value for the company by resolution, any individual who capitalizes the corporation in increments less than the par value could be issued scrip in bearer form. Thus the corporation can be capitalized with legal, anonymous ownership.

In my efforts to research the legal status of the use of bearer scrip, my office contacted several attorneys who served on the committees established by the American Bar Association to draft the 1984 revision of the Model Business Corporation Act. These attorneys had never considered the possibility of capitalizing a corporation entirely through the use of bearer scrip, but they each admitted that there was nothing in the statute, nor in case law that would prohibit such an action.

Here is how to issue corporate scrip:

The Board of Directors of a Wyoming corporation establishes a par value for the stock in either a) the Articles of Incorporation, or b) a resolution, if the Articles provide for no par value stock. This par value should be set high enough to make it easy to incrementally capitalize a corporation with amounts less than the par value. For example, if a corporation had a par value of $5000 per share, a $1000 capital contribution can result in the issuance of scrip representing the equivalent of 1/5 of a share in bearer form. The corporation may or may not actually issue scrip certificates, but should keep a record of the transaction in a scrip ledger.

A WORD ABOUT "OFFSHORE" CORPORATE HAVENS

A great deal has been written about the benefits of incorporating in international corporate havens. Places like the Cayman Islands, the Bahamas, Isle of Man, Nevis, Panama, Gibraltar and many others are frequently used by promoters of offshore strategies as the ideal solution to protecting assets and eliminating taxes. The reason for this phenomenon is in the strict secrecy laws, and favorable tax climate used in many of these jurisdictions.

While it is true that there can be tremendous benefits realized by using an offshore corporation, it is not as easy, or inexpensive, to do properly as many promoters would have us believe. Here are some of the problems:

- A foreign corporation that is more than 50% owned by a U.S. citizen, resident, corporation, partnership, estate or trust is called a **Controlled Foreign Corporation (CFC).** U.S. shareholders of a CFC are taxed on his pro rata share of the corporations earnings, whether distributed or not, for that year.

- A foreign corporation is taxed at a flat **30%** rate on any income, without any deduction, that has a U.S. source, and is not **"effectively connected"** with a U.S. business. This includes interest, dividends, rents, salaries, wages, premiums, annuities, compensation, remuneration, emoluments and other fixed or determinable annual or periodical gains, profits and income, gains from lump-sum distributions from qualified employee plans, gains on sale or exchange of patents, copyrights, and the like, certain types of gambling winnings, or gains from the disposal of timber, coal or iron ore.

- **The IRS requires disclosure** of U.S. taxpayers who own controlling interest in a foreign corporation, or who sign on a foreign bank account. Failure to do so constitutes tax fraud.

Yet many people use offshore corporations every day in a manner that constitutes tax fraud, without getting caught. They are relying solely on the strength of the secrecy laws of the country in which they are incorporated. For many of these people, if the facts were known, they would be serving prison time.

Because of these and other technical problems with offshore incorporation, I generally advise my clients that unless they are or can be engaged in international trade or business, they should not consider using an offshore corporation. Without international trade or business present, the use of an offshore corporation will, in all probability, constitute a sham.

Chapter

4

CONDUCTING INTERSTATE COMMERCE WITH A FOREIGN OR TAX-HAVEN CORPORATION

Dual corporation strategies, tax nexus, domestication, and a bunch of other fun stuff.

When two corporations start transacting business across state lines, it creates interstate commerce, which is a wholesome, healthy and positive thing. It is also the point at which things get a lot more complicated. If a corporation from a tax haven is one of the corporations being used to some strategic advantage, it is vital that the corporate officers understand some important principles if they don't want to end up with more problems than they need.

WHAT'S A "FOREIGN" CORPORATION?

> *"The act of becoming a member (of a corporation) is something more than a contract, - it is entering into a complex and abiding relation, - and as marriage looks to domicile, membership looks to and must be governed by the law of the state granting the incorporation." - Oliver Wendall Holmes, in Modern Woodmen of America v. Mixer*

Consider the use of the terms "domestic" and "foreign" in relation to corporations the same way that various countries handle their immigration and naturalization. In Europe, for instance, the countries are in such close proximity to each other that it is extremely common for individuals to regularly travel from one country to another.

A citizen of Spain, however, does not lose his Spanish citizenship when he visits Paris, although he must obey the laws of France during his visit. As far as France is concerned, he is a "foreigner." (Having been a foreigner in France, I can personally attest that this is the case.)

Similarly, a corporation is "domestic" to the state that formed it, and "foreign" to all other states. Citizenship rights for corporations are not immediately transferable from the state that formed it. If, for example, you have a Texas corporation and try to conduct business in Oklahoma, the Texas corporation, as a citizen of Texas, becomes foreign when it crosses the state line.

MANY PEOPLE MAKE THE FALSE ASSUMPTION THAT A DOMESTIC CORPORATION IS ANY CORPORATION FORMED IN THE UNITED STATES, AND THAT FOREIGN CORPORATIONS COME FROM FOREIGN COUNTRIES.

Corporations formed in foreign countries are called "offshore" corporations, while foreign corporations, together with domestic corporations are collectively called "onshore" corporations. Even Mexican and Canadian corporations are "offshore," although the United States technically shares coastlines.

Remember, for this discussion (as opposed to a discussion of Federal taxation) foreign corporations have nothing to do with other countries, and offshore corporations have nothing to do with shores.

STATE TAXATION

There are a number of reasons why state governments look to tax corporations. The various states deal with the economic consequences of the occasional recession, which translate into lower revenues from sales and other taxes. Further, they have to deal with federal mandates to provide services with a dramatic reduction in federal aid, especially in areas of health-care and aid to dependent children. The resulting budget deficits have forced a number of states to lay off state employees, reduce spending, and find new or additional sources of tax revenue. Because the corporation is viewed by politicians as a nonvoting resident of the state, they are often the first to be targeted.

Recent tax reform has had a tremendous impact on the significance of state corporate taxation. Currently, 41 of the 46 states that have state corporate income tax use federal corporate taxable income as the starting point in computing the state tax. So, when the federal tax laws disallow lobbying expenses, or a greater portion of meal and entertainment expense, it effects the amount of income tax the corporation will have to pay at both the state and federal levels. The reduction in federal tax rates included in the Tax Reform Act of 1986 substantially increased the after-tax cost of state and local taxes. These taxes are a larger percentage of a corporation's total tax liability than ever before.

TAX NEXUS

When a corporation is formed, the state in which it is formed has the proper right to tax the corporation on activity conducted within that state. If the corporation's income comes from business activity or property owned in other states, those states may claim, for tax purposes, a portion of the corporation's income. If a corporation is to be subject to tax in another state, that state must establish sufficient connection, or "nexus" with the corporation's business activity.

> *A corporation that once was subject to a 46% federal tax rate and a 5.4 % state tax rate, paid only **10.51%** of its total tax liability to the state. Now, the state income tax is **16.26%** of the total tax liability.*

Under normal circumstances, a corporation will establish enough nexus whenever the corporation derives income from sources within the state, owns or leases property in the state, has employees in the state, or has capital or property in the state. However this is entirely up to state laws, which specifically define the nexus requirements.

There is, however, a federal limitation on a state's right to impose income tax on foreign corporations. Public Law No. 86-272 prevents the states from taxing or regulating interstate commerce when the only connection with another state is the solicitation of orders (which is defined by each state) for sales of tangible personal property that are sent outside the state for approval or rejection and, if approved, are filled and shipped by the business from a point outside the state.

But, under this law only the sale of **tangible personal property** is immune from taxation. Leases, rentals, and other dispositions of tangible personal property are not protected from taxation. Neither are sales, leases, rentals, etc. of real property or intangible property. Each state may or may not tax this unprotected activity, according to individual state statutes.

"NEXUS" DESCRIBES THE DEGREE OF BUSINESS ACTIVITY THAT MUST BE PRESENT BEFORE A TAXING JURISDICTION HAS THE RIGHT TO IMPOSE A TAX ON THE CORPORATION'S INCOME.

For example, many states have ruled historically that a taxpayer had to have a physical presence in a state before the state may impose an income-based tax. However, the South Carolina Supreme Court , in the case of *Geoffrey, Inc.* (the corporation that owns the Toys "R" Us trademark, named after the company mascot, the giraffe named Geoffrey) held that a Delaware corporation holding a trademark used in South Carolina is subject to income tax, even though Geoffrey, Inc. had no physical presence in South Carolina. The court rejected Geoffrey's claim that it had not purposefully directed it's business activity into South Carolina. Instead, it held that the company had maintained a "minimum connection" and "substantial nexus" with South Carolina by licensing intangibles for use in the state, and receiving income in exchange for their use.

The states are generally free, though, to regulate intrastate commerce. So, unless a foreign corporation is engaged solely in interstate (or foreign) commerce, it must comply with the laws of the host state relating to the conduct of business in that state by foreign corporations, including those related to qualification or registration.

Or it can abandon any business activity that creates a tax nexus by electing an alternative means of accomplishing the same result. This is the most basic element of strategic planning.

Although most planning techniques are used to separate a corporations activities from an undesirable state, they can also be used to create nexus in a corporate haven, such as Nevada or Wyoming. Such activities could include maintaining bank accounts in the desired jurisdiction, maintaining an office address, a corporate telephone (with a Yellow Page listing), obtaining appropriate business licenses, etc.

Whether a particular business activity is exempt from taxation in a particular state is a question of facts. Under Nevada law, which is typical in this regard, a foreign corporation would not generally be found engaged in intrastate commerce in Nevada for qualification purposes if it, for example, it "conducts a single, isolated transaction which is not done in the course of a number of similar transactions."

Qualifying to do Business

In today's global and interstate economy, it is extremely common for a corporation to regularly conduct business in a state other than that of its formation. A Nevada corporation, for example, may conduct business across the country and around the world. How does this corporation go about doing that, since other jurisdictions consider it "foreign?"

The answer is simple. The corporation has to "qualify to do business" in each jurisdiction (except its home state of incorporation - in this case, Nevada) in which it conducts business. In our example, the Nevada corporation does not lose it's Nevada citizenship just because it engages in business activity outside the state. Instead, the business conducted in another state must conform with the laws of that state.

Qualification makes the corporation subject to any reporting, corporate taxes, and fees that the state chooses to place on incoming corporations. Corporations that are engaged in business within the state, that do not go through the qualification process are a sort of "illegal alien," possibly subject to penalties, taxes and interest.

INSTEAD OF PROVIDING A COMPANY OFFICE IN ANOTHER STATE FOR SALES PERSONNEL, THUS CREATING A TAX NEXUS, A CORPORATION COULD PROVIDE SALES REPRESENTATIVES WITH AN OFFICE ALLOWANCE INSTEAD OF AN ACTUAL OFFICE. IF NEXUS IS ESTABLISHED BY CONDUCTING TRAINING SESSIONS OR SEMINARS IN THE STATE, THE CORPORATION COULD SEND THE PERSONNEL INSTEAD TO A NEARBY STATE IN WHICH THE ACTIVITY WOULD NOT CREATE A TAX NEXUS.

This process of conforming with the corporation laws of each state that the corporation conducts business, is called "qualifying to do business."

If your corporation is involved in intrastate business in another state, and does not qualify to do business there, eventually the corporation will get caught. In the never-ending quest for tax revenue, states frequently engage in dragnets that identify companies who are not properly qualified for business in that state. One state has a team of investigators who go from building to building making a list of tenants that are then checked against tax records. If an unqualified company is identified, it is invited to pay back taxes and penalties.

Many states use business directories, property tax rolls, business license information, motor vehicle registration, and information exchange agreements with other states and the Internal Revenue Service to identify unqualified corporations. Data is exchanged on licensing, sales made in a state, names and addresses of employees covered by state unemployment and worker's compensation insurance, and also highway use taxes, sales-use taxes, and other information.

And, if your corporation is not qualified to do business in another state, that state may find the officers and directors of the company personally liable for performance on corporate contracts, or be subject to fines or imprisonment, if they knowingly transact business on behalf of an unqualified corporation. Examples of states with these statutes include Arkansas, California, Colorado, Delaware, Hawaii, Indiana, Kentucky, Louisiana, Maryland, Ohio, Oklahoma, Oregon, Virginia, and Washington.

Typically, a state will require the following information to qualify a foreign corporation:

- The name of the corporation.

- An original certificate of Good Standing from the jurisdiction that incorporated it originally.

- The address of its principal executive office.

- The address of its principal office within that state.

- The name and address of its Resident Agent, upon whom process directed to the corporation may be served within the state, with a Certificate of Acceptance signed by the Resident Agent.

- Certified copies of the articles of incorporation, with the most current amendment, showing the current total authorized number of shares, with the par value of each share, and the number of shares not issued.

- Fees.

- A current list of officers.

- Sometimes, the state will require either a full or partial list of stockholders.

LONG-ARM STATUTES

You need to be aware of your corporation's out of state operations, even if you think all of your business is conducted through interstate commerce. All states have "long-arm statutes" which provide a quick and easy way for a state's citizens to initiate a suit against an out of state corporation. The typical statute provides for suing an out state corporation if it commits a civil wrong within the state, or makes a contract to be performed in whole or in part within the state.

LONG-ARM STATUTES HAVE BEEN ENFORCED IN STRANGE WAYS. IN ONE CASE, (355 US 220) AN INSURANCE COMPANY IN TEXAS WAS SUCCESSFULLY SUED BECAUSE IT ISSUED A SINGLE POLICY IN CALIFORNIA THROUGH THE MAIL.

A resident of New York sued an Illinois corporation because the company manufactured an allegedly defective hammer that had caused injury. The New York Court of Appeals ruled that the suit could be tried in New York because the Illinois company had shipped quantities of the products into the state because of catalog sales, advertisements, and manufacturers' representatives. The court found that the fact that the contracts for sale were all executed in Illinois were not determinative. Nor was it important that the alleged injury took place in Connecticut.

So, when using a corporation in interstate commerce, you must be aware of the fact that long-arm statutes can be used in other jurisdictions to enforce judgment against the corporation. If your corporation is sued under these statutes, and the company is not qualified to do business and has no resident agent in that state, you are not likely to receive notice of the suit because there is no place for service of process to take place. The result can be a default judgment.

Additionally, 45 states have "reciprocal tax collection" statutes, which make a foreign corporation liable for state taxes incurred in outside jurisdictions. Where these statutes exist, a state that thinks that a foreign corporation has a tax liability may go into the courts of the corporation's home state to plead its case and collect on the claim. The court of the corporation's home state has no choice but to hear the case although it involves a tax imposed by another state.

Usually, when you qualify a corporation in another state, you lose something in the translation. For instance, a Nevada corporation is not required to list the stockholders with the Secretary of State, which is an important element in maintaining privacy. But, when that corporation qualifies in another state, suddenly that list of stockholders may be required to be on public record.

"TRANSACTING BUSINESS" – A CALIFORNIA EXAMPLE

Each state defines by exemption what it considers "transacting business." In other words, they usually define "transacting business" in the broadest of terms, and then provide exemptions to the rule. If you are using a corporation in a state other than where it was formed, you need to be familiar with that state's corporation qualification exemptions.

It is possible that the type of business that you are conducting automatically requires your corporation to be qualified. It is also possible that you can structure the business of your corporation so that it does not need to qualify, and is not subject to taxation and reporting requirement of that state. But, if you are not familiar with the exemptions, you'll probably end up qualifying your corporation anyway.

California has perhaps the nation's most refined and scrutinized Corporation Code. Additionally, the California court system is loaded with case law on just about every conceivable twist of a phrase. Many states attempt to emulate the completeness of the California Corporation Code by copying from it and adopting entire sections as their own. So, it usually serves to use the California exemptions to "transacting business" as a proper example of what you are likely to find in your own state.

In California, you are considered to be "transacting business" by the broad definition of having entered into "repeated and successive" transactions of business in that state. But, there are the exemptions by which a foreign corporation is not considered transacting business just because a company is engaged in one or more of the following within California:

> ➤ A foreign corporation shall not be considered to be transacting intrastate business merely because its subsidiary transacts intrastate business.

> ➤ Maintaining or defending any action or suit or any administrative or arbitration proceeding, or effecting the settlement thereof or the settlement of claims or disputes.

> ➤ Holding meetings of its board or shareholders or carrying on other activities concerning its internal affairs.

➢ Maintaining bank accounts.

➢ Maintaining offices or agencies for the transfer, exchange and registration of its securities or depositaries with relation to its securities.

➢ Effecting sales through independent contractors.

➢ Soliciting or procuring orders, whether by mail or through employees or agents or otherwise, where such orders require acceptance without this state before becoming binding contracts.

➢ Creating evidences of debt or mortgages, liens or security interests on real or personal property.

➢ Conducting an isolated transaction completed within a period of 180 days and not in the course of a number of repeated transactions of like nature.

Regarding lending activity, California also specifies what constitutes transacting business within the state. Without excluding other activities which may not constitute transacting intrastate business, any foreign lending institution, which includes any foreign corporation authorized by its charter to invest in loans secured by real and personal property, shall not be considered to be transacting business in California solely "by reason of engaging in any or all of the following activities either on its own behalf or as a trustee of a pension plan, employee profit sharing or retirement plan, testamentary or inter vivos trust, or in any other fiduciary capacity":

➢ The acquisition by purchase, by contract to purchase, by making of advance commitments to purchase or by assignment of loans, secured or unsecured, or any interest therein, if such activities are carried on from outside this state by the lending institution.

➢ The making by an officer or employee of physical inspections and appraisals of real or personal property securing or proposed to secure any loan, if the officer or employee making any physical inspection or appraisal is not a resident of and does not maintain a place of business for such purpose in this state.

➢ The ownership of any loans and the enforcement of any loans by trustee's sale, judicial process or deed in lieu of foreclosure or otherwise.

➢ The modification, renewal, extension, transfer or sale of loans or the acceptance of additional or substitute security therefor or the full or partial release of the security therefor or the acceptance of substitute or additional obligors thereon, if the activities are carried on from outside this state by the lending institution.

➢ The engaging by contractural arrangement of a corporation, firm or association, qualified to do business in this state, which is not a subsidiary or parent of the lending institution and which is not under common management with the lending institution, to make collections and to service loans in any manner whatsoever, including the payment of ground rents, taxes, assessments, insurance and the like and the making, on behalf of the lending institution, of physical inspections and appraisals of real or personal property securing any loans or proposed to secure any loans, and the performance of any such engagement.

➤ The acquisition of title to the real or personal property covered by any mortgage, deed of trust or other security instrument by trustee's sale, judicial sale, foreclosure or deed in lieu of foreclosure, or for the purpose of transferring title to any federal agency or instumentality as the insurer or guarantor of any loan, and the retention of title to any real or personal property so acquired pending the orderly sale or other disposition thereof.

➤ The engaging in activities necessary or appropriate to carry out any of the foregoing activities. Nothing contained in this subdivision shall be construed to permit any foreign banking corporation to maintain an office in this state otherwise than as provided by the laws of this state or to limit the powers conferred upon any foreign banking corporation as set forth in the laws of this state or to permit any foreign lending institution to maintain an office in this state except as otherwise permitted under the laws of this state.

So, if you incorporated in Nevada or Wyoming to take of the particular corporate haven, and transacted business regularly in California, there is your list that describes what you can do in California's borders without having to qualify. In other words, this list contains the activity that is exempted from establishing sufficient tax nexus.

INCORPORATING IN YOUR HOME STATE

Still, corporations often have to qualify to do business in other states because it is neither possible nor practical for most companies to transact business with all those limitations. There are also many instances where it makes sense to incorporate your business in your home state, despite the differences in the Corporation Code.

A small business that depends wholly upon a local, instate market and has no intention toward establishing interstate operations is a prime candidate for local incorporation. It makes no sense for that business to maintain a corporation in another state and qualify it in its home state. In effect, it would often cost more than maintaining two different domestic corporations.

Most local retailers, for example, have a public presence in a local mall or other commercial property, advertise extensively throughout the local area, and have one or more employees. The customers come to the store to make the purchase or engage the service. Obviously, the corporation engages in "repeated and successive" transactions, and would have to qualify itself if it were a foreign corporation. Under these circumstances it makes sense to deal with only one set of state laws, preferably the laws your accountant and attorney are most comfortable with on a daily basis.

> *"As to the astuteness of taxpayers in ordering their affairs so as to minimize taxes, we have said that `the very meaning of a line in the law is that you intentionally may go as close to it as you can if you do not pass it' Superior Oil Company v. Mississippi, 280 US 390, 395,396. This is so because 'nobody owes any public duty to pay more than the law demands: taxes are enforced exactions, not voluntary contributions." - Felix Frankfurter, in Atlantic Coast Line v. Phillips.*

When the time comes that the state corporate tax burden of the business is an issue, it may be appropriate to use a foreign corporation, from a corporate haven jurisdiction such as Nevada or Wyoming in a strategy that will reduce or eliminate them, providing you with a legal and competitive advantage. The discussion of the "dual corporation strategy" will provide additional insight.

THE DUAL CORPORATION STRATEGY

AVOIDING OR ELIMINATING STATE CORPORATE TAXES

Perhaps the most popular use of a corporation from a corporate haven like Nevada or Wyoming is in establishing a planning structure that deals with the reduction or elimination of state corporate taxes. This strategy is commonly promoted by and among the companies that advertise incorporating services in Nevada. It is perhaps the most often used marketing tool for selling Nevada corporation shells. It is extremely effective, not only as a sales tool for incorporating companies, but also in terms of performing as advertised.

The strategy involves the use of a technique called "upstreaming income." This term is used to describe a business structure that allows the company profits to legally accumulate in a jurisdiction that has less of a tax burden.

This practice is common throughout the world of international business, where firms find themselves conducting business in a number of states and countries that each have distinctive tax laws and regulations.

In fact, the practice of upstreaming income is recognized and supported by governments around the world under the umbrella of governmental economic development efforts. Governments know that business will react to the opportunity to reduce costs and increase profits by avoiding taxes. So, jurisdictions that aggressively seek to recruit new industry almost always provide tax breaks and incentives. The largest corporations in the world practice this technique on a daily basis, structuring their business activity so that it takes advantage of different tax structures around the globe. If they have to pay taxes, they want to pay them in a state or country where it costs the least.

As previously stated, Nevada is a good example of a state that has developed aggressive economic development programs and policies. The tax structure of the state provides tremendous incentives for companies to relocate. And, if companies come to Nevada, so do jobs and payrolls.

Nevada cannot be surprised that individuals seek to incorporate in Nevada to take advantage of the favorable tax consequences. However it is common that these individuals reside and conduct their primary business activity in another state. Further, this business activity is often very profitable in these other states, or else tax considerations would not be so motivational.

For purposes of this illustration, lets use the example of Mr. Jones. Assume that Mr. Jones owns a successful manufacturing company in Los Angeles. Besides having to deal with the notorious Southern California regulatory environment, the company exists as a California corporation, and as such is subject to a state corporate tax rate of almost 10 percent on profits.

Mr. Jones had heard quite a bit about "tax-free" Nevada corporations. He originally considered incorporating his business in Nevada entirely. However, he soon learned that taking this step alone this would be self-defeating. His business activity is literally based in California. It has a prominent location at a California address. It employees many people, each of whom are California taxpayers for whom he collects and pays California personal income tax, and the mere use of a Nevada corporation could not possibly result in the company's income being considered as exempt from California taxation. He simply has established too many factors to avoid tax nexus in California.

A Nevada corporation would simply be forced to "qualify to do business" in California, and would be subject to the same state tax rate, and the same regulations. And, he learned that the annual cost for maintaining a Nevada corporation in California is more expensive than maintaining a domestic corporation.

But, Mr. Jones sat with his accountant and reviewed California's statutory exemptions to qualifying a foreign corporation, and discovered that there were certain aspects of his business that could be exempt from California taxation if performed by a Nevada corporation in the proper circumstances. So he went ahead and formed several Nevada corporations to provide those services.

Now, the manufacturing company's research and development will be partially financed by a private Nevada financing company. The Nevada corporation is lending money to fund new product development in increments over several years. The loan is secured by a deed of trust on the California company's real property, and the California company makes regular interest payments to the Nevada corporation.

The note could be constructed any one of a number of ways, but in this instance the loan is structured as interest-only for a five-year term. Since the manufacturing company was fortunate to get this financing package at all, it is willing to pay a higher interest rate than it would pay with a more conventional loan that was basically unavailable anyway.

The California corporation used to maintain an in-house marketing department to produce promotional materials, advertisements, and make media buys for the advertising. Now, it uses an advertising agency in Nevada to provide these services. The advertising agency can purchase printing and advertising at a discount of almost 20 percent under what the California company had paid.

Some of the most talented people who used to work in-house were fortunate to arrange independent contractor agreements with a Nevada ad agency that Mr. Jones had formed and were given responsibility over this account. Many of them were able are now able to work at home, since they are not salaried employees of any California company.

Instead of receiving a salary, they are paid straight commission, based on what the California company spends each month on its advertising. They also work on developing new accounts for the ad agency, and have already had a proposal approved by a certain other corporation in Nevada that provides financing for development projects and several other clients.

The California company has also made changes in their purchasing. They found a new equipment wholesaler in Nevada that is extremely attentive to their needs. And, their new supplier carries virtually every product used by the manufacturing business, including office supplies, lubricants, chemicals, parts, and computers. It may cost more, but the quality of the goods is unsurpassed and the one-stop shopping cuts down on a lot of employee time.

You get the idea. There is no outside evidence of any connection in the ownership of these new firms. In fact, nobody knows who owns each of these Nevada corporations. They each have separate officers and directors. Indeed, they may not be connected at all. Their only similarity is in the fact that each of these Nevada corporations are extremely profitable, and pay no state corporate taxes at all.

On the other hand, the California company, Mr. Jones' primary business, now struggles to make its monthly interest payments to the financing company and owes its main supplier hundreds of thousands of dollars for unpaid bills. The supplier has secured the debt through a series of UCC filings which would place them at the front of the line, in the event the California corporation is unable to pay its obligations. Because the California company is no longer profitable, it no longer pays state corporate income taxes either.

Further, the assets of the California company have a strong measure of protection against other creditors, to the degree that debt to the Nevada corporations is secured by either a deed of trust or a UCC filing. Those assets could be foreclosed upon any time by the Nevada corporations holding the notes and liens.

To successfully carry out this type of strategy may require professional legal and accounting assistance. Because the success of the strategy depends upon meeting or exempting the Nevada business from specific requirements, often an attorney who is familiar with this area is needed. Are your independent contractors really independent contractors? The attorney should be able to resolve this for you.

Note that a Nevada corporation will help reduce only your state taxes. Federal taxes apply in all states. However, if the circumstances support it, a third company in a tax-free jurisdiction outside the United States could be used to administer international business details and needs. This is a very tricky and specialized project that needs experienced professionals, and is far beyond the scope of this book. But it may be possible for some.

ANOTHER BENEFIT: LAWSUIT PROTECTION

No doubt you have read about or experienced the impact of our current liability nightmare. Court calendars around the country are clogged with vengeance and harassment lawsuits -

any one of which could cost a hapless victim everything he or she has earned or saved. But, who is to blame?

Some people blame insurance companies. Others blame the Bar Association or lawyers in general. The real problem behind the liability crunch may be that there are simply too many frivolous lawsuits filed these days. Every community in the country is bombarded by television advertisements for law firms specializing in "personal injury." While there is no question that there are many valid personal injury claims, many competent attorneys readily admit that frivolous claims have increased dramatically.

That means that the more successful your business is, the more risk you run. But if your business is mortgaged and indebted to the extreme, it may be another matter. That explains the advertisements in legal trade publications across the country for individuals who specialize in asset searches. That is the first thing the attorney is likely to check before accepting a case. Where no assets exist, attorneys fear to tread.

This is because they want to be paid for their services, which they should be. If an attorney takes a case on a contingency, it may be a bit of a gamble because he/she only gets paid if the case is won or settled favorably. But the gamble is carefully calculated. They know that if they are pursuing someone with "deep pockets" they are likely to get a favorable settlement from the opposition simply to keep things out of court where anything could happen.

Instead of a contingency-based fee that allows the attorney to collect a percentage of a successful judgment or settlement, the attorney may determine that it is in his or her best interest to require that the client pay a retainer in advance and pay hourly fees regularly. This could be the single most important step in reducing the filing of frivolous lawsuits.

> **MEDICAL PROFESSIONALS, CONTRACTORS, MANUFACTURERS, EMPLOYERS, AND EVEN ATTORNEYS ARE ALL TARGETS FOR LAWSUIT. BUT, ULTIMATELY THERE ARE ONLY TWO REASONS YOU WILL EVER BE SUED: EITHER YOU 1) HAVE MONEY OR OTHER ASSETS OF VALUE THAT ATTRACTS ATTENTION, OR 2) HAVE INSURANCE. IF YOU HAVE NEITHER, YOU'RE SIMPLY NOT A FAT ENOUGH TARGET FOR THE HUNGRY LAWYERS WHO PURSUE THESE CASES ON A CONTINGENCY-FEE BASIS.**

FINANCIAL PRIVACY

Our example, Mr. Jones, is involved in a legal dispute resulting from his primary business activity. Of course, if Mr. Jones' legal adversary knew anything about the Nevada corporations, it might increase the likelihood of litigation. Though the circumstances do not suggest fraudulent conveyance or sham, if it could be proven the Mr. Jones was connected, then the attorney at least knows that assets exist. He would probably be sued in Nevada as well as California, and make the judge decide what sticks and what doesn't.

However, as we have already seen, a primary advantage to incorporating in Nevada is that the reporting and disclosure requirements are minimal. While the officers and directors are a matter of public record, shareholders are not. As a result, it can be extremely difficult indeed to discover who the real owners are. As we have discussed, Nevada law allows corporations to issue stock in the form best suited to guarantee an owner's anonymity: Bearer Shares.

Mr. Jones legal adversary might get as far as a Nevada corporation's resident agent. But, when he asks after the stock ledger, he may find that it is kept by an attorney (who maintains attorney/client privilege), in a bank lock box in Switzerland, or in the deposit box of a chop account in Hong Kong. The resident agent might be the source of all kinds of absolutely useless information. The Nevada corporation structure provides Mr. Jones with an invaluable tool for ensuring his personal and financial privacy.

So, by using this basic dual-corporation strategy, businesses can accomplish the three things that are most important to many business owners:

1. They can lower their taxes,

2. Protect themselves from personal liability, and

3. Maintain their financial privacy.

Additionally, while there is some cost associated with setting this type of structure in place, this strategy is flexible enough to be incorporated into their everyday business affairs without radical and expensive business reorganization of your primary business activity.

Chapter

5

CORPORATE TAXATION

"The wisdom of man never yet contrived a system of taxation that would operate with perfect equality." - Andrew Jackson

FEDERAL CORPORATE INCOME TAX

Corporate income tax rates are designed around a graduated tax structure. In addition, a penalty is applied when the corporation retains earnings beyond the reasonable needs of the business. This penalty is called the accumulated earnings tax. The alternative minimum tax may also apply on some tax preferences.

Figure 1.2, below is based on the 2000 Federal Tax Rates, and will give some idea about the disparity of the current tax system. It also reveals the levels of income where it would be advantageous to receive income into a corporation instead of personally. As you can see, the Internal Revenue Code frequently favors incorporation. There are also more tax deductions available to the corporation than to any other form of business.

> *The corporation's taxable income is calculated as gross income, minus deductions allowed to corporations. Income includes gross profit from sales, interest and dividends, rents and royalties, and gains and losses. Capital contributions are not considered income.*

Possible deductions include life insurance premiums, health and disability insurance, cafeteria plans, 401K pensions and profit sharing plans, travel expenses, entertainment, and qualified personal expenses. So, the corporate taxable income figures can be a bit deceiving when compared to individual taxable income. The corporation is allowed to take a full deduction for many expenses that provide benefits to individuals involved with the corporation, while those same expenses are not deductible to sole proprietorships or partnerships.

Additionally, a corporation may select a fiscal year other than the calendar year. This can create tremendous tax advantages, especially in multiple corporation structures. It may be possible to defer taxes for a period of time by using different corporations that provide different services, with individual fiscal tax years.

Figure 1.2 Taxes payable at various net income levels for different taxpayers

Taxable Income	Married, Filing Separately	Married, Filing Jointly	Head of Household	Individual	Corporation
$15,000		$2,250	$2,250	$2,250	$2,250
$30,000	$5,930	$4,500	$4,500	$5,443	$4,500
$40,000	$8,730	$6,260	$7,235	$8,243	$6,000
$50,000	$11,652	$9,060	$10,035	$11,043	$7,500
$60,000	$14,752	$11,860	$12,835	$13,990	$10,000
$70,000	$17,852	$14,660	$15,635	$17,090	$12,500
$80,000	$21,452	$17,460	$18,474	$20,190	$15,450
$90,000	$25,052	$20,260	$21,574	$23,290	$18,850
$100,000	$28,652	$23,305	$24,674	$26,390	$22,250
$120,000	$35,852	$29,505	$30,874	$32,840	$30,050
$150,000	$47,552	$39,305	$41,299	$43,640	$41,750
$200,000	$67,352	$57,305	$59,299	$61,640	$61,250
$350,000	$126,752	$114,905	$116,899	$119,240	$119,000
$500,000	$186,152	$174,305	$176,299	$178,640	$170,000

CORPORATIONS ARE TREATED AS A SEPARATE TAXPAYER UNDER US INCOME TAX LAWS. BUT IF ONE CORPORATION OWNS AT LEAST 80% OF THE OUTSTANDING SHARES OF ANOTHER CORPORATION, THE INCOME AND LOSSES OF THE TWO CORPORATIONS CAN BE COMBINED FOR TAX PURPOSES AS IF THEY WERE A SINGLE CORPORATION.

"What is the difference between a taxidermist and a tax collector? The taxidermist takes only your skin." - Mark Twain

STATE TAXES

State corporate income taxes currently apply in 46 of the 50 states. The tax is generally applied against income determined to be "sourced" within a state that has a corporate income tax. The use of a corporation from State A, which does not have a state corporate income tax, will not exempt that corporation from paying state corporate income taxes in State B, if State B's corporate and franchise tax laws define the income of the corporation as having its taxable source in State B.

In other words, if Bill incorporates his muffler repair shop in the tax haven of Nevada, but his place of business is located in Sacramento, California, the corporate income will be taxable in California. That is a simple example of what can be an extremely complicated problem when conducting interstate business. Experienced planners can probably assist either an incorporated or unincorporated business in another state by separating elements of the business that are considered "trader business" by the appropriate state tax authority from business activity that would not be considered "trader business."

For example, a California business that currently provides its bookkeeping in-house, may be able to provide that service to the business through a Nevada corporation utilizing independent contractors instead of employees.

Then, whatever the California business pays the Nevada corporation for bookkeeping, it creates a deductible expense to the California business, and transfers money to the Nevada corporation - free of the California state taxes.

LOOK OUT! IT IS GETTING MORE DIFFICULT TO USE INDEPENDENT CONTRACTORS.. YOU NEED TO BE INTIMATELY FAMILIAR WITH IRS INDEPENDENT CONTRACTOR RULES TO SET THIS TYPE OF ARRANGEMENT UP PROPERLY.

Remember, the Nevada corporation is entitled to make a profit. The California business can transfer more money to the Nevada corporation than it was spending for bookkeeping in-house. And, the owners of the Nevada business - generally are the same people who own the primary business - can generate corporate profits free of any state corporate taxes.

> *"Logic and taxation are not always the best of friends."* - James C. McReynolds, Sonneborn Bros. v. Cureton.

DOUBLE TAXATION

One of the challenges of owning stock in a corporation is the problem of taking profits out without being taxed twice. A corporation may build profits over a period, and pay taxes on those proceeds at the appropriate corporate rate, but when the corporation distributes the profits to the shareholders, it becomes taxable as income to the shareholder. This can apply at both the federal and state level.

Although the negative impact of this may be partially offset in a variety of ways, the unwary will face double taxation on declared dividends. Perhaps more significant in terms of dollars, if the corporation is later sold in either whole or part, it can result in a substantial double tax on the capital gain of the sale.

NOT ONLY ARE THE RULES AND REGULATIONS QUITE SPECIFIC ABOUT WHAT IS AND IS NOT DEDUCTIBLE, BUT VIRTUALLY EVERY ITEM MUST BE SUBSTANTIATED BY A SPECIFIC TYPE OF RECORD. MEMORY, OR RULE-OF-THUMB POLICIES ARE NOT CONSIDERED ADEQUATE REPORTING METHODS.

The United States Treasury has been increasingly strict in imposing the letter of the law where corporate tax deductions are concerned, and will continue to do so through the continuing evolution of "tax reform" that Congress keeps attempting. Expenses incurred in the conduct of a trade or business or in the production or collection of income, are ordinarily deductible for tax purposes, although that advantage has been and will probably continue to be significantly reduced in coming years.

The purpose of this chapter is to provide the owners, officers and directors of a corporation with general guidelines to follow that will aid in establishing corporate policies that make corporate deductions stick. This chapter is not a complete reference guide on this matter. Indeed, the entire volume of this handbook would be insufficient to detail the intricacies of our current tax law. For specific information, please consult a qualified tax advisor.

ACCOUNTABLE PLANS

The term "accountable plan" refers to a plan that qualifies under rules on what the IRS will accept as a reimbursement arrangement for business expenses. The difference between an accountable plan and a nonaccountable plan can mean a lot of tax dollars. If your plan is accountable, the corporation does not report reimbursements to employees as income. The reimbursements and the employees expenses are considered a wash.

With a nonaccountable plan, all reimbursements must be included in the income that appears on the employees W-2, and must have income taxes, unemployment taxes, and Social Security taxes withheld on it. The employee must then deduct his business expenses on his or her tax return as miscellaneous itemized deductions. But, they are only deductible to the extent that they exceed 2 percent of adjusted gross income. This usually results in a situation where the additional income exceeds the deductions and the employee owes additional taxes.

If you are both the shareholder of the corporation and the employee, this means you get hit twice. The corporation has additional employment taxes, and you have additional personal income taxes.

The IRS requires that your reimbursements meet three requirements:

1. Reimbursements must have a direct business connection.

2. Expenses must be properly substantiated.

3. Excess reimbursements must be returned to the corporation. Let's look at these requirements one at a time.

BUSINESS CONNECTION.

Reimbursements must be directly related to expenses incurred by the employee while conducting business. These reimbursements may be made in advance to prevent employees from using their personal money for anticipated expenses, and can be made in regular payments to employees who have regular travel and entertainment costs.

It is important that you don't provide advances when the employee isn't expected to immediately incur expense, or the IRS might rule that the money should be counted as income to the employee. Also, it is a good idea to pay these reimbursements with a separate check that identifies it as such. Remember to keep wages as separate as possible.

SUBSTANTIATION.

Most of the expenses that would be normally incurred in the course of business have special substantiation rules in the tax code. The rules require that employees provide the corporation with the proof of the expense, including the time, place, and business purpose. When an employee has expenses that are not covered by the IRS rules, the corporation is expected to get information that enables it to identify the nature of each expense and conclude that it's substantiated.

RETURN EXCESS.

An accountable plan requires employees to return any and all amounts that exceed the substantiated expenses. You should not advance money any more than 30 days before the expense is incurred, and the employee should provide substantiation within 60 days and provide any returns within 120 days. Also, it is a good idea to provide employees with a expense account report every quarter that allows them to substantiate or return any appropriate amounts.

TRAVEL EXPENSES

The IRS distinguishes "travel" expenses from "transportation" expenses. Travel expenses are those incurred by an employee while traveling away from home, including meals and lodging. Transportation expenses include only the costs of travel - not meals and lodging - which are incurred in the conduct of business while the employee is not away from home.

"Home" is defined for travel purposes by the IRS as the taxpayer's place of business, employment station, or post of duty, no matter where the taxpayer lives. So, if you live in St. Louis, but work in Detroit, you cannot deduct any of the expenses for traveling, meals or lodging in Detroit since that is his tax home, and travel home over the weekend is not for a business purpose. Both "travel" and "transportation" expenses are deductible, but must be separated for IRS purposes.

What Is Deductible.

Travel expenses are considered to be normal and necessary, and can include such items as:

- Meals and lodging (either en route or at the destination);

- Baggage charges;

- Cost of maintaining an automobile;

- Air, rail and bus fares;

- Reasonable cleaning and laundry expense;

- Telephone, telegraph, and fax expenses;

- Cost of transporting sample cases or display materials;

- Cost of display or conference rooms;

- Cost of maintaining and operating an airplane, including depreciation on the hangar;

- Cost of secretarial help;

- Taxi fares;

- Reasonable tips incident to any of the above expenses;

- Other similar expenses related to travel.

The IRS allows full deductibility of all travel expenses incurred while looking after income-producing property, including travel to consult with investment advisors and brokers. However, a stockholder generally cannot deduct the cost of travel expenses in attending stockholder meetings of companies in which he or she owns shares.

All travel and transportation expenses incurred in the process of looking for employment in the same line of work are fully deductible. But, any payments made by a prospective employer as an inducement to accept employment is considered income.

ANY TRAVEL COSTS INCURRED TRAVELING ABROAD TO ESTABLISH FOREIGN MARKETS FOR EXISTING PRODUCTS MAY BE DEDUCTED AS LONG AS THEY ARE REASONABLE AND NECESSARY. LAVISH AND EXTRAVAGANT EXPENDITURES ARE NOT DEDUCTIBLE.

What Is Not Deductible.

If you travel away from home, but do not stay overnight, the IRS rules that you cannot deduct meals and lodging. This has been upheld by the Supreme Court. So, any per diem allowances you receive in this situation must be included in your income.

When traveling in the US, and your trip consists of both business and personal interests, the IRS says you cannot deduct the costs associated with the trip unless there is clear evidence that the primary nature of your trip was related primarily to the taxpayer's trade or business. But, expenses incurred at the destination which are properly associated with the taxpayer's trade or business are deductible even though the travel to and from that destination are not.

If a taxpayer travels outside the US for primarily business purposes, but there were some nonbusiness activities, the cost of travel from home to the place of business and back may not be deductible by an individual. The cost may have to be allocated between business and nonbusiness activities, unless any one of the following tests is met:

- Travel outside the US is for one week or less;

- Employees are not related to their employers and are not managing executives;

- The employee did not have substantial control over making the trip arrangements;

- Less that 25% of the time outside the US is spent on personal activity;

- Personal vacation was not a major consideration in scheduling the trip.

If you intend to deduct registration fees and travel and transportation costs associated with attending conventions, seminars or trade shows, you should be prepared to prove that the income-producing purposes are directly related to your trade or business. Usually, the expenses incurred in connection with financial planning or investment seminars and meetings are not deductible.

Deductions for travel incurred for educational purposes are not deductible, unless the travel is necessary to engage in activities that promote deductible education. For example, a high school French teacher may not deduct the expenses of traveling to Paris during summer vacation to improve his or her knowledge of French culture and language. But, if the teacher conducts an educational tour of high school students through the French countryside, those expenses could be deducted since teacher incurs them while educating her students, which is, of course, his or her trade.

If you incur travel expenses while identifying a new domestic location for an established business, or if you incur expenses trying to go into a new business, these costs are not deductible. Instead, the travel expenses must be capitalized into the cost of the new property. (If you want to take a personal deduction for all of your costs, set up a new corporation for the specific purpose of identifying a new location, and follow the rules for treating its stock as Section 1244 stock. Then buy the stock from the corporation in the amount you expect the search will cost. Have the corporation take on the expenses for the search, then if you fail to find the right business location, you can liquidate your corporation and take your losses as an ordinary deduction instead of a capital loss. If you do find a new location, your new corporation is ready to go.)

ENTERTAINMENT

Entertainment costs must be ordinary and necessary for carrying on the trade or business, and are not deductible unless business is discussed before, during, or after the meal, or the meal is "directly related" to, or "associated with," the conduct of business. The deduction is limited to 50 percent of the tab, as long as it is not determined to be lavish or extravagant. The only exceptions to the 50 percent rule are expenses that fall in the following categories:

- Any amount treated as compensation to the recipients, whether they are employees or not;

- Minor fringe benefits such as holiday gifts;

- Employer paid recreation for company picnics, holiday parties, etc.

- Items that are made available to the public, such as promotional samples and materials;

- Charitable sports event tickets, to the extent it meets three conditions: (i) the event's primary purpose is to benefit a qualified non-profit organization, (ii) the entire net proceeds go the charity, and (iii) the event uses volunteers to perform the event's work. This rule applies to cover the entire cost of the event, including parking and meals, and is often used to deduct the cost of charity golf tournaments.

Deductions taken at what the tax code describes as "entertainment facilities" are usually thrown out. This includes hunting lodges, yachts, tennis courts, swimming pools, beach houses, ski lodges, hotel suites, or other housing located in recreational areas. Dues paid to social and athletic clubs no longer qualify as ordinary and necessary expenses to the extent that the club is used as a source of valuable business contacts.

BUSINESS GIFTS

Expenses for ordinary and necessary business gifts are deductible to the extent they do not exceed $25 in a year to any one person. The $25 limitation does not apply to any item that costs no more than $4 and has the giver's name permanently imprinted, promotional material, or any item awarded to an employee because of length of service, productivity, or safety achievements (that does not cost more than $400).

KEEPING RECORDS

TRAVEL.

A taxpayer must prove the following elements to support a deduction for travel expenses:

- The separate amount of each expenditure;

- Dates of departure and return home for each trip;

- The travel destination for each portion of each trip;

- The business reason for the travel, or the expected business benefit derived from the trip.

ENTERTAINMENT.

In addition to the above information, a taxpayer must provide the following elements to support a deduction for entertainment expenses:

- The name, address, or location of the place of entertainment, and the type of entertainment if that is not apparent by the name;

- The purpose for entertaining, or the expected benefit derived for the business;

- The occupation, title, name, and other designation to establish the business relationship of the persons entertained to the taxpayer.

BUSINESS GIFTS.

For business gifts, the following information must be provided:

- The cost of the gift to the taxpayer.

- The date the gift was made.

- The reason the gift was made, or the expected benefit derived for the business.

- The occupation, title, name, and other designation to establish the business relationship of the person receiving the gift to the taxpayer.

- A description of the gift.

- Generally, each employee should keep a detailed expense diary on a timely basis that outlines the above information. In addition, it is useful to keep receipts on file for three years from the date of filing an income tax return on which the deduction was claimed.

MEDICAL EXPENSES

Corporations can deduct 100% on all of the following medical expenses:

- Accident & health insurance.

- Acupuncture.

- Adoption.

- Air conditioner (for allergy relief).

- Alcoholism treatment.
- Ambulance costs.
- Birth control pills.
- Blind persons; attendant to accompany student, Braille books and magazines, seeing-eye dog, special education and educational aids.
- Capital Expenditures; home modifications for handicapped individuals, primary purpose medical care.
- Car; equipped to accommodate wheelchair passengers, handicapped controls.
- Childbirth preparation classes for the mother.
- Chiropractors.
- Christian Science treatment.
- Clarinet & lessons (to alleviate severe teeth malocclusion).
- Computer data bank, storage and retrieval of medical records.
- Contact lenses.
- Contraceptives.
- Cosmetic Surgery.
- Crutches.
- Deaf Persons; hearing aids, hearing aid animal, lip-reading expenses, note taker for deaf student
- Dental Fees.
- Dentures.
- Doctor's Fees.
- Domestic Aid.
- Drug Addition recovery.

- Drugs, prescriptions.
- Dyslexia language training.
- Electrolysis.
- Elevator to alleviate cardiac condition.
- Eye examination and prescription glasses.
- Hair transplants.
- Halfway house.
- Health club dues prescribed by physician for medical condition.
- Health Maintenance Organization.
- Hospital Care.
- Hospital Services (outpatient)
- Indian Medicine Man.
- Insulin.
- Iron Lung.
- Laboratory Fees.
- Laetrile (legal use).
- Lead paint removal.
- Legal expenses. (Authorization for treatment)
- Lifetime Medical Care.
- Limbs (artificial).
- Mattress (prescribed to alleviate arthritis).
- Nursing Home.
- Nursing Services.
- Obstetrical Expenses.
- Operations.
- Orthopedic Shoes.
- Osteopaths.
- Oxygen Equipment.

- Patterning exercises for handicapped child.
- Prosthesis.
- Psychiatric Care.
- Psychologists.
- Psychotherapists.
- Reclining Chair for cardiac patient.
- Remedial Reading.
- Schools (Special, relief of handicap).
- Sexual Dysfunction.
- Sterilization operation.

- Swimming Pool for treatment of polio or arthritis.
- Taxicab to doctor's office.
- Telephone, equipped for deaf persons.
- Television, close caption decoder.
- Transplant.
- Vasectomy.
- Vitamins.
- Wheel Chair.
- Wigs (for alleviation of physical or mental discomfort).
- X-Rays.

Other Expenses Allowed to Corporations. Within certain guidelines, a corporation is allowed to deduct 100% of the following expenses:

- Advertising Expenses.
- Auto Expenses.
- Awards.
- Cleaning Expenses.
- Depreciation and Section 179 Expenses.
- Convention Expenses.
- Delivery Expenses.
- Dues and Publication Expenses.
- Entertainment Expenses.
- Foreign Conventions.
- Gas & Oil Expenses.
- Gifts Expenses.
- Insurance Expenses.
- Legal & Professional Expenses.
- License Fees.
- Mailers Expenses.

- Meals on Premises Expenses.
- Miscellaneous Expenses.
- Office Expenses.
- Pension Expenses.
- Per Diem Meals, including incidental expenses.
- Per Diem Lodging, including incidental expenses.
- Postage & Freight Expenses
- Summer Day Camp.
- Trade Shows & Conference Expenses.
- Tax Expenses, including payroll, property, sales, etc.
- Travel Expenses.
- Utilities, such as phone, electric, gas, water, and garbage.

- Wages and Salaries

Expenses.

THE 1993 DEFICIT REDUCTION TAX LAW

THE INTERNAL REVENUE CODE

The discussion of the impact of the 1993 Deficit Reduction Act upon corporate tax rates should begin with a brief explanation of the Internal Revenue Code (IRC) and how it works. Though it seems unbelievably complex, the basics of the Internal Revenue Code are really quite simple.

In Section 162 of the IRC, it says that "(t)here shall be allowed as a deduction all the ordinary and necessary expenses paid or incurred during the taxable year in carrying on any trade or business . . . " So, the key to getting a deduction for business-related expenses is to qualify an expense as "ordinary and necessary." This is where the tax code becomes complicated, as it requires thousands of pages of technical language in the IRC, and in thousands of court cases, to specify what is and is not "ordinary and necessary."

SECTION 62 OF THE INTERNAL REVENUE CODE SETS THE STAGE WHERE IT SAYS, "(E)XCEPT AS OTHERWISE PROVIDED . . . , GROSS INCOME MEANS ALL INCOME FROM WHATEVER SOURCE DERIVED . . .," WHICH BASICALLY SAYS THAT ALL INCOME WILL BE TAXABLE UNLESS THERE IS A SPECIFIC EXCEPTION WRITTEN INTO THE CODE.

CORPORATE TAX RATES

While the top corporate tax rate has been increased from 34% to 35% for all corporate taxable income (including capital gains), for most companies, that rate only applies to taxable corporate income above $10 million. The significant exception applies to personal service corporations, which will pay federal income tax at the new 35% rate, regardless of size or income.

For corporations with taxable income in the $100,000 to $335,000 range, the tax rate applies a 5% surtax on the 34% rate for an effective tax rate of 39%. A second surtax is created by the new law for corporations with taxable income in the $15 million to $18.3 million range. By adding a 3% surtax to the 35% tax rate, corporations in this range will pay tax at a 38% rate.

The good news is that not all of the changes in the tax law are detrimental for small corporations. The first $50,000 of taxable income - remember, that's net income that takes into consideration the broader deductions that are available to the corporation, not gross income - is still taxable at the attractive rate of 15% rate. That 15% rate disappears at $43,050 for married taxpayers filing joint returns, at $34,550 for heads of households, at $25,750 for single taxpayers, and at $21,525 for married individuals filing separate returns.

CAPITAL GAINS TAX BREAKS (1202 STOCK)

One of the biggest tax breaks available through the new tax law is the incentive for individuals to invest in small corporations. Investors who buy "small business stock" issued after August 10, 1993 can escape tax on their profit when they sell their shares later. The impact of this tax break is almost unbelievable. Since long-term capital gains have a tax rate cap of 28%, small business stock that qualifies for this break is taxed at an effective rate of 14%.

During the 1992 presidential campaign, then-candidate Clinton promised that his election would be accompanied by substantial changes in the Internal Revenue Code. The 1993 Deficit Reduction Act fulfills that promise. As predicted, a significant part of the tax change results in income tax rate hikes for high income taxpayers, especially individuals.

Small business stock that qualifies for this tax break is often referred to as "1202 stock," named after the section in the Internal Revenue Code that describes this mechanism. Further, the shareholder that takes advantage of this break may be another C corporation, an S corporation, individual, partnership, limited liability company, or mutual fund.

To qualify for this break, the stock must be issued by a regular C corporation that meets the following requirements:

- The stock must be (a) newly issued stock, and (b) issued after August 10, 1993.

- The shareholder must hold the stock for at least five years before selling the shares. Stock transfers that occur under the federal estate and gift tax transfer rules may add the time the stock was owned by the transferor to the time the stock is owned by the transferee. Stock owned by a pass-through entity, such as an S corporation or partnership, requires that the owners of the pass-through entity be owners of the entity at the time it purchased the stock and for the following five year period to take advantage of this tax break.

- The issuing corporation must have gross assets of $50 million or less when the stock is issued. The corporation can grow to have gross assets over that figure later without losing the tax break, however if it grows to over $50 million in gross assets and then decreases in value to below that level, it can no longer issue qualified small business stock subject to this tax break.

IF THE TAXPAYER HAS RELATIVELY MODEST INCOME, IT IS POSSIBLE THAT THE CAPITAL GAINS COULD BE TAXED AS ORDINARY INCOME AT A RATE AS LOW AS 15%, WHICH RESULTS IN AN EFFECTIVE TAX OF 7.5% ON THE CAPITAL GAIN ON THE SALE OF QUALIFIED SMALL BUSINESS STOCK.

- The issuing corporation must participate in an active business. This is defined as having at least 80% of its assets used by businesses that do not qualify as professional services.

- The issuing corporation cannot hold more than 10% of its total assets as real estate, or hold more than 10% of its net assets as securities.

- The stock must be purchased with money, awarded to an employee in lieu of compensation, or exchanged for property other than stock in the issuing corporation. There are other technical restrictions here, too. The corporation cannot buy back old shares (issued prior to August 10, 1993) from a shareholder within two years of issuing shares that qualify as "1202 Small Business Stock" without losing the tax break on the newly issued shares, nor can the corporation redeem more than 5% of its stock within one year of issuing qualified stock.

- The shareholder is limited to $10 million per year in the amount of gain he or she can exclude each year. Or, if the amount is greater, he or she can exclude ten times the purchase price of the stock.

PERSONAL SERVICE CORPORATIONS AND FISCAL YEARS

If a personal service corporation uses a fiscal year, it may use a blended rate for the year that includes January 1, 1993. To determine the appropriate tax for fiscal year corporations, begin by counting the number of days of the fiscal year that were in 1992 and divide that by 365. Call this A.

Then figure the tax on the year's income using the old rates, and multiply the tax by A. Next, repeat the process by determining the number of days in the fiscal year that fall in 1993, divide by 365, and multiply by the tax on the entire year's income using the new rates. Call that B. Add A and B together, and you have determined the weighted corporate tax liability for the fiscal year that includes January 1, 1993.

EXPENSING DEDUCTIONS FOR NEW EQUIPMENT PURCHASES INCREASED

Under the previous tax law, a corporation was allowed an expensing deduction (also called a Sec. 179 deduction) for the first $10,000 of new equipment purchased and placed into service during the tax year. Above that limit, the property was depreciated under the Modified Accelerated Cost Recovery System (MACRS).

The new law increases that expensing deduction to a maximum of $20,000, which can be allocated to any one of a number of individual assets in any manner you choose. And, there is a carry-over provision for deductions that are disallowed because of the taxable income limitations outlined below:

- There is a $200,000 limit on the cost of the equipment and property the corporation can place in service during a single tax year. If the value exceeds that figure, then the $20,000 maximum deduction is reduced $1 for each $1 of excess. This effectively phases out this expensing deduction when the cost of the equipment equals $220,000.

- The dollar limitations described above apply not only to a single corporation, but also to a "controlled group" of corporations, and, with an S corporation, to the corporation and its individual shareholders.

- The property or equipment can only be expensed if it is used actively (more than 50%) in a trade or business. Investment property generally is not eligible for this expensing deduction.

- Your expensing deduction cannot exceed the corporation's taxable income for the year.

- Property acquired in a nontaxable exchange will have the adjusted basis of the old asset excluded when computing the expense deduction for the new asset.

DEDUCTING GOODWILL AND OTHER INTANGIBLE ASSETS

The tax law has long provided for the depreciation of all equipment and property used in a trade or business with a limited useful life of one year or more. Generally, if the expected life span of the asset is one year or less, you can deduct the entire cost of asset. But because intangible assets had a life span that was inherently difficult to determine, no deduction was previously allowed.

If a corporation is used to purchase an existing business or the assets of a business, this deduction can have obvious tax benefits. The intangible assets that can be deducted over the 15-year period are often called "Section 197 Intangibles," which includes:

- The value of business goodwill (defined as the value of continued customer patronage);

- Employment contracts and other workforce obligations;

- Customer lists;

- Proprietary computer software;

- Training manuals, internal operating procedures and systems;

- Patents, copyrights, proprietary procedures, formulas, etc.;

- Trademarks, trade names, franchises;

- No-compete agreements;

- Permits, licenses, and other government-granted rights;

- Customer-based contracts and agreements; and

- Favorable supplier-based contracts and agreements.

UNDER THE NEW LAW, MANY INTANGIBLE ASSETS, WITH A LIFE SPAN THAT IS USUALLY DIFFICULT, IF NOT IMPOSSIBLE TO DETERMINE, CAN BE WRITTEN OFF OVER A 15 YEAR PERIOD. THIS STRAIGHT-LINE AMORTIZATION OF THE DEDUCTION APPLIES TO MANY INTANGIBLE ASSETS ACQUIRED AFTER AUGUST 10, 1993, AND MAY BE ELECTED FOR SOME ASSETS ACQUIRED BETWEEN JULY 25, 1991 AND AUGUST 10, 1993.

Chapter

6

CORPORATIONS WITH SPECIAL TAX TREATMENT

> *"It is true that the existence of a corporation is a fiction, but the very meaning of that fiction is that the liability of its members shall be determined as if the fiction were the truth." - Oliver Wendall Holmes, in Remington v. Samana Bay Co.*

The Internal Revenue Service also has its own classifications for corporations that conduct certain types of activity or are organized a certain way. You may want to incorporate a particular service that you feel has potential to fill a market niche, but do you really want to be classified by the IRS as a Personal Services Corporation?

CORPORATIONS MAY BE CLASSIFIED IN SEVERAL WAYS: (1) IN TERMS OF MEMBERSHIP (AGGREGATE V. SOLE, ETC.); (2) IN TERMS OF PURPOSE (PROFIT V. NONPROFIT); (3) IN TERMS OF INTEREST SERVED (PUBLIC, PRIVATE, OR QUASI-PUBLIC); (4) IN TERMS OF FORM (STOCK OR NON STOCK), AND; (5) IN TERMS OF TAX TREATMENT (C V. S CORPORATION).

S CORPORATIONS

An S corporation (also known as a Subchapter S corporation) is a hybrid entity that offers protection of limited liability to corporate shareholders, and yet it is not a taxable entity at all (except certain types of capital gains). Instead, the income, whether distributed or not is transferred directly to the stockholders, who pay taxes on the corporate income at their personal income tax rate - essentially treating the stockholders for tax purposes as if they were partners. This results in having a wider range of corporate deductions applied against the individual stockholder's income. One of the advantages of this arrangement is that any potential for double taxation is eliminated.

TAX DRAWBACKS OF C CORPORATIONS

Obviously, double taxation can have a huge financial impact on the company and its shareholders. Over the years, a variety of methods have been attempted to avoid the double tax. The simplest method is not to declare a dividend: No dividend, no double tax. Unfortunately, shareholders soon realized that no dividend also means..., well, no dividend.

Because many corporations were circumventing the double taxation by not distributing profits, Congress passed Section 531 et seq. of the Internal Revenue Code, which penalizes a corporation that accumulates profits "for the purpose of avoiding the income tax with respect to its shareholders". Under this law, a corporation may only accumulate profits which are "reasonably" necessary for business. It also provides for an amount that may be accumulated without regard to the needs of the business, currently $250,000.

Once this law passed, business strategists set about trying to avoid paying this accumulation penalty while still avoiding a taxable distribution to shareholders. Many closely held corporations attempt to distribute corporate profits to employee/shareholders in the form of nontaxable fringe benefits. These benefits include health, life, and disability insurance, meals, automobiles, gasoline, parking, business entertainment, etc. Congress has repeatedly reduced or eliminated the availability of these opportunities to limited degrees.

Another tax problem associated with the C corporation is that the tax benefit of net business losses do not, generally, pass through to the shareholders. True, shareholders don't usually like to see net operating losses, but if it happens they would like to be able to take the deduction against income they earn in other areas. This is especially true if a corporation has "paper" losses that result from loopholes in depreciation schedules.

These problems, and the impact they created for closely-held corporations, led to the existence of the Subchapter S corporation. For the purpose of maintaining limited personal liability, the S corporation allows shareholders the insulation that they seek. Yet the income or loss passes untaxed through the corporation.

ADVANTAGES OF SUBCHAPTER S STATUS

If ABC Corporation were a C corporation and had a taxable income of $30,000 it would pay $4,500 in federal corporate income taxes at the corporate tax rate. Assume the remaining $25,500 would be distributed to the shareholder, John. In addition to John's salary, the dividend brings his total (net) taxable income for the year to $50,500. Since he files jointly, his personal income tax for the year would be $9,200. Thus, the total liability for the year for both John and the corporation is $13,700 ($4,500 + $9,200).

OTHER ADVANTAGES INCLUDE THE FACT THAT S CORPORATIONS ARE NOT SUBJECT TO THE ACCUMULATED EARNINGS PENALTIES DESCRIBED EARLIER, OR THE PERSONAL HOLDING COMPANY TAX, WHICH AUTOMATICALLY RESULTS IN THE HIGHEST POSSIBLE CORPORATE TAX RATE IF THE CORPORATION QUALIFIES.

But, if the corporation had elected S status, there would be no $4,500 tax. John's taxable income would be $55,500, ($30,000 passed through from the corporation). Now his total tax bill is $10,500. The S corporation saved him $3,200.

In addition to the pass through described above, the S corporation has no corporate tax on the sale of corporate assets, or upon the liquidation of the company. Corporate losses, with some restrictions, pass through to the shareholder as well. This means that a shareholder can offset income derived from other sources with corporate losses.

S CORPORATION DISADVANTAGES

While the S corporation is simpler to operate for some tax reasons, there can be some limitations and drawbacks. For one thing, the stockholders of an S corporation are subject to tax on the income of the corporation whether they receive a distribution of profits or not. If the corporation decides to retain some of the income, the shareholder still must pay the tax out of pocket.

There are other limitations on S election of a corporation. No more than seventy-five stockholders may participate in an S corporation, but a husband and wife are counted only once. Generally stockholders are "natural persons," but certain specified types of corporations, trusts and estates also may own stock. Non-resident aliens, corporations and partnerships are not eligible to hold stock.

S corporations can technically have only one class of stock, although that one class of stock can include both voting and non-voting shares. IRS regulation allows for S corporations to issue stock options, which allows individuals to retain a distant interest in the corporation without endangering the S corporation election.

Shareholders must be revealed to the Internal Revenue Service to determine the proper Federal Income Tax obligation of the individual shareholders. This disclosure includes how much stock they own, when it was acquired, and their individual Social Security numbers. This eliminates a great measure of privacy that would otherwise be possible.

Because the taxes are paid by the individuals, the S corporation is limited in that it usually cannot typically elect a fiscal year other than the calendar year. There are some exceptions to this. The corporation can make a Section 444 election, which generally allows for a tax year ending September 30, October 31, or November 30, but estimated tax payments must be made that would offset any advantage a shareholder might gain by having an offsetting fiscal year. Also, the application form for S election provides for requesting a fiscal year, but the IRS approval rate of fiscal year applications is not high. And, the IRS charges a $200 fee when you submit Form 1128, which is the application for a change of tax year.

The corporation must prove a reasonable business purpose or natural business year for fiscal year approval. To prove that you have cause for a fiscal year, at least twenty-five percent of the corporation's gross receipts must be received in the last two months of the selected tax year for the last three years.

Recent changes in the administrative requirements of the tax law may have real negative effects on S corporations who successfully acquire a fiscal year. Because they are not subject to the calendar-year deadlines, these corporations must make tax-like deposits each May 15. The rate is one percentage point above the prior year's top personal-income tax rate. Because the 1993 tax act raised the top 1993 personal rate to 39.6% from 31%, the rate for deposits due on May 15 jumps to 40.6%. Worse, the deposits don't earn interest.

It is not difficult to convert a C corporation into an S corporation. Simply fill out IRS form 2553, which must be signed by each stockholder (see sample in the Appendix), and mail it to the Internal Revenue Service within 75 days of starting business. An existing corporation can elect S corporation status within 75 days of the start of any corporate tax year.

There can be tax consequences associated with turning an existing C corporation that holds assets into an S corporation, especially in two specific instances:

> **MANY SHAREHOLDERS IN S CORPORATIONS ARE LIKELY TO PAY TAXES IN A MUCH LOWER RATE, BUT THE DEPOSIT REQUIREMENTS DON'T ALLOW FOR AN OWNER'S PERSONAL-TAX RATE.**

1. If a corporate asset has a fair market value at the time of the S election which is greater than the tax basis, and the asset is sold within 10 years of S election, the IRS will tax the "built-in" gain at the maximum corporate tax rate for the year the sale occurs.

2. If a corporation's passive income (interest, dividends, royalties, annuities, gains, etc.) exceeds 25% of gross receipts, it is taxed at the top corporate rate.

> *Speaking of tax basis, the stockholder cannot deduct corporate losses that exceed his tax basis in the shares (which includes capital contributions plus direct loans to the corporation.) If the corporation's losses exceed the stockholder's tax basis, the stockholder can carry the loss forward to a year when his basis increases.*

Because the tax obligation flows through to the shareholders, it is important to remember that the shareholders are taxed on their portion of corporate income, whether or not the income is distributed to the shareholders. If income is not distributed, then the shareholder's basis is adjusted to reflect undistributed income (which has the same tax impact as if the income was distributed to the shareholder, but immediately reinvested in additional shares.)

To determine the income tax obligation of each shareholder, the IRS uses a per-share, per-day formula. If the stock ownership remains the same throughout the tax year, the calculation is easy: Divide each tax item by the percentage of outstanding shares issued to each stockholder.

But, if the ownership changes, it gets more complicated. First, divide each tax item by the number of days in the year (365, except leap years) to find its daily value. Then multiply the daily value by the percentage of outstanding shares issued to each stockholder. Finally multiply this figure by the number of days each stockholder owned the stock. (Aren't tax calculations fun?)

> **THERE ARE NO PENALTY TAXES ON EXCESSIVE ACCUMULATED EARNINGS FOR S CORPORATIONS.**

A C corporation can avoid the accumulated earnings penalties by electing S corporation status and making a timely dividend distribution to the stockholders. This is true for the life of the S corporation election, and applies to the preceding tax year as well, if handled properly. The S corporation also might eliminate the personal holding company penalties, which are equivalent to the top individual tax rate, and problems with unreasonable compensation.

There are some significant differences between fringe benefits available to S corporations, as opposed to C corporations. While the C corporation can deduct the entire cost of health insurance premiums and group-term life insurance (within certain limits) without resulting in taxable income to shareholder/employees, the S corporation shareholder must report the paid premiums as taxable income if he owns more than 2% of the stock. The S corporation shareholder/employee may only deduct 25% of the cost of medical insurance as adjustment to income. Additional amounts may be deductible if itemized, but only to the extent they exceed 7.5% of the shareholder's adjusted gross income.

Keep in mind the fact that not all states recognize S corporation status. In some states, the S corporation is subject to tax in the same manner as regular C corporations. Therefore, it is incumbent upon you to determine what the tax law is in a particular state or states in which the S corporation may be doing business.

Unless and until the S election is terminated, the corporation can keep the status as long as it likes. There are several ways to cancel S election. The most obvious is to have more than 50% of the ownership vote to terminate the election. This is called an elective termination. Otherwise, the termination may be forced by corporate activity that is not allowed under S status. This could include having more shareholders than is allowed, creating a second class of stock, having too much passive income for three consecutive years, etc.

If an S corporation operates in more than one state, the tax laws of each affected state must be checked to see whether state law recognizes S corporations, whether any special state or city elections are required, and whether all of the shareholders of the corporation need to be residents of a particular state. In addition, problems may arise in connection with the apportionment of income among the various states. Some states provide that nonresident individuals must be subject to state income taxes on income from an S corporation operating in that state. Some states require nonresident shareholders to file written consents or agreements to pay income tax on their shares of the S corporation's taxable income.

Fortunately, since Nevada does not impose any corporate or personal income tax, you can avoid this entire question by incorporating your S corporation in Nevada and maintaining all of its business activity within the State.

Once you lose your S status, whether willingly or otherwise, you cannot elect it again for five years unless the majority of ownership changes hands. An accidental termination may be corrected if the IRS allows you to use special waiver provisions and you agree to necessary tax adjustments.

IMPACT OF THE 1993 TAX LAW

The 1993 Deficit Reduction Tax Law creates, for the first time in years, a situation where the top personal income tax rate is higher than the top corporate rate. Naturally, this results in many S corporations wondering if they should terminate their election. If the strategy is to eliminate double taxation, then the answer is probably "no." The double tax is still a stiff penalty, the only change being that the rates of taxation that apply are probably higher in each instance than they were before the change in the tax law.

S CORPORATION STATUS IS APPROPRIATE FOR:

- Companies expecting start-up losses during initial years of operation.

- Companies with no intent of going public in the future.

- Companies that do not expect to issue multiple classes of stock.

- Companies whose shareholder-employees under C corporation status might be subject to charges by the IRS of excessive compensation.

- Companies that might be subject to tax on excessive accumulated earnings.

- Companies that otherwise would be subject to the Alternative Minimum Tax.

S CORPORATION STATUS IS NOT APPROPRIATE FOR:

- Companies that would violate eligibility requirements (having more than 75 shareholders, or ineligible shareholders, etc.)

- Companies that need a tax deduction for significant employee fringe benefits for shareholder-employees, including: $5,000 in death benefits for the employee's estate; Accident and health insurance plans; Up to $50,000 of group term life insurance on the employee's life; The cost of meals or lodging furnished for the convenience of the employer;

- Companies with substantial amounts of earnings and profits who must pay a dividend to shareholders within three years of election or election will be terminated, AND who have more than 25% of gross receipts because of passive investment income such as rents, royalties, interest and dividends.

PERSONAL SERVICES CORPORATION

Many small business owners operate as a regular C corporation to take advantage of the many benefits we have described above. Unfortunately the tax laws classify the work of some service-oriented businesses so that they can lose all the tax advantages associated with incorporating. This classification is known as the Personal Service Corporation (PSC).

Section 448 of the Internal Revenue Code defines the PSC that is subject to the flat 35% tax rate. First, at least 95% of the employee's time is spent working in one of several specified fields. This includes doctors, nurses, dentists, veterinarians, singers, actors, musicians, and consultants paid for their advice and counsel (as opposed to commissions). Second, at least of 95% of the value of the stock is held, either directly or indirectly, by employees who provide the services, retired employees, their estates or heirs within two years of getting their inheritance. As you can see, many small corporations meet this test.

The personal service corporation must generally use a calendar year, with the same exceptions that apply to an S corporation as was discussed earlier. And, the limitation on accumulated earnings for a PSC is $150,000, which is $100,000 less than is available to a C corporation. Like an individual, a PSC cannot offset business income with passive losses.

HOLDING CORPORATIONS

A holding corporation is any corporation that owns or "holds" control of other corporations, which are called subsidiaries. According to the Internal Revenue Service, a corporation maintains control of a subsidiary when it owns at least 80 percent of its stock. At that point, the corporations can combine their income and expenses and either file a consolidated tax return or put together a consolidated financial statement when applying for bank financing.

The assumption that a holding corporation is only involved in the passive business of owning other companies is not necessarily true. Often, the holding company is the primary business, and by virtue of its business activities decides to separately incorporate individual aspects of its business.

PERSONAL HOLDING COMPANIES

The Internal Revenue Service designates any corporation with over 60 percent passive income, whose stock is owned (more than 50%) by not more than five people at any time during the last half of the tax year as a **personal holding company**. To determine the stock ownership requirement, the rules consider stock owned by a corporation, partnership or estate to be owned proportionately by its shareholders, partners, or beneficiaries.

Income to a personal holding company is taxed at personal income tax rates instead of corporate income tax rates, as long as it is being distributed. If it is not distributed, a surtax is 39.6% of undistributed earnings. (Note: Computer software companies may be exempt from the personal holding company tax under the Internal Revenue Code.) Personal holding company income includes the following:

- Rent adjusted for the use of, or the right to use corporate property, with certain exceptions.

- Dividends, interest, royalties, and annuities, including royalties from mineral, oil, gas and copyrights.

- Payments under personal service contracts.

- Taxable income from estates and trusts.

NONPROFIT CORPORATIONS

A nonprofit corporation is one recognized by the Internal Revenue Service as tax exempt under section 501(c)(3) of the Internal Revenue Code, and is organized for a public or charitable purpose. A nonprofit corporation must have at least five directors or trustees, and upon dissolution must either distribute its assets to the state or federal government, or another entity recognized as exempt under Section 501(c)(3).

THE TAX IMPACT OF HAVING THE DESIGNATION OF PERSONAL SERVICE CORPORATION IS THAT THE CORPORATE TAX RATE IS A FLAT 35%, INSTEAD OF THE GRADUATED RATE THAT STARTS AT 15% REPRESENTED ON THE CHART IN THE PREVIOUS CHAPTER. AND, THIS APPLIES TO ALL INCOME, BEGINNING WITH THE FIRST DOLLAR. THEN, WHEN PROFITS ARE DISTRIBUTED TO SHAREHOLDERS, THEY WILL BE TAXED AGAIN AT THE SHAREHOLDER'S PERSONAL RATE.

The American Cancer Society and the Muscular Dystrophy Association are two notable entities organized as nonprofit corporations, and each city in the US is host to many local nonprofit corporations organized to meet local needs. For private purposes, however the nonprofit has severe limitations.

Most corporations that are formed "for-profit" are allowed to engage in "any lawful business activity." Nonprofit corporations are required to state a specific purpose that benefits either the public at large, a segment of the community, or a particular membership-based group.

It is possible to use a nonprofit corporation for charitable purposes and realize favorable tax treatment and benefits. Where the situation is right, an individual could form a nonprofit corporation for some specific or general charitable activity, and hire the grown children to administer to company affairs. There is nothing wrong with a nonprofit corporation paying a salary to its employees.

Contributions to 501(c)(3) corporations are exempt from federal estate taxation. Many wealthy individuals make substantial contributions in their estate plans for qualified nonprofit corporations. These estate plan contributions are actively pursued by many nonprofits as part of their campaign for public support.

For tax purposes, the nonprofit corporation must be formed for religious, charitable, scientific, educational or literary purposes in order to claim 501(c)(3) tax-exempt status. Only with that status is a corporation eligible to receive tax deductible contributions from donors.

UNRELATED INCOME: While the primary purpose of a nonprofit corporation is limited to specific activities, the nonprofit is allowed to make money in ways unrelated to their nonprofit purposes. This unrelated income is often subject to taxation as unrelated business income under state and federal corporate tax laws

ADVANTAGES OF NONPROFIT STATUS

Aside from the obvious tax advantages, 501(c)(3) corporations enjoy many advantages over regular corporations. These advantages are helpful, if not necessary, to the success of the nonprofit organization. They include:

- Lower postal rates on third class bulk mailings.

- Less expensive advertising rates.

- Eligibility for many state and/or federal grants.

- Nonprofits are exclusive beneficiaries of free radio and television Public Service Announcements (PSA's) provided by media outlets.

- Employees may be eligible to participate in a variety of job-training, student intern, work-study, and other federal, state and local employment incentive programs where salaries are substantially paid out of government funds.

501(C)(3) ELIGIBILITY RULES

The Internal Revenue Code places a number of restrictions and limitations that apply to nonprofit corporations. It is essential that the nonprofit corporation meet these rules to maintain their tax exempt status. To be eligible for nonprofit tax exemption, the corporation must:

- be organized and operated for charitable, educational, religious, literary or scientific purposes;

- not distribute gains to directors, officers or members;

- distribute any assets remaining upon dissolution to another qualified tax-exempt entity or group;

- not participate in political campaigns for or against candidates for public office; and

- not substantially engage in grass-roots legislative or political activities except as permitted under federal tax rules.

APPLICATION FOR FEDERAL TAX EXEMPTION

The forms and procedures for applying for 501(c)(3) tax exemption are not simple. You will need to obtain the following federal tax forms and publications by stopping by your local IRS office or calling 1-800-TAX-FORM:

Form 8718: User Fee for Exempt Organization Determination Letter Request. This form is used to compute and pay the fees that are due for applying for tax exemption and should be included in the 1023 application that is submitted to the IRS.

Package 1023: Application for Recognition of Exemption with instructions. This one is the monster. The 1023 package includes two copies of the form. One should be used as a draft until the application is ready. The second copy is for the final application.

Publication 557: Tax-Exempt Status for your Organization

Publication 558: Tax Information for Private Foundations and Foundation Managers

THE IRS ESTIMATES THAT IT TAKES THE AVERAGE PERSON 4 HOURS AND 41 MINUTES TO LEARN ABOUT THE APPLICATION FORM. THEN IT TAKES ANOTHER 9 HOURS AND 22 MINUTES TO PREPARE THE FORM.

Chapter

7

FUNDING THE CORPORATION

Getting the assets in

CAPITALIZING A CORPORATION

A corporation usually needs cash or other assets in order begin functioning as viable business. To obtain money to finance its operations, a corporation may issue interests in itself that are commonly known as securities.

Corporate securities are of two basic types which will be discussed in greater detail in this chapter, they are:

Debt Securities, in which the corporation is in debt to the person holding the security, and;

Equity Securities, in which the holder has purchased an ownership interest in the business.

> *"An investment contract for purposes of the Securities Act means a contract, transaction or scheme whereby a person invests his money in a common enterprise and is let to expect profits solely from the efforts of the promoter or a third party... It embodies a flexible rather than a static principle, one that is capable of adaptation to meet the countless and variable schemes devised by those who seek the use of the money of others on the promise of profits." - Frank Murphy, in SEC v. Howey Co.*

Debt Securities

A debt security is created when a corporation borrows money. The most obvious sources for these borrowed funds is the corporation's organizers or their families, or a bank. These private loans occur when the corporation issues a promissory note to the lender, documenting the terms of the loan.

THE DIFFERENCE BETWEEN BONDS AND DEBENTURES IS THAT A BOND IS SECURED BY THE PROPERTY OF THE CORPORATION, AND A DEBENTURE IS UNSECURED.

Debt securities may be solicited from public sources as well. These securities are called "bonds" or "debentures". Just as the promissory note documents the terms of the debt, bonds and debentures have maturity dates, when the corporation must pay back the face value to the bond holder. The corporation also must make periodic interest charges, which are calculated as a percentage of the face value of the bond.

These instruments are usually issued in amounts of $1,000.00. As a security, the holder can transfer or sell his interest in the security. If a bond is sold for more than its face value, it is said to have been be sold "at a premium". If it is sold at less than face value, it is sold "at a discount."

Advantages of Debt Financing

- A corporation can deduct the interest payments on the debt, while dividends paid to stockholders are not deductible.

- Debt repayment has priority over equity contributions. The bills must be paid before profits are distributed.

- Repayment schedules can be predicted and planned for.

- Repayment is not taxable income to the debt holder.

- In the event of business failure, losses are treated as ordinary business bad debt deductions, instead of as capital loss from worthless stock.

- A debt investor has even less liability than a stockholder. There is less chance of using Alter Ego Theory on debt holders.

Disadvantages of Debt Financing

- If the corporation has too high of a debt-to-equity ratio, and the debt holders are insiders, the courts might rule that the debt is actually hidden equity ownership.

- The IRS takes a close look at shareholder loans in order to identify disguised dividends.

- A corporation with marginal equity may have the claims of stockholder-creditors subordinated by a court.

EQUITY SECURITIES

When a corporation issues an equity security, it is known as shares or stock in a corporation. Stockholders are the owners of the corporation. The Articles of Incorporation state the number of shares that a corporation may issue. The corporation may issue fewer shares than it is authorized, but may not issue more.

The corporation will issue a certificate to each shareholder which states the precise characteristics of the stock it represents. This provides each shareholder with notice of rights, duties, obligations of the shares he or she owns.

To issue stock is to sell corporate securities. The corporation's board of directors may decide when and to whom stock may be sold. When the stock is issued, it is called "outstanding shares." Shareholders generally invest in corporate stock with the expectation that the corporation will generate profits, which will be distributed to the shareholders as dividends.

Advantages of Equity Financing

- Greater potential for growth. Equity financing provides an opportunity to raise more money than is possible through debt financing, since most debt financing requires security against corporation assets.

- A corporation with equity financing is in a stronger financial position than one that relies heavily on debt financing. A better credit rating translates into more potential for additional outside financing.

- Equity financing eliminates cash-flow problems that can be created by the requirement to make interest payments on debt.

Disadvantages of Equity Financing

- Dividends are not deductible expenses for the corporation, while they are taxable to the shareholder. This results in double taxation on corporate profits.

- Dividends are paid only after the corporation has met is other obligations, including debt repayment.

- Dividends may not be paid consistently.

- Shareholders are more likely to have Alter Ego Theory applied in an attempt to pierce the corporate veil.

A MORE DETAILED DISCUSSION OF SECURITIES ISSUES WILL BE COVERED IN THE NEXT CHAPTER.

Whether a corporation sells stock or bonds, it is subject to a number of requirements relative to the value it must receive and the type of payment it may accept. For example, the corporation may not sell its shares for less than the stated par value of the stock. However, once a third party has purchased the stock from the corporation, it may be resold for whatever price is desired.

In addition, the corporation is generally restricted as to the form of payment it may accept. When selling stock, the corporation may receive only money, property, or services actually rendered to it. This requirement may vary from state to state.

FRAUDULENT CONVEYANCE

> "A conveyance for purpose of avoiding collection of damages in a pending action for a tort is fraudulent." Anglo-American Packing & Provision Co. v. Baier.

When you are sued, there may be a temptation to attempt to transfer some or all or your assets to your corporation to keep them protected. This will almost universally get you into trouble. The courts refer to this type of transaction as "fraudulent conveyance," and this term is used to describe any attempt to improperly transfer assets for avoiding lawsuits and liens.

Fraudulent conveyance is based on a principal that a creditor has a right of remedy against a debtor. If the creditor's right to collect the debt is infringed, based on the available assets of the debtor and due to transfer or conveyance of assets, the entire transaction can be set aside.

Even the wisest and most experienced attorney is unable to provide a complete and proper definition of fraudulent conveyance. This is because, ultimately, it is defined by a judge's interpretation, and based on specific circumstances. The courts can only rely on the existence or nonexistence of certain facts. For instance, a judge may look at the amount of time that separates the transfer of assets from an event that results in liability.

The basic rules that define fraudulent conveyance are set forth in one of two legislative acts that are adopted by all of the states. The Uniform Fraudulent Conveyance Act (UFCA) is in effect in most states, and the Uniform Fraudulent Transfers Act (UFTA) is used in the remaining states. The laws are virtually identical in that they define two categories of fraudulent transfers:

> **Fraud-in-law**, or constructive fraud, which occurs when there is a gift or sale of the debtor's property for less than fair market value, in the face of a known liability, which renders the debtor insolvent or unable to pay the creditor. Fraud-in-law can only exist when all the above elements are present, but notably there is no need to prove that the debtor had intentions to defraud the creditor.

> **Fraud-in-fact**, or actual fraud, which occurs when the creditor proves that the debtor intended to hinder, delay or defraud your creditors.

THE THEORY IS THAT WHEN A DEBTOR IS INSOLVENT, HIS PROPERTY CONSTRUCTIVELY BELONGS TO HIS CREDITORS.

TIME FRAME

Creditors must act within a specific time frame if they are to challenge a transfer under fraudulent conveyance statutes. In most states, the statute of limitations is four years after the transfer is made or the debt is incurred, or one year after it could have reasonably been discovered, whichever occurs last.

UNDER FEDERAL BANKRUPTCY LAW, THE BANKRUPTCY TRUSTEE GENERALLY HAS TWO YEARS FROM THE FIRST MEETING OF CREDITORS TO BEGIN A FRAUDULENT TRANSFER CLAIM. THE EXCEPTION TO THIS IS IF THE TRUSTEE CHOOSES TO BRING A FRAUDULENT TRANSFER ACTION UNDER STATE LAW INSTEAD.

Remember that any transfer of your assets needs to be supported by legitimate business reasons. And, the transfer must be made prior to any event or situation that results in a lawsuit. Once the event has actually occurred, the transaction will be subject to intense scrutiny. If the transfer of assets takes place after you have been served with the lawsuit, it is virtually impossible to justify the transaction to the satisfaction of the court.

The best way to avoid fraudulent conveyance is to put a strategy in place before you have reason to expect trouble. When this type of planning is put in place well in advance, the strategy has a much better chance of being upheld by the court.

If a transfer is found to be fraudulent, the court can force a re-transfer of the asset to the creditors. If the party which receives the fraudulent transfer is an innocent third-party, unaware of any fraudulent intent, he or she can place a lien against the transferred asset up to the amount paid.

Chapter

8

STOCK

Ownership IS three-fourths of the law.

T he terms "stock" and "shares" are used synonymously and represent the basic elements of ownership in the corporation. Stockholders "share" in the benefits and risks of the business of the corporation. So, a share of stock represents the right to a distribution of surplus profits of the corporation, and the right to part of the funds left over after all the debt of the corporation has been paid after dissolution.

The ownership of shares of stock is physically manifest by stock certificates. The stock certificate is a written acknowledgment from the corporation that the holder has an interest in the corporation's property and assets.

In some ways, a stock certificate is similar to a bank check. When someone writes you a check, they have not given you something of monetary value per se, but have given you a piece of paper that represents the value of money. When you present the check, properly endorsed, to the appropriate party, they will exchange the piece of paper for the value of the money stated on the check. A stock certificate functions in the same way.

The primary difference between a bank check and a stock certificate is that the value of the check is fixed (a $5 dollar check will always be exchanged for $5) while the value of the stock certificate is variable. But, the fact that the stock certificate, like the check, can be exchanged for value makes it a negotiable instrument. This fact requires that you treat stock certificates with particular care since negotiable instruments are frequent devices for fraud.

It is a common misconception to believe that the stock certificate is the stock itself. The stock certificate is not stock itself, but is merely paper indicative of ownership of the amount of stock stated on it. In most states, Nevada included, the stockholder owns the stock, whether he has the certificate or not.

TYPES OF STOCK - DEFINITIONS

1) **Capital Stock.** Capital stock refers to the total amount of money and property authorized to be paid in to the corporation. The total capital stock is set for each corporation in the articles of incorporation. To arrive at the total capital stock, multiply the number of shares authorized in the articles of incorporation by the par value of each share. The result will be a dollar figure that represents the total capital stock of the corporation. This figure remains the same unless the articles of

incorporation are amended in this regard, and has no bearing on the actual value of the corporation's assets.

2) **Authorized Stock.** The articles of incorporation state the number of individual shares that the corporation is authorized to issue. The total authorized stock includes all shares, whether issued or not.

3) **Common Stock.** Corporations that issue only one class of stock, generally issue common stock. Common stock is sold to raise sufficient capital to provide for the growth of the corporation. Holders of common stock all share identical rights and responsibilities, and have rights to annual dividends in an amount equal to the prorated percentage of their ownership of shares, but are not guaranteed that an annual distribution will take place in any given year. Common stock is often divided into separate classes, the most common division being between voting and non-voting shares. Since the natural assumption is that all stock is voting, any non-voting shares should clearly indicate the fact on the stock certificate to avoid confusion. When common stock is divided into voting and non-voting shares, the classes of common stock are usually called "Class A - Voting Common Capital Stock," and "Class B - Non-Voting Common Capital Stock."

4) **Preferred Stock.** Preferred stock is a class of stock given a preferred status in distribution of dividends. They receive their dividends before any holders of common stock. Occasionally, the bylaws of the corporation guarantee that preferred stockholders will receive a specific annual return on their shares. For example, if there is ten percent preferred stock, that ten percent dividend must be paid before anything is paid on common stock. This creates the possibility that a dividend distribution to preferred stockholders will absorb all of the available dividend distribution, leaving nothing for common stockholders.

5) **Treasury Stock.** The term "treasury stock" refers to shares issued to individuals, and subsequently reacquired by the corporation. When it does no harm to the creditors of the corporation, the stock may be repurchased and held in the corporate treasury, where it can remain for some time. The stock can also be retired or reissued later. Shares of treasury stock do not give the company it's own voting rights.

6) **Deferred Stock.** This term refers to any class of stock to which dividend payments are deferred until after dividend payments have been made to some senior class of stock. By this definition, common stock is deferred when preferred stock is present. Because the Nevada Corporation Code allows for the creation of an unlimited number of stock classes, it is possible to create an extended queue of stock classes deferred until all prior classes are paid.

7) **Convertible Stock.** Convertible stock is stock that may be converted at the option of the corporation to another class of stock. The most common use of convertible stock involves preferred stock that may be converted to common stock.

8) **Redeemable Stock.** When a corporation retains the option to purchase stock from the stockholders, that stock is called "redeemable stock." Depending upon

> PREFERRED STOCK MAY BE CATEGORIZED AS EITHER "CUMULATIVE," OR "NON-CUMULATIVE." CUMULATIVE STOCK MEANS THAT, IN A YEAR IN WHICH THE PREFERRED STOCKHOLDERS DO NOT RECEIVE THEIR GUARANTEED DIVIDEND (BECAUSE OF POOR EARNINGS, ETC.) THE GUARANTEED DIVIDEND IS ADDED TO THE NEXT YEAR'S DIVIDEND, AND SO ON UNTIL THE ACCUMULATED DIVIDEND IS PAID IN ENTIRETY. NON-CUMULATIVE STOCKHOLDERS LOSE THEIR RIGHT TO THEIR DIVIDEND IN ANY YEAR IN WHICH THE CORPORATION ELECTS NOT TO PAY DIVIDENDS.

the bylaws, the corporation may either have the right to exercise its option any time, or may be limited to exercising its option in only certain circumstances. Usually, the stock is redeemed at par value, unless otherwise stated.

9) **Assessable/Non-Assessable Stock.** When a corporation wants to retain the right to assess, or "bill," its stockholders in the event it needs cash resources beyond the available capital stock, it may assign a class of stock as "assessable" stock. Capital stock may be made assessable when the articles of incorporation provide that "the capital stock of the corporation shall be subject to assessment." Holders of assessable stock may be called upon at any time to provide additional financial resources to the corporation. Most stock, however, is non-assessable stock, meaning that the corporation cannot request additional cash from the stockholders without issuing additional stock.

10) **Restricted Stock.** A corporation may choose to restrict the transfer of its shares by specifying the desired restriction in either the articles of incorporation or the bylaws. It is required that certificates representing restricted stock contain a legend that either states the restriction or refers the holder to the provisions in the articles or bylaws that contain them. Common restrictions include giving either the corporation or a specified class of stockholder the first rights of refusal on the stock when it is transferred.

IN NEVADA, FOR EXAMPLE, USING **NO-PAR VALUE** STOCK CAN INCREASE THE COST OF FILING THE ARTICLES OF INCORPORATION. FOR THE PURPOSES OF DECIDING THE FILING FEE, THE SECRETARY OF STATE ASSIGNS A VALUE OF $1 PER SHARE ON STOCK OF NOMINAL VALUE. THE GREATER THE PAR VALUE OF YOUR STOCK, THE HIGHER THE FEE WILL BE TO THE SECRETARY OF STATE.

11) **No-par Value Stock**. No-par stock is stock that has no specific par value attributed to it in the corporations Articles of Incorporation. Although no-par value stock is not addressed in Nevada's Corporation Code, a 1956 Attorney General's opinion says that "corporations may organize, provide for and issue no-par stock for varying considerations." The value of no-par stock depends entirely upon what the market will bear, and on the actual value of the corporation. In reality, all stock is supposed to act that way, no matter its stated value. The exception being when dealing with redeemable stock. (Since redeemable stock is usually paid at par value, when that stock has a stated value the corporation may be forced to redeem shares for more or less than what it is actually worth.) The board of directors has the authority to determine a set value for its no-par value shares. This is done by resolution. The cost of filing a Nevada corporation with 25,000 shares of stock with a value of $50 per share will be $650, while 25,000 shares of no-par value stock will cost $125. The corporation could incorporate with no-par value stock, and then by resolution of the board of directors set the value of those shares at $50, by that accomplishing the same thing, while saving $525 in filing fees.

12) **Bearer Shares**. If stock certificates can be compared to bank checks, then bearer shares can be compared to a check written to "cash." The stock certificate is issued to the "bearer," and anyone with the physical possession of those certificates is technically the owner of the stock. Although the name of that original bearer must be recorded in the books of the corporation, it is possible that the certificates have been transferred several times since they were originally issued, making them very

difficult to track. In theory, the holder of the bearer shares would eventually surface, and provide the corporate secretary with the record of transfers that prove he has the right to the stock. However, until that happens it may be impossible to prove who owns that stock at any given moment. Until the holder of the certificate does register his ownership with the corporation, he does not have any voting rights or right to dividends declared during that period of his ownership.

13) **"Participating" Preferred Stock.** This stock entitles the holder to all the rights of the preferred stockholder, but also participates with the common stock in any earnings above the percentage agreed upon for preferred stockholders.

14) **"Watered" Stock.** This is stock issued gratuitously, or by agreement under which the holder pays less than its par value. This type of stock issuance is binding upon the corporation and any of the stockholders that agree or acquiesce to the transaction. Any dissenting stockholders have the right to sue for cancellation of the stock. When watered stock is part of the original stock issued, it technically represents fraud on future creditors of the corporation who deal in the good faith that the stock has been fully paid. So, if the corporation becomes insolvent, the holders of watered stock may be held liable for its par value to pay to creditors. By using no par value stock, the problems of dealing with watered stock can be decreased or avoided.

CLOSE CORPORATIONS

Some states allow for the formation of corporations that are specifically designated as "close corporations." The close corporation idea is designed for small groups of investors, who may function for all intents and purposes as a partnership, while retaining corporate liability protection and corporate income tax deductions and rates. The close corporation is used to essentially "close" the company from outsiders through restrictions on ownership and information.

A statutory **close corporation** may have no more than 30 stockholders, and is prohibited from making a public stock offering as defined by the Securities Act of 1933. A close corporation also must identify itself as such on all corporate records and when entering into contracts. In other words, the company must include "a close corporation" in or after its name on all documents and records.

Stockholders in close corporations may have materially different rights from stockholders in other corporations. Usually this takes the form of allowing stockholders free access to all corporate records and agreements that may not be as readily accessible to stockholders in other corporations. Additionally, there are limitations placed on the transfer of shares of the close corporation that would not exist otherwise. For example, a close corporation is commonly used to ensure that a particular business activity remains in the family.

The stock would properly have a restriction that provides only for a transfer of shares between family members. (Be sure you can work with that arrangement before you get locked into a messy situation.) Naturally, this depends upon the Corporation Code of the state of origin.

In many states, shareholders of a close corporation may even eliminate the board of directors, (but not officers) and make all management decisions themselves. For example, Nevada's Corporation Code allows the stockholders to "treat the corporation as if it were a partnership or to arrange relations among the stockholders or between the stockholders and the corporation in a way that would be appropriate only among partners."

If the shareholders do away with the directors, they may appoint one among them to sign documents as designated directors, if needed. These "pseudo-directors" are relieved of all personal liability that could be assigned to them because of not observing the usual corporate formalities.

If the close corporation does have a board of directors, their powers can be limited by shareholder agreement to only certain tasks. This generally relieves the directors of all liability imposed by law but transfers what would otherwise have been director's liability to the shareholders that have the voting rights to regulate the board of directors. Check your corporate laws, as this can vary between states.

ISSUANCE OF SHARES

Each state has its own rules concerning what type of asset may be used to capitalize a corporation. The most restrictive approach would require the corporation to issue its shares of stock only in exchange for cash or some other physical asset.

Some states, for instance, do not allow the issuance of shares for intangible assets. So, you should check with the Corporation Code of the state in which your are incorporating to see what considerations are allowed.

The fact that Nevada allows stock to be issued for intangible assets is another advantage that creates flexibility in managing the corporation. Just as the nature of intangible assets is somewhat indeterminate, so is the value of intangible assets difficult to pin down. Who is to say what an intangible asset is worth? Why, the board of directors can decide that issue. And, Nevada law says that their decision is final.

This is a tremendous advantage to a corporation that starts-up with a large amount of "sweat equity." Those who have sacrificed their time and talents to make the corporation succeed can be issued stock for the value of their labor. And that value will be determined by the board. Although this might seem like an unusual way to capitalize a corporation, it is quite effective with a Nevada corporation, and just as binding as a cash capitalization.

Naturally, corporations that need to develop banking relationships for lines of credit, etc. are better off issuing stock only for cash. But even then, it is helpful to have the flexibility of issuing stock for other considerations if the situation requires.

NOT ISSUING SHARES
In order for a corporation that is organized for a profitable purpose to exist, it must necessarily have shareholders. Without shareholders, it is possible that the corporate

TO TREAT THE CLOSE CORPORATION "AS IF IT WERE A PARTNERSHIP" AS ALLOWED UNDER NEVADA'S CORPORATE LAWS IS NOT THE SAME AS A CORPORATION HAVING FLOW-THROUGH TAX STATUS. THAT IS A SEPARATE ISSUE, AND WOULD REQUIRE SUBCHAPTER S ELECTION.

UNDER THE NEVADA CORPORATION CODE, A CORPORATION MAY ISSUE SHARES IN CONSIDERATION OF ANY TANGIBLE OR INTANGIBLE ASSET. THIS MAY INCLUDE, BUT IS NOT LIMITED TO, CASH, SERVICES, PROPERTY, PROMISSORY NOTES, CONTRACTS TO PERFORM SERVICES, OR ANY OTHER SECURITY. NOT EVERY STATE HAS SUCH A BROAD ALLOWANCE FOR THE ISSUANCE OF STOCK.

existence could be set aside under scrutiny. Nevertheless, many states corporate laws do not require that stock be issued within any specified period of time.

There is a common **misconception** perpetrated by some within Nevada's incorporation industry. That is, that you do not have to issue stock if you don't want to because Nevada law does not specifically require it. Although this is technically accurate, following this advise can have dire consequences.

Remember what stock represents. It represents ownership. To own part of a corporation, there must be some form of exchange of assets. When an exchange of assets takes place, you have in reality created a stockholder. To think that you can avoid liability and connection to the corporation because the stock was not issued is pure folly. Even if you intended the exchange of assets to be a loan, if no stockholders exist, it is probable under those circumstances that a judge would rule that the loan in reality represented a capital exchange and de facto stock ownership.

If an exchange of assets does not take place, then the corporation itself has no assets or owners. If the corporation has no assets or owners, it cannot act and becomes a useless entity. If the corporation begins functioning without shareholders, there is the risk that the court may rule that, without shareholders, the corporation was not acting like a corporation at all, thus holding personally liable the individuals who directed the corporate activity.

Just because the Corporation Code does not require that stock be issued, does not mean that you can get away with it for any period of time. Stock issuance is a necessary corporate formality that, if it is handled properly, will offer virtually the same liability protection to the stockholder that he would have if he did not own stock in the first place. The only reason not to issue stock is if you are interested in keeping a corporation shell on the shelf gathering dust for some specific reason.

FEDERAL SECURITIES LIMITATIONS ON PUBLIC OFFERINGS

It is important to remember that the public issuance of stock exposes the corporation and associated individuals with a complex web of state and federal laws that regulate their sale and distribution. A corporation must take great care in planning and executing a public sale of stock to guarantee the validity of the sale and steer clear of the legal violations. It is highly recommended that a professional advisor be consulted when dealing in the sale of corporate securities.

The primary federal statutes regulating securities transactions are the Securities Act of 1933 and the Securities Exchange Act of 1934. It is the intent of these legislative Acts that there be a disclosure of information to potential investors to prevent fraud in securities transactions.

THE SECURITIES ACT OF 1933
The 1933 Act requires that any person or issuing corporation who attempts any sale of a security, file a registration statement that discloses a broad range of information about the security, the company, and the seller. However the Act also lists several exemptions from the registration requirement. For example, there are exemptions for most, but not all, sales

of securities that are made by parties other than the original "issuer", which is generally the company creating the security.

There are other exemptions that remove the registration requirement from some securities sales made by the "issuer" as well. The main exemptions are:

1. **Private Placements**. A private placement is defined as a sale *or solicitation* to not more than 35 persons. There can be no general promotion or advertising of the solicitation to potential investors.

2. **Small Offerings**. This exemption deals with the value of the offering rather than the number of investors. Sales of less than $5 million worth of securities currently need not register.

3. **Intrastate Offerings**. If the corporation is incorporated in and is conducting business solely in one state, and sells its securities only to residents of that state, it is exempt from registration. This rule has some tricky implications because a violation can occur if a nonresident is offered a security, or if a resident purchases a security and subsequently sells the security to a nonresident.

THE SECURITIES EXCHANGE ACT OF 1934

The 1934 Act has broader registration and disclosure requirements and contains provisions designed to reduce the risk of market manipulation, insider-trading, and the like. Companies that are either listed on a national securities exchange, or that have more than 500 shareholders and more than $3 million in assets (typically this applies to stock that trades Over The Counter, or OTC) must be registered. The requirements include registration statements for classes of securities offered for sale and SEC approved updates through annual reports.

STATE SECURITIES ISSUES

"BLUE SKY LAWS"
REFER TO THE
MISCELLANEOUS STATE
LAWS THAT HAVE BEEN
DEVELOPED TO PROHIBIT
FRAUD IN SECURITIES
TRANSACTIONS, AND THE
REQUIRED DISCLOSURE
THROUGH STATE
REGISTRATION. IF A
COMPANY SELLS ITS STOCK
IN SEVERAL STATES, THE
COMPANY MUST COMPLY
WITH THE BLUE SKY LAWS OF
EACH STATE, OR QUALIFY
FOR AN EXEMPTION UNDER
THEM.

Although the federal securities laws apply consistently to all US corporations, each state has its own securities laws that not only differ dramatically, but may also contradict the federal restrictions. Some states, for instance, regulate the sale of corporate stock to any individual outside the original group of incorporators in order for the state to follow and keep track of all transactions that may be taxable events under state income tax laws.

A Nevada corporation may sell stock to up to twenty-five stockholders per year without needing additional authorization from the state. After stockholder number twenty-five, a corporation must meet the Secretary of State's requirements for an intrastate offering that will allow additional sale of stock, as long as the sale takes place within the boundaries of the state. This involves putting together a formal prospectus for the stock offering and filling it with the Securities Division of the Secretary of State's office. Nevada charges a $500 filing and processing fee for this process.

INDIVIDUAL STOCK SALE VS. CORPORATE STOCK SALE

There are restrictions in some states that require that the individuals who are originally issued the stock hold it for a specified period of time. So, you should still check with a knowledgeable securities attorney before using this method to sell your corporate shares.

While a corporation can be strictly regulated in its ability to sell stock, the restrictions on an individual selling stock issued in his name may differ. Since Nevada's Corporation Code specifically says that shares of stock are personal property, the individual could theoretically sell his shares at a garage sale along with the mismatched set of golf clubs and broken lawn furniture.

The result of this is that a corporation could conceivably issue all of its stock - let's say 25,000 shares - to a half dozen people, who could then sell those shares as their personal property. If the stock was originally issued for $5 per share, they could sell them for $10 a share and by that prove that they had the natural profit motive for the transactions. The corporation has sold all of its stock, but the following transfers may result in possibly hundreds or thousands of individual stockholders.

CUMULATIVE VOTING

Nevada corporation code allows corporations to use a procedure known as "cumulative voting" to elect the board of directors. Cumulative voting is not mandated by the state, and is required to be in the articles of incorporation to be legal. This procedure is not available to shareholders when voting on any other issue.

When cumulative voting is in effect, each shareholder is entitled to cast a number of votes equal to the total number of shares he owns, multiplied by the total number of directors to be elected. So, if a shareholder owned 100 shares and the corporation was electing 35 directors, the shareholder is allowed 3500 votes. The shareholder may either cast all of his votes for one candidate or spread his vote out among several candidates.

This system allows for minority representation on the board of directors because often the minority investors will have enough votes to elect their own representative to the board. Though he may be a minority on the board, their representative will have full access to the corporation's records and affairs.

Unless cumulative voting exists, the holder of a majority of the voting rights is entitled to control the election of all open positions on the board. Majority shareholders can then make the votes of minority investors ineffective.

VOTING TRUSTS

Nevada allows for multiple stockholders to form a voting trust, which allows the shareholders to give their voting power to a trustee. The trustee may be given the power to either vote on all matters, or may be limited to voting on only certain subjects.

The voting trust is formed by trust agreement, which specifically outlines all of the powers that are included in the trust. Nevada limits voting trusts to a period of ten years or less, although the term can be extended at anytime during the last two years of the agreement.

VOTING AGREEMENTS

A voting agreement is similar to a voting trust, except no trustee is appointed by the shareholders. Instead, the shareholders retain their own vote, with the agreement to cast them according to the terms of their agreement. This results in a situation in which a shareholder can theoretically break his agreement any time. When this happens, it generally requires litigation to enforce it's terms. Like a voting trust, a voting agreement is limited to a ten-year term, with the same extension rights in the last two years.

PROXIES

Proxies are a commonly-used device by shareholders who want to cast their vote, but are unable to attend the shareholders meeting. The proxy is actually a written document that is similar in nature to a power-of-attorney. The shareholder that signs a proxy appoints another person to act as his agent to vote his shares.

Depending upon the wording of the proxy document, it's power may be general in nature, or may limit the person holding the proxy to votes taken on specific matters. Further, the proxy may allow the person holding it to vote as his own discretion, or to vote in a specific way. The shareholder is usually able to revoke the proxy any time.

Proxies are only valid for six months from its execution unless the instrument states differently. Proxies are no longer valid after seven years from execution. Nevada does not allow directors to use proxies, but require them to use their best judgment in managing the corporation's affairs.

Chapter

9

TAKING CASH OUT OF THE CORPORATION

Procedures, Pitfalls and Precautions

Perhaps the greatest challenge to owner/managers of closely held corporations is in reaping the greatest possible financial benefit that the corporation can afford to pay, while paying the least amount of tax. If you own your own business, there's no question that you have the right to the money the corporation earns. However, if you are not careful about how you put the money in your pocket, you could jeopardize the protection the corporate veil provides.

We have previously examined the tax consequences of incorporating. As previously discussed, Subchapter S can play a major role in reducing the negative tax consequences of double taxation to which a corporation can otherwise be subjected.

AVOIDING DOUBLE TAXATION

One of the potential pitfalls of using a regular, C corporation is the possibility of running into the double taxation trap. As a corporation generates income, it pays tax on the taxable portion of the proceeds at the applicable corporate tax rate. The corporation can deduct necessary expenses, which will include payroll expenses.

But if, after salaries and expenses have been paid, the company has a profit, there is going to be a taxable result. The size of the taxable result depends upon what the company intends to do with the profits. If the corporation keeps the profits as reserves to finance some new project or development, it will pay the appropriate corporate income taxes.

But, if the company wants to declare a dividend to the shareholders, which is often expected by the shareholders, the income will be taxed twice. First it will be taxed as corporate profits at the appropriate corporate income tax rate. Then, it will be taxed as personal income to the shareholders, subject to their respective rates of taxation. What is worse, when a corporation declares dividends, it is not a deductible business expense.

As a rough illustration of the impact of double taxation, if a corporation makes $1 in taxable income, it might pay $.15 of federal corporate tax, based on the minimum rate. That leaves the corporation with $.85 after tax. If that amount is then paid in salaries or dividends to an individual at the 28% rate, he or she pays $.24 in taxes, leaving $.61 of the original dollar.

The other significant impact of the double taxation trap is seen upon the sale of a business organized as a C corporation. This works the same way, but the numbers are usually much larger.

For example, a young entrepreneur sets up a corporation out of his garage to make and sell some gizmo that he believes in. He builds up the business successfully over a period of years through sacrifice, sweat, and ingenuity. He hopes to work hard for a while, but his goal is to cash in on his business and retire to play golf in the Bahamas someday. Eventually he is approached by Monolith Corporation about buying the business. There is enormous profit for him built into the purchase offer. That is, until his accountant points out that the corporation must pay taxes on the huge capital gain, and then he must pay taxes again on the same amount if he hopes to put any of it into his pocket. Suddenly it is easy to see how 60 percent or more of the profit on the sale of the company will go just to pay taxes on the sale. Perhaps, our young entrepreneur thinks, he will stick to playing golf in the summer at the local municipal course when he can squeeze it in his busy work schedule. Just like last year.

There are two specific taxes referred to when double taxation is discussed. Both taxes represent penalties for using a C corporation under the wrong circumstances.

THE IDEAL SITUATION TO AVOIDING THESE PENALTY TAXES IS TO HAVE THE CORPORATION SPEND THOSE EXCESS EARNINGS IN AREAS THAT WILL BENEFIT THE OWNER/EMPLOYEE, YET WILL NOT BE TAXABLE TO THE OWNER/EMPLOYEE, BUT ARE DEDUCTIBLE TO THE CORPORATION.

- **Accumulated Earnings Tax.** One way to avoid double taxation is to leave the money in the corporation. That may work for a while, but at some point you will end up dealing with the Accumulated Earnings Tax, which penalizes corporations of amassing cash reserves in order to avoid income tax on shareholders. Besides the regular corporate income tax, a penalty is imposed equal to 39.6% of the accumulated income.

- **Distributed Earning Tax.** As mentioned above, this is the double tax that occurs when earnings from the corporation are distributed to the shareholders as dividends.

TEN WAYS TO TAKE CASH OR BENEFITS

There are ten basic ways to get cash, compensation or benefits out of your company. Each method may have different tax implications. There is no single set of tax-savings strategies that work for everyone. And remember, the IRS has the right to disallow claimed deductions even though they are not fraudulent, but are viewed as unreasonable under the circumstances.

If that happens, the corporation may be faced with increased taxes, additional interest charges, and tax penalties. That's why it is such a good idea to carefully document and plan your expenditures carefully.

The ten methods for taking cash or benefits are:

1. Dividends, or profit distribution.

2. Fixed Salaries.

3. Bonuses.

4. Commissions.

5. Loans.

6. Leases.

7. Sale of corporate assets.

8. Employee Benefit Plans.

9. Independent Contractor fees for services.

10. Fringe Benefits and Expense Accounts.

DIVIDENDS

IF THERE IS NO SURPLUS, A DIVIDEND DISTRIBUTION COULD BE DECLARED ILLEGAL, ESPECIALLY IF THE DIVIDEND PAYMENT MAKES THE CORPORATION INSOLVENT.

A dividend is a distribution of the corporation's profits to the shareholders. Most corporations are formed for profitable purposes, and the IRS expects to see a corporation pay out profits when there is a surplus on the corporations year-end books. However, there may be other important uses for corporate profits. Even where it is legally permissible to distribute corporate profits, the decision to distribute them is within the reasonable discretion of the corporation's Board of Directors.

To determine if a "surplus" exists, the corporation needs that have an annual income statement and a year-end balance sheet. These standard financial statements can provide you the "reasonable basis" you may need to show that a dividend is available. Likewise, the financial statements can be your defense for not paying dividends.

It is generally a good idea for a corporation to establish a formal dividend policy and record it by way of resolution in the corporate record books. Regular dividends help establish the corporation's credit worthiness and credibility to both outside creditors and the IRS.

While it is not usually necessary to enter a resolution declaring a dividend, it is still a good idea in order to avoid disputes down the road. The corporation must file an informational tax return and provide IRS Form 1099-DIV to each stockholder receiving a dividend over $10 during the year.

A dividend may be paid even when there is not profit in the current year, if there is still a surplus from previous years. However, if the corporation has accumulated a deficit, that deficit must be erased before the dividends can be paid.

If a dividend is declared illegal, the corporate officers could be prosecuted for authorizing their payment. Depending upon the state, the penalties could include fines and imprisonment. Further, if creditors can't be paid because of an improper dividend, the officers can be held personally liable, and the dividend could be subject to forced repayment by the shareholders.

A corporation may distribute three types of dividends:

1. **A cash dividend**, which is a payment of money;

2. **A share dividend**, which is a distribution of additional shares of stock in the corporation itself, which is usually a fractional share of stock already owned by the shareholder; or

3. **A property dividend**, which could include distribution of tangible property, such as real estate, stock in another corporation, or inventory. This is known as an "in kind" distribution.

SALARIES

The salary package for owner/employees can be critical in avoiding double taxation. Ideally, an owner/employee who is threatened with double taxation will want to take out as much money in salary as possible. Maybe his personal income tax rate will be higher than he'd like, but remember that salary is a deductible expense to the corporation. To the extent that the owner/employee receives salary, the corporation does not pay taxes on that amount and double taxation is avoided.

The IRS will want to determine the individual's importance to the business. If your role is "hands-on," meeting with clients, coordinating activities, setting the company's goals and directions, then you can prove you have a personal impact on the entire operations of the business and are crucial to the company. But, if your role is "hands-off," and could be accomplished by someone else, your role might be considered less vital and perhaps not worth the extra salary.

The IRS understands that many personal sacrifices are often necessary to establish a business: dedication, hard work, a scant salary during the early years. Your role in building the company over a period of years, including expanding the company's market, adding to the product line, and building the employee base while being underpaid can be additional proof that you are worth your current salary.

However, the IRS will take a long, hard look at high salaries, because if they can prove that the high salaries were in place simply to avoid declaring dividends, they can collect more taxes. They apply a series of standards to compensation packages to determine if disguised dividends really exist. This is called the "**Reasonableness Test**."

- **What do you do?** The most natural measurement used to justify your executive salary is your role in managing and directing the affairs of the business. Some businesses are more specialized and complex than others, which may be a good reason for higher salary levels.

- **What would you be paid if you performed the same duties for another firm?** If you can prove that you would be paid the same by another company, you would likely win any dispute with the IRS. Perhaps the best evidence in this regard is if you can prove that you have received an offer to run a similar company at a similar salary. To find out what others are paying, consult the statistics compiled by the state agency that oversees unemployment claims. Libraries, newspaper classified ad, and industry trade associations may also provide useful information. When that type of information is still hard to come by, expert testimony is generally accepted.

- **How much time do you put in?** The IRS usually finds that executives that receive full-time pay for part-time work are actually receiving disguised dividends. Most entrepreneurs don't have to worry about working too little, and as long as they keep accurate records of their regular workday, they will have no trouble proving it.

- **What is your background experience and education?** The more specialized your training and experience, the higher you can justify your salary. Maintain a file of all education credits, seminars, degrees, certificates, notable accomplishments, honors and achievements that relate to your business. All these things will be considered when the IRS evaluates your salary.

- **What is the corporation's history and present situation?** Your compensation should be appropriate for the size and type of business of the corporation. Further, your salary should be in line historically with the company's growth in profit. When those two situations exist, the IRS usually accepts your raises as justified.

- **How much did you earn in other jobs?** Your previous employment record is a good indicator of how much the corporation was expecting to pay you to secure your services. You can build a credible basis for your salary by showing an extended record of promotions and salary increases, even in unrelated companies. This type of information proves your worth to other companies in which you are not an owner.

- **What are the prevailing economic conditions?** Your compensation should be analyzed with the current economic conditions of your industry in mind. The government's attitude toward your salary will depend in part on whether the national economy and comparable corporations are going through a period of prosperity or struggle.

- **Does your salary stay up, compared to other employees, when income is down?** Even if your company can afford to pay your salary when income is down, you may have to explain the decision not to cut your pay. This is easiest when you can prove that other workers who own no stock have been paid generously by the company and have not had to take a cut in pay.

- **Is your salary a percentage of sales?** Tying executive salaries to sales is perfectly acceptable as long as the company does not raise the percentage in the middle of a year of high earnings. It is less suspicious if the company keeps the percentage constant, allowing salaries to rise or fall with income or sales.

A SUCCESSFUL CAR DEALER FOR A SMALLER AUTOMOBILE MANUFACTURER PAID HIMSELF $110,000 IN ONE YEAR AND $142,000 IN THE NEXT YEAR. WHEN THE IRS CUT HIS SALARY TO $78,000 AND $90,000 FOR THOSE YEARS BECAUSE OF UNREASONABLE COMPENSATION, HE TOOK THEM TO COURT WHERE HE PROVED HE AVERAGED A MINIMUM OF 65 HOURS PER WEEK, RECEIVED NO BENEFITS AND TOOK NO VACATION DURING THAT TIME. AFTER CONSIDERING THE FACTS, INCLUDING WHAT HE WOULD HAVE MADE AS A DEALER FOR ONE OF THE MAJOR AUTO MANUFACTURERS, THE COURT SET HIS REASONABLE COMPENSATION AT $89,000 FOR THE FIRST YEAR AND $117,000 FOR THE SECOND.

- **What is your company's dividend and bonus history?** Since the IRS uses a magnifying glass on dividend and bonus practices of corporations, it makes it a point to uncover bonuses disguised as dividends. Low dividends to stockholders in years of high bonuses are virtually indefensible to the IRS.

OF COURSE, THE BEST WAY TO OVERCOME CHARGES OF **DISGUISED DIVIDENDS** IS TO SHOW THAT THE CORPORATION PAYS REASONABLE DIVIDENDS IN MOST MONEYMAKING YEARS. IF CURRENT EXPENSES OR PROJECTED EXPANSIONS WARRANT IT, DIVIDENDS MAY BE LOW, BUT THEY SHOULD STILL BE PAID REGULARLY TO AVOID IRS SCRUTINY.

Timing is everything. Don't get caught in the trap of setting or adjusting your salary in midyear when sales trends become evident. If salaries are set after the company's income can be projected accurately, the IRS suspects disguised dividends. Set your salary levels at the start of the year and stick to it if possible. Raises given during midyear should include nonstockholder employee as well. If you keep the percentages in proportion, the stockholders' raises won't appear excessive compared to those of nonstockholder employees.

Even if your salary looks reasonable on the surface, certain practices raise "red flags" to IRS that you may be using illegal tax strategies. Carefully structure your corporation so that the following pitfalls will not snare you:

There is more to it than just salary figures. The IRS is interested in the total compensation package. This includes pension and profit-sharing plans, insurance, perks, and other company programs in which you participate. Use of company cars, boats, airplanes and other corporate privileges such as company-paid vacations will add to the value of your compensation package.

Salaries shouldn't always use all of the company's earnings. If the combined salaries of the shareholders frequently leave the company with minimal net earnings, the IRS may presume the salaries to represent disguised dividends. To overcome this, make certain that the situation does not occur every year. Net earnings should fluctuate with the company income.

Make certain shareholders salaries do not reflect percentages of ownership. Any time that salaries are proportionate to the amount of stock held, the IRS will consider it as evidence that part of the salary is actually dividend. Make certain to set stockholders salaries without regard to percentage of ownership.

Stockholders' salaries should not increase any faster than other high-level employees. If stockholders salaries increase 25% during a period that other employees received raises of, say, 10%, the IRS may see disguised dividends.

Putting your Spouse on the Payroll

Another way that shareholders can legitimately take deductible dollars out of a corporation is by hiring family members to work for the company. As long as the work is actually being performed by the family member, and the salary is reasonable for the position, the compensation is deductible. This technique is called "**income splitting**". Income splitting can keep income in the family at a lower tax rate than if it were earned by the shareholders directly.

Whenever the spouse of the owner of a closely held corporation helps in the business, an opportunity exists to take advantage of valuable tax deductions. Too often, the spouse is not given a salary because the business fails to see any advantage to adding another person to the payroll. Usually, the couple files a joint tax return so half the family income is taxed to each of them, no matter who earns it.

But, adding a spouse to the payroll can add tax-sheltered dollars to the family bankroll. As an employee, the spouse can participate in a variety of tax-sheltered corporate benefits, including:

- **Pension and Profit-Sharing Plans**. The corporation gets a full deduction for its contribution to you and your spouse each year, and the contributions are not taxable income to your spouse until he or she actually cashes in on the fund. Upon retirement, these funds receive favorable tax treatment from the IRS.

- **Group Life Insurance.** A corporation can purchase life insurance for its employees - including you and your spouse - and deduct the cost of the premiums. Additionally, the premiums covering the first $50,000 of insurance are not income to you or your spouse.

- **Company Paid Travel Expenses.** While it is difficult to deduct the travel expenses incurred by your spouse on business trips or conventions, if the spouse is an employee it may be easier to show a legitimate business purpose for the trip. At that point, the spouse's expenses are deductible.

Placing Children on the Payroll

Often, the children of the owners of small, family-oriented corporations are involved in a variety of odd jobs for the business. It may make sense to formally hire the child in those circumstances and pay him or her reasonable wages for the work they perform. Beyond the tax-sheltered benefits outlined above, the employed children can use the full standard deduction to shield their income from taxes on the first $4,400 of earned income.

IT IS ALSO IMPORTANT TO COMPLY WITH ANY REQUIREMENTS OF YOUR STATE'S **CHILD LABOR LAW** AND MAINTAIN COMPLETE AND ACCURATE RECORDS. BUT, AS LONG AS YOU DO, CASE LAW EXISTS IN THE TAX COURTS THAT SUPPORT THE CORPORATE DEDUCTIONS FOR WAGES PAID TO A SEVEN YEAR OLD CHILD. (ELLER, 77 TC 934 ACQ., IRB 1984-52.)

As explained above, the company can pay money that would otherwise be paid at a higher tax bracket in salary or dividends and shift it into your children's lower bracket. The tax on children's wages starts in the 15% range and stays there for a while.

Naturally, it is very important that everything is completely businesslike when your children work for you. If the wages are not reasonable, or the work actually performed, your children may owe taxes on their earnings and the corporation could lose its deduction.

Also, no matter how much your child is paid, you can still claim him or her as a dependency deduction on your income tax return. (Although the child cannot claim a personal exemption on his or her own return if he or she is claimed as a dependent on your return.) The IRS determines that your child is still your dependent as long as you provide more than half the child's support and he or she either (i) won't reach the age of 19 this year, or (ii) is between 18 and 24 and is a full time student during any five calendar months of the year.

The only way you can lose your deduction is if the child spends enough on his or her own support that at least half of it is self-provided. To avoid this, make sure the child puts enough of his or her earnings in the bank so that you can meet the criteria for providing at least half support.

One of the negatives to this strategy for corporations is that Social Security, unemployment taxes, and other state taxes that may apply must be paid for all employees, regardless of their age. These taxes can swallow a significant percentage of workers wages.

TAX-FREE COLLEGE FUNDS.

If you used a traditional investment plan to place $10,000 of taxable income every year into your child's college savings account (assuming the child is under 14 years of age), the taxes would fall into place as follows: After the $500 standard deduction, the next $500 will be taxed at 15% ($75) and the rest at the parent's personal tax rate, say, 33% (another $2,970). The total tax is $3,045.

Now, if instead you paid the child $10,000 over the course of a year to clean the office and do other odd jobs, your child will pay $1,012.50 in tax on the remaining $6,750 of earned income. The tax savings every year is $2,032.50.

Owners of Personal Service Corporations (PSC's) should also appreciate the opportunity to place another worker on the payroll because PSC's must pay a flat tax rate of 34%. So, the more compensation the firm pays out to family members, the less of its income can be taxed at that top rate.

BONUSES

A bonus must be considered as part of the overall compensation package, especially when it comes to the "Reasonableness Test". It has been the attitude of the courts that a sole shareholder has no right to pay himself a bonus as an incentive to do his best in managing the company.

Bonuses need to be supported by established criteria. Usually, you can give yourself a bonus without attracting too much attention, as long as you tie it to established, logical criteria. As with salary increases, bonuses awarded late in the year are suspicious. But, if the bonus criteria is established early in the year, and is based on sensible results like sales quotas or year-over improvements, you should have no trouble.

> You HAVE TO BE VERY CAREFUL ABOUT AWARDING A BONUS SIMPLY BECAUSE YOU HAD A GOOD YEAR. THE IRS CALLS THAT "DISGUISED DIVIDENDS", WHICH ARE SUBJECT TO DOUBLE TAXATION.

COMMISSIONS

If your corporation depends heavily on sales (and what corporation doesn't), you may consider a compensation package that is based on commissions for sales you generate. Put together a commission structure in advance and stick to it. Your commissions should be comparable to those paid to salesmen in competing businesses.

LOANS

Loans from Shareholders

In an earlier discussion in Chapter 6, a distinction was made between capitalizing a corporation with equity or with debt. While a debt holder has no opportunity for growth regarding the money lent to the corporation, he is in a much more secure position than a shareholder. The debt holder gets repaid before any of the shareholders receive a return of their capital.

In many closely held corporations, it is not unusual for shareholders to lend money to the corporation in addition to their capital investment. There should be a board of directors resolution authorizing the corporation to borrow the money and a promissory note evidencing the debt. The note should carry an interest rate on the loan, and the terms of payment should be followed closely.

There can be favorable tax consequences for a shareholder to loan money to the corporation in addition to his capital investment. Remember, while dividends are not tax deductible, interest payments are deductible, with some limitations.

THE IRS HAS THE POWER TO DISALLOW SOME OR ALL OF THE DEDUCTIONS ASSOCIATED WITH THE DEBT AS "CONSTRUCTIVE DIVIDENDS."

Suppose a corporation had been capitalized with $100,000 of paid in capital. If the corporation has a gross income of $70,000 and deductible expenses of $55,000, the $15,000 excess is taxable to the corporation. Any distribution of the profit to shareholders will result in a second tax on the proceeds. If, instead of capitalizing the corporation with $100,000, the shareholders invested $25,000 in capital stock and provided a $75,000 loan at a 12% interest rate, the scenario changes dramatically.

The corporation still has a gross income of $70,000, but the deductible expenses have increased because of the interest being paid on the note. With $9,000 in deductible interest, the expenses now total $64,000. Instead of a taxable income of $15,000, the corporation now has $6,000 in taxable income. The shareholders receive as much, or more, than they would if the original profit had been distributed through a dividend. However the interest is deductible to the corporation and therefore not subject to double taxation.

When a corporation borrows money, it could result in what is known as a "thin incorporation." The IRS is likely to be interested in looking at the ratio of debt to equity that would be reasonable under the existing circumstances of the corporation. They will also want to determine whether the debt is actually just another form of equity, and the interest payments are actually camouflaged dividends.

The Tax Code uses several factors in determining if loans by a shareholder are valid, including:

- The existence of a formal written loan document that details of the loan, including due date, unconditional promise to pay, and interest rate.

- Has the corporation established a valid corporate reason for making the loan? Perhaps the reason might be to keep a key employee who might otherwise seek other employment to meet cash needs, etc. The corporate minutes should reflect that corporate purpose.

- Is there a limit to the loan, or does the loan provide unlimited access to the corporate cookie jar?

- Is the debt subordinated to other indebtedness of the corporation, or does the debt have preference?

- The ratio of corporate debt to equity.

- Is the debt convertible into stock?

Loans to Shareholders

Until the Tax Reform Act was passed, it was quite common for companies to provide interest-free demand loans to key executives as a tax-free fringe benefit. Under the new law, a corporate executive that receives an interest-free loan from his company is treated as having received "phantom" taxable compensation equal to the value of what the company would have charged on the loan. The company executive can then deduct the "phantom" interest expense for the same amount. The net effect of this is that the extra compensation and the deduction cancel each other and the executive pays no tax on the interest-free loan.

But, under the Tax Reform Act, the deduction is subject to new scrutiny that eliminates many of possibilities of the previous law. Fortunately, that tax-free benefit can still be achieved with some types of interest free loans.

> *You can borrow up to $10,000 from your corporation, tax-free, without paying interest or suffering tax consequences. This is called a de minimis exception, and should the loan ever go over the $10,000 ceiling, you could lose the exception and be taxed accordingly.*

For low or no-interest loans over $10,000, the IRS generally assumes an interest rate equal to the Applicable Federal Rate (AFR), which is the rate based on the average market yield on US obligations. If the AFR is 7% and you've borrowed $100,000 at no interest, the imputed interest is $7,000, which the IRS says is additional income to you and is therefore taxable. You can't get around the AFR by charging low interest either. The IRS will impute as additional income the difference between the rate the corporation charges you and the AFR.

Since interest on home mortgages can still be deducted, the corporation can give you an interest-free loan secured by your home. The "phantom compensation" and "phantom interest" should be a wash for tax purposes. Also, interest on business loans is deductible, so an interest-free loan could be used by you to start a company that purchases and develops raw land or residential rentals, etc.

It is important that any loan over $10,000 is structured at arms' length, so the IRS does not have grounds to disallow the loans and declare them as taxable corporate dividends. To prove that the loan is an actual transaction that you intend to repay, make certain to put all of the terms in writing, including the repayment schedule and record the date and amount of the loan on the business books. The corporation's minutes should also reflect approval of the loan.

LEASES

One method of taking cash out of a corporation is by leasing arrangements. A shareholder who has assets that can be leased to the corporation has a tremendous range of options in this regard. Instead of leasing the equipment directly, the shareholder may want to use a partnerships or corporation as the leasing company. If the shareholder, as an individual, enters into a leasing arrangement with his corporation to lease buildings, equipment, etc. to the company, he may be exposing himself to liability he doesn't need.

There are really three types of goods that can be leased effectively: equipment, real estate/building, and employees. Leasing any of these products will put you into a type of business that is widely accepted and recognized for its value to the business world as a whole. It provides an excellent opportunity to transfer taxable profits out of your primary business and into your pocket.

Commercial Property

A 1981 Tax Court decision shows how an owner can set up a special tax shelter opportunity by tying the lease of a commercial property to the gross sales of the company. This type of percentage lease is becoming quite common in commercial real estate. Here is how it worked:

When a food distribution company could not obtain financing for a badly needed warehouse, the company's shareholders, a married couple, bought land and built a warehouse to lease to the company for 20 years. The company paid all of the property taxes and maintenance costs during that term.

According to the lease, the company was to pay to the couple an annual rent of $60,000, plus 1 percent of the company's annual gross sales over $4 million. At the time, the company's gross sales were only $2.3 million, so the couple only received the $60,000 of rent. But within eight years, the company's sales had reached nearly $10 million and the couple received a total payment of $118,000.

Naturally, the IRS attempted to disallow the company's rent deduction over the fixed amount on the basis that it represented a disguised dividend to the shareholders, but the Tax Court disagreed. The court ruled that the couple had a legitimate business purpose in entering into the lease agreement, and were entitled to use the same technique with their own company as they would with any other business tenant. When the lease was drawn up, the court said the provisions were fair.

To effectively carry out this strategy, keep the transaction at arms' length, prove a legitimate business purpose, and make the terms reasonable. Perhaps even have a certified real estate appraiser give you an estimate of a fair rental value for the property in question.

Equipment

Any equipment your business needs can be leased in today's business world. In fact, some of it probably is. If, however, you have traditionally purchased the equipment you need, and even if you already have, you may consider transferring them to a leasing corporation to take additional profit out of your business.

Instead of capitalizing your manufacturing business with the amount of money it needs to purchase equipment, you could capitalize your S corporation to purchase the equipment, which would then be leased to the manufacturing business. The monthly lease payments are deductible to the manufacturing company, and their original cost and depreciation are deductible to the S corporation, which should offset any profit. And, with the S corporation you eliminate the double-taxation issue associated with other forms of taking money out of a corporation.

A LIST OF EQUIPMENT THAT COULD BE LEASED WOULD INCLUDE: COMPUTERS AND PERIPHERALS, PRINTERS, TYPEWRITERS, PHONE SYSTEMS, OFFICE FURNITURE, FAX MACHINES, PHOTOCOPY MACHINES, AUTOMOBILES, AIRPLANES, CARGO SHIPS, TRUCKS AND TRAILERS, OFF-ROAD EQUIPMENT, BULLDOZERS, FORKLIFTS, MACHINE TOOLS, AND OTHER SPECIALIZED EQUIPMENT.

Employees

Employee leasing is a fast-growing trend in the business community. Virtually every city in the country has several companies devoted solely to that enterprise. There is no reason you can't do it as well.

The corporation that leases employees is generally responsible for all of the elements of human resources management for client companies. That includes testing, training, hiring and firing, payroll (including payroll taxes), and benefits. The leasing company charges a fee, naturally, that is usually based on the total payroll for which it is responsible.

So, your primary business would lease all of its employees from another company, at a cost that is slightly higher than the original payroll, but is still fully deductible. The leasing corporation then deducts the total salaries of the employees, along with training costs and other miscellaneous deductions.

The net result is that you have been able to take a little more than twice the deduction for salaries than you have been able to take previously. And, you have more flexibility in your human resource management than you had before.

SALE OF CORPORATE ASSETS

Similar to a corporate leasing arrangement, a shareholder can take cash out of a corporation by selling assets to the corporation. The shareholder will show a gain or loss on the sale.

For the sale to stand up to scrutiny, the transaction should be at a fair price, the corporation should be able to use the assets, and be able to afford payment. A significant difference between sales and leasing is in the ability of corporate creditors to attach the assets. In a sale, the assets could be attached, whereas in a lease, the assets belong to the lessor.

EMPLOYEE BENEFIT PLANS

Changes in the tax laws have created a surge in the popularity of employee benefit plans in recent years. While not providing cash directly, these plans have the indirect benefit of eliminating the need for employee/owners to pay out of pocket for the same benefits. Additionally, if the plan qualifies, the corporation can deduct the contributions or expenses as they are made, rather than later.

Employee benefit plans can include:

- Medical and dental reimbursement plans.

- Retirement plans.

- Group life and accident insurance.

- Professional financial planning assistance.

- Health Insurance.

- Stock option plans and Employee Stock Ownership Plans (ESOP's)

Medical and Dental Reimbursement Plans

Many closely-held corporations are discovering the benefits of setting up medical reimbursement plans for company owner-employees. Since medical costs for an individual are only deductible to the extent their total cost exceeds 7.5 percent of adjusted gross income, many high-wage earners fail to get any deduction at all for these expenses. The more you make, the harder it is to deduct any medical expenses at all.

> *The corporation can fully deduct all costs it incurs in covering medical expenses under a medical reimbursement plan, from the first dollar.*

By putting a medical reimbursement plan in writing, the corporation can reimburse employees for their family's medical expenses. This can save owner/employees thousands of dollars, and is a tax-free benefit, as long as the plan is nondiscriminatory in favor of key people.

The reimbursement is not generally included in the income of the employee, as long as the reimbursement is not more than the cost of the care, and is not attributed to amounts taken by the employee as a medical expense deduction in a prior year.

Retirement Plans

The corporation has a tremendous variety of options to consider when analyzing retirement and pension plans. A well-designed pension plan can serve both as a tax deduction to the company and as a tax deferred nest egg that can compound over time. Often, the literature that promotes pension funds uses the term "tax-free" in describing the pension product. Technically, that is not correct. The proper term is "tax deferred."

The income taxes on your initial contributions and the interest and dividend earnings they generate, are not taxed until the cash is actually withdrawn from the fund. However, the corporation takes the deduction when the pension contributions are made to the plan.

Upon retirement of an employee, the amounts withdrawn are taxed at the appropriate rate. Usually, the withdrawal will take place in a period of your life where you may be in a lower tax bracket as compared to your years of active employment. So, the taxes that are eventually paid may be in actuality less than you would have otherwise paid.

The benefits of compounding retirement funds without tax consequences are obvious. The fund grows faster and earns higher interest than comparable investments taxed each year. It is possible, that the value of the tax-deferred contributions and interest could amount to 500% more than if you paid taxes immediately on the contributions and interest.

One drawback to setting up some pension plans is the tremendous expense in time and money it requires to administer. Government approval and reporting may be required, along with extensive bookkeeping and supervision. Some companies even find themselves having to hire an actuary in-house.

THE SIMPLIFIED PENSION PLAN

THE EMPLOYEE BENEFIT RESEARCH INSTITUTE FOUND THAT ONLY 12% OF EMPLOYEES WORKING FOR COMPANIES WITH TEN OR FEWER EMPLOYEES HAVE A COMPANY PENSION. THAT COMPARES TO 82% OF THE COMPANIES THAT HAVE MORE THAN 250 WORKERS.

For these reasons, the Simplified Employee Pension (SEP) can be an attractive alternative. The SEP provides an avenue to save for your retirement on a tax-deferred basis without the degree of paperwork, administration fees, and other time that other plans require. Additionally, the SEP offers a level of flexibility that most smaller companies need. For instance, most pension plans require that the employer make specified contributions each year, but the SEP allows the employer to skip a year if earnings or poor, or delay the contribution until after the tax return has been settled with the IRS.

A SEP is somewhat like an Individual Retirement Account (IRA), because each employee makes their own decision about their particular investment vehicle, such as banks, mutual funds, bond funds, or brokerage house accounts. The corporation essentially finances an IRA for each employee. But, no longer is the company responsible for the supervision or performance of the retirement fund. There are no complicated nondiscrimination rules to comply with. All the company does is make the contribution.

A significant difference between a SEP and an IRA is that the IRA limits the annual contribution to $2,000 ($2,250 if your spouse doesn't work) per year. With a SEP, the contribution is based on a percentage of the employee's compensation for that year. Even the percentage of contribution can be changed from year to year. However, the maximum contribution an employee may make to a SEP is 15% of his or her wages, up to $24,000.

The contributions from the corporation are tax deductible, and yet are not subject to Social Security or unemployment taxes. There is a 10% penalty if the funds are withdrawn before age 59 ½, and you are required to begin withdrawing the funds upon age 70 ½.

The maximum allowable annual contribution to a SEP is $24,000, or up to 15% of the employee's compensation.

A SEP can be set up easily, using the IRS model form, 5305-SEP, which contains all of the rules for the employees and the employer. And, strangely enough, you don't even send that form in to the IRS - just keep it on file. In addition, most financial institutions have ready-made SEP products that you can also use.

SEC. 401(K) PLANS

Many corporations take advantage of 401(k) plans, which is, essentially, a salary reduction mechanism that reduces your immediate income tax by deferring the tax on the retirement portion. The maximum contribution to a 401(k) in 1999 is 25% of compensation, up to $30,000. This amount will be increased in future years by cost of living adjustments in $500 increments.

Since 401(k) contributions reduce the employee's salary, if you earn $35,000 a year and contribute $2,000 to your plan, you will be taxed as if your salary were only $33,000.

KEOGH PLANS

A Keogh plan is available to anyone with self-employment income, so anyone that receives a paycheck from a corporation does not qualify. However, to the degree that you earn freelance income from the corporation for work you do outside your role as an employee, you might be eligible to participate.

To set up a Keogh, you can adopt an IRS approved plan available at a bank, financial institution or insurance company. Or, you could write your own plan that meets your specific needs. You can apply for approval of your plan by requesting a determination letter from the IRS. As long as your Keogh plan is set up by the end of the year, you have until your tax deadline, usually April 15, to make the contribution.

There are two kinds of Keoghs:

- **Defined Contribution Plans**, and

- **Defined Benefit Plans**.

Under a Defined Contribution Plan, the maximum you can contribute is the lesser of 25% of the self-employment income up to $30,000 if you are an employee of a sole proprietor. If you are self-employed, the maximum you can contribute is the lessor of $30,000 or 20% of your compensation. The minimum amount you must contribute in either case is 1% of compensation

With a Defined Benefit Plan, you have a maximum annual benefit upon retiring at the Social Security retirement age of $130,000 or 100% of the average of your three best earning years. Then you figure out how much you need to contribute to get that "defined" benefit.

Group Life and Accident Insurance

Premiums on group life insurance are deductible expenses to a corporation. They are also excluded from inclusion in the employees taxable income if the insurance coverage provided is less than $50,000 for that employee. If the employee has coverage greater than that amount, the portion of the premium for the excess will be subject to tax.

For a group term life insurance plan to qualify for the employee exclusion, it must cover at least 10 full-time employees, or, if the company has less than 10 employees, all insurable employees must be covered. The plan must also meet the nondiscrimination requirements of the Tax Code.

SPLIT-DOLLAR INSURANCE

When a corporation participates in a split-dollar arrangement, it cannot deduct its premium contribution or the value of the economic benefit enjoyed by the employee, even though the economic benefit is taxable to the employee. The corporation will, however, receive its share of the insurance proceeds tax-free upon the death of the employee.

With split-dollar coverage, the corporation pays premiums on the policy to the extent of the annual increase in the cash surrender value. The employee pays the balance. Upon the death of the employee, the corporation is entitled to the cash surrender value, and the rest of the policy proceeds are distributed to the beneficiaries.

Professional Financial Planning Assistance

The corporation can pay for financial counseling for key employees. The cost of the counseling is deductible to the corporation, but is included in the taxable income of the employee. The corporation may also put a group legal services plan into place. Under this plan, the corporation would make payments directly to a legal service provider. Services used by an employee are fully taxable and included in income.

Health Insurance

Employer-paid health insurance premiums are excluded from an employee's gross income. However, the tax treatment of benefit claims depends upon the type of coverage the corporation paid for. The employee is taxed on disability benefits that are based on the duration of work missed. But the employee can exclude from his gross income any reimbursements he receives for medical expenses.

Stock Option Plans and Employee Stock Ownership Plans (ESOP)

Stock option/bonus plans are commonly used in executive compensation packages. However they are of limited value in a closely held corporation where the executive is also a shareholder of the company. If he already has 100% ownership, what value is there in receiving additional stock?

An ESOP is the most widely known type of stock plan. It has evolved from a novel academic concept into a sophisticated tool of corporate finance that is well integrated into the mainstream of the American business community. Many publicly held corporations have used ESOP's as an employee benefits tool, as a takeover defense measure, and as a means of going private. Owners of closely held companies have used ESOPs not only for ownership succession and capital formation, but also their ultimate exit strategy.

For more information on ESOP's contact: Robert W. Smiley, Jr., of The Benefit Capital Companies, Inc. PO Box 542, Logandale, NV 89021 (702) 398-3222

It consists of a trust designed primarily to invest in and hold stock issued by the corporation for participating employees. Usually, the stock held by the trust must be traded in an established market, but that is not always possible for a closely held company. In such cases, the law provides for corporate stock that has voting and dividend rights at least equal to the highest available on the common stock to be used instead of stock that is publicly traded.

Here's how an ESOP works: The corporation contributes stock to the ESOP and takes a tax deduction for its value, up to 25% of the employee's compensation or $30,000. (These limits may be increased to the lessor of $60,000 or the amount of stock contributed to the plan.) The stock is held in an account for each participating employee, who is allowed to control the voting of his or her shares.

An ESOP may be a better method of corporate finance than a sale, merger, or public offering for the following reasons:

1. If you sell your company to another company, you will pay immediate capital gains tax, lose control, and probably not be able to retain any residual equity.

2. If you sell your stock to the public, you will incur an immediate capital gains tax, become subject to the jurisdiction of the Securities and Exchange Commission (SEC) and risk the possible loss of control.

3. If you enter into a tax-free merger, the capital gains tax will be deferred, but you will lose control and still have all your eggs in one basket.

4. If you sell to an ESOP, you can defer the federal capital gains tax, maintain control of the company, retain residual equity, and invest the proceeds in a diversified portfolio of stocks and bonds without incurring a capital gains tax. All while rewarding the loyal people who helped you build your business.

The corporation benefits from this in many ways. In addition to the tax deductions, the ESOP is able to generate capital through tax-deductible loans. The corporation's deductible cash contributions to the ESOP are used by the ESOP to repay loans which were used to buy corporate stock. Other advantages include:

- An ESOP can borrow to purchase stock contributed to the plan, even if the stock is purchased directly from the corporation. The loan can be used to purchase more stock than is needed for contributions to the plan, and the balance of the proceeds can be used for annual expenses.

- Any lender to an ESOP is able to receive 50% of the interest tax-free.

- The corporation can claim a deduction for dividends paid on its stock held in an ESOP if the dividends are paid in cash directly to participants within 90 days of the end of the plan year, or the dividends are used to repay a loan used to purchase additional stock.

- The corporation can get a deduction for ESOP contributions of company stock, without cash outlay.

- Employees are motivated and productive, enhancing the value for every shareholder.

These benefits are achievable as a result of Internal Revenue Code Section 1042, which provides a road map for the tax-free rollover of proceeds from the sale of stock to an ESOP. The ESOP is required to purchase 30% or more of the common equity in the corporation and that the seller has had at least a three-year holding period. The seller must reinvest the proceeds in other US domestic securities within a period of 12 months.

Independent Contractor Fees for Services
It is common in a closely held corporation for the shareholders also to be the directors. When this is the case, the director's may be paid fees for serving in that capacity and for

attending director's meetings. The fees are obviously income to the director, but they may be deductible to the corporation as long as they are reasonable in light of the size and nature of the corporation.

In addition, shareholders who have professional skills, such as attorneys or accountants, may provide services to the corporation. If these services are outside the scope of their employment with the company, the corporation may pay reasonable fees for the services.

Directors Fees

The corporation should adopt a formal policy in the minutes of the corporate meetings establishing the fee schedule for directors. Fees of $25 to $100 per meeting have been found reasonable, while fees of $250 have been disallowed.

Fringe Benefits and Expense Accounts

The corporation can provide a variety of other tax-favored benefits to employees. Assuming the nondiscrimination rules are met, these miscellaneous benefits may be deductible to the corporation as well as excluded from the income of the employee. These benefits can be generally categorized into one of four groups:

1. **De Minimus Benefits**. These are incidental benefits that are too small, or too inconvenient or costly to monitor. Examples of these benefits include:

   - Personal use of photocopy machines

   - Personal letters by company secretary or on company computers

   - Occasional parties or picnics for employees and guests

   - Traditional holiday gifts with a low value (usually under $25)

   - Flowers, fruit, books, etc. provided under special circumstances.

2. **Employee Discounts**. Many companies, particularly retailers, permit their employees to purchase the products of the corporation at a discount from the price charged to the general public. In theory, the amount saved by the employee could be treated as taxable income, but there will be no tax assessed.

3. **Working Condition Fringe Benefits.** These benefits are provided by the corporation to an employee for business use. If the employee could have taken a deduction for the item if he or she had paid for it, it will qualify as a working condition fringe benefit.

4. **"No Additional Cost" Services.** Similar to the employee discount, this type of benefit involves services that the corporation provides to the public for a fee that an employee is entitled to use at a reduced cost or for free. An example would be an airline that allows employees to fly for free.

The corporation can also provide key employees with substantial expense accounts, allowing the employee to conduct business in expensive restaurants, country clubs, and the like. The corporate expense account has become subject to tightening restrictions in recent tax changes. To the extent that expenses are deductible, the IRS will require detailed substantiation of the expense, including the date, place, and specific business purpose of the expense. Failure to keep proper records will invite the IRS to treat the expenses as non-deductible personal expenses.

Chapter

10

MAINTAINING THE CORPORATE VEIL

> *"The diligent director is the one who exhibits in the performance of his trust 'the same degree of care and prudence that men prompted by self-interest generally exercise in their own affairs.'" - Benjamin N. Cardozo, in People v. Mancuso.*

Acting like a corporation

All states have established case law that provides an avenue to pierce the corporate veil in certain circumstances. When the courts "pierce the corporate veil," they assign liability to individuals for actions that the corporation had taken. It is a common practice for lawyers to name any individuals associated with a corporation, including the officers, directors and employees, as defendants in any litigation against a corporation.

They do this to make the court determine if the corporate veil can be breached, in which case the individuals can be held personally responsible. If the corporate veil is intact, the court will not be able to hold individuals responsible in legal actions against the corporation.

Obviously, if the individuals are held personally liable, it could cost them potentially millions of dollars. In most cases where this occurs, the common thread was gross carelessness by the owners.

ALTER EGO

This has often been called the "alter ego doctrine," and is applied when a court rules that the stockholders have used the corporation so that there is no distinction between the corporation and themselves. In order for the alter ego theory to be applied, the following requirements must generally be met:

- The corporation must be influenced and governed by an individual.

- There must be such a unity of interest and ownership between the individual and the corporation so as to make them indistinguishable.

- The presence of a corporation in a given situation would sanction fraud or promote injustice, even if fraud is not necessarily proven.

When a judge decides that the corporation was simply the "alter ego" of the stockholders, the stockholders can be held personally liable for all of the debts and obligations of the corporation.

Therefore, it is important for every corporation to have a corporate record book. This should be the very first thing that you do after you incorporate. Most attorneys and incorporating companies provide a corporate kit that usually includes a few sample forms to be used for resolutions, minutes. Although these forms will generally get you off the ground, their limited scope and number almost never provide a broad enough variety of forms to be effective in all of the situations that require their use.

IF THE OFFICERS, DIRECTORS AND SHAREHOLDERS DO NOT TREAT THE CORPORATION AS A SEPARATE PERSON, THEY SHOULD NOT EXPECT THE COURTS TO HONOR THE CORPORATE VEIL.

However, the more you understand about the use of corporate records, the more likely it is that you can modify a template document for your situation. Even so, it is a good idea to invest in a complete set of sample corporate records that deals with a variety of situations, or consult with an attorney.

As indicated, the various states have different standards that are used to determine if the corporation was properly maintained. For example, some states do not honor or recognize a "one-man" corporation, in which a single person is the President, Secretary, Treasurer, Director, and stockholder. The state may have a statutory requirement that a minimum of two or three individuals combine to form a corporation. I know of one instance where a California corporation was pierced because it had not maintained more than five shareholders, even though California laws do not require that many.

The issue of piercing the corporate veil is one of the most important reasons to incorporate in a haven, such as Nevada or Wyoming, where a one-man corporation is allowed. These states also have other established factors that make it extremely difficult to pierce the corporate veil.

Nevada case law sets the standard that we wish other states would follow on this subject. A good example of Nevada advantages in this area is found in the case of Rowland v. Lepire, which is printed in its entirety in Appendix A. By reading the case carefully, you can clearly see how difficult it is to pierce the corporate veil in Nevada.

There are five basic issues that can be used, depending upon the jurisdiction, to pierce the corporate veil. Sometimes, the presence of one of these problems is not enough to bring about personal liability. However, sometimes it is. The point is that you never want to go to court with one of these five red flags:

UNDERCAPITALIZATION

If your corporation is not prepared to pay for any potential damage which could normally arise out of the ordinary course of its business, the corporation is undercapitalized. If your corporation has some responsibility for damages caused to other people and does not have enough assets to deal with the liability, there may be an appetite to go after the assets of the owners. While this has not proven to be a valid reason for piercing the corporation veil in all states, it is significant enough that you need to be aware of the potential problem, no matter what state you are incorporated in.

The simplest way to avoid having your corporate veil pierced on the grounds that it is undercapitalized is to buy enough insurance to cover the type of risk that are common to your type of business. That way, when something goes wrong, there is no need for the court to concern itself with the issue of the corporate veil, since there are enough assets available to cover the damages.

> IN ROWLAND V. LEPIRE, THE CORPORATION WAS WOEFULLY UNDERCAPITALIZED. THE DEBT-TO-EQUITY RATIO WAS FAR TOO HIGH. THE DISTRICT COURT HAD PREVIOUSLY RULED THE ROWLAND BROTHERS WERE SIMPLY THE ALTER-EGO OF THE CORPORATION, EFFECTIVELY PIERCING THE CORPORATE VEIL.

Undercapitalization was an issue in Rowland v. Lepire, ruled on by the Nevada Supreme Court in April of 1983. In the case, two brothers formed a Nevada corporation, Rowland Corp., and went into the construction business as a general contractor. The total capitalization of the corporation was $1,100 for eleven shares of stock. Additionally, one of the principals provided an unsecured personal loan to the corporation for fifteen thousand dollars. With that and a $5,000 surety bond, the brothers were in the construction business.

At the time of the trial, the corporation had no other assets and negative net worth. The attorney for Lepire tried to have the Rowland brothers held personally responsible for the damages in dispute. The attorney raised the issue of undercapitalization in an attempt to pierce the corporate veil. The court ruled that although there was evidence that the company was severely undercapitalized, it was insufficient to pierce the corporate veil.

FAILURE TO FOLLOW MINIMAL CORPORATE PROCEDURES

To avoid this time-bomb, religiously attend to the corporate formalities outlined at the end of this chapter. The only way the corporation can defend the actions of its officers and directors is through the corporate records that detail the fact that the individuals were properly authorized by the corporation to carry out their activities. Keep your corporate minutes current, and record every extraordinary activity, such as:

- Changes in corporate bylaws.

- Changes in the location of the principal corporate office.

- Personal loans from the corporation to directors, stockholders, or officers.

- Sale of substantially all of the corporate assets.

- Changes in executive compensation.

- Any action concerning retirement or pension plans.

- All step transactions.

- Reasons for accumulating excessive earnings.

In the case of Rowland v. Lepire, mentioned above, the attorney for Lepire was able to show that the Rowland's corporation not only kept no corporate minutes, but had, in fact, never had any formal meetings, as is required. Even so, the Nevada court ruled that the corporate veil was still to be kept intact. Undoubtedly, this decision would have been different in most other states.

FAILURE TO KEEP BANK ACCOUNTS SEPARATE

IN ROWLAND V. LEPIRE, THIS IS ABOUT THE ONLY THING THAT ROWLAND CORP. DID PROPERLY. BECAUSE THE CORPORATE OFFICERS AND DIRECTORS KEPT THE CORPORATE CHECKING ACCOUNTS SEPARATE, THE SUPREME COURT OVERTURNED THE RULING OF THE DISTRICT COURT IN WHICH THE CORPORATE VEIL WAS PIERCED AND LET THE CORPORATION STAND.

Never commingle funds! This means that you never pay personal expenses from the corporate checking account, and you don't pay corporate bills from your own checking account. If things are getting a little tight, there are proper ways to deal with the situation, such as executing loans or purchasing additional stock. And of course, remember to put those transactions into the minutes.

OPERATE THROUGH EMPLOYEES OR AGENTS OF THE CORPORATION

If the daily activities of the corporation are consistently carried out by an individual, and the corporate records do not authorize that person to carry them out, the corporate veil concerning the individual's liability for personal injuries or damages caused by the business activity, is nonexistent. If, on the other hand, you attend to the corporation's daily activities as an employee or officer of the corporation and have been authorized by the directors to carry out those tasks, you keep the corporate veil in place.

SIGNING YOUR NAME FOR THE CORPORATION

This rule of keeping corporate formalities might be the most commonly abused of all. Remember that you are acting as a corporation. The corporation cannot and does not sign anything - not contracts, purchase orders, agreements, leases, etc. - without an authorized officer of the corporation signing on behalf of it.

How is the public to know that an individual has signed on behalf of a corporation and is not representing himself? The answer is that if you simply sign your name -John Smith - you have represented only yourself. But, if you sign your name and include your corporate title - John Smith, President - you have represented the corporation. If John Smith forgets and signs anything without including his corporate title, he could be held personally responsible for the fulfillment of the obligation.

Also, make sure your suppliers, customers and clients know that when they deal with you, they are dealing with a corporation. The best way to do this is to include a corporate designation in the name of the company, and use it always. When a business is named ABC, Inc., there is no question that the company is incorporated. If the company is named J. Marshall, for example, it is unclear whether the corporation is a person or not.

CORPORATE FORMALITIES OUTLINE

The following is not meant to be an exhaustive list of all corporate formalities and operations, but is merely an overview of basic and minimum requirements which are important for your corporation to follow to be viewed as a legitimate corporation.

Maintenance Formalities

- Understand and follow the articles of incorporation and bylaws in all dealings.

- Hold annual meetings of stockholders.

- Give proper notice of any meetings, or use appropriate waiver of notice.

- Gather reports of officers and committees for inclusion in the corporate minute book.

- Elect directors as necessary and conduct other business in meetings.

- Record proper minutes that reflect the decisions made during meetings.

- Hold regular meetings of the board of directors at least annually.

- Give proper notice.

- Elect Officers and conduct other business.

- Record proper minutes.

- File Tax Returns for the corporation, even if no profit was shown.

- File annual list of officers and directors (or Annual Report) with Secretary of State, or appropriate state agency.

- Retain the services of a Resident Agent and be sure he receives any changes in location of the stock ledger or any amendments to articles or bylaws.

- Be sure all actions of stockholders are done by vote and recorded in minutes of meeting.

- Be sure that all major decisions by the directors are recorded in minutes.

CORPORATE FORMALITIES REFER TO THOSE PROCEDURES THAT MUST BE IN PLACE TO ENSURE THAT THE CORPORATION IS BEING PROPERLY MAINTAINED. THESE PROCEDURES CAN VARY, DEPENDING UPON THE STATE OF INCORPORATION.

- Be sure that a proper contract actually exists for any services contracted for by the corporation.

- Be sure that funds and assets are properly conveyed between the corporation and other entities or individuals.

- Never commingle corporate and personal funds.

- Record all corporate loans in corporate minutes.

- Maintain current accounting and other records for the corporation.

- Keep stock ledger properly. Issue new stock certificates and redeem transferred certificates as such transactions take place, always recording same in stock ledger.

- Whenever signing official corporate instruments or documents, sign on behalf of the corporation and indicate title, rather than as an individual.

Always be sure that the corporation looks and acts as a corporation. Keep records proper and up to date and maintain a traceable paper trail to prove that all actions were performed by a corporation and not just by individuals.

ARM'S LENGTH TRANSACTIONS

For tax purposes, the IRS says that when you are conducting business between related taxpayers you may not be motivated solely by business considerations. It is important to keep all these types of transactions - such as those between you and your corporation - at arms' length. This means that you conduct business under the same terms that would prevail if the parties to the transactions were not related to each other in any way.

Chapter

11

PAPERWORK & RECORDKEEPING

Details, details, details…

A corporation consists of many different parts. Some parts are made of paper, and others are made of flesh and blood; Some parts are stationary, while others may be in constant change. All are extremely important to the life and functionality of the corporation itself.

> *"In business, as in all of life, a small number of events account for most of the obtainable results." - Peter F. Drucker.*

This chapter discusses all of the various parts that make up a Nevada corporation, why they are needed and what they do. All of the corporate documents are addressed in detail, including the articles of incorporation, bylaws, resolutions, minutes, stock certificates and stock ledger. The role of the officers, directors and stockholders is outlined, as are the responsibilities of the resident agent.

The recordkeeping becomes even more important when a corporation has few stockholders. Indeed, the corporate records may be the only things that prove that a one-man corporation is not simply acting as the individual.

Without the paperwork, or corporate records, a corporation could not prove that the board of directors was acting properly when it made decisions for the corporation to carry out. Without the records, the court could determine that the board of directors did not act at all, and since the board of directors was not functioning, neither was the corporation.

Without proper corporate records the protection of the corporate veil is jeopardized. Most of the horror stories that you hear about courts attaching the personal assets of the directors or stockholders arise from situations where the corporate records were not kept properly.

ARTICLES OF INCORPORATION

Articles of incorporation is a document that must be filed with the Secretary of State to be recognized as a corporation. It is considered a form of a contract between the incorporators, the state, and the shareholders regarding the functions, responsibilities, and duties of the corporation to the others.

The Secretary of State has no authority to mandate any changes in the articles of incorporation as long as the articles meet certain requirements. Outside those requirements, the articles may contain virtually any provision that is within the bounds of the law.

In addition to the requirements outlined in the adjacent box, the Nevada Corporation Code allows for the inclusion of a provision discussed in the previous chapter that eliminates the personal liability of a director or stockholder of a corporation to its stockholders. While this provision is technically optional, any clear-thinking director or officer should consider this mandatory in the articles of any corporation on which they serve.

The articles of incorporation also may include provisions that are not mandatory as far as the state is concerned, but are needed by the incorporators to regulate the affairs among stockholders, directors and officers. These provisions might include limitations on the powers of individuals associated with the corporation, or even limitations on the purpose of the corporation itself. Additionally, the articles may limit the life span of the corporation to a specific period instead of allowing for perpetual existence.

When the Secretary of State receives articles of incorporation that have included the mandatory provisions listed above and the appropriate fees, the articles will be officially filed and a certificate of authorization to transact business will be issued to the corporation. At this point the corporation is recognized as a corporate entity by the state.

> **IN NEVADA, THE ARTICLES OF INCORPORATION MUST CONTAIN THE FOLLOWING:**
> **1.** THE NAME OF THE CORPORATION. **2.** THE NAME AND ADDRESS OF THE PERSON OR CORPORATION THAT WILL BE DESIGNATED AS THE RESIDENT AGENT FOR THE CORPORATION. **3.** THE NUMBER OF SHARES THE CORPORATION IS AUTHORIZED TO ISSUE, AND THE SERIES AND NUMBER OF SHARES OF EACH DIFFERENT CLASS OF SHARES AUTHORIZED. **4.** THE NAMES AND ADDRESSES OF THE FIRST BOARD OF DIRECTORS. **5.** THE NAME AND ADDRESS OF EACH INCORPORATOR SIGNING THE ARTICLES.

FIRST ARTICLE

The first section of the Articles of Incorporation should state the name of the corporation. This name should include the word "corporation," "company," "incorporated," "limited," or an abbreviation of one of these terms. One of these terms must be included if the corporate name resembles the name of a person. The name of the corporation may not resemble the name of another corporation conducting business in the state in such a way that would cause confusion.

SECOND ARTICLE

The corporation must declare the period of the corporation's existence. One of the most basic corporate characteristics is the ability to have a perpetual existence. While the corporation can declare a specific period of time, such as ten years, most corporations declare a perpetual existence. A corporation that declares a limited timeframe can be subject to fines if the corporation operates after the expiration date.

THIRD ARTICLE

The corporation must state the purpose or purposes for which the corporation is organized. Under the Model Corporation Act, a business corporation may be organized "for any lawful purpose or purposes, except for the purpose of banking or insurance."

Some organizers choose specific language in stating the corporate purpose, such as, "owning, investing, and managing real estate." If, however, the corporation engages in any business activity outside of that limitation, it must amend the articles of incorporation or else face fines. For that reason, it is common for corporations to be organized "for any lawful purpose."

FOURTH ARTICLE

NEVADA NOTES: A NEVADA CORPORATION MAY HAVE 25,000 SHARES OF NO PAR VALUE STOCK FOR THE MINIMUM FILING FEE.

The corporation must describe the corporation's stock, including the number of available shares, any classification, preference or other rights, and par value. A small corporation may have no need for a large number of authorized shares, but it is usually preferable to organize the corporation with the largest number of shares that the Secretary of State will allow for the minimal filing fee.

The corporation may provide for a certain number of voting and a certain number of non-voting shares. When more investment is needed, but dilution of control is a concern, the corporation could issue the non-voting shares, if they are available. The corporation can divide the corporation's stock into as many different classes of stock as they need to provide for the planning goals of the organizers.

The corporation is also able to declare a specific par value, such as $.001 per share or $100 per share. Many closely held corporations prefer to use No Par Value shares, which allow the Directors to determine the selling price of the shares.

FIFTH ARTICLE

The corporation may issue classes of stock in **"series"**. That means that the Articles may provide for a portion of a class of shares to be issued with a certain dividend rate, redemption privilege, liquidation preference, conversion privileges, etc. and that another portion of shares of the same class may be issued with a different set of variables.

SIXTH ARTICLE

The Articles may provide for **"preemptive rights"** of shareholders. This means that the shareholder has a right to buy a corresponding percentage of his or her current shareholdings of any new stock of the same class. The corporation may offer to sell the shares to other investors only if the shareholders with preemptive rights are not interested or are unable to purchase the offering.

SEVENTH ARTICLE

The corporation may provide for indemnification of the officers, directors, employees and agents for any liability to which they may be subject as a result of the performance of their corporate duties. The ability of a corporation to indemnify individuals may be controlled or limited by state law.

EIGHTH ARTICLE

The corporation must provide the street address of the registered office and resident agent located within the state of incorporation. The resident agent is responsible to receive service of process and official correspondence in the name of the corporation, and forward such communications to the appropriate corporate officer.

NINTH ARTICLE

The corporation must state the number of directors required. Some states, such as Nevada and Wyoming, allow one director, while many states require a minimum of three. The directors who will comprise the initial Board of Directors must be listed by name, with street address in the articles of incorporation.

TENTH ARTICLE

The corporation must have one or more organizer, or "incorporator". The incorporators sign the Articles of incorporation when they are submitted for filing. They are responsible, and potentially liable, if they have made any knowing misstatement of fact in the Articles of incorporation. Otherwise, they have no responsibility to the corporation.

AMENDMENT TO ARTICLES OF INCORPORATION

The original incorporators may amend the articles of incorporation before stock is issued by filing a certificate with the Secretary of State with the detailed changes. The opening paragraph of the certificate of amendment must:

- State that the signers of the certificate are at least two-thirds of the original incorporators.

- State the date the original articles of incorporation were filed with the Secretary of State.

- Certify that no stock has been issued to date.

Upon receipt of the certificate of amendment and appropriate fees, the Secretary of State will file the amended version of the articles of incorporation. All amendments made to articles of incorporation before the issuance of stock will be considered as the original articles of incorporation.

A corporation that has already issued its stock also may make amendments to the articles of incorporation. However, there are only five areas in which the articles of incorporation may be changed:

- The existing powers and purposes of the corporation may be either broadened or narrowed.

- The other powers and purposes may be substituted for the existing powers and purposes of the corporation.

- Amendments may change the number or classification of its authorized stock, including changes to the par value, restrictions, options, etc.

- The corporation's name may be changed.

- The optional provisions may be changed as needed.

BYLAWS

The bylaws of a corporation are a separate document from the Articles of incorporation, and usually deal with matters of internal corporate procedure. The bylaws are considered a contract between the stockholders, directors, and officers and typically contain the terms that are not required in the articles of incorporation regarding the regulation of their rights and the affairs of the corporation.

The bylaws usually state the place and time of the annual meetings of the stockholders and directors, and detail the procedures for notifying these individuals of these meetings. The bylaws also will define what makes up a voting majority and a quorum for the purposes of the corporation. The procedures for calling special meetings are usually described, as is the standard order of business. The bylaws are also the place where the specific duties of the officers of the corporation are described.

While many of these terms could be otherwise stated in the articles of incorporation, it is usually easier to adopt them as bylaws.

Since bylaws are drafted by the directors and adopted by the shareholders as their internal operating procedure, the directors may draft changes to the bylaws any time. The changes must then be adopted by the shareholders. Neither the bylaws nor any amendments to them are filed with the Secretary of State.

The bylaws generally contain the following features:

- They identify the location of the corporation's offices.

- They specify the date and time of annual shareholder's meetings.

- They provide for calling "special meetings" of the shareholders.

- They define a voting quorum of shareholders.

- They provide for the use of proxies.

- They provide for informal actions, not requiring a formal meeting.

- They provide for cumulative voting procedures.

- They set the number, tenure and qualifications of the directors.

- They specify the date and time of annual directors meetings.

- They establish the directors fees for meeting attendance.

- They define a quorum of the Board of Directors.

- They provide for filling vacancies on the Board of Directors.

- They establish procedures for removal or discharge of directors.

- They describe the corporation's officers and their specific duties.

- They establish procedures for removal or discharge of officers.

- They describe the share certificate.

- They establish a fiscal year for the corporation.

- They provide for the use of a corporate seal.

- They provide for the use of committees.

- They provide for amending the bylaws.

If a corporation functions without bylaws, the articles of incorporation become the sole document that regulates the affairs of the corporation. Since amendments to the articles of incorporation require more procedure and cost, it is advisable for a corporation to adopt bylaws as a way of maintaining some flexibility in the functions of the corporation.

MINUTES

The minutes of a corporation's meetings provide a complete record of corporate formalities, and provide decisive proof that the corporation was functioning properly. "Put it in writing" should be the adage for a corporation to live by. In small corporations, it is too easy to make important decisions during the day over the telephone, during coffee breaks, or on the golf course.

Even if you feel that you are too busy managing the corporation to attend to the detail of the corporate minutes, you need to realize that accurate, written reports of your corporate proceedings may be your only defense. Without accurate minutes, a judge or IRS agent may disallow many corporations' actions, including executive compensation and bonuses, retirement plans, and dividend disbursements.

For every action that is taken during a meeting, the minutes should show that the matter was properly introduced, seconded, discussed, and agreed to by a voting majority as defined in the bylaws. The complete text of any resolution, contract, report, or other document adopted or ratified in a meeting also should appear in the minutes.

The minutes of any meeting should show that the meeting was properly called, and that everyone there received adequate notice as required by the corporate bylaws. If a written notice of the meeting was sent out, a copy should be included, and if no notice was given, the appropriate waiver of notice should accompany the minutes. The minutes should be signed by all attending, showing agreement that the minutes accurately reflect what took place in the meeting.

There is no standard format for minutes, but such items as the time, date, and place of the meeting, along with a list of all attending should be included. All actions by the board should be recorded. Although minutes should be specific, they need not record every word of debate on every subject. They should concentrate on final decisions rather than discussion.

Officers and directors can defend themselves in some very important areas by detailing the following corporate decisions in the minutes:

1. **Executive Salaries.** If the IRS feels that your salary or the salary of your employees is excessive, they may suspect you of trying to distribute profits as compensation instead of dividends. Compensation is tax-deductible and dividends are not. The IRS keeps a close eye on small corporations in this regard, since it is easier to hide profits as deductible compensation when there are only a few employee-stockholders. If the minutes of the corporate meetings show that the company compared the salaries of similar talent for comparable companies in the area, including benefits, and considered each specific employee's training and experience, then a strong case can be made for the high compensation levels. But, when these factors won't adequately explain high compensation levels, the minutes could show that the company's growth potential was a factor and that agreements existed for substantial bonuses when the employee produced significant results. When the corporate minutes adequately reflect this, the IRS probably will agree that increased compensation was proper in a profitable year. The minutes could also contain a "hedge agreement" that covers the corporation in case you're not sure you can justify the salary levels. To do this, before any salaries are paid, the directors enter a resolution into the minutes stating that if the IRS rules any stockholder-employee's salary is too high in any year, that individual will return the excess to the corporation. As a result, the stockholder won't be taxed on that amount (although the returned amount will be taxable to the corporation.)

2. **Accumulating Excessive Earnings.** Corporations that accumulate over $250,000 in earnings may be penalized by additional taxes on top of those that apply to corporate profits. The reason for this is that the Internal Revenue Service assumes that you are holding the money to avoid distributing taxable dividends. However, if your corporation plans to make significant equipment purchases, or is planning on expanding or diversifying, then reasonable grounds exist for retaining excess earnings. But your minutes must record the reasons for the accumulation, including the cost estimates for putting the plans into place. Your reasons do not have to be immediate. They can be long-range, since your minutes reflect your long-term corporate needs.

Other possible reasons for accumulating excessive earnings are:

- For building inventory.

- To protect against loss of profits when the corporation depends on a small number of customers.

- To reserve funds for profit-sharing and pension plan obligations.

- To invest or lend money to suppliers or customers that are necessary to maintain their business.

- To build reserves against actual or potential lawsuits.

3. **Consolidations and Mergers.** Accurate minutes are mandatory during corporate mergers and consolidations. They must specifically outline the plan for selling and acquiring assets and putting new management and control in place. Used in these circumstances, the minutes are usually required to be filed with the corporate tax returns of the involved corporations.

4. **Dissolution and Liquidation.** The minutes of the meetings at which the liquidation plan of a corporation was discussed and adopted is also filed with the corporate tax return. Since the tax consequences of this type of action are extremely complicated, it is advisable to seek counsel with competent professionals in drafting the minutes, as they play a critical part in determining how the IRS looks at various distributions.

5. **Dividends.** If a stockholder receives a dividend as stock instead of cash, it isn't considered taxable until the stock is sold. That is, unless the stockholder can choose between stock and cash, in which case it is taxable. So, the minutes should clearly state whether stockholders have this option.

6. **Step Transactions.** Any time that a corporation involves itself with several transactions over a period of time that are "steps" toward a larger transaction, the company's minutes should reflect that each of these "steps" were taken with the larger goal in mind.

7. **Qualified Retirement Plans**. If your corporation plans to offer employee pension, profit-sharing or stock-bonus plans, the corporate minutes will be necessary to gain IRS approval. When your plan meets IRS requirements, employees won't be taxed on corporate contributions or gains until they receive the money. Once the plan is in place and operational, the minutes also should indicate the amount of corporate contributions each year. Also, if you have to abandon the plan, the minutes should document the reasons why that action was deemed necessary.

RESOLUTIONS

NEVADA NOTES:
NEVADA'S CORPORATION
CODE ALLOWS THE BOARD
OF DIRECTORS TO TAKE AN
ACTION WITHOUT AN
OFFICIAL DIRECTORS
MEETING, AS LONG AS ALL
THE DIRECTORS SIGN A
RESOLUTION IN SUPPORT OF
THE ACTION, AND THAT
RESOLUTION IS RATIFIED AT
THE NEXT MEETING AND
FILED WITH THE MINUTES.

The use of resolutions provides another way to manage the formalities of a Nevada corporation. By definition, a resolution is a document that records actions that the directors (or is some cases, stockholders) "resolve" to take on behalf of the corporation. Resolutions may be included as part of the minutes of either directors or stockholders meetings, or they may be included separately into a Resolutions section of the corporate record book.

The stockholders also may take action without a meeting as long as at least a majority of the voting rights consent in writing to the action. In other words, a Nevada corporation can conduct nearly all of its business with resolutions. Simply keep the corporate resolutions in chronological order, and you will maintain a complete record of all the corporate activities. Then, at each annual meeting, the shareholders will ratify all of the actions taken by resolution by the board of directors. You may find this method of maintaining corporate formalities to be much simpler and faster, and equally effective as holding special meetings and recording their minutes.

The typical resolutions will contain the following:

- An indication about whose resolution it is (i.e., directors or shareholders).

- The name of the corporation.

- The state of incorporation.

- An indication that the resolution contains the direction of at least a majority of those empowered to make decisions at this level.

- The text of the resolution itself.

- The date of the adoption of the resolution.

- The signatures of all of individuals who have approved the resolution.

THE CORPORATE SEAL

It was once a common practice for a corporation to "seal" any formal document or contract that it executed. While a corporate seal is a nice touch, it is not legally required in most states. A corporate seal may, however, be required when executing documents from other countries, such as foreign contracts, etc.

Any requirement to use a corporate seal is completely voluntary, and may be written into the corporate bylaws. The legality of any corporate document that does not bear the impression of a corporate seal is not affected.

STOCK

STOCK CERTIFICATE

Most states require that every stockholder be entitled to have a certificate, signed by the appropriate corporate officers or agents, which certifies the number of shares owned by him in the corporation. After the stock certificate has been issued, the corporation is required to send to the stockholder a written statement that contains all of the information of the stock certificate. The corporation must usually confirm all of this information in writing to the stockholders on at least an annual basis.

When the corporation is authorized to issue different classes or series of shares, the certificate should reflect the kind and class of stock represented by the certificate. Other useful information for the stock certificate includes:

- The state of incorporation,

- The number of the stock certificate,

- The authorized capitalization of the corporation,

- The date the certificate is issued to the owner,

- The name of the resident agent, and

- Any other term that the bylaws or articles of incorporation apply to the issuance of stock, (such as whether the stock can be assessed by the corporation when funds run short.)

When the corporate officer or agent issues the stock certificate, it will show how many shares the certificate is worth. Like a checkbook, each stock certificate has a stub that remains a permanent part of the corporate record, indicating the number of shares issued to that particular person on that date.

Also like a check, the back of the stock certificate is left blank, to be reserved for the time that the certificate is endorsed and either transferred or redeemed ("cashed"). When shares are transferred from one individual to another, it is customary to record those changes in the official ledger. Nevada case law suggests that transfers of stock between individuals are not recognized by the corporation until the transfer is registered upon the books of the corporation.

The important thing about stock ownership is not the number of shares owned, but the percentage of ownership and voting rights those shares represent. To find this information

IN NEVADA, THE ONLY CORPORATION REQUIRED TO USE A SEAL IS THE **CORPORATION SOLE. A** CORPORATION SOLE IS REQUIRED NOT ONLY TO USE A CORPORATION SEAL ON ALL DOCUMENTS, BUT ALSO TO REGISTER ITS IMPRESSION WITH THE SECRETARY OF STATE'S OFFICE.

IT IS NOT NECESSARY TO ISSUE A STOCK CERTIFICATE FOR EVERY SHARE. JUST AS A CHECK CAN BE WRITTEN FOR ANY AMOUNT, A STOCK CERTIFICATE CAN REPRESENT ANY NUMBER SHARES.

out, the corporate secretary can tell you how many shares of stock are authorized by the state to be issued, and how many shares have actually been issued. Remember that the control of the corporation rests ultimately with the stockholder, and when a stockholder or group of stockholders control the majority of ownership and voting rights, they can do essentially what they want with the corporation.

STOCK LEDGER

The stock ledger is the official record of the corporation concerning the issuance and transfer of shares. All transfers of corporate shares between individuals must eventually be registered upon the books of the corporation. Until that is done, all of the rights of ownership remain with the original holder of the shares. That includes the right to vote and the right to receive dividends. The purpose for this is to protect the officers of the corporation in determining these rights among the stockholders. Any use of "bearer" shares should be made with this in mind.

The stock ledger should contain information regarding each stockholder:

- Their name and address.

- The date and time that they became owners of the shares.

- The number and class of shares they received.

- The amount they paid for the shares.

- The number of the stock certificate that they received to evidence their ownership in the shares.

- The name of the person the shares were transferred from, if applicable.

- The number of the stock certificate of the person from whom the stock was transferred.

NEVADA NOTES:
WHILE SOME STATES REQUIRE A COPY OF THE OFFICIAL STOCK LEDGER TO BE MAINTAINED AT THE OFFICE OF THE RESIDENT AGENT, NEVADA HAS NO SUCH REQUIREMENT. IN FACT, THE STOCK LEDGER CAN BE MAINTAINED ANYWHERE IN THE WORLD, AND STILL BE VALID.

Any person who has been a stockholder for at least six months is entitled to inspect the stock ledger either in person or by agent or attorney during usual business hours and on five days written notice. Some states require that the resident agent have a current copy of the corporation's stock ledger at all times.

A corporation that refuses to open the stock ledger for inspection to a qualified stockholder may be fined by the state $25 for every day that access is denied. Additionally, the corporation is liable to the person for all damages resulting from the period of denied access.

STOCK LEDGER STATEMENT

Some states, such as Nevada, requires that in lieu of keeping a copy of the stock ledger, the resident agent have on file a "stock ledger statement," that provides the name and address of the person that has the official stock ledger in their custody.

Under Nevada law, that person could be located anywhere in the world. So, to find the official records of ownership of a Nevada corporation, you would have to subpoena the resident agent, which will only provide information that will require another subpoena, probably in another jurisdiction. By the time the second subpoena was obtained and served, it is possible that the location of the stock ledger would have changed. Of course, you would have to serve the resident agent all over to find out that new location. The use of the stock ledger statement provides another advantage to the owners of a Nevada corporation.

Chapter

12

THE PEOPLE BEHIND THE CORPORATION

And the meetings they have to attend

A corporation needs people in order to fill specific roles that are necessary in allowing the corporation to act like a corporation. The presence of these individuals acting properly in defined roles allows the corporation to retain its separate corporate identity, for without them, the corporation cannot exist.

The various states each have a mechanism through which the identities of these individuals are revealed to the public. Typically, a state might require the corporation to file an "annual report" that, in addition to naming the corporate officers and directors, might also require disclosure of shareholders and usually requires some information regarding the value of corporate assets. Alternatively, some states may have this information included in the annual state tax return.

Nevada may have the simplest, and most favorable disclosure requirements. A one-page form requires the disclosure of the President, Secretary, Treasurer, and at least one Director of the corporation. Since Nevada allows for a one-man corporation, the name of the same individual may be used in each instance. No other information is required.

Although that list is then filed annually, the Nevada corporation is not required to file a list of officers and directors more frequently than on an annual basis, even if there is a mid-year changing of the guard. The corporation is not required to keep any officer or director for the entire year. They can be removed from office and replaced at any time.

So, the corporation could file its list of officers on July 1, and on July 2 replace those officers with different people entirely. The new officers could, theoretically serve 364 days a year without ever being listed with the state. On the 365th day of every year, the officers whose names you would like to appear on public records are re-appointed for the purpose of the filing, and serve their one day term. Thus, it is possible for officers and directors to serve without ever being listed on the records of the state.

NEVADA & WYOMING NOTES. WITHIN 60 DAYS OF INCORPORATING, YOU ARE REQUIRED TO SUBMIT TO THE SECRETARY OF STATE A LIST OF OFFICERS AND DIRECTORS FOR THE COMING YEAR. WYOMING, ON THE OTHER HAND, DOES NOT REQUIRE THAT THE CORPORATION FILE AN ANNUAL REPORT FOR ONE FULL YEAR.

OFFICERS

The officers of a corporation are elected by the board of directors, and are assigned responsibilities in the bylaws to conduct the regular, day-to-day business of the corporation. A Nevada corporation must have a president, a secretary, a treasurer and a resident agent, and has the option to have one or more vice presidents and any other officer or assistant officer that it wants. So, if the need exists, the corporation may have an assistant-secretary, or assistant-treasurer that is authorized to sign all documents and conduct all business that the original officer is otherwise assigned.

Under the law, the secretary or other officer of a private corporation has only the authority specifically delegated to him by the bylaws and board of directors. They are not personally liable for the regular debts of the corporation, but may have exposure to the IRS for payroll taxes or other specific tax obligations.

PRESIDENT

It is generally the president's responsibility to oversee the actions of the other officers. He is the person that reports to the board of directors and is responsible for carrying out their wishes.

SECRETARY

The secretary is generally responsible for maintaining the corporate records and formalities. His duties involve executing and recording the minutes of meetings and resolutions, maintaining the corporate stock ledger and overseeing the issuance and transfer of corporate shares. It is often the responsibility of the corporate secretary to see to it that the corporation abides by its internal rules and bylaws, including the timely distribution of the appropriate notices and waivers, and that some form of parliamentary procedure is followed in all corporate meetings. The secretary acts as voting inspector during stockholders meetings, and announces the winning vote.

TREASURER

The treasurer is responsible for all financial records and transactions. The treasurer will usually present the Treasurer's Report at all regular meetings, and oversees all bank accounts, investments and liabilities of the corporation. It is his responsibility to see to it that the board of directors has the information available to make educated decisions concerning the corporation's financial future.

VICE PRESIDENT

One or more vice presidents may be allowed by the corporate bylaws or by a resolution of the board of directors. They may be assigned any specific or general duty necessary to fulfill the needs of the corporation.

OFFICER'S ROLE IN CORPORATE MANAGEMENT.

NEVADA & WYOMING NOTE:
NEVADA CORPORATION CODE ALLOWS ONE PERSON TO ACT IN ALL THESE CAPACITIES, AND THAT PERSON MAY ALSO SERVE ON THE BOARD OF DIRECTORS. THIS ALLOWS FOR A TRUE ONE-MAN CORPORATION THAT IS NOT POSSIBLE IN MANY OTHER STATES.

A corporation must have a president, a secretary, and a treasurer. These people comprise the mandatory officers of the corporation. Additionally, a corporation may have one or more vice-presidents, assistant secretaries, and any other officers as the board of directors sees fit. Officers must generally be at least 18 years of age and need not be a resident of the state of incorporation or the United States.

The responsibility of the board of directors to manage the affairs of the corporation is generally delegated to the officers. Each officer is given the authority and assigned specific duties in the management of the corporation by provisions in the bylaws or by resolution of the board of directors. The board of directors may remove an officer any time.

> *"Obviously, the only justification for the director's existence is that he should direct."* - Louis Brandeis.

DIRECTORS

The management and control of the affairs of the private corporation are vested in the board of directors by the stockholders, as limited by the articles of incorporation and the Nevada Corporation Code. If a director does not meet the standards of care and loyalty in carrying out his duties, he may be held personally liable to the corporation or its stockholders.

Directors have the responsibility to be informed concerning all of the decisions they are asked to make for the corporation. In making their decisions, they should consider:

- The interests of the corporation's employees, suppliers, creditors and customers;

- The economy of the state and nation;

- The interests of the community and of society, and;

- The long-term and short-term interests of the corporation and its stockholders.

All decisions of the board must be defensible by one of those criteria. A director also must not use his office to make a personal profit (ever hear of "insider trading?") or gain any other personal advantage.

If the shareholders cannot break a deadlock of the board of directors, the matter can be referred to a court of proper jurisdiction to wind up the affairs of the corporation and liquidate its assets.

While the Nevada corporation must have one director, the articles of incorporation might stipulate either a fixed number of directors, or a minimum and maximum number of directors that the corporation must stay within. Directors must be at least eighteen years of age, but are not required to be a citizen of Nevada or the United States.

The Nevada Corporation Code provides for the formation of committees within the board of directors. As long as the bylaws or articles of incorporation provide for their existence, a committee of the board of directors may be formed to exercise the powers of the board in the management of the business and affairs of the corporation. Each committee must include at least one director, and unless the articles of incorporation state otherwise, the board may appoint other persons who are not directors to serve on the committees.

The board of directors may reach a deadlock when it is unable to make a decision on a matter due to a split in the vote, and no shareholder has enough voting power to reconstruct the membership of the board. It is advisable for the bylaws to refer deadlocked issues to the stockholders.

DIRECTOR'S ROLE IN CORPORATE MANAGEMENT

NEVADA NOTE:
ASSUMING THEY WERE ACTING DILIGENTLY AND HONESTLY IN THEIR ROLE, THE BOARD OF DIRECTORS CAN BE INDEMNIFIED UNDER NEVADA REVISED STATUTE FROM BEING HELD PERSONALLY LIABLE FOR THEIR ACTIONS ON BEHALF OF THE CORPORATION.

The board of directors has the responsibility to manage the corporation's affairs within the boundaries of the Corporation Code and the articles of incorporation. Directors must act prudently in their role, and have reason to believe that their actions are lawful, in order to be indemnified from personal liability for their actions.

If the stockholders choose not to hold a director liable for his actions, a court may or may not let that decision stand, depending upon the legal precedent of the state. When the court follows the decision of the stockholders to not hold the directors liable for their actions, it is often referred to as the "business-judgment" rule.

STOCKHOLDERS

Stockholders are owners of the corporation, and ultimately have the power to regulate and control its affairs. The power of the stockholders is manifest through the directors, who are elected by the stockholders and are then delegated the powers necessary to conduct the business of the corporation. Each share of voting stock is allowed one vote.

The rights of the stockholder are dependent upon the type of stock that he is issued. A more complete discussion of the variety of rights and responsibilities of a stockholder depending upon the type of stock he holds is included in the review of "stock" in this handbook.

SHAREHOLDER'S ROLE IN CORPORATE MANAGEMENT

The investor that controls the voting majority of the issued stock can ultimately maintain control over all corporate decisions. However, the primary method by which a shareholder exercises control is in his ability to elect directors. When only one investor exists, the process is simple. However when there are many shareholders the issue can be a little more complicated. The fact that different classes of stock can exist, as discussed above, means that it is possible for a stockholder to have a minority interest in the corporation, but a majority of the voting rights of the shareholders.

In these cases, special planning is required to ensure that minority shareholders will have enough voting rights to give them a level of participation that the Corporation Code guarantees them, without giving them inappropriate control. Several methods can be used to allocate voting powers between different groups of investors. Some of these result in permanent allocations of control, while other methods allow for temporary allocations of control for special circumstances.

The possibilities for allocating different levels of power among shareholders by using different classes of stock are virtually limitless. For instance, a majority stockholder may own all of the shares of one class of stock, which authorizes him to elect all of the directors except one. The minority stockholders may own all of the shares of another class of stock, which may equal or exceed the total investment of the majority stockholder, and only be allowed to elect one director among them. Stockholders of one class may not be allowed to elect any of the directors, but may have total control over the sale of corporate assets.

RESIDENT or REGISTERED AGENT

Each corporation is required to maintain a registered office within the boundaries of the state in which it is incorporated. This office is referred to in the Corporation Code as a "resident agent" or "registered agent." A resident agent may be either a corporation or a natural person, and is required to have an actual street address, not just a post office box.

In Nevada, the resident agent, although appointed by the corporation, must file an acceptance of that appointment with the Secretary of State before it is officially considered the resident agent of that corporation.

The purpose of the resident agent is that it requires the corporation to maintain a form of physical presence in the state to insure the availability of legal process service or notice upon the corporation. Your resident agent will be acting for you, and his actions have a binding influence on the corporation. This is not a difficult job, but it requires an agent that knows what he is doing.

In other words, if your corporation gets sued, the resident agent will be served with the papers.

Here is a true example that provides a great deal of insight about the importance of having a qualified resident agent: A customer falls inside a store and sues for $15,000 plus costs. When the case went to trial, no one appeared to defend the company that owned the store, so a default judgment was entered. Upon appeal, the Supreme Court of Arizona refused to overturn the judgment. When the legal papers were originally served upon the store manager, he called the legal department at the company headquarters and was told to forward them in the company mail pouch. Then, days later, they were returned to the store manager without comment. The manager assumed they were a copy for his files, when they actually had been mishandled by the mail room.

The court decision said that "having received the summons and complaint back with no communication whatsoever accompanying same, it seems careless, in retrospect at least to file them away and do nothing more. (The manager) testified that the reason he had treated them as lightly as he did was because he received them back in the morning when he was in a hurry to open up his store. Day-to-day operations were held in higher regard than court process."

The decision went on to say that "the failure to answer was clearly a fault on the part of the defendants that ordinary prudence would recommend be cured as soon as possible after discovery. The persons concerned are in the commercial world and should be able to take legal action promptly."

A Nevada corporation is required to maintain certain records at the office of the resident agent. This includes:

- A copy of the articles of incorporation, complete with all amendments, as certified by the Secretary of State;

- A copy of the bylaws, certified by an officer of the corporation, and;

- Either the original stock ledger, a duplicate stock ledger, or

- A statement that sets forth the name and address of the custodian of the stock ledger.

YOUR CORPORATION IS RESPONSIBLE FOR THE ACTS OF YOUR RESIDENT AGENT, INCLUDING ERRORS IN JUDGMENT, DELAY IN HANDLING LEGAL SERVICE, AND A LACK OF KNOWLEDGE ABOUT HOW TO HANDLE EMERGENCIES. REMEMBER THAT IT IS LIKELY THAT THE ONLY TIME WHEN YOUR RESIDENT AGENT WILL BE USED IS IN SITUATIONS OF IMPORTANCE.

The selection of your resident agent is one of the most important decisions you will make when first setting up your Nevada corporation. It is important that your resident agent has established, regular office hours, and is familiar with the implications and procedures of receiving legal service of process.

Another vital factor in selecting a resident agent is in determining the stability of the company. During 1993, one of the largest resident agents in Nevada filed for protection under Federal Bankruptcy statutes, throwing thousands of corporations into confusion regarding their status while the office was administered by a California law firm.

In late 1995, a Nevada resident agent simply closed his doors and walked away from his hundreds of corporate clients. Many of these corporations have no access to their corporate mail or other correspondence, are unable to deposit checks that have been mailed to their Nevada office. Several corporations that this company formed in the weeks prior to the office closing were terminated by the Nevada Secretary of State because this resident agent was bouncing the checks that were intended to pay the state filing fees. That is a headache nobody needs.

There are many examples of companies that have unknowingly incurred default judgments because they were not notified properly by their resident agent. If the agent does not perform it's function properly, the legal responsibility for the service of process in still the corporation's.

In Nevada, the resident agent business is extremely competitive. Some companies aggressively market their services or seminars using direct mail and telemarketing to all

Nevada corporations filed with the Secretary of State. Many resident agents also provide additional services which may or may not be useful or necessary, depending upon your corporate circumstances.

ORGANIZERS

The organizers of the corporation are the individuals who prepare and file the organizational documents. The organizer may be an attorney, a prospective shareholder or director of the corporation, or a consultant or advisor to the parties involved. It is not required that a corporation be formed by an attorney. In Nevada, there are many firms that specialize in forming Nevada entities and providing the necessary resident agent service. These companies act as the organizer by drafting the Articles of Incorporation. They have a responsibility to accurately prepare the Articles, but have no ongoing obligation or liability once the corporation is formed.

MEETINGS

While all corporations are required to hold annual stockholder's meetings, public corporations must follow federal laws and private corporations must follow state laws that regulate these meetings. It can be very crucial that the applicable laws are followed, as one slip-up can give a disgruntled stockholder ammunition for creating trouble.

Nevada's Corporation Code requires only two meetings to be held each year. Those meetings are the annual meeting of stockholders and the annual meeting of directors. These meetings may be held anywhere in the world, in a manner provided for in the bylaws of the corporation. Nevada also allows for these meetings to be held via teleconference or computer link, unless restricted otherwise by the articles of incorporation or bylaws.

STOCKHOLDERS MEETINGS
Election of Directors.

THE IRS HAS BEEN KNOWN TO DISALLOW LEGITIMATE CORPORATE DEDUCTIONS ON FINDING THAT SOME ASPECT OF THE MEETING IN WHICH THE MATTER WAS DISCUSSED WAS IN VIOLATION OF THE LAW.

Generally, the purpose of the stockholders meeting is to elect the board of directors for the following year. In many small, family-owned corporations, this is probably just a formality. But, when outside stockholders exist, the Corporation Code must be strictly followed.

The secretary, who monitors the election process, is usually prepared with a current list of stockholders and, when applicable, a separate list of stockholders who are entitled to vote. The secretary is responsible for the proper execution of the voting plan adopted by the corporation.

If the stockholders fail or are unable to elect directors within eighteen months after the last election of directors, the district court has the jurisdiction to order the election of the directors. To do this, a group of stockholders representing at least fifteen percent of the voting power of the corporation must file a petition in the county where the resident agent is located.

Approval of Changes in Bylaws or Articles of Incorporation.

Any change in the written rules of the corporation should be approved by the stockholders. This includes any proposed amendments to the bylaws or the articles of incorporation. When approving these changes, cumulative voting does not apply.

Other Issues.

There are other situations that may require stockholder approval. For instance, if one of the corporate officers would like to borrow money from the corporation or have the corporation guarantee a loan, the stockholders must approve the action. If the corporation would like to offer stock options or stock benefits to the officers, directors, or employees, that too must be approved by the stockholders. Any major purchase or sale of corporate assets should be approved by a majority of the stockholders.

DIRECTORS MEETINGS

The primary purpose of directors' meeting is to make the decisions that have been delegated to the directors by the stockholders. The directors also should use this opportunity to ratify all of the actions they may have taken by resolution since their last meeting.

THE CORPORATION MAY BE ABLE TO DEDUCT THE TRAVEL AND LODGING EXPENSES FOR DIRECTORS REQUIRED TO ATTEND ANNUAL MEETINGS.

The directors are also given the responsibility in their meeting to elect the corporate officers for the following year. The bylaws should contain all of the procedural direction necessary for the directors to conduct the business of their meetings, including the applicable definitions of a working majority and quorum.

Since the current tax law does not allow the corporation to deduct the travel and lodging expenses for stockholders to attend their annual meetings, you may choose (either instead or in addition) to act as a director for your family-held corporation to take those corporate deductions. In that situation, it may be desirable to stretch the annual meeting out for a full week, if the meeting is scheduled at a particularly alluring location, like Hawaii.

Your written agenda can provide sufficient documentation that the meeting warranted the extra time. Here is one idea for a ten-day schedule:

Day One.

Order of Business.
Review of minute book.
Ratification of Directors actions.
Location of Stock Ledger

Day Two.

Review of first quarter's financial statements.

Day Three.

Review of second quarter's financial statements.

Day Four.

Review of third quarter's financial statements.

Day Five.

Review of fourth quarter's financial statements.

Day Six.

Review of year end financial statements.

Day Seven.
> Review and discussion of assets.
> Review and discussion of leases.
> Review and discussion of liabilities.
> Review and discussion of payroll.

Day Eight.
> Plans for next twelve months.

Day Nine.
> Election of officers for next twelve months.

Day Ten.
> Review discussion of the actions of the last nine days.
> Miscellaneous items of business.
> Discussion and scheduling of next board meeting.
> Meeting is closed.

STEPS TO TAKE BEFORE AND AFTER MEETINGS

Before Your Meeting

> IT MAY NOT BE REQUIRED FOR A SMALL COMPANY THAT HAS NO STOCKHOLDERS OUTSIDE THE FAMILY TO PREPARE AND SEND AN ANNUAL REPORT, BUT IT IS ALWAYS A GOOD IDEA TO PROVIDE THIS INFORMATION ANNUALLY TO THE STOCKHOLDERS ANYWAY.

1. **Send the annual report to the stockholders.** In a small company, this may simply be a financial statement that details the profit and loss, and assets and liabilities of the corporation. The accuracy of all financial documents should be attested to by either the treasurer or company accountant.

2. **Have an agenda.** Whatever the number of items to be discussed, and whatever the number of stockholders or directors of the corporation, it is a good idea to go through the motions of putting an agenda together. The presence of an agenda notifies everyone involved of the topics of discussion for the meeting.

3. **Update the list of stockholders**. If there have been any changes or transfers of stock, make sure the corporate books reflect the current situation. Where there are many stockholders, this list is required to verify the voting rights of those attending the meetings.

4. **Notify stockholders.** In Nevada, stockholders must be notified of any meetings not less than ten nor more than sixty days before the meeting is held. This notification must include the purpose for the meeting, as well as the time and place where it is to be held.

5. **Issue proxy statements.** When the notifications are sent out, it is a good idea to include proxy statements that will allow stockholders who will be unable to attend the meeting to participate by designating someone else to cast their votes for them.

6. **Prepare yourself to answer questions.** Small corporations will usually be able to anticipate controversial topics, but larger corporations can be "blind-sided" by stockholders who may be unknown to any of the officers and directors. When a large number of stockholders will be present, it is a good idea to arrange for your attorneys and accountants to be at the meeting with

any documentation they may need to consult. This material is likely to include all corporate records, contracts, leases, and tax data.

After Your Meeting

1. **Write and distribute the meeting's minutes.** File your corporate minutes with your corporate records. The minutes should contain accurate and specific records about all decisions made during the meeting, and should be attested to by those attending.

2. **Follow up on all approved actions.** Some actions taken in a meeting may not take effect until the Secretary of State is notified. This includes any changes to the articles of incorporation.

Chapter

13

MAXIMIZING CORPORATE ADVANTAGES

Corporate Strategies for Achieving Success

ESTATE PLANNING STRATEGIES

One of the most practical uses of a corporation is in providing for a convenient transfer of wealth and assets to one's heirs. The corporation allows for assets that would otherwise be difficult to split up evenly because of their very nature, to be divided and controlled in precise increments. It may be difficult to split up a rental duplex among three children, but it is easy to split the ownership of a corporation which owns the duplex into three equally beneficial units.

"Estate planning" is frequently considered to be an art in contemplation of death to protect from death's negative tax consequences. The corporation can provide planning options that, in addition to those tax concerns, also deals well with such issues as protecting the ownership of assets from creditors.

There are many ways that a corporation can be used to accomplish these goals. Here are but a few, intended to start you thinking about the possibilities that exist.

THE FAMILY-OWNED CORPORATION

An individual who is planning on starting a new business could utilize a very simple technique to reduce estate taxes on any gain that might occur as a result of the business success. For example, Joe has a great business idea and wants to see if he can make a go of it. He forms a corporation that has Class A, Voting stock and Class B Non Voting Stock and transfers $10,000 into the company to get it off the ground. Of that, $1,000 is capitalization in exchange for Class A, Voting stock, and $9,000 is a loan to the company.

He then issues himself stock, representing 5% of the company. Since the company is essentially worthless, he issues 30% of the corporation to each of his three children. However, they are issued Class B, Non Voting stock. He also issues 5% to his wife, of the Class A variety.

By using the two different classes of stock, Joe and his wife have assured themselves of control of the company. Their children can't kick them out when they reach 18 years old, since they don't control anything.

> THE CORPORATE CHARACTERISTIC THAT IS MOST HELPFUL IN ACCOMPLISHING ESTATE PLANNING GOALS IS THAT OF AN UNLIMITED LIFESPAN. BECAUSE A CORPORATION CAN TECHNICALLY LIVE FOREVER, IT DOES NOT CEASE TO EXIST WHEN THE SHAREHOLDERS DIE.

The corporation commences business, and to his delight, Joe finds out that his business intuition was right. The corporation is a success. Five years later, it is worth $2 million, and Joe dies unexpectedly. (Nobody told him that running your own business is very stressful, and cuts down on your lifespan.)

Instead of his estate containing a business worth $2 million, which would leave his family with a federal estate tax bill of $512,800, his estate contains only 5% of a $2 million business, or $100,000. Since the $100,000 value of his business ownership is well under the $600,000 lifetime exemption, he will have no estate tax to pay. He saved his family over a half million dollars in taxes!

THE CORPORATION OWNED BY A LIMITED PARTNERSHIP

This strategy is good for individuals who want to transfer assets of enduring value to their heirs.

1. Form a corporation with No Par Stock in a corporate haven, such as Nevada or Wyoming. This corporation exists solely as a "shell", without any assets, liabilities or value.

2. After the corporation is properly organized, have the Board of Directors pass a resolution that sets a par value for corporate shares at a nominal amount, such as a penny per share.

3. Sell the shares to your heirs at the price determined in the corporate resolution. Because they are purchasing the shares, the corporation is not being "gifted" to your heirs, and there is no taxable event.

4. Form a limited partnership for the purpose of owning the shares of the corporation. The partnership should have an extended lifespan, such as fifty years. The limited partnership agreement should provide for a termination of the partnership upon the death of the general partner. You become a one percent general partner and will have the exclusive right to vote the shares of the corporation. The limited partners are your heirs.

5. Your heirs, the stockholders of the corporation, transfer their shares into the limited partnership in exchange for an ownership interest in the partnership. The general partner owns one percent, you own an additional one percent as a limited partner, and your heirs become 98% limited partners.

6. Sell your personal assets to the corporation for the lowest fair market value that you can defend. Take back a demand promissory note with a long maturity period. The note should bear interest at a market rate, and can provide that in the event of your death, the corporation will forgive any debt still owed.

7. The corporation pays the interest as it becomes due under the note. You will have taxable interest income as a result.

8. When you die, your heirs will already own the assets you intend to leave them.

THE CORPORATION OWNED BY AN IRREVOCABLE TRUST

This strategy is a vehicle to minimize estate taxes on appreciating assets or on profits generated by a particular business deal, by transferring the capital gains to the irrevocable trust.

1. Form a corporation shell, without assets, liabilities, or value. You (and possibly your spouse) are the shareholder(s). The purpose of this corporation is to own appreciating assets, or to be the beneficial party in profitable business dealing.

2. Form an irrevocable trust, using an independent trustee, naming your heirs as beneficiaries.

3. Transfer the corporation shares into the trust under the $10,000 federal annual exclusion from estate and gift tax. Because the corporation is worthless, this transfer will not trigger a taxable event (assuming, of course, no other transfers have been made the would approach the $10,000 exclusion limitation.) Now the trust owns the corporation, and the Trustee controls the shares for the benefit of your heirs.

4. If you are dealing with appreciating assets, the assets can be sold to the corporation for the lowest defensible fair market value, in exchange for a demand note bearing interest (similar to the scenario outlined above).

5. If you are dealing with a new business opportunity or enterprise, the corporation is now able entertain that business activity, since any value the enterprise builds will take place outside of your estate. Any gain that occurs will be passed on to the trust.

BUY-SELL AGREEMENTS

The death of a shareholder in a closely held corporation can cause real problems. These problems effect not only the estate of the shareholder, but in some cases can have severe ramifications regarding whether the corporation continues to exist or not.

Other problems include:

- The estate of the shareholder will have the burden of proof in establishing the value of the corporate shares. The IRS will probably establish as high a figure as possible for the stock, which the executor will have to dispute with proof.

- The beneficiaries of the deceased shareholder may need money, which could induce the executor to make a hasty distribution. However, that could put the executor in the position of having personal liability for unpaid taxes.

- The employees of the corporation may wonder if the corporation will be liquidated due to dissension between remaining shareholders, or lack of cash.

- Creditors of the corporation could pressure the company for early repayment of any loans, or could impose additional restrictions or requirements on the company's operations.

A solution to these problems is in having the corporation establish a form of a buy-out agreement to protect against the loss of key shareholders. One of the most popular forms of a buy-out agreement is called a "buy-sell agreement" in which other stockholders agree to purchase the shares of any party who dies at a predetermined price.

Then, on the death of a shareholder, his or her shares would be sold to the other shareholders who were parties under the plan. The value of the shares for estate tax purposes would the price used at the time of the transfer, because it represented an actual sale at arm's length between two shareholders who didn't know at the time they signed the agreement, whether they would be purchasers or sellers of stock.

The IRS will honor the value of the deceased owner's shares under the buy-sell agreement if you follow a few simple guidelines:

- Be reasonable. If you use a reasonable and realistic method to arrive at the value of shares, such as basing it on the earnings, or appraised value, etc., the IRS will agree with the value you agree upon. Fixed prices can create problems because the real value of the corporation is likely to change over time.

- State your business reason for the agreement. The IRS will not allow buy-sell agreements that are designed simply to pass on corporate shares at less than their full value. However, they do recognize that maintaining family control and ownership of a corporation is a valid business purpose for a buy-sell agreement.

- The deceased's estate must have an obligation to sell the shares at the specified price. And, either the corporation or the shareholders must be obligated to purchase the shares. An option to buy or to sell the stock is not enough

The buy-sell agreement must restrict stock transfers while the shareholder is alive, as well. The corporation and/or the shareholders must have the right of first refusal on the transfer of shares, at the price specified in the agreement.

One method of providing guaranteed funding for the purchase of the shares is to have each shareholder take out a life insurance policy on the other shareholder for this specific purpose. The policies can be assigned to a trustee to ensure that the proceeds will only be used to purchase shares from the estate. While the insurance premiums paid for this purpose are not tax deductible, any legal expense incurred to set up the plan and draft the agreement may be deductible.

THE AGREED PRICE PER SHARE MAY BE ON THE BASIS OF SOME APPRAISED VALUE OR, BETTER YET, WOULD USE A SELF-ADJUSTING FORMULA, SUCH AS THE AVERAGE EARNINGS OF THE PAST THREE YEARS CAPITALIZED AT A DEFINED PERCENTAGE.

The other type of buy-out agreement is called a **"redemption agreement."** With a redemption agreement there is a form of a contract between the shareholders holding redeemable shares and their corporation. When a shareholder dies, the corporation retains the right to purchase the deceased's shares from the estate at a specified price. The corporation funds the stock purchase with life insurance that it takes out on the shareholder. The corporation becomes both the owner and the beneficiary of the policy.

The corporation's premium payments under a redemption agreement are not deductible, but are also not taxable to the stockholders. The proceeds of the policy are tax-free to the corporation.

ASSET FREEZE

There have been provisions available in the tax code for many years that have provided for what is often called an "asset freeze," which essentially freezes the value of a certain class of stock of a corporation. However these provisions have undergone several dramatic changes in the last few years which has essentially re-written the way an asset freeze works.

Boiled down to its essence, an asset freeze allows a corporation that has more than one class of stock to freeze the value of one of the classes, and allow any gain to accrue in the remaining classes of stock. This technique has been promoted by several estate planning experts as a mechanism for dramatically reducing the estate taxes on an individual who owns stock of a corporation that is experiencing growth in value.

The most common way in which an asset freeze is promoted using a corporation is as follows:

1. Form a Nevada corporation with 25 million authorized shares with a par value of $.001 per share.

2. Of the 25 million authorized shares, 1 million is designated as Preferred, Voting stock, and 24 million is designated as Common, Non Voting stock.

3. The owner/principal of the corporation is issued Preferred, Voting shares, while his heirs or beneficiaries are issued Common, Non Voting shares.

4. The Board of Directors passes a resolution wherein the corporation "freezes" the value of the Preferred stock at a predetermined value, based on the actual value of the stock at that moment in time, thus causing all future appreciation or gain to occur with the Common, Non Voting stock.

Having done this, the corporation limits the gain that would otherwise be attributed to the Preferred shareholder as the corporation builds value over the years. Theoretically, a corporation worth $10,000 today, that has issued 50% of the stock to Preferred, Voting shareholders and 50% to Common, Non Voting shareholders, could freeze $5,000 of value forever. Fifty years from now, when the corporation is worth $20 million, the Preferred, Voting stock is still worth only $5,000, and the Common, Non Voting stock is worth $19,995,000.

ONE WARNING ON THE USE OF A **BUY-SELL AGREEMENT** IS TO BE CAREFUL THAT THE OPERATION OF A BUY-SELL AGREEMENT DOES NOT REDUCE THE NUMBER OF SHAREHOLDERS TO A LEVEL WHERE A PERSONAL HOLDING COMPANY WILL EXIST. THIS COULD HAPPEN IN A SITUATION WHERE THERE ARE UNDISTRIBUTED EARNINGS OR IF THE INCOME IS FROM PASSIVE SOURCES.

Sounds good, doesn't it? When the Preferred, Voting shareholder dies, there will be no estate tax on his $5,000 worth of stock. And, this scenario is technically correct. It is also fatally flawed when used with a regular, C corporation.

The problem with this scenario is that tax advisors strongly advise against building significant value in a C corporation, unless the corporation intends to go public. Any time you build value in a C corporation, you add an additional layer of income tax. You also face the Accumulated Earnings Tax penalty of 39.6% *in addition* to the regular corporate income tax. The scenario that is widely promoted will generate estate tax savings, but there will be substantial income tax penalties that are likely to more than offset any estate tax saving that might be realized.

An asset freeze cannot be accomplished with an S corporation, because an S corporation is not allowed to have more than one class of shares that is required to make the strategy work. Sophisticated tax planners are using limited partnerships and limited liability companies as the proper vehicle for an asset freeze, due to the single level of federal income taxation they enjoy.

TAX STRATEGIES

TWELVE YEARS OF TAX DEFERRAL = ZERO TAXES

The real value of tax deferral is often misunderstood. If you can borrow $1,000 (interest free) and invest it (at compound interest) for 12 years at a 6% rate of interest, you will have $2,000. You can then pay back the original $1,000 and have an extra $1,000 to keep. There is a simple "rule of thumb" with which you can estimate the time it takes for any amount of money to double in value. It's called the Rule of 72. Money will double when the interest rate times the period of years multiplies to equal 72.

- At 12% interest, money will double in 6 years.

- At 10% interest, money will double in 7.2 years.

- At 8% interest, money will double in 9 years.

- At 6% interest, money will double in 12 years.

If you can defer $1,000 of taxes for nine years and invest those tax dollars to earn 8% a year (compounded), you will have $2,000 at the end of the nine years. However, if you cash in then, you will owe taxes on the accumulated earnings of $1,000. Assuming you are in the 33% tax bracket, you would only have $1,667 left after taxes. When you pay back the original $1,000, you only have an extra $667.

Here is how long it will take to make 2.5 times your initial investment at different interest rates.

- At 6%, it will take about 16 years.

- At 8%, it will take about 12 years.

- At 10%, it will take about 10 years.

- At 12%, it will take about 9 years.

Thus, if you can defer $1,000 of taxes for 12 years and invest that money to earn 8% compounded, you will have $2,500. You can then pay 33% in taxes on the $1,500 of income and have $2,000 left. When you pay the $1,000 of deferred taxes to the IRS, you still have $1,000 left. Deferring taxes for 12 years at 8% is like not paying the taxes at all.

BEATING THE "SELF-EMPLOYMENT" TAX

Many owners of closely held corporations struggle with the burden of "self-employment" taxes, and often don't realize their obligation until it is too late to do anything about it. Fortunately, the Nevada corporation provides a terrific solution to reducing these taxes.

Your Nevada S corporation can pay you a reasonable salary which is comparable to the average salary for your position and type of work. This salary should be the lowest amount that you can defend as reasonable. (These figures can be found in the Nevada Wage Survey, published by the Nevada Employment Security Department, 500 East 3rd Street, Carson City, Nevada, 89710.) Of course, any salary you take will be subject to FICA and Medicare taxes.

After the corporation deducts all corporate expenses, it pays out the remaining net earnings as dividends. These dividends will not be subject to FICA or Medicare, which eliminates the self-employment tax trap.

1244 STOCK LOSS

Under usual circumstances, when you are operating a business as a C corporation, any losses you suffer when you sell your stock are treated as capital losses. They are deductible only against capital gains and up to $3,000 a year in ordinary income. However, if you would like an ordinary loss deduction for you corporate stock, the solution is to treat your stock as "Section 1244 stock."

To qualify for Section 1244 stock treatment, the stock must have been issued to you by the corporation in exchange for cash or (not in exchange for stock or securities). In addition, the corporation must have received more than half of its gross receipts from sources other than royalties, rents, dividends, interest, annuities, and sales or exchanges of securities during the five most recent tax years. Also, the corporation cannot have received more than $1,000,000 as a contribution to capital or paid in surplus.

This deduction can be taken for any class of stock, including nonvoting, restricted, and preferred shares. Any loss in excess of the $50,000-per-individual limit is treated as a capital loss. There are no real disadvantages to using 1244 stock treatment, and most corporations should consider its use as standard practice.

INTERNAL REVENUE CODE 351 TREATMENT

The Internal Revenue Code allows stockholders who contribute non-cash assets for shares to make the transfer without any effect on capital gains or loss. The tax basis of the assets becomes the tax basis of the shares. This type of treatment is only available if the contribution results in the shareholder owning at least 80 percent of the control of the corporation.

CORPORATIONS AND AUTOMOBILES

In the past, a common corporate perk was the use of a company car. Salespeople, in particular have become use to this as part of their compensation package. Studies have recently shown, however, that frequently employees are driving their own cars these days. And the reasons have been easy to pinpoint. Companies can eliminate a tremendous amount of internal paperwork and have less trouble with the IRS if employees drive their own cars.

The fact is, virtually every employee that has a company car will use that car for personal reasons and business purposes. The IRS even considers commuting to and from work a person use of the automobile. Employers are expected to keep track of all of this personal use and treat it as taxable income to the employee. Hence, the additional paperwork and recordkeeping.

- **Corporate Deductions**. The corporation can write off the cost of any car it gives to an employee. The mileage the employee puts on the vehicle is not a factor, nor is the breakdown of business to personal mileage. The employee's personal use is considered a compensation expense.

- **Reimbursements.** By requiring employees to use their own vehicles and reimbursing them for the expense, a corporation can reduce their paperwork requirements and potential face-off with the IRS. Unfortunately, the IRS only allows reimbursements up to 32.5 cents per mile (31 cents per mile after March 31, 1999), which is frankly not sufficient to operate and care for most automobiles - particularly older models that require more maintenance and repairs.

The corporation should adopt a standard procedure that requires the employee to submit expense-account forms regularly that details the mileage usage of the employee on behalf of the business each week or month. The IRS treats this type of reimbursement (32.5 cents per mile or less) as a wash. The corporation does not show the reimbursement as taxable income to the employee and the employee is not required to show detailed records of expenses on his or her tax return

COMPANIES THAT REIMBURSE MORE THAN $.28 PER MILE MUST EITHER REPORT THE EXCESS AS INCOME TO THE EMPLOYEE, OR REQUIRE THAT THE EMPLOYEES PROVIDE PROOF OF THEIR ADDITIONAL EXPENSES.

If the corporation sticks to the 32.5 cents per mile rule, any employee who requires additional reimbursement can attempt to deduct them on Form 2106, "Employee Business Expenses," and is treated as a miscellaneous itemized expense. Many employees, however, will get either no deduction or partial deduction because these expenses are only deductible to the extent that they exceed 2% of adjusted gross income.

Here is and example of how this might work: Mr. Johnson purchases a new car for $30,000 and drives in 12,000 miles per year, strictly for business use. The car gets 25 miles per gallon, and gas has cost him an average of $1.50 per gallon. Maintenance, service and repairs come to $850; insurance costs $1,000; and other expenses, $350. Mr. Johnson depreciated $6,000 on the vehicle (20 percent of $30,000).

Mr. Johnson should seriously consider claiming his actual expenses on the car. He keeps a diary that records when and where he travels, for what purpose, and the number of miles traveled. His company pays him a reimbursement based on the 32.5 cents mile rule of $3,900. If he adds another item in his expense diary - the actual dollar amount of his expenses, supported by documentation - he gains an additional tax deduction.

If he reports the $3,900 reimbursement on his tax return, he can deduct 100 percent of his documented expenses - in this case $8,920 - as long as his miscellaneous expenses exceed 2 percent of his adjusted gross income. This deduction not only covers his reimbursement, but $5,020 of his other income as well.

The corporation may choose to adopt a reimbursement plan that is not based on a **cents-per-mile formula**. The company could pay a flat rate that they have proven approximates the average monthly employee costs, or could combine a flat allowance and a lesser mileage reimbursement, say $350 per month and $.12 per mile. Although there is increased reporting and recordkeeping for a corporation using this type of plan, there is less risk of expense padding.

Since the use of a company-owned car is considered a taxable fringe benefit, the value of the personal use is subject to federal income and state unemployment taxes. This requires the corporation to place a dollar amount on the value of the personal usage. There are a couple of ways to do this.

Automobile Lease Value Method

Consult the lease tables in IRS Publication 535 to learn the lease value of a particular car. That publication places the lease value of a $30,000 car at $8,250. If the employee only uses the car part of the year, you can use the daily value listed in the Publication 535, or the value can be prorated. Using records submitted by the employee, the company must find the percentage of time the employee drives the car on personal business.

Then, calculate the personal value of the car by multiplying the percentage of personal use by the annual lease value of the car. On a car driven 10,000 miles per year, which the employee shows he uses 15 percent of the time on personal business, 1,500 miles are personal miles.

Assuming the car had an annual lease value of $8,250, 15% of that - or $1,237.50 - is taxable to the employee. Since the annual lease value doesn't include the cost of gasoline, the employee can be reimbursed for either the actual cost of the gas. So, if the employee has been reimbursed $550 for gas, he would have to include that in his gross income, which he could offset with an itemized deduction for gas expenses.

Cents Per Mile Valuation

The company can use the standard mileage rate of 32.5 cents per mile to figure the value of personal use of a car. In the example above, the 1,500 personal miles would be reported as $487.50 of taxable income. This type of reimbursement is not available for what the IRS considers luxury cars, and obviously nobody at the IRS has bought a new car recently, since their definition of a luxury car is one that costs over $15,000.

Federal Tax Withholding on the Value of the Company Car.

The corporation has several choices about how it wants to withhold on the taxable income an employee has due to the use of a company car. The company can either withhold using a flat 20 percent rate or use the normal withholding method for supplemental wages.

The other option is to not withhold at all, although you must notify the employee before January 21 of that tax year (or within 30 days of providing the car) so he or she has a chance to change the W-4 to accommodate additional withholding from his paycheck to cover the additional taxes. Additionally, the company will be responsible for Social Security and unemployment taxes on the value of the company car if the employee's wages are below $72,600.

Special Rule on Commuting.

The corporation can establish a policy that limits the use of a company car to commuting, and can set the value of the commute each way at $1.50. You must establish reasonable business reasons for requiring the employee to commute in the company vehicle, and the employee must be prohibited from using the car for any other personal driving.

Purchasing Luxury Cars for the Price of an Economy Car.

It is possible to use your corporation and the current tax law to purchase a new luxury car each year at a relatively small cost. Naturally, the first step is to pick out a new car that is commensurate with your position and need. For purposes of example, suppose the car that has caught your eye has a sticker price of $40,000.

THE CORPORATION CAN LEND YOU THE ENTIRE AMOUNT, INTEREST-FREE, AND SECURES THE LOAN WITH A SECOND MORTGAGE ON YOUR HOME. THIS ALLOWS YOU TO BUY THE CAR WITH CASH, WHICH SHOULD BE A FACTOR IN ALLOWING YOU TO NEGOTIATE A GREAT DEAL.

The tax law considers the additional compensation that you have received to be equivalent to the interest you would have had to pay to the corporation on the loan. In other words, you are paying the interest on the loan with the extra compensation you are receiving. So, the tax consequences are a wash. Although the compensation is taxable, you get an offsetting deduction because the interest that you should be paying is deductible as long as the mortgage doesn't exceed $100,000.

Additionally, the corporation can pay you 75 percent of the maximum allowed first year depreciation on the business-use portion of the car. That amounts to $1,995, which is tax-free to you and deductible by your corporation

After a year, you can sell the car for, say, $34,000, and use the proceeds plus an additional $6,000 out of pocket to pay off the loan to the corporation. Then you go out and pick out another new car and get another interest-free loan from the company. This strategy can allow you to drive a new car every year at a net cost to you of around $4,005 per year

($6,000 out of pocket minus $1,995 depreciation reimbursement). Just try purchasing or leasing a new, $40,000 car every year for around $334 per month!

INTEREST-FREE, TAX-FREE LOANS FROM YOUR CORPORATION

Until the Tax Reform Act was passed, it was quite common for companies to provide interest-free demand loans to key executives as a tax-free fringe benefit. Under the new law, a corporate executive that receives an interest-free loan from his company is treated as having received "phantom" taxable compensation equal to the value of what the company would have charged on the loan. The company executive can then deduct the "phantom" interest expense for the same amount. The net effect of this is that the extra compensation and the deduction cancel each other and the executive pays no tax on the interest-free loan.

But, under the Tax Reform Act, the deduction is subject to new scrutiny that eliminates many of possibilities of the previous law. Fortunately, that tax-free benefit can still be achieved with some types of interest free loans.

You can borrow up to $10,000 from your corporation, tax-free, without paying interest or suffering tax consequences. This is called a "de minimis" exception, and should the loan ever go over the $10,000 ceiling, you could lose the exception and be taxed accordingly.

For low or no-interest loans over $10,000, the IRS generally assumes an interest rate equal to the Applicable Federal Rate (AFR), which is the rate based on the average market yield on US obligations. If the AFR is 7% and you've borrowed $100,000 at no interest, the imputed interest is $7,000, which the IRS says is additional income to you and is therefore taxable. You can't get around the AFR by charging low interest either. The IRS will impute as additional income the difference between the rate the corporation charges you and the AFR.

Since interest on home mortgages can still be deducted, the corporation can give you an interest-free loan secured by your home. The "phantom compensation" and "phantom interest" should be a wash for tax purposes. Also, interest on business loans is deductible, so an interest-free loan could be used by you to start a company that purchases and develops raw land or residential rentals, etc.

It is important that any loan over $10,000 is structured at arms' length, so the IRS does not have grounds to disallow the loans and declare them as taxable corporate dividends. To prove that the loan is an actual transaction that you intend to repay, make certain to put all of the terms in writing, including the repayment schedule and record the date and amount of the loan on the business books. The corporation's minutes should also reflect approval of the loan.

CHARITABLE DEDUCTIONS FOR INVENTORY

S CORPORATIONS, PARTNERSHIPS, AND SOLE PROPRIETORSHIPS EARN A STRAIGHT COST DEDUCTION.

Business owners should take advantage of a Federal tax deduction that lets you clear out excess or inactive inventory and help schools and charities at the same time. Regular C corporations may deduct the cost of the inventory donated, plus half the difference between the cost and fair market value. The total deduction may be up to twice the original cost.

Double-dipping is prohibited. Many businesses give old computers to charity and expect a tax deduction. If that computer has already been written off, no deduction is allowed. Double deduction on a single business asset is prohibited.

It is very easy to find a Qualified Charity to receive the donation. Many schools will be more than happy to accept outdated stationery, business forms, or miscellaneous office supplies for use in the classroom. However, any donations over $250.00 should be supported by a written acknowledgment.

Also, check out a charity before making a major contribution. See whether the charity is on the IRS's list of organizations approved to receive tax-deductible contribution. Simply requesting the IRS determination letter may not be enough. Your tax advisor may want to request audited financial statements to see if the charity spends funds on charitable activities instead of salaries.

SECTION 1202 STOCK: CUT CAPITAL GAINS IN HALF

One of the biggest tax breaks available through the new tax law is the incentive for individuals to invest in small corporations. Individuals who purchase "small business stock" issued after August 10, 1993 and hold the shares for at least five years can escape tax on half their profit when they sell their shares later.

The impact of this tax break is almost unbelievable. Since long-term capital gains have a tax rate cap of 28%, small business stock that qualifies for this break is taxed at an effective rate of 14%.

Small business stock that qualifies for this break is often referred to as "1202 stock", after the section in the Internal Revenue Code that describes this mechanism. And, the shareholder that can take advantage of this break may be another C corporation, an S corporation, individual, partnership, limited liability company or mutual fund.

CORPORATE DISSOLUTION TO AVOID BUILDING LENGTHY AUDIT TRAILS

The timing of the dissolution of your corporation is a factor that should be given some consideration. With some foresight and planning you may be able to dissolve your corporation periodically and gain a strategic advantage.

One highly respected tax attorney recently said that he rarely allowed a client to maintain a corporation for longer than three to five years. So, if a client starts a corporation in year one and operates it for three or four years, he would then terminate, liquidate and dissolve the corporation while starting a new company to handle new or recurring business opportunities.

The primary reason for doing this is to keep the track record of the corporation to a minimum to reduce or eliminate the likelihood of problems. For example, the longer a corporation exists, the more likely it is to be audited by the IRS. And, considering the cost and aggravation of an IRS audit, the cost and trouble of dissolving an old corporation and starting a new one was "cheap insurance."

This strategy doesn't always work and isn't always possible. However, with proper advance planning, it is possible in many circumstances.

In addition, replacing one corporation with another will only complicate matters for any potential judgment creditors or auditors of state agencies. This is especially effective if, say, you use a Nevada corporation originally and replace it with a corporation from a different jurisdiction, such as Wyoming and so on.

LIABILITY PROTECTION STRATEGIES

DIRECTOR'S INSURANCE

Even though Nevada law provides unmatched liability protection for corporate officers and directors, it is nevertheless a good strategy for knowledgeable directors to insist upon indemnification by the corporation for any suit brought against them resulting from their corporate duties. To make the indemnification even stronger, the company could consider obtaining director liability insurance. Without this type of insurance, few outside directors would be willing to take the risk of service.

When the corporation purchases the insurance, instead of requiring the individual director to purchase his or her own policy, the defense of claims is less complicated, the writing-off the cost of the premiums is less problematic, and the policy is generally less expensive.

When shopping for director insurance, look carefully at the following items:

- How much coverage does the policy provide? In today's litigious world, a policy should provide a minimum of $1 million in coverage per occurrence. Larger corporations involved in riskier activity, such as hazardous waste, will need more.

- What is excluded from coverage? Does the policy exclude claims based on dishonesty, fraud, libel, slander, securities violations, insider trading, or other activities. These exclusions may be negotiated back into the coverage at a certain cost.

- What are the deductibles? Many policies use a "split deductible" approach to claims, where the policy only provides, for example, 95% coverage on any claim. However, if a large judgment exists, 5 percent can amount to a lot of money. Also common are policies that have a flat deductible of $5,000 per director.

- Must the company notify the directors upon cancellation of the insurance coverage?

- Will any supplemental insurance exist to cover deductibles, lapses in coverage or exclusions?

- Is the insurance company stable and highly rated?

ULTIMATE PRIVACY: PROFESSIONAL OFFICERS & DIRECTORS

A great way to avoid unnecessary lawsuits is to keep your name off the corporation records in the first place. In Nevada, only the officers and directors are on any public record, which means if you can find someone else to provide those services, your name needn't appear at all.

Some Nevada incorporating companies and resident agents can provide nominee officers and directors for corporations that they form. Fees for this service generally range from $750 per year to $2,000 per year. However if you are considering using these services,

> **ALMOST 90 PERCENT OF ALL PUBLICLY TRADED CORPORATIONS PROTECT THEIR BOARDS WITH INDEMNIFICATION AND INSURANCE.**

carefully read any contracts before you sign them because there are frequently additional costs for certain activities, or excessive use of time.

If confidentiality is a priority, have your attorney hire the nominee officers on your behalf. The nominee officers and directors never need to know who you are if they take all instruction from your attorney. Your attorney gives you additional protection through the attorney-client privilege.

PLANNING FOR PROFESSIONALS: LOOKING FOR THE RIGHT STRUCTURE

Many professionals, such as physicians, dentists, lawyers, architects, and accountants, struggle to find the proper mix of tax breaks, liability protections, and corporate practicality. As a result, many professionals use a professional corporation, which provides a degree of liability protection, and provides tax benefits - especially with regard to pensions. But it is not the total answer.

The limitation of the professional corporation is in the body of law that exists that defines the relationship between the provider and recipient of a professional service. In many circumstances, the professional is still held personally liable, regardless of his corporate status.

The solution to this problem can be in an innovative strategy that was designed specifically to help structure a medical practice:

1. The practicing professional sets up his or her own professional corporation through which the professional service is performed.

2. A second, regular business corporation is formed for the purpose of managing the practice, and which will also own the client base.

3. The stock of the business corporation is issued to the professional's spouse as his or her separate property. (An option would be to issue the stock to an irrevocable trust as described earlier.)

4. The Business Corporation "hires" the professional corporation, by contract, to provide the professional service in return for a set annual fee.

5. The client, or patient, pays the business corporation, which handles the billing, for services received.

This structure provides liability protection by isolating the risk associated with the professional service from the assets of the business. If the professional is involved in a lawsuit or receives a judgment, the business corporation could exercise a provision in the contract between the two companies that allows it "fire" the professional corporation and replace it with another professional service provider.

STANDING UP TO SCRUTINY

The success of many corporate strategies is dependent upon the corporation's ability to demonstrate that it has a valid, viable business purpose. With a valid business purpose, the corporation should always function as if it were any other business competing within its industry. Anyone who has reason to investigate the corporations business activities will expect a viable business to have met certain established criteria.

One of the services readily available from a number of professional Resident Agent companies is a variation of the "contract office service" or "corporate headquarters service." These services differ depending upon the provider, but typically include a combination of mail-forwarding, telephone answering and messaging, use of FAX, assistance with state and local business licenses, assistance with obtaining Nevada bank accounts, and use of office and/or conference facilities. The companies that provide these services charge monthly, quarterly, or annual fees that can be as high as $3000.00 per year.

These services are commonly sold as if they were an insurance policy of sorts, providing "proof" of the corporation's bona fide existence in order to dissuade frivolous lawsuits. They also are used to establish the facts of the corporation's domicile and base of business operations when the corporation is used as part of a strategy to eliminate or reduce state corporate income taxes. They can be critical in the corporation's ability to prove the existence of interstate commerce instead of intrastate commerce.

There is no standardized litmus test used to test whether or not a corporation is legitimately conducting business any one place. Nevertheless, it has been suggested that the following should be considered:

> THE MODEL BUSINESS CORPORATION ACT, ANNOTATED [SEC. 202(A)(3)] STATES THAT "A MAILING ADDRESS CONSISTING ONLY OF A POST OFFICE BOX IS NOT SUFFICIENT" FOR DEMONSTRATING A BUSINESS BASE.

- **The company should have an actual business address**. While today's office technology make this a very fine line to deal with, it has been traditionally held that if the corporation does not have a real office, it is often determined to be merely a shell or a holding company, and not a legitimate business establishment. The existence of the office should be supported for tax purposes by canceled corporate checks in payment of rent.

- **The company should have a telephone listing in the corporate name**, at the office address. This should be supported similarly by canceled corporate checks for payment of monthly phone bills.

- **The company should have the appropriate licenses** to engage in business activity as required by local jurisdictions.

- The company should handle all financial transactions through **corporate bank accounts** established in the local area.

- All contracts, agreements, transactions, purchases, sales, etc. should be signed, notarized, and consummated **at the corporate office**.

- **The company should have employees or representatives available** at the local office to greet visitors, distribute mail, and answer the phone.

The contract office facilities that are available meet these criteria to different degrees. The obvious question is whether there is value in using these services. Are they worth it? Clearly, the answer is: It depends upon the circumstances.

I believe that in order for these services to be worthwhile one of several circumstances should be present:

1. You actually need the service, and it provides an affordable alternative to renting an office. Perhaps it is more convenient for you to operate your business through a stable address and working environment than to operate out of hotel rooms and taxi cabs. You like the idea of having someone take messages for you, instead of using impersonal voice mail or paging.

2. The nature of the corporation's activity is regulated or licensed, such as a talent agency, and as such must have an office in the local jurisdiction.

3. You need to draw all attention regarding the corporation away from you. Maybe the corporation engages in activity that would be in competition with your employer, and you are bound by a non-competition clause in your employee agreement. Or, the company is involved in real estate investment, and you don't want to show that you are a licensed real estate agent.

4. You want to project a more stable, professional appearance than you would otherwise be able to display.

5. Your corporate strategy depends upon not having to qualify to do business as a foreign corporation in another state, and you recognize the possibility of being investigated or audited by state revenue agents in your home state.

6. The corporation is used for asset protection purposes, and needs to appear completely unconnected to you or your personal affairs. The corporate location in Nevada can be a tremendous aid in maintaining that separation.

7. The corporation will file for bankruptcy, and you don't want it to file in your hometown district. By demonstrating that the corporation has based its business operations in Nevada, it would file for federal bankruptcy protection in a Nevada district.

HOWEVER, EVEN WHEN THESE SITUATIONS ARE PRESENT, IT DOES NOT NECESSARILY MEAN THAT YOU NEED THESE SERVICES. THERE MAY BE OTHER WAYS OF DEALING WITH THESE CIRCUMSTANCES THAT DO NOT INVOLVE LONG-TERM COMMITMENT OR THE ASSOCIATED COSTS.

If these circumstances exist, then you might be wise to consider using an office service that will provide the Nevada base. There is no question that maintaining the appearance of a fully staffed office may strengthen your corporate appearance. And, we all know that appearance means a lot. Even so, if your corporation has to defend itself in court, the fact that you used a contract office service may not mean a whole lot if the other facts are not in your favor.

APPENDIX A: COURT CASES

Legal Support for Successful Corporate Strategies

T he following cases have been selected to assist you in obtaining a feel for how the court system deals with many aspects relating to the corporation structure. The topics that these cases discuss include piercing the corporate veil (and cases where the veil of corporate protection was left intact), the rights of a stockholder to view the stock ledger and other corporate records, the transfer of shares of stock, the limitation of a state's authority to tax multistate corporations, the legal right of a taxpayer to decrease his or taxes, and the "Alter Ego Theory."

ALSO INCLUDED ARE SEVERAL TAX COURT OPINIONS AND MEMOS THAT ESTABLISH PRECEDENT FOR USING CERTAIN TAX STRATEGIES THAT ARE DISCUSSED IN THE PRECEDING CHAPTER. THE CASE LAW REPRESENTED HERE IS BY NO MEANS COMPLETE. YOU WILL FIND ADDITIONAL LEGAL REFERENCES CITED WITHIN MOST OF THE CASES WE HAVE ENCLOSED, AS WELL AS IN THE LEGAL REFERENCES PROVIDED IN OTHER CHAPTERS.

PIERCING THE CORPORATE VEIL

The following two cases are from the Nevada Supreme Court, and represent instances where the court has both pierced the corporate veil, and left the corporate veil intact. The circumstances in each case that caused the court to rule as it did are informative to anyone associated with a Nevada corporation. The cases quoted below omit portions of the decision that involve other issues, such as slander, libel, and damages, etc.

ROWLAND V LEPIRE

GLEN E. ROWLAND, MARTIN L. ROWLAND and ROWLAND CORPORATION, Appellants, v. EUGENE LEPIRE and JUDY LEPIRE, Respondents.

April 29, 1983

662 P.2d 1332

Appeal from judgment awarding damages and providing other relief, First Judicial District Court, Carson City; Michael E. Fondi, Judge.

Appeal was taken from a judgment of the district court in favor of homeowners in suit against builders alleging breach of contract and slander of title. The Supreme Court, held that: (1) substantial evidence supported findings of trial court and did not require conclusion as a matter of law that express contract was abandoned; (2) evidence failed to establish element of malice, and therefore owners could not recover under theory of slander of title; (3) owners were not entitled to award of attorney fees; and (4) evidence was insufficient to support finding that the two officers, directors and shareholders off construction corporation were its alter ego so as to justify piercing corporate veil.

Affirmed in part; reversed in part.

In order to apply alter ego doctrine to pierce corporate veil, following requirements must be met: corporation must be influenced and governed by person asserted to be its alter ego; there must be such unity of interest and ownership that one is inseparable from the other; and facts must be such that adherence to fiction of separate entity would, under circumstances, sanction fraud or promote injustice.

Although evidence did show that the construction corporation was undercapitalized and that there was little existence separate and apart from the two officers, directors and shareholder, evidence was insufficient to support finding that the latter were alter ego of the corporation so as to justify piercing of corporate veil.

Opinion

This is an appeal involving construction of a substantial residence by appellant, Rowland Corporation, for respondents, Eugene and Judy Lepire, husband and wife. Appellants contend that the trial court committed several errors in (1) finding that the express contract between appellants and respondents was modified rather than abandoned; (2) finding that sufficient evidence supported respondents' claim of slander of title; (3) awarding respondents punitive damages; (4) awarding respondents attorney's fees; and (5) finding sufficient evidence upon which to base application of the alter ego doctrine.

Appellants Glen Rowland and Martin Rowland are officers, directors and shareholders of the Rowland Corporation. In July of 1977, the Rowland Corporation was issued a class B-2 general contractor's license with an authorized limit of $60,000. In April of 1978, appellants entered into a contract with the Lepires to construct a home for them in Carson City. The contract was for a total price of $119,000, less certain offsets and plus any extras the Lepires might request during the course of construction. The contract provided for four progress payments through completion. It did not provide for a completion date.

Construction began in April of 1978. During the course of construction, numerous changes were requested by the Lepires. Among other things, these changes increased the floor space in the house from 4,500 square feet to 6,500 square feet and raised the house several inches. The foundations and outside dimensions remained the same. The Lepires made payments on the contract ahead of schedule and paid for extra labor and materials as requested.

In early December, problems began developing between the parties. A lien claim by a subcontractor hired pursuant to a contract with the Rowland Corporation had been filed in October of 1978. In addition, the Meek Lumber Company gave notice of its intent to file a lien against the residence. During this same period, Glen Rowland prematurely requested an additional payment.

These events precipitated a meeting between Glen Rowland and the Lepires on December 13, 1978. The district court found that an oral modification of the contract resulted from that meeting. Shortly thereafter, a controversy arose at the job site, causing the Rowlands to refuse further performance despite requests for completion by the Lepires. Instead, the Rowlands, upon advice of their attorney, filed a lien against the project for $68,000 on December 22, 1978. Recordation of the lien resulted in the Lepires' loss of an anticipated loan to be secured by the home. They were, nevertheless, able to obtain a personal loan at a higher interest rate.

As a consequence, the Lepires commenced this action in April of 1979, alleging breach of contract, slander of title and defamation. The defamation claim was later dismissed. In August 1979, the Rowland Corporation filed suit against the Lepires, alleging breach of contract, unjust enrichment and abuse of process. The two cases were eventually consolidated and the Rowland Corporation complaint was treated as a counterclaim in the Lepires' suit. Subsequently, a bench trial was conducted. The lower court found that the express contract had been modified and that appellants had materially breached the contract. Predicated on the foregoing findings and conclusions, the court awarded damages for the cost of completion, for the cost of correcting defective construction and for paying bills which the Rowland Corporation had incurred and was obligated to pay. Additionally, the court found that the lien made of record by the corporation constituted slander of title and awarded special damages and punitive damages in the amount of $15,000. Further the court awarded the Lepires $12,000 in attorney's fees. Finally, the court found that the Rowland Corporation was the alter ego of Glen Rowland and Martin Rowland and entered a personal judgment against the Rowlands in the approximate sum of $65,000. Appellants appeal, challenging every portion of the judgment.

The Alter Ego Doctrine.

Appellant's final contention is that the trial court erred in finding that sufficient evidence existed to justify piercing the corporate veil. We (the court) agree.

In order to apply the alter ego doctrine, the following requirements must be met: (1) the corporation must be influenced and governed by the person asserted to be its alter ego; (2) there must be such unity of interest and ownership that one is inseparable from the other; and (3) the facts must be such that adherence to the fiction of a separate entity would, under the circumstances, sanction a fraud or promote injustice. In North Arlington Med. v. Sanchez Constr., 86 Nev. 515,522, 471 P.2d 240, 244 (1970), we stated:

Undercapitalization, where it is clearly shown, is an important factor in determining whether the doctrine of alter ego should be applied. However, in the absence of fraud or injustice to the aggrieved party, it is not an absolute ground for disregarding a corporate entity. In any event, it is incumbent upon the one seeking to pierce the corporate veil, to show by a preponderance of the evidence, that the financial setup of the corporation is only a sham and caused an injustice.

In the instant case, the record reveals that the Rowland Corporation was incorporated by Martin Rowland in 1974. The directors at the time of incorporation were Martin Rowland, Glen Rowland and Gerald Rowland. Martin Rowland acted as president, performing the bookkeeping duties, and Glen Rowland acted as vice president, handling the construction. Shares of stock were first issued in 1977: one share for $100 issued to Martin Rowland and his wife; one share for $100 issued to Glen Rowland and his wife; one share of $100 issued to Darlene Rowland (Martin's daughter); and one share of $100 issued to Gerald Rowland (Martin's son.) and his wife. Several months later, an additional five shares were issued to Martin and his wife for $500 and two shares issued to Glen and his wife for $200. In addition to this paid-in capital, Martin Rowland made an unsecured personal loan of $15,000 to the corporation in 1977. The corporation had no other assets, and, as of the time of trial, had a negative net worth. Although no formal directors or shareholders meetings were ever held, Martin testified that in lieu thereof, he personally phoned the directors and shareholders regarding corporate business. No dividends were paid to shareholders, nor did the officers or directors receive salaries. The corporation did not have a minute book, nor is there evidence that any minutes were kept. The corporation did obtain a general contractor's license and a framing contractor's license, both in its name. It also obtained a surety bond in the amount of $5,000. The corporation also obtained workmen's compensation insurance and transacted business with the Employment Security Department. In addition, there was a corporate checking account. Martin also testified that other directors and shareholders besides Glen and he were involved in the corporation business. Martin and Glen did not, however, confer with the other stockholders or directors when they entered into the Lepire contract, nor when they filed the lien.

Although the evidence does show that the corporation was undercapitalized and that there was little existence separate and apart from Martin and Glen Rowland, we conclude that the evidence was insufficient to support a finding that appellants were the alter ego of the Rowland Corporation.

Appellants' remaining claims either lack merit or need not be addressed.

The trial court's judgment is affirmed with the exception of its findings of slander of title, alter ego and its award of punitive damages and attorney's fees. We reverse the latter determinations.

MCCLEARY CATTLE CO. V SEWELL

FRANK McCLEARY CATTLE COMPANY, a corporation, Appellant, v. C.A. SEWELL and ORENE H. SEWELL, his wife, Respondents.

November 12, 1957

Appeal from special order of the Sixth Judicial District Court, Humboldt County; Frank B. Gregory, Presiding Judge.

Proceedings supplemental to execution. From an order of the lower court making assets of another corporation available to execution upon the judgment, that corporation appealed. The Supreme Court, Merrill, J., held that appellant corporation, which was owned by sole owners of judgment debtor corporation and to which all assets of judgment debtor corporation had been transferred, was properly treated as alter ego of judgment debtor corporation and that its assets were properly made available to execution upon the judgment without an independent action against transferee corporation, but that judgment should be corrected to run against transferee corporation.

Affirmed.

Where all assets of judgment debtor corporation had been transferred to another corporation, which bore costs of litigation against judgment debtor corporation, had the same president and was owned by sole owners of judgment debtor corporation, and charter of judgment debtor corporation had been revoked, corporate fiction was properly disregarded and transferee corporation was properly treated as "alter ego" of judgment debtor corporation.

In order to invoke "alter ego" doctrine, corporation must be influenced and governed by person asserted to be its alter ego, there must be such unity of interest and ownership that one is inseparable from the other, and facts must be such that adherence to fiction of separate entity would, under the circumstances, sanction a fraud or promote injustice, though actual fraud need not be shown.

Assets of corporation to which assets of judgment debtor corporation had been transferred and which was alter ego of judgment debtor corporation were properly made available to execution upon judgment by special order entered in proceedings supplemental to execution without independent action and judgment against transferee corporation, but judgment should be corrected to run against transferee corporation.

Judgment debtor corporation and corporation which was its alter ego should be regarded as identical for purposes of execution issued upon the judgment.

Opinion

By the Court, MERRILL, J.:

This action was brought by respondents against Henry McCleary Timber Company, a Washington corporation.. Judgment in favor of respondents was affirmed upon appeal to this court. The present appeal is taken by Frank McCleary Cattle Company, a Nevada corporation, from a special order after judgement, by which order the assets of appellant were made available to execution upon the judgment against the timber company. The order followed hearing in proceedings supplemental to execution. Appellant contends that the only method by which its assets can be subjected to judgment against the timber company is through an independent action brought against appellant.

It may be conceded that appellant's contentions would have merit in the ordinary case where property in the hands of a third party is sought to be subjected to a judgment debt. The court below, disregarding corporate entities, held that the cattle company was the alter ego of the timber company. The questions before us on this appeal are whether this ruling was justified by the evidence and, if so, whether the necessity for an independent action and judgment against the cattle company was thereby eliminated.

The evidence establishes the following facts: The action below was based upon an agreement entered into between respondents and the timber company on February 14, 1951. The cattle company was incorporated February 9, 1952. In December 1952 an obligation of the timber company under its agreement with respondents in the sum of approximately $25,000 was paid by the cattle company. In March of 1956 the charter of the timber company, both in Washington, the state of its domicile, and in Nevada, was revoked by official state action. Prior to that date all the assets of the timber company had been transferred to the cattle company. The value of the assets so transferred amounted to several million dollars, and the transfer was for tax reasons. All stock in each corporation was owned by Frank McCleary and Catherine McCleary. As to each stockholder the number of shares held in the cattle company was the same as the number held in the timber company. Frank McCleary was president of both corporations. Costs of the litigation with the timber company were borne by the cattle company.

There can be no question but that, under these circumstances, the trial court was justified in disregarding the corporate fiction and in holding the cattle company to be the alter ego of the timber company. Minifie v. Rowley, 187 Cal. 481,202 P. 673, sets forth the requirements for application of the alter ego doctrine. (Editors note: See above.)

Under these circumstances it is not necessary that a separate action be brought against the cattle company. Respondents are not seeking to read assets in the hands of a third party. Respondents are not seeking to substitute or add a new party to the old action. For the purposes of execution the timber company and the cattle company are to be regarded as identical. Mirabito v. San Francisco Dairy Co.l, 8 Cal. App.2d 54, 47 P.2d 530, is squarely in point upon this proposition. This was an action brought against the San Francisco Dairy Company. The corporation was then in existence but was nonoperative, having transferred substantially all of is assets to the Dairy Dale Company. The latter transferred the assets to the Dairy Delivery Company for consideration. It was held that the San Francisco Dairy Company was the alter ego of the Dairy Delivery Company. The court stated, p. 532, "The basis of the rule is, of course, that the court having acquired jurisdiction of the person of the defendant and of the subject of the action, it necessarily possessed the power to correct a misnomer. * * * Where * * *, as here, * * * the evidence is sufficient to warrant the conclusion that in effect the two corporations are identical; where, as here the action was fully and fairly tried with at least the direct financial assistance of appellant; and where as here, nothing appears in the record to show that Dairy Delivery Company could have produced a scintilla of evidence that would have, in any way , affected the results of the trial, there is no basis for a different rule. The trial court having acquired jurisdiction of the San Francisco Dairy Company must, likewise, be held to have acquired jurisdiction of its alter ego, the appellant herein." To the same effect: Leviston V. Swan, 33 Cal. 480.

In the case before us the court below did not direct that the judgment in favor of respondents be corrected to run against the cattle company. This, we feel, should be done if the judgment is properly to support the execution.

The trial court is affirmed. This matter is remanded with instructions that an order be entered by the court below correcting the written judgment in action number 5003 in the Sixth Judicial District Court of the State of Nevada in and for the county of Humboldt, to show that judgment is rendered against the Frank McCleary Cattle Company, a Nevada corporation. Costs to respondents.

LIMITATION ON STATE'S POWER TO TAX MULTISTATE CORPORATIONS

RATHER THAN INCLUDE THE ENTIRE DECISIONS, WHICH WOULD TAKE MANY PAGES, ONLY THE CASE SUMMARIES HAVE BEEN INCLUDED.

The following two cases were appealed to the United States Supreme Court in the early 1980's. Although these cases each came from different states, the issues involved were similar. In these cases the Supreme Court ruled that if a company is not based within a state, that state may not tax the dividends, interest income and capital gains earned by the corporation's foreign subsidiaries. Prior to these rulings, many states required multistate and multinational corporations to pay taxes on earnings of their independent subsidiaries, no matter where they were based.

WOOLWORTH V. NEW MEXICO

F.W. WOOLWORTH CO. v. TAXATION AND REVENUE DEPARTMENT OF NEW MEXICO

June 29, 1982

Appellant's principal place of business and commercial domicile are in New York, but it engages in chain store retailing throughout the United States. Under its income tax laws, New Mexico distinguishes between "business" income, which it apportions between it and other States, and "nonbusiness" income, which it generally allocates to a single State on the basis of commercial domicile. Appellant reported its dividend income from four of its foreign subsidiaries, which engage in chain store retailing in foreign countries, as "nonbusiness" income, none of which was to be allocated to New Mexico. Similarly, appellant did not report as New Mexico "business" income a sum, commonly known as "gross-up," that it never actually received from its foreign subsidiaries but that the Federal Government (for purposes of calculating appellant's federal foreign tax credit) deemed it to have received. On audit, appellee determined that appellant should have included in its apportionable New Mexico income both the dividends and the gross-up figure. Appellant's protest was denied but appellee's decision was reversed by the New Mexico Court of Appeals. However, the New Mexico Supreme Court in turn reversed, holding that both the dividends and the gross-up figure were apportionable New Mexico income.

Held:

1. New Mexico's tax on a portion of the dividends received by appellant from its foreign subsidiaries fails to meet established due process standards.

> (a) The linchpin of apportionability for state income taxation of an interstate enterprise is the "unitary-business principle." Appellant - as owner of all of the stock of three of its subsidiaries and a majority interest in the fourth - potentially has the authority to operate these companies as integrated divisions of a single unitary business. But the potential to operate a company as part of a unitary business is not dispositive when, as here, the dividend income from the subsidiaries in fact is derived from unrelated business activity of the subsidiaries, each of which operates a discrete business enterprise.

> (b) For due process purposes, the income attributed to a State must be rationally related to values connected with the taxing State. This limitation is not satisfied merely because the nondomiciliary parent corporation derives some economic benefit from its ownership of stock in another corporation.

> (c) None of the factors relevant to a State's right to tax dividends from foreign subsidiaries' operations - such as a store site selection, advertising, accounting, purchasing, warehousing, and personnel training - were not functionally integrated. And except for the type of occasional oversight - with

respect to capital structure, major debt, and dividends - that any parent gives to an investment in a subsidiary, there was little or no integration of business activities or centralization of management. Thus, the subsidiaries were not a part of a "unitary business."

(d) New Mexico's efforts to tax the "gross-up" income also contravenes the Due Process Clause. The "fictitious" gross-up figure is treated for federal foreign tax credit purposes as a dividend in the same manner as a dividend actually received by the domestic corporation from a foreign corporation. In this case the foreign tax credit arose from the taxation by foreign nations of appellant's foreign subsidiaries that had no unitary business relationship with New Mexico.

POWELL, J., delivered the opinion of the Court, in which BURGER, C.J., and BRENNAN, WHITE, MARSHALL, and STEVENS, JJ., joined. Burger, C.J., filed a concurring opinion. O'CONNOR, J., filed a dissenting opinion, in which BLACKMUN and REHNQUIST, JJ., joined.

ASARCO V. IDAHO

ASARCO INC. v. IDAHO STATE TAX COMMISSION

June 29, 1982

Held:

The State of Idaho may not constitutionally include within the taxable income of appellant nondomiciliary parent corporation doing some business (primarily silver mining) in the State a portion of intangible income (dividends, interest payments, and capital gains from the sale of stock) that appellant received from subsidiary corporations having no other connection with the State.

(a) As a general principle, a State may not tax value earned outside its borders. "The linchpin of apportionability in the field of state income taxation is the unitary-business principle." Mobile Oil Corp. v. Commissioner of Taxes of Vermont, 445 U.S. 425, 439; Exxon Corp. v. Wisconsin Dept. of Revenue, 447 U.S. 207, 223.

(b) Here, based on the findings in the state trial court and the undisputed facts, appellant succeeded in proving that no unitary business relationship existed between appellant and its subsidiaries.

(c) To have, as Idaho proposes, corporate purpose define unitary business - i.e., to consider intangible income as part of a unitary business if the intangible property (shares of stock) is "acquired, managed or disposed of for purposes relating or contributing to the taxpayer's business" - would destroy the concept of unitary business. Such a definition, which would permit nondomiciliary States to apportion and tax dividends "where the business activities of the dividend payor have nothing to do with the activities of the recipient in the taxing State," Mobil Oil Corp., supra, cannot be accepted consistently with recognized due process standards. While the dividend-paying subsidiaries in this case "add to the riches" of appellant, Wallace v. Hines, 253 U.S. 66, 70 (1920), they are "discrete business enterprises" that in "any business or economic sense" have "nothing to do with the activities" of appellant in Idaho. Therefore, there is no "rational relationship between [appellant's dividend] income attributed to the State and the intrastate values of the enterprise." The Due Process Clause bars Idaho's effort to levy upon income that is not properly within the reach of its taxing power.

(d) Under the same unitary-business standard applied to the dividend income in question, Idaho's attempt to tax the interest and capital gains income derived from its subsidiaries also violates the Due Process Clause.

POWELL, J., delivered the opinion of the Court, in which BURGER, C.J., and BRENNAN, WHITE, MARSHALL, and STEVENS, JJ., joined. BURGER, C.J., filed a concurring opinion. O'CONNOR, J., filed a dissenting opinion, in which BLACKMUN and REHNQUIST, JJ., joined.

SHAREHOLDER'S RIGHT TO INSPECT RECORDS

The following case discusses many of the considerations related to a shareholder's right to inspect the stock ledger and related materials of a Nevada Corporation.

CENERGY V. BRYSON

CENERGY CORPORATION, a Nevada corporation, Plaintiff, v. BRYSON OIL & GAS P.L.C., a public limited company organized under the laws of Northern Ireland, Defendant.

United States District Court, D. Nevada.

April 28, 1987

Corporation brought declaratory judgment action seeking declaration that its refusal to release stock ledgers was proper. The District Court, Edward C. Reed, Jr., Chief Judge, held that: (1)shareholder's possible solicitation of proxies was proper purpose for inspection of stock ledgers, and (2) corporation was required to permit inspection of all materials which corporation used regularly to communicate with its shareholders, including list of nonobjecting and official owners.

Ordered accordingly.

See also 657 F. Supp. 867.

In diversity case, where state's highest court has not decided issue, task of federal court is to predict how state court would resolve it.

Although at time affidavit accompanying request to inspect stock ledgers was submitted, request was improper because equitable owner of stock was not shareholder who could demand inspection, change in status of equitable owner to that of shareholder was not such that it would change shareholder's purpose in seeking stock ledgers, as stated in original affidavit accompanying first request, and thus affidavit fulfilled requirements of statute, notwithstanding fact that new affidavit was not submitted along with second request for inspection.

Statute allowing for inspection of stock ledgers does not require affidavit regarding purpose of inspection to accompany every shareholder request to inspect stock ledgers; rather statute only provides that if shareholder refuses to provide affidavit regarding purpose, shareholder may be denied ledgers, and thus statute requires that corporation from which shareholder seeks stock ledgers may demand affidavit regarding purpose, and if corporation demands affidavit, shareholder seeking to inspect stock ledgers may not refuse to provide one or stock ledgers may be withheld.

In absence of evidence of demand on part of corporation that shareholder produce affidavit other than affidavit accompanying original improper demand for inspection of stock ledgers, no duty arose on part of shareholder to further support request by new affidavit.

In determining whether shareholder is seeking to inspect stock ledgers for proper purpose, court may look beyond shareholder's statement of purpose.

Notwithstanding shareholder's equivocal statement of purpose, that he wished to inspect stock ledgers "to consider communicating" with fellow stockholders to enable stockholder to consider soliciting proxies from fellow stockholders, shareholder had formed intention to solicit proxies, and thus shareholder's purpose in seeking to inspect stock ledgers was proper purpose, not adverse to interests of corporations.

Shareholder who made proper request to inspect stock ledgers was entitled to inspect all materials which corporation used regularly to communicate with its shareholders, including list of nonobjecting beneficial owners and breakdowns in computer records, which corporation had in its possession, in order to wage proxy fight.

Order

EDWARD C. REED, Jr., Chief Judge.

On March 2, 1987, the defendant in this case, Bryson, filed with the plaintiff, Cenergy, a demand to inspect Cenergy's stock ledger. Bryson at that time was a beneficial owner of approximately 13% of Cenergy's shares. In this demand, Bryson stated that its purpose in securing the shareholder information was to consider mounting a proxy fight against Cenergy's incumbent management. Cenergy refused to allow Bryson access to the shareholder material, contending that such demands had to be made by record shareholder. As Bryson was only a beneficial owner, Cenergy decided not to release the stock ledger.

On March 10, 1987, Cenergy filed a declaratory relief action in this Court, seeking a declaration that its refusal to release the stock ledger was proper. Subsequently, Bryson had six percent of the outstanding Cenergy shares transferred from the nominal owner back into its own name. As it was now the record owner of six percent of Cenergy, Bryson renewed its demand for the stock ledger. Once again, Cenergy refused this demand, arguing that Bryson had failed to articulate a proper purpose for access to the shareholder list. In that Bryson's demand stated that the list was needed to "consider" a possible proxy fight, Cenergy felt that Bryson had not reached the present intent to wage the proxy battle.

Because of this equivocation on Bryson's part, Cenergy found that no proper purpose had been stated for release of the stock ledger.

Additionally, Bryson's demand also requested that all NOBO materials be turned over, as well as the stock ledger itself. NOBO is the shorthand designation for "non-objecting beneficial owners," and is commonly used in the cases. Bryson contends that the simple stock ledger is useless in waging a proxy fight, in that a large percentage of the shares are held by nominal holders, such as Cede & Co. In that these nominal holders have no power to execute proxies on behalf of their beneficiaries, Bryson contends that a simple list of the shareholders would be useless, as it would merely refer Bryson to a variety of nominal owners, who have no power to effect change in the management of the company. Cenergy, on the other hand, argues that a shareholder has the right to inspect the stock ledger, and nothing more.

[1] Nevada substantive law applies in this diversity case. The task of this Court is to approximate state law as closely as possible. Gee v. Tenneco, Inc., 615 F.2d 857, 861 (9th Cir. 1980). Where the state's highest court has not decided the issue, the task of the federal court is to predict how the state high court would resolve it. Dimidowich v. Bell & Howell, 803 F.2d 1473, 1482 (9th Cir.1986).

Both parties have moved for summary judgment, and have indicated that there are no facts in dispute in this case. Additionally, both parties have waived oral arguments on their motions, requesting that the Court resolve the cross-motions for summary judgment as soon as possible. On the basis of the factual record currently before the Court, and on the basis of the pleadings filed in this action, it appears that Bryson is entitled to inspect the shareholder material and that summary judgment should be entered it its favor.

PROPER PURPOSE

> An inspection...[of a stock ledger] may be denied to such stockholder or other person upon his refusal to furnish to the corporation an affidavit that such inspection is not desired for a purpose which is in the interest of a business or object other than the business of the corporation and that he has not at any time sold or offered for sale any list of stockholders of any domestic or foreign corporation or aided or abetted any person in procuring any such record of stockholders for any such purpose.

NRS 78.105(3) provides:

[2] NRS 78.105(3) provides that the shareholder seeking the ledger may not refuse to supply an affidavit regarding the shareholder's purposes. On March 2, 1987, Bryson provided such an affidavit. The March 2, 1987 affidavit, however, was provided in conjunction with a request to inspect stock ledgers which was improper in that at that time Bryson was not a shareholder which, under NRS 78.105(2), could demand inspection. In

the following weeks, Bryson changed its position such that it qualified under 78.105(2). On March 16, 1987, Bryson again requested inspection of the stock ledgers. This time no affidavit was provided. The March 2, 1987 affidavit arguably does not support the March 16, 1987, request for inspection. The Court finds this argument to be weak. Bryson's change of position as a shareholder between March 2 and March 16 was not such that it would change Bryson's purposes in seeking the stock ledgers. The March 2, 1987, affidavit fulfills the requirements of NRS 78.105(3).

[3] Technically, however, the question of the adequacy of the March 2 affidavit need not be reached. NRS 78.105(3) does not require an affidavit regarding purpose of inspection to accompany every shareholder request to inspect stock ledgers. That statute only provides that if a shareholder refuses to provide an affidavit regarding purpose, the shareholder may be denied the ledger. A fair reading of the statute is that a corporation from which a shareholder seeks a stock ledger may demand an affidavit regarding purpose. If the corporation demands an affidavit, the shareholder seeking to inspect the stock ledger may not refuse to provide one. If the shareholder does refuse, the stock ledger may be withheld.

[4] There is no evidence of a demand on the part of Cenergy that Bryson produce an affidavit other than the March 2, 1987, affidavit produced. Therefore, no duty arose on the part of Bryson to further support by affidavit its request to inspect the stock ledgers.

The burden is now upon Cenergy to show that Bryson seeks to inspect the stock ledgers for an improper purpose. The Court finds that Bryson seeks the stock ledger for a proper purpose. Bryson stated its purpose as follows:

The purpose of this demand is to permit the Stockholder to consider communicating with its fellow stockholders on matters relating to their mutual interest as stockholders, and to enable the stockholder (should it determine to do so) to consider soliciting proxies from its fellow stockholders in connection with the next meeting of stockholders, including to solicit proxies with respect to the election of directors of the Company or other matters to be voted on by the Stockholders.

The cases on the subject consistently hold that proxy solicitation is a proper purpose for the inspection of stock ledgers. An intent antagonistic toward present management does not necessarily indicate an interest detrimental to the corporation itself.

[5,6] The opinion in Hatleigh Corp. v. Lane Bryant, Inc., 428 A.2d 350 (Del.Ch.1981), pg. 1146 requires that, in order for proxy solicitation to be a proper purpose for the inspection of stock ledgers, the shareholder seeking the ledgers must have formed a bona fide intention to solicit proxies. Cenergy argues that Bryson had not formed such a bona fide intention when it sought the stock ledger. Cenergy points to the equivocal nature of the language in the demand by Bryson. It is true that Bryson's language was less than clear about its intention. The Court, however, may look beyond the shareholder's statement of purpose to determine whether a shareholder had a proper purpose in seeking a stock ledger. The surrounding circumstances are relevant. Notwithstanding Bryson's equivocal statement of purpose, the Court finds that Bryson had formed an intention to solicit proxies. Most significant is the fact that Bryson had retained D.F. King Co., Inc.; D.F. King is a proxy solicitation firm. Also significant is the fact that the annual shareholders' meeting was imminent when Bryson made its demand.

The Court finds that Bryson seeks to inspect the stock ledgers of Cenergy for a proper purpose, one not adverse to the interests of Cenergy. Under Nevada law, therefore, Bryson is entitled to inspect the stock ledger.

NOBO MATERIALS

The question of exactly what materials Bryson is entitled to inspect still remains. As noted above, Bryson argues that it must have access to the NOBO materials, which would include the names and addresses of the beneficial owners of Cenergy stock, in order to wage a proxy battle. There is no doubt that this is true. Without the names and addresses of the beneficial owners of the shares, Bryson could not contact them, and therefore could not run a proxy campaign.

Cenergy does not dispute the fact that access to the NOBO materials is critical to the waging of a proxy fight. It does maintain that Nevada law restricts the insurgents' inquiry solely to the stock ledger. On balance, it appears that Bryson should be allowed access to the NOBO materials.

The Nevada Supreme Court has not ruled on this topic. Several cases from Delaware, however, are instructive. In Shamrock Assoc's v. Texas American Energy Corp., 517 A. 2d 658 (Del.Ch.1986) the plaintiff had begun a proxy fight against the defendant's incumbent management. In so doing, the plaintiff made a demand for the stock ledger, and also demanded access to the NOBO list which the corporation had acquired to contact its shareholders. The defendant refused to deliver the NOBO list, claiming among other things that Delaware law only required delivery of the stock ledger, and that any other material, such as a NOBO list, was merely ancillary, and need not be produced.

The Delaware court rejected this argument. In interpreting the relevant section of the Delaware Code, the court found it had repeatedly recognized that "the stock-list materials provided to a shareholder should include all of those forms of shareholder data readily available to the corporation." If the corporation were allowed to shield the names of the actual owners of the corporation from other shareholders, the court found, it would have an unfair advantage in the proxy solicitation battle. By requiring the corporation to divulge all of the shareholder information in its possession, the court concluded that the goal of fairness in proxy solicitation would be effectuated. Therefore, the court ordered that the defendant allow the plaintiff access to any NOBO list which the corporation might have acquired in the course of proxy solicitation. In addition, the court impliedly held that the plaintiff would be allowed access to all other forms of ancillary shareholder information used by the corporation to contact its shareholders, such as Cede & Co. breakdowns and magnetic tapes.

[7] Based upon the preceding authority, it appears that Bryson is entitled to inspect all materials which Cenergy uses regularly to communicate with its shareholders. This would include the NOBO list, as well as any Cede & Co. breakdowns and computer records which Cenergy has in its possession. Cenergy argues, however, that the Court cannot read the Nevada statute as to allow this broader type of inspection rights, for the Nevada Supreme Court has given this statute a very narrow construction. In that the state's highest court has narrowly construed the inspection rights, Cenergy argues that this Court must similarly construe them.

Initially, the state supreme court opinion cited by Cenergy, Crown-Zellerbach Corp. v. General Oriental Securities Ltd., No. 16417 (Nev. May 1, 1985), is an unpublished opinion. As such, it does not constitute authority, even in the state system. See Nevada Employment Security Dep't v. Weber, 100 Nev. 121, 122, 676 P.2d 1318 (1984) (citation of unpublished orders of the state supreme court is prohibited); Supreme Court Rule 123 (unpublished opinions shall not be regarded as precedent and shall not be cited as legal authority). Even if the Court were to consider this case, it would not alter the decision made here. At issue in Crown-Zellerbach was the interpretation of the qualifications for giving access to shareholder lists under 78.105(2). In that case, the court held that it would require all parties to be shareholders of record in order to gain access to the stock ledger. Because some states do not require shareholders to be of record to see the list, the court found its reading of the statute to be comparatively narrow.

That the supreme court has limited the class of shareholders entitled to see the stock ledger to only record owners does not mean that the information which those shareholders will receive is also necessarily limited. The factors to be taken into consideration are quite different in the two questions. As regards access to the stock ledger, a court might reasonably conclude that only record shareholders ought to be allowed access, so as to simplify corporate record-keeping, and prevent the list from being distributed wrongly. At the same time, however, a court could also require that the corporation turn over all information it uses to contact shareholders along with the stock ledger, in order to facilitate corporate democracy. A strict reading of the access question does not therefore necessarily imply a strict reading on the information question.

Cenergy nonetheless stoutly protests that it has never used a NOBO list or any such ancillary material in communicating with its shareholders. Although it is difficult to imagine that a corporation does not have a good idea of who its actual owners are, the Court will not order Cenergy to acquire specially any shareholder information which it does not already possess in order to then distribute it to Bryson. Cenergy must, however, allow Bryson access to any and all shareholder information, such as NOBO lists and Cede & Co. breakdowns, which it has in its possession at this time for the purpose of contacting its shareholders.

IT IS, THEREFORE, HEREBY ORDERED that defendant Bryson's motion for summary judgment is GRANTED.

IT IS FURTHER ORDERED that plaintiff Cenergy shall allow Bryson to inspect its stock ledger, and all other information in Cenergy's possession for the purpose of contacting and communicating with its shareholders. This inspection shall take place at the place of business where these records are normally kept, and shall take place during normal business hours. The inspection shall take place within ten days of the issuance of this order.

IT IS FURTHER ORDERED that Cenergy's motion for leave to cite an unpublished opinion is DENIED.

IT IS FURTHER ORDERED that Cenergy's motion for summary judgment is DENIED.

IT IS FURTHER ORDERED that the Clerk shall enter judgment in favor of defendant and against plaintiff in accordance with the foregoing orders.

THE RIGHT TO MINIMIZE YOUR TAXES

The following case was a landmark decision by the United States Supreme Court in 1935 concerning a taxpayers right to legally organize his affairs so as to reduce or eliminate his taxes at every opportunity. Excerpts from Gregory v. Helvering have been quoted extensively by business professionals for years. Here, in its entirety, is that landmark case.

GREGORY V. HELVERING

GREGORY v. HELVERING, COMMISSIONER OF INTERNAL REVENUE.

Argued December 4, 5, 1934 - Decided January 7, 1935.

1. A corporation wholly owned by a taxpayer transferred 1000 shares of stock in another corporation held by it among its assets to a new corporation, which thereupon issued all of its shares to the taxpayer. Within a few days the new corporation was dissolved and was liquidated by the distribution of the 1000 shares to the taxpayer, who immediately sold them for her individual profit. No other business was transacted, or intended to be transacted, by the new corporation. The whole plan was designed to conform to Section 112 of the Revenue Act of 1928 as a "reorganization," but for the sole purpose of transferring the shares in question to the taxpayer, with a resulting tax liability less than that which would have ensued from a direct transfer by way of dividend. Held: while the plan conformed to the terms of the statute, there was no reorganization within the intent of the statute.

2. By means which the law permits, a taxpayer has the right to decrease the amount of what otherwise would be his taxes, or to altogether avoid them.

3. The rule which excludes from consideration the motive of tax avoidance is not pertinent to the situation here, because the transaction upon its face lies outside the plain intent of the statute.

69 F. (2d) 809, affirmed.

Opinion of the Court

MR. JUSTICE SUTHERLAND delivered the opinion of the court.

Petitioner in 1928 was the owner of all the stock of United Mortgage Corporation. That corporation held among its assets 1,000 shares of the Monitor Securities Corporation. For the sole purpose of procuring a transfer of these shares to herself in order to sell them for her individual profit, at, at the same time, diminish the amount of income tax which would result from a direct transfer by way of dividend, she sought to bring about a "reorganization" under Sec. 112 (g) of the Revenue Act of 1928, c. 852, 45 Stat. 791, 818, set forth later in this opinion.

To that end, she caused the Averill Corporation to be organized under the laws of Delaware on September 18, 1928. Three days later, the United Mortgage Corporation transferred to the Averill Corporation the 1,000 shares of Monitor stock, for which all the shares of the Averill Corporation were issued to the petitioner. On September 24, the Averill Corporation was dissolved, and liquidated by distributing all its assets, namely, the Monitor shares, to the petitioner. No other business was ever transacted, or intended to be transacted, by that company. Petitioner immediately sold the Monitor shares for $133,333.33. She returned for taxation as capital net gain the sum of $76,007.88, based upon an apportioned cost of $57,325.45. Further details are necessary. It is not disputed that if the interposition of the so-called reorganization was ineffective, petitioner became liable for a much larger tax as a result of the transaction.

The Commissioner of Internal Revenue, being of opinion that the reorganization attempted was without substance and must be disregarded, held that petitioner was liable for a tax as though the United corporation had paid her a dividend consisting of the amount realized from the sale of the Monitor shares. In a proceeding before the Board of Tax Appeals, that body rejected the commissioner's view and upheld that of petitioner. Upon a review of the latter decision, the circuit court of appeals sustained the commissioner and reversed the board, holding that there had been no "reorganization" within the meaning of the statute. Petitioner applied to this court for a writ of certiorari, which the government, considering the question one of importance, did not oppose. We granted the writ.

Section 112 of the Revenue Act of 1928 deals with the subject of gain or loss resulting from the sale or exchange of property. Such gain or loss is to be recognized in computing the tax, except as provided in that section. The provisions of the section, so far as they are pertinent to the question here presented, follow:

It is earnestly contended on behalf of the taxpayer that since every element required by the foregoing subdivision (B) is to be found in what was done, a statutory reorganization was effected; and that the motive of the taxpayer thereby to escape payment of a tax will not alter the result or make unlawful what the statute allows. It is quite true that if a reorganization in reality was effected within the meaning of subdivision (B), the ulterior purpose mentioned will be disregarded. The legal right of a taxpayer to decrease the amount of what otherwise would be his taxes, or altogether avoid them, by means which the law permits, cannot be doubted. United States v. Isham, 17 Wall. 496, 506; Superior Oil Co. v. Mississippi, 280 U.S. 390, 395-6; Jones v. Helvering, 63 App. D.C. 204; 71 F. (2d) 214, 217. But the question for determination is whether what was done, apart from the tax motive, was the thing which the statute intended. The reasoning of the court below in justification of a negative answer leaves little to be said.

When subdivision (B) speaks of a transfer of assets by one corporation to another, it means a transfer made "in pursuance of a plan of reorganization" of corporate business; and not a transfer of assets by one corporation to another in pursuance of a plan having no relation to the business of either, as plainly is the case here. Putting aside, then, the question of motive in respect to taxation altogether, and fixing the character of the proceedings by what actually occurred, what do we find? Simply an operation having no business or corporate purpose - a mere device which put on the form of a corporate reorganization as a disguise for concealing its real character, and the sole object and accomplishment of which was the consummation of a preconceived plan, not to reorganize a business or any part of a business, but to transfer a parcel of corporate shares to the petitioner. No doubt, a new and valid corporation was created. But that corporation was nothing more than a contrivance to the end last described. It was brought into existence for no other purpose; it performed, as it was intended from the beginning it should perform, no other function. When that limited function had been exercised, it immediately was put to death.

In these circumstances, the facts speak for themselves and are susceptible of but one interpretation. The whole undertaking, though conducted according to the terms of subdivision (B), was in fact an elaborate and devious form of conveyance masquerading as a corporate reorganization, and nothing else. The rule which excludes from consideration the motive of tax avoidance is not pertinent to the situation, because the transaction upon its face lies outside the plain intent of the statute. To hold otherwise would be to exalt artifice above reality and to deprive the statutory provision in question of all serious purpose.

Judgment affirmed.

ENFORCEABILITY OF CORPORATE ACTIONS TAKEN IN INFORMAL MEETINGS, WHERE NO MINUTES WERE PRESENT

SORGE V. SIERRA AUTO SUPPLY COMPANY

October 4, 1923

218 Pac. 735

APPEAL from Second Judicial District Court, Washoe County; Thomas F. Moran, Judge.

Suite by Nick Sorge against the Sierra Auto Supply Company and others. From a judgment for plaintiff, the defendant Fred Stadtmuller, as trustee in bankruptcy of the Sierra Auto Supply Company, appeals. Remanded for modification. Petition for rehearing denied.

Price & Hawkins, for Appellant Stadtmuller:

Where a corporate resolution authorizing borrowing of money and execution of note and mortgage does not expressly authorize attorney's fees, such fees are not recoverable. Defanti v. Allen Clark Co., 45 Nev. 120; Harden v. I.R. & C. Co., 43 N.W. 544.

Trustees represent corporation only when assembled together and acting as board. Yellow Jacket M.Co. v. Stevenson, 5 Nev. 232; Rev. Laws, 1127.

A board of directors should act in official meetings, and by its records. Being only artificial, corporation can act only in manner provided by law. A corporation may by custom become estopped and it may be held for acts of its officers ultra vires when it ratifies them, or receives benefits of unauthorized acts. Star Mills v. Bailey, 130 S.W. 1079.

According to Prescott v. Grady, 27 Pac. 756, attorney's fees are damages resulting from breach of special contract, and should be specially averred.

W.M. Kearney, for Respondent:

The ruling in Defanti case, on which counsel so strongly rely, was apparently made because there were no facts upon which lower court could have found ratification, estoppel, or approval of mortgages by board as to form, such as we find in case at bar, and the very pertinent reservations of court in Thomas v. Wentworth, 117 Pac. 1041, where similar situation arose, indicate clearly that rule stated in Defanti case refers only to abstract proposition of law when standing alone, and that, if evidence had shown that it was usual and customary for officers to execute mortgages providing for payment of attorney's fees, court would have allowed them.

In Gribble v. Columbus Brewing Co., 35 Pac. 530, where facts were very similar to those in instant case, the court said: "The note and mortgage were such as corporation had right to authorize, and consequently were not ultra vires." If all persons in corporation having right to object to unauthorized act knowingly acquiesce in it, contract is as binding as if originally authorized. Taylor, Corporations, sec. 211.

In Gribble case, Harden v. Ry. Co., cited by counsel, was construed and distinguished and court refused to follow it, though facts are not nearly so strong on ratification or estoppel as in case at bar.

Lack of formality of corporate procedure does not invalidate corporate act where there has been ratification. Murray v. Beal, 65 Pac. 726; 4 Thompson, Corporations, par. 4624.

In absence of evidence to contrary it will be presumed that corporation's note and mortgage were authorized at lawful meeting of board. Clark Realty Co. v. Douglas, 46 Nev. 378; 4 Thompson, Corporations, 5105.

Mortgage by corporation is not invalid merely because of some informality in corporate procedure. Bank v. Coats, 205 Fed. 618.

Informality of corporate acts does not affect third persons acting in good faith with corporation. Miners Ditech Co. v. Zellerbach, 37 Cal. 543.

If all directors happen to be together and agree to hold meeting for particular object within their jurisdiction, their action cannot be impeached for want of notice of meeting. Chase v. Tuttle, 12 Atl. 874.

Where it has been custom of corporation to function without minutes, it is bound nevertheless by its acts.

By the Court, COLEMAN, J.:

There is but one question presented on this appeal, and that is whether the trial court erred in adjudging the plaintiff in the foreclosure of a mortgage to be entitled to recover an attorney's fee. In determining this question we need consider only the contention of the appellants that the defendant corporation did not authorize its officers to embody in the notes and mortgages executed the provision therein contained authorizing a court, in case of foreclosure, to award to the mortgagee such fee. On this point the facts are few. The defendant company executed two notes, one for $20,000, dated May 6 1920, and another for $4,000, dated May 20, 1921, both containing the following provision:

"And in case suit or action is instituted to collect this note, or any portion thereof, we promise and agree to pay, in addition to the costs and disbursements provided by state, such additional sum in like lawful money of the United States, as the court may adjudge reasonable for attorney's fees to be allowed in said suit or action."

These notes were secured by mortgages containing provisions to the effect that in case of foreclosure thereof the court could adjudge the plaintiff to be entitled to recover such a sum as attorney's fee as it might deem reasonable.

The only defendant which appeared in the trial court and contested plaintiff's right to an attorney's fee is the defendant, Fred Stadtmuller, as trustee, etc. From a judgment in favor of plaintiff, he has appealed.

1.   Counsel for appellant insist that the judgment must be reversed for the reason that there was no meeting of the trustees of the defendant company, duly called, at which the officers of the company were authorized to execute the note and mortgage in question. No contention is made as to the incorrectness of the judgment as to the money loaned since the company received the benefit thereof, but upon authority of Defanti v. Clark, 45 Nev. 120, 198 Pac. 549, it is said that the court erred in awarding the plaintiff an attorney's fee. We do not think that case is in point. There is a wide difference between the facts that in case and in the instant one. In that case we held that Defanti could not recover attorney's fee for the reason that there was no legal meeting of the board of trustees authorizing the execution of the note and mortgage, and that no such transaction had ever been ratified. In that case there was no meeting of the board of trustees at which all the trustees were present and acting, whereas in the instant case, so far as the $20,000 note and mortgage are concerned, they were all present and acting. It is true it does not appear that a meeting was held pursuant to notice, but they all assembled, for the sole purpose evidently of considering the proposition of borrowing the money obtained and of giving a note and mortgage to secure payment thereof. The trustees knew that the company could not get the desired money unless these papers were authorized. The note and mortgage had been prepared by an attorney for the respondent. They embodied the terms and conditions upon which respondent was willing to part with the money. There is in evidence a resolution purporting to have been adopted at a meeting of the board of directors of the defendant company on May 6, which authorizes the officers of the company to borrow from Nick Sorge the sum of $20,000 on behalf of the company and to execute a note therefore and a mortgage to secure the same. The evidence shows that at the meeting at which the resolution mentioned was adopted the note and mortgage to which we have referred, and which were sued upon, were read over by all of the directors, and their execution authorized. It was the particular note and mortgage in question here which the board of directors were acting upon. In such circumstances we see no escape from the conclusion that the note and mortgage in question are valid and binding in every particular. In Hubbard v. University Bank of Los Angeles, 125 Cal. 684, 58 Pac. 297, the court said:

> *"The averments above quoted are sufficient to charge the corporation with the execution of this particular mortgage, and, as they are not denied, the defendants are bound by them."*

This holding seems to be squarely in point and decisive of the contention made.

2.   It is said that the evidence does not show that the board of directors acted as such. The resolution adopted confutes this contention. The fact that the minutes of the meeting were not written up and attested by the officers of the company is not a circumstance which can be invoked to defeat the mortgage given pursuant to the resolution.

3.   The $4,000 note and mortgage were not authorized at a meeting of which notice was given or at which all of the trustees attended, nor has the execution thereof been ratified. That note and mortgage are controlled by the law as declared in the Defanti case, supra. It follows that the court could not take into consideration in fixing an attorney's fee the services rendered in the foreclosing of the $4,000 note.

It is ordered that the case be remanded, and that the trial court modify its judgment in accordance with the views above expressed.

APPENDIX B: NEVADA REVISED STATUTES CHAPTER 78

PRIVATE CORPORATIONS

NRS 78.010 **Definitions; construction.**

1. As used in this chapter:

(a) "Approval" and "vote" as describing action by the directors or stockholders mean the vote of directors in person or by written consent or of stockholders in person, by proxy or by written consent.

(b) "Articles," "articles of incorporation" and "certificate of incorporation" are synonymous terms and unless the context otherwise requires, include all certificates filed pursuant to NRS 78.030, 78.1955, 78.209, 78.380, 78.385 and 78.390 and any articles of merger or exchange filed pursuant to NRS 92A.200 to 92A.240, inclusive. Unless the context otherwise requires, these terms include restated articles and certificates of incorporation.

(c) "Directors" and "trustees" are synonymous terms.

(d) "Receiver" includes receivers and trustees appointed by a court as provided in this chapter or in chapter 32 of NRS.

(e) "Registered office" means the office maintained at the street address of the resident agent.

(f) "Resident agent" means the agent appointed by the corporation upon whom process or a notice or demand authorized by law to be served upon the corporation may be served.

(g) "Sign" means to affix a signature to a document.

(h) "Signature" means a name, word or mark executed or adopted by a person with the present intention to authenticate a document. The term includes, without limitation, a digital signature as defined in NRS 720.060.

(i) "Stockholder of record" means a person whose name appears on the stock ledger of the corporation.

(j) "Street address" of a resident agent means the actual physical location in this state at which a resident agent is available for service of process.

2. General terms and powers given in this chapter are not restricted by the use of special terms, or by any grant of special powers contained in this chapter.

[Part 47:177:1925; NCL § 1646] + [83:177:1925; A 1931, 415; 1931 NCL § 1682]—(NRS A 1965, 216; 1977, 184; 1989, 871; 1991, 1207; 1993, 944; 1995, 2093; 1997, 695; 1999, 1576)

NRS 78.015 **Applicability of chapter; effect on corporations existing before April 1, 1925.**

1. The provisions of this chapter apply to:

(a) Corporations organized in this state on or after October 1, 1991, except:

(1) Where the provisions of chapters 80, 84 and 89 of NRS are inconsistent with the provisions of this chapter;

(2) Corporations expressly excluded by the provisions of this chapter; and

(3) Corporations governed by the provisions of NRS 81.170 to 81.540, inclusive, and chapter 82 of NRS.

(b) Corporations whose charters are renewed or revived in the manner provided in NRS 78.730.

(c) Corporations organized and still existing under this chapter before October 1, 1991, or any prior act or any amendment thereto.

(d) Close corporations, unless otherwise provided in chapter 78A of NRS.

(e) All insurance companies, mutual fire insurance companies, surety companies, express companies, railroad companies, and public utility companies now existing and formed before October 1, 1991, under any other act or law of this state, subject to any special provisions concerning any class of corporations inconsistent with the provisions of this chapter, in which case the special provisions continue to apply.

2. Neither the existence of corporations formed or existing before April 1, 1925, nor any liability, cause of action, right, privilege or immunity validly existing in favor of or against any such corporation on April 1, 1925, are affected, abridged, taken away or impaired by this chapter, or by any change in the requirements for the formation of corporations provided by this chapter, nor by the amendment or repeal of any laws under which such prior existing corporations were formed or created.

[1:177:1925; A 1935, 146; 1937, 4; 1945, 196; 1943 NCL § 1600]—(NRS A 1989, 948; 1991, 1207; 1995, 2094)

NRS 78.020 **Limitations on incorporation under chapter; compliance with other laws.**

1. Insurance companies, mutual fire insurance companies, surety companies, express companies and railroad companies may be formed under this chapter, but such a corporation may not:

(a) Transact any such business within this state until it has first complied with all laws concerning or affecting the right to engage in such business.

(b) Infringe the laws of any other state or country in which it may intend to engage in business, by so incorporating under this chapter.

2. No trust company, savings and loan association, thrift company or corporation organized for the purpose of conducting a banking business may be organized under this chapter.

[Part 4:177:1925; A 1929, 413; 1931, 415; 1949, 158; 1955, 402]—(NRS A 1975, 1; 1983, 117; 1997, 1014)

NRS 78.025 **Reserved power of state to amend or repeal chapter; chapter part**

of corporation's charter. This chapter may be amended or repealed at the pleasure of the legislature, and every corporation created under this chapter, or availing itself of any of the provisions of this chapter, and all stockholders of such corporation shall be bound by such amendment; but such amendment or repeal shall not take away or impair any remedy against any corporation, or its officers, for any liability which shall have been previously incurred. This chapter, and all amendments thereof, shall be a part of the charter of every corporation, except so far as the same are inapplicable and inappropriate to the objects of the corporation.

[2:177:1925; NCL § 1601]

NRS 78.027 Corporate documents: Microfilming and return. The secretary of state may microfilm any document which is filed in his office by a corporation pursuant to this chapter and may return the original document to the corporation.

(Added to NRS by 1977, 572)

NRS 78.028 Filing of documents written in language other than English. No document which is written in a language other than English may be filed or submitted for filing in the office of the secretary of state pursuant to the provisions of this chapter unless it is accompanied by a verified translation of that document into the English language.

(Added to NRS by 1995, 1112)

NRS 78.029 Procedure to submit replacement page to secretary of state before filing of document. Before the issuance of stock an incorporator, and after the issuance of stock an officer, of a corporation may authorize the secretary of state in writing to replace any page of a document submitted for filing, on an expedited basis, before the actual filing, and to accept the page as if it were part of the originally signed filing.

(Added to NRS by 1997, 2807; A 1999, 1577)

NRS 78.0295 Incorrect or defective document: Certificate of correction; effective date of correction.

1. A corporation may correct a document filed by the secretary of state if the document contains an incorrect statement or was defectively executed, attested, sealed, verified or acknowledged.

2. To correct a document, the corporation shall:

(a) Prepare a certificate of correction which:

(1) States the name of the corporation;

(2) Describes the document, including, without limitation, its filing date;

(3) Specifies the incorrect statement and the reason it is incorrect or the manner in which the execution or other formal authentication was defective;

(4) Corrects the incorrect statement or defective execution; and

(5) Is signed by an officer of the corporation; and

(b) Deliver the certificate to the secretary of state for filing.

3. A certificate of correction is effective on the effective date of the document it corrects except as to persons relying on the uncorrected document and adversely affected by the correction. As to those persons, the certificate is effective when filed.

(Added to NRS by 1997, 693)

FORMATION

NRS 78.030 Filing of articles of incorporation and certificate of acceptance of appointment of resident agent.

1. One or more persons may establish a corporation for the transaction of any lawful business, or to promote or conduct any legitimate object or purpose, pursuant and subject to the requirements of this chapter, by:

(a) Executing and filing in the office of the secretary of state articles of incorporation; and

(b) Filing a certificate of acceptance of appointment, executed by the resident agent of the corporation, in the office of the secretary of state.

2. The articles of incorporation must be as provided in NRS 78.035, and the secretary of state shall require them to be in the form prescribed. If any articles are defective in this respect, the secretary of state shall return them for correction.

[3:177:1925; A 1931, 415; 1931 NCL § 1602]—(NRS A 1963, 70; 1979, 394; 1981, 1888; 1989, 948; 1991, 1208; 1995, 2095; 1999, 1577)

NRS 78.035 Articles of incorporation: Required provisions. The articles of incorporation must set forth:

1. The name of the corporation. A name appearing to be that of a natural person and containing a given name or initials must not be used as a corporate name except with an additional word or words such as "Incorporated," "Limited," "Inc.," "Ltd.,"

"Company," "Co.," "Corporation," "Corp.," or other word which identifies it as not being a natural person.

2. The name of the person designated as the corporation's resident agent, the street address of the resident agent where process may be served upon the corporation, and the mailing address of the resident agent if different from the street address.

3. The number of shares the corporation is authorized to issue and, if more than one class or series of stock is authorized, the classes, the series and the number of shares of each class or series which the corporation is authorized to issue, unless the articles authorize the board of directors to fix and determine in a resolution the classes, series and numbers of each class or series as provided in NRS 78.195 and 78.196.

4. The number, names and post office box or street addresses, either residence or business, of the first board of directors or trustees, together with any desired provisions relative to the right to change the number of directors as provided in NRS 78.115.

5. The name and post office box or street address, either residence or business of each of the incorporators executing the articles of incorporation.

[Part 4:177:1925; A 1929, 413; 1931, 415; 1949, 158; 1955, 402]—(NRS A 1957, 75; 1967, 769; 1981, 1888; 1985, 1785; 1987, 81, 574, 1054; 1991, 1208; 1993, 945; 1995, 2095; 1999, 1577)

NRS 78.037 Articles of incorporation: Optional provisions. The articles of incorporation may also contain:

1. A provision eliminating or limiting the personal liability of a director or officer to the corporation or its stockholders for damages for breach of fiduciary duty as a director or officer, but such a provision must not eliminate or limit the liability of a director or officer for:

(a) Acts or omissions which involve intentional misconduct, fraud or a knowing violation of law; or

(b) The payment of distributions in violation of NRS 78.300.

2. Any provision, not contrary to the laws of this state, for the management of the business and for the conduct of the affairs of the corporation, and any provision creating, defining, limiting or regulating the powers of the corporation or the rights, powers or duties of the directors, and the stockholders, or any class of the stockholders, or the holders of bonds or other obligations of the corporation, or governing the distribution or division of the profits of the corporation.

(Added to NRS by 1987, 80; A 1991, 1210; 1993, 945)

NRS 78.039 Name of corporation: Distinguishable name required; availability of name of revoked, merged or otherwise terminated corporation; regulations.

1. The name proposed for a corporation must be distinguishable on the records of the secretary of state from the names of all other artificial persons formed, organized, registered or qualified pursuant to the provisions of this Title that are on file in the office of the secretary of state and all names that are reserved in the office of the secretary of state pursuant to the provisions of this Title. If a proposed name is not so distinguishable, the secretary of state shall return the articles of incorporation containing the proposed name to the incorporator, unless the written, acknowledged consent of the holder of the name on file or reserved name to use the same name or the requested similar name accompanies the articles of incorporation.

2. For the purposes of this section and NRS 78.040, a proposed name is not distinguishable from a name on file or reserved name solely because one or the other contains distinctive lettering, a distinctive mark, a trade-mark or a trade name, or any combination of these.

3. The name of a corporation whose charter has been revoked, which has merged and is not the surviving entity or whose existence has otherwise terminated is available for use by any other artificial person.

4. The secretary of state may adopt regulations that interpret the requirements of this section.

(Added to NRS by 1975, 477; A 1987, 1056; 1991, 1210; 1993, 945; 1997, 2807; 1999, 1578)

NRS 78.040 Name of corporation: Reservation; injunctive relief.

1. The secretary of state, when requested so to do, shall reserve, for a period of 90 days, the right to use any name available under NRS 78.039, for the use of any proposed corporation. During the period, a name so reserved is not available for use or reservation by any other artificial person forming, organizing, registering or qualifying in the office of the secretary of state pursuant to the provisions of this Title without the written, acknowledged consent of the person at whose request the reservation was made.

2. The use by any other artificial person of a name in violation of subsection 1 or NRS 78.039 may be enjoined, even if the document under which the artificial person is formed, organized, registered or qualified has been filed by the secretary of state.

[4a:177:1925; added 1931, 415; 1931 NCL § 1603.01] + [4b:177:1925; added 1931, 415; 1931 NCL § 1603.02]—(NRS A 1963, 64; 1979, 395; 1981, 472; 1987, 1056; 1993, 946; 1999, 1578)

NRS 78.045 Articles of incorporation: Approval or certification required before filing of certain articles or amendments.

1. The secretary of state shall not accept for filing any articles of incorporation or any certificate of amendment of articles of incorporation of any corporation formed pursuant to the laws of this state which provides that the name of the corporation contains the word "bank" or "trust," unless:

(a) It appears from the articles or the certificate of amendment that the corporation proposes to carry on business as a banking or trust company, exclusively or in connection with its business as a bank or savings and loan association; and

(b) The articles or certificate of amendment is first approved by the commissioner of financial institutions.

2. The secretary of state shall not accept for filing any articles of incorporation or any certificate of amendment of articles of incorporation of any corporation formed pursuant to the provisions of this chapter if it appears from the articles or the certificate of amendment that the business to be carried on by the corporation is subject to supervision by the commissioner of insurance or by the commissioner of financial institutions, unless the articles or certificate of amendment is approved by the commissioner who will supervise the business of the corporation.

3. Except as otherwise provided in subsection 5, the secretary of state shall not accept for filing any articles of incorporation or any certificate or amendment of articles of incorporation of any corporation formed pursuant to the laws of this state if the name of the corporation contains the words "engineer," "engineered," "engineering," "professional engineer" "registered engineer" or "licensed engineer" unless:

(a) The state board of professional engineers and land surveyors certifies that the principals of the corporation are licensed to practice engineering pursuant to the laws of this state; or

(b) The state board of professional engineers and land surveyors certifies that the corporation is exempt from the prohibitions of NRS 625.520.

4. The secretary of state shall not accept for filing any articles of incorporation or any certificate of amendment of articles of incorporation of any corporation formed pursuant to the laws of this state which provides that the name of the corporation contains the words "accountant," "accounting," "accountancy," "auditor" or "auditing" unless the Nevada state board of accountancy certifies that the corporation:

(a) Is registered pursuant to the provisions of chapter 628 of NRS; or

(b) Has filed with the state board of accountancy under penalty of perjury a written statement that the corporation is not engaged in the practice of accounting and is not offering to practice accounting in this state.

5. The provisions of subsection 3 do not apply to any corporation, whose securities are publicly traded and regulated by the Securities Exchange Act of 1934, which does not engage in the practice of professional engineering.

6. The commissioner of financial institutions and the commissioner of insurance may approve or disapprove the articles or amendments referred to them pursuant to the provisions of this section.

[4.5:177:1925; added 1949, 520; 1943 NCL § 1603.1]—(NRS A 1977, 1056; 1979, 1102; 1983, 467, 1696; 1987, 1873; 1993, 128; 1995, 1112; 1997, 1058; 1999, 1706, 2441)

NRS 78.050 Commencement of corporate existence.

1. Upon the filing of the articles of incorporation and the certificate of acceptance pursuant to NRS 78.030, and the payment of the filing fees, the secretary of state shall issue to the corporation a certificate that the articles, containing the required statement of facts, have been filed. From the date the articles are filed, the corporation is a body corporate, by the name set forth in the articles of incorporation, subject to the forfeiture of its charter or dissolution as provided in this chapter.

2. Neither an incorporator nor a director designated in the articles of incorporation thereby becomes a subscriber or stockholder of the corporation.

3. The filing of the articles of incorporation does not, by itself, constitute commencement of business by the corporation.

[Part 5:177:1925; NCL § 1604]—(NRS A 1989, 948; 1991, 1211; 1993, 946)

NRS 78.055 Acceptable evidence of incorporation. A copy of any articles of incorporation filed pursuant to this chapter, and certified by the secretary of state under his official seal, or, with respect to a corporation organized before October 1, 1991, a copy of the copy thereof, filed with the county clerk, or microfilmed by the county clerk, under the county seal, certified by the clerk, must be received in all courts and places as prima facie evidence of the facts therein stated, and of the existence and incorporation of the corporation therein named.

[Part 5:177:1925; NCL § 1604]—(NRS A 1963, 70; 1991, 1211)

POWERS

NRS **78.060** General powers.

1. Any corporation organized under the provisions of this chapter:

(a) Has all the rights, privileges and powers conferred by this chapter.

(b) Has such rights, privileges and powers as may be conferred upon corporations by any other existing law.

(c) May at any time exercise those rights, privileges and powers, when not inconsistent with the provisions of this chapter, or with the purposes and objects for which the corporation is organized.

(d) Unless otherwise provided in its articles, has perpetual existence.

2. Every corporation, by virtue of its existence as such, is entitled:

(a) To have succession by its corporate name until dissolved and its affairs are wound up according to law.

(b) To sue and be sued in any court of law or equity.

(c) To make contracts.

(d) To hold, purchase and convey real and personal estate and to mortgage or lease any such real and personal estate with its franchises. The power to hold real and personal estate includes the power to take it by devise or bequest in this state, or in any other state, territory or country.

(e) To appoint such officers and agents as the affairs of the corporation require, and to allow them suitable compensation.

(f) To make bylaws not inconsistent with the constitution or laws of the United States, or of this state, for the management, regulation and government of its affairs and property, the transfer of its stock, the transaction of its business, and the calling and holding of meetings of its stockholders.

(g) To wind up and dissolve itself, or be wound up or dissolved, in the manner mentioned in this chapter.

(h) Unless otherwise provided in the articles, to engage in any lawful activity.

[Part 8:177:1925; NCL § 1607] + [91:177:1925; NCL § 1690]— (NRS A 1969, 99; 1991, 1211)

NRS **78.065** Adoption and use of corporate seal or stamp.

1. Every corporation, by virtue of its existence as such, shall have power to adopt and use a common seal or stamp, and alter the same at pleasure.

2. The use of a seal or stamp by a corporation on any corporate documents is not necessary. The corporation may use a seal or stamp, if it desires, but such use or nonuse shall not in any way affect the legality of the document.

[Part 8:177:1925; NCL § 1607] + [85:177:1925; A 1953, 180]— (NRS A 1967, 102; 1971, 1100)

NRS **78.070** Specific powers.
Subject to such limitations, if any, as may be contained in its articles of incorporation, every corporation has the following powers:

1. To borrow money and contract debts when necessary for the transaction of its business, or for the exercise of its corporate rights, privileges or franchises, or for any other lawful purpose of its incorporation; to issue bonds, promissory notes, bills of exchange, debentures, and other obligations and evidences of indebtedness, payable at a specified time or times, or payable upon the happening of a specified event or events, whether secured by mortgage, pledge or other security, or unsecured, for money borrowed, or in payment for property purchased, or acquired, or for any other lawful object.

2. To guarantee, purchase, hold, take, obtain, receive, subscribe for, own, use, dispose of, sell, exchange, lease, lend, assign, mortgage, pledge, or otherwise acquire, transfer or deal in or with bonds or obligations of, or shares, securities or interests in or issued by, any person, government, governmental agency or political subdivision of government, and to exercise all the rights, powers and privileges of ownership of such an interest, including the right to vote, if any.

3. To purchase, hold, sell, pledge and transfer shares of its own stock, and use therefor its property or money.

4. To conduct business, have one or more offices, and hold, purchase, mortgage and convey real and personal property in this state, and in any of the several states, territories, possessions and dependencies of the United States, the District of Columbia, Puerto Rico and any foreign countries.

5. To do everything necessary and proper for the accomplishment of the objects enumerated in its articles of incorporation or necessary or incidental to the protection and benefit of the corporation, and, in general, to carry on any lawful business necessary or incidental to the attainment of the objects of the corporation, whether or not the business is similar in nature to the objects set forth in the articles of incorporation, except that:

(a) A corporation created under the provisions of this chapter does not possess the power of issuing bills, notes or other evidences of debt for circulation of money; and

(b) This chapter does not authorize the formation of banking corporations to issue or circulate money or currency within this state, or outside of this state, or at all, except the federal currency, or the notes of banks authorized under the laws of the United States.

6. To make donations for the public welfare or for charitable, scientific or educational purposes.

7. To enter into any relationship with another person in connection with any lawful activities.

[9:177:1925; A 1931, 415; 1949, 158; 1953, 180]—(NRS A 1959, 690; 1963, 1146; 1969, 117; 1987, 576; 1991, 1212; 1993, 947; 1997, 696)

NRS **78.075** Railroad companies: Powers.
In furtherance of and in addition to the powers which railroad companies organized under this chapter are entitled to exercise, but not in limitation of any of the powers granted by this chapter, every railroad company may:

1. Cause such examination and surveys for the proposed railroad to be made as may be necessary to the selection of the most advantageous route for the railroad, and for such purposes, by their officers, agents and employees, to enter upon the lands or waters of any persons, but subject to responsibility for all damages which they do thereto.

2. Receive, hold, take and convey, by deed or otherwise, as a natural person might or could do, such voluntary grants and donations of real estate, and other property of every description, as may be made to it to aid and encourage the construction, maintenance and accommodation of the railroad.

3. Purchase, and by voluntary grants and donations receive and take, and by its officers, engineers, surveyors and agents, enter upon and take possession of, and hold and use, in any manner they may deem proper, all such lands and real estate, and

other property as the directors may deem necessary and proper for the construction and maintenance of the railroad, and for the stations, depots and other accommodations and purposes, deemed necessary to accomplish the object for which the corporation is formed.

4. Lay out its road or roads, not exceeding 200 feet wide, and construct and maintain the road with such tracks and with such appendages as may be deemed necessary for the convenient use of it. The company may make embankments, excavations, ditches, drains, culverts or otherwise, and procure timber, stone and gravel, or other materials, and may take as much more land, whenever they may think proper, as may be necessary for the purposes aforesaid, in the manner hereinafter provided, for the proper construction and security of the road.

5. Construct their road across, along or upon any stream of water, watercourse, roadstead, bay, navigable stream, street, avenue or highway, or across any railway, canal, ditch or flume which the route of its road intersects, crosses or runs along, in such manner as to afford security for life and property. The corporation shall restore the stream or watercourse, road, street, avenue, highway, railroad, canal, ditch or flume thus intersected to its former state, as near as may be, or in a sufficient manner not to have impaired unnecessarily its usefulness or injured its franchises.

6. Cross, intersect, join and unite its railroad with any other railroad, either before or after constructed, at any point upon its route, and upon the grounds of such other railroad company, with the necessary turnouts, sidings and switches, and other conveniences, in furtherance of the objects of its connections; and every company whose railroad is, or will be hereafter, intersected by any new railroad in forming such intersections and connection, and grant the facilities aforesaid. If the two corporations cannot agree upon the amount of compensation to be made therefor, or the points or the manner of such crossings, intersections and connections, the same must be ascertained and determined by commissioners, to be appointed as is provided hereinafter in respect to the taking of lands, but this section is not to affect the rights and franchises heretofore granted.

7. Purchase lands, timber, stone, gravel or other materials to be used in the construction and maintenance of its road, or take them in the manner provided by this chapter. The railroad company may change the line of its road, in whole or in part, whenever a majority of the directors determine, as is provided hereinafter, but no such change may vary the general route of a road, as contemplated in the articles of incorporation of the company.

8. Receive by purchase, donation or otherwise, any lands, or other property, of any description, and hold and convey it in any manner the directors may think proper, the same as natural persons might or could do, that may be necessary for the construction and maintenance of its road, or for the erection of depots, turnouts, workshops, warehouses or for any other purposes necessary for the convenience of railroad companies, in order to transact the business usual for railroad companies.

9. Take, transport, carry and convey persons and property on their railroad, by the force and power of steam, of animals, or any mechanical power, or by any combinations of them, and receive tolls or compensation therefor.

10. Erect and maintain all necessary and convenient buildings, stations, depots and fixtures and machinery for the accommodation and use of their passengers, freight and business, obtain and hold the lands and other property necessary therefor, and acquire additional lands and rights of way and build and operate extensions or branches of its line of railroad.

11. Regulate the time and manner in which passengers and property are transported, and the tolls and compensation to be paid therefor, within the limits prescribed by law.

12. Regulate the force and speed of their locomotives, cars, trains or other machinery used and employed on their road, and establish, execute and enforce all needful and proper rules and regulations fully and completely for the management of its business transactions usual and proper for railroad companies.

13. Purchase, hold, sell and transfer shares of its own stock, bonds, debentures, or other securities issued by it, except that:

(a) No corporation may use its funds or property for the purchase of its own shares of stock when such use would cause any impairment of the capital of the corporation; and

(b) Shares of its own stock belonging to the corporation must not be voted upon, directly or indirectly, nor counted as outstanding for the purpose of any stockholders' quorum or vote.

14. Acquire, own, and operate motor vehicles, and air transportation facilities, and transport persons and property along and over the streets and highways of this state, for the transportation, for hire, of passengers, property and freight, either directly or through a subsidiary company or companies, subject to all relevant provisions of law concerning permits, licenses, franchises and the regulation of such form of transportation by motor vehicles or other agencies.

Whenever the track of a railroad crosses a railroad or highway, such railroad or highway may be carried under, over or on a level with the track, as may be most expedient, and in cases where an embankment or cutting makes a change in the line of such railroad or highway desirable, with a view to a more easy ascent or descent, the company may take such additional lands and materials, if needed for the construction of such road or highway, on such new line, as may be deemed requisite by the railroad. Unless the lands and materials so taken are purchased, or voluntarily given for the purpose aforesaid, compensation therefor must be ascertained in the manner provided by law.

[9(a):177:1925; added 1945, 196; 1943 NCL § 1608.01]—(NRS A 1993, 2762)

NRS 78.080 Railroad companies: Rights of way granted by the state, counties and municipalities; limitations; reversion on abandonment; duties of companies.

1. The right of way is hereby given and granted to all railroad companies that are now organized, or may be organized under the provisions of this chapter, or under the laws of any other state or territory, or under any act of Congress, to locate, construct and maintain their roads, or any part or parcel thereof, over and through any of the swamp or overflowed lands belonging to this state, or any other public lands which are now or may be the property of the state, at the time of constructing the railroad.

2. Such railroad companies are hereby authorized to survey and mark through the lands of the state, to be held by them for the track of their respective railroads, 200 feet in width, for the whole length the roads may be located over the lands of the state; and the right is hereby further given and granted to the companies to locate, occupy and hold all necessary sites and grounds for watering places, depots or other buildings, for the convenient use of the same, along the line of the road or roads, so far as the places convenient for the same may fall upon the lands belonging to the state, except within the limits of any incorporated city or town, or within 3 miles where the same shall be taken, on paying to the state the value of the same.

3. No one depot, watering place, machine or workshop, or other buildings for the convenient use of such roads, shall cover over 6 acres each, and the sites or places on the lands of this state shall not be nearer to

each other than 5 miles along the line of the roads.

4. The right is hereby further given and granted to the companies to take from any of the lands belonging to this state all such materials of earth, wood, stone or other materials whatever, as may be necessary or convenient, from time to time, for the first construction or equipment of the road or roads, or any part thereof.

5. If any road, at any time after its location, shall be discontinued or abandoned by the company or companies, or the location of any part thereof be so changed as not to cover the lands of the state thus previously occupied, then the lands so abandoned or left shall revert to this state.

6. When the location of the route of either of the railroads, or sites or places for depots, watering places, machine or workshops or other buildings for the convenient use of the same, shall be selected, the secretary of the company shall transmit to the director of the state department of conservation and natural resources, and to the state controller, and to the recorder of the county in which the lands so selected are situated, to each of the officers, a correct plot of the location of the railroad, or sites or places, before such selection shall become operative.

7. When any such company shall, for its purposes aforesaid, require any of the lands belonging to any of the counties, cities or towns in this state, the county, city and town officers, respectively, having charge of such lands, may grant and convey such land to such company, for a compensation which shall be agreed upon between them, or may donate and convey the same without any compensation; and if they shall not agree upon the sale and price, the same may be taken by the company as is provided in other cases of taking lands by condemnation.

8. Before any corporation incorporated or organized otherwise than under the laws of this state shall be entitled to any of the rights granted by this chapter, it shall file in the office of the county recorder of each county in which the railroad, or any part, extension or branch thereof shall be situate, a copy of its certificate or articles of incorporation, or of the act or law by which it was created, with the certified list of its officers, in the manner and form required by law.

[9(b):177:1925; added 1945, 196; 1943 NCL § 1608.02]—(NRS A 1957, 653)

NRS 78.085 **Railroad companies: Filing of certified maps and profiles.**

1. Every railroad company in this state shall, within 90 days after its road is finally located:

(a) Cause to be made a map and profile thereof, and of the land taken and obtained for the use thereof, and the boundaries of the several counties through which the road may run;

(b) File the same in the office of the secretary of state and a duplicate thereof with the public utilities commission of Nevada; and

(c) Cause to be made like maps of the parts thereof located in different counties, and file the same in the office of the recorder of the county in which such parts of the road are located.

2. The maps and profiles must be certified by the chief engineer, the acting president, and secretary of such company and copies of the same, so certified and filed as required by subsection 1, must be kept in the office of the company, subject to examination by all interested persons.

[9(d):177:1925; added 1945, 196; 1943 NCL § 1608.04]—(NRS A 1997, 1963)

REGISTERED OFFICE AND RESIDENT AGENT

NRS 78.090 **Resident agent required; address of registered office; powers of bank or corporation who is resident agent; penalty for noncompliance; service of documents on resident agent.**

1. Except during any period of vacancy described in NRS 78.097, every corporation must have a resident agent who resides or is located in this state. Every resident agent must have a street address for the service of process, and may have a separate mailing address such as a post office box, which may be different from the street address. The street address of the resident agent is the registered office of the corporation in this state.

2. If the resident agent is a bank or corporation, it may:

(a) Act as the fiscal or transfer agent of any state, municipality, body politic or corporation and in that capacity may receive and disburse money.

(b) Transfer, register and countersign certificates of stock, bonds or other evidences of indebtedness and act as agent of any corporation, foreign or domestic, for any purpose required by statute, or otherwise.

(c) Act as trustee under any mortgage or bond issued by any municipality, body politic or corporation, and accept and execute any other municipal or corporate trust not inconsistent with the laws of this state.

(d) Receive and manage any sinking fund of any corporation, upon such terms as may be agreed upon between the corporation and those dealing with it.

3. Every corporation organized pursuant to this chapter which fails or refuses to comply with the requirements of this section is subject to a fine of not less than $100 nor more than $500, to be recovered with costs by the state, before any court of competent jurisdiction, by action at law prosecuted by the attorney general or by the district attorney of the county in which the action or proceeding to recover the fine is prosecuted.

4. All legal process and any demand or notice authorized by law to be served upon a corporation may be served upon the resident agent of the corporation in the manner provided in subsection 2 of NRS 14.020. If any demand, notice or legal process, other than a summons and complaint, cannot be served upon the resident agent, it may be served in the manner provided in NRS 14.030. These manners and modes of service are in addition to any other service authorized by law.

[78:177:1925; A 1929, 413; NCL § 1677] + [Part 79:177:1925; NCL § 1678]—(NRS A 1959, 682; 1969, 571; 1987, 1057; 1989, 949, 975, 1971; 1991, 1213; 1993, 948; 1995, 2095)

NRS 78.095 **Change of address of resident agent and registered office.**

1. Within 30 days after changing the location of his office from one address to another in this state, a resident agent shall execute a certificate setting forth:

(a) The names of all the corporations represented by the resident agent;

(b) The address at which the resident agent has maintained the registered office for each of such corporations; and

(c) The new address to which the resident agency will be transferred and at which the resident agent will thereafter maintain the registered office for each of the corporations recited in the certificate.

2. Upon the filing of the certificate in the office of the secretary of state the registered office in this state of each of the corporations recited in the certificate is located at the new address of the resident agent thereof as set forth in the certificate.

[1:17:1931; 1931 NCL § 1677.01]—(NRS A 1983, 261;

1989, 871; 1991, 1214; 1993, 948; 1995, 1112)

NRS 78.097 Resignation of resident agent; notice to corporation of resignation; appointment of successor.

1. A resident agent who desires to resign shall file with the secretary of state a signed statement for each corporation that he is unwilling to continue to act as the agent of the corporation for the service of process. A resignation is not effective until the signed statement is filed with the secretary of state.

2. The statement of resignation may contain a statement of the affected corporation appointing a successor resident agent for that corporation. A certificate of acceptance executed by the new resident agent, stating the full name, complete street address and, if different from the street address, mailing address of the new resident agent, must accompany the statement appointing a successor resident agent.

3. Upon the filing of the statement of resignation with the secretary of state the capacity of the resigning person as resident agent terminates. If the statement of resignation contains no statement by the corporation appointing a successor resident agent, the resigning resident agent shall immediately give written notice, by mail, to the corporation of the filing of the statement and its effect. The notice must be addressed to any officer of the corporation other than the resident agent.

4. If a resident agent dies, resigns or removes from the state, the corporation, within 30 days thereafter, shall file with the secretary of state a certificate of acceptance executed by the new resident agent. The certificate must set forth the full name and complete street address of the new resident agent for the service of process, and may have a separate mailing address, such as post office box, which may be different from the street address.

5. A corporation that fails to file a certificate of acceptance executed by the new resident agent within 30 days after the death, resignation or removal of its former resident agent shall be deemed in default and is subject to the provisions of NRS 78.170 and 78.175.

(Added to NRS by 1959, 681; A 1967, 89; 1969, 11; 1989, 949; 1991, 1214; 1993, 949; 1999, 1579)

NRS 78.105 Maintenance of records at registered office; inspection and copying of records; civil liability; penalties.

1. A corporation shall keep a copy of the following records at its registered office:

(a) A copy certified by the secretary of state of its articles of incorporation, and all amendments thereto;

(b) A copy certified by an officer of the corporation of its bylaws and all amendments thereto; and

(c) A stock ledger or a duplicate stock ledger, revised annually, containing the names, alphabetically arranged, of all persons who are stockholders of the corporation, showing their places of residence, if known, and the number of shares held by them respectively. In lieu of the stock ledger or duplicate stock ledger, the corporation may keep a statement setting out the name of the custodian of the stock ledger or duplicate stock ledger, and the present and complete post office address, including street and number, if any, where the stock ledger or duplicate stock ledger specified in this section is kept.

2. A corporation shall maintain the records required by subsection 1 in written form or in another form capable of conversion into written form within a reasonable time.

3. Any person who has been a stockholder of record of a corporation for at least 6 months immediately preceding his demand, or any person holding, or thereunto authorized in writing by the holders of, at least 5 percent of all of its outstanding shares, upon at least 5 days' written demand is entitled to inspect in person or by agent or attorney, during usual business hours, the records required by subsection 1 and make copies therefrom. Holders of voting trust certificates representing shares of the corporation must be regarded as stockholders for the purpose of this subsection. Every corporation that neglects or refuses to keep the records required by subsection 1 open for inspection, as required in this subsection, shall forfeit to the state the sum of $25 for every day of such neglect or refusal.

4. If any corporation willfully neglects or refuses to make any proper entry in the stock ledger or duplicate copy thereof, or neglects or refuses to permit an inspection of the records required by subsection 1 upon demand by a person entitled to inspect them, or refuses to permit copies to be made therefrom, as provided in subsection 3, the corporation is liable to the person injured for all damages resulting to him therefrom.

5. When the corporation keeps a statement in the manner provided for in paragraph (c) of subsection 1, the information contained thereon must be given to any stockholder of the corporation demanding the information, when the demand is made during business hours. Every corporation that neglects or refuses to keep a statement available, as in this subsection required, shall forfeit to the state the sum of $25 for every day of such neglect or refusal.

6. In every instance where an attorney or other agent of the stockholder seeks the right of inspection, the demand must be accompanied by a power of attorney executed by the stockholder authorizing the attorney or other agent to inspect on behalf of the stockholder.

7. The right to copy records under subsection 3 includes, if reasonable, the right to make copies by photographic, xerographic or other means.

8. The corporation may impose a reasonable charge to recover the costs of labor and materials and the cost of copies of any documents provided to the stockholder.

[80:177:1925; A 1951, 332]— (NRS A 1959, 29; 1963, 217; 1965, 978; 1991, 1214; 1997, 697)

NRS 78.107 Denial of request for inspection of records; defense to action for penalties or damages; authority of court to compel production of records.

1. An inspection authorized by NRS 78.105 may be denied to a stockholder or other person upon his refusal to furnish to the corporation an affidavit that the inspection is not desired for a purpose which is in the interest of a business or object other than the business of the corporation and that he has not at any time sold or offered for sale any list of stockholders of any domestic or foreign corporation or aided or abetted any person in procuring any such record of stockholders for any such purpose.

2. It is a defense to any action for penalties or damages under NRS 78.105 that the person suing has at any time sold, or offered for sale, any list of stockholders of the corporation, or any other corporation, or has aided or abetted any person in procuring any such stock list for any such purpose, or that the person suing desired inspection for a purpose which is in the interest of a business or object other than the business of the corporation.

3. This section does not impair the power or jurisdiction of any court to compel the production for examination of the books of a corporation in any proper case.

(Added to NRS by 1997, 693)

NRS 78.110 Change of resident agent.

1. If a corporation created pursuant to this chapter desires to change its resident agent, the change may be effected by filing with the secretary of state a certificate of

change signed by an officer of the corporation which sets forth:

(a) The name of the corporation;

(b) The name and street address of its present resident agent; and

(c) The name and street address of the new resident agent.

2. The new resident agent's certificate of acceptance must be a part of or attached to the certificate of change.

3. A change authorized by this section becomes effective upon the filing of the certificate of change.

[89:177:1925; NCL § 1688]— (NRS A 1959, 683; 1989, 950; 1991, 1216; 1995, 2096; 1999, 1579)

DIRECTORS AND OFFICERS

NRS 78.115 Board of directors: Number and qualifications. The business of every corporation must be managed by a board of directors or trustees, all of whom must be natural persons who are at least 18 years of age. A corporation must have at least one director, and may provide in its articles of incorporation or in its bylaws for a fixed number of directors or a variable number of directors within a fixed minimum and maximum, and for the manner in which the number of directors may be increased or decreased. Unless otherwise provided in the articles of incorporation, directors need not be stockholders.

[Part 31:177:1925; NCL § 1630]—(NRS A 1965, 1012; 1981, 384; 1987, 577; 1993, 949; 1995, 1113)

NRS 78.120 Board of directors: General powers.

1. Subject only to such limitations as may be provided by this chapter, or the articles of incorporation of the corporation, the board of directors has full control over the affairs of the corporation.

2. Subject to the bylaws, if any, adopted by the stockholders, the directors may make the bylaws of the corporation.

3. The selection of a period for the achievement of corporate goals is the responsibility of the directors.

[Part 31:177:1925; NCL § 1630]—(NRS A 1991, 1217)

NRS 78.125 Committees of board of directors: Designation; powers; names; membership.

1. Unless it is otherwise provided in the articles of incorporation, the board of directors may designate one or more committees which, to the extent provided in the resolution or resolutions or in the bylaws of the corporation, have and may exercise the powers of the board of directors in the management of the business and affairs of the corporation, and may have power to authorize the seal of the corporation to be affixed to all papers on which the corporation desires to place a seal.

2. The committee or committees must have such name or names as may be stated in the bylaws of the corporation or as may be determined from time to time by resolution adopted by the board of directors.

3. Each committee must include at least one director. Unless the articles of incorporation or the bylaws provide otherwise, the board of directors may appoint natural persons who are not directors to serve on committees.

[32:177:1925; A 1929, 413; NCL § 1631]—(NRS A 1971, 1100; 1991, 1217; 1993, 949)

NRS 78.130 Officers of corporation: Selection; qualifications; terms; powers and duties; filling of vacancies.

1. Every corporation must have a president, a secretary and a treasurer.

2. Every corporation may also have one or more vice presidents, assistant secretaries and assistant treasurers, and such other officers and agents as may be deemed necessary.

3. All officers must be natural persons and must be chosen in such manner, hold their offices for such terms and have such powers and duties as may be prescribed by the bylaws or determined by the board of directors. Any natural person may hold two or more offices.

4. An officer holds office after the expiration of his term until a successor is chosen or until his resignation or removal before the expiration of his term. A failure to elect officers does not require the corporation to be dissolved. Any vacancy occurring in an office of the corporation by death, resignation, removal or otherwise, must be filled as the bylaws provide, or in the absence of such a provision, by the board of directors.

[36:177:1925; A 1937, 291; 1931 NCL § 1635]—(NRS A 1960, 152; 1991, 1217; 1993, 950)

NRS 78.135 Authority of directors and representatives of corporation.

1. The statement in the articles of incorporation of the objects, purposes, powers and authorized business of the corporation constitutes, as between the corporation and its directors, officers or stockholders, an authorization to the directors and a limitation upon the actual authority of the representatives of the corporation. Such limitations may be asserted in a proceeding by a stockholder or the state to enjoin the doing or continuation of unauthorized business by the corporation or its officers, or both, in cases where third parties have not acquired rights thereby, or to dissolve the corporation, or in a proceeding by the corporation or by the stockholders suing in a representative suit against the officers or directors of the corporation for violation of their authority.

2. No limitation upon the business, purposes or powers of the corporation or upon the powers of the stockholders, officers or directors, or the manner of exercise of such powers, contained in or implied by the articles may be asserted as between the corporation or any stockholder and any third person.

3. Any contract or conveyance, otherwise lawful, made in the name of a corporation, which is authorized or ratified by the directors, or is done within the scope of the authority, actual or apparent, given by the directors, binds the corporation, and the corporation acquires rights thereunder, whether the contract is executed or is wholly or in part executory.

[Part 31(a):177:1925; added 1949, 158; 1943 NCL § 1630.01]— (NRS A 1961, 94; 1993, 950)

NRS 78.138 Directors and officers: Exercise of powers, performance of duties, presumptions and considerations.

1. Directors and officers shall exercise their powers in good faith and with a view to the interests of the corporation.

2. In performing their respective duties, directors and officers are entitled to rely on information, opinions, reports, books of account or statements, including financial statements and other financial data, that are prepared or presented by:

(a) One or more directors, officers or employees of the corporation reasonably believed to be reliable and competent in the matters prepared or presented;

(b) Counsel, public accountants, or other persons as to matters reasonably believed to be within the preparer's or presenter's professional or expert competence; or

(c) A committee on which the director or officer relying thereon does not serve, established in accordance with NRS 78.125, as to matters within the committee's designated authority and matters on which the committee is reasonably believed to merit confidence,

but a director or officer is not entitled to rely on such information, opinions, reports, books of account or statements if he has knowledge concerning the matter in question that would cause reliance thereon to be unwarranted.

3. Directors and officers, in deciding upon matters of business, are presumed to act in good faith, on an informed basis and with a view to the interests of the corporation.

4. Directors and officers, in exercising their respective powers with a view to the interests of the corporation, may consider:

(a) The interests of the corporation's employees, suppliers, creditors and customers;

(b) The economy of the state and nation;

(c) The interests of the community and of society; and

(d) The long-term as well as short-term interests of the corporation and its stockholders, including the possibility that these interests may be best served by the continued independence of the corporation.

5. Directors and officers are not required to consider the effect of a proposed corporate action upon any particular group having an interest in the corporation as a dominant factor.

6. The provisions of subsections 4 and 5 do not create or authorize any causes of action against the corporation or its directors or officers.

(Added to NRS by 1991, 1184; A 1993, 951; 1999, 1580)

NRS 78.139 Directors and officers: Duties, presumptions and powers when confronted with change or potential change in control of corporation.

1. Except as otherwise provided in subsection 2 or the articles of incorporation, directors and officers confronted with a change or potential change in control of the corporation have:

(a) The duties imposed upon them by subsection 1 of NRS 78.138; and

(b) The benefit of the presumptions established by subsection 3 of that section.

2. If directors and officers take action to resist a change or potential change in control of a corporation which impedes the exercise of the right of stockholders to vote for or remove directors:

(a) The directors must have reasonable grounds to believe that a threat to corporate policy and effectiveness exists; and

(b) The action taken which impedes the exercise of the stockholders' rights must be reasonable in relation to that threat.

If those facts are found, the directors and officers have the benefit of the presumption established by subsection 3 of NRS 78.138.

3. The provisions of subsection 2 do not apply to:

(a) Actions that only affect the time of the exercise of stockholders' voting rights; or

(b) The adoption or execution of plans, arrangements or instruments that deny rights, privileges, power or authority to a holder of a specified number or fraction of shares or fraction of voting power.

4. The provisions of subsections 2 and 3 do not permit directors or officers to abrogate any right conferred by statute or the articles of incorporation.

5. Directors may resist a change or potential change in control of the corporation if the directors by a majority vote of a quorum determine that the change or potential change is opposed to or not in the best interest of the corporation:

(a) Upon consideration of the interests of the corporation's stockholders and any of the matters set forth in subsection 4 of NRS 78.138; or

(b) Because the amount or nature of the indebtedness and other obligations to which the corporation or any successor to the property of either may become subject, in connection with the change or potential change in control, provides reasonable grounds to believe that, within a reasonable time:

(1) The assets of the corporation or any successor would be or become less than its liabilities;

(2) The corporation or any successor would be or become insolvent; or

(3) Any voluntary or involuntary proceeding pursuant to the federal bankruptcy laws concerning the corporation or any successor would be commenced by any person.

(Added to NRS by 1999, 1575)

NRS 78.140 Restrictions on transactions involving interested directors or officers; compensation of directors.

1. A contract or other transaction is not void or voidable solely because:

(a) The contract or transaction is between a corporation and:

(1) One or more of its directors or officers; or

(2) Another corporation, firm or association in which one or more of its directors or officers are directors or officers or are financially interested;

(b) A common or interested director or officer:

(1) Is present at the meeting of the board of directors or a committee thereof

which authorizes or approves the contract or transaction; or

(2) Joins in the execution of a written consent which authorizes or approves the contract or transaction pursuant to subsection 2 of NRS 78.315; or

(c) The vote or votes of a common or interested director are counted for the purpose of authorizing or approving the contract or transaction,

if one of the circumstances specified in subsection 2 exists.

2. The circumstances in which a contract or other transaction is not void or voidable pursuant to subsection 1 are:

(a) The fact of the common directorship, office or financial interest is known to the board of directors or committee, and the board or committee authorizes, approves or ratifies the contract or transaction in good faith by a vote sufficient for the purpose without counting the vote or votes of the common or interested director or directors.

(b) The fact of the common directorship, office or financial interest is known to the stockholders, and they approve or ratify the contract or transaction in good faith by a majority vote of stockholders holding a majority of the voting power. The votes of the common or interested directors or officers must be counted in any such vote of stockholders.

(c) The fact of the common directorship, office or financial interest is not known to the director or officer at the time the transaction is brought before the board of directors of the corporation for action.

(d) The contract or transaction is fair as to the corporation at the time it is authorized or approved.

3. Common or interested directors may be counted in determining the presence of a quorum at a meeting of the board of directors or a committee thereof which authorizes, approves or ratifies a contract or transaction, and if the votes of the common or interested directors are not counted at the meeting, then a majority of the disinterested directors may authorize, approve or ratify a contract or transaction.

4. Unless otherwise provided in the articles of incorporation or the bylaws, the board of directors, without regard to personal interest, may establish the compensation of directors for services in any capacity. If the board of directors establishes the compensation of directors pursuant to this subsection, such compensation is presumed to be fair to the corporation unless proven unfair by a preponderance of the evidence.

[31(b):177:1925; added 1951, 328]—(NRS A 1959, 683; 1969, 113; 1989, 872; 1991, 1218; 1993, 952; 1997, 698)

ANNUAL LIST OF OFFICERS AND DIRECTORS; DEFAULTING CORPORATIONS

NRS 78.150 Filing requirements; fee; forms. [Effective through June 30, 2000.]

1. A corporation organized under the laws of this state shall, on or before the first day of the second month after the filing of its articles of incorporation with the secretary of state, file with the secretary of state a list, on a form furnished by him, containing:

(a) The name of the corporation;

(b) The file number of the corporation, if known;

(c) The names and titles of the president, secretary, treasurer and of all the directors of the corporation;

(d) The mailing or street address, either residence or business, of each officer and director listed, following the name of the officer or director; and

(e) The signature of an officer of the corporation certifying that the list is true, complete and accurate.

2. The corporation shall annually thereafter, on or before the last day of the month in which the anniversary date of incorporation occurs in each year, file with the secretary of state, on a form furnished by him, an amended list containing all of the information required in subsection 1.

3. Upon filing a list of officers and directors, the corporation shall pay to the secretary of state a fee of $85.

4. The secretary of state shall, 60 days before the last day for filing the annual list required by subsection 2, cause to be mailed to each corporation which is required to comply with the provisions of NRS 78.150 to 78.185, inclusive, and which has not become delinquent, a notice of the fee due pursuant to subsection 3 and a reminder to file a list of officers and directors. Failure of any corporation to receive a notice or form does not excuse it from the penalty imposed by law.

5. If the list to be filed pursuant to the provisions of subsection 1 or 2 is defective in any respect or the fee required by subsection 3 or 7 is not paid, the secretary of state may return the list for correction or payment.

6. An annual list for a corporation not in default which is received by the secretary of state more than 60 days before its due date shall be deemed an amended list for the previous year and does not satisfy the requirements of subsection 2 for the year to which the due date is applicable.

7. If the corporation is an association as defined in NRS 116.110315, the secretary of state shall not accept the filing required by this section unless it is accompanied by the fee required to be paid pursuant to NRS 116.31155.

[Part 1:180:1925; A 1929, 122; 1931, 408; 1931 NCL § 1804]—(NRS A 1957, 315; 1959, 684; 1977, 401; 1979, 185; 1983, 689; 1985, 233; 1989, 976; 1991, 2460; 1993, 952; 1995, 2096; 1997, 2808, 3126; 1999, 639, 1581)

NRS 78.150 Filing requirements; fee; forms. [Effective July 1, 2000.]

1. A corporation organized under the laws of this state shall, on or before the first day of the second month after the filing of its articles of incorporation with the secretary of state, file with the secretary of state a list, on a form furnished by him, containing:

(a) The name of the corporation;

(b) The file number of the corporation, if known;

(c) The names and titles of the president, secretary, treasurer and of all the directors of the corporation;

(d) The mailing or street address, either residence or business, of each officer and director listed, following the name of the officer or director; and

(e) The signature of an officer of the corporation certifying that the list is true, complete and accurate.

2. The corporation shall annually thereafter, on or before the last day of the month in which the anniversary date of incorporation occurs in each year, file with the secretary of state, on a form furnished by him, an amended list containing all of the information required in subsection 1.

3. Upon filing a list of officers and directors, the corporation shall pay to the secretary of state a fee of $85.

4. The secretary of state shall, 60 days before the last day for filing the annual list required by subsection 2, cause to be mailed to each corporation which is required to comply with the provisions of NRS 78.150 to 78.185, inclusive, and which has not become delinquent, a notice of the fee due pursuant to subsection 3 and a reminder to file a list of officers and directors. Failure of any corporation to receive a notice or form does not excuse it from the penalty imposed by law.

5. If the list to be filed pursuant to the provisions of subsection 1 or 2 is defective in any respect or the fee required by subsection 3 or 7 is not paid, the secretary of state may return the list for correction or payment.

6. An annual list for a corporation not in default which is received by the secretary of state more than 60 days before its due date shall be deemed an amended list for the previous year and does not satisfy the requirements of subsection 2 for the year to which the due date is applicable.

7. If the corporation is an association as defined in NRS 116.110315, the secretary of state shall not accept the filing required by this section unless it is accompanied by evidence of the payment of the fee required to be paid pursuant to NRS 116.31155 that is provided to the association pursuant to subsection 4 of that section.

[Part 1:180:1925; A 1929, 122; 1931, 408; 1931 NCL § 1804]—(NRS A 1957, 315; 1959, 684; 1977, 401; 1979, 185; 1983, 689; 1985, 233; 1989, 976; 1991, 2460; 1993, 952; 1995, 2096; 1997, 2808, 3126; 1999, 639, 1581, 3018, effective July 1, 2000)

NRS 78.155 Certificate of authorization to transact business. If a corporation has filed the initial or annual list of officers and directors and designation of resident agent in compliance with NRS 78.150 and has paid the appropriate fee for the filing, the canceled check received by the corporation constitutes a certificate authorizing it to transact its business within this state until the last day of the month in which the anniversary of its incorporation occurs in the next succeeding calendar year. If the corporation desires a formal certificate upon its payment of the initial or annual fee, its payment must be accompanied by a self-addressed, stamped envelope.

[2:180:1925; A 1931, 408; 1931 NCL § 1805]—(NRS A 1959, 684; 1981, 62; 1983, 689; 1993, 953; 1999, 1582)

NRS 78.165 Addresses of officers and directors required; failure to file.

1. Every list required to be filed under the provisions of NRS 78.150 to 78.185, inclusive, must, after the name of each officer and director listed thereon, set forth the post office box or street address, either residence or business, of each officer and director.

2. If the addresses are not stated for each person on any list offered for filing, the secretary of state may refuse to file the list, and the corporation for which the list has

been offered for filing is subject to all the provisions of NRS 78.150 to 78.185, inclusive, relating to failure to file the list within or at the times therein specified, unless a list is subsequently submitted for filing which conforms to the provisions of NRS 78.150 to 78.185, inclusive.

[3(a):180:1925; added 1951, 280]—(NRS A 1959, 685; 1985, 233; 1991, 1219)

NRS 78.170 Defaulting corporations: Identification; penalty.

1. Each corporation required to make a filing and pay the fee prescribed in NRS 78.150 to 78.185, inclusive, which refuses or neglects to do so within the time provided shall be deemed in default.

2. For default there must be added to the amount of the fee a penalty of $15. The fee and penalty must be collected as provided in this chapter.

[4:180:1925; A 1931, 408; 1931 NCL § 1807]—(NRS A 1977, 401, 606; 1979, 185; 1983, 690; 1985, 233; 1989, 976; 1991, 1219; 1995, 1113)

NRS 78.175 Defaulting corporations: Duties of secretary of state; revocation of charter and forfeiture of right to transact business; distribution of assets.

1. The secretary of state shall notify, by letter addressed to its resident agent, each corporation deemed in default pursuant to NRS 78.170. The notice must be accompanied by a statement indicating the amount of the filing fee, penalties and costs remaining unpaid.

2. On the first day of the ninth month following the month in which the filing was required, the charter of the corporation is revoked and its right to transact business is forfeited.

3. The secretary of state shall compile a complete list containing the names of all corporations whose right to do business has been forfeited. The secretary of state shall forthwith notify, by letter addressed to its resident agent, each such corporation of the forfeiture of its charter. The notice must be accompanied by a statement indicating the amount of the filing fee, penalties and costs remaining unpaid.

4. If the charter of a corporation is revoked and the right to transact business is forfeited as provided in subsection 2, all of the property and assets of the defaulting domestic corporation must be held in trust by the directors of the corporation as for insolvent corporations, and the same proceedings may be had with respect thereto

as are applicable to insolvent corporations. Any person interested may institute proceedings at any time after a forfeiture has been declared, but if the secretary of state reinstates the charter the proceedings must at once be dismissed and all property restored to the officers of the corporation.

5. Where the assets are distributed they must be applied in the following manner:

(a) To the payment of the filing fee, penalties and costs due to the state;

(b) To the payment of the creditors of the corporation; and

(c) Any balance remaining to distribution among the stockholders.

[Part 5:180:1925; NCL § 1808]—(NRS A 1957, 152; 1959, 59; 1973, 1026; 1977, 606; 1979, 185; 1991, 1219; 1995, 1113)

NRS 78.180 Defaulting corporations: Conditions and procedure for reinstatement.

1. Except as otherwise provided in subsections 3 and 4, the secretary of state shall reinstate a corporation which has forfeited its right to transact business under the provisions of this chapter and restore to the corporation its right to carry on business in this state, and to exercise its corporate privileges and immunities, if it:

(a) Files with the secretary of state the list required by NRS 78.150; and

(b) Pays to the secretary of state:

(1) The annual filing fee and penalty set forth in NRS 78.150 and 78.170 for each year or portion thereof during which its charter was revoked; and

(2) A fee of $50 for reinstatement.

2. When the secretary of state reinstates the corporation, he shall:

(a) Immediately issue and deliver to the corporation a certificate of reinstatement authorizing it to transact business as if the filing fee had been paid when due; and

(b) Upon demand, issue to the corporation one or more certified copies of the certificate of reinstatement.

3. The secretary of state shall not order a reinstatement unless all delinquent fees and penalties have been paid, and the revocation of the charter occurred only by reason of failure to pay the fees and penalties.

4. If a corporate charter has been revoked pursuant to the provisions of this chapter and has remained revoked for a period of 5 consecutive years, the charter must not be reinstated.

[6:180:1925; A 1927, 42; NCL § 1809]—(NRS A 1959, 60; 1973, 1027; 1975, 477; 1977, 402; 1985,

234, 1871; 1991, 1220; 1993, 953; 1995, 1114; 1997, 2808)

NRS 78.185 Defaulting corporations: Reinstatement under old or new name; regulations.

1. Except as otherwise provided in subsection 2, if a corporation applies to reinstate or revive its charter but its name has been legally reserved or acquired by another artificial person formed, organized, registered or qualified pursuant to the provisions of this Title whose name is on file with the office of the secretary of state or reserved in the office of the secretary of state pursuant to the provisions of this Title, the corporation shall in its application for reinstatement submit in writing to the secretary of state some other name under which it desires its corporate existence to be reinstated or revived. If that name is distinguishable from all other names reserved or otherwise on file, the secretary of state shall issue to the applying corporation a certificate of reinstatement or revival under that new name.

2. If the applying corporation submits the written, acknowledged consent of the artificial person having a name, or the person who has reserved a name, which is not distinguishable from the old name of the applying corporation or a new name it has submitted, it may be reinstated or revived under that name.

3. For the purposes of this section, a proposed name is not distinguishable from a name on file or reserved name solely because one or the other contains distinctive lettering, a distinctive mark, a trade-mark or a trade name, or any combination of these.

4. The secretary of state may adopt regulations that interpret the requirements of this section.

[7:180:1925; NCL § 1810]—(NRS A 1961, 94; 1987, 1057; 1991, 1221; 1993, 953; 1997, 2809; 1999, 1582)

STOCK AND OTHER SECURITIES; DISTRIBUTIONS

NRS 78.191 "Distribution" defined. As used in NRS 78.195 to 78.307, inclusive, unless the context otherwise requires, the word "distribution" means a direct or indirect transfer of money or other property other than its own shares or the incurrence of indebtedness by a corporation to or for the benefit of its stockholders with respect to any of its shares. A distribution may be in the form of a declaration or payment of a dividend, a purchase, redemption or other acquisition of shares, a distribution of indebtedness, or otherwise.

(Added to NRS by 1991, 1185)

NRS 78.195 Issuance of more than one class or series of stock; rights of stockholders.

1. If a corporation desires to have more than one class or series of stock, the articles of incorporation must prescribe, or vest authority in the board of directors to prescribe, the classes, series and the number of each class or series of stock and the voting powers, designations, preferences, limitations, restrictions and relative rights of each class or series of stock. If more than one class or series of stock is authorized, the articles of incorporation or the resolution of the board of directors passed pursuant to a provision of the articles must prescribe a distinguishing designation for each class and series. The voting powers, designations, preferences, limitations, restrictions, relative rights and distinguishing designation of each class or series of stock must be described in the articles of incorporation or the resolution of the board of directors before the issuance of shares of that class or series.

2. All shares of a series must have voting powers, designations, preferences, limitations, restrictions and relative rights identical with those of other shares of the same series and, except to the extent otherwise provided in the description of the series, with those of other series of the same class.

3. Unless otherwise provided in the articles of incorporation, no stock issued as fully paid up may ever be assessed and the articles of incorporation must not be amended in this particular.

4. Any rate, condition or time for payment of distributions on any class or series of stock may be made dependent upon any fact or event which may be ascertained outside the articles of incorporation or the resolution providing for the distributions adopted by the board of directors if the manner in which a fact or event may operate upon the rate, condition or time of payment for the distributions is stated in the articles of incorporation or the resolution.

5. The provisions of this section do not restrict the directors of a corporation from taking action to protect the interests of the corporation and its stockholders, including, but not limited to, adopting or executing plans, arrangements or instruments that deny rights, privileges, power or authority to a holder of a specified number of shares or percentage of share ownership or voting power.

[11:177:1925; A 1929, 413; 1941, 374; 1931 NCL § 1610]—

(NRS A 1961, 195; 1985, 1787; 1987, 577; 1989, 873; 1991, 1221; 1993, 954; 1995, 2097; 1999, 1582)

NRS 78.1955 Establishment of matters regarding class or series of stock by resolution of board of directors.

1. If the voting powers, designations, preferences, limitations, restrictions and relative rights of any class or series of stock have been established by a resolution of the board of directors pursuant to a provision in the articles of incorporation, a certificate of designation must be filed with the secretary of state setting forth the resolution. The certificate of designation must be executed by the president or vice president and secretary or assistant secretary and acknowledged by the president or vice president before a person authorized by the laws of Nevada to take acknowledgments of deeds. The certificate of designation so executed and acknowledged must be filed before the issuance of any shares of the class or series.

2. Unless otherwise provided in the articles of incorporation or the certificate of designation being amended, if no shares of a class or series of stock established by a resolution of the board of directors have been issued, the designation of the class or series, the number of the class or series and the voting powers, designations, preferences, limitations, restrictions and relative rights of the class or series may be amended by a resolution of the board of directors pursuant to a certificate of amendment filed in the manner provided in subsection 4.

3. Unless otherwise provided in the articles of incorporation or the certificate of designation, if shares of a class or series of stock established by a resolution of the board of directors have been issued, the designation of the class or series, the number of the class or series and the voting powers, designations, preferences, limitations, restrictions and relative rights of the class or series may be amended by a resolution of the board of directors only if the amendment is approved as provided in this subsection. Unless otherwise provided in the articles of incorporation or the certificate of designation, the proposed amendment adopted by the board of directors must be approved by the vote of stockholders holding shares in the corporation entitling them to exercise a majority of the voting power, or such greater proportion of the voting power as may be required by the articles of incorporation or the certificate of designation, of:

(a) The class or series of stock being amended; and

(b) Each class and each series of stock which, before amendment, is senior to the class or series being amended as to the payment of distributions upon dissolution of the corporation, regardless of any limitations or restrictions on the voting power of that class or series.

4. A certificate of amendment to a certificate of designation must be filed with the secretary of state and must:

(a) Set forth the original designation and the new designation, if the designation of the class or series is being amended;

(b) State that no shares of the class or series have been issued or state that the approval of the stockholders required pursuant to subsection 3 has been obtained; and

(c) Set forth the amendment to the class or series or set forth the designation of the class or series, the number of the class or series and the voting powers, designations, preferences, limitations, restrictions and relative rights of the class or series, as amended.

The certificate of amendment must be executed by the president or vice president and secretary or assistant secretary and acknowledged by the president or vice president before a person authorized by the laws of Nevada to take acknowledgments of deeds. NRS 78.380, 78.385 and 78.390 do not apply to certificates of amendment filed pursuant to this section.

(Added to NRS by 1995, 2092)

NRS 78.196 Required and authorized classes or series of stock.

1. Each corporation must have:

(a) One or more classes or series of shares that together have unlimited voting rights; and

(b) One or more classes or series of shares that together are entitled to receive the net assets of the corporation upon dissolution.

If the articles of incorporation provide for only one class of stock, that class of stock has unlimited voting rights and is entitled to receive the net assets of the corporation upon dissolution.

2. The articles of incorporation, or a resolution of the board of directors pursuant thereto, may authorize one or more classes or series of stock that:

(a) Have special, conditional or limited voting powers, or no right to vote, except to the extent otherwise provided by this Title;

(b) Are redeemable or convertible:

(1) At the option of the corporation, the stockholders or another person, or upon the occurrence of a designated event;

(2) For cash, indebtedness, securities or other property; or

(3) In a designated amount or in an amount determined in accordance with a designated formula or by reference to extrinsic data or events;

(c) Entitle the stockholders to distributions calculated in any manner, including dividends that may be cumulative, noncumulative or partially cumulative;

(d) Have preference over any other class or series of shares with respect to distributions, including dividends and distributions upon the dissolution of the corporation;

(e) Have par value; or

(f) Have powers, designations, preferences, limitations, restrictions and relative rights dependent upon any fact or event which may be ascertained outside of the articles of incorporation or the resolution if the manner in which the fact or event may operate on such class or series of stock is stated in the articles of incorporation or the resolution.

3. The description of voting powers, designations, preferences, limitations, restrictions and relative rights of the classes or series of shares contained in this section is not exclusive.

(Added to NRS by 1991, 1185; A 1999, 1583)

NRS 78.197 **Rights of persons holding obligations of corporation.** A corporation may provide in its articles of incorporation that the holder of a bond, debenture or other obligation of the corporation may have any of the rights of a stockholder in the corporation.

(Added to NRS by 1987, 574; A 1993, 955)

NRS 78.200 **Rights or options to purchase stock.** A corporation may create and issue, whether in connection with the issue and sale of any shares of stock or other securities of the corporation, rights or options entitling the holders thereof to purchase from the corporation any shares of its stock of any class or classes, to be evidenced by or in such instrument or instruments as are approved by the board of directors. The terms upon which, the time or times, which may be limited or unlimited in duration, at or within which, and the price or prices at which any such shares may be purchased from the corporation upon the exercise of any such a right or option must be fixed and stated in the articles of incorporation or in a resolution or resolutions adopted by the board of directors providing for the creation and issue of the rights or options, and, in every case, set forth or incorporated by reference in the instrument or instruments evidencing the rights or options.

[11(a):177:1925; added 1949, 158; 1943 NCL § 1610.01]—(NRS A 1991, 1223; 1993, 955)

NRS 78.205 **Fractions of shares: Issuance; alternatives to issuance.**

1. A corporation is not obliged to but may execute and deliver a certificate for or including a fraction of a share.

2. In lieu of executing and delivering a certificate for a fraction of a share, a corporation may:

(a) Pay to any person otherwise entitled to become a holder of a fraction of a share:

(1) The appraised value of that share if the appraisal was properly demanded; or

(2) If no appraisal was demanded or an appraisal was not properly demanded, an amount in cash specified for that purpose as the value of the fraction in the articles, plan of reorganization, plan of merger or exchange, resolution of the board of directors, or other instrument pursuant to which the fractional share would otherwise be issued, or, if not specified, then as may be determined for that purpose by the board of directors of the issuing corporation;

(b) Issue such additional fraction of a share as is necessary to increase the fractional share to a full share; or

(c) Execute and deliver registered or bearer scrip over the manual or facsimile signature of an officer of the corporation or of its agent for that purpose, exchangeable as provided on the scrip for full share certificates, but the scrip does not entitle the holder to any rights as a stockholder except as provided on the scrip. The scrip may provide that it becomes void unless the rights of the holders are exercised within a specified period and may contain any other provisions or conditions that the corporation deems advisable. Whenever any scrip ceases to be exchangeable for full share certificates, the shares that would otherwise have been issuable as provided on the scrip are deemed to be treasury shares unless the scrip contains other provisions for their disposition.

[11(b):177:1925; added 1953, 180]—(NRS A 1979, 1160; 1993, 956)

NRS 78.207 **Increase or decrease in number of authorized shares of class and series: Resolution by board of directors; vote of stockholders required under certain circumstances.**

1. Unless otherwise provided in the articles of incorporation, a corporation organized and existing under the laws of this state that desires to change the number of shares of a class and series, if any, of its authorized stock by increasing or decreasing the number of authorized shares of the class and series and correspondingly increasing or decreasing the number of issued and outstanding shares of the same class and series held by each stockholder of record at the effective date and time of the change, may, except as otherwise provided in subsections 2 and 3, do so by a resolution adopted by the board of directors, without obtaining the approval of the stockholders. The resolution may also provide for a change of the par value, if any, of the same class and series of the shares increased or decreased. After the effective date and time of the change, the corporation may issue its stock in accordance therewith.

2. A proposal to increase or decrease the number of authorized shares of any class and series, if any, that includes provisions pursuant to which only money will be paid or scrip will be issued to stockholders who:

(a) Before the increase or decrease in the number of shares becomes effective, in the aggregate hold 10 percent or more of the outstanding shares of the affected class and series; and

(b) Would otherwise be entitled to receive fractions of shares in exchange for the cancellation of all of their outstanding shares,

must be approved by the vote of stockholders holding a majority of the voting power of the affected class and series, or such greater proportion as may be provided in the articles of incorporation, regardless of limitations or restrictions on the voting power thereof.

3. If a proposed increase or decrease in the number of authorized shares of any class or series would alter or change any preference or any relative or other right given to any other class or series of outstanding shares, then the increase or decrease must be approved by the vote, in addition to any vote otherwise required, of the holders of shares representing a majority of the voting power of each class or series whose preference or rights are affected by the increase or decrease, regardless of limitations or restrictions on the voting power thereof.

4. Any proposal to increase or decrease the number of authorized shares of any class and series, if any, that includes provisions pursuant to which only money will be paid or scrip will be issued to stockholders who:

(a) Before the increase or decrease in the number of shares becomes effective, hold 1 percent or more of the outstanding shares of the affected class and series; and

(b) Would otherwise be entitled to receive a fraction of a share in exchange for the cancellation of all of their outstanding shares, is subject to the provisions of NRS 92A.300 to 92A.500, inclusive. If the proposal is subject to those provisions, any stockholder who is obligated to accept money or scrip rather than receive a fraction of a share resulting from the action taken pursuant to this section may dissent in accordance with those provisions and obtain payment of the fair value of the fraction of a share to which the stockholder would otherwise be entitled.

[Part 6:177:1925; A 1951, 28]— (NRS A 1959, 688; 1991, 1224; 1993, 956; 1995, 2098; 1997, 699)

NRS 78.209 **Filing certificate of change in number of authorized shares of class and series; contents of certificate; articles of incorporation deemed amended.**

1. A change pursuant to NRS 78.207 is not effective until after the filing in the office of the secretary of state of a certificate, signed by the corporation's president, or a vice president, and its secretary, or an assistant secretary, and acknowledged by the president or vice president before a person authorized by the laws of this state to take acknowledgments of deeds, setting forth:

(a) The current number of authorized shares and the par value, if any, of each class and series, if any, of shares before the change;

(b) The number of authorized shares and the par value, if any, of each class and series, if any, of shares after the change;

(c) The number of shares of each affected class and series, if any, to be issued after the change in exchange for each issued share of the same class or series;

(d) The provisions, if any, for the issuance of fractional shares, or for the payment of money or the issuance of scrip to stockholders otherwise entitled to a fraction of a share and the percentage of outstanding shares affected thereby;

(e) That any required approval of the stockholders has been obtained; and

(f) Whether the change is effective on filing the certificate or, if not, the date and time at which the change will be effective, which must not be more than 90 days after the certificate is filed.
The provisions in the articles of incorporation of the corporation regarding the authorized number and par value, if any, of the changed class and series, if any, of shares shall be deemed amended as provided in the certificate at the effective date and time of the change.

2. Unless an increase or decrease of the number of authorized shares pursuant to NRS 78.207 is accomplished by an action that otherwise requires an amendment to the corporation's articles of incorporation, such

an amendment is not required by that section.

(Added to NRS by 1997, 694)

NRS 78.211 **Consideration for shares: Types; adequacy; effect of receipt; actions of corporation pending receipt in future.**

1. The board of directors may authorize shares to be issued for consideration consisting of any tangible or intangible property or benefit to the corporation, including, but not limited to, cash, promissory notes, services performed, contracts for services to be performed or other securities of the corporation.

2. Before the corporation issues shares, the board of directors must determine that the consideration received or to be received for the shares to be issued is adequate. The judgment of the board of directors as to the adequacy of the consideration received for the shares issued is conclusive in the absence of actual fraud in the transaction.

3. When the corporation receives the consideration for which the board of directors authorized the issuance of shares, the shares issued therefor are fully paid.

4. The corporation may place in escrow shares issued for a contract for future services or benefits or a promissory note, or make any other arrangements to restrict the transfer of the shares. The corporation may credit distributions made for the shares against their purchase price, until the services are performed, the benefits are received or the promissory note is paid. If the services are not performed, the benefits are not received or the promissory note is not paid, the shares escrowed or restricted and the distributions credited may be canceled in whole or in part.

(Added to NRS by 1991, 1186; A 1993, 958)

NRS 78.215 **Issuance of shares for consideration or as share dividend.**

1. A corporation may issue and dispose of its authorized shares for such consideration as may be prescribed in the articles of incorporation or, if no consideration is so prescribed, then for such consideration as may be fixed by the board of directors.

2. If a consideration is prescribed for shares without par value, that consideration must not be used to determine the fees required for filing articles of incorporation pursuant to NRS 78.760.

3. Unless the articles of incorporation provide otherwise, shares may be issued pro rata and without consideration to the corporation's stockholders or to the

stockholders of one or more classes or series. An issuance of shares under this subsection is a share dividend.

4. Shares of one class or series may not be issued as a share dividend in respect of shares of another class or series unless:

(a) The articles of incorporation so authorize;

(b) A majority of the votes entitled to be cast by the class or series to be issued approve the issue; or

(c) There are no outstanding shares of the class or series to be issued.

5. If the board of directors does not fix the record date for determining stockholders entitled to a share dividend, it is the date the board of directors authorizes the share dividend.

[13:177:1925; NCL § 1612]— (NRS A 1975, 478; 1991, 1225; 1993, 958)

NRS 78.220 **Subscription for corporate shares: Payment; collection on default; irrevocability.**

1. Subscriptions to the shares of a corporation, whether made before or after its organization, shall be paid in full at such time or in such installments at such times as determined by the board of directors. Any call made by the board of directors for payment on subscriptions shall be uniform as to all shares of the same class or series.

2. If default is made in the payment of any installment or call, the corporation may proceed to collect the amount due in the same manner as any debt due the corporation. In addition, the corporation may sell a sufficient number of the subscriber's shares at public auction to pay for the installment or call and any incidental charges incurred as a result of the sale. No penalty causing a forfeiture of a subscription, of stock for which a subscription has been executed, or of amounts paid thereon, may be declared against any subscriber unless the amount due remains unpaid for 30 days after written demand. Such written demand shall be deemed made when it is mailed by registered or certified mail, return receipt requested, to the subscriber's last known address. If any of the subscriber's shares are sold at public auction, any excess of the proceeds over the total of the amount due plus any incidental charges of the sale shall be paid to the subscriber or his legal representative. If an action is brought to recover the amount due on a subscription or call, any judgment in favor of the corporation shall be reduced by the amount

of the net proceeds of any sale by the corporation of the subscriber's stock.

3. If a receiver of a corporation has been appointed, all unpaid subscriptions shall be paid at such times and in such installments as the receiver or the court may direct, subject, however, to the provisions of the subscription contract.

4. A subscription for shares of a corporation to be organized is irrevocable for 6 months unless otherwise provided by the subscription agreement or unless all of the subscribers consent to the revocation of the subscription.

[14:177:1925; NCL § 1613]—(NRS A 1977, 651)

NRS 78.225 Stockholder's liability: No individual liability except for payment for which shares were authorized to be issued or which was specified in subscription agreement. Unless otherwise provided in the articles of incorporation, no stockholder of any corporation formed under the laws of this state is individually liable for the debts or liabilities of the corporation. A purchaser of shares of stock from the corporation is not liable to the corporation or its creditors with respect to the shares, except to pay the consideration for which the shares were authorized to be issued or which was specified in the written subscription agreement.

[15:177:1925; A 1929, 413; NCL § 1614]—(NRS A 1991, 1225)

NRS 78.230 Liability of holder of stock as collateral security; liability of executors, administrators, guardians and trustees.

1. No person holding shares in any corporation as collateral security shall be personally liable as a stockholder.

2. No executor, administrator, guardian or trustee, unless he, without authorization, shall have voluntarily invested the trust funds in such shares, shall be personally liable as a stockholder, but the estate and funds in the hands of such executor, administrator, guardian or trustee shall be liable.

[16:177:1925; NCL § 1615]

NRS 78.235 Stock certificates: Validation; facsimile signatures; uncertificated shares and informational statements.

1. Except as otherwise provided in subsection 4, every stockholder is entitled to have a certificate, signed by officers or agents designated by the corporation for the purpose, certifying the number of shares owned by him in the corporation.

2. Whenever any certificate is countersigned or otherwise authenticated by a transfer agent or transfer clerk, and by a registrar, then a facsimile of the signatures of the officers or agents, the transfer agent or transfer clerk or the registrar of the corporation may be printed or lithographed upon the certificate in lieu of the actual signatures. If a corporation uses facsimile signatures of its officers and agents on its stock certificates, it cannot act as registrar of its own stock, but its transfer agent and registrar may be identical if the institution acting in those dual capacities countersigns or otherwise authenticates any stock certificates in both capacities.

3. If any officer or officers who have signed, or whose facsimile signature or signatures have been used on, any certificate or certificates for stock cease to be an officer or officers of the corporation, whether because of death, resignation or other reason, before the certificate or certificates have been delivered by the corporation, the certificate or certificates may nevertheless be adopted by the corporation and be issued and delivered as though the person or persons who signed the certificate or certificates, or whose facsimile signature or signatures have been used thereon, had not ceased to be an officer or officers of the corporation.

4. A corporation may provide in its articles of incorporation or in its bylaws for the issuance of uncertificated shares of some or all of the shares of any or all of its classes or series. The issuance of uncertificated shares has no effect on existing certificates for shares until surrendered to the corporation, or on the respective rights and obligations of the stockholders. Unless otherwise provided by a specific statute, the rights and obligations of stockholders are identical whether or not their shares of stock are represented by certificates.

5. Within a reasonable time after the issuance or transfer of shares without certificates, the corporation shall send the stockholder a written statement containing the information required on the certificates pursuant to subsection 1. At least annually thereafter, the corporation shall provide to its stockholders of record, a written statement confirming the information contained in the informational statement previously sent pursuant to this subsection.

[Part 18:177:1925; A 1929, 413; 1937, 8; 1931 NCL § 1617]—(NRS A 1965, 1012; 1987, 579; 1991, 1226; 1993, 959)

NRS 78.240 Shares of stock are personal property; transfers. The shares of stock in every corporation shall be personal property and shall be transferable on the books of the corporation, in such manner and under such regulations as may be provided in the bylaws, and as provided in chapter 104 of NRS.

[Part 18:177:1925; A 1929, 413; 1937, 8; 1931 NCL § 1617]—(NRS A 1965, 917)

NRS 78.242 Restrictions on transfer of stock.

1. Subject to the limitation imposed by NRS 104.8204, a written restriction on the transfer or registration of transfer of the stock of a corporation, if permitted by this section, may be enforced against the holder of the restricted stock or any successor or transferee of the holder, including an executor, administrator, trustee, guardian or other fiduciary entrusted with like responsibility for the person or estate of the holder.

2. A restriction on the transfer or registration of transfer of the stock of a corporation may be imposed by the articles of incorporation or by the bylaws or by an agreement among any number of stockholders or between one or more stockholders and the corporation. No restriction so imposed is binding with respect to stocks issued before the adoption of the restriction unless the stockholders are parties to an agreement or voted in favor of the restriction.

3. A restriction on the transfer or the registration of transfer of shares is valid and enforceable against the transferee of the stockholder if the restriction is not prohibited by other law and its existence is noted conspicuously on the front or back of the stock certificate or is contained in the statement of information required by NRS 78.235. Unless so noted, a restriction is not enforceable against a person without knowledge of the restriction.

4. A restriction on the transfer or registration of transfer of stock of a corporation is permitted, without limitation by this enumeration, if it:

(a) Obligates the stockholder first to offer to the corporation or to any other stockholder or stockholders of the corporation or to any other person or persons or to any combination of the foregoing a prior opportunity, to be exercised within a reasonable time, to acquire the stock;

(b) Obligates the corporation or any holder of stock of the corporation or any other person or any combination of the foregoing to purchase stock which is the subject of an agreement respecting the purchase and sale of the stock;

(c) Requires the corporation or any stockholder or stockholders to consent to any proposed transfer of the stock or to approve the proposed transferee of stock;

(d) Prohibits the transfer of the stock to designated persons or classes of persons, and such designation is not manifestly unreasonable; or

(e) Prohibits the transfer of stock:

(1) To maintain the corporation's status when it is dependent on the number or identity of its stockholders;

(2) To preserve exemptions under federal or state laws governing taxes or securities; or

(3) For any other reasonable purpose.

5. For the purposes of this section, "stock" includes a security convertible into or carrying a right to subscribe for or to acquire stock.

(Added to NRS by 1969, 112; A 1991, 1226)

NRS 78.245 Corporate stocks, bonds and securities not taxed when owned by nonresidents or foreign corporations. No stocks, bonds or other securities issued by any corporation organized under this chapter, nor the income or profits therefrom, nor the transfer thereof by assignment, descent, testamentary disposition or otherwise, shall be taxed by this state when such stocks, bonds or other securities shall be owned by nonresidents of this state or by foreign corporations.

[87:177:1925; A 1929, 413; NCL § 1686]

NRS 78.250 Cancellation of outstanding certificates or change in informational statements: Issuance of new certificates or statements; order for surrender of certificates; penalties for failure to comply.

1. When the articles of incorporation are amended in any way affecting the statements contained in certificates for outstanding shares or informational statements sent pursuant to NRS 78.235, or it becomes desirable for any reason, in the discretion of the board of directors, to cancel any outstanding certificate for shares and issue a new certificate therefor conforming to the rights of the holder, the board of directors may send additional informational statements as provided in NRS 78.235 and order any holders of outstanding certificates for shares to surrender and exchange them for new certificates within a reasonable time to be fixed by the board of directors.

2. Such an order may provide that the holder of any certificate so ordered to be surrendered is not entitled to vote or to receive distributions or exercise any of the other rights of stockholders of record until he has complied with the order, but the order operates to suspend such rights only after notice and until compliance.

3. The duty to surrender any outstanding certificates may also be enforced by action at law.

[18a:177:1925; added 1937, 8; 1931 NCL § 1617.01]—(NRS A 1987, 580; 1993, 960)

NRS 78.257 Right of stockholders to inspect and audit financial records; exceptions.

1. Any person who has been a stockholder of record of any corporation and owns not less than 15 percent of all of the issued and outstanding shares of the stock of such corporation or has been authorized in writing by the holders of at least 15 percent of all its issued and outstanding shares, upon at least 5 days' written demand, is entitled to inspect in person or by agent or attorney, during normal business hours, the books of account and all financial records of the corporation, to make extracts therefrom, and to conduct an audit of such records. Holders of voting trust certificates representing 15 percent of the issued and outstanding shares of the corporation shall be regarded as stockholders for the purpose of this subsection. The right of stockholders to inspect the corporate records may not be limited in the articles or bylaws of any corporation.

2. All costs for making extracts of records or conducting an audit must be borne by the person exercising his rights under subsection 1.

3. The rights authorized by subsection 1 may be denied to any stockholder upon his refusal to furnish the corporation an affidavit that such inspection, extracts or audit is not desired for any purpose not related to his interest in the corporation as a stockholder. Any stockholder or other person, exercising rights under subsection 1, who uses or attempts to use information, documents, records or other data obtained from the corporation, for any purpose not related to the stockholder's interest in the corporation as a stockholder, is guilty of a gross misdemeanor.

4. If any officer or agent of any corporation keeping records in this state willfully neglects or refuses to permit an inspection of the books of account and financial records upon demand by a person entitled to inspect them, or refuses to permit an audit to be conducted, as provided in subsection 1, the corporation shall forfeit to the state the sum of $100 for every day of such neglect or refusal, and the corporation,

officer or agent thereof is jointly and severally liable to the person injured for all damages resulting to him.

5. A stockholder who brings an action or proceeding to enforce any right under this section or to recover damages resulting from its denial:

(a) Is entitled to costs and reasonable attorney's fees, if he prevails; or

(b) Is liable for such costs and fees, if he does not prevail,

in the action or proceeding.

6. Except as otherwise provided in this subsection, the provisions of this section do not apply to any corporation listed and traded on any recognized stock exchange nor do they apply to any corporation that furnishes to its stockholders a detailed, annual financial statement. A person who owns, or is authorized in writing by the owners of, at least 15 percent of the issued and outstanding shares of the stock of a corporation that has elected to be governed by subchapter S of the Internal Revenue Code and whose shares are not listed or traded on any recognized stock exchange is entitled to inspect the books of the corporation pursuant to subsection 1 and has the rights, duties and liabilities provided in subsections 2 to 5, inclusive.

(Added to NRS by 1971, 863; A 1977, 659; 1997, 3092)

NRS 78.265 Preemptive rights of stockholders in corporations organized before October 1, 1991.

1. The provisions of this section apply to corporations organized in this state before October 1, 1991.

2. Except to the extent limited or denied by this section or the articles of incorporation, shareholders have a preemptive right to acquire unissued shares, treasury shares or securities convertible into such shares.

3. Unless otherwise provided in the articles of incorporation:

(a) A preemptive right does not exist:

(1) To acquire any shares issued to directors, officers or employees pursuant to approval by the affirmative vote of the holders of a majority of the shares entitled to vote or when authorized by a plan approved by such a vote of shareholders;

(2) To acquire any shares sold for a consideration other than cash;

(3) To acquire any shares issued at the same time that the shareholder who claims a preemptive right acquired his shares;

(4) To acquire any shares issued as part of the same offering in which the shareholder who claims a preemptive right acquired his shares; or

(5) To acquire any shares, treasury shares or securities convertible into such shares, if the shares or the shares into which the convertible securities may be converted are upon issuance registered pursuant to section 12 of the Securities Exchange Act of 1934 (15 U.S.C. § 78l).

(b) Holders of shares of any class that is preferred or limited as to dividends or assets are not entitled to any preemptive right.

(c) Holders of common stock are not entitled to any preemptive right to shares of any class that is preferred or limited as to dividends or assets or to any obligations, unless convertible into shares of common stock or carrying a right to subscribe to or acquire shares of common stock.

(d) Holders of common stock without voting power have no preemptive right to shares of common stock with voting power.

(e) The preemptive right is only an opportunity to acquire shares or other securities upon such terms as the board of directors fixes for the purpose of providing a fair and reasonable opportunity for the exercise of such right.

[23:177:1925; NCL § 1622]— (NRS A 1977, 909; 1987, 581; 1991, 1227)

NRS 78.267 Preemptive rights of stockholders in corporations organized on or after October 1, 1991.

1. The provisions of this section apply to corporations organized in this state on or after October 1, 1991.

2. The stockholders of a corporation do not have a preemptive right to acquire the corporation's unissued shares except to the extent the articles of incorporation so provide.

3. A statement included in the articles of incorporation that "the corporation elects to have preemptive rights" or words of similar import have the following effects unless the articles of incorporation otherwise provide:

(a) The stockholders of the corporation have a preemptive right, granted on uniform terms and conditions prescribed by the board of directors to provide a fair and reasonable opportunity to exercise the right, to acquire proportional amounts of the corporation's unissued shares upon the decision of the board of directors to issue them.

(b) A stockholder may waive his preemptive right. A waiver evidenced by a writing is irrevocable even though it is not supported by consideration.

(c) There is no preemptive right with respect to:

(1) Shares issued as compensation to directors, officers, agents or employees of the corporation, its subsidiaries or affiliates;

(2) Shares issued to satisfy rights of conversion or options created to provide compensation to directors, officers, agents or employees of the corporation, its subsidiaries or affiliates;

(3) Shares authorized in articles of incorporation which are issued within 6 months from the effective date of incorporation; or

(4) Shares sold otherwise than for money.

(d) Holders of shares of any class without general voting rights but with preferential rights to distributions or assets have no preemptive rights with respect to shares of any class.

(e) Holders of shares of any class with general voting rights but without preferential rights to distributions or assets have no preemptive rights with respect to shares of any class with preferential rights to distributions or assets unless the shares with preferential rights are convertible into or carry a right to subscribe for or acquire shares without preferential rights.

(f) Shares subject to preemptive rights that are not acquired by stockholders may be issued to any person for 1 year after being offered to stockholders at a consideration set by the board of directors that is not lower than the consideration set for the exercise of preemptive rights. An offer at a lower consideration or after the expiration of one year is subject to the stockholders' preemptive rights.

4. As used in this section, "shares" includes a security convertible into or carrying a right to subscribe for or acquire shares.

(Added to NRS by 1991, 1187)

NRS 78.275 Assessments on stock: Levy and collection; sale after default in payment.

1. The directors may at such times and in such amount, as they may from time to time deem the interest of the corporation to require, levy and collect assessments upon the assessable stock of the corporation in the manner provided in this section.

2. Notice of each assessment must be given to the stockholders personally, or by publication once a week for at least 4 weeks, in some newspaper published in the county in which the registered office or place of business of the corporation is located, and in a newspaper published in the county wherein the property of the corporation is situated if in this state, and if no paper is published in either of those counties, then the newspaper published nearest to the registered office in the state.

3. If after the notice has been given, any stockholder defaults in the payment of the assessment upon the shares held by him, so many of those shares may be sold as will be necessary for the payment of the assessment upon all the shares held by him, together with all costs of advertising and expenses of sale. The sale of the shares must be made at the office of the corporation at public auction to the highest bidder, after a notice thereof published for 4 weeks as directed in this section, and a copy of the notice mailed to each delinquent stockholder if his address is known 4 weeks before the sale. At the sale the person who offers to pay the assessment so due, together with the expenses of advertising and sale, for the smallest number of shares, or portion of a share, as the case may be, shall be deemed the highest bidder.

[Part 74:177:1925; NCL § 1673]—(NRS A 1993, 960)

NRS 78.280 Purchase by corporation of its own stock at assessment sale when no other available purchaser.

1. Every corporation in this state may, whenever at any assessment sale of the stock of the corporation no person will take the stock and pay the assessment, or amount unpaid and due thereon and costs, purchase such stock and hold the stock for the benefit of the corporation.

2. All purchases of its own stock by any corporation in this state which have been previously made at assessment sales whereat outside persons have failed to bid, and which purchases were for the amount of assessments due, and costs or otherwise, are valid, and vest the legal title to the stock in the corporation.

3. The stock so purchased is subject to the control of the remaining stockholders, who may dispose of the stock as they may deem fit.

4. Whenever any portion of the stock of any corporation is held by the corporation by purchase or otherwise, a majority of the remaining shares of stock in the corporation is a majority of the shares of the stock in the incorporated company, for all purposes of election or voting on any question before a stockholders' meeting.

[Part 74:177:1925; NCL § 1673]—(NRS A 1993, 2764)

NRS 78.283 Treasury shares: Definition; limitations; retirement and disposal.

1. As used in this section, "treasury shares" means shares of a corporation issued and thereafter acquired by the corporation or another entity, the majority of whose

outstanding voting power to elect its general partner, directors, managers or members of the governing body is beneficially held, directly or indirectly, by the corporation, which have not been retired or restored to the status of unissued shares.

2. Treasury shares do not carry voting rights or participate in distributions, may not be counted as outstanding shares for any purpose and may not be counted as assets of the corporation for the purpose of computing the amount available for distributions. Unless the articles of incorporation provide otherwise, treasury shares may
be retired and restored to the status of authorized and unissued shares without an amendment to the articles of incorporation or may be disposed of for such consideration as the board of directors may determine.

3. This section does not limit the right of a corporation to vote its shares held by it in a fiduciary capacity.

(Added to NRS by 1959, 682; A 1981, 1890; 1991, 1228; 1997, 701)

NRS **78.288** Distributions to stockholders.

1. Except as otherwise provided in subsection 2 and the articles of incorporation, a board of directors may authorize and the corporation may make distributions to its stockholders.

2. No distribution may be made if, after giving it effect:

(a) The corporation would not be able to pay its debts as they become due in the usual course of business; or

(b) Except as otherwise specifically allowed by the articles of incorporation, the corporation's total assets would be less than the sum of its total liabilities plus the amount that would be needed, if the corporation were to be dissolved at the time of distribution, to satisfy the preferential rights upon dissolution of stockholders whose preferential rights are superior to those receiving the distribution.

3. The board of directors may base a determination that a distribution is not prohibited under subsection 2 on:

(a) Financial statements prepared on the basis of accounting practices that are reasonable in the circumstances;

(b) A fair valuation, including, but not limited to, unrealized appreciation and depreciation; or

(c) Any other method that is reasonable in the circumstances.

4. The effect of a distribution under subsection 2 must be measured:

(a) In the case of a distribution by purchase, redemption or other acquisition of the corporation's shares, as of the earlier of:

(1) The date money or other property is transferred or debt incurred by the corporation; or

(2) The date upon which the stockholder ceases to be a stockholder with respect to the acquired shares.

(b) In the case of any other distribution of indebtedness, as of the date the indebtedness is distributed.

(c) In all other cases, as of:

(1) The date the distribution is authorized if the payment occurs within 120 days after the date of authorization; or

(2) The date the payment is made if it occurs more than 120 days after the date of authorization.

5. A corporation's indebtedness to a stockholder incurred by reason of a distribution made in accordance with this section is at parity with the corporation's indebtedness to its general unsecured creditors except to the extent subordinated by agreement.

6. Indebtedness of a corporation, including indebtedness issued as a distribution, is not considered a liability for purposes of determinations under subsection 2 if its terms provide that payment of principal and interest are made only if and to the extent that payment of a distribution to stockholders could then be made pursuant to this section. If the indebtedness is issued as a distribution, each payment of principal or interest must be treated as a distribution, the effect of which must be measured on the date the payment is actually made.

(Added to NRS by 1991, 1187)

NRS **78.295** Liability of directors for declaration of distributions.
A director is fully protected in relying in good faith upon the books of account of the corporation or statements prepared by any of its officials as to the value and amount of the assets, liabilities or net profits of the corporation, or any other facts pertinent to the existence and amount of money from which distributions may properly be declared.

[Part 26:177:1925; A 1931, 415; 1949, 158; 1943 NCL § 1625]— (NRS A 1991, 1229)

NRS **78.300** Liability of directors for unlawful distributions.

1. The directors of a corporation shall not make distributions to stockholders except as provided by this chapter.

2. In case of any willful or grossly negligent violation of the provisions of this section, the directors under whose administration the violation occurred, except those who caused their dissent to be entered upon the minutes of the meeting of the directors at the time, or who not then being present caused their dissent to be entered on learning of such action, are jointly and severally liable, at any time within 3 years after each violation, to the corporation, and, in the event of its dissolution or insolvency, to its creditors at the time of the violation, or any of them, to the lesser of the full amount of the distribution made or of any loss sustained by the corporation by reason of the distribution to stockholders.

[75:177:1925; A 1931, 415; 1949, 158; 1943 NCL § 1674]— (NRS A 1987, 83; 1991, 1229)

NRS **78.307** "Investment company" and "open-end investment company" defined; redemption of shares by open-end investment company.

1. As used in this section, unless the context requires otherwise:

(a) "Investment company" means any corporation, trust, association or fund which is engaged or proposes to engage in the business of investing, reinvesting, owning, holding or trading in securities, and whose assets are invested principally in cash or in securities of other issuers.

(b) "Open-end investment company" means any investment company which issues one or more series or classes of securities under the terms of which the holder of the security, upon presentation thereof to the issuer, is entitled to receive approximately his proportionate share of the current net assets of the issuer applicable to such series or class, or the cash equivalent thereof.

2. An open-end investment company may, from time to time, redeem its shares, in accordance with their terms, at approximately the proportionate share of the current net assets of the issuer applicable to such shares, or the cash equivalent thereof.

(Added to NRS by 1961, 174)

MEETINGS, ELECTIONS, VOTING AND NOTICE

NRS **78.310** Place of stockholders' and directors' meetings.
Meetings of stockholders and directors of any corporation organized under the provisions of this chapter may be held within or without this state, in the manner provided by the bylaws of the corporation. The articles of incorporation may designate any place or places where such stockholders' or directors' meetings may be held, but in the absence of any provision therefor in the articles of incorporation, then the meetings must be held within or without this state, as directed from time to time by the bylaws of the corporation.

[Part 31:177:1925; NCL § 1630]—(NRS A 1993, 961)

NRS 78.315 Directors' meetings: Quorum; consent for actions taken without meeting; participation by telephone or similar method.

1. Unless the articles of incorporation or the bylaws provide for a different proportion, a majority of the board of directors of the corporation then in office, at a meeting duly assembled, is necessary to constitute a quorum for the transaction of business, and the act of directors holding a majority of the voting power of the directors, present at a meeting at which a quorum is present, is the act of the board of directors.

2. Unless otherwise restricted by the articles of incorporation or bylaws, any action required or permitted to be taken at a meeting of the board of directors or of a committee thereof may be taken without a meeting if, before or after the action, a written consent thereto is signed by all the members of the board or of the committee.

3. Unless otherwise restricted by the articles of incorporation or bylaws, members of the board of directors or the governing body of any corporation, or of any committee designated by such board or body, may participate in a meeting of the board, body or committee by means of a telephone conference or similar method of communication by which all persons participating in the meeting can hear each other. Participation in a meeting pursuant to this subsection constitutes presence in person at the meeting.

[Part 31:177:1925; NCL § 1630]—(NRS A 1957, 75; 1959, 685; 1977, 412; 1991, 1229; 1993, 961; 1997, 701)

NRS 78.320 Stockholders' meetings: Quorum; consent for actions taken without meeting; participation by telephone or similar method.

1. Unless this chapter, the articles of incorporation or the bylaws provide for different proportions:

(a) A majority of the voting power, which includes the voting power that is present in person or by proxy, regardless of whether the proxy has authority to vote on all matters, constitutes a quorum for the transaction of business; and

(b) Action by the stockholders on a matter other than the election of directors is approved if the number of votes cast in favor of the action exceeds the number of votes cast in opposition to the action.

2. Unless otherwise provided in the articles of incorporation or the bylaws, any action required or permitted to be taken at a meeting of the stockholders may be taken without a meeting if, before or after the action, a written consent thereto is signed by stockholders holding at least a majority of the voting power, except that if a different proportion of voting power is required for such an action at a meeting, then that proportion of written consents is required.

3. In no instance where action is authorized by written consent need a meeting of stockholders be called or notice given.

4. Unless otherwise restricted by the articles of incorporation or bylaws, stockholders may participate in a meeting of stockholders by means of a telephone conference or similar method of communication by which all persons participating in the meeting can hear each other. Participation in a meeting pursuant to this subsection constitutes presence in person at the meeting.

[29(a):177:1925; added 1949, 158; 1943 NCL § 1628.01]—(NRS A 1959, 686; 1987, 581; 1989, 875; 1991, 1229; 1993, 961; 1997, 702; 1999, 1584)

NRS 78.325 Actions at meetings not regularly called: Ratification and approval.

1. Whenever all persons entitled to vote at any meeting, whether of directors, trustees or stockholders, consent, either by:

(a) A writing on the records of the meeting or filed with the secretary; or

(b) Presence at such meeting and oral consent entered on the minutes; or

(c) Taking part in the deliberations at such meeting without objection;

the doings of such meeting shall be as valid as if had at a meeting regularly called and noticed.

2. At such meeting any business may be transacted which is not excepted from the written consent or to the consideration of which no objection for want of notice is made at the time.

3. If any meeting be irregular for want of notice or of such consent, provided a quorum was present at such meeting, the proceedings of the meeting may be ratified and approved and rendered likewise valid and the irregularity or defect therein waived by a writing signed by all parties having the right to vote at such meeting.

4. Such consent or approval of stockholders or creditors may be by proxy or attorney, but all such proxies and powers of attorney must be in writing.

[Part 92:177:1925; A 1929, 413; NCL § 1691]

NRS 78.330 Directors: Election; classification; voting power.

1. Unless elected pursuant to NRS 78.320, directors of every corporation must be elected at the annual meeting of the stockholders by a plurality of the votes cast at the election. Unless otherwise provided in the bylaws, the board of directors have the authority to set the date, time and place for the annual meeting of the stockholders. If for any reason directors are not elected pursuant to NRS 78.320 or at the annual meeting of the stockholders, they may be elected at any special meeting of the stockholders which is called and held for that purpose.

2. The articles of incorporation or the bylaws may provide for the classification of directors as to the duration of their respective terms of office or as to their election by one or more authorized classes or series of shares, but at least one-fourth in number of the directors of every corporation must be elected annually. If an amendment reclassifying the directors would otherwise increase the term of a director, unless the amendment is to the articles of incorporation and otherwise provides, the term of each incumbent director on the effective date of the amendment terminates on the date it would have terminated had there been no reclassification.

3. The articles of incorporation may provide that the voting power of individual directors or classes of directors may be greater than or less than that of any other individual directors or classes of directors, and the different voting powers may be stated in the articles of incorporation or may be dependent upon any fact or event that may be ascertained outside the articles of incorporation if the manner in which the fact or event may operate on those voting powers is stated in the articles of incorporation. If the articles of incorporation provide that any directors may have voting power greater than or less than other directors, every reference in this chapter to a majority or other proportion of directors shall be deemed to refer to a majority or other proportion of the voting power of all of the directors or classes of directors, as may be required by the articles of incorporation.

[Part 33:177:1925; A 1929, 413; NCL § 1632]—(NRS A 1967, 267; 1979, 215; 1987, 582; 1989, 875; 1993, 962; 1999, 1585)

NRS 78.335 Directors: Removal; filling of vacancies.

1. Except as otherwise provided in this section, any director or one or more of the incumbent directors may be removed from office by the vote of stockholders representing not less than two-thirds of the voting power of the issued and outstanding stock entitled to voting power.

2. In the case of corporations which have provided in their articles of incorporation for the election of directors by cumulative voting, any director or directors who constitute fewer than all of the incumbent directors may not be removed from office at any one time or as the result of any one transaction under the provisions of this section except upon the vote of stockholders owning sufficient shares to prevent each director's election to office at the time of removal.

3. The articles of incorporation may require the concurrence of more than two-thirds of the voting power of the issued and outstanding stock entitled to voting power in order to remove one or more directors from office.

4. Whenever the holders of any class or series of shares are entitled to elect one or more directors, unless otherwise provided in the articles of incorporation, removal of any such director requires only the proportion of votes, specified in subsection 1, of the holders of that class or series, and not the votes of the outstanding shares as a whole.

5. All vacancies, including those caused by an increase in the number of directors, may be filled by a majority of the remaining directors, though less than a quorum, unless it is otherwise provided in the articles of incorporation.

6. Unless otherwise provided in the articles of incorporation, when one or more directors give notice of his or their resignation to the board, effective at a future date, the board may fill the vacancy or vacancies to take effect when the resignation or resignations become effective, each director so appointed to hold office during the remainder of the term of office of the resigning director or directors.

[Part 33:177:1925; A 1929, 413; NCL § 1632]—(NRS A 1989, 875; 1991, 1230; 1993, 962; 1999, 1585)

NRS 78.340 Failure to hold election of directors on regular day does not dissolve corporation. If the directors shall not be elected on the day designated for the purpose, the corporation shall not for that reason be dissolved; but every director shall continue to hold his office and discharge his duties until his successor has been elected.

[34:177:1925; NCL § 1633]

NRS 78.345 Election of directors by order of court upon failure of regular election.

1. If any corporation fails to elect directors within 18 months after the last election of directors required by NRS 78.330, the district court has jurisdiction in equity, upon application of any one or more stockholders holding stock entitling them to exercise at least 15 percent of the voting power, to order the election of directors in the manner required by NRS 78.330.

2. The application must be made by petition filed in the county where the registered office of the corporation is located and must be brought on behalf of all stockholders desiring to be joined therein. Such notice must be given to the corporation and the stockholders as the court may direct.

3. The directors elected pursuant to this section have the same rights, powers and duties and the same tenure of office as directors elected by the stockholders at the annual meeting held at the time prescribed therefor, next before the date of the election pursuant to this section, would have had.

[35:177:1925; NCL § 1634]— (NRS A 1991, 1231)

NRS 78.347 Application by stockholder for order of court appointing custodian or receiver; authority of custodian.

1. Any stockholder may apply to the district court to appoint one or more persons to be custodians of the corporation, and, if the corporation is insolvent, to be receivers of the corporation when:

(a) The business of the corporation is suffering or is threatened with irreparable injury because the directors are so divided respecting the management of the affairs of the corporation that a required vote for action by the board of directors cannot be obtained and the stockholders are unable to terminate this division; or

(b) The corporation has abandoned its business and has failed within a reasonable time to take steps to dissolve, liquidate or distribute its assets in accordance with this chapter.

2. A custodian appointed pursuant to this section has all the powers and title of a trustee appointed under NRS 78.590, 78.635 and 78.650, but the authority of the custodian is to continue the business of the corporation and not to liquidate its affairs or distribute its assets, except when the district court so orders and except in cases arising pursuant to paragraph (b) of subsection 1.

(Added to NRS by 1991, 1188)

NRS 78.350 Voting rights of stockholders; determination of stockholders entitled to notice of and to vote at meeting.

1. Unless otherwise provided in the articles of incorporation, or in the resolution providing for the issuance of the stock adopted by the board of directors pursuant to authority expressly vested in it by the provisions of the articles of incorporation, every stockholder of record of a corporation is entitled at each meeting of stockholders thereof to one vote for each share of stock standing in his name on the records of the corporation. If the articles of incorporation, or the resolution providing for the issuance of the stock adopted by the board of directors pursuant to authority expressly vested in it by the articles of incorporation, provides for more or less than one vote per share for any class or series of shares on any matter, every reference in this chapter to a majority or other proportion of stock shall be deemed to refer to a majority or other proportion of the voting power of all of the shares or those classes or series of shares, as may be required by the articles of incorporation, or in the resolution providing for the issuance of the stock adopted by the board of directors pursuant to authority expressly vested in it by the provisions of the articles of incorporation, or the provisions of this chapter.

2. Unless contrary provisions are contained in the articles of incorporation, the directors may prescribe a period not exceeding 60 days before any meeting of the stockholders during which no transfer of stock on the books of the corporation may be made, or may fix, in advance, a record date not more than 60 or less than 10 days before the date of any such meeting as the date as of which stockholders entitled to notice of and to vote at such meetings must be determined. Only stockholders of record on that date are entitled to notice or to vote at such a meeting. If a record date is not fixed, the record date is at the close of business on the day before the day on which notice is given or, if notice is waived, at the close of business on the day before the meeting is held. A determination of stockholders of record entitled to notice of or to vote at a meeting of stockholders applies to an adjournment of the meeting unless the board of directors fixes a new record date for the adjourned meeting. The board of directors must fix a new record date if the meeting is adjourned to a date more than 60 days later than the date set for the original meeting.

3. The provisions of this section do not restrict the directors from taking action to protect the interests of the corporation and its stockholders, including, but not limited to, adopting or executing plans, arrangements or instruments that deny rights, privileges, power or authority to a holder or holders of a specified number of shares or percentage of share ownership or voting power.

[28:177:1925; NCL § 1627]— (NRS A 1965, 1012; 1989, 876; 1991, 1231; 1993, 963; 1999, 1586)

NRS **78.355** Stockholders' proxies.

1. At any meeting of the stockholders of any corporation any stockholder may designate another person or persons to act as a proxy or proxies. If any stockholder designates two or more persons to act as proxies, a majority of those persons present at the meeting, or, if only one is present, then that one has and may exercise all of the powers conferred by the stockholder upon all of the persons so designated unless the stockholder provides otherwise.

2. Without limiting the manner in which a stockholder may authorize another person or persons to act for him as proxy pursuant to subsection 1, the following constitute valid means by which a stockholder may grant such authority:

(a) A stockholder may execute a writing authorizing another person or persons to act for him as proxy. The proxy may be limited to action on designated matters. Execution may be accomplished by the signing of the writing by the stockholder or his authorized officer, director, employee or agent or by causing the signature of the stockholder to be affixed to the writing by any reasonable means, including, but not limited to, a facsimile signature.

(b) A stockholder may authorize another person or persons to act for him as proxy by transmitting or authorizing the transmission of a telegram, cablegram or other means of electronic transmission to the person who will be the holder of the proxy or to a firm which solicits proxies or like agent who is authorized by the person who will be the holder of the proxy to receive the transmission. Any such telegram, cablegram or other means of electronic transmission must either set forth or be submitted with information from which it can be determined that the telegram, cablegram or other electronic transmission was authorized by the stockholder. If it is determined that the telegram, cablegram or other electronic transmission is valid, the persons appointed by the corporation to count the votes of stockholders and determine the validity of proxies and ballots or other persons making

those determinations must specify the information upon which they relied.

3. Any copy, communication by telecopier, or other reliable reproduction of the writing or transmission created pursuant to subsection 2, may be substituted for the original writing or transmission for any purpose for which the original writing or transmission could be used, if the copy, communication by telecopier, or other reproduction is a complete reproduction of the entire original writing or transmission.

4. No such proxy is valid after the expiration of 6 months from the date of its creation, unless it is coupled with an interest, or unless the stockholder specifies in it the length of time for which it is to continue in force, which may not exceed 7 years from the date of its creation. Subject to these restrictions, any proxy properly created is not revoked and continues in full force and effect until another instrument or transmission revoking it or a properly created proxy bearing a later date is filed with or transmitted to the secretary of the corporation or another person or persons appointed by the corporation to count the votes of stockholders and determine the validity of proxies and ballots.

[29:177:1925; A 1953, 180]— (NRS A 1991, 1232; 1997, 702)

NRS **78.360** Cumulative voting.

1. The articles of incorporation of any corporation may provide that at all elections of directors of the corporation each holder of stock possessing voting power is entitled to as many votes as equal the number of his shares of stock multiplied by the number of directors to be elected, and that he may cast all of his votes for a single director or may distribute them among the number to be voted for or any two or more of them, as he may see fit. To exercise the right of cumulative voting, one or more of the stockholders requesting cumulative voting must give written notice to the president or secretary of the corporation that the stockholder desires that the voting for the election of directors be cumulative.

2. The notice must be given not less than 48 hours before the time fixed for holding the meeting, if notice of the meeting has been given at least 10 days before the date of the meeting, and otherwise not less than 24 hours before the meeting. At the meeting, before the commencement of voting for the election of directors, an announcement of the giving of the notice must be made by the chairman or the secretary of the meeting or by or on behalf of the stockholder giving the notice. Notice to stockholders of the requirement of this

subsection must be contained in the notice calling the meeting or in the proxy material accompanying the notice.

[30:177:1925; NCL § 1629]— (NRS A 1969, 101; 1991, 1233; 1993, 963)

NRS **78.365** Voting trusts.

1. A stockholder, by agreement in writing, may transfer his stock to a voting trustee or trustees for the purpose of conferring the right to vote the stock for a period not exceeding 15 years upon the terms and conditions therein stated. Any certificates of stock so transferred must be surrendered and canceled and new certificates for the stock issued to the trustee or trustees in which it must appear that they are issued pursuant to the agreement, and in the entry of ownership in the proper books of the corporation that fact must also be noted, and thereupon the trustee or trustees may vote the stock so transferred during the terms of the agreement. A duplicate of every such agreement must be filed in the registered office of the corporation and at all times during its terms be open to inspection by any stockholder or his attorney.

2. At any time within the 2 years next preceding the expiration of an agreement entered into pursuant to the provisions of subsection 1, or the expiration of an extension of that agreement, any beneficiary of the trust may, by written agreement with the trustee or trustees, extend the duration of the trust for a time not to exceed 15 years after the scheduled expiration date of the original agreement or the latest extension. An extension is not effective unless the trustee, before the expiration date of the original agreement or the latest extension, files a duplicate of the agreement providing for the extension in the registered office of the corporation. An agreement providing for an extension does not affect the rights or obligations of any person not a party to that agreement.

3. An agreement between two or more stockholders, if in writing and signed by them, may provide that in exercising any voting rights the stock held by them must be voted:

(a) Pursuant to the provisions of the agreement;

(b) As they may subsequently agree; or

(c) In accordance with a procedure agreed upon.

4. An agreement entered into pursuant to the provisions of subsection 3 is not effective for a term of more than 15 years, but at any time within the 2 years next preceding the expiration of the agreement the parties thereto may extend its duration for as many additional periods, each not to exceed 15 years, as they wish.

5. An agreement entered into pursuant to the provisions of subsection 1 or 3 is not invalidated by the fact that by its terms its duration is more than 15 years, but its duration shall be deemed amended to conform with the provisions of this section.

[22:177:1925; A 1929, 413; 1951, 328]—(NRS A 1987, 582; 1989, 976; 1991, 1234; 1993, 964)

NRS 78.370 Notice to stockholders.

1. If under the provisions of this chapter stockholders are required or authorized to take any action at a meeting, the notice of the meeting must be in writing and signed by the president or a vice president, or the secretary, or an assistant secretary, or by such other natural person or persons as the bylaws may prescribe or permit or the directors may designate.

2. The notice must state the purpose or purposes for which the meeting is called and the time when, and the place, which may be within or without this state, where it is to be held.

3. A copy of the notice must be delivered personally or mailed postage prepaid to each stockholder of record entitled to vote at the meeting not less than 10 nor more than 60 days before the meeting. If mailed, it must be directed to the stockholder at his address as it appears upon the records of the corporation, and upon the mailing of any such notice the service thereof is complete, and the time of the notice begins to run from the date upon which the notice is deposited in the mail for transmission to the stockholder. Personal delivery of any such notice to any officer of a corporation or association, or to any member of a partnership, constitutes delivery of the notice to the corporation, association or partnership.

4. The articles of incorporation or the bylaws may require that the notice be also published in one or more newspapers.

5. Notice delivered or mailed to a stockholder in accordance with the provisions of this section and the provisions, if any, of the articles of incorporation or the bylaws is sufficient, and in the event of the transfer of his stock after such delivery or mailing and before the holding of the meeting it is not necessary to deliver or mail notice of the meeting to the transferee.

6. Any stockholder may waive notice of any meeting by a writing signed by him, or his duly authorized attorney, either before or after the meeting.

7. Unless otherwise provided in the articles of incorporation or the bylaws, if notice is required to be given, under any provision of this chapter or the articles of incorporation or bylaws of any corporation, to any stockholder to whom:

(a) Notice of two consecutive annual meetings, and all notices of meetings or of the taking of action by written consent without a meeting to him during the period between those two consecutive annual meetings; or

(b) All, and at least two, payments sent by first-class mail of dividends or interest on securities during a 12-month period,

have been mailed addressed to him at his address as shown on the records of the corporation and have been returned undeliverable, the giving of further notices to him is not required. Any action or meeting taken or held without notice to such a stockholder has the same effect as if the notice had been given. If any such stockholder delivers to the corporation a written notice setting forth his current address, the requirement that notice be given to him is reinstated. If the action taken by the corporation is such as to require the filing of a certificate under any of the other sections of this chapter, the certificate need not state that notice was not given to persons to whom notice was not required to be given pursuant to this subsection.

8. Unless the articles of incorporation or bylaws otherwise require, and except as otherwise provided in this subsection, if a stockholders' meeting is adjourned to another date, time or place, notice need not be given of the date, time or place of the adjourned meeting if they are announced at the meeting at which the adjournment is taken. If a new record date is fixed for the adjourned meeting, notice of the adjourned meeting must be given to each stockholder of record as of the new record date.

[27:177:1925; A 1941, 110; 1931 NCL § 1626]—(NRS A 1991, 1235; 1993, 965; 1999, 1587)

NRS 78.375 Waiver of notice.
Whenever any notice whatever is required to be given under the provisions of this chapter, a waiver thereof in writing, signed by the person or persons entitled to the notice, whether before or after the time stated therein, shall be deemed equivalent thereto.

[Part 92:177:1925; A 1929, 413; NCL § 1691]

ACQUISITION OF CONTROLLING INTEREST

NRS 78.378 Applicability; imposition of stricter requirements; protection of corporation and its stockholders.

1. The provisions of NRS 78.378 to 78.3793, inclusive, apply to any acquisition of a controlling interest in an issuing corporation unless the articles of incorporation or bylaws of the corporation in effect on the 10th day following the acquisition of a controlling interest by an acquiring person provide that the provisions of those sections do not apply to the corporation or to an acquisition of a controlling interest specifically by types of existing or future stockholders, whether or not identified.

2. The articles of incorporation, the bylaws or a resolution adopted by the directors of the issuing corporation may impose stricter requirements on the acquisition of a controlling interest in the corporation than the provisions of NRS 78.378 to 78.3793, inclusive.

3. The provisions of NRS 78.378 to 78.3793, inclusive, do not restrict the directors of an issuing corporation from taking action to protect the interests of the corporation and its stockholders, including, but not limited to, adopting or executing plans, arrangements or instruments that deny rights, privileges, power or authority to a holder of a specified number of shares or percentage of share ownership or voting power.

(Added to NRS by 1987, 755; A 1989, 877; 1999, 1588)

NRS 78.3781 Definitions.
As used in NRS 78.378 to 78.3793, inclusive, unless the context otherwise requires, the words and terms defined in NRS 78.3782 to 78.3788, inclusive, have the meanings ascribed to them in those sections.

(Added to NRS by 1987, 756)

NRS 78.3782 "Acquiring person" defined.
"Acquiring person" means any person who, individually or in association with others, acquires or offers to acquire, directly or indirectly, a controlling interest in an issuing corporation. The term does not include any person who, in the ordinary course of business and without an intent to avoid the requirements of NRS 78.378 to 78.3793, inclusive, acquires voting shares for the benefit of others, in respect of which he is not specifically authorized to exercise or direct the exercise of voting rights.

(Added to NRS by 1987, 756)

NRS 78.3783 "Acquisition" defined.

1. Except as otherwise provided in subsection 2, "acquisition" means the direct or indirect acquisition of a controlling interest.

2. "Acquisition" does not include any acquisition of shares in good faith, and without an intent to avoid the requirements of NRS 78.378 to 78.3793, inclusive:

(a) By an acquiring person authorized pursuant to NRS 78.378 to 78.3793, inclusive, to exercise voting rights, to the extent that the new acquisition does not result in the acquiring person obtaining a controlling interest greater than that previously authorized; or

(b) Pursuant to:

(1) The laws of descent and distribution;

(2) The enforcement of a judgment;

(3) The satisfaction of a pledge or other security interest; or

(4) A merger or reorganization effected in compliance with the provisions of NRS 78.622 or 92A.200 to 92A.240, inclusive, to which the issuing corporation is a party.

(Added to NRS by 1987, 756; A 1991, 1236; 1995, 2099)

NRS 78.3784 "Control shares" defined. "Control shares" means those outstanding voting shares of an issuing corporation which an acquiring person and those persons acting in association with an acquiring person:

1. Acquire in an acquisition or offer to acquire in an acquisition; and

2. Acquire within 90 days immediately preceding the date when the acquiring person became an acquiring person.

(Added to NRS by 1987, 756)

NRS 78.3785 "Controlling interest" defined. "Controlling interest" means the ownership of outstanding voting shares of an issuing corporation sufficient, but for the provisions of NRS 78.378 to 78.3793, inclusive, to enable the acquiring person, directly or indirectly and individually or in association with others, to exercise:

1. One-fifth or more but less than one-third;

2. One-third or more but less than a majority; or

3. A majority or more,

of all the voting power of the corporation in the election of directors.

(Added to NRS by 1987, 756)

NRS 78.3786 "Fair value" defined. "Fair value" means a value not less than the highest price per share paid by the acquiring person in an acquisition.

(Added to NRS by 1987, 756)

NRS 78.3787 "Interested stockholder" defined. "Interested stockholder" means a person who directly or indirectly exercises voting rights in the shares of an issuing corporation and who is:

1. An acquiring person;

2. An officer or a director of the corporation; or

3. An employee of the corporation.

(Added to NRS by 1987, 757; A 1999, 1588)

NRS 78.3788 "Issuing corporation" defined. "Issuing corporation" means a corporation which is organized in this state and which:

1. Has 200 or more stockholders of record, at least 100 of whom have addresses in this state appearing on the stock ledger of the corporation; and

2. Does business in this state directly or through an affiliated corporation.

(Added to NRS by 1987, 757; A 1989, 877; 1999, 1588)

NRS 78.3789 Delivery of offeror's statement by acquiring person; contents of statement. An acquiring person who has made or offered to make an acquisition of a controlling interest in an issuing corporation may deliver an offeror's statement to the registered office of the corporation. The acquiring person may request in the statement that the directors of the corporation call a special meeting of the stockholders of the corporation, as provided in NRS 78.379. The statement must set forth:

1. A recital that the statement is given pursuant to this section;

2. The name of the acquiring person and of every person associated with him in the acquisition;

3. The number of shares in any class of voting securities owned, as of the date of the statement, by the acquiring person and each person with whom he is associated, or which the acquiring person intends to acquire;

4. The percentage of the voting securities of the corporation owned, as of the date of the statement, by the acquiring person and each person with whom he is associated, or which the acquiring person intends to acquire; and

5. If the acquiring person has not yet acquired the securities of the corporation, a detailed description of:

(a) The terms and conditions of the proposed acquisition; and

(b) The means by which any required consideration, and any indebtedness incurred to consummate the transaction, are to be paid.

(Added to NRS by 1987, 757; A 1993, 966)

NRS 78.379 Voting rights of acquiring person; meeting of stockholders; statements to accompany notice of meeting.

1. An acquiring person and those acting in association with an acquiring person obtain only such voting rights in the control shares as are conferred by a resolution of the stockholders of the corporation, approved at a special or annual meeting of the stockholders.

2. If an acquiring person so requests in an offeror's statement delivered pursuant to NRS 78.3789, and if he gives an undertaking to pay the expenses of the meeting, the directors of the corporation shall, within 10 days after delivery of the statement, call a special meeting of the stockholders to determine the voting rights to be accorded the control shares.

3. A notice of any meeting of stockholders at which the question of voting rights is to be determined must be accompanied by:

(a) A complete copy of the offeror's statement; and

(b) A statement of the board of directors of the corporation setting forth the position of the board with respect to the acquisition or, if it is the case, stating that the board makes no recommendation concerning the matter.

4. A special meeting of stockholders called pursuant to this section:

(a) Must not be held before the expiration of 30 days after the delivery of the offeror's statement, unless the statement contains a request that the meeting be held sooner.

(b) Must be held within 50 days after the delivery of the statement, unless the acquiring person otherwise agrees in writing that the meeting may be held after that time.

5. If the offeror's statement does not include a request that a special meeting be called, the question of voting rights must be presented to the next special or annual meeting of the stockholders.

(Added to NRS by 1987, 757)

NRS 78.3791 Approval of voting rights of acquiring person. Except as otherwise provided by the articles of incorporation of the issuing corporation, a resolution of the stockholders granting voting rights to the control shares acquired by an acquiring person must be approved by:

1. The holders of a majority of the voting power of the corporation; and

2. If the acquisition will result in any change of the kind described in subsection 3 of NRS 78.390, the holders of a majority of each class or series affected,

excluding those shares as to which any interested stockholder exercises voting rights.

(Added to NRS by 1987, 758; A 1991, 1236; 1999, 1589)

NRS 78.3792 Redemption of control shares.

1. If so provided in the articles of incorporation or the bylaws of the issuing corporation in effect on the 10th day following the acquisition of a controlling interest by an acquiring person, the issuing corporation may call for redemption of not less than all the control shares at the average price paid for the control shares, if:

(a) An offeror's statement is not delivered with respect to the acquisition as provided in NRS 78.3789 on or before the 10th day after the acquisition of the control shares; or

(b) An offeror's statement is delivered, but the control shares are not accorded full voting rights by the stockholders.

2. The issuing corporation shall call for redemption within 30 days after the occurrence of the event prescribed in paragraph (a) or (b) of subsection 1, and the shares must be redeemed within 60 days after the call.

(Added to NRS by 1987, 758; A 1989, 877)

NRS 78.3793 Notice to stockholders; purchase of shares by corporation.

1. Unless otherwise provided in the articles of incorporation or the bylaws of the issuing corporation in effect on the 10th day following the acquisition of a controlling interest by an acquiring person, if the control shares are accorded full voting rights pursuant to NRS 78.378 to 78.3793, inclusive, and the acquiring person has acquired control shares with a majority or more of all the voting power, any stockholder of record, other than the acquiring person, who has not voted in favor of authorizing voting rights for the control shares is entitled to demand payment for the fair value of his shares.

2. The board of directors of the issuing corporation shall, within 20 days after the vote of the stockholders authorizing voting rights for the control shares, cause a notice to be sent to any stockholder, other than the acquiring person, who has not voted in favor of authorizing voting rights for the control shares, advising him of the fact and of his right to receive fair value for his shares as provided in subsection 3.

3. Within 20 days after the mailing of the notice described in subsection 2, any stockholder of the corporation, other than the acquiring person, who has not voted in favor of authorizing voting rights for the control shares, may deliver to the registered office of the corporation a written demand that the corporation purchase, for fair value, all or any portion of his shares. The corporation shall comply with the demand within 30 days after its delivery.

(Added to NRS by 1987, 758; A 1989, 877; 1993, 966)

AMENDMENT AND RESTATEMENT OF ARTICLES OF INCORPORATION

NRS 78.380 Amendment of articles before issuing stock.

1. At least two-thirds of the incorporators or of the board of directors of any corporation, before issuing any stock, may amend the original articles of incorporation thereof as may be desired by executing or proving in the manner required for original articles of incorporation, and filing with the secretary of state a certificate amending, modifying, changing or altering the original articles, in whole or in part. The certificate must:

(a) Declare that the signers thereof are at least two-thirds of the incorporators or of the board of directors of the corporation, and state the corporation's name.

(b) State the date upon which the original articles thereof were filed with the secretary of state.

(c) Affirmatively declare that to the date of the certificate, no stock of the corporation has been issued.

2. The amendment is effective upon the filing of the certificate with the secretary of state.

3. This section does not permit the insertion of any matter not in conformity with this chapter.

[Part 6:177:1925; A 1951, 28]—(NRS A 1959, 686; 1991, 1236; 1993, 966; 1999, 1589)

NRS 78.385 Amendment of articles after issuing stock: Scope of amendments.

1. Any corporation having stock may amend its articles of incorporation in any of the following respects:

(a) By addition to its corporate powers and purposes, or diminution thereof, or both.

(b) By substitution of other powers and purposes, in whole or in part, for those prescribed by its articles of incorporation.

(c) By increasing, decreasing or reclassifying its authorized stock, by changing the number, par value, preferences, or relative, participating, optional or other rights, or the qualifications, limitations or restrictions of such rights, of its shares, or of any class or series of any class thereof whether or not the shares are outstanding at the time of the amendment, or by changing shares with par value, whether or not the shares are outstanding at the time of the amendment, into shares without par value or by changing shares without par value, whether or not the shares are outstanding at the time of the amendment, into shares with par value, either with or without increasing or decreasing the number of shares, and upon such basis as may be set forth in the certificate of amendment.

(d) By changing the name of the corporation.

(e) By making any other change or alteration in its articles of incorporation that may be desired.

2. All such changes or alterations may be effected by one certificate of amendment; but any articles of incorporation so amended, changed or altered, may contain only such provisions as it would be lawful and proper to insert in original articles of incorporation, pursuant to NRS 78.035 and 78.037, if the original articles were executed and filed at the time of making the amendment.

[Part 7:177:1925; A 1931, 415; 1937, 8; 1949, 158; 1943 NCL § 1606]—(NRS A 1989, 878; 1991, 1237; 1999, 1589)

NRS 78.390 Amendment of articles after issuing stock: Procedure.

1. Every amendment adopted pursuant to the provisions of NRS 78.385 must be made in the following manner:

(a) The board of directors must adopt a resolution setting forth the amendment proposed and declaring its advisability, and call a meeting, either annual or special, of the stockholders entitled to vote for the consideration thereof.

(b) At the meeting, of which notice must be given to each stockholder entitled to vote pursuant to the provisions of this section, a vote of the stockholders entitled to vote in person or by proxy must be taken for and against the proposed amendment. If it appears upon the canvassing of the votes that stockholders holding shares in the corporation entitling them to exercise at least a majority of the voting power, or such greater proportion of the voting power as may be required in the case of a vote by classes or series, as provided in subsections 3 and 5, or as may be required by the provisions of the articles of incorporation, have voted in favor of the amendment, the president, or vice president, and secretary, or assistant secretary, shall execute a certificate setting forth the amendment, or setting forth the articles of incorporation as amended, and the vote by which the amendment was adopted.

(c) The certificate so executed must be filed in the office of the secretary of state.

2. Upon filing the certificate the articles of incorporation are amended accordingly.

3. If any proposed amendment would alter or change any preference or any relative or other right given to any class or series of outstanding shares, then the amendment must be approved by the vote, in addition to the affirmative vote otherwise required, of the holders of shares representing a majority of the voting power of each class or series affected by the amendment regardless of limitations or restrictions on the voting power thereof.

4. Provision may be made in the articles of incorporation requiring, in the case of any specified amendments, a larger proportion of the voting power of stockholders than that required by this section.

5. Different series of the same class of shares do not constitute different classes of shares for the purpose of voting by classes except when the series is adversely affected by an amendment in a different manner than other series of the same class.

[Part 7:177:1925; A 1931, 415; 1937, 8; 1949, 158; 1943 NCL § 1606]—(NRS A 1959, 686; 1971, 1101; 1979, 395; 1991, 1238; 1993, 967; 1997, 703; 1999, 1590)

NRS **78.403** Restatement of articles.

1. A corporation may restate, or amend and restate, in a single certificate the entire text of its articles of incorporation as amended by filing with the secretary of state a certificate entitled "Restated Articles of Incorporation of ....," which must set forth the articles as amended to the date of the certificate. If the certificate alters or amends the articles in any manner, it must comply with the provisions of this chapter governing such amendments and must be accompanied by:

(a) A resolution; or

(b) A form prescribed by the secretary of state,

setting forth which provisions of the articles of incorporation on file with the secretary of state are being altered or amended.

2. If the certificate does not alter or amend the articles, it must be signed by the president or vice president and the secretary or assistant secretary of the corporation and state that they have been authorized to execute the certificate by resolution of the board of directors adopted on the date stated, and that the certificate correctly sets forth

the text of the articles of incorporation as amended to the date of the certificate.

3. The following may be omitted from the restated articles:

(a) The names, addresses, signatures and acknowledgments of the incorporators;

(b) The names and addresses of the members of the past and present boards of directors; and

(c) The name and address of the resident agent.

4. Whenever a corporation is required to file a certified copy of its articles, in lieu thereof it may file a certified copy of the most recent certificate restating its articles as amended, subject to the provisions of subsection 2, together with certified copies of all certificates of amendment filed subsequent to the restated articles and certified copies of all certificates supplementary to the original articles.

(Added to NRS by 1959, 682; A 1985, 1789; 1989, 977; 1995, 2100; 1997, 704)

COMBINATIONS WITH INTERESTED STOCKHOLDERS

NRS **78.411** Definitions. As used in NRS 78.411 to 78.444, inclusive, unless the context otherwise requires, the words and terms defined in NRS 78.412 to 78.432, inclusive, have the meanings ascribed to them in those sections.

(Added to NRS by 1991, 1200)

NRS **78.412** "Affiliate" defined. "Affiliate" means a person that directly, or indirectly through one or more intermediaries, is controlled by, or is under common control with, a specified person.

(Added to NRS by 1991, 1200)

NRS **78.413** "Associate" defined. "Associate," when used to indicate a relationship with any person, means:

1. Any corporation or organization of which that person is an officer or partner or is, directly or indirectly, the beneficial owner of 10 percent or more of any class of voting shares;

2. Any trust or other estate in which that person has a substantial beneficial interest or as to which he serves as trustee or in a similar fiduciary capacity; and

3. Any relative or spouse of that person, or any relative of the spouse, who has the same home as that person.

(Added to NRS by 1991, 1200)

NRS **78.414** "Beneficial owner" defined. "Beneficial owner," when used

with respect to any shares, means a person that:

1. Individually or with or through any of its affiliates or associates, beneficially owns the shares, directly or indirectly;

2. Individually or with or through any of its affiliates or associates, has:

(a) The right to acquire the shares, whether the right is exercisable immediately or only after the passage of time, under any agreement, arrangement or understanding, whether or not in writing, or upon the exercise of rights to convert or exchange, warrants or options, or otherwise, but a person is not considered the beneficial owner of shares tendered under an offer for a tender or exchange made by the person or any of his affiliates or associates until the tendered shares are accepted for purchase or exchange; or

(b) The right to vote the shares under any agreement, arrangement or understanding, whether or not in writing, but a person is not considered the beneficial owner of any shares under this paragraph if the agreement, arrangement or understanding to vote the shares arises solely from a revocable proxy or consent given in response to a solicitation made in accordance with the applicable regulations under the Securities Exchange Act and is not then reportable on a Schedule 13D under the Securities Exchange Act, or any comparable or successor report; or

3. Has any agreement, arrangement or understanding, whether or not in writing, for the purpose of acquiring, holding, voting, except voting under a revocable proxy or consent as described in paragraph (b) of subsection 2, or disposing of the shares with any other person who beneficially owns, or whose affiliates or associates beneficially own, directly or indirectly, the shares.

(Added to NRS by 1991, 1200)

NRS **78.416** "Combination" defined. "Combination," when used in reference to any resident domestic corporation and any interested stockholder of the resident domestic corporation, means any of the following:

1. Any merger or consolidation of the resident domestic corporation or any subsidiary of the resident domestic corporation with:

(a) The interested stockholder; or

(b) Any other corporation, whether or not itself an interested stockholder of the resident domestic corporation, which is, or after the merger or consolidation would be, an affiliate or associate of the interested stockholder.

2. Any sale, lease, exchange, mortgage, pledge, transfer or other disposition, in one transaction or a series of transactions, to or

with the interested stockholder or any affiliate or associate of the interested stockholder of assets of the resident domestic corporation or any subsidiary of the resident domestic corporation:

(a) Having an aggregate market value equal to 5 percent or more of the aggregate market value of all the assets, determined on a consolidated basis, of the resident domestic corporation;

(b) Having an aggregate market value equal to 5 percent or more of the aggregate market value of all the outstanding shares of the resident domestic corporation; or

(c) Representing 10 percent or more of the earning power or net income, determined on a consolidated basis, of the resident domestic corporation.

3. The issuance or transfer by the resident domestic corporation or any subsidiary of the resident domestic corporation, in one transaction or a series of transactions, of any shares of the resident domestic corporation or any subsidiary of the resident domestic corporation that have an aggregate market value equal to 5 percent or more of the aggregate market value of all the outstanding shares of the resident domestic corporation to the interested stockholder or any affiliate or associate of the interested stockholder except under the exercise of warrants or rights to purchase shares offered, or a dividend or distribution paid or made, pro rata to all stockholders of the resident domestic corporation.

4. The adoption of any plan or proposal for the liquidation or dissolution of the resident domestic corporation proposed by, or under any agreement, arrangement or understanding, whether or not in writing, with, the interested stockholder or any affiliate or associate of the interested stockholder.

5. Any:

(a) Reclassification of securities, including, without limitation, any splitting of shares, dividend distributed in shares, or other distribution of shares with respect to other shares, or any issuance of new shares in exchange for a proportionately greater number of old shares;

(b) Recapitalization of the resident domestic corporation;

(c) Merger or consolidation of the resident domestic corporation with any subsidiary of the resident domestic corporation; or

(d) Other transaction, whether or not with or into or otherwise involving the interested stockholder, proposed by, or under any agreement, arrangement or understanding, whether or not in writing, with, the interested stockholder or any affiliate or associate of the interested stockholder, which has the effect, directly or

indirectly, of increasing the proportionate share of the outstanding shares of any class or series of voting shares or securities convertible into voting shares of the resident domestic corporation or any subsidiary of the resident domestic corporation which is directly or indirectly owned by the interested stockholder or any affiliate or associate of the interested stockholder, except as a result of immaterial changes because of adjustments of fractional shares.

6. Any receipt by the interested stockholder or any affiliate or associate of the interested stockholder of the benefit, directly or indirectly, except proportionately as a stockholder of the resident domestic corporation, of any loan, advance, guarantee, pledge or other financial assistance or any tax credit or other tax advantage provided by or through the resident domestic corporation.

(Added to NRS by 1991, 1200)

NRS 78.417 "Common shares" defined. "Common shares" means any shares other than preferred shares.

(Added to NRS by 1991, 1202)

NRS 78.418 "Control," "controlling," "controlled by" and "under common control with" defined; presumption of control.

1. Except as otherwise provided in subsection 2:

(a) "Control," used alone or in the terms "controlling," "controlled by" and "under common control with," means the possession, directly or indirectly, of the power to direct or cause the direction of the management and policies of a person, whether through the ownership of voting securities, by contract or otherwise.

(b) A person's beneficial ownership of 10 percent or more of the voting power of a corporation's outstanding voting shares creates a presumption that the person has control of the corporation.

2. A person is not considered to have control of a corporation if he holds voting power, in good faith and not for the purpose of circumventing the provisions of this chapter, as an agent, bank, broker, nominee, custodian or trustee for one or more beneficial owners who do not individually or as a group have control of the corporation.

(Added to NRS by 1991, 1202)

NRS 78.419 "Date of acquiring shares" defined. "Date of acquiring shares," with respect to any person and any resident domestic corporation, means the date that the person first becomes an interested stockholder of the resident domestic corporation.

(Added to NRS by 1991, 1202)

NRS 78.421 "Date of announcement" defined. "Date of announcement," when used in reference to any combination, means the date of the first public announcement of the final, definitive proposal for the combination.

(Added to NRS by 1991, 1202)

NRS 78.422 "Date of consummation" defined. "Date of consummation," with respect to any combination, means the date of the consummation of the combination or, in the case of a combination as to which a vote of stockholders is taken, the later of:

1. The business day before the vote; or

2. Twenty days before the date of consummation of the combination.

(Added to NRS by 1991, 1202)

NRS 78.423 "Interested stockholder" defined.

1. "Interested stockholder," when used in reference to any resident domestic corporation, means any person, other than the resident domestic corporation or any subsidiary of the resident domestic corporation, who is:

(a) The beneficial owner, directly or indirectly, of 10 percent or more of the voting power of the outstanding voting shares of the resident domestic corporation; or

(b) An affiliate or associate of the resident domestic corporation and at any time within 3 years immediately before the date in question was the beneficial owner, directly or indirectly, of 10 percent or more of the voting power of the then outstanding shares of the resident domestic corporation.

2. To determine whether a person is an interested stockholder, the number of voting shares of the resident domestic corporation considered to be outstanding includes shares considered to be beneficially owned by that person through the application of NRS 78.414, but does not include any other unissued shares of a class of voting shares of the resident domestic corporation which may be issuable under any agreement, arrangement or understanding, or upon exercise of rights to convert, warrants or options, or otherwise.

(Added to NRS by 1991, 1202; A 1993, 968)

NRS 78.424 "Market value" defined. "Market value," when used in reference to the shares or property of any resident domestic corporation, means:

1. In the case of shares, the highest closing sale price of a share during the 30 days immediately preceding the date in question on the composite tape for shares listed on the New York Stock Exchange, or,

if the shares are not quoted on the composite tape or not listed on the New York Stock Exchange, on the principal United States securities exchange registered under the Securities Exchange Act on which the shares are listed, or, if the shares are not listed on any such exchange, the highest closing bid quoted with respect to a share during the 30 days preceding the date in question on the National Association of Securities Dealers, Inc.'s, Automated Quotations System or any system then in use, or if no such quotation is available, the fair market value on the date in question of a share as determined by the board of directors of the resident domestic corporation in good faith.

2. In the case of property other than cash or shares, the fair market value of the property on the date in question as determined by the board of directors of the resident domestic corporation in good faith.

(Added to NRS by 1991, 1203)

NRS 78.426 "Preferred shares" defined. "Preferred shares" means any class or series of shares of a resident domestic corporation that under the bylaws or articles of incorporation of the resident domestic corporation:

1. Is entitled to receive payment of dividends before any payment of dividends on some other class or series of shares; or

2. Is entitled in the event of any voluntary liquidation, dissolution or winding up of the corporation to receive payment or distribution of a preferential amount before any payments or distributions are received by some other class or series of shares.

(Added to NRS by 1991, 1203)

NRS 78.427 "Resident domestic corporation" defined.

1. "Resident domestic corporation" is limited to a domestic corporation that has 200 or more stockholders of record.

2. A resident domestic corporation does not cease to be a resident domestic corporation by reason of events occurring or actions taken while the resident domestic corporation is subject to NRS 78.411 to 78.444, inclusive.

(Added to NRS by 1991, 1203; A 1999, 1591)

NRS 78.428 "Securities Exchange Act" defined. "Securities Exchange Act" means the Act of Congress known as the Securities Exchange Act of 1934, as amended (15 U.S.C. §§ 78a et seq.).

(Added to NRS by 1991, 1203)

NRS 78.429 "Share" defined. "Share" means:

1. Any share or similar security, any certificate of interest, any participation in any profit-sharing agreement, any voting-trust certificate, or any certificate of deposit for a share; and

2. Any security convertible, with or without consideration, into shares, or any warrant, call or other option or privilege of buying shares without being bound to do so, or any other security carrying any right to acquire, subscribe to, or purchase shares.

(Added to NRS by 1991, 1203)

NRS 78.431 "Subsidiary" defined. "Subsidiary" of any resident domestic corporation means any other corporation of which a majority of the outstanding voting shares whose votes are entitled to be cast are owned, directly or indirectly, by the resident domestic corporation.

(Added to NRS by 1991, 1203)

NRS 78.432 "Voting shares" defined. "Voting shares" means shares of stock of a corporation entitled to vote generally in the election of directors.

(Added to NRS by 1991, 1204)

NRS 78.433 Applicability: Generally. NRS 78.411 to 78.444, inclusive, do not apply to any combination of a resident domestic corporation:

1. Which does not, as of the date of acquiring shares, have a class of voting shares registered with the Securities and Exchange Commission under section 12 of the Securities Exchange Act, unless the corporation's articles of incorporation provide otherwise.

2. Whose articles of incorporation have been amended to provide that the resident domestic corporation is subject to NRS 78.411 to 78.444, inclusive, and which did not have a class of voting shares registered with the Securities and Exchange Commission under section 12 of the Securities Exchange Act on the effective date of the amendment, if the combination is with an interested stockholder whose date of acquiring shares is before the effective date of the amendment.

(Added to NRS by 1991, 1206)

NRS 78.434 Applicability: Election not to be governed by provisions. NRS 78.411 to 78.444, inclusive, do not apply to any combination of a resident domestic corporation:

1. Whose original articles of incorporation contain a provision expressly electing not to be governed by NRS 78.411 to 78.444, inclusive;

2. Which, within 30 days after October 1, 1991, adopts an amendment to its bylaws expressly electing not to be governed by NRS 78.411 to 78.444, inclusive, which may

be rescinded by subsequent amendment of the bylaws; or

3. Which adopts an amendment to its articles of incorporation, approved by the affirmative vote of the holders, other than interested stockholders and their affiliates and associates, of a majority of the outstanding voting power of the resident domestic corporation, excluding the voting shares of interested stockholders and their affiliates and associates, expressly electing not to be governed by NRS 78.411 to 78.444, inclusive, but the amendment to the articles of incorporation is not effective until 18 months after the vote of the resident domestic corporation's stockholders and does not apply to any combination of the resident domestic corporation with an interested stockholder whose date of acquiring shares is on or before the effective date of the amendment.

(Added to NRS by 1991, 1206)

NRS 78.436 Applicability: Combination with inadvertent interested stockholder. NRS 78.411 to 78.444, inclusive, do not apply to any combination of a resident domestic corporation with an interested stockholder of the resident domestic corporation who became an interested stockholder inadvertently, if he:

1. As soon as practicable, divests himself of a sufficient amount of the voting power of the corporation so that he no longer is the beneficial owner, directly or indirectly, of 10 percent or more of the outstanding voting power of the resident domestic corporation; and

2. Would not at any time within 3 years preceding the date of announcement with respect to the combination have been an interested stockholder but for the inadvertent acquisition.

(Added to NRS by 1991, 1207; A 1993, 968)

NRS 78.437 Applicability: Combination with stockholder who became interested before January 1, 1991. NRS 78.411 to 78.444, inclusive, do not apply to any combination with an interested stockholder who was an interested stockholder on January 1, 1991.

(Added to NRS by 1991, 1207)

NRS 78.438 Combination prohibited within 3 years after stockholder becomes interested; exception; action on proposal.

1. Except as otherwise provided in NRS 78.433 to 78.437, inclusive, a resident domestic corporation may not engage in any combination with any interested stockholder of the resident domestic corporation for 3 years after the interested stockholder's date

of acquiring shares unless the combination or the purchase of shares made by the interested stockholder on the interested stockholder's date of acquiring shares is approved by the board of directors of the resident domestic corporation before that date.

2. If a proposal in good faith regarding a combination is made in writing to the board of directors of the resident domestic corporation, the board of directors shall respond, in writing, within 30 days or such shorter period, if any, as may be required by the Securities Exchange Act, setting forth its reasons for its decision regarding the proposal.

3. If a proposal in good faith to purchase shares is made in writing to the board of directors of the resident domestic corporation, the board of directors, unless it responds affirmatively in writing within 30 days or such shorter period, if any, as may be required by the Securities Exchange Act, is considered to have disapproved the purchase.

(Added to NRS by 1991, 1204; A 1993, 968)

NRS 78.439 Authorized combinations: General requirements. A resident domestic corporation may not engage in any combination with an interested stockholder of the resident domestic corporation after the expiration of 3 years after his date of acquiring shares other than a combination meeting all of the requirements of the articles of incorporation of the resident domestic corporation and either the requirements specified in subsection 1 or 2 or all of the requirements specified in NRS 78.441 to 78.444, inclusive:

1. A combination approved by the board of directors of the resident domestic corporation before the interested stockholder's date of acquiring shares, or as to which the purchase of shares made by the interested stockholder on that date had been approved by the board of directors of the resident domestic corporation before that date.

2. A combination approved by the affirmative vote of the holders of stock representing a majority of the outstanding voting power not beneficially owned by the interested stockholder proposing the combination, or any affiliate or associate of the interested stockholder proposing the combination, at a meeting called for that purpose no earlier than 3 years after the interested stockholder's date of acquiring shares.

(Added to NRS by 1991, 1204; A 1993, 969)

NRS 78.441 Authorized combinations: Consideration to be received by disinterested holders of common shares. A combination engaged in with an interested stockholder of the resident domestic corporation more than 3 years after the interested stockholder's date of acquiring shares may be permissible if the aggregate amount of the cash and the market value, as of the date of consummation, of consideration other than cash to be received per share by all of the holders of outstanding common shares of the resident domestic corporation not beneficially owned by the interested stockholder immediately before that date is at least equal to the higher of the following:

1. The highest price per share paid by the interested stockholder, at a time when he was the beneficial owner, directly or indirectly, of 5 percent or more of the outstanding voting shares of the resident domestic corporation, for any common shares of the same class or series acquired by him within 3 years immediately before the date of announcement with respect to the combination or within 3 years immediately before, or in, the transaction in which he became an interested stockholder, whichever is higher, plus, in either case, interest compounded annually from the earliest date on which the highest price per share was paid through the date of consummation at the rate for one-year obligations of the United States Treasury from time to time in effect, less the aggregate amount of any dividends paid in cash and the market value of any dividends paid other than in cash, per common share since the earliest date, but no more may be subtracted than the amount of the interest.

2. The market value per common share on the date of announcement with respect to the combination or on the interested stockholder's date of acquiring shares, whichever is higher, plus interest compounded annually from that date through the date of consummation at the rate for one-year obligations of the United States Treasury from time to time in effect, less the aggregate amount of any dividends paid in cash and the market value of any dividends paid other than in cash, per common share since that date, but no more may be subtracted than the amount of the interest.

(Added to NRS by 1991, 1204; A 1993, 969)

NRS 78.442 Authorized combinations: Consideration to be received by disinterested holders of class or series of shares other than common shares. A combination engaged in with an interested stockholder of the resident domestic corporation more than 3 years after the interested stockholder's date of acquiring shares may be permissible if the aggregate amount of the cash and the market value, as of the date of consummation, of consideration other than cash to be received per share by all of the holders of outstanding shares of any class or series of shares, other than common shares, of the resident domestic corporation not beneficially owned by the interested stockholder immediately before that date is at least equal to the highest of the following, whether or not the interested stockholder has previously acquired any shares of the class or series of shares:

1. The highest price per share paid by the interested stockholder, at a time when he was the beneficial owner, directly or indirectly, of 5 percent or more of the outstanding voting shares of the resident domestic corporation, for any shares of that class or series of shares acquired by him within 3 years immediately before the date of announcement with respect to the combination or within 3 years immediately before, or in, the transaction in which he became an interested stockholder, whichever is higher, plus, in either case, interest compounded annually from the earliest date on which the highest price per share was paid through the date of consummation at the rate for one-year obligations of the United States Treasury from time to time in effect, less the aggregate amount of any dividends paid in cash and the market value of any dividends paid other than in cash, per share of the class or series of shares since the earliest date, but no more may be subtracted than the amount of the interest.

2. The highest preferential amount per share to which the holders of shares of the class or series of shares are entitled in the event of any voluntary liquidation, dissolution or winding up of the resident domestic corporation, plus the aggregate amount of any dividends declared or due to which the holders are entitled before payment of the dividends on some other class or series of shares, unless the aggregate amount of the dividends is included in the preferential amount.

3. The market value per share of the class or series of shares on the date of announcement with respect to the combination or on the interested stockholder's date of acquiring shares, whichever is higher, plus interest compounded annually from that date through the date of consummation at the rate for one-year obligations of the United States Treasury from time to time in effect, less the aggregate amount of any dividends paid in cash and the market value of any dividends paid other than in cash, per share of the class or series of shares since that date, but no

more may be subtracted than the amount of the interest.

(Added to NRS by 1991, 1205; A 1993, 970)

NRS 78.443 Authorized combinations: Required form and distribution of consideration. The consideration to be received by holders of a particular class or series of outstanding shares, including common shares, of the resident domestic corporation in the combination pursuant to NRS 78.441 and 78.442, must be in cash or in the same form as the interested stockholder has used to acquire the largest number of shares of the class or series of shares previously acquired by it, and the consideration must be distributed promptly.

(Added to NRS by 1991, 1206)

NRS 78.444 Authorized combinations: Restrictions on beneficial ownership of additional voting shares by interested stockholder. A combination may be permissible if after the interested stockholder's date of acquiring shares and before the date of consummation with respect to the combination, the interested stockholder has not become the beneficial owner of any additional voting shares of the resident domestic corporation except:

1. As part of the transaction that resulted in his becoming an interested stockholder;

2. By virtue of proportionate splitting of shares, dividends distributed in shares, or other distributions of shares in respect of shares not constituting a combination;

3. Through a combination meeting all of the conditions of NRS 78.439; or

4. Through a purchase at any price that, if the price had been paid in an otherwise permissible combination whose date of announcement and date of consummation were the date of the purchase, would have satisfied the requirements of NRS 78.441, 78.442 and 78.443.

(Added to NRS by 1991, 1206; A 1993, 971)

SALE OF ASSETS; DISSOLUTION AND WINDING UP

NRS 78.565 Sale, lease or exchange of assets: Conditions. Every corporation may, by action taken at any meeting of its board of directors, sell, lease or exchange all of its property and assets, including its good will and its corporate franchises, upon such terms and conditions as its board of directors may deem expedient and for the best interests of the corporation, when and as authorized by the affirmative vote of stockholders holding stock in the corporation entitling them to exercise at least a majority of the voting power given at a stockholders' meeting called for that purpose but:

1. The articles of incorporation may require the vote of a larger proportion of the stockholders and the separate vote or consent of any class of stockholders; and

2. Unless the articles of incorporation provide otherwise, no vote of stockholders is necessary for a transfer of assets by way of mortgage, or in trust or in pledge to secure indebtedness of the corporation.

[37:177:1925; NCL § 1636]— (NRS A 1989, 886; 1993, 973)

NRS 78.570 Sale of property and franchise under decree of court. Sales of the property and franchises of corporations that may be sold under a decree of court shall be made after such notice of the time and place as the court may deem proper. If the sales are made in the foreclosure of one or more mortgages, the court may order the sale to be made for the whole amount of indebtedness secured by the mortgage or mortgages, or for the amount of interest due under the mortgage or mortgages, subject to the payment by the purchaser of the outstanding indebtedness and interest secured thereby as they become due. In the latter event the court may, by proper orders, secure the assumption thereof by the purchaser. When a sale shall be ordered to be made, subject as aforesaid, the court shall direct the officer making such sale, in the event that the property and franchises offered do not sell for enough to pay the amount aforesaid, to sell the same free from encumbrances. Sales under this section shall be made on such credits as the court may deem proper.

[38:177:1925; NCL § 1637]

NRS 78.575 Procedure for dissolution before payment of capital and beginning of business. Before the payment of any part of the capital and before beginning the business for which the corporation was created, the incorporators or the board of directors named in the articles of incorporation may dissolve a corporation by filing in the office of the secretary of state a certificate, signed by a majority of the incorporators or of the board of directors named in the articles of incorporation, stating that no part of the capital has been paid and the business has not begun, and thereupon the corporation is dissolved.

[73:177:1925; NCL § 1672]— (NRS A 1993, 973; 1995, 1114; 1999, 1591)

NRS 78.580 Procedure for dissolution after issuance of stock or beginning of business.

1. If the board of directors of any corporation organized under this chapter, after the issuance of stock or the beginning of business, decides that the corporation should be dissolved, the board may adopt a resolution to that effect. If the corporation has issued no stock, only the directors need to approve the dissolution. If the corporation has issued stock, the directors must recommend the dissolution to the stockholders. The corporation shall notify each stockholder entitled to vote on dissolution and the stockholders entitled to vote must approve the dissolution.

2. If the dissolution is approved by the directors or both the directors and stockholders, as respectively provided in subsection 1, the corporation shall file a certificate setting forth that the dissolution has been approved by the directors, or by the directors and the stockholders, and a list of the names and post office box or street addresses, either residence or business, of the corporation's president, secretary and treasurer and all of its directors, certified by the president, or a vice president, and the secretary, or an assistant secretary, in the office of the secretary of state. The secretary of state, upon being satisfied that these requirements have been complied with and that the corporate charter has not been revoked, shall issue a certificate that the corporation is dissolved.

[64:177:1925; NCL § 1663]— (NRS A 1963, 1391; 1979, 397; 1991, 1239; 1993, 973)

NRS 78.585 Continuation of corporation after dissolution for winding up business; limitation on actions by or against dissolved corporation. The dissolution of a corporation does not impair any remedy or cause of action available to or against it or its directors, officers or shareholders arising before its dissolution and commenced within 2 years after the date of the dissolution. It continues as a body corporate for the purpose of prosecuting and defending suits, actions, proceedings and claims of any kind or character by or against it and of enabling it gradually to settle and close its business, to collect and discharge its obligations, to dispose of and convey its property, and to distribute its assets, but not for the purpose of continuing the business for which it was established.

[65:177:1925]—(NRS A 1949, 170; 1955, 165; 1985, 1793)

NRS 78.590 Trustees of dissolved corporation: Powers of directors.

1. Upon the dissolution of any corporation under the provisions of NRS 78.580, or upon the expiration of the period of its corporate existence, limited by its articles of incorporation, the directors become trustees thereof, with full power to settle the affairs, collect the outstanding debts, sell and convey the property, real and personal, and divide the money and other property among the stockholders, after paying or adequately providing for the payment of its liabilities and obligations.

2. After paying or adequately providing for the liabilities and obligations of the corporation, the trustees, with the written consent of stockholders holding stock in the corporation entitling them to exercise at least a majority of the voting power, may sell the remaining assets or any part thereof to a corporation organized under the laws of this or any other state, and take in payment therefor the stock or bonds, or both, of that corporation and distribute them among the stockholders of the liquidated corporation, in proportion to their interest therein. No such sale is valid as against any stockholder who, within 30 days after the mailing of notice to him of the sale, applies to the district court for an appraisal of the value of his interest in the assets so sold, and unless within 30 days after the appraisal is confirmed by the court the stockholders consenting to the sale, or some of them, pay to the objecting stockholder or deposit for his account, in the manner directed by the court, the amount of the appraisal. Upon the payment or deposit the interest of the objecting stockholder vests in the person or persons making the payment or deposit.

[66:177:1925; NCL § 1665]— (NRS A 1993, 974)

NRS 78.595 Trustees of dissolved corporation: Authority to sue and be sued; joint and several responsibility. The persons constituted trustees as provided in NRS 78.590 shall have authority to sue for and recover the debts and property therein mentioned, by the name of the trustees of the corporation, describing it by its corporate name, and shall be suable by the same name for the debts owing by the corporation at the time of its dissolution, and shall be jointly and severally responsible for such debts, to the amounts of the moneys and property of the corporation which shall come into their hands or possession.

[67:177:1925; NCL § 1666]

NRS 78.600 Trustees or receivers for dissolved corporations: Appointment; powers. When any corporation organized under this chapter shall be dissolved or cease to exist in any manner whatever, the district court, on application of any creditor or stockholder of the corporation, at any time, may either continue the directors trustees as provided in NRS 78.590, or appoint one or more persons to be receivers of and for the corporation, to take charge of the estate and effects thereof, and to collect the debts and property due and belonging to the corporation, with power to prosecute and defend, in the name of the corporation, or otherwise, all such suits as may be necessary or proper for the purposes aforesaid, and to appoint an
agent or agents under them, and to do all other acts which might be done by the corporation, if in being, that may be necessary for the final settlement of the unfinished business of the corporation. The powers of the trustees or receivers may be continued as long as the district court shall think necessary for the purposes aforesaid.

[68:177:1925; NCL § 1667]

NRS 78.605 Jurisdiction of district court. The district court shall have jurisdiction of the application prescribed in NRS 78.600 and of all questions arising in the proceedings thereon, and may make such orders and decrees and issue injunctions therein as justice and equity shall require.

[69:177:1925; NCL § 1668]

NRS 78.610 Duties of trustees or receivers; payment and distribution to creditors and stockholders. The trustees or receivers, after payment of all allowances, expenses and costs, and the satisfaction of all special and general liens upon the funds of the corporation to the extent of their lawful priority, shall pay the other debts due from the corporation, if the funds in their hands shall be sufficient therefor, and if not, they shall distribute the same ratably among all the creditors who shall prove their debts in the manner that shall be directed by an order or decree of the court for that purpose. If there shall be any balance remaining after the payment of the debts and necessary expenses (or the making of adequate provision therefor), they shall distribute and pay the same to and among those who shall be justly entitled thereto, as having been stockholders of the corporation, or their legal representatives.

[70:177:1925; NCL § 1669]

NRS 78.615 Abatement of pending actions; substitution of dissolution trustees or receivers. If any corporation organized under this chapter becomes dissolved by the expiration of its charter or otherwise, before final judgment obtained in any action pending or commenced in any court of record of this state against the corporation, the action shall not abate by reason thereof, but the dissolution of the corporation being suggested upon the record, and the names of the trustees or receivers of the corporation being entered upon the record, and notice thereof served upon the trustees or receivers, or if such service be impracticable upon the counsel of record in such case, the action shall proceed to final judgment against the trustees or receivers by the name of the corporation.

[71:177:1925; NCL § 1670]

NRS 78.620 Dissolution or forfeiture of charter by decree of court; filing. Whenever any corporation is dissolved or its charter forfeited by decree or judgment of the district court, the decree or judgment shall be forthwith filed by the clerk of the court in the office of the secretary of state.

[72:177:1925; NCL § 1671]

INSOLVENCY; RECEIVERS AND TRUSTEES

NRS 78.622 Reorganization under federal law: Powers of corporation.

1. If a corporation is under reorganization in a federal court pursuant to Title 11 of U.S.C., it may take any action necessary to carry out any proceeding and do any act directed by the court relating to reorganization, without further action by its directors or stockholders. This authority may be exercised by:

(a) The trustee in bankruptcy appointed by the court;

(b) Officers of the corporation designated by the court; or

(c) Any other representative appointed by the court,
with the same effect as if exercised by the directors and stockholders of the corporation.

2. By filing a certified copy of the confirmed plan of reorganization with the secretary of state, the corporation may:

(a) Alter, amend or repeal its bylaws;

(b) Constitute or reconstitute and classify or reclassify its board of directors;

(c) Name, constitute or appoint directors and officers in place of or in addition to all or some of the directors or officers then in office;

(d) Amend its articles of incorporation;

(e) Make any change in its authorized and issued stock;

(f) Make any other amendment, change, alteration or provision authorized by this chapter; and

(g) Be dissolved, transfer all or part of its assets or merge or consolidate or make any other change authorized by this chapter.

3. In any action taken pursuant to subsections 1 and 2, a stockholder has no right to demand payment for his stock.

4. Any amendment of the articles of incorporation made pursuant to subsection 2 must be signed under penalty of perjury by the person authorized by the court and filed with the secretary of state. If the amendment is filed in accordance with the order of reorganization, it becomes effective when it is filed unless otherwise ordered by the court.

5. Any filing with the secretary of state pursuant to this section must be accompanied by the appropriate fee, if any.

(Added to NRS by 1985, 1042; A 1993, 2765)

NRS 78.626 Notice: Petition in bankruptcy. Repealed. (See chapter 357, Statutes of Nevada 1999, at page 1639.)

NRS 78.627 Notice: Application for appointment of receiver or trustee. Repealed. (See chapter 357, Statutes of Nevada 1999, at page 1639.)

NRS 78.628 Notice: Application for dissolution of corporation. Repealed. (See chapter 357, Statutes of Nevada 1999, at page 1639.)

NRS 78.630 Application of creditors or stockholders of insolvent corporation for injunction and appointment of receiver or trustee; hearing.

1. Whenever any corporation becomes insolvent or suspends its ordinary business for want of money to carry on the business, or if its business has been and is being conducted at a great loss and greatly prejudicial to the interest of its creditors or stockholders, any creditors holding 10 percent of the outstanding indebtedness, or stockholders owning 10 percent of the outstanding stock entitled to vote, may, by petition setting forth the facts and circumstances of the case, apply to the district court of the county in which the registered office of the corporation is located for a writ of injunction and the appointment of a receiver or receivers or trustee or trustees.

2. The court, being satisfied by affidavit or otherwise of the sufficiency of the application and of the truth of the allegations contained in the petition and upon hearing after such notice as the court by order may direct, shall proceed in a summary way to hear the affidavits, proofs and allegations which may be offered in behalf of the parties.

3. If upon such inquiry it appears to the court that the corporation has become insolvent and is not about to resume its business in a short time thereafter, or that its business has been and is being conducted at a great loss and greatly prejudicial to the interests of its creditors or stockholders, so that its business cannot be conducted with safety to the public, it may issue an injunction to restrain the corporation and its officers and agents from exercising any of its privileges or franchises and from collecting or receiving any debts or paying out, selling, assigning or transferring any of its estate, money, lands, tenements or effects, except to a receiver appointed by the court, until the court otherwise orders.

[46:177:1925; NCL § 1645]—(NRS A 1993, 974, 2765, 2820)

NRS 78.635 Appointment of receiver or trustee of insolvent corporation: Powers.

1. The district court, at the time of ordering the injunction, or at any time afterwards, may appoint a receiver or receivers or a trustee or trustees for the creditors and stockholders of the corporation.

2. The receiver or receivers or trustee or trustees shall have full power and authority:

(a) To demand, sue for, collect, receive and take into his or their possession all the goods and chattels, rights and credits, moneys and effects, lands and tenements, books, papers, choses in action, bills, notes and property, of every description of the corporation; and

(b) To institute suits at law or in equity for the recovery of any estate, property, damages or demands existing in favor of the corporation; and

(c) In his or their discretion to compound and settle with any debtor or creditor of the corporation, or with persons having possession of its property or in any way responsible at law or in equity to the corporation at the time of its insolvency or suspension of business, or afterwards, upon such terms and in such manner as he or they shall deem just and beneficial to the corporation; and

(d) In case of mutual dealings between the corporation and any person to allow just

setoffs in favor of such person in all cases in which the same ought to be allowed according to law and equity.

3. A debtor who shall have in good faith paid his debt to the corporation without notice of its insolvency or suspension of business, shall not be liable therefor, and the receiver or receivers or trustee or trustees shall have power to sell, convey and assign all the estate, rights and interests, and shall hold and dispose of the proceeds thereof under the directions of the district court.

[Part 47:177:1925; NCL § 1646]—(NRS A 1969, 93)

NRS 78.640 Property and privileges of insolvent corporation vest in appointed receiver. All real and personal property of an insolvent corporation, wheresoever situated, and all its franchises, rights, privileges and effects shall, upon the appointment of a receiver, forthwith vest in him, and the corporation shall be divested of the title thereto.

[48:177:1925; NCL § 1647]

NRS 78.645 Corporation may resume control upon payment of debts and receipt of capital to conduct business; order of court dissolving corporation and forfeiting charter.

1. Whenever a receiver shall have been appointed as provided in NRS 78.635 and it shall afterwards appear that the debts of the corporation have been paid or provided for, and that there remains or can be obtained by further contributions sufficient capital to enable it to resume its business, the district court may, in its discretion, a proper case being shown, direct the receiver to reconvey to the corporation all its property, franchises, rights and effects, and thereafter the corporation may resume control of and enjoy the same as fully as if the receiver had never been appointed.

2. In every case in which the district court shall not direct such reconveyance, the court may, in its discretion, make a decree dissolving the corporation and declaring its charter forfeited and void.

[49:177:1925; NCL § 1648]

NRS 78.650 Stockholders' application for injunction and appointment of receiver when corporation mismanaged.

1. Any holder or holders of one-tenth of the issued and outstanding stock may apply to the district court, held in the district where the corporation has its principal place of business, for an order dissolving the corporation and appointing a receiver to

wind up its affairs, and by injunction restrain the corporation from exercising any of its powers or doing business whatsoever, except by and through a receiver appointed by the court, whenever:

(a) The corporation has willfully violated its charter;

(b) Its trustees or directors have been guilty of fraud or collusion or gross mismanagement in the conduct or control of its affairs;

(c) Its trustees or directors have been guilty of misfeasance, malfeasance or nonfeasance;

(d) The corporation is unable to conduct the business or conserve its assets by reason of the act, neglect or refusal to function of any of the directors or trustees;

(e) The assets of the corporation are in danger of waste, sacrifice or loss through attachment, foreclosure, litigation or otherwise;

(f) The corporation has abandoned its business;

(g) The corporation has not proceeded diligently to wind up its affairs, or to distribute its assets in a reasonable time;

(h) The corporation has become insolvent;

(i) The corporation, although not insolvent, is for any cause not able to pay its debts or other obligations as they mature; or

(j) The corporation is not about to resume its business with safety to the public.

2. The application may be for the appointment of a receiver, without at the same time applying for the dissolution of the corporation, and notwithstanding the absence, if any there be, of any action or other proceeding in the premises pending in such court.

3. In any such application for a receivership, it is sufficient for a temporary appointment if notice of the same is given to the corporation alone, by process as in the case of an application for a temporary restraining order or injunction, and the hearing thereon may be had after 5 days' notice unless the court directs a longer or different notice and different parties.

4. The court may, if good cause exists therefor, appoint one or more receivers for such purpose, but in all cases directors or trustees who have been guilty of no negligence nor active breach of duty must be preferred in making the appointment. The court may at any time for sufficient cause make a decree terminating the receivership, or dissolving the corporation and terminating its existence, or both, as may be proper.

5. Receivers so appointed have, among the usual powers, all the functions, powers, tenure and duties to be exercised under the direction of the court as are conferred on receivers and as provided in NRS 78.635, 78.640 and 78.645, whether the corporation is insolvent or not.

[49a:177:1925; added 1941, 405; 1931 NCL § 1648.01]—(NRS A 1993, 2766)

NRS 78.655 Reorganization of corporation by majority of stockholders during receivership. Whenever stockholders holding stock entitling them to exercise at least a majority of the voting power of the corporation shall have agreed upon a plan for the reorganization of the corporation and a resumption by it of the management and control of its property and business, the corporation may, with the consent of the district court:

1. Upon the reconveyance to it of its property and franchises, mortgage the same for such amount as may be necessary for the purposes of reorganization; and

2. Issue bonds or other evidences of indebtedness, or additional stock of one or more classes, with or without nominal or par value, or both, or both bonds and stock, or certificates of investment or participation certificates, and use the same for the full or partial payment of the creditors who will accept the same, or otherwise dispose of the same for the purposes of the reorganization.

[50:177:1925; NCL § 1649]

NRS 78.660 Powers of district court.

1. The court shall have power to send for persons and papers and to examine any persons, including the creditors and claimants, and the president, directors and other officers and agents of the corporation, on oath or affirmation, respecting its affairs and transactions and its estate, money, goods, chattels, credits, notes, bills and choses in action, real and personal estate and effects of every kind, and also respecting its debts, obligations, contracts and liabilities, and the claims against it.

2. If any person shall refuse to be sworn or affirmed, or to make answers to such questions as shall be put to him, or refuse to declare the whole truth touching the subject matter of the examination, the district court may commit such person to a place of confinement, there to remain until he shall submit himself to be examined, and pay all the costs of the proceedings against him.

[51:177:1925; NCL § 1650]

NRS 78.665 Receiver to take possession of corporate assets upon court order. The receiver, upon order of the court, with the assistance of a peace officer, may break open, in the daytime, the houses, shops, warehouses, doors, trunks, chests or other places of the corporation where any of its goods, chattels, choses in action, notes, bills, moneys, books, papers or other writings or effects have been usually kept, or shall be, and take possession of the same and of the lands and tenements belonging to the corporation.

[52:177:1925; NCL § 1651]

NRS 78.670 Inventory, list of debts and reports by receiver. The receiver, as soon as convenient, shall lay before the district court a full and complete inventory of all the estate, property and effects of the corporation, its nature and probable value, and an account of all debts due from and to it, as nearly as the same can be ascertained, and make a report to the court of his proceedings at least every 3 months thereafter during the continuance of the trust, and whenever he shall be so ordered.

[53:177:1925; NCL § 1652]

NRS 78.675 Creditors' proofs of claims; when participation barred; notice. All creditors shall present and make proof to the receiver of their respective claims against the corporation within 6 months from the date of appointment of the receiver or trustee for the corporation, or sooner if the court shall order and direct, and all creditors and claimants failing to do so within the time limited by this section, or the time prescribed by the order of the court, shall by the direction of the court be barred from participating in the distribution of the assets of the corporation. The court shall also prescribe what notice, by publication or otherwise, shall be given to creditors of such limitation of time.

[54:177:1925; A 1949, 158; 1943 NCL § 1653]

NRS 78.680 Creditors' claims to be in writing under oath; examination of claimants. Every claim against any corporation for which a receiver has been appointed shall be presented to the receiver in writing and upon oath. The claimant, if required, shall submit himself to such examination in relation to the claim as the court shall direct, and shall produce such books and papers relating to the claim as shall be required. The court shall have power to authorize the receiver to examine, under oath or affirmation, all witnesses produced before him touching the claim or any part thereof.

[55:177:1925; NCL § 1654]

NRS 78.685   Action on creditors' claims; appeal of disallowed claims.

1.   The clerk of the district court, immediately upon the expiration of the time fixed for the filing of claims, shall notify the trustee or receiver of the filing of the claims. The trustee or receiver shall inspect the claims and within 30 days notify each claimant of his decision. The trustee or receiver may require all creditors whose claims are disputed to submit themselves to an examination in relation to their claims, and to produce such books and papers relating to their claims as the trustee or receiver requests. The trustee or receiver may examine, under oath or affirmation, all witnesses produced before him regarding the claims, and shall pass upon and allow or disallow the claims, or any part thereof, and notify the claimants of his determination.

2.   Every creditor or claimant who has received notice from the receiver or trustee that his claim has been disallowed in whole or in part may appeal to the district court within 30 days thereafter. The court, after a hearing, shall determine the rights of the parties.

[56:177:1925; NCL § 1655] + [Part 57:177:1925; NCL § 1656]— (NRS A 1991, 1239)

NRS 78.695   Substitution of receiver as a party; abatement of actions.

1.   A receiver, upon application by him, shall be substituted as party plaintiff or complainant in the place and stead of the corporation in any suit or proceeding at law or in equity which was pending at the time of his appointment.

2.   No action against a receiver of a corporation shall abate by reason of his death, but, upon suggestion of the facts on the record, shall be continued against his successor, or against the corporation in case no new receiver be appointed.

[58:177:1925; NCL § 1657] + [59:177:1925; NCL § 1658]

NRS 78.700   Sales of encumbered or deteriorating property.   Where property of an insolvent corporation is at the time of the appointment of a receiver encumbered with mortgages or other liens, the legality of which is brought in question, or the property is of a character which will materially deteriorate in value pending the litigation, the district court may order the receiver to sell the same, clear of encumbrances, at public or private sale, for the best price that can be obtained, and pay the money into court, there to remain subject to the same liens and equities of all parties in interest as

was the property before sale, to be disposed of as the court shall direct.

[60:177:1925; NCL § 1659]

NRS 78.705   Compensation, costs and expenses of receiver.   Before distribution of the assets of an insolvent corporation among the creditors or stockholders, the district court shall allow a reasonable compensation to the receiver for his services and the costs and expenses of the administration of the trust, and the cost of the proceedings in the court, to be first paid out of the assets.

[61:177:1925; NCL § 1660]

NRS 78.710   Distribution of money to creditors and stockholders.   After payment of all allowances, expenses and costs, and the satisfaction of all special and general liens upon the funds of the corporation to the extent of their lawful priority, the creditors shall be paid proportionately to the amount of their respective debts, excepting mortgage and judgment creditors when the judgment has not been by confession for the purpose of preferring creditors. The creditors shall be entitled to distribution on debts not due, making in such case a rebate of interest, when interest is not accruing on the same. The surplus funds, if any, after payment of the creditors and the costs, expenses and allowances, shall be distributed among the stockholders or their legal representatives in proportion to their interests.

[62:177:1925; NCL § 1661]

NRS 78.715   Acts of majority of receivers effectual; removal and vacancies.

1.   Every matter and thing by this chapter required to be done by receivers or trustees shall be good and effectual, to all intents and purposes, if performed by a majority of them.

2.   The district court may remove any receiver or trustee and appoint another or others in his place to fill any vacancy which may occur.

[63:177:1925; NCL § 1662]

NRS 78.720   Employees' liens for wages when corporation insolvent.

1.   Whenever any corporation becomes insolvent or is dissolved in any way or for any cause, the employees doing labor or service, of whatever character, in the regular employ of the corporation, have a lien upon the assets thereof for the amount of wages due to them, not exceeding $1,000, which have been earned within 3 months before the date of the insolvency or dissolution, which must be paid before any other debt of the corporation.

2.   The word "employees" does not include any of the officers of the corporation.

[86:177:1925; NCL § 1685]— (NRS A 1959, 607; 1983, 1362)

REINCORPORATION; RENEWAL AND REVIVAL OF CHARTERS

NRS 78.725   Domestic corporations in existence on April 1, 1925, may reincorporate under this chapter.

1.   Any corporation organized and existing under the laws of this state on April 1, 1925, may reincorporate under this chapter, either under the same or a different name, by:

(a) Filing with the secretary of state a certificate executed by its president and attested by its secretary and duly authorized by a meeting of the stockholders called for that purpose, setting forth the statements required in an original certificate of incorporation by NRS 78.035; and

(b) Surrendering the existing charter or certificate of incorporation of the corporation, and accepting the provisions of this chapter.

2.   Upon the filing of the certificate, the corporation shall be deemed to be incorporated under this chapter and shall be entitled to and be possessed of all the privileges, franchises and powers as if originally incorporated under this chapter. All the properties, rights and privileges theretofore belonging to the corporation, which were acquired by gift, grant, conveyance, assignment or otherwise, shall be and the same are hereby ratified, approved and confirmed and assured to the corporation with like effect and to all intents and purposes as if the same had been originally acquired through incorporation under this chapter.

3.   Any corporation reincorporating under this chapter shall be subject to all the contracts, duties and obligations theretofore resting upon the corporation whose charter or certificate of incorporation is thus surrendered or to which the corporation shall then be in any way liable.

[82:177:1925; NCL § 1681]— (NRS A 1971, 1105)

NRS 78.730   Renewal or revival: Procedure; fee; certificate as evidence.

1.   Any corporation which did exist or is existing under the laws of this state may, upon complying with the provisions of NRS 78.180, procure a renewal or revival of its

charter for any period, together with all the rights, franchises, privileges and immunities, and subject to all its existing and preexisting debts, duties and liabilities secured or imposed by its original charter and amendments thereto, or existing charter, by filing:

(a) A certificate with the secretary of state, which must set forth:

(1) The name of the corporation, which must be the name of the corporation at the time of the renewal or revival, or its name at the time its original charter expired.

(2) The name of the person designated as the resident agent of the corporation, his street address for the service of process, and his mailing address if different from his street address.

(3) The date when the renewal or revival of the charter is to commence or be effective, which may be, in cases of a revival, before the date of the certificate.

(4) Whether or not the renewal or revival is to be perpetual, and, if not perpetual, the time for which the renewal or revival is to continue.

(5) That the corporation desiring to renew or revive its charter is, or has been, organized and carrying on the business authorized by its existing or original charter and amendments thereto, and desires to renew or continue through revival its existence pursuant to and subject to the provisions of this chapter.

(b) A list of its president, secretary and treasurer and all of its directors and their post office box or street addresses, either residence or business.

2. A corporation whose charter has not expired and is being renewed shall cause the certificate to be signed by its president or vice president and secretary or assistant secretary. The certificate must be approved by a majority of the voting power of the shares.

3. A corporation seeking to revive its original or amended charter shall cause the certificate to be signed by a person or persons designated or appointed by the stockholders of the corporation. The execution and filing of the certificate must be approved by the written consent of stockholders of the corporation holding at least a majority of the voting power and must contain a recital that this consent was secured. If no stock has been issued, the certificate must contain a statement of that fact, and a majority of the directors then in office may designate the person to sign the certificate. The corporation shall pay to the secretary of state the fee required to establish a new corporation pursuant to the provisions of this chapter.

4. The filed certificate, or a copy thereof which has been certified under the hand and seal of the secretary of state, must be received in all courts and places as prima facie evidence of the facts therein stated and of the existence and incorporation of the corporation therein named.

[93:177:1925]—(NRS A 1937, 4; 1953, 314; 1985, 1872; 1993, 975; 1995, 2100; 1997, 705; 1999, 1591)

NRS 78.740 Renewal or revival: Status of corporation. Any corporation existing on or incorporated after April 1, 1925, desiring to renew or revive its corporate existence, upon complying with the provisions of this chapter, is and continues for the time stated in its certificate of renewal to be a corporation, and in addition to the rights, privileges and immunities conferred by its original charter, possesses and enjoys all the benefits of this chapter that are applicable to the nature of its business, and is subject to the restrictions and liabilities by this chapter imposed on such corporations.

[95:177:1925; NCL § 1694]—(NRS A 1993, 976)

SUITS AGAINST CORPORATIONS, DIRECTORS, OFFICERS, EMPLOYEES, AGENTS AND STOCKHOLDERS

NRS 78.745 Action against stockholder for unpaid subscriptions; limitation of action. No action shall be brought by the corporation against any stockholder for any unpaid subscription unless within 2 years after the debt becomes due, and no action shall be brought against the stockholder after he shall cease to be the owner of the shares, unless brought within 2 years from the time he shall have ceased to be a stockholder.

[17:177:1925; NCL § 1616]

NRS 78.750 Service of process on corporations.

1. In any action commenced against any corporation in any court of this state, service of process may be made in the manner provided by law and rule of court for the service of civil process.

2. Service of process on a corporation which has been continued as a body corporate under NRS 78.585 may be made by mailing copies of the process and any associated documents by certified mail, with return receipt requested, to:

(a) The resident agent of the corporation, if there is one; and

(b) Each officer and director of the corporation as named in the list last filed with the secretary of state before the dissolution or expiration of the corporation or the forfeiture of its charter.

The manner of serving process described in this subsection does not affect the validity of any other service authorized by law.

[81:177:1925; NCL § 1680]—(NRS A 1979, 568; 1997, 474)

NRS 78.7502 Discretionary and mandatory indemnification of officers, directors, employees and agents: General provisions.

1. A corporation may indemnify any person who was or is a party or is threatened to be made a party to any threatened, pending or completed action, suit or proceeding, whether civil, criminal, administrative or investigative, except an action by or in the right of the corporation, by reason of the fact that he is or was a director, officer, employee or agent of the corporation, or is or was serving at the request of the corporation as a director, officer, employee or agent of another corporation, partnership, joint venture, trust or other enterprise, against expenses, including attorneys' fees, judgments, fines and amounts paid in settlement actually and reasonably incurred by him in connection with the action, suit or proceeding if he acted in good faith and in a manner which he reasonably believed to be in or not opposed to the best interests of the corporation, and, with respect to any criminal action or proceeding, had no reasonable cause to believe his conduct was unlawful. The termination of any action, suit or proceeding by judgment, order, settlement, conviction or upon a plea of nolo contendere or its equivalent, does not, of itself, create a presumption that the person did not act in good faith and in a manner which he reasonably believed to be in or not opposed to the best interests of the corporation, and that, with respect to any criminal action or proceeding, he had reasonable cause to believe that his conduct was unlawful.

2. A corporation may indemnify any person who was or is a party or is threatened to be made a party to any threatened, pending or completed action or suit by or in the right of the corporation to procure a judgment in its favor by reason of the fact that he is or was a director, officer, employee or agent of the corporation, or is or was serving at the request of the corporation as a director, officer, employee

or agent of another corporation, partnership, joint venture, trust or other enterprise against expenses, including amounts paid in settlement and attorneys' fees actually and reasonably incurred by him in connection with the defense or settlement of the action or suit if he acted in good faith and in a manner which he reasonably believed to be in or not opposed to the best interests of the corporation. Indemnification may not be made for any claim, issue or matter as to which such a person has been adjudged by a court of competent jurisdiction, after exhaustion of all appeals therefrom, to be liable to the corporation or for amounts paid in settlement to the corporation, unless and only to the extent that the court in which the action or suit was brought or other court of competent jurisdiction determines upon application that in view of all the circumstances of the case, the person is fairly and reasonably entitled to indemnity for such expenses as the court deems proper.

3. To the extent that a director, officer, employee or agent of a corporation has been successful on the merits or otherwise in defense of any action, suit or proceeding referred to in subsections 1 and 2, or in defense of any claim, issue or matter therein, the corporation shall indemnify him against expenses, including attorneys' fees, actually and reasonably incurred by him in connection with the defense.

(Added to NRS by 1997, 694)

NRS 78.751 Authorization required for discretionary indemnification; advancement of expenses; limitation on indemnification and advancement of expenses.

1. Any discretionary indemnification under NRS 78.7502 unless ordered by a court or advanced pursuant to subsection 2, may be made by the corporation only as authorized in the specific case upon a determination that indemnification of the director, officer, employee or agent is proper in the circumstances. The determination must be made:

(a) By the stockholders;

(b) By the board of directors by majority vote of a quorum consisting of directors who were not parties to the action, suit or proceeding;

(c) If a majority vote of a quorum consisting of directors who were not parties to the action, suit or proceeding so orders, by independent legal counsel in a written opinion; or

(d) If a quorum consisting of directors who were not parties to the action, suit or proceeding cannot be obtained, by independent legal counsel in a written opinion.

2. The articles of incorporation, the bylaws or an agreement made by the corporation may provide that the expenses of officers and directors incurred in defending a civil or criminal action, suit or proceeding must be paid by the corporation as they are incurred and in advance of the final disposition of the action, suit or proceeding, upon receipt of an undertaking by or on behalf of the director or officer to repay the amount if it is ultimately determined by a court of competent jurisdiction that he is not entitled to be indemnified by the corporation. The provisions of this subsection do not affect any rights to advancement of expenses to which corporate personnel other than directors or officers may be entitled under any contract or otherwise by law.

3. The indemnification and advancement of expenses authorized in or ordered by a court pursuant to this section:

(a) Does not exclude any other rights to which a person seeking indemnification or advancement of expenses may be entitled under the articles of incorporation or any bylaw, agreement, vote of stockholders or disinterested directors or otherwise, for either an action in his official capacity or an action in another capacity while holding his office, except that indemnification, unless ordered by a court pursuant to NRS 78.7502 or for the advancement of expenses made pursuant to subsection 2, may not be made to or on behalf of any director or officer if a final adjudication establishes that his acts or omissions involved intentional misconduct, fraud or a knowing violation of the law and was material to the cause of action.

(b) Continues for a person who has ceased to be a director, officer, employee or agent and inures to the benefit of the heirs, executors and administrators of such a person.

(Added to NRS by 1969, 118; A 1987, 83; 1993, 976; 1997, 706)

NRS 78.752 Insurance and other financial arrangements against liability of directors, officers, employees and agents.

1. A corporation may purchase and maintain insurance or make other financial arrangements on behalf of any person who is or was a director, officer, employee or agent of the corporation, or is or was serving at the request of the corporation as a director, officer, employee or agent of another corporation, partnership, joint venture, trust or other enterprise for any liability asserted against him and liability and expenses incurred by him in his capacity as a director, officer, employee or agent, or arising out of his status as such, whether or not the corporation has the authority to indemnify him against such liability and expenses.

2. The other financial arrangements made by the corporation pursuant to subsection 1 may include the following:

(a) The creation of a trust fund.

(b) The establishment of a program of self-insurance.

(c) The securing of its obligation of indemnification by granting a security interest or other lien on any assets of the corporation.

(d) The establishment of a letter of credit, guaranty or surety.

No financial arrangement made pursuant to this subsection may provide protection for a person adjudged by a court of competent jurisdiction, after exhaustion of all appeals therefrom, to be liable for intentional misconduct, fraud or a knowing violation of law, except with respect to the advancement of expenses or indemnification ordered by a court.

3. Any insurance or other financial arrangement made on behalf of a person pursuant to this section may be provided by the corporation or any other person approved by the board of directors, even if all or part of the other person's stock or other securities is owned by the corporation.

4. In the absence of fraud:

(a) The decision of the board of directors as to the propriety of the terms and conditions of any insurance or other financial arrangement made pursuant to this section and the choice of the person to provide the insurance or other financial arrangement is conclusive; and

(b) The insurance or other financial arrangement:

(1) Is not void or voidable; and

(2) Does not subject any director approving it to personal liability for his action,

even if a director approving the insurance or other financial arrangement is a beneficiary of the insurance or other financial arrangement.

5. A corporation or its subsidiary which provides self-insurance for itself or for another affiliated corporation pursuant to this section is not subject to the provisions of Title 57 of NRS.

(Added to NRS by 1987, 80)

SECRETARY OF STATE: DUTIES AND FEES

NRS 78.755 Duties: Collection of fees; employment of new technology to aid in performance.

1. The secretary of state, for services relating to his official duties and the records of his office, shall charge and collect the fees designated in NRS 78.760 to 78.785, inclusive.

2. The secretary of state may accept the filing of documents by facsimile machine and employ new technology, as it is developed, to aid in the performance of all duties required by law. The secretary of state may establish rules, fee schedules and regulations not inconsistent with law, for filing documents by facsimile machine and for the adoption, employment and use of new technology in the performance of his duties.

[Part 1:52:1933; A 1949, 363; 1951, 393] + [Part 2:52:1933; A 1949, 409; 1943 NCL § 7421.02]— (NRS A 1979, 76; 1991, 1239; 1997, 2810)

NRS 78.760 Filing fees: Articles of incorporation.

1. The fee for filing articles of incorporation is prescribed in the following schedule:

If the amount represented by the total number of shares provided for in the articles or agreement is:

$25,000 or less - $125
Over $25,000 and not over $75,000 - $175
Over $75,000 and not over $200,000 - $225
Over $200,000 and not over $500,000 - $325
Over $500,000 and not over $1,000,000 - $425
Over $1,000,000:
    For the first $1,000,000 - $425
    For each additional $500,000 or fraction thereof - $225

2. The maximum fee which may be charged under this section is $25,000 for:

(a) The original filing of articles of incorporation.

(b) A subsequent filing of any instrument which authorizes an increase in stock.

3. For the purposes of computing the filing fees according to the schedule in subsection 1, the amount represented by the total number of shares provided for in the articles of incorporation is:

(a) The aggregate par value of the shares, if only shares with a par value are therein provided for;

(b) The product of the number of shares multiplied by $1, regardless of any lesser amount prescribed as the value or consideration for which shares may be issued and disposed of, if only shares without par value are therein provided for; or

(c) The aggregate par value of the shares with a par value plus the product of the number of shares without par value multiplied by $1, regardless of any lesser amount prescribed as the value or consideration for which the shares without par value may be issued and disposed of, if shares with and without par value are therein provided for.

For the purposes of this subsection, shares with no prescribed par value shall be deemed shares without par value.

4. The secretary of state shall calculate filing fees pursuant to this section with respect to shares with a par value of less than one-tenth of a cent as if the par value were one-tenth of a cent.

[Part 1:52:1933; A 1949, 363; 1951, 393]—(NRS A 1975, 478; 1977, 402; 1983, 690; 1989, 978; 1991, 1240; 1993, 555, 978; 1995, 1115)

NRS 78.765 Filing fees: Certificate changing number of authorized shares; amendment of articles; certificate of correction.

1. The fee for filing a certificate changing the number of authorized shares pursuant to NRS 78.209 or a certificate of amendment to articles of incorporation that increases the corporation's authorized stock or a certificate of correction that increases the corporation's authorized stock is the difference between the fee computed at the rates specified in NRS 78.760 upon the total authorized stock of the corporation, including the proposed increase, and the fee computed at the rates specified in NRS 78.760 upon the total authorized capital, excluding the proposed increase. In no case may the amount be less than $75.

2. The fee for filing a certificate of amendment to articles of incorporation that does not increase the corporation's authorized stock or a certificate of correction that does not increase the corporation's authorized stock is $75.

3. The fee for filing a certificate or an amended certificate pursuant to NRS 78.1955 is $75.

[Part 1:52:1933; A 1949, 363; 1951, 393]—(NRS A 1983, 691; 1989, 978; 1991, 1240; 1993, 979; 1995, 1115, 2101; 1997, 708; 1999, 1592)

NRS 78.767 Filing fees: Certificates of restated articles of incorporation.

1. The fee for filing a certificate of restated articles of incorporation that does not increase the corporation's authorized stock is $75.

2. The fee for filing a certificate of restated articles of incorporation that increases the corporation's authorized stock is the difference between the fee computed pursuant to NRS 78.760 based upon the total authorized stock of the corporation, including the proposed increase, and the fee computed pursuant to NRS 78.760 based upon the total authorized stock of the corporation, excluding the proposed increase. In no case may the amount be less than $75.

(Added to NRS by 1959, 682; A 1983, 691; 1989, 979; 1993, 979; 1995, 1116)

NRS 78.770 Filing fees: Articles of merger; articles of exchange.

1. The fee for filing articles of merger of two or more domestic corporations is the difference between the fee computed at the rates specified in NRS 78.760 upon the aggregate authorized stock of the corporation created by the merger and the fee so computed upon the aggregate amount of the total authorized stock of the constituent corporations.

2. The fee for filing articles of merger of one or more domestic corporations with one or more foreign corporations is the difference between the fee computed at the rates specified in NRS 78.760 upon the aggregate authorized stock of the corporation created by the merger and the fee so computed upon the aggregate amount of the total authorized stock of the constituent corporations which have paid fees as required by NRS 78.760 and 80.050.

3. In no case may the amount paid be less than $125, and in no case may the amount paid pursuant to subsection 2 exceed $25,000.

4. The fee for filing articles of exchange is $125.

[Part 1:52:1933; A 1949, 363; 1951, 393]—(NRS A 1960, 226; 1961, 398; 1983, 691; 1989, 979; 1991, 1241; 1999, 1592)

NRS 78.780 Filing fees: Certificates of extension and dissolution.

1. The fee for filing a certificate of extension of corporate existence of any corporation is an amount equal to one-fourth of the fee computed at the rates specified in NRS 78.760 for filing articles of incorporation.

2. The fee for filing a certificate of dissolution whether it occurs before or after payment of capital and beginning of business is $30.

[Part 1:52:1933; A 1949, 363; 1951, 393]—(NRS A 1981, 1890; 1989, 979; 1993, 979)

NRS 78.785 Miscellaneous fees.

1. The fee for filing a certificate of change of location of a corporation's registered office and resident agent, or a new designation of resident agent, is $15.

2. The fee for certifying articles of incorporation where a copy is provided is $10.

3. The fee for certifying a copy of an amendment to articles of incorporation, or to a copy of the articles as amended, where a copy is furnished, is $10.

4. The fee for certifying an authorized printed copy of the general corporation law as compiled by the secretary of state is $10.

5. The fee for reserving a corporate name is $20.

6. The fee for executing a certificate of corporate existence which does not list the previous documents relating to the corporation, or a certificate of change in a corporate name, is $15.

7. The fee for executing a certificate of corporate existence which lists the previous documents relating to the corporation is $20.

8. The fee for executing, certifying or filing any certificate or document not provided for in NRS 78.760 to 78.785, inclusive, is $20.

9. The fee for copies made at the office of the secretary of state is $1 per page.

10. The fee for filing articles of incorporation, articles of merger, or certificates of amendment increasing the basic surplus of a mutual or reciprocal insurer must be computed pursuant to NRS 78.760, 78.765 and 78.770, on the basis of the amount of basic surplus of the insurer.

11. The fee for examining and provisionally approving any document at any time before the document is presented for filing is $100.

[Part 1:52:1933; A 1949, 363; 1951, 393]—(NRS A 1959, 689; 1975, 565; 1977, 403; 1979, 398; 1981, 141; 1983, 692; 1985, 1873; 1987, 1058; 1989, 979; 1991, 1241; 1993, 979; 1995, 1116)

MISCELLANEOUS PROVISIONS

NRS 78.795 Registration of natural person or corporation willing to serve as resident agent for corporation, limited-liability company or limited partnership.

1. Any natural person or corporation residing or located in this state may, on or after January 1 of any year but before January 31 of that year, register his willingness to serve as the resident agent of a domestic or foreign corporation, limited-liability company or limited partnership with the secretary of state. The registration must be accompanied by a fee of $250 per office location of the resident agent.

2. The secretary of state shall maintain a list of those persons who are registered pursuant to subsection 1 and make the list available to persons seeking to do business in this state.

(Added to NRS by 1995, 1111; A 1999, 1593)

APPENDIX C: NEVADA REVISED STATUTES CHAPTER 78A

CLOSE CORPORATIONS

GENERAL PROVISIONS

NRS 78A.010 Applicability of chapter. The provisions of this chapter apply to all close corporations formed pursuant to NRS 78A.020. Unless otherwise provided by this chapter, the provisions of chapter 78 of NRS are applicable to all close corporations.

(Added to NRS by 1989, 940)

NRS 78A.015 Filing of documents written in language other than English. No document which is written in a language other than English may be filed or submitted for filing in the office of the secretary of state pursuant to the provisions of this chapter unless it is accompanied by a verified translation of that document into the English language.

(Added to NRS by 1995, 1117)

FORMATION

NRS 78A.020 Procedure; requirements concerning stock; contents of articles of incorporation.

1. A close corporation must be formed in accordance with NRS 78.030 to 78.055, inclusive, subject to the following requirements:

(a) All of the issued stock of the corporation of all classes, exclusive of treasury shares, must be represented by certificates and must be held of record by a specified number of persons, not to exceed 30.

(b) All of the issued stock of all classes must be subject to one or more of the restrictions on transfer pursuant to NRS 78A.050.

(c) The corporation shall not offer any of its stock of any class that would constitute a public offering within the meaning of the Securities Act of 1933, 15 U.S.C. §§ 77 et seq.

2. The articles of incorporation of a close corporation must:

(a) Set forth the matters required by NRS 78.035 except that the articles must

state that there will be no board of directors if so agreed pursuant to NRS 78A.070.

(b) Contain a heading stating the name of the corporation and that it is a close corporation.

3. The articles of incorporation of a close corporation may set forth the qualifications of stockholders by specifying the classes of persons who are entitled to be holders of record of stock of any class, the classes of persons who are not entitled to be holders of record of stock of any class, or both.

4. To determine the number of holders of record of the stock of a close corporation, stock that is held in joint or common tenancy or by community property must be treated as held by one stockholder.

(Added to NRS by 1989, 941; A 1993, 980)

NRS 78A.030 Procedure for existing corporation to become close corporation.

1. Any corporation organized under chapter 78 of NRS may become a close corporation pursuant to this chapter by executing, filing and recording, in accordance with NRS 78.390, a certificate of amendment of the certificate of incorporation which must:

(a) Contain a statement that the corporation elects to become a close corporation; and

(b) Meet the requirements of subsection 2 of NRS 78A.020.

2. Except as otherwise provided in subsection 3, the amendment must be adopted in accordance with the requirements of NRS 78.390.

3. The amendment must be approved by a vote of the holders of record of at least two-thirds of the shares of each class of stock of the corporation that are outstanding and entitled to vote, unless the articles of incorporation or bylaws require approval by a greater proportion.

(Added to NRS by 1989, 941; A 1999, 1593)

SHARES OF STOCK

NRS 78A.040 Notice required on share certificates; effect of notice and restrictions on transfer of shares; shareholders to be provided with copies of provisions restricting rights.

1. The following statement must appear conspicuously on each share certificate issued by a close corporation:

> The rights of stockholders in a close corporation may differ materially from the rights of shareholders in other corporations. Copies of the certificate of incorporation, bylaws, shareholders' agreements and other documents, any of which may restrict transfers of stock and affect voting and other rights, may be obtained by a shareholder on written request to the corporation.

2. A person claiming an interest in the shares of a close corporation that has complied with the requirement of subsection 1 is bound by the documents referred to in the notice. A person claiming an interest in the shares of a close corporation that has not complied with the requirement of subsection 1 is bound by any document that he or a person through whom he claims has knowledge or notice.

3. A close corporation shall provide to any shareholder upon his written request and without charge, copies of the provisions that restrict transfer or affect voting or other rights of shareholders appearing in the articles of incorporation, bylaws, shareholders' agreements or voting trust agreements filed with the corporations.

4. Except as otherwise provided in subsection 5, the close corporation may refuse to register the transfer of stock into the name of a person to whom the stock of a close corporation has been transferred if the person has, or is presumed to have, notice that the transfer of the stock is in violation of a restriction on the transfer of stock. If the close corporation refuses to register the

transfer of stock into the name of the transferee, the close corporation must notify the transferee of its refusal and state the reasons therefor.

5. Subsection 4 does not apply if:

(a) The transfer of stock, even if contrary to the restrictions on transfer of stock, has been consented to by all the stockholders of the close corporation; or

(b) The close corporation has amended its certificate of incorporation in accordance with NRS 78A.180.

6. The provisions of this section do not impair any rights of a transferee to:

(a) Rescind the transaction by which he acquired the stock; or

(b) Recover under any applicable warranty.

7. As used in this section, "transfer" is not limited to a transfer for value.

(Added to NRS by 1989, 941)

NRS 78A.050 Transfer of shares prohibited; exceptions.

1. An interest in the shares of a close corporation may not be transferred, except to the extent permitted by the certificate of incorporation, the bylaws, a shareholders' agreement or a voting trust agreement.

2. Except as otherwise provided by the certificate of incorporation, the provisions of this section do not apply to a transfer:

(a) To the corporation or to any other shareholder of the same class or series of shares.

(b) To heirs at law.

(c) That has been approved in writing by all of the holders of the shares of the corporation having voting rights.

(d) To an executor or administrator upon the death of a shareholder or to a trustee or receiver as a result of a bankruptcy, insolvency, dissolution or similar proceeding brought by or against a shareholder.

(e) By merger or share exchange or an exchange of existing shares for other shares of a different class or series in the corporation.

(f) By a pledge as collateral for a loan that does not grant the pledgee any voting rights possessed by the pledgor.

(g) Made after the termination of the status of the corporation as a close corporation.

(Added to NRS by 1989, 942)

NRS 78A.060 Effect of attempt to transfer shares in violation of prohibition.

1. An attempt to transfer shares in a close corporation in violation of a prohibition against such a transfer is ineffective.

2. An attempt to transfer shares in a close corporation in violation of a prohibition against transfer that is not binding on the transferee because:

(a) The notice required by NRS 78A.040 was not given; or

(b) The prohibition is held unenforceable by a court of competent jurisdiction,

gives the corporation an option to purchase the shares from the transferee for the same price and on the same terms that he purchased them. To exercise the option, the corporation must give the transferee written notice within 30 days after they receive a share certificate for registration in the name of the transferee.

(Added to NRS by 1989, 943)

POWERS AND DUTIES

NRS 78A.070 Shareholders' agreements: Authority to enter; effect; amendment.

1. All shareholders of a close corporation who are entitled to vote may agree in writing to regulate the exercise of the corporate powers and the management of the business and affairs of the corporation or the relationship among the shareholders of the corporation.

2. An agreement authorized by this section is effective even if the agreement:

(a) Eliminates a board of directors.

(b) Restricts the discretion or powers of the board of directors or authorizes director proxies or weighted voting rights.

(c) Treats the corporation as a partnership.

(d) Creates a relationship among the shareholders or between the shareholders and the corporation that would otherwise be appropriate among partners.

3. If the corporation has a board of directors, an agreement authorized by this section that restricts the discretion or powers of the board of directors:

(a) Relieves directors of liability imposed by law; and

(b) Imposes that liability on each person in whom the discretion or power of the board is vested,

to the extent that the discretion or power of the board of directors is governed by the agreement.

4. A provision eliminating a board of directors in an agreement authorized by this section is not effective unless the articles of incorporation contain a statement to that effect.

5. A provision entitling one or more shareholders to dissolve the corporation under NRS 78A.160 is effective if a statement of this right is contained in the articles of incorporation.

6. To amend an agreement authorized by this section, all shareholders entitled to vote must approve the amendment in writing, unless the agreement provides otherwise.

7. Subscribers for shares may act as shareholders with respect to an agreement authorized by this section if shares are not issued when the agreement was made.

8. This section does not prohibit any other agreement between or among shareholders in a close corporation.

(Added to NRS by 1989, 944)

NRS 78A.080 Shareholders' agreements: Validity.

A written agreement among stockholders of a close corporation or any provision of the certificate of incorporation or of the bylaws of the corporation that relates to any phase of the affairs of the corporation, including, but not limited to, the management of its business, the declaration and payment of dividends or other division of profits, the election of directors or officers, the employment of stockholders by the corporation or the arbitration of disputes is not invalid on the ground that it is an attempt by the parties to the agreement or by the stockholders of the corporation to treat the corporation as if it were a partnership or to arrange relations among the stockholders or between the stockholders and the corporation in a manner that would be appropriate only among partners.

(Added to NRS by 1989, 947)

NRS 78A.090 Operation without board of directors; elimination and reinstatement of board.

1. A close corporation may operate without a board of directors if the certificate of incorporation contains a statement to that effect.

2. An amendment to the certificate of incorporation eliminating a board of directors must be approved:

(a) By all the shareholders of the corporation, whether or not otherwise entitled to vote on amendments; or

(b) If no shares have been issued, by all subscribers for shares, if any, or if none, by the incorporators.

3. While a corporation is operating without a board of directors as authorized by subsection 1:

(a) All corporate powers must be exercised by or under the authority of, and the business and affairs of the corporation managed under the direction of, the shareholders.

(b) Unless the articles of incorporation provide otherwise:

(1) Action requiring the approval of the board of directors or of both the board of directors and the shareholders is authorized if approved by the shareholders; and

(2) Action requiring a majority or greater percentage vote of the board of directors is authorized if approved by the majority or greater percentage of votes of the shareholders entitled to vote on the action.

(c) A requirement by a state or the United States that a document delivered for filing contain a statement that specified action has been taken by the board of directors is satisfied by a statement that the corporation is a close corporation without a board of directors and that the action was approved by the shareholders.

(d) The shareholders by resolution may appoint one or more shareholders to sign documents as designated directors.

4. An amendment to the articles of incorporation that deletes the provision which eliminates a board of directors must be approved by the holders of at least two-thirds of the votes of each class or series of shares of the corporation, voting as separate voting groups, whether or not otherwise entitled to vote on amendments. The amendment must specify the number, names and mailing addresses of the directors of the corporation or describe who will perform the duties of the board of directors.

5. As used in this section, "sign" means to execute or adopt a name, word or mark, including, without limitation, a digital signature as defined in NRS 720.060, with the present intention to authenticate a document.

(Added to NRS by 1989, 944: A 1999, 1593)

NRS 78A.100 Annual meeting. A close corporation shall hold an annual meeting if one or more shareholders delivers a written notice to the corporation requesting a meeting. Upon receipt of a notice, the close corporation must hold a meeting within 30 days.

(Added to NRS by 1989, 945)

NRS 78A.110 Execution of documents by person acting in more than one capacity. Notwithstanding any law to the contrary, a person who holds more than one office in a close corporation may execute, acknowledge or verify in more than one capacity any document required to be executed, acknowledged or verified by the holders of two or more offices.

(Added to NRS by 1989, 945)

NRS 78A.120 Limitation on liability of shareholders. Personal liability may not be imposed upon shareholders of a close corporation solely as a result of the failure of the close corporation to observe the usual corporate formalities or requirements relating to the exercise of corporate powers or management of its business and affairs, where such failure results from the distinct nature and permissible functioning of a close corporation.

(Added to NRS by 1989, 945)

NRS 78A.130 Merger or share exchange; sale, lease or exchange of assets.

1. A plan of merger or share exchange that if effected would:

(a) Terminate the close corporation status must be approved by the holders of at least two-thirds of the votes of each class or series of shares of the close corporation, voting as separate voting groups, whether or not the holders are entitled to vote on the plan.

(b) Create the surviving corporation as a close corporation must be approved by the holders of at least two-thirds of the votes of each class or series of shares of the surviving corporation, voting as separate voting groups, whether or not the holders are entitled to vote on the plan.

2. If not made in the usual and regular course of business, a sale, lease, exchange or other disposition of all or substantially all of the property of a close corporation must be approved by the holders of at least two-thirds of the votes of each class or series of shares of the corporation, voting as separate voting groups, whether or not the holders are entitled to vote on the transaction.

(Added to NRS by 1989, 945)

NRS 78A.140 Appointment of custodian, receiver or provisional director. 1. Upon application of a stockholder, the court may appoint one or more persons to be custodians and, if the corporation is insolvent, to be receivers of any close corporation when:

(a) The business and affairs of the close corporation are managed by the stockholders who are so divided that the business of the corporation is suffering or is threatened with irreparable injury and any remedy with respect to such a deadlock provided in the certificate of incorporation or bylaws or in any written agreement of the stockholders has failed; or

(b) The petitioning stockholder has the right to the dissolution of the corporation under a provision of the certificate of incorporation permitted by NRS 78A.160.

2. If the court determines that it would be in the best interest of the corporation, the court may appoint a provisional director in lieu of appointing a custodian or receiver for a close corporation. Such an appointment does not preclude any subsequent order of the court appointing a custodian or receiver for the corporation.

(Added to NRS by 1989, 946)

NRS 78A.150 Provisional director: Requirements for appointment; qualifications, rights and powers; compensation.

1. Notwithstanding any contrary provision of the certificate of incorporation, the bylaws or an agreement of the stockholders, the court may appoint a provisional director for a close corporation if the shareholders or directors, if any, are so divided concerning the management of the business and affairs of the corporation that the votes required for action by the board of directors cannot be obtained, with the consequence that the business and affairs of the corporation cannot be conducted to the advantage of the stockholders generally.

2. An application for relief pursuant to this section must be filed:

(a) By at least one-half of the number of directors then in office;

(b) By the holders of at least one-third of all stock then entitled to elect directors; or

(c) If there is more than one class of stock then entitled to elect one or more directors, by the holders of two-thirds of the stock of each class.

The certificate of incorporation of a close corporation may provide that a lesser proportion of the directors, the stockholders or a class of stockholders may apply for relief under this section.

3. A provisional director:

(a) Must be an impartial person who is not a stockholder or a creditor of the corporation or of any subsidiary or affiliate of the corporation and whose further qualifications, if any, may be determined by the court.

(b) Is not a custodian or receiver of the corporation and does not have the title and powers of a custodian or receiver appointed under NRS 78A.140.

(c) Has the rights and powers of an elected director of the corporation, including the right to notice of and to vote at meetings of directors, until such time as he may be removed by order of the court.

4. The compensation of a provisional director must be determined by agreement between the provisional director and the corporation subject to the approval of the court, which may fix his compensation in the absence of agreement or in the event of disagreement between the provisional director and the corporation.

(Added to NRS by 1989, 946)

NRS 78A.160 Option of stockholder to dissolve corporation: Inclusion in certificate of incorporation; exercise of option; notice on stock certificate.

1. The certificate of incorporation of any close corporation may include a provision granting to any stockholder or to the holder of any specified number or percentage of shares of any class of stock an option to have the corporation dissolved at will or upon the occurrence of any specified event or contingency. Whenever any option to dissolve is exercised, the stockholders who exercise the option shall give written notice thereof to all other stockholders. Thirty days after the notice is sent, the dissolution of the corporation must proceed as if the required number of stockholders having voting power consented in writing to dissolution of the corporation as provided by NRS 78.320.

2. If the certificate of incorporation as originally filed does not contain a provision authorized by subsection 1, the certificate may be amended to include such a provision if adopted by the affirmative vote of the holders of all the outstanding stock, whether or not otherwise entitled to vote, unless the certificate of incorporation specifically authorizes such an amendment by a vote which is not less than two-thirds of all the outstanding stock, whether or not otherwise entitled to vote.

3. Each stock certificate in any corporation whose certificate of incorporation authorizes dissolution as permitted by this section must conspicuously note on the face of the certificate the existence of the provision or the provision is ineffective.

(Added to NRS by 1989, 947)

TERMINATION OF STATUS AS CLOSE CORPORATION

NRS 78A.170 Time of termination of status. A close corporation is subject to the provisions of this chapter until:

1. The corporation files with the secretary of state a certificate of amendment deleting from the certificate of incorporation the provisions required or permitted by NRS 78A.020, to be stated in the certificate of incorporation; or

2. A provision or condition required or permitted by NRS 78A.020 to be stated in a certificate of incorporation has been breached and the corporation or any stockholder has not acted pursuant to NRS 78A.190 to prevent the loss of status or remedy the breach.

(Added to NRS by 1989, 941)

NRS 78A.180 Voluntary termination of status.

1. A corporation may voluntarily terminate its status as a close corporation, and cease to be subject to the provisions of this chapter, by amending the certificate of incorporation to delete therefrom the additional provisions required or permitted by NRS 78A.020 to be stated in the certificate of incorporation of a close corporation. An amendment must be adopted and become effective in accordance with NRS 78.390, except that it must be approved by a vote of the holders of record of at least two-thirds of the voting shares of each class of stock of the corporation that are outstanding.

2. The certificate of incorporation of a close corporation may provide that on any amendment to terminate the status as a close corporation, a vote greater than two-thirds or a vote of all shares of any class may be required. If the certificate of incorporation contains such a provision, that provision may not be amended, repealed or modified by any vote less than that required to terminate the status of the corporation as a close corporation.

(Added to NRS by 1989, 943)

NRS 78A.190 Involuntary termination of status; intervention by court.

1. The status of a corporation as a close corporation terminates if one or more of the provisions or conditions of this chapter cease to exist or be fulfilled unless:

(a) Within 30 days after the occurrence of the event, or within 30 days after the event has been discovered by the corporation, whichever is later, the corporation files with the secretary of state an executed certificate stating that a specified provision or condition included in the certificate of incorporation to qualify the corporation as a close corporation has ceased to be applicable and furnishes a copy of the certificate to each stockholder; and

(b) The corporation, concurrently with the filing of a certificate, takes such steps as are necessary to correct the situation that threatens the status as a close corporation, including the refusal to register the transfer of stock which has been wrongfully transferred as provided by NRS 78A.050 or commencing a proceeding under subsection 2.

2. Upon the suit of the close corporation or any stockholder, the court has jurisdiction to:

(a) Issue all orders necessary to prevent the corporation from losing its status as a close corporation.

(b) Restore the status of the corporation as a close corporation by enjoining or setting aside any act or threatened act on the part of the corporation or a stockholder that would be inconsistent with any of the provisions or conditions required or permitted by this chapter to be stated in the certificate of incorporation of a close corporation, unless it is an act approved in accordance with NRS 78A.050.

(c) Enjoin or set aside any transfer or threatened transfer of stock of a close corporation that is contrary to the terms of the certificate of incorporation or of any permitted restriction on transfer.

(d) Enjoin any public offering or threatened public offering of stock of the close corporation.

(Added to NRS by 1989, 943; A 1999, 1594)

NRS 78A.200 Effect of termination of status.

1. A corporation that terminates its status as a close corporation is subject to the provisions of chapter 78 of NRS.

2. Termination of the status of a close corporation does not affect any right of a shareholder or of the corporation under an agreement or the articles of incorporation unless invalidated by law.

(Added to NRS by 1989, 946)

APPENDIX D: NEVADA REVISED STATUTES CHAPTER 80

FOREIGN CORPORATIONS

NRS 80.001 Definitions. As used in this chapter, unless the context otherwise requires, the words and terms defined in NRS 80.003 and 80.004 have the meanings ascribed to them in those sections.

(Added to NRS by 1999, 1595)

NRS 80.003 "Signed" defined. "Signed" means to have executed or adopted a name, word or mark, including, without limitation, a digital signature as defined in NRS 720.060, with the present intention to authenticate a document.

(Added to NRS by 1999, 1595)

NRS 80.004 "Street address" defined. "Street address" of a resident agent means the actual physical location in this state at which a resident agent is available for service of process.

(Added to NRS by 1999, 1595)

NRS 80.005 Corporate documents: Microfilming and return. The secretary of state may microfilm any document which is filed in his office by a foreign corporation pursuant to this chapter and may return the original document to the corporation.

(Added to NRS by 1977, 572)

NRS 80.007 Incorrect or defective document: Certificate of correction; effective date of correction.

1. A foreign corporation may correct a document filed by the secretary of state if the document contains an incorrect statement or was defectively executed, attested, sealed or verified.

2. To correct a document, the corporation shall:

(a) Prepare a certificate of correction which:

(1) States the name of the corporation;

(2) Describes the document, including, without limitation, its filing date;

(3) Specifies the incorrect statement and the reason it is incorrect or the manner in which the execution was defective;

(4) Corrects the incorrect statement or defective execution; and

(5) Is signed by an officer of the corporation; and

(b) Deliver the certificate to the secretary of state for filing.

3. A certificate of correction is effective on the effective date of the document it corrects except as to persons relying on the uncorrected document and adversely affected by the correction. As to those persons, the certificate is effective when filed.

(Added to NRS by 1997, 708; A 1999, 1595)

NRS 80.010 Requirements to do business in Nevada; filings; limitations on name; certification of authority to engage in certain businesses; regulations.

1. Before commencing or doing any business in this state, each corporation organized pursuant to the laws of another state, territory, the District of Columbia, a possession of the United States or a foreign country, that enters this state to do business must:

(a) File in the office of the secretary of state of this state:

(1) A certificate of corporate existence issued not more than 90 days before the date of filing by an authorized officer of the jurisdiction of its incorporation setting forth the filing of documents and instruments related to the articles of incorporation, or the governmental acts or other instrument or authority by which the corporation was created. If the certificate is in a language other than English, a translation, together with the oath of the translator and his attestation of its accuracy, must be attached to the certificate.

(2) A certificate of acceptance of appointment executed by its resident agent, who must be a resident or located in this state. The certificate must set forth the name of the resident agent, his street address for the service of process, and his mailing address if different from his street address. The street address of the resident agent is the registered office of the corporation in this state.

(3) A statement executed by an officer of the corporation setting forth:

(I) A general description of the purposes of the corporation; and

(II) The authorized stock of the corporation and the number and par value of shares having par value and the number of shares having no par value.

(b) Lodge in the office of the secretary of state a copy of the document most recently filed by the corporation in the jurisdiction of its incorporation setting forth the authorized stock of the corporation, the number of par-value shares and their par value, and the number of no-par-value shares.

2. The secretary of state shall not file the documents required by subsection 1 for any foreign corporation whose name is not distinguishable on the records of the secretary of state from the names of all other artificial persons formed, organized, registered or qualified pursuant to the provisions of this Title that are on file in the office of the secretary of state and all names that are reserved in the office of the secretary of state pursuant to the provisions of this Title, unless the written, acknowledged consent of the holder of the name on file or reserved name to use the same name or the requested similar name accompanies the articles of incorporation.

3. The secretary of state shall not accept for filing the documents required by subsection 1 or NRS 80.110 for any foreign corporation if the name of the corporation contains the words "engineer," "engineered," "engineering," "professional engineer," "registered engineer" or "licensed engineer" unless the state board of professional engineers and land surveyors certifies that:

(a) The principals of the corporation are licensed to practice engineering pursuant to the laws of this state; or

(b) The corporation is exempt from the prohibitions of NRS 625.520.

4. The secretary of state shall not accept for filing the documents required by subsection 1 or NRS 80.110 for any foreign corporation if it appears from the documents that the business to be carried on by the corporation is subject to supervision by the commissioner of financial institutions, unless the commissioner certifies that:

(a) The corporation has obtained the authority required to do business in this state; or

(b) The corporation is not subject to or is exempt from the requirements for obtaining such authority.

5. The secretary of state shall not accept for filing the documents required by subsection 1 or NRS 80.110 for any foreign corporation if the name of the corporation contains the words "accountant," "accounting," "accountancy," "auditor" or "auditing" unless the Nevada state board of accountancy certifies that the foreign corporation:

(a) Is registered pursuant to the provisions of chapter 628 of NRS; or

(b) Has filed with the state board of accountancy under penalty of perjury a written statement that the foreign corporation is not engaged in the practice of accounting and is not offering to practice accounting in this state.

6. The secretary of state may adopt regulations that interpret the requirements of this section.

[Part 1:89:1907; A 1949, 503; 1951, 203; 1955, 404]—(NRS A 1957, 74; 1959, 839; 1965, 600; 1977, 404; 1979, 398; 1981, 385; 1985, 1874; 1987, 1059; 1989, 950, 980, 1972; 1991, 99, 1243, 2248; 1993, 129, 980; 1995, 1117, 2102; 1997, 1059; 1999, 1595, 1707, 2442)

NRS 80.012 Reservation of corporate name; injunctive relief.

1. The secretary of state, when requested so to do, shall reserve, for a period of 90 days, the right to use any name available pursuant to NRS 80.010, for the use of any foreign corporation. During the period, a name so reserved is not available for use or reservation by any other artificial person forming, organizing, registering or qualifying in the office of the secretary of state pursuant to the provisions of this Title without the written, acknowledged consent of the person at whose request the reservation was made.

2. The use by any other artificial person of a name in violation of subsection 1 or NRS 80.010 may be enjoined, even if the document under which the artificial person

is formed, organized, registered or qualified has been filed by the secretary of state.

(Added to NRS by 1991, 1242; A 1993, 982; 1999, 1597)

NRS 80.015 Activities that do not constitute doing business in Nevada; persons not doing business in Nevada exempted from certain provisions.

1. For the purposes of this chapter, the following activities do not constitute doing business in this state:

(a) Maintaining, defending or settling any proceeding;

(b) Holding meetings of the board of directors or stockholders or carrying on other activities concerning internal corporate affairs;

(c) Maintaining accounts in banks or credit unions;

(d) Maintaining offices or agencies for the transfer, exchange and registration of the corporation's own securities or maintaining trustees or depositaries with respect to those securities;

(e) Making sales through independent contractors;

(f) Soliciting or receiving orders outside of this state through or in response to letters, circulars, catalogs or other forms of advertising, accepting those orders outside of this state and filling them by shipping goods into this state;

(g) Creating or acquiring indebtedness, mortgages and security interests in real or personal property;

(h) Securing or collecting debts or enforcing mortgages and security interests in property securing the debts;

(i) Owning, without more, real or personal property;

(j) Isolated transactions completed within 30 days and not a part of a series of similar transactions;

(k) The production of motion pictures as defined in NRS 231.020;

(l) Transacting business as an out-of-state depository institution pursuant to the provisions of Title 55 of NRS; and

(m) Transacting business in interstate commerce.

2. The list of activities in subsection 1 is not exhaustive.

3. A person who is not doing business in this state within the meaning of this section need not qualify or comply with any provision of NRS 80.010 to 80.280, inclusive, chapter 645A, 645B or 645E of NRS or Title 55 or 56 of NRS unless he:

(a) Maintains an office in this state for the transaction of business; or

(b) Solicits or accepts deposits in the state, except pursuant to the provisions of chapter 666 or 666A of NRS.

(Added to NRS by 1989, 980; A 1991, 1244; 1993, 982; 1995, 1561; 1997, 708; 1999, 1455, 1597, 3803, 3814)

NRS 80.016 Determination of whether solicitation is made or accepted in Nevada. For the purposes of NRS 80.015:

1. A solicitation of a deposit is made in this state, whether or not either party is present in this state, if the solicitation:

(a) Originates in this state; or

(b) Is directed by the solicitor to a destination in this state and received where it is directed, or at a post office in this state if the solicitation is mailed.

2. A solicitation of a deposit is accepted in this state if acceptance:

(a) Is communicated to the solicitor in this state; and

(b) Has not previously been communicated to the solicitor, orally or in writing, outside this state.

Acceptance is communicated to the solicitor in this state, whether or not either party is present in this state, if the depositor directs it to the solicitor reasonably believing the solicitor to be in this state and it is received where it is directed, or at any post office in this state if the acceptance is mailed.

3. A solicitation made in a newspaper or other publication of general, regular and paid circulation is not made in this state if the publication:

(a) Is not published in this state; or

(b) Is published in this state but has had more than two-thirds of its circulation outside this state during the 12 months preceding the solicitation.

If a publication is published in editions, each edition is a separate publication except for material common to all editions.

4. A solicitation made in a radio or television program or other electronic communication received in this state which originates outside this state is not made in this state. A radio or television program or other electronic communication shall be deemed to have originated in this state if the broadcast studio or origin of the source of transmission is located within the state, unless:

(a) The program or communication is syndicated and distributed from outside this state for redistribution to the general public in this state;

(b) The program is supplied by a radio, television or other electronic network whose electronic signal originates outside this state for redistribution to the general public in this state;

(c) The program or communication is an electronic signal that originates outside this state and is captured for redistribution to the general public in this state by a community antenna or cable, radio, cable television or other electronic system; or

(d) The program or communication consists of an electronic signal which originates within this state, but which is not intended for redistribution to the general public in this state.

(Added to NRS by 1991, 1242)

NRS **80.025** Modification of corporate name to qualify to do business in this state: Requirements; procedure.

1. If a foreign corporation cannot qualify to do business in this state because its name does not meet the requirements of subsection 2 or 3 of NRS 80.010, it may apply for a certificate to do business by having its board of directors adopt a resolution setting forth the name under which the corporation elects to do business in this state. The resolution may:

(a) Add to the existing corporate name a word, abbreviation or other distinctive element; or

(b) Adopt a name different from its existing corporate name that is available for use in this state.

2. In addition to the documents required by subsection 1 of NRS 80.010, the corporation shall file a certified copy of the resolution adopting the modified name.

3. If the secretary of state determines that the modified corporate name complies with the provisions of subsection 2 or 3 of NRS 80.010, he shall issue the certificate in the foreign corporation's modified name if the foreign corporation otherwise qualifies to do business in this state.

4. A foreign corporation doing business in this state under a modified corporate name approved by the secretary of state shall use the modified name in its dealings and communications with the secretary of state.

(Added to NRS by 1985, 1873; A 1991, 2249)

NRS **80.030** Filing of amendatory documents after qualification.

1. Each foreign corporation admitted to do business in this state shall, within 30 days after the filing of any document amendatory or otherwise relating to the original articles in the place of its creation, file in the office of the secretary of state:

(a) A copy of the document certified by an authorized officer of the place of its creation, or a certificate evidencing the filing, issued by the authorized officer of the

place of its creation with whom the document was filed; and

(b) A statement of an officer of the corporation of the change reflected by the filing of the document, showing its relation to the name, authorized capital stock, or general purposes.

2. When a foreign corporation authorized to do business in this state becomes a constituent of a merger permitted by the laws of the state or country in which it is incorporated, it shall, within 30 days after the merger becomes effective, file a copy of the agreement of merger filed in the place of its creation, certified by an authorized officer of the place of its creation, or a certificate, issued by the proper officer of the place of its creation, attesting to the occurrence of the event, in the office of the secretary of state.

3. The secretary of state may revoke the right of a foreign corporation to transact business in this state if it fails to file the documents required by this section or pay the fees incident to that filing.

[Part 1:89:1907; A 1949, 503; 1951, 203; 1955, 404]—(NRS A 1977, 405; 1979, 399; 1981, 21; 1999, 1598)

NRS **80.040** Qualification: English translations to accompany documents in foreign language.

If the papers required by NRS 80.010 and 80.030 to be filed in this state are of record in a language other than English in the place of creation of the corporation, the certified papers in that language shall be accompanied by a verified translation into the English language.

[Part 1:89:1907; A 1949, 503; 1951, 203; 1955, 404]—(NRS A 1977, 406)

NRS **80.050** Fees payable by foreign corporations.

1. Except as otherwise provided in subsection 3, foreign corporations shall pay the same fees to the secretary of state as are required to be paid by corporations organized pursuant to the laws of this state, but the amount of fees to be charged must not exceed:

(a) The sum of $25,000 for filing documents for initial qualification; or

(b) The sum of $25,000 for each subsequent filing of a certificate increasing authorized capital stock.

2. If the corporate documents required to be filed set forth only the total number of shares of stock the corporation is authorized to issue without reference to value, the authorized shares shall be deemed to be

without par value and the filing fee must be computed pursuant to paragraph (b) of subsection 3 of NRS 78.760.

3. Foreign corporations which are nonprofit corporations and do not have or issue shares of stock shall pay the same fees to the secretary of state as are required to be paid by nonprofit corporations organized pursuant to the laws of this state.

4. The fee for filing a notice of withdrawal from the State of Nevada by a foreign corporation is $30.

[2:89:1907; RL § 1349; NCL § 1842] + [Part 1:52:1933; A 1949, 363; 1951, 393]—(NRS A 1960, 177; 1961, 398; 1977, 406; 1983, 692; 1989, 981; 1995, 1118)

NRS **80.060** Resident agent: Appointment.

Every foreign corporation owning property or doing business in this state shall appoint and keep in this state a resident agent as provided in NRS 14.020.

[Part 1911 CPA § 82; A 1933, 191; 1939, 66; 1931 NCL § 8580]

NRS **80.070** Resident agent: Revocation of appointment; resignation, death or removal from state; filing new certificate of acceptance of appointment.

1. A foreign corporation may change its resident agent by filing with the secretary of state:

(a) A certificate of change, signed by an officer of the corporation, setting forth:

(1) The name of the corporation;

(2) The name and street address of the present resident agent; and

(3) The name and street address of the new resident agent; and

(b) A certificate of acceptance executed by the new resident agent, which must be a part of or attached to the certificate of change.

The change authorized by this subsection becomes effective upon the filing of the certificate of change.

2. A person who has been designated by a foreign corporation as resident agent may file with the secretary of state a signed statement that he is unwilling to continue to act as the agent of the corporation for the service of process.

3. Upon the filing of the statement of resignation with the secretary of state, the capacity of the resigning person as resident agent terminates. If the statement of resignation is not accompanied by a statement of the corporation appointing a successor resident agent, the resigning resident agent shall give written notice, by mail, to the corporation, of the filing of the

statement and its effect. The notice must be addressed to any officer of the corporation other than the resident agent.

4. If a resident agent dies, resigns or moves from the state, the corporation, within 30 days thereafter, shall file with the secretary of state a certificate of acceptance executed by the new resident agent. The certificate must set forth the name of the new resident agent, his street address for the service of process, and his mailing address if different from his street address.

5. A corporation that fails to file a certificate of acceptance executed by a new resident agent within 30 days after the death, resignation or removal of its resident agent shall be deemed in default and is subject to the provisions of NRS 80.150 and 80.160.

[1:127:1939; 1931 NCL § 1813.01] + [2:127:1939; 1931 NCL § 1813.02]—(NRS A 1959, 840; 1969, 33; 1989, 951; 1993, 983; 1999, 1598)

NRS 80.080 **Service of process on foreign corporation in this state.** Service of process on a foreign corporation owning property or doing business in this state shall be made in the manner provided in NRS 14.020 and 14.030.

[Part 1911 CPA § 83; A 1921, 107; 1939, 66; 1931 NCL § 8581]

NRS 80.090 **Limitations of actions.** If a foreign corporation doing business in this state maintains and keeps in the state a resident agent as provided by NRS 80.060 and files or has microfilmed the papers, documents and instruments required by NRS 80.010 to 80.040, inclusive, it shall be entitled to the benefit of the laws of this state limiting the time for the commencement of civil actions.

[Part 1:165:1907; A 1921, 88; 1933, 24; 1931 NCL § 1848]— (NRS A 1965, 601)

NRS 80.100 **Authority of directors and representatives: Contracts and conveyances.** The provisions of NRS 78.135 apply to contracts and conveyances made by foreign corporations in this state and to all conveyances by foreign corporations of real property situated in this state.

[Part 31(a):177:1925; added 1949, 158; 1943 NCL § 1630.01]

NRS 80.110 **Annual list of officers and directors and designation of resident agent: Filing requirements; fee; forms.**

1. Each foreign corporation doing business in this state shall, on or before the first day of the second month after the filing of its certificate of corporate existence with the secretary of state, and annually thereafter on or before the last day of the month in which the anniversary date of its qualification to do business in this state occurs in each year, file with the secretary of state, on a form furnished by him, a list of its president, secretary and treasurer or their equivalent, and all of its directors and a designation of its resident agent in this state, signed by an officer of the corporation.

2. Upon filing the list and designation, the corporation shall pay to the secretary of state a fee of $85.

3. The secretary of state shall, 60 days before the last day for filing the annual list required by subsection 1, cause to be mailed to each corporation required to comply with the provisions of NRS 80.110 to 80.170, inclusive, which has not become delinquent, the blank forms to be completed and filed with him. Failure of any corporation to receive the forms does not excuse it from the penalty imposed by the provisions of NRS 80.110 to 80.170, inclusive.

4. An annual list for a corporation not in default which is received by the secretary of state more than 60 days before its due date shall be deemed an amended list for the previous year and does not satisfy the requirements of subsection 1 for the year to which the due date is applicable.

[Part 1:180:1925; A 1929, 122; 1931, 408; 1931 NCL § 1804]— (NRS A 1957, 296; 1959, 840; 1977, 406; 1979, 186, 400, 401; 1983, 693; 1985, 234; 1989, 981; 1991, 2460; 1993, 983; 1995, 2103; 1999, 1599)

NRS 80.120 **Certificate authorizing corporation to transact business.** If a corporation has filed the initial or annual list of officers and directors and designation of resident agent in compliance with NRS 80.110 and has paid the appropriate fee for the filing, the canceled check received by the corporation constitutes a certificate authorizing it to transact its business within this state until the last day of the month in which the anniversary of its qualification to transact business occurs in the next succeeding calendar year. If the corporation desires a formal certificate upon its payment of the initial or annual fee, its payment must be accompanied by a self-addressed, stamped envelope.

[2:180:1925; A 1931, 408; 1931 NCL § 1805]—(NRS A 1959, 841; 1983, 693; 1993, 984; 1999, 1599)

NRS 80.140 **Contents of annual list: Names and addresses; penalties.**

1. Every list required to be filed under the provisions of NRS 80.110 to 80.170, inclusive, must, after the name of each officer and director listed thereon, set forth the post office box or street address, either residence or business, of each officer and director.

2. If the addresses are not stated for each person on any list offered for filing, the secretary of state may refuse to file the list, and the corporation for which the list has been offered for filing is subject to all the provisions of NRS 80.110 to 80.170, inclusive, relating to failure to file the list within or at the times therein specified, unless a list is subsequently submitted for filing which conforms to the provisions of this section.

[3(a):180:1925; added 1951, 280]—(NRS A 1959, 841; 1985, 235; 1993, 984)

NRS 80.150 **Defaulting corporations: Identification; penalty and forfeiture.**

1. Any corporation required to make a filing and pay the fee prescribed in NRS 80.110 to 80.170, inclusive, which refuses or neglects to do so within the time provided, is in default.

2. For default there must be added to the amount of the fee a penalty of $15, and unless the filing is made and the fee and penalty are paid on or before the first day of the ninth month following the month in which filing was required, the defaulting corporation by reason of its default forfeits its right to transact any business within this state. The fee and penalty must be collected as provided in this chapter.

[4:180:1925; A 1931, 408; 1931 NCL § 1807]—(NRS A 1977, 407; 1979, 186; 1983, 694; 1985, 235; 1989, 982; 1993, 984; 1995, 1118)

NRS 80.160 **Defaulting corporations: Duties of secretary of state.**

1. The secretary of state shall notify, by letter addressed to its resident agent, each corporation deemed in default pursuant to NRS 80.150. The notice must be accompanied by a statement indicating the amount of the filing fee, penalties and costs remaining unpaid.

2. Immediately after the first day of the ninth month following the month in which filing was required, the secretary of state shall compile a full and complete list containing the names of all corporations whose right to do business has been forfeited.

3. The secretary of state shall notify, by letter addressed to its resident agent, each corporation specified in subsection 2 of the forfeiture of its right to do business. The notice must be accompanied by a statement indicating the amount of the filing fee, penalties and costs remaining unpaid.

[Part 5:180:1925; NCL § 1808]—(NRS A 1959, 60, 575; 1965, 601; 1973, 1028; 1979, 187, 400, 402; 1993, 984; 1995, 1119)

NRS 80.170 Defaulting corporations: Conditions and procedure for reinstatement.

1. Except as otherwise provided in subsections 3 and 4, the secretary of state shall reinstate a corporation which has forfeited or which forfeits its right to transact business under the provisions of this chapter and restore to the corporation its right to transact business in this state, and to exercise its corporate privileges and immunities if it:

(a) Files with the secretary of state a list of officers and directors as provided in NRS 80.110 and 80.140; and

(b) Pays to the secretary of state:

(1) The annual filing fee and penalty set forth in NRS 80.110 and 80.150 for each year or portion thereof that its right to transact business was forfeited; and

(2) A fee of $50 for reinstatement.

2. If payment is made and the secretary of state reinstates the corporation to its former rights he shall:

(a) Immediately issue and deliver to the corporation so reinstated a certificate of reinstatement authorizing it to transact business in the same manner as if the filing fee had been paid when due; and

(b) Upon demand, issue to the corporation one or more certified copies of the certificate of reinstatement.

3. The secretary of state shall not order a reinstatement unless all delinquent fees and penalties have been paid, and the revocation of the right to transact business occurred only by reason of failure to pay the fees and penalties.

4. If the right of a corporation to transact business in this state has been forfeited pursuant to the provisions of NRS 80.160 and has remained forfeited for a period of 5 consecutive years, the right is not subject to reinstatement.

[6:180:1925; A 1927, 42; NCL § 1809]—(NRS A 1959, 61; 1965, 602; 1973, 1029; 1975, 478; 1985, 235; 1987, 1060; 1991, 1245; 1993, 985; 1995, 1119)

NRS 80.190 Publication of annual statement; recovery of penalty.

1. Except as otherwise provided in subsection 2, each foreign corporation doing business in this state shall, not later than the month of March in each year, publish a statement of its last calendar year's business in two numbers or issues of a newspaper published in this state.

2. If the corporation keeps its records on the basis of a fiscal year other than the calendar, the statement required by subsection 1 must be published not later than the end of the third month following the close of each fiscal year.

3. A corporation which neglects or refuses to publish a statement as required by this section is liable to a penalty of $100 for each month that the statement remains unpublished.

4. Any district attorney in the state or the attorney general may sue to recover the penalty. The first county suing through its district attorney shall recover the penalty, and if no suit is brought for the penalty by any district attorney, the state may recover through the attorney general.

[1:108:1901; A 1913, 270; 1939, 169; 1949, 86; 1955, 751] + [2:108:1901; A 1907, 39; RL § 1352; NCL § 1845]—(NRS A 1969, 147; 1977, 607, 1354; 1993, 986)

NRS 80.200 Surrender of right to transact intrastate business.

1. Any foreign corporation qualified to do business in this state under the provisions of this chapter may withdraw therefrom and surrender its right by:

(a) Filing with the secretary of state a notice of its purpose so to do, duly authorized to be given by resolution of its board of directors and executed under its corporate seal by the proper officers thereof; and

(b) Paying the fee required by NRS 80.050 for filing notice.

2. The provisions of subsection 1 apply only when the corporation's right to do business in this state at the time the notice is submitted for filing has not been forfeited.

[1(a):89:1907; added 1949, 503; 1943 NCL § 1841.01]—(NRS A 1993, 986)

NRS 80.210 Penalties for failure to comply with requirements for qualification; enforcement.

1. Every corporation which fails or neglects to comply with the provisions of NRS 80.010 to 80.040, inclusive:

(a) Is subject to a fine of not less than $500, to be recovered in a court of competent jurisdiction; and

(b) Except as otherwise provided in subsection 2, may not commence or maintain any action or proceeding in any court of this state until it has fully complied with the provisions of NRS 80.010 to 80.040, inclusive.

2. An action or proceeding may be commenced by such a corporation if an extraordinary remedy available pursuant to chapter 31 of NRS is all or part of the relief sought. Such an action or proceeding must be dismissed without prejudice if the corporation does not comply with the provisions of NRS 80.010 to 80.040, inclusive, within 45 days after the action or proceeding is commenced.

3. When the secretary of state is advised that a corporation is doing business in contravention of NRS 80.010 to 80.040, inclusive, he shall report that fact to the governor. The governor shall, as soon as practicable, instruct the district attorney of the county where the corporation has its principal place of business or the attorney general, or both, to institute proceedings to recover any applicable fine provided for in this section.

[3:89:1907; RL § 1350; NCL § 1843]—(NRS A 1989, 17; 1993, 986)

NRS 80.220 Suspension of statute of limitations for failure to comply. The benefit of NRS 80.090 shall be suspended during any period or periods when the corporation is in default in complying with the requirements of NRS 80.090; and no such corporation can maintain any action or proceeding in any court of this state while so in default.

[Part 1:165: 1907; A 1921, 88; 1933, 24; 1931 NCL § 1848]

NRS 80.270 Notice of certain proceedings concerning insolvency or mismanagement of corporation. Repealed. (See chapter 357, Statutes of Nevada 1999, at page 1639.)

NRS 80.280 License required for corporation to render professional service. A foreign corporation organized to render a professional service may not render that service in this state unless the person rendering it is licensed to do so by the appropriate regulating board of this state.

(Added to NRS by 1995, 2102)

APPENDIX E: NEVADA REVISED STATUTES CHAPTER 86

LIMITED LIABILITY COMPANIES

NRS 86.011 Definitions. As used in this chapter, unless the context otherwise requires, the words and terms defined in NRS 86.021 to 86.128, inclusive, have the meanings ascribed to them in those sections.

(Added to NRS by 1991, 1292; A 1993, 1012; 1995, 2107; 1999, 1611)

NRS 86.021 "Articles of organization" defined. "Articles of organization" means the articles of organization filed with the secretary of state for the purpose of forming a limited-liability company pursuant to this chapter.

(Added to NRS by 1991, 1292)

NRS 86.031 "Bankrupt" defined. "Bankrupt" is limited to the effect of the federal statutes codified as Title 11 of the United States Code.

(Added to NRS by 1991, 1292)

NRS 86.051 "Foreign limited-liability company" defined. "Foreign limited-liability company" means a limited-liability company formed under the laws of any jurisdiction other than this state.

(Added to NRS by 1991, 1292)

NRS 86.061 "Limited-liability company" and "company" defined. "Limited-liability company" or "company" means a limited-liability company organized and existing under this chapter.

(Added to NRS by 1991, 1292)

NRS 86.065 "Majority in interest" defined. "Majority in interest" means a majority of the interests in the current profits of a limited-liability company.

(Added to NRS by 1995, 2106; A 1997, 715)

NRS 86.071 "Manager" defined. "Manager" means a person, or one of several persons, designated in or selected pursuant to the articles of organization or operating agreement of a limited-liability company to manage the company.

(Added to NRS by 1991, 1293; A 1997, 715)

NRS 86.081 "Member" defined. "Member" means the owner of an interest in a limited-liability company.

(Added to NRS by 1991, 1293; A 1997, 715)

NRS 86.091 "Member's interest" defined. "Member's interest" means his share of the economic interests in a limited-liability company, including profits, losses and distributions of assets.

(Added to NRS by 1991, 1293; A 1997, 715)

NRS 86.101 "Operating agreement" defined. "Operating agreement" means any valid written agreement of the members as to the affairs of a limited-liability company and the conduct of its business.

(Added to NRS by 1991, 1293)

NRS 86.111 "Real property" defined. "Real property" includes land, any interest, leasehold or estate in land, and any improvements on it.

(Added to NRS by 1991, 1293)

NRS 86.121 "Registered office" defined. "Registered office" of a limited-liability company means the office maintained at the street address of its resident agent.

(Added to NRS by 1991, 1293; A 1993, 1012; 1995, 1126)

NRS 86.125 "Resident agent" defined. "Resident agent" means the agent appointed by the company upon whom process or a notice or demand authorized by law to be served upon the company may be served.

(Added to NRS by 1995, 2106)

NRS 86.126 "Sign" defined. "Sign" means to affix a signature to a document.

(Added to NRS by 1999, 1610)

NRS 86.127 "Signature" defined. "Signature" means a name, word or mark executed or adopted by a person with the present intention to authenticate a document. The term includes, without limitation, a digital signature as defined in NRS 720.060.

(Added to NRS by 1999, 1610)

NRS 86.128 "Street address" defined. "Street address" of a resident agent means the actual physical location in this state at which a resident agent is available for service of process.

(Added to NRS by 1999, 1610)

NRS 86.131 Applicability of chapter to foreign and interstate commerce. The provisions of this chapter apply to commerce with foreign nations and among the several states. It is the intention of the legislature by enactment of this chapter that the legal existence of limited-liability companies formed under this chapter be recognized beyond the limits of this state and that, subject to any reasonable requirement of registration, any such company transacting business outside this state be granted protection of full faith and credit under Section 1 of Article IV of the Constitution of the United States.

(Added to NRS by 1991, 1304)

ORGANIZATION

NRS 86.141 Purpose for organization. A limited-liability company may be organized under this chapter for any lawful purpose, except insurance.

(Added to NRS by 1991, 1293; A 1995, 496)

NRS 86.151 Method of formation; issuance of certificate by secretary of state; membership.

1. One or more persons may form a limited-liability company by:

(a) Executing and filing with the secretary of state articles of organization for the company; and

(b) Filing with the secretary of state a certificate of acceptance of appointment, executed by the resident agent of the company.

2. Upon the filing of the articles of organization and the certificate of acceptance with the secretary of state, and the payment to him of the required filing fees, the secretary of state shall issue to the company a certificate that the articles, containing the required statement of facts, have been filed.

3. A signer of the articles of organization or a manager designated in the articles does not thereby become a member of the company. At all times after commencement of business by the company, the company must have one or more members. The filing of the articles does not, by itself, constitute commencement of business by the company.

(Added to NRS by 1991, 1293; A 1993, 1012; 1995, 1126, 2107; 1997, 715; 1999, 1611)

NRS 86.155 Perpetual existence of company. Unless otherwise provided in its articles of organization or operating agreement, a limited-liability company has perpetual existence.

(Added to NRS by 1997, 714)

NRS 86.161 Articles of organization: Contents.

1. The articles of organization must set forth:

(a) The name of the limited-liability company;

(b) The name and complete street address of its resident agent, and the mailing address of the resident agent if different from the street address;

(c) The name and post office or street address, either residence or business, of each of the organizers executing the articles; and

(d) If the company is to be managed by:

(1) One or more managers, the name and post office or street address, either residence or business, of each manager; or

(2) The members, the name and post office or street address, either residence or business, of each member.

2. The articles may set forth any other provision, not inconsistent with law, which the members elect to set out in the articles of organization for the regulation of the internal affairs of the company, including any provisions which under this chapter are required or permitted to be set out in the operating agreement of the company.

3. It is not necessary to set out in the articles of organization:

(a) The rights, if any, of the members to contract debts on behalf of the limited-liability company; or

(b) Any of the powers enumerated in this chapter.

(Added to NRS by 1991, 1293; A 1993, 1012; 1995, 1126, 2107; 1997, 716; 1999, 1612)

NRS 86.171 Name of company: Distinguishable name required; availability of name of revoked, merged or otherwise terminated company; limitations; regulations.

1. The name of a limited-liability company formed under the provisions of this chapter must contain the words "Limited-Liability Company," "Limited Company," or "Limited" or the abbreviations "Ltd.," "L.L.C.," "L.C.," "LLC" or "LC." The word "Company" may be abbreviated as "Co."

2. The name proposed for a limited-liability company must be distinguishable on the records of the secretary of state from the names of all other artificial persons formed, organized, registered or qualified pursuant to the provisions of this Title that are on file in the office of the secretary of state and all names that are reserved in the office of the secretary of state pursuant to the provisions of this Title. If a proposed name is not so distinguishable, the secretary of state shall return the articles of organization to the organizer, unless the written, acknowledged consent of the holder of the name on file or reserved name to use the same name or the requested similar name accompanies the articles of organization.

3. For the purposes of this section and NRS 86.176, a proposed name is not distinguishable from a name on file or reserved name solely because one or the other contains distinctive lettering, a distinctive mark, a trade-mark or a trade name, or any combination of these.

4. The name of a limited-liability company whose charter has been revoked, which has merged and is not the surviving entity or whose existence has otherwise terminated is available for use by any other artificial person.

5. The secretary of state shall not accept for filing any articles of organization for any limited-liability company if the name of the limited-liability company contains the words "accountant," "accounting," "accountancy," "auditor" or "auditing" unless the Nevada state board of accountancy certifies that the limited-liability company:

(a) Is registered pursuant to the provisions of chapter 628 of NRS; or

(b) Has filed with the state board of accountancy under penalty of perjury a written statement that the limited-liability company is not engaged in the practice of accounting and is not offering to practice accounting in this state.

6. The secretary of state may adopt regulations that interpret the requirements of this section.

(Added to NRS by 1991, 1294; A 1993, 1013; 1995, 2108; 1997, 2812; 1999, 1612, 1709)

NRS 86.176 Name of company: Reservation; injunctive relief.

1. The secretary of state, when requested so to do, shall reserve, for a period of 90 days, the right to use any name available under NRS 86.171, for the use of any proposed limited-liability company. During the period, a name so reserved is not available for use or reservation by any other artificial person forming, organizing, registering or qualifying in the office of the secretary of state pursuant to the provisions of this Title without the written, acknowledged consent of the person at whose request the reservation was made.

2. The use by any other artificial person of a name in violation of subsection 1 or NRS 86.171 may be enjoined, even if the document under which the artificial person is formed, organized, registered or qualified has been filed by the secretary of state.

(Added to NRS by 1993, 1009; A 1999, 1613)

NRS 86.201 Articles of organization: Filing.

1. Upon filing the articles of organization and the certificate of acceptance of the resident agent, and the payment of filing fees, the limited-liability company is considered legally organized pursuant to this chapter.

2. A limited-liability company must not transact business or incur indebtedness, except that which is incidental to its organization or to obtaining subscriptions for or payment of contributions, until the secretary of state has filed the articles of organization and the certificate of acceptance.

(Added to NRS by 1991, 1294; A 1993, 1014; 1995, 1127, 2108)

NRS 86.211 Articles of organization: Notice imparted by filing. The fact that the articles of organization are on file in the office of the secretary of state is notice that the limited-liability company is a limited-liability company and is notice of all other facts sets forth therein which are required to be set forth in the articles of organization, unless the existence and facts set forth have been rebutted and made a part of a record of any court of competent jurisdiction.

(Added to NRS by 1991, 1294)

NRS 86.221 Amendment of articles of organization; restated articles of organization.

1. The articles of organization of a limited-liability company may be amended for any purpose, not inconsistent with law, as determined by all of the members or permitted by the articles or an operating agreement.

2. An amendment must be made in the form of a certificate setting forth:

(a) The name of the limited-liability company;

(b) The date of filing of the articles of organization; and

(c) The amendment to the articles of organization.

3. The certificate of amendment must be signed by a manager of the company, or if management is not vested in a manager, by a member.

4. Restated articles of organization may be executed and filed in the same manner as a certificate of amendment.

(Added to NRS by 1991, 1304; A 1993, 1014; 1995, 1127, 2108; 1997, 716; 1999, 1613)

NRS 86.226 Filing of certificate of amendment or judicial decree of amendment.

1. A signed certificate of amendment, or a certified copy of a judicial decree of amendment, must be filed with the secretary of state. A person who executes a certificate as an agent, officer or fiduciary of the limited-liability company need not exhibit evidence of his authority as a prerequisite to filing. Unless the secretary of state finds that a certificate does not conform to law, upon his receipt of all required filing fees he shall file the certificate.

2. Upon the filing of a certificate of amendment or judicial decree of amendment in the office of the secretary of state, the articles of organization are amended as set forth therein.

(Added to NRS by 1993, 1009; A 1995, 2109; 1997, 717; 1999, 1613)

OPERATION

NRS 86.231 Resident agent and registered office: Maintenance; change of address.

1. Except during any period of vacancy described in NRS 86.251, a limited-liability company shall have a resident agent who must have a street address for the service of process. The street address of the resident agent is the registered office of the limited-liability company in this state.

2. Within 30 days after changing the location of his office from one address to another in this state, a resident agent shall file a certificate with the secretary of state setting forth the names of the limited-liability companies represented by him, the address at which he has maintained the office for each of the limited-liability companies, and the new address to which the office is transferred.

(Added to NRS by 1991, 1295; A 1993, 1015; 1995, 1127, 2109)

NRS 86.235 Change of resident agent.

1. If a limited-liability company formed pursuant to this chapter desires to change its resident agent, the change may be effected by filing with the secretary of state a certificate of change signed by a manager of the company or, if management is not vested in a manager, by a member, that sets forth:

(a) The name of the limited-liability company;

(b) The name and street address of its present resident agent; and

(c) The name and street address of the new resident agent.

2. The new resident agent's certificate of acceptance must be a part of or attached to the certificate of change.

3. The change authorized by this section becomes effective upon the filing of the certificate of change.

(Added to NRS by 1995, 1125; A 1997, 717; 1999, 1614)

NRS 86.241 Records: Maintenance at office in state; inspection and copying.

1. Each limited-liability company shall continuously maintain in this state an office, which may but need not be a place of its business in this state, at which it shall keep, unless otherwise provided by an operating agreement:

(a) A current list of the full name and last known business address of each member and manager, separately identifying the members in alphabetical order and the managers, if any, in alphabetical order;

(b) A copy of the filed articles of organization and all amendments thereto, together with executed copies of any powers of attorney pursuant to which any document has been executed; and

(c) Copies of any then effective operating agreement of the company.

2. Records kept pursuant to this section are subject to inspection and copying at the reasonable request, and at the expense, of any member during ordinary business hours, unless otherwise provided in an operating agreement.

(Added to NRS by 1991, 1295; A 1993, 1015; 1995, 2110)

NRS 86.251 Resident agent: Resignation; designation of successor after death, resignation or movement from state.

1. A resident agent who desires to resign shall file with the secretary of state a signed statement for each limited-liability company that he is unwilling to continue to act as the agent of the limited-liability company for the service of process. A resignation is not effective until the signed statement is filed with the secretary of state.

2. The statement of resignation may contain a statement of the affected limited-liability company appointing a successor resident agent for that limited-liability company, giving the agent's full name, street address for the service of process, and mailing address if different from the street address. A certificate of acceptance executed by the new resident agent must accompany the statement appointing a successor resident agent.

3. Upon the filing of the statement of resignation with the secretary of state the capacity of the resigning person as resident agent terminates. If the statement of resignation contains no statement by the limited-liability company appointing a successor resident agent, the resigning agent shall immediately give written notice, by mail, to the limited-liability company of the filing of the statement and its effect. The notice must be addressed to any manager or, if none, to any member, of the limited-liability company other than the resident agent.

4. If a resident agent dies, resigns or moves from the state, the limited-liability company, within 30 days thereafter, shall file with the secretary of state a certificate of acceptance executed by the new resident agent. The certificate must set forth the name, complete street address and mailing address, if different from the street address, of the new resident agent.

5. Each limited-liability company which fails to file a certificate of acceptance executed by the new resident agent within 30 days after the death, resignation or removal of its resident agent as provided in subsection 4, shall be deemed in default and is subject to the provisions of NRS 86.272 and 86.274.

(Added to NRS by 1991, 1296; A 1993, 1016; 1995, 1128; 1999, 1614)

NRS 86.261 **Service of process, notice or demand upon resident agent.**

1. The resident agent appointed by a limited-liability company is an agent of the company upon whom any process, notice or demand required or permitted by law to be served upon the company may be served.

2. This section does not limit or affect the right to serve any process, notice or demand required or permitted by law to be served upon a limited-liability company in any other manner permitted by law.

(Added to NRS by 1991, 1296; A 1995, 1128; 1997, 474)

NRS 86.263 **Annual filing of list of managers or managing members; fee; notice.**

1. A limited-liability company shall, on or before the last day of the month in which the anniversary date of its formation occurs, file with the secretary of state, on a form furnished by him, a list containing:

(a) The name of the limited-liability company;

(b) The file number of the limited-liability company, if known;

(c) The names and titles of all of its managers or, if there is no manager, all of its managing members;

(d) The mailing or street address, either residence or business, of each manager or managing member listed, following the name of the manager or managing member; and

(e) The signature of a manager or managing member of the limited-liability company certifying that the list is true, complete and accurate.

2. The limited-liability company shall annually thereafter, on or before the last day of the month in which the anniversary date of organization occurs, file with the secretary of state, on a form furnished by him, an amended list containing all of the information required in subsection 1. If the limited-liability company has had no changes in its managers or, if there is no manager, its managing members, since its previous list was filed, no amended list need be filed if a manager or managing member of the limited-liability company certifies to the secretary of state as a true and accurate statement that no changes in the managers or managing members have occurred.

3. Upon filing the list of managers or managing members, or certifying that no changes have occurred, the limited-liability company shall pay to the secretary of state a fee of $85.

4. The secretary of state shall, 60 days before the last day for filing the list required by subsection 1, cause to be mailed to each limited-liability company required to comply with the provisions of this section, which has not become delinquent, a notice of the fee due under subsection 3 and a reminder to file a list of managers or managing members or a certification of no change. Failure of any company to receive a notice or form does not excuse it from the penalty imposed by law.

5. If the list to be filed pursuant to the provisions of subsection 1 or 2 is defective or the fee required by subsection 3 is not paid, the secretary of state may return the list for correction or payment.

6. An annual list for a limited-liability company not in default received by the secretary of state more than 60 days before its due date shall be deemed an amended list for the previous year.

(Added to NRS by 1993, 1010; A 1995, 1129, 2110; 1997, 2813)

NRS 86.266 **Certificate authorizing company to transact business.** If a limited-liability company has filed the annual list of managers or members and designation of a resident agent in compliance with NRS 86.263 and has paid the appropriate fee for the filing, the canceled check received by the limited-liability company constitutes a certificate authorizing it to transact its business within this state until the last day of the month in which the anniversary of its formation occurs in the next succeeding calendar year. If the company desires a formal certificate upon its payment of the annual fee, its payment must be accompanied by a self-addressed, stamped envelope.

(Added to NRS by 1993, 1010; A 1995, 1129; 1999, 1615)

NRS 86.269 **Contents of annual list: Names and addresses; penalties.**

1. Every list required to be filed under the provisions of NRS 86.263 must, after the name of each manager and member listed thereon, set forth the post office box or street address, either residence or business, of each manager or member.

2. If the addresses are not stated for each person on any list offered for filing, the secretary of state may refuse to file the list, and the limited-liability company for which the list has been offered for filing is subject to the provisions of NRS 86.272 and 86.274 relating to failure to file the list within or at the times therein specified, unless a list is subsequently submitted for filing which conforms to the provisions of this section.

(Added to NRS by 1993, 1010)

NRS 86.272 **Defaulting companies: Identification; penalty.**

1. Each limited-liability company required to make a filing and pay the fee prescribed in NRS 86.263 which refuses or neglects to do so within the time provided is in default.

2. For default there must be added to the amount of the fee a penalty of $15. The fee and penalty must be collected as provided in this chapter.

(Added to NRS by 1993, 1010; A 1995, 1129)

NRS 86.274 **Defaulting companies: Duties of secretary of state; forfeiture; distribution of assets.**

1. The secretary of state shall notify, by letter addressed to its resident agent, each limited-liability company deemed in default pursuant to the provisions of this chapter. The notice must be accompanied by a statement indicating the amount of the filing fee, penalties and costs remaining unpaid.

2. On the first day of the ninth month following the month in which the filing was required, the charter of the company is revoked and its right to transact business is forfeited.

3. The secretary of state shall compile a complete list containing the names of all limited-liability companies whose right to do business has been forfeited. The secretary of state shall forthwith notify each limited-liability company by letter addressed to its resident agent of the forfeiture of its charter. The notice must be accompanied by a statement indicating the amount of the filing fee, penalties and costs remaining unpaid.

4. If the charter of a limited-liability company is revoked and the right to transact business is forfeited, all of the property and assets of the defaulting company must be held in trust by the managers or, if none, by the members of the company, and the same proceedings may be had with respect to its property and assets as apply to the dissolution of a limited-liability company. Any person interested may institute proceedings at any time after a forfeiture has been declared, but if the secretary of state reinstates the charter the proceedings must be dismissed and all property restored to the company.

5. If the assets are distributed they must be applied in the following manner:

(a) To the payment of the filing fee, penalties and costs due to the state; and

(b) To the payment of the creditors of the company.

Any balance remaining must be distributed among the members as provided in subsection 1 of NRS 86.521.

(Added to NRS by 1993, 1011; A 1995, 1130)

NRS 86.276 Defaulting companies: Procedure and conditions for reinstatement.

1. Except as otherwise provided in subsections 3 and 4, the secretary of state shall reinstate any limited-liability company which has forfeited its right to transact business under the provisions of this chapter and restore to the company its right to carry on business in this state, and to exercise its privileges and immunities, if it:

(a) Files with the secretary of state the list required by NRS 86.263; and

(b) Pays to the secretary of state:

(1) The annual filing fee and penalty set forth in NRS 86.263 and 86.272 for each year or portion thereof during which its charter has been revoked; and

(2) A fee of $50 for reinstatement.

2. When the secretary of state reinstates the limited-liability company, he shall:

(a) Immediately issue and deliver to the company a certificate of reinstatement authorizing it to transact business as if the filing fee had been paid when due; and

(b) Upon demand, issue to the company one or more certified copies of the certificate of reinstatement.

3. The secretary of state shall not order a reinstatement unless all delinquent fees and penalties have been paid, and the revocation of the charter occurred only by reason of failure to pay the fees and penalties.

4. If a company's charter has been revoked pursuant to the provisions of this chapter and has remained revoked for a period of 5 consecutive years, the charter must not be reinstated.

(Added to NRS by 1993, 1011; A 1995, 1130; 1997, 2814)

NRS 86.278 Defaulting companies: Reinstatement under old or new name; regulations.

1. Except as otherwise provided in subsection 2, if a limited-liability company applies to reinstate its charter but its name has been legally acquired or reserved by any other artificial person formed, organized, registered or qualified pursuant to the provisions of this Title whose name is on file with the office of the secretary of state or reserved in the office of the secretary of state pursuant to the provisions of this Title, the company shall submit in writing to the secretary of state some other name under which it desires its existence to be reinstated. If that name is distinguishable from all other names reserved or otherwise on file, the secretary of state shall issue to the applying limited-liability company a certificate of reinstatement under that new name.

2. If the applying limited-liability company submits the written, acknowledged consent of the artificial person having the name, or the person reserving the name, which is not distinguishable from the old name of the applying company or a new name it has submitted, it may be reinstated under that name.

3. For the purposes of this section, a proposed name is not distinguishable from a name on file or reserved name solely because one or the other contains distinctive lettering, a distinctive mark, a trade-mark or a trade name or any combination of these.

4. The secretary of state may adopt regulations that interpret the requirements of this section.

(Added to NRS by 1993, 1012; A 1997, 2814; 1999, 1615)

NRS 86.281 General powers. A limited-liability company organized and existing under this chapter may:

1. Sue and be sued, complain and defend, in its name;

2. Purchase, take, receive, lease or otherwise acquire, own, hold, improve, use and otherwise deal in and with real or personal property, or an interest in it, wherever situated;

3. Sell, convey, mortgage, pledge, lease, exchange, transfer and otherwise dispose of all or any part of its property and assets;

4. Lend money to and otherwise assist its members;

5. Purchase, take, receive, subscribe for or otherwise acquire, own, hold, vote, use, employ, sell, mortgage, lend, pledge or otherwise dispose of, and otherwise use and deal in and with shares, member's interests or other interests in or obligations of domestic or foreign limited-liability companies, domestic or foreign corporations, joint ventures or similar associations, general or limited partnerships or natural persons, or direct or indirect obligations of the United States or of any government, state, territory, governmental district or municipality or of any instrumentality of it;

6. Make contracts and guarantees and incur liabilities, borrow money at such rates of interest as the company may determine, issue its notes, bonds and other obligations and secure any of its obligations by mortgage or pledge of all or any part of its property, franchises and income;

7. Lend, invest and reinvest its money and take and hold real property and personal property for the payment of money so loaned or invested;

8. Conduct its business, carry on its operations and have and exercise the powers granted by this chapter in any state, territory, district or possession of the United States, or in any foreign country;

9. Appoint managers and agents, define their duties and fix their compensation;

10. Cease its activities and surrender its articles of organization;

11. Exercise all powers necessary or convenient to effect any of the purposes for which the company is organized; and

12. Hold a license issued pursuant to the provisions of chapter 463 of NRS.

(Added to NRS by 1991, 1297; A 1993, 2011; 1997, 718)

NRS 86.286 Operating agreement. A limited-liability company may, but is not required to, adopt an operating agreement. An operating agreement may be adopted only by the unanimous vote or unanimous written consent of the members, and the operating agreement must be in writing. Unless otherwise provided in the operating agreement, amendments to the agreement may be adopted only by the unanimous vote or unanimous written consent of the persons who are members at the time of amendment.

(Added to NRS by 1995, 2106; A 1997, 718)

NRS 86.291 Management. Except as otherwise provided in this section, the articles of organization or the operating agreement, management of a limited-liability company is vested in its members in proportion to their contribution to its capital, as adjusted from time to time to reflect properly any additional contributions or withdrawals by the members. If provision is made in the articles of organization, management of the company may be vested in a manager or managers, who may but need not be members, in the manner prescribed by the operating agreement of the company. The manager or managers also hold the offices and have the responsibilities accorded to them by the members and set out in the operating agreement.

(Added to NRS by 1991, 1300; A 1993, 1017; 1995, 1131; 1997, 719)

NRS 86.301 Limitation on authority to contract debt or incur liability. Except as otherwise provided in this chapter or in its articles of organization, no debt may be contracted or liability incurred by or on behalf of a limited-liability company, except by one or more of its managers if management of the limited-liability company has been vested by the members in a manager or managers or, if management of the limited-liability company is retained by the members, then as provided in the articles of organization or the operating agreement.

(Added to NRS by 1991, 1300; A 1997, 719; 1999, 1615)

NRS 86.311 Acquisition, ownership and disposition of property. Real and personal property owned or purchased by a limited-liability company must be held and owned, and conveyance made, in the name of the company. Except as otherwise provided in the articles of organization, instruments and documents providing for the acquisition, mortgage or disposition of property of the company are valid and binding upon the company if executed by one or more managers of a company which has a manager or managers or as provided by the articles of organization of a company in which management has been retained by the members.

(Added to NRS by 1991, 1300; A 1997, 719)

NRS 86.321 Contributions to capital: Form. The contributions to capital of a member to a limited-liability company may be in cash, property or services rendered, or a promissory note or other binding obligation to contribute cash or property or to perform services.

(Added to NRS by 1991, 1300; A 1997, 719)

NRS 86.331 Resignation or withdrawal of member: Limitation; payment to member who rightfully resigns or withdraws.

1. Except as otherwise provided in chapter 463 of NRS, other applicable law, the articles of organization or the operating agreement, a member may not resign or withdraw as a member from a limited-liability company before the dissolution and winding up of the company.

2. If a member has a right to resign or withdraw, the amount that a resigning or withdrawing member is entitled to receive from the company for his interest must be determined pursuant to the provisions of this chapter, chapter 463 of NRS, the articles of organization or the operating agreement. If not otherwise provided therein, a resigning or withdrawing member is entitled to receive, within a reasonable time after resignation or withdrawal, the fair market value of his interest on the date of resignation or withdrawal.

(Added to NRS by 1991, 1301; A 1993, 2012; 1995, 2111; 1997, 719)

NRS 86.335 Resignation or withdrawal of member in violation of operating agreement; loss of rights to

participate upon resignation or withdrawal. Except as otherwise provided in this chapter, chapter 463 of NRS, the articles of organization or the operating agreement:

1. If the resignation or withdrawal of a member violates the operating agreement:

(a) The amount payable to the member who has resigned or withdrawn is the fair market value of his interest reduced by the amount of all damages sustained by the company or its other members as a result of the violation; and

(b) The company may defer the payment for so long as necessary to prevent unreasonable hardship to the company.

2. Except as otherwise provided in chapter 463 of NRS, the articles of organization or the operating agreement, a member who resigns or withdraws ceases to be a member, has no voting rights and has no right to participate in the management of the company, even if under this section a payment due him from the company is deferred.

(Added to NRS by 1997, 714)

NRS 86.341 Distribution of profits. A limited-liability company may, from time to time, divide the profits of its business and distribute them to its members, and any transferee as his interest may appear, upon the basis stipulated in the operating agreement. If the operating agreement does not otherwise provide, profits and losses must be allocated proportionately to the value, as shown in the records of the company, of the contributions made by each member and not returned.

(Added to NRS by 1991, 1301; A 1997, 720)

NRS 86.343 Prohibition on distribution of profits.

1. A distribution of the profits of a limited-liability company must not be made if, after giving it effect:

(a) The company would not be able to pay its debts as they become due in the usual course of business; or

(b) Except as otherwise specifically permitted by the articles of organization, the total assets of the company would be less than the sum of its total liabilities.

2. The manager or, if management of the company is not vested in a manager or managers, the members may base a determination that a distribution is not prohibited under this section on:

(a) Financial statements prepared on the basis of accounting practices that are reasonable in the circumstances;

(b) A fair valuation, including unrealized appreciation and depreciation; or

(c) Any other method that is reasonable in the circumstances.

3. The effect of a distribution under this section must be measured:

(a) In the case of a distribution by purchase, redemption or other acquisition by the company of member's interests, as of the earlier of:

(1) The date on which money or other property is transferred or debt incurred by the company; or

(2) The date on which the member ceases to be a member with respect to his acquired interest.

(b) In the case of any other distribution of indebtedness, as of the date on which the indebtedness is distributed.

(c) In all other cases, as of:

(1) The date on which the distribution is authorized if the payment occurs within 120 days after the date of authorization; or

(2) The date on which the payment is made if it occurs more than 120 days after the date of authorization.

4. Indebtedness of the company, including indebtedness issued as a distribution, is not considered a liability for purposes of determinations under this section if its terms provide that payment of principal and interest are to be made only if and to the extent that payment of a distribution to the members could then be made pursuant to this section. If the indebtedness is issued as a distribution, each payment of principal or interest must be treated as a distribution, the effect of which must be measured as of the date of payment.

(Added to NRS by 1997, 713)

NRS 86.346 Distributions: Form; status of member or transferee.

1. Unless otherwise provided in the operating agreement, a member, regardless of the nature of his contributions, or a transferee, regardless of the nature of his predecessor's contributions, has no right to demand or receive any distribution from a limited-liability company in any form other than cash.

2. Except as otherwise provided in NRS 86.391 and 86.521, and unless otherwise provided in the operating agreement, at the time a member or transferee becomes entitled to receive a distribution he has the status of and is entitled to all remedies available to a creditor of the company with respect to the distribution.

(Added to NRS by 1995, 2106; A 1997, 720)

NRS 86.351 Transfer or assignment of member's interest; rights of transferee; substituted members.

1. The interest of each member of a limited-liability company is personal property. The articles of organization or operating agreement may prohibit or regulate the transfer of a member's interest. Unless otherwise provided in the articles or agreement, a transferee of a member's interest has no right to participate in the management of the business and affairs of the company or to become a member unless a majority in interest of the other members approve the transfer. If so approved, the transferee becomes a substituted member. The transferee is only entitled to receive the share of profits or other compensation by way of income, and the return of contributions, to which his transferor would otherwise be entitled.

2. A substituted member has all the rights and powers and is subject to all the restrictions and liabilities of his transferor, except that the substitution of the transferee does not release the transferor from any liability to the company.

(Added to NRS by 1991, 1302; A 1995, 2112; 1997, 720)

LIABILITY, INDEMNIFICATION AND INSURANCE

NRS 86.361 Liability of persons assuming to act as company without authority. All persons who assume to act as a limited-liability company without authority to do so are jointly and severally liable for all debts and liabilities of the company.

(Added to NRS by 1991, 1304)

NRS 86.371 Liability of member or manager for debts or liabilities of company. Unless otherwise provided in the articles of organization or an agreement signed by the member or manager to be charged, no member or manager of any limited-liability company formed under the laws of this state is individually liable for the debts or liabilities of the company.

(Added to NRS by 1991, 1300; A 1995, 2112)

NRS 86.381 Member of company is not proper party in proceeding by or against company; exception. A member of a limited-liability company is not a proper party to proceedings by or against the company, except where the object is to enforce the member's right against or liability to the company.

(Added to NRS by 1991, 1304)

NRS 86.391 Liability to company of member or contributor to capital.

1. A member is liable to a limited-liability company:

(a) For a difference between his contributions to capital as actually made and as stated in the articles of organization or operating agreement as having been made; and

(b) For any unpaid contribution to capital which he agreed in the articles of organization or operating agreement to make in the future at the time and on the conditions stated in the articles of organization or operating agreement.

2. A member holds as trustee for the company:

(a) Specific property stated in the articles of organization or operating agreement as contributed by him, but which was not contributed or which has been wrongfully or erroneously returned; and

(b) Money or other property wrongfully paid or conveyed to him on account of his contribution or the contribution of a predecessor with respect to his member's interest.

3. The liabilities of a member as set out in this section can be waived or compromised only by the consent of all of the members, but a waiver or compromise does not affect the right of a creditor of the company to enforce the liabilities if he extended credit or his claim arose before the effective date of an amendment of the articles of organization or operating agreement effecting the waiver or compromise.

4. When a contributor has rightfully received the return in whole or in part of his contribution to capital, the contributor is liable to the company for any sum, not in excess of the return with interest, necessary to discharge its liability to all of its creditors who extended credit or whose claims arose before the return.

(Added to NRS by 1991, 1301; A 1997, 721)

NRS 86.401 Rights of judgment creditor of member. On application to a court of competent jurisdiction by a judgment creditor of a member, the court may charge the member's interest with payment of the unsatisfied amount of the judgment with interest. To the extent so charged, the judgment creditor has only the rights of an assignee of the member's interest. This section does not deprive any member of the benefit of any exemption applicable to his interest.

(Added to NRS by 1991, 1302)

NRS 86.411 Indemnification of manager, member, employee or agent: Proceeding other than by company. A limited-liability company may indemnify any person who was or is a party or is threatened to be made a party to any threatened, pending or completed action, suit or proceeding, whether civil, criminal, administrative or investigative, except an action by or in the right of the company, by reason of the fact that he is or was a manager, member, employee or agent of the company, or is or was serving at the request of the company as a manager, member, employee or agent of another limited-liability company, corporation, partnership, joint venture, trust or other enterprise, against expenses, including attorney's fees, judgments, fines and amounts paid in settlement actually and reasonably incurred by him in connection with the action, suit or proceeding if he acted in good faith and in a manner which he reasonably believed to be in or not opposed to the best interests of the company, and, with respect to any criminal action or proceeding, had no reasonable cause to believe his conduct was unlawful. The termination of any action, suit or proceeding by judgment, order, settlement or conviction, or upon a plea of nolo contendere or its equivalent, does not, of itself, create a presumption that the person did not act in good faith and in a manner which he reasonably believed to be in or not opposed to the best interests of the limited-liability company, and that, with respect to any criminal action or proceeding, he had reasonable cause to believe that his conduct was unlawful.

(Added to NRS by 1991, 1297; A 1997, 721)

NRS 86.421 Indemnification of manager, member, employee or agent: Proceeding by company. A limited-liability company may indemnify any person who was or is a party or is threatened to be made a party to any threatened, pending or completed action or suit by or in the right of the company to procure a judgment in its favor by reason of the fact that he is or was a manager, member, employee or agent of the company, or is or was serving at the request of the company as a manager, member, employee or agent of another limited-liability company, corporation, partnership, joint venture, trust or other enterprise against expenses, including amounts paid in settlement and attorneys' fees actually and reasonably incurred by him in connection with the defense or settlement of the action or suit if he acted in good faith and in a manner in which he reasonably believed to be in or not opposed to the best interests of the company. Indemnification may not be made for any claim, issue or matter as to which such a person has been adjudged by a court of competent jurisdiction, after exhaustion of all appeals therefrom, to be liable to the company or for amounts paid in settlement to the company, unless and only to the extent that the court in which the action or suit was brought or other court of competent jurisdiction determines upon application that in view of all the circumstances of the case, he is fairly and reasonably entitled to indemnity for such expenses as the court deems proper.

(Added to NRS by 1991, 1298; A 1997, 722)

NRS 86.431 **Indemnification of manager, member, employee or agent: Scope; authorization.**

1. To the extent that a manager, member, employee or agent of a limited-liability company has been successful on the merits or otherwise in defense of any action, suit or proceeding described in NRS 86.411 and 86.421, or in defense of any claim, issue or matter therein, the company shall indemnify him against expenses, including attorney's fees, actually and reasonably incurred by him in connection with the defense.

2. Any indemnification under NRS 86.411 and 86.421, unless ordered by a court or advanced pursuant to NRS 86.441, may be made by the limited-liability company only as authorized in the specific case upon a determination that indemnification of the manager, member, employee or agent is proper in the circumstances. The determination must be made:

(a) By the members or managers as provided in the articles of organization or the operating agreement;

(b) If there is no provision in the articles of organization or the operating agreement, by a majority in interest of the members who are not parties to the action, suit or proceeding;

(c) If a majority in interest of the members who are not parties to the action, suit or proceeding so order, by independent legal counsel in a written opinion; or

(d) If members who are not parties to the action, suit or proceeding cannot be obtained, by independent legal counsel in a written opinion.

(Added to NRS by 1991, 1298; A 1993, 1017; 1997, 722)

NRS 86.441 **Indemnification of member or manager: Advancement of expenses.** The articles of organization, the operating agreement or a separate agreement made by a limited-liability company may provide that the expenses of members and managers incurred in defending a civil or criminal action, suit or proceeding must be

paid by the company as they are incurred and in advance of the final disposition of the action, suit or proceeding, upon receipt of an undertaking by or on behalf of the manager or member to repay the amount if it is ultimately determined by a court of competent jurisdiction that he is not entitled to be indemnified by the company. The provisions of this section do not affect any rights to advancement of expenses to which personnel of the company other than managers or members may be entitled under any contract or otherwise by law.

(Added to NRS by 1991, 1299; A 1997, 723)

NRS 86.451 **Indemnification of manager, member, employee or agent: Effect of provisions on other rights; continuation after cessation of status.** Indemnification or advancement of expenses authorized in or ordered by a court pursuant to NRS 86.411 to 86.441, inclusive:

1. Does not exclude any other rights to which a person seeking indemnification or advancement of expenses may be entitled under the articles of organization or any operating agreement, vote of members or disinterested managers, if any, or otherwise, for an action in his official capacity or an action in another capacity while holding his office, except that indemnification, unless ordered by a court pursuant to NRS 86.421 or for the advancement of expenses made pursuant to NRS 86.441, may not be made to or on behalf of any member or manager if a final adjudication establishes that his acts or omissions involved intentional misconduct, fraud or a knowing violation of the law and was material to the cause of action.

2. Continues for a person who has ceased to be a member, manager, employee or agent and inures to the benefit of his heirs, executors and administrators.

(Added to NRS by 1991, 1299; A 1997, 723)

NRS 86.461 **Maintenance of insurance or other financial arrangements against liability of member, manager, employee or agent.**

1. A limited-liability company may purchase and maintain insurance or make other financial arrangements on behalf of any person who is or was a member, manager, employee or agent of the company, or is or was serving at the request of the company as a manager, member, employee or agent of another corporation, limited-liability company, partnership, joint venture, trust or other enterprise for any liability asserted against him and liability and expenses incurred by him in his capacity as a manager, member, employee or agent,

or arising out of his status as such, whether or not the company has the authority to indemnify him against such liability and expenses.

2. The other financial arrangements made by the company pursuant to subsection 1 may include:

(a) The creation of a trust fund.

(b) The establishment of a program of self-insurance.

(c) The securing of its obligation of indemnification by granting a security interest or other lien on any assets of the company.

(d) The establishment of a letter of credit, guaranty or surety.

No financial arrangement made pursuant to this subsection may provide protection for a person adjudged by a court of competent jurisdiction, after exhaustion of all appeals therefrom, to be liable for intentional misconduct, fraud or a knowing violation of law, except with respect to the advancement of expenses or indemnification ordered by a court.

3. Any insurance or other financial arrangement made on behalf of a person pursuant to this section may be provided by the company or any other person approved by the managers, if any, or by the members, if no managers exist, even if all or part of the other person's member's interest in the company is owned by the company.

(Added to NRS by 1991, 1299)

NRS 86.471 **Effect of providing insurance or other financial arrangements against liability of member, manager, employee or agent.** In the absence of fraud:

1. The decision of a limited-liability company as to the propriety of the terms and conditions of any insurance or other financial arrangement made pursuant to NRS 86.461 and the choice of the person to provide the insurance or other financial arrangement is conclusive; and

2. The insurance or other financial arrangement:

(a) Is not void or voidable; and

(b) Does not subject any manager or member approving it to personal liability for his action,

even if a manager or member approving the insurance or other financial arrangement is a beneficiary of the insurance or other financial arrangement.

(Added to NRS by 1991, 1300)

NRS 86.481 **Exclusion of company which provides self-insurance from Title 57 of NRS.** A limited-liability company or its subsidiary which provides self-insurance for itself or for an affiliated limited-liability company pursuant to NRS 86.461 is not subject to the provisions of Title 57 of NRS.

(Added to NRS by 1991, 1300)

DISSOLUTION

NRS 86.491 Events requiring dissolution and winding up of affairs. A limited-liability company organized under this chapter must be dissolved and its affairs wound up:

1. At the time, if any, specified in the articles of organization;

2. Upon the occurrence of an event specified in an operating agreement; or

3. By the unanimous written agreement of all members.

(Added to NRS by 1991, 1302; A 1995, 2112; 1997, 723)

NRS 86.505 Continuation of company after dissolution for winding up of affairs; limitation on actions by or against dissolved company. The dissolution of a limited-liability company does not impair any remedy or cause of action available to or against it or its managers or members arising before its dissolution and commenced within 2 years after the date of the dissolution. A dissolved company continues as a company for the purpose of prosecuting and defending suits, actions, proceedings and claims of any kind or nature by or against it and of enabling it gradually to settle and close its business, to collect and discharge its obligations, to dispose of and convey its property, and to distribute its assets, but not for the purpose of continuing the business for which it was established.

(Added to NRS by 1995, 2106; A 1997, 724)

NRS 86.521 Distribution of assets after dissolution.

1. In settling accounts after dissolution, the liabilities of a limited-liability company are entitled to payment in the following order:

(a) Those to creditors, including members who are creditors, in the order of priority as provided and to the extent otherwise permitted by law, except those to members of the limited-liability company on account of their contributions;

(b) Those to members of the limited-liability company in respect of their share of the profits and other compensation by way of income on their contributions; and

(c) Those to members of the limited-liability company in respect of their contributions to capital.

2. Subject to any statement in the operating agreement, members share in the company's assets in respect to their claims for capital and in respect to their claims for profits or for compensation by way of

income on their contributions, respectively, in proportion to the respective amounts of the claims.

(Added to NRS by 1991, 1303; A 1995, 2113)

NRS 86.531 Articles of dissolution: Preparation and contents; execution.

1. When all debts, liabilities and obligations have been paid and discharged or adequate provision has been made therefor and all of the remaining property and assets have been distributed to the members, articles of dissolution must be prepared and signed setting forth:

(a) The name of the limited-liability company;

(b) That all debts, obligations and liabilities have been paid and discharged or that adequate provision has been made therefor;

(c) That all the remaining property and assets have been distributed among its members in accordance with their respective rights and interests; and

(d) That there are no suits pending against the company in any court or that adequate provision has been made for the satisfaction of any judgment, order or decree which may be entered against it in any pending suit.

2. The articles must be signed by a manager, or if there is no manager by a member, of the company.

(Added to NRS by 1991, 1303; A 1995, 2113; 1999, 1616)

NRS 86.541 Articles of dissolution: Filing; duties of secretary of state; effect of filing.

1. The signed articles of dissolution must be filed with the secretary of state. Unless the secretary of state finds that the articles of dissolution do not conform to law, he shall when all fees and license taxes prescribed by law have been paid issue a certificate that the limited-liability company is dissolved.

2. Upon the filing of the articles of dissolution the existence of the company ceases, except for the purpose of suits, other proceedings and appropriate action as provided in this chapter. The manager or managers in office at the time of dissolution, or the survivors of them, are thereafter trustees for the members and creditors of the dissolved company and as such have authority to distribute any property of the company discovered after dissolution, convey real estate and take such other action as may be necessary on behalf of and in the name of the dissolved company.

(Added to NRS by 1991, 1303; A 1995, 2113; 1999, 1616)

MISCELLANEOUS PROVISIONS

NRS 86.551 Registration of foreign limited-liability company. A foreign limited-liability company may register with the secretary of state by complying with the provisions of NRS 88.570 to 88.605, inclusive, which provide for registration of foreign limited partnerships, except that:

1. The provisions of subsection 7 of NRS 88.575 do not apply; and

2. Cancellation is accomplished by filing articles of dissolution signed by all managers, if any, or by all members, if there are no managers.

(Added to NRS by 1991, 1305)

NRS 86.555 Issuance of occupational or professional license to limited-liability company by board or commission; regulations.

1. Except as otherwise provided by statute, an agency, board or commission that regulates an occupation or profession pursuant to Title 54, 55 or 56 of NRS may grant a license to a limited-liability company or a foreign limited-liability company if the agency, board or commission is authorized to grant a license to a corporation formed pursuant to chapter 78 of NRS.

2. An agency, board or commission that makes a license available to a limited-liability company or foreign limited-liability company pursuant to subsection 1 shall adopt regulations:

(a) Listing the persons in the limited-liability company or foreign limited-liability company who must qualify for the license or indicating that the agency, board or commission will use other means to determine whether the limited-liability company or foreign limited-liability company qualifies for a license;

(b) Listing the persons who may engage in the activity for which the license is required on behalf of the limited-liability company or foreign limited-liability company;

(c) Indicating whether the limited-liability company or foreign limited-liability company may engage in a business other than the business for which the license is required;

(d) Listing the changes, if any, in the management or control of the limited-liability company or foreign limited-liability company that require notice, review, approval or other action by the agency, board or commission; and

(e) Setting forth the conditions under which a limited-liability company or foreign limited-liability company may obtain a license.

3. An agency, board or commission that adopts regulations pursuant to subsection 2 shall not impose a restriction or requirement on a limited-liability company or foreign limited-liability company which is significantly different from or more burdensome than the restrictions or requirements imposed on a partnership or corporation.

(Added to NRS by 1997, 714)

NRS 86.561 Secretary of state: Fees.
1. The secretary of state shall charge and collect for:
(a) Filing the original articles of organization, or for registration of a foreign company, $125;
(b) Amending or restating the articles of organization, or amending the registration of a foreign company, $75;
(c) Filing the articles of dissolution of a domestic or foreign company, $30;
(d) Filing a statement of change of address of a records or registered office, or change of the resident agent, $15;
(e) Certifying articles of organization or an amendment to the articles, in both cases where a copy is provided, $10;
(f) Certifying an authorized printed copy of this chapter, $10;
(g) Reserving a name for a limited-liability company, $20;
(h) Executing, filing or certifying any other document, $20; and
(i) Copies made at the office of the secretary of state, $1 per page.
2. The secretary of state shall charge and collect at the time of any service of process on him as agent for service of process of a limited-liability company, $10 which may be recovered as taxable costs by the party to the action causing the service to be made if the party prevails in the action.
3. Except as otherwise provided in this section, the fees set forth in NRS 78.785 apply to this chapter.

(Added to NRS by 1991, 1305; A 1993, 1017; 1995, 1131)

NRS 86.563 Secretary of state: Procedure to submit replacement page before filing of document. Before the issuance of members' interests an organizer, and after the issuance of members' interests, a manager, of a limited-liability company may authorize the secretary of state in writing to replace any page of a document submitted for filing on an expedited basis, before the actual filing, and to accept the page as if it were part of the originally signed filing. The signed authorization of the organizer or manager to the secretary of state permits, but does not require, the secretary of state to alter the original document as requested.

(Added to NRS by 1997, 2812; 1999, 1611)

NRS 86.566 Secretary of state: Filing of documents written in language other than English. No document which is written in a language other than English may be filed or submitted for filing in the office of the secretary of state pursuant to the provisions of this chapter unless it is accompanied by a verified translation of that document into the English language.

(Added to NRS by 1995, 1126)

NRS 86.571 Waiver of notice. When, under the provisions of this chapter or under the provisions of the articles of organization or operating agreement of a limited-liability company, notice is required to be given to a member or to a manager of the company, if it has a manager or managers, a waiver in writing signed by the person or persons entitled to the notice, whether before or after the time stated in it, is equivalent to the giving of notice.

(Added to NRS by 1991, 1304)

NRS 86.580 Renewal or revival of charter: Procedure; fee; certificate as evidence.
1. A limited-liability company which did exist or is existing under the laws of this state may, upon complying with the provisions of NRS 86.276, procure a renewal or revival of its charter for any period, together with all the rights, franchises, privileges and immunities, and subject to all its existing and preexisting debts, duties and liabilities secured or imposed by its original charter and amendments thereto, or existing charter, by filing:
(a) A certificate with the secretary of state, which must set forth:
(1) The name of the limited-liability company, which must be the name of the limited-liability company at the time of the renewal or revival, or its name at the time its original charter expired.
(2) The name of the person designated as the resident agent of the limited-liability company, his street address for the service of process, and his mailing address if different from his street address.
(3) The date when the renewal or revival of the charter is to commence or be effective, which may be, in cases of a revival, before the date of the certificate.
(4) Whether or not the renewal or revival is to be perpetual, and, if not

perpetual, the time for which the renewal or revival is to continue.
(5) That the limited-liability company desiring to renew or revive its charter is, or has been, organized and carrying on the business authorized by its existing or original charter and amendments thereto, and desires to renew or continue through revival its existence pursuant to and subject to the provisions of this chapter.
(b) A list of its managers, or if there are no managers, all its managing members and their post office box or street addresses, either residence or business.
2. A limited-liability company whose charter has not expired and is being renewed shall cause the certificate to be signed by its manager, or if there is no manager, by a person designated by its members. The certificate must be approved by a majority of the members.
3. A limited-liability company seeking to revive its original or amended charter shall cause the certificate to be signed by a person or persons designated or appointed by the members. The execution and filing of the certificate must be approved by the written consent of a majority of the members and must contain a recital that this consent was secured. The limited-liability company shall pay to the secretary of state the fee required to establish a new limited-liability company pursuant to the provisions of this chapter.
4. The filed certificate, or a copy thereof which has been certified under the hand and seal of the secretary of state, must be received in all courts and places as prima facie evidence of the facts therein stated and of the existence of the limited-liability company therein named.

(Added to NRS by 1999, 1610)

NRS 86.590 Renewal or revival of charter: Status of company. A limited-liability company that has revived or renewed its charter pursuant to the provisions of this chapter:
1. Is a limited-liability company and continues to be a limited-liability company for the time stated in the certificate of revival or renewal;
2. Possesses the rights, privileges and immunities conferred by the original charter and by this chapter; and
3. Is subject to the restrictions and liabilities set forth in this chapter.

(Added to NRS by 1999, 1611)

APPENDIX F: NEVADA REVISED STATUTES CHAPTER 88A

BUSINESS TRUSTS

NRS 88A.010 Definitions. As used in this chapter, unless the context otherwise requires, the words and terms defined in NRS 88A.020 to 88A.110, inclusive, have the meanings ascribed to them in those sections.

(Added to NRS by 1999, 1561)

NRS 88A.020 "Beneficial owner" defined. "Beneficial owner" means the owner of a beneficial interest in a business trust.

(Added to NRS by 1999, 1561)

NRS 88A.030 "Business trust" defined. "Business trust" means an unincorporated association which:

1. Is created by a trust instrument under which property is held, managed, controlled, invested, reinvested or operated, or any combination of these, or business or professional activities for profit are carried on, by a trustee for the benefit of the persons entitled to a beneficial interest in the trust property; and

2. Files a certificate of trust pursuant to NRS 88A.210.

The term includes, without limitation, a trust of the type known at common law as a business trust or Massachusetts trust, a trust qualifying as a real estate investment trust pursuant to 26 U.S.C. §§ 856 et seq., as amended, or any successor provision, or a trust qualifying as a real estate mortgage investment conduit pursuant to 26 U.S.C. § 860D, as amended, or any successor provision. The term does not include a corporation as that term is defined in 11 U.S.C. § 101(9).

(Added to NRS by 1999, 1561)

NRS 88A.040 "Foreign business trust" defined. "Foreign business trust" means a business trust formed pursuant to the laws of a foreign nation or other foreign jurisdiction and denominated as such pursuant to those laws.

(Added to NRS by 1999, 1561)

NRS 88A.050 "Governing instrument" defined. "Governing instrument" means the trust instrument that creates a business trust and provides for the governance of its affairs and the conduct of its business.

(Added to NRS by 1999, 1561)

NRS 88A.060 "Registered office" defined. "Registered office" means the office of a business trust maintained at the street address of its resident agent.

(Added to NRS by 1999, 1561)

NRS 88A.070 "Resident agent" defined. "Resident agent" means the agent appointed by a business trust upon whom process or a notice or demand authorized by law to be served upon the business trust may be served.

(Added to NRS by 1999, 1561)

NRS 88A.080 "Sign" defined. "Sign" means to affix a signature to a document.

(Added to NRS by 1999, 1561)

NRS 88A.090 "Signature" defined. "Signature" means a name, word or mark executed or adopted by a person with the present intention to authenticate a document. The term includes, without limitation, a digital signature as defined in NRS 720.060

(Added to NRS by 1999, 1562)

NRS 88A.100 "Street address" defined. "Street address" of a resident agent means the actual physical location in this state at which a resident agent is available for service of process.

(Added to NRS by 1999, 1562)

NRS 88A.110 "Trustee" defined. "Trustee" means the person or persons appointed as trustee in accordance with the governing instrument of a business trust.

(Added to NRS by 1999, 1562)

APPLICABILITY

NRS 88A.150 Applicability of chapter to foreign and interstate commerce. The provisions of this chapter apply to commerce with foreign nations and among the several states. It is the intention of the legislature by enactment of this chapter that the legal existence of business trusts formed pursuant to this chapter be recognized beyond the limits of this state and that, subject to any reasonable requirement of registration, any such business trust transacting business outside this state be granted protection of full faith and credit pursuant to section 1 of article IV of the Constitution of the United States.

(Added to NRS by 1999, 1562)

NRS 88A.160 Applicability of laws pertaining to trusts; principle of freedom of contract and enforceability of governing instruments.

1. Except as otherwise provided in the certificate of trust, the governing instrument or this chapter, the laws of this state pertaining to trusts apply to a business trust.

2. In applying the provisions of this chapter, the court shall give the greatest effect to the principle of freedom of contract and the enforceability of governing instruments.

(Added to NRS by 1999, 1573)

NRS 88A.170 Provisions of chapter may be altered or repealed. All provisions of this chapter may be altered from time to time or repealed, and all rights of business trusts, trustees, beneficial owners and other persons are subject to this reservation.

(Added to NRS by 1999, 1574)

FORMATION

NRS 88A.200 Purpose. A business trust may be formed to carry on any lawful business or activity.

(Added to NRS by 1999, 1562)

NRS 88A.210 Procedure; required provisions of certificate of trust; issuance of certificate by secretary of state.

1. One or more persons may form a business trust by executing and filing with the secretary of state a certificate of trust and a certificate of acceptance of appointment signed by the resident agent of the business trust. The certificate of trust must set forth:

(a) The name of the business trust;

(b) The name and the post office box or street address, either residence or business, of at least one trustee;

(c) The name of the person designated as the resident agent for the business trust, the street address of the resident agent where process may be served upon the business trust and the mailing address of the resident agent if different from the street address;

(d) The name and post office box or street address, either residence or business, of each person signing the certificate of trust; and

(e) Any other information the trustees determine to include.

2. Upon the filing of the certificate of trust and the certificate of acceptance with the secretary of state and the payment to him of the required filing fee, the secretary of state shall issue to the business trust a certificate that the required documents with the required content have been filed. From the date of that filing, the business trust is legally formed pursuant to this chapter.

(Added to NRS by 1999, 1562)

NRS 88A.220 Procedure for amending or restating certificate of trust.

1. A certificate of trust may be amended by filing with the secretary of state a certificate of amendment signed by at least one trustee. The certificate of amendment must set forth:

(a) The name of the business trust;

(b) The date of filing of the original certificate of trust; and

(c) The amendment to the certificate of trust.

2. A certificate of trust may be restated by integrating into a single instrument all the provisions of the original certificate, and all amendments to the certificate, which are then in effect or are to be made by the restatement. The restated certificate of trust must be so designated in its heading, must be signed by at least one trustee and must set forth:

(a) The present name of the business trust and, if the name has been changed, the name under which the business trust was originally formed;

(b) The date of filing of the original certificate of trust;

(c) The provisions of the original certificate of trust, and all amendments to the certificate, which are then in effect; and

(d) Any further amendments to the certificate of trust.

3. A certificate of trust may be amended or restated at any time for any purpose determined by the trustees.

(Added to NRS by 1999, 1562)

NRS 88A.230 Name of trust: Distinguishable name required; availability of name of revoked, merged or otherwise terminated trust; regulations.

1. The name of a business trust formed pursuant to the provisions of this chapter must contain the words "Business Trust" or the abbreviation "B.T." or "BT."

2. The name proposed for a business trust must be distinguishable on the records of the secretary of state from the names of all other artificial persons formed, organized, registered or qualified pursuant to the provisions of this Title that are on file in the office of the secretary of state and all names that are reserved in the office of the secretary of state pursuant to the provisions of this Title. If a proposed name is not so distinguishable, the secretary of state shall return the certificate of trust containing it to the signers of the certificate, unless the written, acknowledged consent of the holder of the name on file or reserved name to use the same name or the requested similar name accompanies the certificate.

3. For the purposes of this section and NRS 88A.240, a proposed name is not distinguishable from a name on file or reserved name solely because one or the other contains distinctive lettering, a distinctive mark, a trade-mark or trade name, or any combination of these.

4. The name of a business trust whose certificate of trust has been revoked, which has merged and is not the surviving entity or whose existence has otherwise terminated is available for use by any other artificial person.

5. The secretary of state may adopt regulations that interpret the requirements of this section.

(Added to NRS by 1999, 1563)

NRS 88A.240 Name of trust: Reservation; injunctive relief.

1. The secretary of state, when requested to do so, shall reserve, for a period of 90 days, the right to use a name available pursuant to NRS 88A.230 for the use of a proposed business trust. During the period, the name so reserved is not available for use or reservation by any other artificial person forming, organizing, registering or qualifying in the office of the secretary of state pursuant to the provisions of this Title without the written, acknowledged consent of the person at whose request the reservation was made.

2. The use by any artificial person of a name in violation of subsection 1 or NRS 88A.230 may be enjoined, even if the document under which the artificial person is formed, organized, registered or qualified has been filed by the secretary of state.

(Added to NRS by 1999, 1563)

NRS 88A.250 Effect of filing certificate of amendment, restatement or cancellation or of filing articles of merger. Upon the filing of a certificate of amendment or restatement with the secretary of state, or upon the future effective date of such a certificate as provided for therein, the certificate of trust is amended or restated as set forth. Upon the filing of a certificate of cancellation, or articles of merger in which the business trust is not a surviving entity, with the secretary of state, or upon the future effective date of the certificate or articles, the certificate of trust is canceled.

(Added to NRS by 1999, 1563)

NRS 88A.260 Perpetual existence of trust; artificial person formed pursuant to other laws who is beneficial owner or trustee; inapplicability of certain laws.

1. Except as otherwise provided in the certificate of trust, the governing instrument or this chapter, a business trust has perpetual existence and may not be terminated or revoked by a beneficial owner or other person except in accordance with the certificate of trust or governing instrument.

2. Except as otherwise provided in the certificate of trust or the governing instrument, the death, incapacity, dissolution, termination or bankruptcy of a beneficial owner does not result in the termination or dissolution of a business trust.

3. An artificial person formed or organized pursuant to the laws of a foreign nation or other foreign jurisdiction or the laws of another state shall not be deemed to be doing business in this state solely because it is a beneficial owner or trustee of a business trust.

4. The provisions of NRS 662.245 do not apply to the appointment of a trustee of a business trust formed pursuant to this chapter.

(Added to NRS by 1999, 1564)

NRS 88A.270 Optional contents and provisions of governing instrument. A governing instrument may consist of one or more agreements, instruments or other writings and may include or incorporate bylaws containing provisions relating to the business of the business trust, the conduct of its affairs, and its rights or powers or the rights or powers of its trustees, beneficial owners, agents or employees. The governing instrument may provide that one or more of the beneficial owners may serve as trustee.

(Added to NRS by 1999, 1564)

NRS 88A.280 Optional provisions of governing instrument relating to management of trust and rights, duties and obligations of trustees, beneficial owners and other persons. A governing instrument may contain any provision relating to the management or the business or affairs of the business trust and the rights, duties and obligations of the trustees, beneficial owners and other persons which is not contrary to a provision or requirement of this chapter and may:

1. Provide for classes, groups or series of trustees or beneficial owners, or of beneficial interests, having such relative rights, powers and duties as the governing instrument provides, and may provide for the future creation in the manner provided in the governing instrument of additional such classes having such relative rights, powers and duties as may from time to time be established, including rights, powers and duties senior or subordinate to existing classes, groups or series.

2. Provide that a person becomes a beneficial owner and bound by the governing instrument if he, or his representative authorized orally, in writing or by action such as payment for a beneficial interest, complies with the conditions for becoming a beneficial owner set forth in the governing instrument or any other writing and acquires a beneficial interest.

3. Establish or provide for a designated series of trustees, beneficial owners or beneficial interests having separate rights, powers or duties with respect to specified property or obligations of the business trust or profits and losses associated with specified property or obligations, and, to the extent provided in the governing instrument, any such series may have a separate business purpose or investment objective.

4. Provide for the taking of any action, including the amendment of the governing instrument, the accomplishment of a merger, the appointment of one or more trustees, the sale, lease, transfer, pledge or other disposition of all or any part of the assets of the business trust or the assets of any series, or the dissolution of the business trust, and the creation of a class, group or series of beneficial interests that was not previously outstanding, without the vote or approval of any particular trustee or beneficial owner or class, group or series of trustees or beneficial owners.

5. Grant to or withhold from all or certain trustees or beneficial owners, or a specified class, group or series of trustees or beneficial owners, the right to vote, separately or with one or more of the trustees, beneficial owners or classes, groups or series thereof, on any matter. Voting power may be apportioned per capita, proportionate to financial interest, by class, group or series, or on any other basis.

6. If and to the extent that voting rights are granted under the certificate of trust or governing instrument, set forth provisions relating to notice of the time, place or purpose of a meeting at which a matter will be voted on, waiver of notice, action by consent without a meeting, the establishment of record dates, requirement of a quorum, voting in person, by proxy or otherwise, or any other matter with respect to the exercise of the right to vote.

7. Provide for the present or future creation of more than one business trust, including the creation of a future business trust to which all or any part of the assets, liabilities, profits or losses of any existing business trust are to be transferred, and for the conversion of beneficial interests in an existing business trust, or series thereof, into beneficial interests in the separate business trust or a series thereof.

8. Provide for the appointment, election or engagement, either as agents or independent contractors of the business trust or as delegates of the trustees, of officers, employees, managers or other persons who may manage the business and affairs of the business trust and have such titles and relative rights, powers and duties as the governing instrument provides. Except as otherwise provided in the governing instrument, the trustees shall choose and supervise those officers, managers and other persons.

(Added to NRS by 1999, 1569)

OPERATION

NRS 88A.300 General powers. A business trust formed and existing pursuant to this chapter has such powers as are necessary or convenient to effect any of the purposes for which the business trust is formed.

(Added to NRS by 1999, 1569)

NRS 88A.310 Management of business and affairs by trustees; giving directions to trustees.

1. Except as otherwise provided in this section, the certificate of trust or the governing instrument, the business and affairs of a business trust must be managed by or under the direction of its trustees. To the extent provided in the certificate of trust

or the governing instrument, any person, including a beneficial owner, may direct the trustees or other persons in the management of the business trust.

2. Except as otherwise provided in the certificate of trust or the governing instrument, neither the power to give direction to a trustee or other person nor the exercise thereof by any person, including a beneficial owner, makes him a trustee. To the extent provided in the certificate of trust or the governing instrument, neither the power to give direction to a trustee or other person nor the exercise thereof by a person, including a beneficial owner, causes him to have duties, fiduciary or other, or liabilities relating to the power or its exercise to the business trust or a beneficial owner thereof.

(Added to NRS by 1999, 1569)

NRS 88A.320 Ownership of beneficial interest in trust: Participation in profits and losses; creditor of beneficial owner; personal property; evidence of interest; transferability; distributions.

1. Except as otherwise provided in the governing instrument, a beneficial owner participates in the profits and losses of a business trust in the proportion of his beneficial interest to the entire beneficial interest. A governing instrument may provide that the business trust, or the trustees on its behalf, hold beneficial ownership of income earned on securities owned by the business trust.

2. A creditor of a beneficial owner has no right to obtain possession of, or otherwise exercise legal or equitable remedies with respect to, property of the business trust.

3. A beneficial interest in a business trust is personal property regardless of the nature of the property of the business trust. Except as otherwise provided in the certificate of trust or the governing instrument, a beneficial owner has no interest in specific property of the business trust.

4. A beneficial interest in a business trust may be evidenced by the issuance of certificates of ownership or by other means set forth in the certificate of trust or the governing instrument.

5. Except as otherwise provided in the certificate of trust or the governing instrument, a beneficial interest in a business trust is freely transferable.

6. Except as otherwise provided in the certificate of trust or the governing instrument, if a beneficial owner becomes entitled to receive a distribution, he has the status of, and is entitled to all remedies available to, a creditor of the business trust with respect to the distribution. The governing instrument may provide for the establishment of record dates with respect to

allocations and distributions by a business trust.

7. The fact of ownership of a beneficial interest in a business trust is determined, and the means of evidencing it are set forth, by the applicable provisions of the certificate of trust or the governing instrument.

(Added to NRS by 1999, 1564)

NRS 88A.330 Beneficial owner of trust: Contribution to trust; obligations; penalties.

1. A contribution of a beneficial owner to a business trust may be any tangible or intangible property or benefit to the business trust, including cash, a promissory note, services performed, a contract for services to be performed, or a security of the business trust. A person may become a beneficial owner of a business trust and may receive a beneficial interest in a business trust without making, or being obligated to make, a contribution to the business trust.

2. Except as otherwise provided in the certificate of trust or the governing instrument, a beneficial owner is obligated to the business trust to perform a promise to make a contribution even if he is unable to perform because of death, disability or any other reason. If a beneficial owner does not make a promised contribution of property or services, he is obligated at the option of the business trust to contribute cash equal to that portion of the agreed value, as stated in the records of the business trust, of the contribution which has not been made. The foregoing option is in addition to any other rights, including specific performance, that the business trust may have against the beneficial owner under the governing instrument or applicable law.

3. A certificate of trust or governing instrument may provide that the interest of a beneficial owner who fails to make a contribution that he is obligated to make is subject to specific penalties for, or specified consequences of, such failure. The penalty or consequence may take the form of reducing or eliminating the defaulting beneficial owner's proportionate interest in the business trust, subordinating that beneficial interest to those of nondefaulting owners, a forced sale of the beneficial interest, forfeiture of the beneficial interest, the lending by other beneficial owners of the amount necessary to meet the defaulter's commitment, a fixing of the value of the beneficial interest by appraisal or formula and redemption or sale of the beneficial interest at that value, or any other form.

(Added to NRS by 1999, 1571)

NRS 88A.340 Maintenance of records at registered office.

1. A business trust shall keep a copy of the following records at its registered office:

(a) A copy certified by the secretary of state of its certificate of trust and all amendments thereto or restatements thereof;

(b) A copy certified by one of its trustees of its governing instrument and all amendments thereto; and

(c) A ledger or duplicate ledger, revised annually, containing the names, alphabetically arranged, of all its beneficial owners, showing their places of residence if known. Instead of this ledger, the business trust may keep a statement containing the name of the custodian of the ledger and the present complete address, including street and number, if any, where the ledger is kept.

2. A business trust shall maintain the records required by subsection 1 in written form or in another form capable of conversion into written form within a reasonable time.

(Added to NRS by 1999, 1566)

NRS 88A.350 Right of certain beneficial owners to inspect and copy ledger; denial of inspection.

1. A person who has been a beneficial owner of record of a business trust for at least 6 months immediately preceding his demand, or a person holding, or authorized in writing by the holders of, at least 5 percent of its beneficial ownership, is entitled, upon at least 5 days' written demand, to inspect in person or by agent or attorney, during usual business hours, the ledger or duplicate ledger, whether kept in the registered office of the business trust or elsewhere, and to make copies therefrom.

2. An inspection authorized by subsection 1 may be denied to a beneficial owner or other person upon his refusal to furnish to the business trust an affidavit that the inspection is not desired for a purpose which is in the interest of a business or object other than the business of the business trust and that he has not at any time sold or offered for sale any list of beneficial owners of a domestic or foreign business trust, stockholders of a domestic or foreign corporation or members of a domestic or foreign limited-liability company, or aided or abetted any person in procuring such a list for such a purpose.

(Added to NRS by 1999, 1567)

NRS 88A.360 Duties and liabilities of trustee. To the extent that, at law or in equity, a trustee has duties, fiduciary or otherwise, and liabilities relating thereto to a business trust or beneficial owner:

1. If he acts pursuant to a governing instrument, he is not liable to the business trust or to a beneficial owner for his reliance in good faith on the provisions of the governing instrument; and

2. His duties and liabilities may be expanded or restricted by provisions in the governing instrument.

(Added to NRS by 1999, 1571)

NRS 88A.370 Duties and liabilities of officer, employee, manager or other person acting pursuant to certificate of trust or governing instrument. To the extent that, at law or in equity, an officer, employee, manager or other person acting pursuant to the certificate of trust or a governing instrument has duties, fiduciary or otherwise, and liabilities relating thereto to a business trust, beneficial owner or trustee:

1. If he acts pursuant to a governing instrument, he is not liable to the business trust, a beneficial owner or a trustee for his reliance in good faith on the provisions of the governing instrument; and

2. His duties and liabilities may be expanded or restricted by provisions in the governing instrument.

(Added to NRS by 1999, 1571)

NRS 88A.380 Enforceability of debts, liabilities, obligations and expenses against assets of series of trustees, beneficial owners or beneficial interests. The debts, liabilities, obligations and expenses incurred, contracted for or otherwise existing with respect to a particular series of trustees, beneficial owners or beneficial interests are enforceable against the assets of only that series only if:

1. The governing instrument of the business trust creates one or more series of trustees, beneficial owners or beneficial interests;

2. Separate records are maintained for the series;

3. The assets associated with the series are held and accounted for separately from the other assets of the business trust or any other series of the business trust and the governing instrument requires separate holding and accounting; and

4. Notice of the limitation on liability of the series is set forth in the certificate of trust, or an amendment thereto, filed with the secretary of state before the series is established.

(Added to NRS by 1999, 1571)

NRS 88A.390 Beneficial owner, trustee, officer, agent, manager or employee not personally liable.

1. Unless otherwise provided in the certificate of trust, the governing instrument or an agreement signed by the person to be charged, a beneficial owner, trustee, officer,

agent, manager or employee of a business trust formed pursuant to the laws of this state is not personally liable for the debts or liabilities of the business trust.

2. Except as otherwise provided in the certificate of trust or the governing instrument, a trustee acting in that capacity is not personally liable to any person other than the business trust or a beneficial owner for any act or omission of the business trust or a trustee thereof.

3. Except as otherwise provided in the certificate of trust or the governing instrument, an officer, employee, agent or manager of a business trust or another person who manages the business and affairs of a business trust, acting in that capacity, is not personally liable to any person other than the business trust or a beneficial owner for any act or omission of the business trust or a trustee thereof.

4. Except as otherwise provided in the certificate of trust or the governing instrument, a trustee, officer, employee, agent or manager of a business trust or another person who manages the business and affairs of a business trust is not personally liable to the business trust or a beneficial owner for damages for breach of fiduciary duty in such capacity except for acts or omissions that involve intentional misconduct, fraud or a knowing violation of law.

(Added to NRS by 1999, 1572)

NRS 88A.400 **Indemnification of trustee, beneficial owner or other person.**

1. Subject to the standards and restrictions, if any, set forth in the certificate of trust or the governing instrument, a business trust may indemnify and hold harmless a trustee, beneficial owner or other person from and against all claims and demands.

2. The absence of a provision for indemnity in the certificate of trust or governing instrument does not deprive a trustee or beneficial owner of any right to indemnity which is otherwise available to him pursuant to the laws of this state.

(Added to NRS by 1999, 1572)

NRS 88A.410 **Derivative action maintained by beneficial owner in right of trust.**

1. A beneficial owner may maintain an action in the right of a business trust to recover a judgment in its favor if trustees having authority to do so have refused to bring the action or if an effort to cause those trustees to bring the action is unlikely to succeed.

2. In a derivative action, the plaintiff must be a beneficial owner at the time of bringing the action and:

(a) He must have been a beneficial owner at the time of the transaction of which he complains; or

(b) His status as a beneficial owner must have devolved upon him by operation of law or pursuant to a provision of the certificate of trust or the governing instrument from a person who was a beneficial owner at the time of the transaction.

3. In a derivative action, the complaint must state with particularity the effort, if any, of the plaintiff to cause the trustees to bring the act, or the reasons for not making the effort.

4. If a derivative action is successful, in whole or in part, or if anything is received by the business trust through judgment or settlement of the action, the court may award the plaintiff reasonable expenses, including attorney's fees. If the plaintiff receives any proceeds of judgment or settlement, the court shall make the award of his expenses payable from those proceeds and remit the remainder to the business trust. If the proceeds received by the plaintiff are less than the expenses awarded, the court may direct all or part of the remainder of the award to be paid by the business trust.

5. A beneficial owner's right to bring a derivative action may be subject to additional standards and restrictions set forth in the governing instrument, including, without limitation, a requirement that beneficial owners of a specified beneficial interest join in the action.

(Added to NRS by 1999, 1573)

NRS 88A.420 **Cancellation of certificate of trust upon termination of trust.** A certificate of trust must be canceled upon the completion or winding up of the business trust and its termination. A certificate of cancellation must be signed by a trustee, filed with the secretary of state, and set forth:

1. The name of the business trust;

2. The date of filing of its certificate of trust;

3. A future effective date of the certificate of cancellation, if it is not to be effective upon filing, which may not be more than 90 days after the certificate is filed; and

4. Any other information the trustee determines to include.

(Added to NRS by 1999, 1573)

RESIDENT AGENT

NRS 88A.500 **Requirement; address; penalty for noncompliance.**

1. Except during any period of vacancy described in NRS 88A.530, a business trust shall have a resident agent who resides or is located in this state. A resident agent shall

have a street address for the service of process and may have a mailing address such as a post office box, which may be different from the street address.

2. A business trust formed pursuant to this chapter that fails or refuses to comply with the requirements of this section is subject to a fine of not less than $100 nor more than $500, to be recovered with costs by the state, before any court of competent jurisdiction, by action at law prosecuted by the attorney general or by the district attorney of the county in which the action or proceeding to recover the fine is prosecuted.

(Added to NRS by 1999, 1565)

NRS 88A.510 **Change of address.**

1. Within 30 days after changing the location of his office from one address to another in this state, a resident agent shall execute a certificate setting forth:

(a) The names of all the business trusts represented by him;

(b) The address at which he has maintained the registered office for each of those business trusts; and

(c) The new address to which his office is transferred and at which he will maintain the registered office for each of those business trusts.

2. Upon the filing of the certificate with the secretary of state, the registered office of each of the business trusts listed in the certificate is located at the new address set forth in the certificate.

(Added to NRS by 1999, 1565)

NRS 88A.520 **Powers; service of process, demand or notice.**

1. If the resident agent is a bank or an artificial person formed or organized pursuant to this Title, it may:

(a) Act as the fiscal or transfer agent of a state, municipality, body politic or business trust, and in that capacity may receive and disburse money.

(b) Transfer, register and countersign certificates evidencing a beneficial owner's interest in a business trust, bonds or other evidences of indebtedness and act as agent of any business trust, foreign or domestic, for any purpose required by statute or otherwise.

2. All legal process and any demand or notice authorized by law to be served upon a business trust may be served upon its resident agent in the manner provided in subsection 2 of NRS 14.020. If a demand, notice or legal process, other than a summons and complaint, cannot be served upon the resident agent, it may be served in the manner provided in NRS 14.030. These manners of service are in addition to any other service authorized by law.

(Added to NRS by 1999, 1565)

NRS 88A.530 **Resignation; notice to trust of resignation; designation of successor after death, resignation or movement from state.**

1. A resident agent who desires to resign shall file with the secretary of state a signed statement for each business trust for which he is unwilling to continue to act. A resignation is not effective until the signed statement is so filed.

2. The statement of resignation may contain a statement of the affected business trust appointing a successor resident agent. A certificate of acceptance executed by the new resident agent, stating the full name, complete street address and, if different from the street address, mailing address of the new resident agent, must accompany the statement appointing a successor resident agent.

3. Upon the filing of the statement of resignation with the secretary of state, the capacity of the resigning person as resident agent terminates. If the statement of resignation contains no statement by the business trust appointing a successor resident agent, the resigning agent shall immediately give written notice, by mail, to the business trust of the filing of the statement of resignation and its effect. The notice must be addressed to a trustee of the business trust other than the resident agent.

4. If its resident agent dies, resigns or removes from the state, a business trust, within 30 days thereafter, shall file with the secretary of state a certificate of acceptance executed by a new resident agent. The certificate must set forth the full name and complete street address of the new resident agent, and may contain a mailing address, such as a post office box, different from the street address.

5. A business trust that fails to file a certificate of acceptance executed by its new resident agent within 30 days after the death, resignation or removal of its former resident agent shall be deemed in default and is subject to the provisions of NRS 88A.630 to 88A.660, inclusive.

(Added to NRS by 1999, 1566)

NRS 88A.540 **Change of resident agent.**

1. If a business trust formed pursuant to this chapter desires to change its resident agent, the change may be effected by filing with the secretary of state a certificate of change, signed by at least one trustee of the business trust, setting forth:

(a) The name of the business trust;

(b) The name and street address of the present resident agent; and

(c) The name and street address of the new resident agent.

2. A certificate of acceptance executed by the new resident agent must be a part of or attached to the certificate of change.

3. The change authorized by this section becomes effective upon the filing of the certificate of change.

(Added to NRS by 1999, 1566)

ANNUAL LIST OF RESIDENT AGENT AND TRUSTEES; DEFAULTING TRUSTS

NRS 88A.600 **Filing requirements; fee; notice.**

1. A business trust formed pursuant to this chapter shall annually, on or before the last day of the month in which the anniversary date of the filing of its certificate of trust with the secretary of state occurs, file with the secretary of state on a form furnished by him a list signed by at least one trustee containing the name and mailing address of its resident agent and at least one trustee. Upon filing the list, the business trust shall pay to the secretary of state a fee of $85.

2. The secretary of state shall, 60 days before the last day for filing the annual list required by subsection 1, cause to be mailed to each business trust which is required to comply with the provisions of NRS 88A.600 to 88A.660, inclusive, and which has not become delinquent, the blank forms to be completed and filed with him. Failure of a business trust to receive the forms does not excuse it from the penalty imposed by law.

3. An annual list for a business trust not in default which is received by the secretary of state more than 60 days before its due date shall be deemed an amended list for the previous year.

(Added to NRS by 1999, 1567)

NRS 88A.610 **Certificate authorizing trust to transact business.** When the fee for filing the annual list has been paid, the canceled check received by the business trust constitutes a certificate authorizing it to transact its business within this state until the last day of the month in which the anniversary of the filing of its certificate of trust occurs in the next succeeding calendar year. If the business trust desires a formal certificate upon its payment of the annual fee, its payment must be accompanied by a self-addressed, stamped envelope.

(Added to NRS by 1999, 1567)

NRS 88A.620 **Address of trustee required; failure to file.**

1. Each list required to be filed pursuant to the provisions of NRS 88A.600 to 88A.660, inclusive, must, after the name of each trustee listed thereon, set forth his post office box or street address, either residence or business.

2. If the addresses are not stated on a list offered for filing, the secretary of state may refuse to file the list, and the business trust for which the list has been offered for filing is subject to all the provisions of NRS 88A.600 to 88A.660, inclusive, relating to failure to file the list when or at the times therein specified, unless a list is subsequently submitted for filing which conforms to the provisions of those sections.

(Added to NRS by 1999, 1568)

NRS 88A.630 **Defaulting trusts: Identification; penalty.**

1. Each business trust required to file the annual list and pay the fee prescribed in NRS 88A.600 to 88A.660, inclusive, which refuses or neglects to do so within the time provided shall be deemed in default.

2. For default, there must be added to the amount of the fee a penalty of $15. The fee and penalty must be collected as provided in this chapter.

(Added to NRS by 1999, 1568)

NRS 88A.640 **Defaulting trusts: Duties of secretary of state; forfeiture; assets held in trust as for insolvent business trusts.**

1. The secretary of state shall notify, by letter addressed to its resident agent, each business trust deemed in default pursuant to the provisions of this chapter. The notice must be accompanied by a statement indicating the amount of the filing fee, penalties and costs remaining unpaid.

2. On the first day of the ninth month following the month in which the filing was required, the certificate of trust of the business trust is revoked and its right to transact business is forfeited.

3. The secretary of state shall compile a complete list containing the names of all business trusts whose right to do business has been forfeited. He shall forthwith notify each such business trust, by letter addressed to its resident agent, of the revocation of its certificate of trust. The notice must be accompanied by a statement indicating the amount of the filing fee, penalties and costs remaining unpaid.

4. If the certificate of trust is revoked and the right to transact business is forfeited, all the property and assets of the defaulting business trust must be held in trust by its trustees as for insolvent business trusts, and the same proceedings may be had with respect thereto as are applicable to insolvent business trusts. Any person interested may institute proceedings at any time after a forfeiture has been declared, but if the secretary of state reinstates the certificate of

trust, the proceedings must at once be dismissed.

(Added to NRS by 1999, 1568)

NRS 88A.650 Defaulting trusts: Procedure and conditions for reinstatement.

1. Except as otherwise provided in subsection 3, the secretary of state shall reinstate a business trust which has forfeited its right to transact business pursuant to the provisions of this chapter and restore to the business trust its right to carry on business in this state, and to exercise its privileges and immunities, if it:

(a) Files with the secretary of state the list and designation required by NRS 88A.600; and

(b) Pays to the secretary of state:

(1) The annual filing fee and penalty set forth in NRS 88A.600 and 88A.630 for each year or portion thereof during which its certificate of trust was revoked; and

(2) A fee of $50 for reinstatement.

2. When the secretary of state reinstates the business trust, he shall:

(a) Immediately issue and deliver to the business trust a certificate of reinstatement authorizing it to transact business as if the filing fee had been paid when due; and

(b) Upon demand, issue to the business trust one or more certified copies of the certificate of reinstatement.

3. The secretary of state shall not order a reinstatement unless all delinquent fees and penalties have been paid, and the revocation of the certificate of trust occurred only by reason of the failure to file the list or pay the fees and penalties.

(Added to NRS by 1999, 1568)

NRS 88A.660 Defaulting trusts: Reinstatement under old or new name.

1. Except as otherwise provided in subsection 2, if a certificate of trust is revoked pursuant to the provisions of this chapter and the name of the business trust has been legally reserved or acquired by another artificial person formed, organized, registered or qualified pursuant to the provisions of this Title whose name is on file with the office of the secretary of state or reserved in the office of the secretary of state pursuant to the provisions of this Title, the business trust shall submit in writing to the secretary of state some other name under which it desires to be reinstated. If that name is distinguishable from all other names reserved or otherwise on file, the secretary of state shall issue to the business trust a certificate of reinstatement under that new name.

2. If the defaulting business trust submits the written, acknowledged consent of the artificial person using a name, or the person who has reserved a name, which is not distinguishable from the old name of the business trust or a new name it has submitted, it may be reinstated under that name.

(Added to NRS by 1999, 1569)

FOREIGN BUSINESS TRUSTS

NRS 88A.700 Laws governing organization, internal affairs and liability of beneficial owners, trustees, officers, employees and managers; registration. Subject to the constitution of this state:

1. The laws of the state under which a foreign business trust is organized govern its organization and internal affairs and the liability of its beneficial owners, trustees, officers, employees or managers; and

2. A foreign business trust may not be denied registration by reason of any difference between those laws and the laws of this state.

(Added to NRS by 1999, 1574)

NRS 88A.710 Application for registration: Requirements; contents. Before transacting business in this state, a foreign business trust shall register with the secretary of state. In order to register, a foreign business trust shall submit to the secretary of state an application for registration as a foreign business trust, signed by a trustee, and a signed certificate of acceptance of a resident agent. The application for registration must set forth:

1. The name of the foreign business trust and, if different, the name under which it proposes to register and transact business in this state;

2. The state and date of its formation;

3. The name and address of the resident agent whom the foreign business trust elects to appoint;

4. The address of the office required to be maintained in the state of its organization by the laws of that state or, if not so required, of the principal office of the foreign business trust; and

5. The name and business address of one trustee.

(Added to NRS by 1999, 1574)

NRS 88A.720 Issuance of certificate of registration by secretary of state. If the secretary of state finds that an application for registration conforms to law and all requisite fees have been paid, he shall issue a certificate of registration to transact business in this state and mail it to the person who filed the application or his representative.

(Added to NRS by 1999, 1575)

NRS 88A.730 Registration of name. A foreign business trust may register with the secretary of state under any name, whether or not it is the name under which it is registered in its state of organization, which includes the words "Business Trust" or the abbreviation "B.T." or "BT" and which could be registered by a domestic business trust.

(Added to NRS by 1999, 1575)

NRS 88A.740 Cancellation of registration. A foreign business trust may cancel its registration by filing with the secretary of state a certificate of cancellation signed by a trustee. The certificate must set forth:

1. The name of the foreign business trust;

2. The date upon which its certificate of registration was filed;

3. The effective date of the cancellation if other than the date of the filing of the certificate of cancellation; and

4. Any other information deemed necessary by the trustee.

A cancellation does not terminate the authority of the secretary of state to accept service of process on the foreign business trust with respect to causes of action arising out of the transaction of business in this state.

(Added to NRS by 1999, 1575)

NRS 88A.750 Transaction of business without certificate of registration: Liability; appointment of secretary of state as agent for service of process.

1. A foreign business trust transacting business in this state may not maintain any action, suit or proceeding in any court of this state until it has registered in this state.

2. The failure of a foreign business trust to register in this state does not impair the validity of any contract or act of the foreign business trust or prevent the foreign business trust from defending any action, suit or proceeding in any court of this state.

3. A foreign business trust, by transacting business in this state without registration, appoints the secretary of state as its agent for service of process with respect to causes of action arising out of the transaction of business in this state.

(Added to NRS by 1999, 1575)

MISCELLANEOUS PROVISIONS

NRS 88A.900 Fees charged by secretary of state. The secretary of state shall charge and collect the following fees for:

1. Filing an original certificate of trust, or for registering a foreign business trust, $125.

2. Filing an amendment or restatement, or a combination thereof, to a certificate of trust, $75.

3. Filing a certificate of cancellation, $125.

4. Certifying a copy of a certificate of trust or an amendment or restatement, or a combination thereof, $10 per certification.

5. Certifying an authorized printed copy of this chapter, $10.

6. Reserving a name for a business trust, $20.

7. Executing a certificate of existence of a business trust which does not list the previous documents relating to it, or a certificate of change in the name of a business trust, $15.

8. Executing a certificate of existence of a business trust which lists the previous documents relating to it, $20.

9. Filing a statement of change of address of the registered office for each business trust, $15.

10. Filing a statement of change of the registered agent, $15.

11. Executing, certifying or filing any certificate or document not otherwise provided for in this section, $20.

12. Examining and provisionally approving a document before the document is presented for filing, $100.

13. Copying a document on file with him, for each page, $1.

(Added to NRS by 1999, 1574)

NRS 88A.910 Facsimile signatures.
A signature on any certificate authorized to be filed with the secretary of state pursuant to a provision of this chapter may be a facsimile. The certificate may be filed by telecopy or similar electronic transmission, but the secretary of state need not accept the filing if the certificate is illegible or otherwise unsuitable for the procedures of his office.

(Added to NRS by 1999, 1564)

APPENDIX G: NEVADA REVISED STATUTES CHAPTER 89

PROFESSIONAL CORPORATIONS AND ASSOCIATIONS

NRS 89.010 Short title. This chapter is known and may be cited as the Professional Corporations and Associations Act.

(Added to NRS by 1963, 865; A 1969, 519)

NRS 89.020 Definitions. As used in this chapter, unless the context requires otherwise:

1. "Employee" means a person licensed or otherwise legally authorized to render professional service within this state who renders such service through a professional corporation or a professional association, but does not include clerks, bookkeepers, technicians or other persons who are not usually considered by custom and practice of the profession to be rendering professional services to the public.

2. "Licensed" means legally authorized by the appropriate regulating board of this state to engage in a regulated profession in this state.

3. "Professional association" means a common law association of two or more persons licensed or otherwise legally authorized to render professional service within this state when created by written articles of association which contain in substance the following provisions characteristic of corporate entities:

(a) The death, insanity, bankruptcy, retirement, resignation, expulsion or withdrawal of any member of the association does not cause its dissolution.

(b) The authority to manage the affairs of the association is vested in a board of directors or an executive board or committee, elected by the members of the association.

(c) The members of the association are employees of the association.

(d) Members' ownership is evidenced by certificates.

4. "Professional corporation" means a corporation organized under this chapter to render a professional service.

5. "Professional service" means any type of personal service which may legally be performed only pursuant to a license, certificate of registration or other legal authorization.

6. "Regulating board" means the body which regulates and authorizes the admission to the profession which a professional corporation or a professional association is authorized to perform.

(Added to NRS by 1963, 865; A 1969, 519; 1995, 2117)

NRS 89.025 Secretary of state: Fees. Except as otherwise provided in NRS 89.200 to 89.270, inclusive, the fees set forth in NRS 78.785 apply to this chapter.

(Added to NRS by 1995, 1139)

NRS 89.027 Secretary of state: Filing of documents written in language other than English. No document which is written in a language other than English may be filed or submitted for filing in the office of the secretary of state pursuant to the provisions of this chapter unless it is accompanied by a verified translation of that document into the English language.

(Added to NRS by 1995, 1137)

PROFESSIONAL CORPORATIONS

NRS 89.030 Applicability of chapter 78 of NRS. The laws applicable to other Nevada private corporations organized under chapter 78 of NRS and all rights, privileges and duties thereunder shall apply to professional corporations, except where such laws are in conflict with or inconsistent with the provisions of this chapter. In case of conflict, the provisions of this chapter shall apply.

(Added to NRS by 1963, 865)

NRS 89.040 Organization: Procedure; limitation; contents of articles of incorporation; corporate name.

1. One or more persons may organize a professional corporation in the manner provided for organizing a private corporation pursuant to chapter 78 of NRS. Each person organizing the corporation must, except as otherwise provided in subsection 2 of NRS 89.050, be authorized to perform the professional service for which the corporation is organized. The articles of incorporation must contain the following additional information:

(a) The profession to be practiced by means of the professional corporation.

(b) The names and post office box or street addresses, either residence or business, of the original stockholders and directors of the professional corporation.

(c) A certificate from the regulating board of the profession to be practiced showing that each of the directors, and each of the stockholders who is a natural person, is licensed to practice the profession.

2. The corporate name of a professional corporation must contain the words "Professional Corporation" or the abbreviation "Prof. Corp.," or the word "Chartered" or "Limited" or the abbreviation "Ltd." The corporate name must contain the last name of one or more of its stockholders. The corporation may render professional services and exercise its authorized powers under a fictitious name if the corporation has first registered the name in the manner required by chapter 602 of NRS.

(Added to NRS by 1963, 865; A 1969, 520; 1979, 122; 1987, 585; 1991, 323, 1305; 1995, 2118)

NRS 89.050 Scope of business; property and investments; professional services by officers and employees.

1. Except as otherwise provided in subsection 2, a professional corporation may be organized only for the purpose of rendering one specific type of professional service and may not engage in any business other than rendering the professional service for which it was organized and services reasonably related thereto, except that a professional corporation may own real and personal property appropriate to its business

and may invest its funds in any form of real property, securities or any other type of investment.

2. A professional corporation may be organized to render a professional service relating to:

(a) Architecture, interior design, engineering and landscape architecture, or any combination thereof, and may be composed of persons:

(1) Engaged in the practice of architecture as provided in chapter 623 of NRS;

(2) Practicing as a registered interior designer as provided in chapter 623 of NRS;

(3) Engaged in the practice of landscape architecture as provided in chapter 623A of NRS; and

(4) Engaged in the practice of professional engineering as provided in chapter 625 of NRS.

(b) Medicine, homeopathy and osteopathy, and may be composed of persons engaged in the practice of medicine as provided in chapter 630 of NRS, persons engaged in the practice of homeopathic medicine as provided in chapter 630A of NRS and persons engaged in the practice of osteopathic medicine as provided in chapter 633 of NRS. Such a professional corporation may market and manage additional professional corporations which are organized to render a professional service relating to medicine, homeopathy and osteopathy.

3. A professional corporation may render a professional service only through its officers and employees, all of whom must be authorized to render that professional service.

(Added to NRS by 1963, 866; A 1969, 705; 1985, 585; 1991, 323, 1306; 1995, 353, 1704; 1997, 206)

NRS 89.060 Professional relationship preserved. The provisions of this chapter relating to professional corporations do not modify any law applicable to the relationship between a person furnishing professional service and a person receiving such service, including liability arising out of such professional service; but nothing contained in this section shall render:

1. A person personally liable in tort for any act in which he has not personally participated.

2. A director, officer or employee of a professional corporation liable in contract for any contract which he executes on behalf

of a professional corporation within the limits of his actual authority.

(Added to NRS by 1963, 866; A 1969, 521)

NRS 89.070 Restrictions on ownership and transfer of shares.

1. Except as otherwise provided in subsections 2 and 3:

(a) No corporation organized under the provisions of this chapter may issue any of its stock to anyone other than a natural person who is licensed to render the same specific professional services as those for which the corporation was incorporated.

(b) No stockholder of a corporation organized under this chapter may enter into a voting trust agreement or any other type of agreement vesting another person with the authority to exercise the voting power of any or all of his stock, unless the other person is licensed to render the same specific professional services as those for which the corporation was incorporated.

(c) No shares of a corporation organized under this chapter may be sold or transferred except to a natural person who is eligible to be a stockholder of the corporation or to the personal representative or estate of a deceased or legally incompetent stockholder. The personal representative or estate of the stockholder may continue to own shares for a reasonable period, but may not participate in any decisions concerning the rendering of professional services.

The articles of incorporation or bylaws may provide specifically for additional restrictions on the transfer of shares and may provide for the redemption or purchase of the shares by the corporation, its stockholders or an eligible individual account plan complying with the requirements of subsection 2 at prices and in a manner specifically set forth. A stockholder may transfer his shares in the corporation or any other interest in the assets of the corporation to a revocable trust if he acts as trustee of the revocable trust and any person who acts as cotrustee and is not licensed to perform the services for which the corporation was incorporated does not participate in any decisions concerning the rendering of those services.

2. A person not licensed to render the professional services for which the corporation was incorporated may own a beneficial interest in any of the assets, including corporate shares, held for his account by an eligible individual account plan sponsored by the professional corporation for the benefit of its employees, which is intended to qualify under section 401 of the Internal Revenue Code (26

U.S.C. § 401) if the terms of the trust are such that the total number of shares which may be distributed for the benefit of persons not licensed to render the professional services for which the corporation was incorporated is less than a controlling interest and:

(a) The trustee of the trust is licensed to render the same specific professional services as those for which the corporation was incorporated; or

(b) The trustee is not permitted to participate in any corporate decisions concerning the rendering of professional services in his capacity as trustee.

A trustee who is individually a stockholder of the corporation may participate in his individual capacity as a stockholder, director or officer in any corporate decision.

3. A professional corporation in which all the stockholders who are natural persons are licensed to render the same specific professional service, may acquire and hold stock in another professional corporation, or in a similar corporation organized pursuant to the corresponding law of another state, if all the stockholders who are natural persons of the corporation whose stock is acquired are licensed in that corporation's state of incorporation to render the same specific professional service as the stockholders who are natural persons of the professional corporation that acquires the stock.

4. Any act in violation of this section is void and does not pass any rights or privileges or vest any powers, except to an innocent person who is not a stockholder and who has relied on the effectiveness of the action.

(Added to NRS by 1963, 866; A 1969, 521; 1977, 643; 1991, 1306; 1995, 2118)

NRS 89.080 Duties upon legal disqualification of officer, stockholder, director or employee; qualifications of officer or director; death of stockholder whose interest is in revocable trust.

1. If any officer, stockholder, director or employee of a corporation organized under this chapter who has been rendering professional service to the public becomes legally disqualified to render such professional services within this state, he shall sever within a reasonable period all professional service with and financial interest in the corporation; but this chapter does not prevent a corporation formed under this chapter from entering into a contract with an employee which provides for severance pay or for compensation for past services upon termination of professional service, whether by death or otherwise.

2. No person may be an officer or director of a corporation organized under

this chapter other than a natural person who is licensed to render the same specific professional services as those for which the corporation was incorporated.

3. Upon the death of a stockholder of a corporation who has transferred his interest in the corporation to a revocable trust as permitted by NRS 89.070, the trustee of the revocable trust may continue to retain any interest so transferred, including corporate shares, for a reasonable period, but may not exercise any authority concerning the rendering of professional services and may not distribute the corporate interest to any person not licensed to render the services for which the corporation was incorporated.

4. A corporation's failure to require compliance with the provisions of this section is a ground for the forfeiture of its charter.

(Added to NRS by 1963, 866; A 1969, 522; 1991, 1307; 1995, 2119)

NRS 89.100 Authority of regulating boards not affected. The provisions of this chapter relating to professional corporations do not bar the regulating board of any profession from taking any action otherwise within its power, nor do they affect the rules of ethics or practice of any profession.

(Added to NRS by 1963, 867; A 1969, 522)

NRS 89.110 Scope of authority. No professional corporation may do any act which is prohibited to be done by natural persons licensed to practice the profession which the professional corporation is organized to practice.

(Added to NRS by 1963, 867; A 1995, 2120)

PROFESSIONAL ASSOCIATIONS

NRS 89.200 Inapplicability of chapter 87 of NRS. The provisions of chapter 87 of NRS (Uniform Partnership Act) do not apply to professional associations.

(Added to NRS by 1969, 523)

NRS 89.210 Articles of association to be filed with secretary of state; filing of amendments; name.

1. Within 30 days following the organization of a professional association under this chapter the association shall file with the secretary of state a copy of the articles of association, duly executed, and shall pay at that time a filing fee of $25. Any such association formed as a common law

association before July 1, 1969, shall file, within 30 days of July 1, 1969, a certified copy of its articles of association, with any amendments thereto, with the secretary of state, and shall pay at that time a filing fee of $25. A copy of any amendments to the articles of association adopted after July 1, 1969, must also be filed with the secretary of state within 30 days after the adoption of such amendments. Each copy of amendments so filed must be certified as true and correct and be accompanied by a filing fee of $10.

2. The name of such a professional association must contain the words "Professional Association," "Professional Organization" or the abbreviations "Prof. Ass'n" or "Prof. Org." The association may render professional services and exercise its authorized powers under a fictitious name if the association has first registered the name in the manner required under chapter 602 of NRS.

(Added to NRS by 1969, 523; A 1979, 123)

NRS 89.220 Professional relationship preserved. The provisions of this chapter relating to professional associations do not modify any law applicable to the relationship between a person furnishing professional service and a person receiving such service, including liability arising out of such professional service, but:

1. A member or employee of a professional association shall not be personally liable in tort for any act in which he has not personally participated.

2. A member or employee of a professional association shall not be personally liable in contract for any contract which he executes on behalf of a professional association within the limits of his actual authority.

(Added to NRS by 1969, 523)

NRS 89.230 Restrictions on membership. Members who organize a professional association must all be natural persons licensed to render the same specific professional services as those for which the professional association is organized. A professional association may render professional service only through its members and employees, all of whom must be licensed to render the professional service.

(Added to NRS by 1969, 523; A 1995, 2120)

NRS 89.240 Duties upon legal disqualification of member or employee; redemption of and restrictions on transfer and ownership of member's interest.

1. If any member or employee of a professional association who has been rendering professional service to the public becomes legally disqualified to render the professional service within this state, he shall sever within a reasonable period all professional service with and financial interest in the association; but this chapter does not prevent a professional association from entering into a contract with a member or employee which provides for severance pay or for compensation for past services upon termination of professional service, whether by death or otherwise. Upon the death of a member of the association who has transferred his interest in the association to a revocable trust as permitted by subsection 2, the trustee of the revocable trust may continue to retain any interest so transferred for a reasonable period, but may not exercise any authority concerning the rendering of professional services and may not distribute the interest in the association or its assets to any person not licensed to render the services for which the association was organized.

2. No membership interest in a professional association may be sold or transferred except to a natural person who is eligible to be a member of the association or to the personal representative or estate of a deceased or legally incompetent member, except as provided in this subsection. The personal representative of such a member may continue to own such interest for a reasonable period, but may not participate in any decisions concerning the rendering of professional service. A member may transfer his interest in the association or any other interest in the assets of the association to a revocable trust if he acts as trustee of the revocable trust and any person who acts as cotrustee and is not licensed to perform the services for which the association is organized does not participate in any decisions concerning the rendering of those professional services.

3. The articles of association may provide specifically for additional restrictions on the transfer of members' interests and may provide for the redemption or purchase of such an interest by the association or its other members at prices and in a manner specifically set forth in the articles.

(Added to NRS by 1969, 523; A 1991, 1308; 1995, 2120)

NRS 89.250 Annual statement regarding members and employees: Filing; contents; execution; fee.

1. A professional association shall, on or before the last day of the month in which the anniversary date of its organization occurs in each year, furnish a statement to the secretary of state showing the names and residence addresses of all members and employees in such association and shall certify that all members and employees are licensed to render professional service in this state.

2. The statement must:

(a) Be made on a form prescribed by the secretary of state and must not contain any fiscal or other information except that expressly called for by this section.

(b) Be signed by the chief executive officer of the association.

3. Upon filing the annual statement required by this section, the association shall pay to the secretary of state a fee of $15.

4. As used in this section, "signed" means to have executed or adopted a name, word or mark, including, without limitation, a digital signature as defined in NRS 720.060, with the present intention to authenticate a document.

(Added to NRS by 1969, 524; A 1995, 1139; 1999, 1625)

NRS 89.252 Defaulting associations: Identification; penalty.

1. Each professional association that is required to make a filing and pay the fee prescribed in NRS 89.250 but refuses to do so within the time provided is in default.

2. For default, there must be added to the amount of the fee a penalty of $5. The fee and penalty must be collected as provided in this chapter.

(Added to NRS by 1995, 1138)

NRS 89.254 Defaulting associations: Duties of secretary of state; forfeiture; distribution of assets.

1. The secretary of state shall notify by letter each professional association which is in default pursuant to the provisions of NRS 89.252. The notice must be accompanied by a statement indicating the amount of the filing fee, penalties and costs remaining unpaid.

2. On the first day of the ninth month following the month in which the filing was required, the articles of association of the professional association is revoked and its right to transact business is forfeited.

3. The secretary of state shall compile a complete list containing the names of all professional associations whose right to do business has been forfeited. The secretary of state shall forthwith notify each such association by letter of the forfeiture of its right to transact business. The notice must be accompanied by a statement indicating the amount of the filing fee, penalties and costs remaining unpaid.

4. If the articles of association of a professional association are revoked and the right to transact business is forfeited, all the property and assets of the defaulting association must be held in trust by its members, as for insolvent corporations, and the same proceedings may be had with respect to its property and assets as apply to insolvent corporations. Any interested person may institute proceedings at any time after a forfeiture has been declared, but if the secretary of state reinstates the articles of association the proceedings must be dismissed and all property restored to the members of the professional association.

5. If the assets of the association are distributed, they must be applied to:

(a) The payment of the filing fee, penalties and costs due to the state; and

(b) The payment of the creditors of the association.

Any balance remaining must be distributed as set forth in the articles of association or, if no such provisions exist, among the members of the association.

(Added to NRS by 1995, 1138)

NRS 89.256 Defaulting associations: Procedure and conditions for reinstatement.

1. Except as otherwise provided in subsections 3 and 4, the secretary of state shall reinstate any professional association which has forfeited its right to transact business under the provisions of this chapter and restore the right to carry on business in this state and exercise its privileges and immunities if it:

(a) Files with the secretary of state the statement and certification required by NRS 89.250; and

(b) Pays to the secretary of state:

(1) The annual filing fee and penalty set forth in NRS 89.250 and 89.252 for each year or portion thereof during which the articles of association have been revoked; and

(2) A fee of $25 for reinstatement.

2. When the secretary of state reinstates the association to its former rights, he shall:

(a) Immediately issue and deliver to the association a certificate of reinstatement authorizing it to transact business, as if the fees had been paid when due; and

(b) Upon demand, issue to the association a certified copy of the certificate of reinstatement.

3. The secretary of state shall not order a reinstatement unless all delinquent fees and penalties have been paid, and the revocation of the association's articles of association occurred only by reason of its failure to pay the fees and penalties.

4. If the articles of association of a professional association have been revoked pursuant to the provisions of this chapter and have remained revoked for 10 consecutive years, the articles must not be reinstated.

(Added to NRS by 1995, 1138)

NRS 89.260 Authority of regulating board not affected. The provisions of this chapter relating to professional associations do not bar the regulating board of any profession from taking any action otherwise within its power, nor do they affect the rules of ethics or practice of any profession.

(Added to NRS by 1969, 524)

NRS 89.270 Scope of authority. No professional association may do any act which is prohibited to be done by natural persons licensed to practice the profession which the professional association is organized to practice.

(Added to NRS by 1969, 524; A 1995, 2121)

APPENDIX H: NEVADA REVISED STATUTES CHAPTER 92A

MERGERS AND EXCHANGES OF INTEREST

NRS 92A.005 Definitions. As used in this chapter, unless the context otherwise requires, the words and terms defined in NRS 92A.007 to 92A.080, inclusive, have the meanings ascribed to them in those sections.

(Added to NRS by 1995, 2079; A 1997, 726; 1999, 1626)

NRS 92A.007 "Approval" and "vote" defined. "Approval" and "vote" as describing action by directors or stockholders mean the vote by directors in person or by written consent, or action of stockholders in person, by proxy or by written consent.

(Added to NRS by 1997, 726)

NRS 92A.008 "Business trust" defined. "Business trust" means:

1. A domestic business trust; or

2. An unincorporated association formed pursuant to, existing under or governed by the law of a jurisdiction other than this state and generally described by NRS 88A.030.

(Added to NRS by 1999, 1626)

NRS 92A.010 "Constituent document" defined. "Constituent document" means the articles of incorporation or bylaws of a corporation, whether or not for profit, the articles of organization or operating agreement of a limited-liability company or the certificate of limited partnership or partnership agreement of a limited partnership.

(Added to NRS by 1995, 2079)

NRS 92A.015 "Constituent entity" defined. "Constituent entity" means, with respect to a merger, each merging or surviving entity and, with respect to an exchange, each entity whose owner's interests will be acquired or each entity acquiring those interests.

(Added to NRS by 1995, 2079)

NRS 92A.020 "Domestic" defined. "Domestic" as applied to an entity means one organized and existing under the laws of this state.

(Added to NRS by 1995, 2079)

NRS 92A.022 "Domestic business trust" defined. "Domestic business trust" means a business trust formed and existing pursuant to the provisions of chapter 88A of NRS.

(Added to NRS by 1999, 1626)

NRS 92A.025 "Domestic corporation" defined. "Domestic corporation" means a corporation organized and existing under chapter 78, 78A or 89 of NRS, or a nonprofit cooperative corporation organized pursuant to NRS 81.010 to 81.160, inclusive.

(Added to NRS by 1995, 2079; A 1997, 726)

NRS 92A.030 "Domestic limited-liability company" defined. "Domestic limited-liability company" means a limited-liability company organized and existing under chapter 86 of NRS.

(Added to NRS by 1995, 2079)

NRS 92A.035 "Domestic limited partnership" defined. "Domestic limited partnership" means a limited partnership organized and existing under chapter 88 of NRS.

(Added to NRS by 1995, 2079)

NRS 92A.040 "Domestic nonprofit corporation" defined. "Domestic nonprofit corporation" means a corporation organized or existing under chapter 82 of NRS, including those listed in NRS 82.051.

(Added to NRS by 1995, 2079)

NRS 92A.045 "Entity" defined. "Entity" means a foreign or domestic corporation, whether or not for profit, limited-liability company, limited partnership or business trust.

(Added to NRS by 1995, 2079; A 1999, 1626)

NRS 92A.050 "Exchange" defined. "Exchange" means the acquisition by one or more foreign or domestic entities of all an owner's interests or one or more classes or series of an owner's interests of one or more foreign or domestic entities.

(Added to NRS by 1995, 2079)

NRS 92A.055 "Foreign" defined. "Foreign" as applied to an entity means one not organized or existing under the laws of this state.

(Added to NRS by 1995, 2079)

NRS 92A.060 "Limited partner" defined. "Limited partner" means a person who has been admitted to a limited partnership as a limited partner in accordance with the partnership agreement.

(Added to NRS by 1995, 2079)

NRS 92A.070 "Member" defined. "Member" means:

1. A person who owns an interest in, and has the right to participate in the management of the business and affairs of a domestic limited-liability company; or

2. A member of a nonprofit corporation which has members.

(Added to NRS by 1995, 2080)

NRS 92A.075 "Owner" defined. "Owner" means the holder of an interest described in NRS 92A.080.

(Added to NRS by 1995, 2080)

NRS 92A.080 "Owner's interest" defined. "Owner's interest" means shares of stock in a corporation, membership in a nonprofit corporation, the interest of a member of a limited-liability company or a beneficial owner of a business trust, or the partnership interest of a general or limited partner of a limited partnership.

(Added to NRS by 1995, 2080; A 1999, 1626)

AUTHORITY, PROCEDURE AND EFFECT

NRS 92A.100 Authority for merger; approval, contents and form of plan of merger.

1. Except as limited by NRS 78.411 to 78.444, inclusive, one or more domestic entities may merge into another entity if the plan of merger is approved pursuant to the provisions of this chapter.

2. The plan of merger must set forth:

(a) The name, address and jurisdiction of organization and governing law of each constituent entity;

(b) The name, jurisdiction of organization and kind of entity or entities that will survive the merger;

(c) The terms and conditions of the merger; and

(d) The manner and basis of converting the owner's interests of each constituent entity into owner's interests, rights to purchase owner's interests, or other securities of the surviving or other entity or into cash or other property in whole or in part.

3. The plan of merger may set forth:

(a) Amendments to the constituent documents of the surviving entity; and

(b) Other provisions relating to the merger.

4. The plan of merger must be in writing.

(Added to NRS by 1995, 2080; A 1997, 726)

NRS 92A.110 Authority for exchange; approval, contents and form of plan of exchange.

1. Except as a corporation is limited by NRS 78.411 to 78.444, inclusive, one or more domestic entities may acquire all of the outstanding owner's interests of one or more classes or series of another entity not already owned by the acquiring entity or an affiliate thereof if the plan of exchange is approved pursuant to the provisions of this chapter.

2. The plan of exchange must set forth:

(a) The name, address and jurisdiction of organization and governing law of each constituent entity;

(b) The name, jurisdiction of organization and kind of each entity whose owner's interests will be acquired by one or more other entities;

(c) The terms and conditions of the exchange; and

(d) The manner and basis of exchanging the owner's interests to be acquired for owner's interests, rights to purchase owner's interests, or other securities of the acquiring or any other entity or for cash or other property in whole or in part.

3. The plan of exchange may set forth other provisions relating to the exchange.

4. This section does not limit the power of a domestic entity to acquire all or part of the owner's interests or one or more class or series of owner's interests of another person through a voluntary exchange or otherwise.

5. The plan of exchange must be in writing.

(Added to NRS by 1995, 2080; A 1997, 726)

NRS 92A.120 Approval of plan of merger or exchange for domestic corporation.

1. After adopting a plan of merger or exchange, the board of directors of each domestic corporation that is a constituent entity in the merger, or the board of directors of the domestic corporation whose shares will be acquired in the exchange, must submit the plan of merger, except as otherwise provided in NRS 92A.130, or the plan of exchange for approval by its stockholders.

2. For a plan of merger or exchange to be approved:

(a) The board of directors must recommend the plan of merger or exchange to the stockholders, unless the board of directors determines that because of a conflict of interest or other special circumstances it should make no recommendation and it communicates the basis for its determination to the stockholders with the plan; and

(b) The stockholders entitled to vote must approve the plan.

3. The board of directors may condition its submission of the proposed merger or exchange on any basis.

4. The domestic corporation must notify each stockholder, whether or not he is entitled to vote, of the proposed stockholders' meeting in accordance with NRS 78.370. The notice must also state that the purpose, or one of the purposes, of the meeting is to consider the plan of merger or exchange and must contain or be accompanied by a copy or summary of the plan.

5. Unless this chapter, the articles of incorporation or the board of directors acting pursuant to subsection 3 require a greater vote or a vote by classes of stockholders, the plan of merger or exchange to be authorized must be approved by a majority of the voting power unless stockholders of a class of shares are entitled to vote thereon as a class. If stockholders of a class of shares are so entitled, the plan must be approved by a majority of all votes entitled to be cast on the plan by each class and representing a majority of all votes entitled to be voted.

6. Separate voting by a class of stockholders is required:

(a) On a plan of merger if the plan contains a provision that, if contained in the proposed amendment to the articles of incorporation, would entitle particular stockholders to vote as a class on the proposed amendment; and

(b) On a plan of exchange by each class or series of shares included in the exchange, with each class or series constituting a separate voting class.

7. Unless otherwise provided in the articles of incorporation or the bylaws of the domestic corporation, the plan of merger may be approved by written consent as provided in NRS 78.320.

(Added to NRS by 1995, 2081)

NRS 92A.130 Approval of plan of merger for domestic corporation: Conditions under which action by stockholders of surviving corporation is not required.

1. Action by the stockholders of a surviving domestic corporation on a plan of merger is not required if:

(a) The articles of incorporation of the surviving domestic corporation will not differ from its articles before the merger;

(b) Each stockholder of the surviving domestic corporation whose shares were outstanding immediately before the effective date of the merger will hold the same number of shares, with identical designations, preferences, limitations and relative rights immediately after the merger;

(c) The number of voting shares outstanding immediately after the merger, plus the number of voting shares issued as a result of the merger, either by the conversion of securities issued pursuant to the merger or the exercise of rights and warrants issued pursuant to the merger, will not exceed by more than 20 percent the total number of voting shares of the surviving domestic corporation outstanding immediately before the merger; and

(d) The number of participating shares outstanding immediately after the merger, plus the number of participating shares issuable as a result of the merger, either by the conversion of securities issued pursuant to the merger or the exercise of rights and warrants issued pursuant to the merger, will not exceed by more than 20 percent the total number of participating shares outstanding immediately before the merger.

2. As used in this section:

(a) "Participating shares" means shares that entitle their holders to participate without limitation in distributions.

(b) "Voting shares" means shares that entitle their holders to vote unconditionally in elections of directors.

(Added to NRS by 1995, 2082)

NRS 92A.140 Approval of plan of merger or exchange for domestic limited partnership; "majority in interest of the partnership" defined.
1. Unless otherwise provided in the partnership agreement or the certificate of limited partnership, a plan of merger or exchange involving a domestic limited partnership must be approved by all general partners and by limited partners who own a majority in interest of the partnership then owned by all the limited partners. If the partnership has more than one class of limited partners, the plan of merger must be approved by those limited partners who own a majority in interest of the partnership then owned by the limited partners in each class.
2. For the purposes of this section, "majority in interest of the partnership" means a majority of the interests in capital and profits of the limited partners of a domestic limited partnership which:
(a) In the case of capital, is determined as of the date of the approval of the plan of merger or exchange.
(b) In the case of profits, is based on any reasonable estimate of profits for the period beginning on the date of the approval of the plan of merger or exchange and ending on the anticipated date of the termination of the domestic limited partnership, including any present or future division of profits distributed pursuant to the partnership agreement.
(Added to NRS by 1995, 2082; A 1997, 727)

NRS 92A.150 Approval of plan of merger or exchange for domestic limited-liability company. Unless otherwise provided in the articles of organization or an operating agreement:
1. A plan of merger or exchange involving a domestic limited-liability company must be approved by members who own a majority of the interests in the current profits of the company then owned by all of the members; and
2. If the company has more than one class of members, the plan of merger must be approved by those members who own a majority of the interests in the current profits of the company then owned by the members in each class.
(Added to NRS by 1995, 2082; A 1997, 727; 1999, 1627)

NRS 92A.160 Approval of plan of merger or exchange for domestic nonprofit corporation.
1. A plan of merger or exchange involving a domestic nonprofit corporation

must be adopted by the board of directors. The plan must also be approved by each public officer or other person whose approval of a plan of merger or exchange is required by the articles of incorporation of the domestic nonprofit corporation.
2. If the domestic nonprofit corporation has members entitled to vote on plans of merger or exchange, the board of directors of the domestic nonprofit corporation must recommend the plan of merger or exchange to the members, unless the board of directors determines that because of a conflict of interest or other special circumstances it should make no recommendation and it communicates the basis for its determination to the members with the plan.
3. The board of directors may condition its submission of the proposed merger or exchange on any basis.
4. The members entitled to vote on a plan of merger or exchange must approve the plan at a meeting of members called for that purpose, by written consent pursuant to NRS 82.276, or by a vote by written ballot pursuant to NRS 82.326.
5. The corporation must notify, in the manner required by NRS 82.336, each nonprofit member of the time and place of the meeting of members at which the plan of merger or exchange will be submitted for a vote.
6. Unless the articles of incorporation of the domestic nonprofit corporation or the board of directors acting pursuant to subsection 3 require a greater vote or a vote by classes of members, the plan of merger or exchange to be authorized must be approved by a majority of a quorum of the members unless a class of members is entitled to vote thereon as a class. If a class of members is so entitled, the plan must be approved by a majority of a quorum of the votes entitled to be cast on the plan by each class.
7. Separate voting by a class of members is required:
(a) On a plan of merger if the plan contains a provision that, if contained in the proposed amendment to articles of incorporation, would entitle particular members to vote as a class on the proposed amendment; and
(b) On a plan of exchange by each class or series of memberships included in the exchange, with each class or series constituting a separate voting class.
(Added to NRS by 1995, 2082)

NRS 92A.165 Approval of merger by trustees and beneficial owners of certain business trusts. Unless otherwise provided in the certificate of trust or governing instrument of a business trust, a merger must be approved by all the trustees

and beneficial owners of each business trust that is a constituent entity in the merger.
(Added to NRS by 1999, 1626)

NRS 92A.170 Abandonment of planned merger or exchange before articles of merger or exchange are filed. After a merger or exchange is approved, and at any time before the articles of merger or exchange are filed, the planned merger or exchange may be abandoned, subject to any contractual rights, without further action, in accordance with the procedure set forth in the plan of merger or exchange or, if none is set forth, in the case of:
1. A domestic corporation, whether or not for profit, by the board of directors;
2. A domestic limited partnership, unless otherwise provided in the partnership agreement or certificate of limited partnership, by all general partners;
3. A domestic limited-liability company, unless otherwise provided in the articles of organization or an operating agreement, by members who own a majority in interest of the company then owned by all of the members or, if the company has more than one class of members, by members who own a majority in interest of the company then owned by the members in each class; and
4. A domestic business trust, unless otherwise provided in the certificate of trust or governing instrument, by all the trustees.
(Added to NRS by 1995, 2083; A 1999, 1627)

NRS 92A.175 Termination of planned merger or exchange after articles of merger or exchange are filed. After a merger or exchange is approved, at any time after the articles of merger or exchange are filed but before an effective date specified in the articles which is later than the date of filing the articles, the planned merger or exchange may be terminated in accordance with a procedure set forth in the plan of merger or exchange by filing articles of termination pursuant to the provisions of NRS 92A.240.
(Added to NRS by 1999, 1626)

NRS 92A.180 Merger of subsidiary into parent.
1. A parent domestic corporation, whether or not for profit, parent domestic limited-liability company or parent domestic limited partnership owning at least 90 percent of the outstanding shares of each class of a subsidiary corporation, 90 percent of the percentage or other interest in the capital and profits of a subsidiary limited partnership then owned by both the general and each class of limited partners or 90 percent of the percentage or other interest in

the capital and profits of a subsidiary limited-liability company then owned by each class of members may merge the subsidiary into itself without approval of the owners of the owner's interests of the parent domestic corporation, domestic limited-liability company or domestic limited partnership or the owners of the owner's interests of a subsidiary domestic corporation, subsidiary domestic limited-liability company or subsidiary domestic limited partnership.

2. The board of directors of the parent corporation, the managers of a parent limited-liability company with managers unless otherwise provided in the operating agreement, all the members of a parent limited-liability company without managers unless otherwise provided in the operating agreement, or all the general partners of the parent limited partnership shall adopt a plan of merger that sets forth:

(a) The names of the parent and subsidiary; and

(b) The manner and basis of converting the owner's interests of the disappearing entity into the owner's interests, obligations or other securities of the surviving or any other entity or into cash or other property in whole or in part.

3. The parent shall mail a copy or summary of the plan of merger to each owner of the subsidiary who does not waive the mailing requirement in writing.

4. The parent may not deliver articles of merger to the secretary of state for filing until at least 30 days after the date the parent mailed a copy of the plan of merger to each owner of the subsidiary who did not waive the requirement of mailing.

5. Articles of merger under this section may not contain amendments to the constituent documents of the surviving entity.

(Added to NRS by 1995, 2083; A 1997, 727; 1999, 1627)

NRS 92A.190 Merger or exchange with foreign entity.

1. One or more foreign entities may merge or enter into an exchange of owner's interests with one or more domestic entities if:

(a) In a merger, the merger is permitted by the law of the jurisdiction under whose law each foreign entity is organized and governed and each foreign entity complies with that law in effecting the merger;

(b) In an exchange, the entity whose owner's interests will be acquired is a domestic entity, whether or not an exchange of owner's interests is permitted by the law

of the jurisdiction under whose law the acquiring entity is organized;

(c) The foreign entity complies with NRS 92A.200 to 92A.240, inclusive, if it is the surviving entity in the merger or acquiring entity in the exchange and sets forth in the articles of merger or exchange its address where copies of process may be sent by the secretary of state; and

(d) Each domestic entity complies with the applicable provisions of NRS 92A.100 to 92A.180, inclusive, and, if it is the surviving entity in the merger or acquiring entity in the exchange, with NRS 92A.200 to 92A.240, inclusive.

2. When the merger or exchange takes effect, the surviving foreign entity in a merger and the acquiring foreign entity in an exchange shall be deemed:

(a) To appoint the secretary of state as its agent for service of process in a proceeding to enforce any obligation or the rights of dissenting owners of each domestic entity that was a party to the merger or exchange. Service of such process must be made by personally delivering to and leaving with the secretary of state duplicate copies of the process and the payment of a fee of $25 for accepting and transmitting the process. The secretary of state shall forthwith send by registered or certified mail one of the copies to the surviving or acquiring entity at its specified address, unless the surviving or acquiring entity has designated in writing to the secretary of state a different address for that purpose, in which case it must be mailed to the last address so designated.

(b) To agree that it will promptly pay to the dissenting owners of each domestic entity that is a party to the merger or exchange the amount, if any, to which they are entitled under or created pursuant to NRS 92A.300 to 92A.500, inclusive.

3. This section does not limit the power of a foreign entity to acquire all or part of the owner's interests of one or more classes or series of a domestic entity through a voluntary exchange or otherwise.

(Added to NRS by 1995, 2086; A 1997, 728; 1999, 1628)

NRS 92A.200 Articles of merger or exchange: Filing and contents. After a plan of merger or exchange is approved as required by this chapter, the surviving or acquiring entity shall deliver to the secretary of state for filing articles of merger or exchange setting forth:

1. The name and jurisdiction of organization of each constituent entity;

2. That a plan of merger or exchange has been adopted by each constituent entity;

3. If approval of the owners of one or more constituent entities was not required, a

statement to that effect and the name of each entity;

4. If approval of owners of one or more constituent entities was required, the name of each entity and a statement for each entity that:

(a) The plan was approved by the unanimous consent of the owners; or

(b) A plan was submitted to the owners pursuant to this chapter including:

(1) The designation, percentage of total vote or number of votes entitled to be cast by each class of owner's interests entitled to vote separately on the plan; and

(2) Either the total number of votes or percentage of owner's interests cast for and against the plan by the owners of each class of interests entitled to vote separately on the plan or the total number of undisputed votes or undisputed total percentage of owner's interests cast for the plan separately by the owners of each class, and the number of votes or percentage of owner's interests cast for the plan by the owners of each class of interests was sufficient for approval by the owners of that class;

5. In the case of a merger, the amendment to the articles of incorporation, articles of organization, certificate of limited partnership or certificate of trust of the surviving entity; and

6. If the entire plan of merger or exchange is not set forth, a statement that the complete executed plan of merger or plan of exchange is on file at the registered office if a corporation, limited-liability company or business trust, or office described in paragraph (a) of subsection 1 of NRS 88.330 if a limited partnership, or other place of business of the surviving entity or the acquiring entity, respectively.

(Added to NRS by 1995, 2084; A 1997, 729; 1999, 1629)

NRS 92A.210 Articles of merger, exchange or termination: Fee for filing. The fee for filing articles of merger, articles of exchange or articles of termination is $125.

(Added to NRS by 1995, 2085; A 1999, 1629)

NRS 92A.220 Articles of merger or exchange: Duty when entire plan of merger or exchange is not set forth. If the entire plan of merger or exchange is not set forth, a copy of the plan of merger or exchange must be furnished by the surviving or acquiring entity, on request and without cost, to any owner of any entity which is a party to the merger or exchange.

(Added to NRS by 1995, 2085)

NRS 92A.230 Articles of merger or exchange: Execution.

1. Articles of merger or exchange must be signed by each domestic constituent entity as follows:

(a) By the president or a vice president of a domestic corporation, whether or not for profit;

(b) By all the general partners of a domestic limited partnership;

(c) By a manager of a domestic limited-liability company with managers or by all the members of a domestic limited-liability company without managers; and

(d) By a trustee of a domestic business trust.

2. If the domestic entity is a corporation, the articles must also be signed by the secretary or an assistant secretary.

3. Articles of merger or exchange must be signed by each foreign constituent entity in the manner provided by the law governing it.

4. As used in this section, "signed" means to have executed or adopted a name, word or mark, including, without limitation, a digital signature as defined in NRS 720.060, with the present intention to authenticate a document.

(Added to NRS by 1995, 2085; A 1997, 730; 1999, 1630)

NRS 92A.240 Effective date of merger or exchange; filing of articles of termination before effective date.

1. A merger or exchange takes effect upon filing the articles of merger or exchange or upon a later date as specified in the articles, which must not be more than 90 days after the articles are filed.

2. If the filed articles of merger or exchange specify such a later effective date, the constituent may file articles of termination before the effective date, setting forth:

(a) The name of each constituent entity; and

(b) That the merger or exchange has been terminated pursuant to the plan of merger or exchange.

3. The articles of termination must be executed in the manner provided in NRS 92A.230.

(Added to NRS by 1995, 2085; A 1999, 1630)

NRS 92A.250 Effect of merger or exchange.

1. When a merger takes effect:

(a) Every other entity that is a constituent entity merges into the surviving entity and the separate existence of every entity except the surviving entity ceases;

(b) The title to all real estate and other property owned by each merging constituent entity is vested in the surviving entity without reversion or impairment;

(c) The surviving entity has all of the liabilities of each other constituent entity;

(d) A proceeding pending against any constituent entity may be continued as if the merger had not occurred or the surviving entity may be substituted in the proceeding for the entity whose existence has ceased;

(e) The articles of incorporation, articles of organization, certificate of limited partnership or certificate of trust of the surviving entity are amended to the extent provided in the plan of merger; and

(f) The owner's interests of each constituent entity that are to be converted into owner's interests, obligations or other securities of the surviving or any other entity or into cash or other property are converted, and the former holders of the owner's interests are entitled only to the rights provided in the articles of merger or any created pursuant to NRS 92A.300 to 92A.500, inclusive.

2. When an exchange takes effect, the owner's interests of each acquired entity are exchanged as provided in the plan, and the former holders of the owner's interests are entitled only to the rights provided in the articles of exchange or any rights created pursuant to NRS 92A.300 to 92A.500, inclusive.

(Added to NRS by 1995, 2085; A 1999, 1630)

NRS 92A.260 Liability of owner. An owner that is not personally liable for the debts, liabilities or obligations of the entity pursuant to the laws and constituent documents under which the entity was organized does not become personally liable for the debts, liabilities or obligations of the surviving entity or entities of the merger or exchange unless the owner consents to becoming personally liable by action taken in connection with the plan of merger or exchange.

(Added to NRS by 1995, 2081)

RIGHTS OF DISSENTING OWNERS

NRS 92A.300 Definitions. As used in NRS 92A.300 to 92A.500, inclusive, unless the context otherwise requires, the words and terms defined in NRS 92A.305 to 92A.335, inclusive, have the meanings ascribed to them in those sections.

(Added to NRS by 1995, 2086)

NRS 92A.305 "Beneficial stockholder" defined. "Beneficial stockholder" means a person who is a beneficial owner of shares held in a voting trust or by a nominee as the stockholder of record.

(Added to NRS by 1995, 2087)

NRS 92A.310 "Corporate action" defined. "Corporate action" means the action of a domestic corporation.

(Added to NRS by 1995, 2087)

NRS 92A.315 "Dissenter" defined. "Dissenter" means a stockholder who is entitled to dissent from a domestic corporation's action under NRS 92A.380 and who exercises that right when and in the manner required by NRS 92A.400 to 92A.480, inclusive.

(Added to NRS by 1995, 2087; A 1999, 1631)

NRS 92A.320 "Fair value" defined. "Fair value," with respect to a dissenter's shares, means the value of the shares immediately before the effectuation of the corporate action to which he objects, excluding any appreciation or depreciation in anticipation of the corporate action unless exclusion would be inequitable.

(Added to NRS by 1995, 2087)

NRS 92A.325 "Stockholder" defined. "Stockholder" means a stockholder of record or a beneficial stockholder of a domestic corporation.

(Added to NRS by 1995, 2087)

NRS 92A.330 "Stockholder of record" defined. "Stockholder of record" means the person in whose name shares are registered in the records of a domestic corporation or the beneficial owner of shares to the extent of the rights granted by a nominee's certificate on file with the domestic corporation.

(Added to NRS by 1995, 2087)

NRS 92A.335 "Subject corporation" defined. "Subject corporation" means the domestic corporation which is the issuer of the shares held by a dissenter before the corporate action creating the dissenter's rights becomes effective or the surviving or acquiring entity of that issuer after the corporate action becomes effective.

(Added to NRS by 1995, 2087)

NRS 92A.340 Computation of interest. Interest payable pursuant to NRS 92A.300 to 92A.500, inclusive, must be computed from the effective date of the action until the date of payment, at the average rate currently paid by the entity on its principal bank loans or, if it has no bank loans, at a rate that is fair and equitable under all of the circumstances.

(Added to NRS by 1995, 2087)

NRS 92A.350 Rights of dissenting partner of domestic limited partnership. A partnership agreement of a domestic limited partnership or, unless otherwise provided in the partnership agreement, an agreement of merger or exchange, may provide that contractual rights with respect to the partnership interest of a dissenting general or limited partner of a domestic limited partnership are available for any class or group of partnership interests in connection with any merger or exchange in which the domestic limited partnership is a constituent entity.

(Added to NRS by 1995, 2088)

NRS 92A.360 Rights of dissenting member of domestic limited-liability company. The articles of organization or operating agreement of a domestic limited-liability company or, unless otherwise provided in the articles of organization or operating agreement, an agreement of merger or exchange, may provide that contractual rights with respect to the interest of a dissenting member are available in connection with any merger or exchange in which the domestic limited-liability company is a constituent entity.

(Added to NRS by 1995, 2088)

NRS 92A.370 Rights of dissenting member of domestic nonprofit corporation.

1. Except as otherwise provided in subsection 2, and unless otherwise provided in the articles or bylaws, any member of any constituent domestic nonprofit corporation who voted against the merger may, without prior notice, but within 30 days after the effective date of the merger, resign from membership and is thereby excused from all contractual obligations to the constituent or surviving corporations which did not occur before his resignation and is thereby entitled to those rights, if any, which would have existed if there had been no merger and the membership had been terminated or the member had been expelled.

2. Unless otherwise provided in its articles of incorporation or bylaws, no member of a domestic nonprofit corporation, including, but not limited to, a cooperative corporation, which supplies services described in chapter 704 of NRS to its members only, and no person who is a member of a domestic nonprofit corporation

as a condition of or by reason of the ownership of an interest in real property, may resign and dissent pursuant to subsection 1.

(Added to NRS by 1995, 2088)

NRS 92A.380 Right of stockholder to dissent from certain corporate actions and to obtain payment for shares.

1. Except as otherwise provided in NRS 92A.370 and 92A.390, a stockholder is entitled to dissent from, and obtain payment of the fair value of his shares in the event of any of the following corporate actions:

(a) Consummation of a plan of merger to which the domestic corporation is a party:

(1) If approval by the stockholders is required for the merger by NRS 92A.120 to 92A.160, inclusive, or the articles of incorporation and he is entitled to vote on the merger; or

(2) If the domestic corporation is a subsidiary and is merged with its parent under NRS 92A.180.

(b) Consummation of a plan of exchange to which the domestic corporation is a party as the corporation whose subject owner's interests will be acquired, if he is entitled to vote on the plan.

(c) Any corporate action taken pursuant to a vote of the stockholders to the event that the articles of incorporation, bylaws or a resolution of the board of directors provides that voting or nonvoting stockholders are entitled to dissent and obtain payment for their shares.

2. A stockholder who is entitled to dissent and obtain payment under NRS 92A.300 to 92A.500, inclusive, may not challenge the corporate action creating his entitlement unless the action is unlawful or fraudulent with respect to him or the domestic corporation.

(Added to NRS by 1995, 2087)

NRS 92A.390 Limitations on right of dissent: Stockholders of certain classes or series; action of stockholders not required for plan of merger.

1. There is no right of dissent with respect to a plan of merger or exchange in favor of stockholders of any class or series which, at the record date fixed to determine the stockholders entitled to receive notice of and to vote at the meeting at which the plan of merger or exchange is to be acted on, were either listed on a national securities exchange, included in the national market system by the National Association of Securities Dealers, Inc., or held by at least 2,000 stockholders of record, unless:

(a) The articles of incorporation of the corporation issuing the shares provide otherwise; or

(b) The holders of the class or series are required under the plan of merger or exchange to accept for the shares anything except:

(1) Cash, owner's interests or owner's interests and cash in lieu of fractional owner's interests of:

(I) The surviving or acquiring entity; or

(II) Any other entity which, at the effective date of the plan of merger or exchange, were either listed on a national securities exchange, included in the national market system by the National Association of Securities Dealers, Inc., or held of record by a least 2,000 holders of owner's interests of record; or

(2) A combination of cash and owner's interests of the kind described in sub-subparagraphs (I) and (II) of subparagraph (1) of paragraph (b).

2. There is no right of dissent for any holders of stock of the surviving domestic corporation if the plan of merger does not require action of the stockholders of the surviving domestic corporation under NRS 92A.130.

(Added to NRS by 1995, 2088)

NRS 92A.400 Limitations on right of dissent: Assertion as to portions only to shares registered to stockholder; assertion by beneficial stockholder.

1. A stockholder of record may assert dissenter's rights as to fewer than all of the shares registered in his name only if he dissents with respect to all shares beneficially owned by any one person and notifies the subject corporation in writing of the name and address of each person on whose behalf he asserts dissenter's rights. The rights of a partial dissenter under this subsection are determined as if the shares as to which he dissents and his other shares were registered in the names of different stockholders.

2. A beneficial stockholder may assert dissenter's rights as to shares held on his behalf only if:

(a) He submits to the subject corporation the written consent of the stockholder of record to the dissent not later than the time the beneficial stockholder asserts dissenter's rights; and

(b) He does so with respect to all shares of which he is the beneficial stockholder or over which he has power to direct the vote.

(Added to NRS by 1995, 2089)

NRS 92A.410 Notification of stockholders regarding right of dissent.

1. If a proposed corporate action creating dissenters' rights is submitted to a vote at a stockholders' meeting, the notice of the meeting must state that stockholders are or may be entitled to assert dissenters' rights under NRS 92A.300 to 92A.500, inclusive, and be accompanied by a copy of those sections.

2. If the corporate action creating dissenters' rights is taken by written consent of the stockholders or without a vote of the stockholders, the domestic corporation shall notify in writing all stockholders entitled to assert dissenters' rights that the action was taken and send them the dissenter's notice described in NRS 92A.430.

(Added to NRS by 1995, 2089; A 1997, 730)

NRS 92A.420 Prerequisites to demand for payment for shares.

1. If a proposed corporate action creating dissenters' rights is submitted to a vote at a stockholders' meeting, a stockholder who wishes to assert dissenter's rights:

(a) Must deliver to the subject corporation, before the vote is taken, written notice of his intent to demand payment for his shares if the proposed action is effectuated; and

(b) Must not vote his shares in favor of the proposed action.

2. A stockholder who does not satisfy the requirements of subsection 1 and NRS 92A.400 is not entitled to payment for his shares under this chapter.

(Added to NRS by 1995, 2089; 1999, 1631)

NRS 92A.430 Dissenter's notice: Delivery to stockholders entitled to assert rights; contents.

1. If a proposed corporate action creating dissenters' rights is authorized at a stockholders' meeting, the subject corporation shall deliver a written dissenter's notice to all stockholders who satisfied the requirements to assert those rights.

2. The dissenter's notice must be sent no later than 10 days after the effectuation of the corporate action, and must:

(a) State where the demand for payment must be sent and where and when certificates, if any, for shares must be deposited;

(b) Inform the holders of shares not represented by certificates to what extent the transfer of the shares will be restricted after the demand for payment is received;

(c) Supply a form for demanding payment that includes the date of the first announcement to the news media or to the stockholders of the terms of the proposed action and requires that the person asserting dissenter's rights certify whether or not he acquired beneficial ownership of the shares before that date;

(d) Set a date by which the subject corporation must receive the demand for payment, which may not be less than 30 nor more than 60 days after the date the notice is delivered; and

(e) Be accompanied by a copy of NRS 92A.300 to 92A.500, inclusive.

(Added to NRS by 1995, 2089)

NRS 92A.440 Demand for payment and deposit of certificates; retention of rights of stockholder.

1. A stockholder to whom a dissenter's notice is sent must:

(a) Demand payment;

(b) Certify whether he acquired beneficial ownership of the shares before the date required to be set forth in the dissenter's notice for this certification; and

(c) Deposit his certificates, if any, in accordance with the terms of the notice.

2. The stockholder who demands payment and deposits his certificates, if any, before the proposed corporate action is taken retains all other rights of a stockholder until those rights are canceled or modified by the taking of the proposed corporate action.

3. The stockholder who does not demand payment or deposit his certificates where required, each by the date set forth in the dissenter's notice, is not entitled to payment for his shares under this chapter.

(Added to NRS by 1995, 2090; A 1997, 730)

NRS 92A.450 Uncertificated shares: Authority to restrict transfer after demand for payment; retention of rights of stockholder.

1. The subject corporation may restrict the transfer of shares not represented by a certificate from the date the demand for their payment is received.

2. The person for whom dissenter's rights are asserted as to shares not represented by a certificate retains all other rights of a stockholder until those rights are canceled or modified by the taking of the proposed corporate action.

(Added to NRS by 1995, 2090)

NRS 92A.460 Payment for shares: General requirements.

1. Except as otherwise provided in NRS 92A.470, within 30 days after receipt of a demand for payment, the subject corporation shall pay each dissenter who complied with

NRS 92A.440 the amount the subject corporation estimates to be the fair value of his shares, plus accrued interest. The obligation of the subject corporation under this subsection may be enforced by the district court:

(a) Of the county where the corporation's registered office is located; or

(b) At the election of any dissenter residing or having its registered office in this state, of the county where the dissenter resides or has its registered office. The court shall dispose of the complaint promptly.

2. The payment must be accompanied by:

(a) The subject corporation's balance sheet as of the end of a fiscal year ending not more than 16 months before the date of payment, a statement of income for that year, a statement of changes in the stockholders' equity for that year and the latest available interim financial statements, if any;

(b) A statement of the subject corporation's estimate of the fair value of the shares;

(c) An explanation of how the interest was calculated;

(d) A statement of the dissenter's rights to demand payment under NRS 92A.480; and

(e) A copy of NRS 92A.300 to 92A.500, inclusive.

(Added to NRS by 1995, 2090)

NRS 92A.470 Payment for shares: Shares acquired on or after date of dissenter's notice.

1. A subject corporation may elect to withhold payment from a dissenter unless he was the beneficial owner of the shares before the date set forth in the dissenter's notice as the date of the first announcement to the news media or to the stockholders of the terms of the proposed action.

2. To the extent the subject corporation elects to withhold payment, after taking the proposed action, it shall estimate the fair value of the shares, plus accrued interest, and shall offer to pay this amount to each dissenter who agrees to accept it in full satisfaction of his demand. The subject corporation shall send with its offer a statement of its estimate of the fair value of the shares, an explanation of how the interest was calculated, and a statement of the dissenters' right to demand payment pursuant to NRS 92A.480.

(Added to NRS by 1995, 2091)

NRS 92A.480 Dissenter's estimate of fair value: Notification of subject corporation; demand for payment of estimate.

1. A dissenter may notify the subject corporation in writing of his own estimate of the fair value of his shares and the amount of interest due, and demand payment of his estimate, less any payment pursuant to NRS 92A.460, or reject the offer pursuant to NRS 92A.470 and demand payment of the fair value of his shares and interest due, if he believes that the amount paid pursuant to NRS 92A.460 or offered pursuant to NRS 92A.470 is less than the fair value of his shares or that the interest due is incorrectly calculated.

2. A dissenter waives his right to demand payment pursuant to this section unless he notifies the subject corporation of his demand in writing within 30 days after the subject corporation made or offered payment for his shares.

(Added to NRS by 1995, 2091)

NRS 92A.490 Legal proceeding to determine fair value: Duties of subject corporation; powers of court; rights of dissenter.

1. If a demand for payment remains unsettled, the subject corporation shall commence a proceeding within 60 days after receiving the demand and petition the court to determine the fair value of the shares and accrued interest. If the subject corporation does not commence the proceeding within the 60-day period, it shall pay each dissenter whose demand remains unsettled the amount demanded.

2. A subject corporation shall commence the proceeding in the district court of the county where its registered office is located. If the subject corporation is a foreign entity without a resident agent in the state, it shall commence the proceeding in the county where the registered office of the domestic corporation merged with or whose shares were acquired by the foreign entity was located.

3. The subject corporation shall make all dissenters, whether or not residents of Nevada, whose demands remain unsettled, parties to the proceeding as in an action against their shares. All parties must be served with a copy of the petition. Nonresidents may be served by registered or certified mail or by publication as provided by law.

4. The jurisdiction of the court in which the proceeding is commenced under subsection 2 is plenary and exclusive. The court may appoint one or more persons as appraisers to receive evidence and recommend a decision on the question of fair value. The appraisers have the powers described in the order appointing them, or any amendment thereto. The dissenters are entitled to the same discovery rights as parties in other civil proceedings.

5. Each dissenter who is made a party to the proceeding is entitled to a judgment:

(a) For the amount, if any, by which the court finds the fair value of his shares, plus interest, exceeds the amount paid by the subject corporation; or

(b) For the fair value, plus accrued interest, of his after-acquired shares for which the subject corporation elected to withhold payment pursuant to NRS 92A.470.

(Added to NRS by 1995, 2091)

NRS 92A.500 Legal proceeding to determine fair value: Assessment of costs and fees.

1. The court in a proceeding to determine fair value shall determine all of the costs of the proceeding, including the reasonable compensation and expenses of any appraisers appointed by the court. The court shall assess the costs against the subject corporation, except that the court may assess costs against all or some of the dissenters, in amounts the court finds equitable, to the extent the court finds the dissenters acted arbitrarily, vexatiously or not in good faith in demanding payment.

2. The court may also assess the fees and expenses of the counsel and experts for the respective parties, in amounts the court finds equitable:

(a) Against the subject corporation and in favor of all dissenters if the court finds the subject corporation did not substantially comply with the requirements of NRS 92A.300 to 92A.500, inclusive; or

(b) Against either the subject corporation or a dissenter in favor of any other party, if the court finds that the party against whom the fees and expenses are assessed acted arbitrarily, vexatiously or not in good faith with respect to the rights provided by NRS 92A.300 to 92A.500, inclusive.

3. If the court finds that the services of counsel for any dissenter were of substantial benefit to other dissenters similarly situated, and that the fees for those services should not be assessed against the subject corporation, the court may award to those counsel reasonable fees to be paid out of the amounts awarded to the dissenters who were benefited.

4. In a proceeding commenced pursuant to NRS 92A.460, the court may assess the costs against the subject corporation, except that the court may assess costs against all or some of the dissenters who are parties to the proceeding, in amounts the court finds equitable, to the extent the court finds that such parties did not act in good faith in instituting the proceeding.

5. This section does not preclude any party in a proceeding commenced pursuant to NRS 92A.460 or 92A.490 from applying the provisions of N.R.C.P. 68 or NRS 17.115.

(Added to NRS by 1995, 2092)

APPENDIX I: MISCELLANEOUS STATUTES

SELECTED SECTIONS OF NEVADA LAW RELATING TO CORPORATIONS THAT ARE NOT FOUND IN THE GENERAL CORPORATION LAW

NRS CHAPTER 14, COMMENCEMENT OF ACTIONS

NRS 14.020 Foreign corporations, limited-liability companies, limited-liability partnerships, limited partnerships, business trusts and municipal corporations doing business in state to appoint resident agents; service of process, demand or notice.

1. Every corporation, limited-liability company, limited-liability partnership, limited partnership, business trust and municipal corporation created and existing under the laws of any other state, territory, or foreign government, or the Government of the United States, doing business in this state shall appoint and keep in this state a resident agent who resides or is located in this state, upon whom all legal process and any demand or notice authorized by law to be served upon it may be served in the manner provided in subsection 2. The corporation, limited-liability company, limited-liability partnership, limited partnership, business trust or municipal corporation shall file with the secretary of state a certificate of acceptance of appointment signed by its resident agent. The certificate must set forth the full name and address of the resident agent. The certificate must be renewed in the manner provided in Title 7 of NRS whenever a change is made in the appointment or a vacancy occurs in the agency.

2. All legal process and any demand or notice authorized by law to be served upon the foreign corporation, limited-liability company, limited-liability partnership, limited partnership, business trust or municipal corporation may be served upon the resident agent personally or by leaving a true copy thereof with a person of suitable age and discretion at the address shown on the current certificate of acceptance filed with the secretary of state.

3. Subsection 2 provides an additional mode and manner of serving process, demand or notice and does not affect the validity of any other service authorized by law.

[1911 CPA § 82; A 1933, 191; 1939, 66; 1931 NCL § 8580]—(NRS A 1969, 570; 1989, 952; 1991, 1309; 1993, 556; 1999, 1631)

NRS 14.030 Service of process, demand or notice when foreign corporation, limited-liability company, limited-liability partnership, limited partnership, business trust or municipal corporation fails to appoint resident agent.

1. If any artificial person described in NRS 14.020 fails to appoint a resident agent, or fails to file a certificate of acceptance of appointment for 30 days after a vacancy occurs in the agency, on the production of a certificate of the secretary of state showing either fact, which is conclusive evidence of the fact so certified to be made a part of the return of service, the artificial person may be served with any and all legal process, or a demand or notice described in NRS 14.020, by delivering a copy to the secretary of state, or, in his absence, to any deputy secretary of state, and such service is valid to all intents and purposes. The copy must:

(a) Include a specific citation to the provisions of this section. The secretary of state may refuse to accept such service if the proper citation is not included.

(b) Be accompanied by a fee of $10.

The secretary of state shall keep a copy of the legal process received pursuant to this section in his office for at least 1 year after receipt thereof and shall make those records available for public inspection during normal business hours.

2. In all cases of such service, the defendant has 40 days, exclusive of the day of service, within which to answer or plead.

3. Before such service is authorized, the plaintiff shall make or cause to be made and filed an affidavit setting forth the facts, showing that due diligence has been used to ascertain the whereabouts of the officers of the artificial person to be served, and the facts showing that direct or personal service on, or notice to, the artificial person cannot be had.

4. If it appears from the affidavit that there is a last known address of the artificial person or any known officers thereof, the plaintiff shall, in addition to and after such service on the secretary of state, mail or cause to be mailed to the artificial person or to the known officer, at such address, by registered or certified mail, a copy of the summons and a copy of the complaint, and in all such cases the defendant has 40 days after the date of the mailing within which to appear in the action.

5. This section provides an additional manner of serving process, and does not affect the validity of any other valid service.

[1911 CPA § 83; A 1921, 107; 1939, 66; 1931 NCL § 8581]—(NRS A 1960, 226; 1969, 17, 95; 1997, 472; 1999, 404, 1632)

NRS 14.040 Service by publication on unknown heirs; plaintiff to file affidavit before entry of judgment.

1. When it appears to the satisfaction of the court or the judge thereof from the verified complaint or from an affidavit in behalf of the plaintiff or plaintiffs in any action that any heir or heirs of a deceased person is or are necessary or proper party or parties defendant, that a cause of action in favor of the plaintiff or plaintiffs exists against him or them, and that due diligence to ascertain the name or names and the place or places of residence of such heir or heirs has

been unsuccessfully exercised by or in behalf of the plaintiff or plaintiffs, the court or judge may grant an order for the service of the summons in such action on such unknown heir or heirs by publication in like manner and for the period of time prescribed by the Nevada Rules of Civil Procedure for the publication of summons in other actions.

2. Such service when made shall as to such unknown heir or heirs be sufficient to confer on the court jurisdiction to hear and determine the issues in such action, and the judgment of the court based on such service and duly made and entered in such action shall bind each and every one of the heirs of such deceased person whose name or names and place or places of residence were so, as aforesaid, unknown to the plaintiff or plaintiffs with like effect as if the name or names of such heir or heirs had been inserted in the complaint and published summons, regardless of whether such heir or heirs shall subsequently appear to have been residents or nonresidents of this state at the time of such publication.

3. Before final judgment in favor of the plaintiff or plaintiffs and against any such unknown heir or heirs shall be entered in any such action, every such plaintiff shall make and file with the clerk of the court in which the action is pending an affidavit showing that since the commencement of the action he has neither learned the name or names of any such heir or heirs nor received any information indicating a line of search or inquiry which if properly pursued might lead to the discovery of such name or names and that the same still remains or remain unknown to such plaintiff; or, if he has received such information, such affidavit shall so state and
show that diligent search and inquiry along the lines indicated had been made by or in behalf of such plaintiff and resulted in failure to learn such name or names and that the same are still unknown to such plaintiff.

[1911 CPA § 86; RL § 5028; NCL § 8584] + [1911 CPA § 87; RL § 5029; NCL § 8585]

NRS 14.050 Service by publication on unknown parties generally. If any plaintiff shall allege that there are, or that he verily believes that there are, persons, other than heirs, interested in the subject matter of the complaint, whose names he cannot insert therein because they are unknown to him, and shall describe the interest of such persons and how derived, so far as his knowledge extends, the court or the judge thereof shall make an order for the publication of summons, reciting, moreover, the substance of the allegations of the complaint in relation to the

interest of such unknown parties; and, after the completion of service by such publication, the court shall have jurisdiction of such persons, and any judgment or decree rendered in the action shall apply to and conclude such persons with respect to such interest in the subject matter of the action.

[1911 CPA § 88; RL § 5030; NCL § 8586]

NRS 14.060 Proceedings where there are several defendants and part only are served. Where the action is against two or more defendants, and the summons is served on one or more but not on all of them, the plaintiff may proceed as follows:

1. If the action be against the defendants jointly indebted upon a contract, he may proceed against the defendant served, unless the court otherwise directs; and if he recover judgment, it may be entered against all the defendants thus jointly indebted, so far only as that it may be enforced against the joint property of all and the separate property of the defendant served; or

2. If the action be against defendants severally liable, he may proceed against the defendants served in the same manner as if they were the only defendants.

[1911 CPA § 89; RL § 5031; NCL § 8587]

NRS 14.065 Exercise of jurisdiction on any basis consistent with state and federal constitutions; service of summons to confer jurisdiction.

1. A court of this state may exercise jurisdiction over a party to a civil action on any basis not inconsistent with the constitution of this state or the Constitution of the United States.

2. Personal service of summons upon a party outside this state is sufficient to confer upon a court of this state jurisdiction over the party so served if the service is made by delivering a copy of the summons, together with a copy of the complaint, to the party served in the manner provided by statute or rule of court for service upon a person of like kind within this state.

3. The method of service provided in this section is cumulative, and may be utilized with, after or independently of other methods of service.

(Added to NRS by 1969, 845; A 1983, 1503; 1993, 865; 1995, 1041)

NRS 14.070 Service of process on operator of motor vehicle involved in accident.

1. The use and operation of a motor vehicle over the public roads, streets or highways, or in any other area open to the public and commonly used by motor vehicles, in the State of Nevada by any person, either as principal, master, agent or servant, shall be deemed an appointment by the operator, on behalf of himself and his principal or master, his executor, administrator or personal representative, of the director of the department of motor vehicles and public safety to be his true and lawful attorney upon whom may be served all legal process in any action or proceeding against him, his principal or master, his executor, administrator or personal representative, growing out of such use or resulting in damage or loss to person or property, and the use or operation signifies his agreement that any process against him which is so served has the same legal force and validity as though served upon him personally within the State of Nevada.

2. Service of process must be made by leaving a copy of the process with a fee of $5 in the hands of the director of the department of motor vehicles and public safety or in his office, and the service shall be deemed sufficient upon the operator if notice of service and a copy of the process is sent by registered or certified mail by the plaintiff to the defendant at the address supplied by the defendant in his accident report, if any, and if not, at the best address available to the plaintiff, and a return receipt signed by the defendant or a return of the United States Postal Service stating that the defendant refused to accept delivery or could not be located, or that the address was insufficient, and the plaintiff's affidavit of compliance therewith are attached to the original process and returned and filed in the action in which it was issued. Personal service of notice and a copy of the process upon the defendant, wherever found outside of this state, by any person qualified to serve like process in the State of Nevada is the equivalent of mailing, and may be proved by the affidavit of the person making the personal service appended to the original process and returned and filed in the action in which it was issued.

3. The court in which the action is pending may order such continuances as may be necessary to afford the defendant reasonable opportunity to defend the action.

4. The fee of $5 paid by the plaintiff to the director of the department of motor vehicles and public safety at the time of the service must be taxed in his costs if he prevails in the suit. The director of the department of motor vehicles and public

safety shall keep a record of all service of process, including the day and hour of service.

5. The foregoing provisions of this section with reference to the service of process upon an operator defendant are not exclusive, except if the operator defendant is found within the State of Nevada, he must be served with process in the State of Nevada.

6. The provisions of this section apply to nonresident motorists and to resident motorists who have left the state or cannot be found within the state following an accident which is the subject of an action for which process is served pursuant to this section.

[1:275:1953; A 1955, 453] + [2:275:1953] + [3:275:1953] + [4:275:1953] + [5:275:1953]—(NRS A 1957, 628; 1961, 155; 1963, 800; 1969, 95, 611; 1981, 1591; 1985, 1971)

NRS 14.080 Service of process on foreign manufacturers, producers and suppliers of products.

1. Any company, firm, partnership, corporation or association created and existing under the laws of any other state, territory, foreign government or the Government of the United States, which manufactures, produces, makes, markets or otherwise supplies directly or indirectly any product for distribution, sale or use in this state may be lawfully served with any legal process in any action to recover damages for an injury to a person or property resulting from such distribution, sale or use in this state by mailing to the last known address of the company, firm, partnership, corporation or association, by registered or certified mail return receipt requested, a copy of the summons and a copy of the complaint.

2. In all cases of such service, the defendant has 40 days, exclusive of the day of service, within which to answer or plead.

3. This section provides an additional manner of serving process and does not invalidate any other service.

(Added to NRS by 1961, 57; A 1969, 18, 95; 1997, 473)

NRS CHAPTER 32, RECEIVERS

NRS 32.010 Cases in which receiver may be appointed. A receiver may be appointed by the court in which an action is pending, or by the judge thereof:

1. In an action by a vendor to vacate a fraudulent purchase of property, or by a creditor to subject any property or fund to his claim, or between partners or others jointly owning or interested in any property or fund, on application of the plaintiff, or of any party whose right to or interest in the property or fund, or the proceeds thereof, is probable, and where it is shown that the property or fund is in danger of being lost, removed or materially injured.

2. In an action by a mortgagee for the foreclosure of his mortgage and sale of the mortgaged property, where it appears that the mortgaged property is in danger of being lost, removed or materially injured, or that the condition of the mortgage has not been performed, and that the property is probably insufficient to discharge the mortgage debt.

3. After judgment, to carry the judgment into effect.

4. After judgment, to dispose of the property according to the judgment, or to preserve it during the pendency of an appeal, or in proceedings in aid of execution, when an execution has been returned unsatisfied, or when the judgment debtor refuses to apply his property in satisfaction of the judgment.

5. In the cases when a corporation has been dissolved, or is insolvent, or in imminent danger of insolvency, or has forfeited its corporate rights.

6. In all other cases where receivers have heretofore been appointed by the usages of the courts of equity.

[1911 CPA § 251; RL § 5193; NCL § 8749]

NRS 32.015 Additional cases in which receiver may be appointed.

1. In addition to the cases enumerated in NRS 32.010, a court or judge may appoint a receiver in an action brought by a secured lender to enforce the right provided in NRS 40.507, or a similar right provided in a mortgage, to enter and inspect real collateral to determine the existence, location, nature and magnitude of any past, present or threatened release or presence of a hazardous substance from, in, into or onto it. A right provided in a mortgage is subject to the same limitations and requirement of notice as are provided in NRS 40.507.

2. As used in this section, "hazardous substance," "release" and "secured lender" have the meanings ascribed to them in NRS 40.504, 40.505 and 40.506, respectively.

(Added to NRS by 1993, 151)

NRS 32.020 Reversion and disposition of unclaimed dividends in receivership.

1. In any receivership proceeding instituted in which a dividend has been declared and ordered paid to creditors, any dividend which remains unclaimed for 5 years reverts to the general fund of the estate and must be applied as follows:

(a) To the payment of costs and expenses of the administration of the estate and receivership.

(b) To a new dividend distributed to creditors whose claims have been allowed but not paid in full. After those claims have been paid in full the balance is presumed abandoned under NRS 120A.210.

2. This section applies to any receivership proceeding which may be brought, and includes any bank, banking corporation, corporation, copartnership, company, association or natural person.

[1:34:1929; NCL § 9422]+[2:34:1929; NCL § 9423]— (NRS A 1979, 1760; 1983, 1476; 1987, 754)

NRS CHAPTER 35, QUO WARRANTO

NRS 35.010 Action in name of state against public officer, association or usurper of public office or franchise. A civil action may be brought in the name of the state:

1. Against a person who usurps, intrudes into, or unlawfully holds or exercises, a public office, civil or military, except the office of assemblyman or state senator, or a franchise, within this state, or an officer in a corporation created by the authority of this state.

2. Against a public officer, civil or military, except the office of assemblyman or state senator, who does or suffers an act which, by the provisions of law, works a forfeiture of his office.

3. Against an association of persons who act as a corporation within this state without being legally incorporated.

[1911 CPA § 714; RL § 5656; NCL § 9203]—(NRS A 1971, 660)

NRS 35.020 Action in name of state against corporation. A like action may be brought against a corporation:

1. When it has offended against a provision of an act by or under which it was created, altered or renewed, or any act altering or amending such acts.

2. When it has forfeited its privileges and franchises by a nonuser.

3. When it has committed or omitted an act which amounts to a surrender or a forfeiture of its corporate rights, privileges and franchises.

4. When it has misused a franchise or privilege conferred upon it by law, or exercised a franchise or privilege not so conferred.

[1911 CPA § 715; RL § 5657; NCL § 9204]

NRS 35.030 Attorney general to begin action. The attorney general, when directed by the governor, shall commence any such action; and when, upon complaint or otherwise, he has good reason to believe that any case specified in NRS 35.020 can be established by proof, he shall commence an action.

[1911 CPA § 716; RL § 5658; NCL § 9205]

NRS 35.040 Action brought on relation of another; security for costs. Such officer may, upon his own relation, bring any such action, or he may, on the leave of the court, or a judge thereof, bring the action upon the relation of another person; and, if the action be brought under subsection 1 of NRS 35.010, he may require security for costs to be given as in other cases.

[1911 CPA § 717; RL § 5659; NCL § 9206]

NRS 35.050 Action for usurpation by claimant in name of state; bond. A person claiming to be entitled to a public office, except the office of assemblyman or state senator, unlawfully held and exercised by another may, by himself or by an attorney and counselor at law, bring an action therefor in the name of the state, as provided in this chapter. On filing the complaint, such person shall enter into an undertaking with two sufficient sureties, to be approved by the judge, or any judge of the court in which the action is brought, conditioned that such person will pay any judgment for costs or damages recovered against him, and all costs and expenses incurred in the prosecution of the action, which undertaking shall be filed with the clerk of the court.

[1911 CPA § 718; RL § 5660; NCL § 9207]—(NRS A 1971, 660)

NRS 35.060 Name of person entitled to office set forth in complaint; judgment may determine rights of both incumbent and claimant. When the action is against a person for usurping, intruding into or unlawfully holding or exercising an office, the complaint shall set forth the name of the person who claims to be entitled thereto, with an averment of his right thereto, and judgment may be rendered upon the right of the defendant, and also upon the right of the person so averred to be entitled, or only upon the right of the defendant, as justice requires.

[1911 CPA § 719; RL § 5661; NCL § 9208]

NRS 35.070 All claimants to same office made defendants. All persons who claim to be entitled to the same office or franchise may be made defendants in the same action to try their respective rights to such office or franchise.

[1911 CPA § 720; RL § 5662; NCL § 9209]

NRS 35.080 Jurisdiction in supreme court or district court. An action under this chapter can be brought in the supreme court or in the district court of the proper county.

[1911 CPA § 721; RL § 5663; NCL § 9210]

NRS 35.090 Application to file complaint; notice to defendant; hearing. Upon application for leave to file a complaint, the court or judge may, in its discretion, direct notice thereof to be given to the defendant previous to granting such leave, and may hear the defendant in opposition thereto; and if leave be granted, an entry thereof shall be made on the minutes of the court, or the fact shall be endorsed by the judge on the complaint, which shall then be filed.

[1911 CPA § 722; RL § 5664; NCL § 9211]

NRS 35.100 Issuance of summons; when unnecessary. When the complaint is filed without leave and notice, or upon leave and notice in case all the defendants do not appear, a summons shall issue and be served as in other cases. When all the defendants appear to oppose the filing of the complaint, no summons need issue.

[1911 CPA § 723; RL § 5665; NCL § 9212]

NRS 35.110 Pleadings. The pleadings shall be as in other cases.

[1911 CPA § 724; RL § 5666; NCL § 9213]

NRS 35.120 Judgment of ouster; relator to recover costs; delivery of books by defendant; violation by corporation.

1. When a defendant is found guilty of usurping, intruding into or unlawfully holding or exercising an office, franchise or privilege, judgment shall be rendered that such defendant be ousted and altogether excluded therefrom, and that the relator recover his costs. The court, after such judgment, shall order the defendant to deliver over all books and papers in his custody or under his control belonging to the office, to the parties entitled thereto.

2. If the defendant be found guilty of unlawfully holding or exercising any office, franchise or privilege, or if a corporation be found to have violated the law by which it holds its existence, or in any other manner to have done acts which amount to a surrender or a forfeiture of its privileges, judgment shall be rendered that such defendant be ousted and altogether excluded from such office, franchise or privilege, and also that he pay the costs of the proceedings.

3. If the defendant be found to have exercised merely certain individual powers and privileges to which he is not entitled, the judgment shall be the same as above directed, but only in relation to those particulars in which he is thus exceeding the lawful exercise of his rights and privileges.

4. In case judgment is rendered against a pretended, but not real, corporation, the costs may be collected from any person who has been acting as an officer or proprietor of such pretended corporation.

[1911 CPA § 725; RL § 5667; NCL § 9214]

NRS 35.130 Judgment ousting director of corporation. When the action is against a director of a corporation and the court finds that at his election, either illegal votes were received or legal votes were rejected, or both, sufficient to change the result, judgment may be rendered that the defendant be ousted, and judgment of induction entered in favor of the person who was entitled to be declared elected at such election.

[1911 CPA § 726; RL § 5668; NCL § 9215]

NRS 35.140 Action for damages within 1 year. Such person may, at any time within 1 year after the date of such judgment, bring an action against the person ousted and recover the damages he sustained by reason of such usurpation.

[1911 CPA § 727; RL § 5669; NCL § 9216]

NRS 35.150 Judgment against corporation; dissolution or restraint. When, in any such action, it is found and adjudged that a corporation has, by an act done or omitted, surrendered or forfeited its corporate rights, privileges or franchises, or has not used the same during a term of 2 years, judgment shall be entered that it be ousted and excluded therefrom, and that it be dissolved; and when it is found and adjudged that a corporation has offended in any matter or manner which does not work such surrender or forfeiture or has misused a franchise, or exercised a power not conferred by law, judgment shall be entered that it be enjoined from the continuance of such offense or the exercise of such power.

[1911 CPA § 728; RL § 5670; NCL § 9217]

NRS 35.160 Court shall appoint trustee for dissolved corporation; trustee's compensation. If a corporation is ousted and dissolved by the proceedings herein authorized, the court shall appoint some disinterested person as trustee of the creditors and stockholders. The trustee shall receive a compensation for his services to be fixed by the court.

[1911 CPA § 729; RL § 5671; NCL § 9218]

NRS 35.170 Bond of trustee. The trustee shall enter into bond in such a penalty and with such security as the court approves, conditioned for the faithful discharge of his duties.

[1911 CPA § 730; RL § 5672; NCL § 9219]

NRS 35.180 Suit on trustee's bond. Suit may be brought on the bond of the trustee by any person injured by the negligence or wrongful act of the trustee in the discharge of his duties.

[1911 CPA § 731; RL § 5673; NCL § 9220]

NRS 35.190 Trustee to collect debts and divide surplus. The trustee shall proceed immediately to collect the debts and pay the liabilities of the corporation, and to divide the surplus among those thereto entitled.

[1911 CPA § 732; RL § 5674; NCL § 9221]

NRS 35.200 Court may order books and effects delivered to trustee. The court shall, upon an application for that purpose, order an officer of such corporation, or any other person having possession of any of the effects, books or papers of the corporation, in anywise necessary for the settlement of its affairs, to deliver the same to the trustee.

[1911 CPA § 733; RL § 5675; NCL § 9222]

NRS 35.210 Trustee to file sworn inventory with clerk. As soon as practicable after his appointment, the trustee shall make and file, in the office of the clerk of the court, an inventory of all the effects, rights and credits which come to his possession or knowledge, the truth of which inventory shall be sworn to.

[1911 CPA § 734; RL § 5676; NCL § 9223]

NRS 35.220 Responsibilities of trustee. The trustee shall sue for and recover the debts and property of the corporation, and shall be responsible to the creditors and stockholders, respectively, to the extent of the effects which come into his hands, in the same manner as though he were the executor of the estate of a deceased person.

[1911 CPA § 735; RL § 5677; NCL § 9224]

NRS 35.230 Liability of corporation directors when judgment of ouster rendered. When judgment of ouster is rendered against a corporation on account of the misconduct of the directors or officers thereof, such officers shall be jointly and severally liable to an action by anyone injured thereby.

[1911 CPA § 736; RL § 5678; NCL § 9225]

NRS 35.240 Penalty for refusal to obey order of court. Any person who, without good reason, refuses to obey an order of the court, as provided in this chapter, shall be deemed guilty of a contempt of court, and shall be fined in any sum not exceeding $5,000, and imprisoned in the county jail until

he comply with the order, and shall be further liable for the damages resulting to any person on account of his refusal to obey such order.

[1911 CPA § 737; RL § 5679; NCL § 9226]

NRS 35.250 Actions in quo warranto take precedence. Actions under this chapter in any court shall have precedence of any civil business pending therein; and the court, if the matter is of public concern, shall, on motion of the attorney general, or of the attorney of the party, require as speedy a trial of the merits of the case as may be consistent with the rights of the parties.

[1911 CPA § 738; RL § 5680; NCL § 9227]

NRS 35.260 Procedure in supreme court same as in district court; determination of issue of fact to be tried by jury in district court. Actions under this chapter commenced in the supreme court shall be conducted in the same manner as if commenced in the district court, and the clerk of the supreme court shall have the same authority to issue process and to enter orders and judgments as the clerk of the district court has in like cases. All pleadings and the conduct of the trial shall be the same as in the district court. If a jury is required to determine an issue of fact, the court shall order the question to be tried before a jury in the district court of any county designated in such order, and that the verdict be certified to the supreme court.

[1911 CPA § 739; RL § 5681; NCL § 9228]

NRS 35.270 Appeal does not stay judgment of ouster. If the action is commenced in the district court, an appeal may be taken from the final judgment by either party to the supreme court as in other cases; but if there is judgment of ouster against the defendant, there shall be no stay of execution or proceedings pending such appeal.

[1911 CPA § 740; RL § 5682; NCL § 9229]

NRS CHAPTER 37, EMINENT DOMAIN

NRS 37.250 Right of eminent domain granted to nonresident or foreign corporations or partnerships; conditions.

The right of eminent domain is hereby granted to nonresident or foreign corporations or partnerships which are now organized or may be organized under the laws of another state or territory, or under any act of Congress, and upon the same terms and conditions as any resident citizen, domestic corporation or partnership. Before any corporation or partnership organized or incorporated otherwise than under the laws of this state is entitled to any of the rights granted by this chapter, it must first comply with all laws of this state prescribing the conditions in which the corporation or partnership may be authorized to do business within the state or within any county of the state in which it seeks to exercise the right of eminent domain.

[1911 CPA § 687; RL § 5629; NCL § 9176]—(NRS A 1989, 549)

NRS Chapter 41, Actions by Shareholders Against Corporations and Associations to Enforce Secondary Rights

NRS 41.520 Contents and verification of complaint; motion to require plaintiff to furnish security; order; recourse of corporation or association to security.

1. As used in this section "corporation" includes an unincorporated associa-tion, and "board of directors" includes the managing body of an unincorporated association.

2. In an action brought to enforce a secondary right on the part of one or more shareholders in a corporation or association, incorporated or unincorporated, because the corporation or association refuses to enforce rights which may properly be asserted by it, the complaint must be verified by oath and must aver that the plaintiff was a shareholder at the time of the transaction of which he complains or that his share thereafter devolved on him by operation of law. The complaint must also set forth with particularity the efforts of the plaintiff to secure from the board of directors or trustees and, if necessary, from the shareholders such action as he desires, and the reasons for his failure to obtain such action or the reasons for not making such effort.

3. In any such action, at any time within 30 days after service of summons upon the corporation or any defendant who is an officer or director of the corporation, or held such office at the time of the acts complained of, the corporation or such defendant may move the court for an order, upon notice and hearing, requiring the plaintiff to furnish security as hereinafter provided. Such motion must be based upon one or more of the following grounds:

(a) That there is no reasonable possibility that the prosecution of the cause of action alleged in the complaint against the moving party will benefit the corporation or its security holders.

(b) That the moving party, if other than the corporation, did not participate in the transaction complained of in any capacity.
The court on application of the corporation or any defendant may, for good cause shown, extend the 30-day period for an additional period or periods not exceeding 60 days.

4. At the hearing upon such motion, the court shall consider such evidence, written or oral, by witnesses or affidavit, as may be material:

(a) To the ground or grounds upon which the motion is based; or

(b) To a determination of the probable reasonable expenses, including attorney's fees, of the corporation and the moving party which will be incurred in the defense of the action. If the court determines, after hearing the evidence adduced by the parties at the hearing, that the moving party has established a probability in support of any of the grounds upon which the motion is based, the court shall fix the nature and amount of security to be furnished by the plaintiff for reasonable expenses, including attorney's fees, which may be incurred by the moving party and the corporation in connection with such action, including expenses which the corporation may incur by reason of any obligation which it may have to indemnify its officers or directors pursuant to NRS 78.7502 or otherwise. A determination by the court that security either must or must not be furnished or must be furnished as to one or more defendants and not as to others shall not be deemed a determination of any one or more issues in the action or of the merits thereof. The corporation and the moving party have recourse to the security in such amount as the court determines upon the termination of the action. The amount of the security may thereafter from time to time be increased or decreased in the discretion of the court upon showing that the security provided has or may become inadequate or is excessive. If the court, upon any such motion, makes a determination that security must be furnished by the plaintiff as to any one or more defendants, the action must be dismissed as to such defendant or defendants, unless the security required by the court is furnished within such reasonable time as may be fixed by the court.

5. If any such motion is filed, no pleadings need be filed by the corporation or any other defendants, and the prosecution of the action must be stayed, until 10 days after the motion has been disposed of.

(Added to NRS by 1965, 1411; A 1969, 116; 1997, 731)

NRS Chapter 104, Uniform Commerical Code

NRS 104.8405 Replacement of lost, destroyed or wrongfully taken security certificate.

1. If an owner of a certificated security, whether in registered or bearer form, claims that the certificate has been lost, destroyed or wrongfully taken, the issuer shall issue a new certificate if the owner:

(a) So requests before the issuer has notice that the security has been acquired by a protected purchaser;

(b) Files with the issuer a sufficient indemnity bond; and

(c) Satisfies other reasonable requirements imposed by the issuer.

2. If, after the issue of a new security certificate, a protected purchaser of the original certificate presents it for registration of transfer, the issuer shall register the transfer unless an overissue would result. In that case, the issuer's liability is governed by NRS 104.8210. In addition to any rights on the indemnity bond, the issuer may recover the new certificate from the person to whom it was issued or any person taking under him except a protected purchaser.

(Added to NRS by 1965, 889; A 1985, 112; 1997, 405)

NRS 104.8406 Obligation to notify issuer of lost, destroyed or wrongfully taken security certificate. If a security certificate has been lost, apparently destroyed or wrongfully taken and the owner fails to notify the issuer of that fact within a reasonable time after the owner has notice of it and the issuer registers a transfer of the security before receiving notification, the owner may not assert against the issuer a claim for registering the transfer under NRS 104.8404 or a claim to a new security certificate under NRS 104.8405.

(Added to NRS by 1997, 366)

NRS 104.8407 Authenticating trustee, transfer agent and registrar. A person acting as authenticating trustee, transfer agent, registrar or other agent for an issuer in the registration of a transfer of its securities, in the issue of new security certificates or uncertificated securities or in the cancellation of surrendered security certificates has the same obligation to the holder or owner of a certificated or uncertificated security with regard to the particular functions performed as the issuer has in regard to those functions.

(Added to NRS by 1965, 889; A 1985, 113; 1997, 406)

NRS 120A, DISPOSITION OF UNCLAIMED PROPERTY

NRS 120A.010 Short title. This chapter may be cited as the Uniform Disposition of Unclaimed Property Act.

(Added to NRS by 1979, 1750; A 1983, 1476)

NRS 120A.020 Definitions. As used in this chapter, unless the context otherwise requires, the words and terms defined in NRS 120A.025 to 120A.120, inclusive, have the meanings ascribed to them in those sections.

(Added to NRS by 1979, 1751; A 1983, 1462)

NRS 120A.025 "Administrator" defined. "Administrator" means the chief of the division of unclaimed property.

(Added to NRS by 1983, 1461)

NRS 120A.030 "Banking organization" defined. "Banking organization" means any bank, trust company, savings bank, industrial bank, land bank, safe-deposit company or a private banker.

(Added to NRS by 1979, 1751; A 1983, 1462)

NRS 120A.040 "Business association" defined. "Business association" means any corporation (other than a public corporation), joint-stock company, investment company, business trust, partnership or any association for business purposes of two or more natural persons, whether or not for profit, including a banking organization, financial organization, insurance company or utility.

(Added to NRS by 1979, 1751; A 1983, 1462)

NRS 120A.050 "Division" defined. "Division" means the division of unclaimed property in the department of business and industry.

(Added to NRS by 1979, 1751; A 1983, 1462; 1993, 1510)

NRS 120A.070 "Financial organization" defined. "Financial organization" means any savings and loan association, building and loan association, thrift company, credit union, cooperative bank or investment company.

(Added to NRS by 1979, 1751; A 1983, 1462; 1985, 242)

NRS 120A.080 "Holder" defined. "Holder" means a person, wherever organized or domiciled, who is:

1. In possession of property belonging to another;

2. A trustee; or
3. Indebted to another on an obligation.

(Added to NRS by 1979, 1751; A 1983, 1462)

NRS 120A.090 "Insurance company" defined. "Insurance company" means an association, corporation, fraternal or mutual benefit organization, whether or not for profit, which is engaged in providing insurance, including the following kinds: Accident, burial, casualty, credit life, contract performance, dental, fidelity, fire, health, hospitalization, illness, life (including endowments and annuities), malpractice, marine, mortgage, surety and wage protection.

(Added to NRS by 1979, 1751; A 1983, 1462)

NRS 120A.095 "Intangible property" defined. "Intangible property" includes:

1. Money, checks, drafts, deposits, interest, dividends and income;
2. Credit balances, customers' overpayments, gift certificates, security deposits, refunds, credit memoranda, unpaid wages, unused airline tickets and unidentified remittances;
3. Stocks and other intangible interests in business associations;
4. Money deposited to redeem stocks, bonds, coupons and other securities or to make distributions;
5. Amounts due under the terms of insurance policies; and
6. Amounts distributable from a trust or custodial fund established under a plan to provide benefits such as health, welfare, pension, vacation, severance, retirement, death, stock purchase, profit sharing, employees' savings, supplemental unemployment insurance or the like.

(Added to NRS by 1983, 1461; A 1985, 116)

NRS 120A.100 "Owner" defined. "Owner" means a depositor in the case of a deposit, a beneficiary in the case of a trust other than a deposit in trust, a creditor, claimant or payee in the case of other intangible property, or a person having a legal or equitable interest in property subject to this chapter, or his legal representative.

(Added to NRS by 1979, 1751; A 1983, 1463)

NRS 120A.110 "Person" defined. "Person" includes a government, a governmental agency and a political subdivision of a government.

(Added to NRS by 1979, 1751; A 1983, 1463; 1985, 508)

NRS 120A.120 "Utility" defined. "Utility" means any person who owns or operates within this state for public use any plant, equipment, property, franchise or license for the transmission of communications or the production, storage, transmission, sale, delivery or furnishing of electricity, water, steam or gas.

(Added to NRS by 1979, 1751; A 1983, 1476)

NRS 120A.130 Uniformity of interpretation. This chapter shall be so construed as to effectuate its general purpose to make uniform the law of those states which enact it.

(Added to NRS by 1979, 1751; A 1983, 1476)

NRS 120A.135 **Inapplicability of chapter to unredeemed gaming chips or tokens.**

1. The provisions of this chapter do not apply to gaming chips or tokens which are not redeemed at an establishment.

2. As used in this section:

(a) "Establishment" has the meaning ascribed to it in NRS 463.0148.

(b) "Gaming chip or token" means any object which may be redeemed at an establishment for cash or any other representative of value.

(Added to NRS by 1989, 418)

NRS 120A.140 **Administration of chapter; regulations.** The administrator shall carry out the provisions of this chapter and may adopt regulations appropriate for this purpose.

(Added to NRS by 1979, 1751; A 1983, 1463)

NRS 120A.145 **Information to remain confidential.** The administrator or any officer, agent or employee of the division shall not use or disclose any information received by the administrator in the course of carrying out the provisions of this chapter which is confidential or which is provided to the division on the basis that the information is to remain confidential, unless the use or disclosure of the information is necessary to locate the owner of unclaimed or abandoned property.

(Added to NRS by 1983, 1462)

NRS 120A.150 **Periods of limitation not bar for purposes of chapter; limitation on actions by administrator.**

1. The expiration, before, on or after January 1, 1980, of any period specified by a contract, statute or court order, during which a claim for money or property can be made or during which an action or proceeding may be commenced or enforced to obtain payment of a claim for money or to recover property, does not prevent the money or property from being presumed abandoned or affect any duty to file a report or to pay or deliver abandoned property to the administrator as required by this chapter.

2. Except as otherwise provided in this subsection, no action or proceeding may be commenced by the administrator with respect to any duty of a holder pursuant to this chapter more than 10 years after the duty arose. The provisions of this subsection do not apply to any action or proceeding against a state or the Federal Government, or any agency or entity thereof.

(Added to NRS by 1979, 1758; A 1983, 1463; 1989, 375; 1997, 1596)

PROPERTY PRESUMED ABANDONED

NRS 120A.160 **Property held by banking or financial organizations or by business associations.** The following property held or owing by a banking or financial organization or by a business association is presumed abandoned:

1. Any demand, savings or matured time deposit or other certificate of deposit with a banking organization, together with any interest or dividend thereon, excluding any charges that may lawfully be withheld, including a deposit that is automatically renewable, and any money paid toward the purchase of a share, a mutual investment certificate or any other interest in a banking or financial organization, unless the owner has within 5 years:

(a) In the case of a deposit, increased or decreased the amount of the deposit, or presented the passbook or other similar evidence of the deposit for the crediting of interest;

(b) Communicated in writing with the banking organization concerning the property;

(c) Otherwise indicated an interest in the property as evidenced by a memorandum or other record on file prepared by an employee of the banking or financial organization;

(d) Owned other property to which paragraph (a), (b) or (c) applies and if the banking or financial organization communicates in writing with the owner with regard to the property that would otherwise be presumed abandoned under this subsection at the address to which communications regarding the other property regularly are sent; or

(e) Had another relationship with the banking or financial organization concerning which the owner has:

(1) Communicated in writing with the banking or financial organization; or

(2) Otherwise indicated an interest as evidenced by a memorandum or other record on file prepared by an employee of the banking or financial organization and if the banking or financial organization communicates in writing with the owner with regard to the property that would otherwise be abandoned under this subsection at the address to which communications regarding the other relationship regularly are sent.

For the purposes of this subsection, "property" includes interest and dividends.

2. Any property described in subsection 1 that is automatically renewable is matured for purposes of subsection 1 upon the expiration of its initial time period, but in the case of any renewal to which the owner consents at or about the time of renewal by communicating in writing with the banking or financial organization or otherwise indicating consent as evidenced by a memorandum or other record on file prepared by an employee of the organization, the property is matured upon the expiration of the last time period for which consent was given. If, at the time provided for delivery in NRS 120A.320, a penalty or forfeiture in the payment of interest would result from the delivery of the property, the time for delivery is extended until the time when no penalty or forfeiture would result.

3. Any sum payable on a check certified in this state or on a written instrument issued in this state on which a banking or financial organization or business association is directly liable, including any draft or cashier's check, which has been outstanding for more than 5 years after the date it was payable, or after the date of its issuance if payable on demand, or any sum payable on a money order which has been outstanding for more than 7 years after its issuance, or any sum payable on a

traveler's check which has been outstanding for more than 15 years after the date of its issuance, unless the owner has within the specified period corresponded in writing with the banking or financial organization or business association concerning it, or otherwise indicated an interest as evidenced by a memorandum on file with the banking or financial organization or business association.

4. Any money or other personal property, tangible or intangible, removed from a safe-deposit box or any other safekeeping repository on which the lease or rental period has expired because of nonpayment of rental charges or other reason, or any surplus amounts arising from the sale thereof pursuant to law, that have been unclaimed by the owner for more than 5 years from the date on which the lease or rental period expired. A safe-deposit box for which no rent is charged or which is provided to the user because of a specific amount deposited with a banking or financial organization or business association is presumed abandoned at the same time as the account for which it was given.

(Added to NRS by 1979, 1751; A 1983, 1463; 1985, 117; 1987, 747)

NRS 120A.170 **Unclaimed money held by insurance companies.**

1. Unclaimed money held and owing by an insurance company is presumed abandoned if the last known address, according to the records of the company, of the person entitled to the money is within this state. If a person other than the insured or annuitant is entitled to the money and no address of such person is known to the company or if it is not definite and certain from the records of the company what person is entitled to the money, it is presumed that the last known address of the person entitled to the money is the same as the last known address of the insured or annuitant according to the records of the company.

2. "Unclaimed money," as used in this section, means all money held and owing by any insurance company unclaimed and unpaid for more than 5 years after the money became due and payable as established from the records of the company under any life or endowment insurance policy or annuity contract which has matured or terminated. A life insurance policy not matured by actual proof of the death of the insured shall be deemed matured and the proceeds thereof deemed due if the policy was in force when the insured attained the limiting age under the mortality table on which the reserve is based, unless the person appearing entitled thereto has within the preceding 5 years:

(a) Assigned, readjusted or paid premiums on the policy or subjected the policy to loan; or

(b) Corresponded in writing with the insurance company concerning the policy.

3. Money otherwise payable according to the records of the company shall be deemed due although the policy or contract has not been surrendered as required.

(Added to NRS by 1979, 1752; A 1983, 1465)

NRS 120A.180 Deposits and advance payments held by utilities. Any money held or owing by any utility is presumed abandoned if it is money deposited by a subscriber with a utility to secure payment for or to pay in advance for utility services, less any lawful deductions, that has remained unclaimed by the person appearing on the records of the utility entitled thereto for more than 1 year after the termination of the services for which the deposit or advance payment was made.

(Added to NRS by 1979, 1753; A 1983, 1466)

NRS 120A.185 Unclaimed wages held by business. All earned but unpaid wages, including wages represented by unpresented checks, owing in the ordinary course of the holder's business that have remained unclaimed by the owner for more than 1 year after becoming payable are presumed abandoned.

(Added to NRS by 1985, 116)

NRS 120A.190 Intangible interest or money held or owing by business associations; exception.

1. Any stock or other intangible interest, or any dividend, profit, distribution, interest, payment on principal or other sum held or owing by a business association is presumed abandoned if, within 5 years after the date prescribed for payment or delivery the shareholder, certificate holder, member, bondholder, other security holder or the participating patron of a cooperative has not claimed the property, corresponded in writing with the business association or otherwise indicated an interest in the property as evidenced by a memorandum or other record on file with the association. As to that property, the business association shall be deemed to be the holder.

2. Any dividend, profit, interest or other distributions held for or owing to a person at the time the stock or other property to which they attach are presumed to be abandoned shall be deemed to be abandoned at the same time as the stock or other property.

3. This section does not apply to any stock or other intangible interest enrolled in a plan that provides for the automatic reinvestment of dividends, distributions, or other sums payable as a result of the interest unless the records available to the administrator of the plan show, with respect to any intangible interest not enrolled in the reinvestment plan, that the owner has not within 5 years communicated in any manner described in subsection 1.

(Added to NRS by 1979, 1753; A 1983, 1466; 1985, 118; 1987, 749)

NRS 120A.200 Intangible personal property distributable in course of dissolution. All intangible personal property distributable in the course of a dissolution of a business association, banking organization or financial organization organized under the laws of or created in this state that is unclaimed by the owner within 1 year after the date for final distribution is presumed abandoned.

(Added to NRS by 1979, 1753; A 1983, 1467)

NRS 120A.210 Intangible personal property held in fiduciary capacity. All intangible personal property and any income or increment thereon held in a fiduciary capacity for the benefit of another person is presumed abandoned unless the owner has, within 5 years after it becomes payable or distributable, increased or decreased the principal, accepted payment of principal or income, corresponded in writing concerning the property or otherwise indicated an interest as evidenced by a memorandum on file with the fiduciary:

1. If the property is held by a banking organization or a financial organization or by a business association organized under the laws of or created in this state;

2. If it is held by a business association doing business in this state but not organized under the laws of or created in this state and the records of the business association indicate that the last known address of the person entitled thereto is in this state; or

3. If it is held in this state by any other person.

(Added to NRS by 1979, 1753; A 1983, 1476; 1987, 749)

NRS 120A.220 Intangible personal property held by court, public corporation or officer, or governmental entity. All intangible personal property held for the owner by any court, public corporation, public authority or public officer, an appointee thereof, a federal or state governmental entity or a political subdivision thereof, that has remained unclaimed by the owner for more than 5 years after it became payable or distributable is presumed abandoned and subject to the provisions of this chapter if:

1. The last known address or residence of the owner of the property is in this state; or

2. The property is otherwise abandoned in this state.

This section does not apply to refunds held by the public utilities commission of Nevada pursuant to NRS 703.375.

(Added to NRS by 1979, 1754; A 1983, 1476; 1987, 750; 1997, 1965)

NRS 120A.225 Intangible personal property held by intermediary in another state.

1. All intangible personal property, including, but not limited to, any income or increment thereon, that is held for the owner outside this state by a court, public corporation, public authority or public officer,

an appointee thereof, a federal or state governmental entity or a political subdivision thereof or any business association, that has remained unclaimed by the owner for more than 3 years after it became payable or distributable by the issuer of the property is presumed abandoned and subject to the provisions of this chapter if:

(a) The last known address of the owner is unknown to the holder of the property; and

(b) The property was issued or originated by:

(1) This state;

(2) A political subdivision of this state; or

(3) An entity or organization that was incorporated or organized under the laws of this state or was otherwise located in this state at the time the property was issued or originated.

2. The provisions of subsection 1 do not apply to property which is or may be presumed abandoned and subject to the custody of this state pursuant to any other specific statute.

(Added to NRS by 1991, 287; A 1993, 116)

NRS 120A.230 **Intangible personal property not otherwise covered by chapter.** All intangible personal property not otherwise covered by this chapter, including any income or increment thereon and deducting any lawful charges, that is held or owing in this state in the ordinary course of the holder's business and has remained unclaimed by the owner for more than 5 years after it became payable or distributable is presumed abandoned.

(Added to NRS by 1979, 1754; A 1983, 1476; 1987, 750)

NRS 120A.240 **Reciprocity for property presumed abandoned or escheated under laws of another state.** If specific property which is subject to the provisions of NRS 120A.160, 120A.190, 120A.200, 120A.210 and 120A.230 is held for or owed or distributable to an owner whose last known address is in another state by a holder who is subject to the jurisdiction of that state, the specific property is not presumed abandoned in this state and subject to this chapter if:

1. It may be claimed as abandoned or escheated under the laws of the other state; and

2. The laws of the other state make reciprocal provision that similar specific property is not presumed abandoned or escheatable by the other state when held for or owed or distributable to an owner whose last known address is within this state by a holder who is subject to the jurisdiction of this state.

(Added to NRS by 1979, 1754; A 1983, 1476)

REPORTS; NOTICES; CHARGES

NRS 120A.250 **Annual report of property presumed abandoned: Filing; contents; verification.**

1. Every person holding money or other property presumed abandoned under this chapter shall make a verified report to the division with respect to the property.

2. The report must include:

(a) Except with respect to traveler's checks and money orders, the name, if known, and last known address, if any, of each person appearing from the records of the holder to be the owner of any property of the value of $50 or more presumed abandoned under this chapter.

(b) In case of unclaimed money held by an insurance company, the full name of the insured or annuitant and his last known address according to the corporation's records.

(c) The nature and identifying number, if any, or description of the property and the amount appearing from the records to be due, except that items of value under $50 each may be reported in the aggregate.

(d) The date when the property became payable, demandable or returnable and the date of the last transaction with the owner with respect to the property.

(e) Other information which the administrator prescribes by regulation as necessary for the administration of this chapter.

3. If the person holding property presumed abandoned is a successor to other persons who previously held the property for the owner, or if the holder has changed his name while holding the property, he shall file with his report all prior known names and addresses of each holder of the property.

4. The report must be filed before November 1 of each year for the preceding fiscal year ending June 30 except that the report of an insurance company must be filed before May 1 of each year for the preceding calendar year. The administrator may, in writing, postpone the reporting date upon written request by any person required to file a report.

5. Verification of the report, if made by:

(a) A partnership, must be executed by a partner.

(b) An unincorporated association or private corporation, must be executed by an officer.

(c) A public entity or corporation, must be executed by its chief fiscal officer.

(Added to NRS by 1979, 1755; A 1983, 1467; 1987, 750)

NRS 120A.260 **Communication with owner before filing annual report.**

1. If the holder of property presumed abandoned under this chapter knows the whereabouts of the owner and if the owner's claim has not been barred by the statute of limitations, the holder shall, before filing the annual report, communicate with the owner and take necessary steps to prevent abandonment from being presumed. The holder shall exercise due diligence to ascertain the whereabouts of the owner.

2. The administrator may, by regulation, prescribe a form on which the owner may indicate his interest in maintaining the deposit, shares or account. If a form is so prescribed, the holder shall send the form to each owner whose balance is more than $50, not less than 6 nor more than 12 months before the holder's report is due. If the owner fills out, signs and returns the form to the holder, this action prevents abandonment from being presumed. The administrator may, by regulation, authorize the holder to impose a charge of not more than a prescribed amount upon the owner's deposit, shares or account for the expense of mailing the form. In the absence of a regulation prescribing the maximum charge, the holder may impose a charge of not more than $2.

(Added to NRS by 1979, 1756; A 1983, 1468; 1987, 751)

NRS 120A.270 **Reports by banking or financial organization or business association not holding property presumed abandoned.** Any banking or financial organization or business association which holds property for another, if it does not hold property presumed to be abandoned, shall file a report with the administrator, on or before November 1 of each 5-year period after November 1, 1984, which indicates that it is not a holder of any property presumed abandoned during that period. The reports of an insurance company under this section must be filed before May 1 of each year for the preceding calendar years.

(Added to NRS by 1979, 1756; A 1983, 1468)

NRS 120A.280 **Notice to owners of abandoned property.**

1. Within 180 days after the filing of the report required by NRS 120A.250 and the payment or delivery of the property required by NRS 120A.360, the administrator shall cause notice to be published in at least one newspaper of general circulation in the county in this state in which is located the last known address of any person to be named in the notice. If no address is listed or if the address is outside this state, the notice must be published in the county in which the holder of the abandoned property has his principal place of business within this state.

2. The published notice must be entitled "Notice of Names of Persons Appearing To Be Owners of Abandoned Property," and must contain:

(a) The names in alphabetical order and last known addresses, if any, of persons listed in the report and entitled to notice within the county.

(b) A statement that information concerning the amount or description of the property and the name and address of the holder may be obtained by any person possessing an interest in the property by addressing an inquiry to the division.

(c) If the property was removed from a safe-deposit box or other safekeeping repository, a statement declaring that the administrator will hold the property for 1 year after the date the property was delivered to the division, and that the property may be destroyed if no claims are made for it within that period.

3. The administrator is not required to publish in the notice any item valued at less than $50 unless he deems the publication to be in the public interest.

4. In addition to the notice required to be published pursuant to this section, the administrator shall take such actions as are reasonably calculated to give actual notice to the owner of property presumed abandoned, including, without limitation, using information obtained from the department of motor vehicles and public safety and other governmental agencies or executing contracts with private businesses to assist in locating such owners of property.

(Added to NRS by 1979, 1756; A 1983, 1469; 1985, 242; 1987, 751; 1995, 279)

NRS 120A.300 Charge upon dormant accounts: Notice; limitation upon rate.

1. A banking or financial organization shall not impose a charge upon a depositor's account based on the dormancy of the account unless the organization has first mailed a notice of its intended charge to the depositor at his last known address and has allowed him 60 days to respond.

2. The administrator may prescribe by regulation the highest rate of charge which a banking or financial organization may impose upon a dormant account.

3. In the absence of such a regulation, a banking or financial institution shall not impose a charge upon a dormant account of more than $5 per month.

(Added to NRS by 1979, 1752; A 1983, 1470)

NRS 120A.310 Charge upon unclaimed property. No service, handling, maintenance or other charge or fee may be deducted or withheld from any property subject to this chapter if, under the holder's policy or practice, the holder would not have excluded, withheld or deducted such a charge or fee if the property had been claimed by the owner before it was paid or delivered to the division.

(Added to NRS by 1979, 1757; A 1983, 1470)

PLACEMENT OF PROPERTY WITH DIVISION

NRS 120A.320 Time for paying or delivering abandoned property to division; delivery of duplicate certificate or other evidence of ownership to administrator.

1. Except as otherwise provided in subsection 3 and NRS 120A.160, every person who files a report under NRS 120A.250 shall, at the time of filing the report, pay or deliver to the division all abandoned property specified in this report.

2. The holder of an interest under NRS 120A.190 shall deliver a duplicate certificate or other evidence of ownership if the holder does not issue certificates of ownership to the division. Upon delivery of a duplicate certificate to the administrator, the holder and any transfer agent, registrar, or other person acting for or on behalf of a holder in executing or delivering the duplicate certificate is relieved of all liability to every person, including any person acquiring the original certificate or the duplicate of the certificate issued to the division, for any losses or damages resulting to any person by the issuance and delivery to the division of the duplicate certificate.

3. Property which in all probability will be presumed abandoned pursuant to NRS 120A.200 may, upon approval of the administrator, be reported and delivered by the holder to the division before the date it is statutorily presumed abandoned.

(Added to NRS by 1979, 1757; A 1983, 1470; 1985, 119; 1987, 752; 1995, 280)

NRS 120A.330 Administrator may decline to receive abandoned property. Except for property that was removed from a safe-deposit box, the administrator may decline to receive any abandoned property which he deems to have a value less than the cost of giving notice and holding a sale, or he may, if he deems it desirable because of the small sum involved, postpone taking possession until a sufficient sum accumulates. Unless it gives notice to the contrary at the time it receives abandoned property, the division shall be deemed to have elected to receive and maintain the custody of the property.

(Added to NRS by 1979, 1759; A 1983, 1470; 1995, 281)

NRS 120A.340 Relief from liability by payment or delivery; reimbursement or indemnification of holder.

1. Upon the payment or delivery to it of abandoned property, the division shall assume custody of the property and is thereafter responsible for its safe-keeping.

2. Any person who pays or delivers abandoned property to the division under this chapter is relieved of all liability to the extent of the value of the property so paid or delivered for any claim which then exists or which thereafter may arise or be made in respect to the property.

3. Any holder who has paid money to the division pursuant to this chapter may make payment to any person appearing to the holder to be entitled thereto, and if the holder files with the division proof of such payment and proof that the payee was entitled thereto, the division shall forthwith reimburse the holder for the payment, without charge. Where reimbursement is sought for a payment made on a negotiable instrument (including a traveler's check or money order), the division shall reimburse the holder upon his filing proof that the instrument was presented to him and that payment was made thereon to a person who appeared to the holder to be entitled to payment.

4. If the holder pays or delivers property to the division in accordance with this chapter and thereafter any person claims the property from the holder, or another state claims the property from the holder under that state's laws, the attorney general shall, upon written request of the holder, defend him against the claim and the administrator shall indemnify him against any liability on the claim.

5. Property removed from a safe-deposit box or other safekeeping repository is received by the administrator subject to the holder's right to be reimbursed for the actual cost of the opening and to any valid lien or contract providing for the holder to be reimbursed for unpaid rent or storage charges. The administrator shall reimburse or pay the holder out of the proceeds remaining after deducting the administrator's selling cost.

(Added to NRS by 1979, 1757; A 1983, 1471)

NRS 120A.350 Interest, dividends and other increments accruing before liquidation or conversion to money. When property other than money is paid or delivered to the division under this chapter, the owner is entitled to receive from the division any dividends, interest or other increments realized or accruing on the property at or before liquidation or conversion thereof into money.

(Added to NRS by 1979, 1758; A 1983, 1471)

NRS 120A.360 Sale or destruction of abandoned property.

1. Except as otherwise provided in subsections 4, 5 and 6, all abandoned property other than money delivered to the division under this chapter must, within 1 year after the delivery, be sold by the administrator to the highest bidder at public sale in whatever city in the state affords in his judgment the most favorable market for the property involved. The administrator may decline the highest bid and reoffer the property for sale if he considers the price bid insufficient.

2. Any sale held under this section must be preceded by a single publication of notice thereof at least 2 weeks in advance of sale in a newspaper of general circulation in the county where the property is to be sold.

3. The purchaser at any sale conducted by the administrator pursuant to this chapter is vested with title to the property purchased, free from all claims of the owner or prior holder and of all persons claiming through or under them. The administrator shall execute all documents necessary to complete the transfer of title.

4. The administrator need not offer any property for sale if in his opinion the probable cost of sale exceeds the value of the property. The administrator may destroy or otherwise dispose of such property or may transfer it to:

(a) The Nevada museum and historical society, the Nevada state museum or the Nevada historical society, upon its written request, if the property has, in the opinion of the requesting institution, historical, artistic or literary value and is worthy of preservation; or

(b) A genealogical library, upon its written request, if the property has genealogical value and is not wanted by the Nevada museum and historical society, the Nevada state museum or the Nevada historical society.

An action may not be maintained by any person against the holder of the property because of that transfer, disposal or destruction.

5. Securities listed on an established stock exchange must be sold at the prevailing price for that security on the exchange at the time of sale. Other securities not listed on an established stock exchange may be sold:

(a) Over the counter at the prevailing price for that security at the time of sale; or

(b) By any other method the administrator deems acceptable.

6. The administrator shall hold property that was removed from a safe-deposit box or other safekeeping repository for 1 year after the date of the delivery of the property to the division, unless that property is a will or a codicil to a will, in which case the administrator shall hold the property for 10 years after the date of the delivery of the property to the division. If no claims are filed for the property within that period, it may be destroyed.

(Added to NRS by 1979, 1758; A 1983, 1471; 1985, 120, 1013; 1987, 753, 1300, 1318; 1995, 281)

NRS 120A.370 Abandoned property trust fund.

1. There is hereby created in the state treasury the abandoned property trust fund.

2. All money received by the division under this chapter, including the proceeds from the sale of abandoned property, must be deposited by the administrator in the state treasury for credit to the abandoned property trust fund.

3. Before making a deposit, the administrator shall record the name and last known address of each person appearing from the holders' reports to be entitled to the abandoned property and of the name and last known address of each insured person or annuitant, and with respect to each policy or contract listed in the report of an insurance company, its number, the name of the company and the amount due. The record must be available for public inspection at all reasonable business hours.

4. The administrator may pay from money available in the abandoned property trust fund:

(a) Any costs in connection with the sale of abandoned property.

(b) Any costs of mailing and publication in connection with any abandoned property.

(c) Reasonable service charges.

(d) Any costs incurred in examining the records of a holder and in collecting the abandoned property.

(e) Any valid claims filed pursuant to this chapter.

5. At the end of each fiscal year the amount of the balance in the fund in excess of $100,500 must be deposited with the state treasurer for credit to the state general fund but remains subject to the valid claims of holders pursuant to NRS 120A.340 or owners pursuant to NRS 120A.380.

6. If there is an insufficient amount of money in the abandoned property trust fund to pay any cost or charge pursuant to subsection 4, the state board of examiners may, upon the application of the administrator, authorize a temporary transfer from the state general fund to the abandoned property trust fund of an amount necessary to pay those costs or charges. The administrator shall repay the amount of the transfer as soon as sufficient money is available in the abandoned property trust fund.

(Added to NRS by 1979, 1759; A 1983, 1472; 1985, 120; 1987, 754)

RECOVERY OF PROPERTY BY OWNER

NRS 120A.380 Claim for property delivered to state. Any person claiming an interest in any property delivered to the state under this chapter may file a claim to the property or to the proceeds from the sale thereof on the form prescribed by the administrator.

(Added to NRS by 1979, 1759; A 1983, 1472)

NRS 120A.390 Determination of claim.

1. The administrator shall review each claim filed under this chapter and may hold a hearing and receive evidence concerning the claim. If a hearing is held, he shall prepare findings of fact and a decision in writing stating the substance of any evidence heard and the reasons for his decision. The decision is a public record.

2. If the administrator allows the claim, he shall pay it, without deduction for costs of notices or sale or for service charges, from the abandoned property trust fund as other claims against the state are paid.

(Added to NRS by 1979, 1759; A 1983, 1473)

NRS 120A.400 Review of administrator's decision; action to establish

claim. Any person aggrieved by a decision of the administrator, or as to whose claim the administrator has failed to render a decision within 90 days after the filing of the claim, may do either of the following, or both:

1. Request the director of the department of business and industry to review the administrative record. The request must be made in writing and must be filed with the director within 90 days after the decision of the administrator or within 180 days after the filing of the claim. The decision of the director constitutes the final decision in a contested case.

2. Commence an action in the district court to establish his claim. The proceeding must be brought within 90 days after the decision of the administrator or within 180 days after the filing of the claim if the administrator has failed to render a decision. The action must be tried without a jury in cases where the administrator has failed to render a decision.

(Added to NRS by 1979, 1759; A 1983, 1473; 1993, 1510)

NRS 120A.405 **Agreements to recover property presumed abandoned.**

1. Any agreement to locate, deliver, recover or assist in the recovery of property presumed abandoned which is entered into by or on behalf of the owner of the property must:

(a) Be in writing.

(b) Be signed by the owner.

(c) Include a description of the property.

(d) Include the value of the property.

(e) Include the name and address of the person in possession of the property, if known.

2. No such agreement is valid unless it is executed:

(a) Before the date on which the property is reported to the division pursuant to NRS 120A.250; or

(b) Two years after the property has been paid or delivered to the division.

3. No fee charged for the location, delivery, recovery or assistance in the recovery of property presumed abandoned may be more than 10 percent of the total value of the property.

(Added to NRS by 1983, 1461)

ENFORCEMENT; PENALTIES

NRS 120A.410 **Reciprocity.**

1. The administrator may enter into an agreement to provide information needed to enable another state to determine the existence of unclaimed property to which it may be entitled if the other state agrees to provide this state with information needed to enable this state to determine the existence of unclaimed property to which this state may be entitled. The administrator may, by regulation, require the reporting of information needed to enable him to comply with agreements made pursuant to this section and may, by regulation, prescribe the form, including verification, of the information to be reported and the times for filing the reports.

2. At the request of another state, the attorney general of this state may bring an action in the name of the other state, in any court of competent jurisdiction of this state or federal court within this state, to enforce the unclaimed property laws of the other state against a holder in this state of property to which the other state is entitled, if:

(a) The courts of the other state cannot obtain jurisdiction over the holder;

(b) The other state has agreed to bring actions in the name of this state at the request of the attorney general of this state to enforce the provisions of this chapter against any person in the other state believed by the administrator to hold property to which this state is entitled, where the courts of this state cannot obtain jurisdiction over that person; and

(c) The other state has agreed to pay reasonable costs incurred by the attorney general in bringing the action on its behalf.

3. If the administrator believes that a person in another state holds property to which this state is entitled under this chapter and the courts of this state cannot obtain jurisdiction over that person, the attorney general of this state may request an officer of the other state to bring an action in the name of this state to enforce the provisions of this chapter against that person. This state shall pay all reasonable costs incurred by the other state in any action brought under the authority of this section. The administrator may agree to pay to the state, a political subdivision of the state, or an agency of either, which employs the officer bringing such an action a reward not to exceed 15 percent of the value, after deducting reasonable costs, of any property recovered for this state as a direct or indirect result of the action. Any costs or rewards paid pursuant to this section must be paid from the abandoned property trust fund and must not be deducted from the amount that is subject to be claimed by the owner in accordance with this chapter.

(Added to NRS by 1979, 1754; A 1983, 1473; 1985, 121)

NRS 120A.420 **Examination of records of holders of abandoned property.**

1. The chief of the division of unclaimed property may at reasonable times and upon reasonable notice examine the records of any person if he has reason to believe that the person has failed to report property which should have been reported pursuant to this chapter.

2. To determine compliance with this chapter, the commissioner of financial institutions may examine the records of any banking organization and any savings and loan association doing business within this state but not organized under the laws of or created in this state.

3. When requested by the chief of the division of unclaimed property, any licensing or regulating agency otherwise empowered by the laws of this state to examine the records of the holder shall include in its examination a determination whether the holder has complied with this chapter.

(Added to NRS by 1979, 1760; A 1983, 1474; 1987, 1874)

NRS 120A.430 **Action to enforce payment or delivery of abandoned property to division; award of costs and attorney's fees; imposition of civil penalty.** If any person refuses to pay or deliver property to the division as required under this chapter, the attorney general, upon request of the administrator, may bring an action in a court of competent jurisdiction to enforce the payment or delivery. In such an action, the court may award costs and reasonable attorney's fees to the prevailing party, and, if the division is the prevailing party, may impose a civil penalty against the losing party in an amount not to exceed 2 percent of the value of the property, or $1,000, whichever is greater.

(Added to NRS by 1979, 1760; A 1983, 1474; 1995, 282)

NRS 120A.440 **Criminal penalties.**

1. Any person who willfully fails to make any report or perform any other duty required under this chapter is guilty of a misdemeanor. Each day such a report is withheld constitutes a separate offense.

2. Any person who willfully refuses to pay or deliver abandoned property to the division as required under this chapter is guilty of a gross misdemeanor.

(Added to NRS by 1979, 1760; A 1983, 1474)

NRS 120A.450 **Interest.**

1. Except as otherwise provided in subsection 2, in addition to any penalties for which he may be liable, any person who fails

to report or to pay or deliver abandoned property within the time prescribed by this chapter shall pay to the division interest at the rate of 18 percent per annum on the money or the value of other property from the date on which the property should have been paid or delivered.

2. The administrator may waive any right to the payment of interest pursuant to this section if:

(a) The person otherwise obligated to make payment files with the division a verified statement of the facts, showing that his failure to report or to make payment or delivery was not willful or negligent but occurred because of circumstances beyond his control; and

(b) The administrator so finds.

(Added to NRS by 1979, 1760; A 1983, 1475; 1989, 375)

NRS Chapter 163, Trusts

NRS 163.080 Voting stock. A trustee owning corporate stock may vote it by proxy, but shall be liable for any loss resulting to the beneficiaries from a failure to use reasonable care in deciding how to vote the stock and in voting it.

[7:136:1941; 1931 NCL § 7718.36]

NRS 163.090 Holding stock in name of nominee. A trustee owning stock may hold it in the name of a nominee without mention of the trust in the stock certificate or stock registration books; providing that:

1. The trust records and all reports or accounts rendered by the trustee clearly show the ownership of the stock by the trustee and the facts regarding its holding; and

2. The nominee shall deposit with the trustee a signed statement showing the trust ownership.

The trustee shall be personally liable for any loss to the trust resulting from any act of such nominee in connection with stock so held.

[8:136:1941; 1931 NCL § 7718.37]—(NRS A 1961, 471)

NRS Chapter 193, Crimes and Punishments

NRS 193.160 Penalty for misdemeanor by corporations when not fixed by statute. In all cases where a corporation is convicted of an offense for the commission of which a natural person would be punishable as for a misdemeanor, and there is no other punishment prescribed by law, the corporation is punishable by a fine not exceeding $1,000.

[1911 C&P § 21; RL § 6286; NCL § 9970]—(NRS A 1981, 652)

NRS Chapter 205, Crimes against Property

NRS 205.090 Forgery of conveyances, negotiable instruments, stock certificates, wills and other instruments; utterance of forged instrument. A person who falsely makes, alters, forges or counterfeits any record, or other authentic matter of a public nature, or any charter, letters patent, deed, lease, indenture, writing obligatory, will, testament, codicil, annuity, bond, covenant, bank bill or note, post note, check, draft, bill of exchange, contract, promissory note, traveler's check, money order, due bill for the payment of money or property or for the payment of any labor claim, receipt for money or property, power of attorney, any auditor's warrant for the payment of the money at the treasury, county order or warrant, or request for the payment of money, or the delivery of goods or chattels of any kind, or for the delivery of any instrument of writing, or acquittance, release, or receipt for money, goods, or labor claim, or any acquittance, release, or discharge for any debt, account, suit, action, demand, or other thing, real or personal, or any transfer or assurance of money, stock, goods, chattels, or other property whatever, or any letter of attorney, or other power to receive money, or to receive or transfer stock or annuities, or to let, lease, dispose of, alien or convey any goods or chattels, lands or tenements, or other estate, real or personal, or any acceptance or

endorsement of any bill of exchange, promissory note, draft, order or assignment of any bond, writing obligatory, or promissory note, for money or other property, or any order, writ or process lawfully issued by any court or public officer, or any document or paper recorded or filed in any court or with any public officer, or in the senate or assembly, or counterfeits or forges the seal or handwriting of another, with the intent to damage or defraud any person, body politic or corporate, whether the person, body politic or corporate, resides in or belongs to this state or not, or utters, publishes, passes or attempts to pass, as true and genuine, any of the above-named false, altered, forged or counterfeited matters, as above specified and described, knowing it to be false, altered, forged or counterfeited with the intent to prejudice, damage or defraud any person, body politic or corporate, whether the person, body politic or corporate, resides in this state or not, is guilty of forgery, and shall be punished for a category D felony as provided in NRS 193.130. In addition to any other penalty, the court shall order the person to pay restitution.

[1911 C&P § 398; A 1941, 308; 1931 NCL § 10350]—(NRS A 1967, 494; 1969, 14; 1973, 174; 1979, 1440; 1995, 1216)

NRS 205.105 Forgery of instrument purporting to have been issued by corporation or state. The false making or forging of an instrument or writing purporting to have been issued by or in behalf of a corporation or association, state or government and bearing the pretended signature of any person therein falsely indicated as an agent or officer of such corporation, association, state or government, is forgery the same as if that person were in truth such officer or agent of such corporation, association, state or government.

[1911 C&P § 401; RL § 6666; NCL § 10353]

NRS 205.435 Fraudulent issue of stock. An officer, agent or other person in the service of a joint-stock company or corporation, domestic or foreign, who, willfully and knowingly with the intent to defraud:

1. Sells, pledges or issues, or causes to be sold, pledged or issued, or signs or executes or causes to be signed or executed, with the intent to sell, pledge or issue, or cause to be sold, pledged or issued, any certificate or instrument purporting to be a certificate or evidence of ownership of any share of that company or corporation, or any conveyance or encumbrance of real or personal property, contract, bond or evidence

of debt, or writing purporting to be a conveyance or encumbrance of real or personal property, contract, bond or evidence of debt of that company or corporation, without being first duly authorized by the company or corporation, or contrary to the charter or laws under which the company or corporation exists, or in excess of the power of the company or corporation, or of the limit imposed by law or otherwise upon its power to create or issue stock or evidence of debt; or

2. Reissues, sells, pledges or disposes of, or causes to be reissued, sold, pledged or disposed of, any surrendered or canceled certificate or other evidence of the transfer of ownership of any such share,

is guilty of a category C felony and shall be punished as provided in NRS 193.130. In addition to any other penalty, the court shall order the person to pay restitution.

[1911 C&P § 457; RL § 6722; NCL § 10410]—(NRS A 1979, 1447; 1995, 1226)

NRS Chapter 364A, Business Tax

NRS 364A.010 Definitions. As used in this chapter, unless the context otherwise requires, the words and terms defined in NRS 364A.020 to 364A.050, inclusive, have the meanings ascribed to them in those sections.

(Added to NRS by 1991, 2448)

NRS 364A.020 "Business" defined.

1. "Business" includes:

(a) A corporation, partnership, proprietorship, business association and any other similar organization that conducts an activity for profit;

(b) The activities of a natural person which are deemed to be a business pursuant to NRS 364A.120; and

(c) A trade show or convention held in this state in which a business described in paragraph (a) or (b) takes part, or which a person who conducts such a business attends, for a purpose related to the conduct of the business.

2. The term includes an independent contractor.

3. The term does not include:

(a) A nonprofit religious, charitable, fraternal or other organization that qualifies as a tax-exempt organization pursuant to 26 U.S.C. § 501(c);

(b) A governmental entity; or

(c) A business that creates or produces motion pictures. As used in this paragraph, "motion pictures" has the meaning ascribed to it in NRS 231.020.

(Added to NRS by 1991, 2449; A 1993, 2422; 1999, 3113)

NRS 364A.030 "Commission" defined. "Commission" means the Nevada tax commission.

(Added to NRS by 1991, 2449)

NRS 364A.040 "Employee" defined.

1. "Employee" includes:

(a) A natural person who receives wages or other remuneration from a business for personal services, including commissions and bonuses and remuneration payable in a medium other than cash; and

(b) A natural person engaged in the operation of a business.

2. The term includes:

(a) A partner or other co-owner of a business; and

(b) Except as otherwise provided in subsection 3, a natural person reported as an employee to the:

(1) Employment security division of the department of employment, training and rehabilitation;

(2) Administrator of the division of industrial relations of the department of business and industry; or

(3) Internal Revenue Service on an Employer's Quarterly Federal Tax Return (Form 941), Employer's Monthly Federal Tax Return (Form 941-M), Employer's Annual Tax Return for Agricultural Employees (Form 943) or any equivalent or successor form.

3. The term does not include:

(a) A business, including an independent contractor, that performs services on behalf of another business.

(b) A natural person who is retired or otherwise receiving remuneration solely because of past service to the business.

(c) A newspaper carrier or the immediate supervisor of a newspaper carrier who is an independent contractor of the newspaper and receives compensation solely from persons who purchase the newspaper.

(d) A natural person who performs all of his duties for the business outside of this state.

4. An independent contractor is not an employee of a business with whom he contracts.

(Added to NRS by 1991, 2449; A 1993, 1576; 1995, 2045)

NRS 364A.050 "Wages" defined. "Wages" means any remuneration paid for personal services, including commissions, and

bonuses and remuneration payable in any medium other than cash.

(Added to NRS by 1991, 2449)

ADMINISTRATION

NRS 364A.060 Regulations of Nevada tax commission. The commission shall adopt such regulations as it deems necessary to carry out the provisions of this chapter.

(Added to NRS by 1991, 2459)

NRS 364A.070 Maintenance and availability of records of business; penalty.

1. Each person responsible for maintaining the records of a business shall:

(a) Keep such records as may be necessary to determine the amount of its liability pursuant to the provisions of this chapter;

(b) Preserve those records for 4 years or until any litigation or prosecution pursuant to this chapter is finally determined, whichever is longer; and

(c) Make the records available for inspection by the department upon demand at reasonable times during regular business hours.

2. Any person who violates the provisions of subsection 1 is guilty of a misdemeanor.

(Added to NRS by 1991, 2454)

NRS 364A.080 Examination of records by department; payment of expenses of department for examination of records outside state.

1. To verify the accuracy of any return filed, or, if no return is filed by a business, to determine the amount required to be paid, the department, or any person authorized in writing by it, may examine the books, papers, and records of any person or business that may be liable for the tax imposed by this chapter.

2. Any person or business which may be liable for the tax imposed by this chapter and which keeps outside of this state its books, papers and records relating thereto, shall pay to the department an amount equal to the allowance provided for state officers and employees generally while traveling outside of the state for each day or fraction thereof during which an employee of the department is engaged in examining those documents, plus any other actual expenses incurred by the employee while he is absent from his regular place of employment to examine those documents.

(Added to NRS by 1991, 2454)

NRS 364A.090 Authority of executive director to request information to carry out chapter. The executive director may request lists of employers, the number of employees employed by each employer and the total wages paid by each employer from the administrator and the employment security division of the department of employment, training and rehabilitation to carry out the provisions of this chapter.

(Added to NRS by 1991, 2454; A 1993, 1576; 1995, 2045)

NRS 364A.100 Confidentiality of records and files of department.

1. Except as otherwise provided in NRS 360.250 and subsections 2 and 3, the records and files of the department concerning the administration of this chapter are confidential and privileged. The department, and any employee engaged in the administration of this chapter, or charged with the custody of any such records or files, shall not disclose any information obtained from the department's records or files or from any examination, investigation or hearing authorized by the provisions of this chapter. Neither the department nor any employee of the department may be required to produce any of the records, files and information for the inspection of any person or for use in any action or proceeding.

2. The records and files of the department concerning the administration of this chapter are not confidential and privileged in the following cases:

(a) Testimony by a member or employee of the department and production of records, files and information on behalf of the department or a taxpayer in any action or proceeding pursuant to the provisions of this chapter if that testimony or the records, files or information, or the facts shown thereby are directly involved in the action or proceeding.

(b) Delivery to a taxpayer or his authorized representative of a copy of any return or other document filed by the taxpayer pursuant to this chapter.

(c) Publication of statistics so classified as to prevent the identification of a particular business or document.

(d) Exchanges of information with the Internal Revenue Service in accordance with compacts made and provided for in such cases.

(e) Disclosure in confidence to the governor or his agent in the exercise of the governor's general supervisory powers, or to any person authorized to audit the accounts of the department in pursuance of an audit, or to the attorney general or other legal representative of the state in connection with an action or proceeding pursuant to this chapter or to any agency of this or any other state charged with the administration or enforcement of laws relating to workers' compensation, unemployment compensation, public assistance, taxation, labor or gaming.

3. The executive director shall periodically, as he deems appropriate, but not less often than annually, transmit to the administrator of the division of industrial relations of the department of business and industry a list of the businesses of which he has a record. The list must include the mailing address of the business and the approximate number of employees of the business as reported to the department.

(Added to NRS by 1991, 2455; A 1993, 777; 1995, 645, 1578)

NRS 364A.110 Business tax account: Deposits; refunds.

1. The department shall deposit all fees, taxes, interest and penalties it receives under this chapter in the state treasury for credit to the business tax account in the state general fund.

2. The money in the business tax account may, upon order of the state controller, be used for refunds under this chapter.

(Added to NRS by 1991, 2459)

BUSINESS LICENSE; IMPOSITION AND COLLECTION OF TAX

NRS 364A.120 Activities constituting business. The activity or activities conducted by a natural person shall be deemed to be a business that is subject to the provisions of this chapter if the person files with the Internal Revenue Service a Schedule C (Form 1040), Profit or Loss from Business Form, or its equivalent or successor form, or a Schedule F (Form 1040), Farm Income and Expenses Form, or its equivalent or successor form, for the activity or activities.

(Added to NRS by 1991, 2449)

NRS 364A.130 Business license required; application for license; activities constituting conduct of business.

1. Except as otherwise provided in subsection 6, a person shall not conduct a business in this state unless he has a business license issued by the department.

2. The application for a business license must:

(a) Be made upon a form prescribed by the department;

(b) Set forth the name under which the applicant transacts or intends to transact business and the location of his place or places of business;

(c) Declare the estimated number of employees for the previous calendar quarter;

(d) Be accompanied by a fee of $25; and

(e) Include any other information that the department deems necessary.

3. The application must be signed by:

(a) The owner, if the business is owned by a natural person;

(b) A member or partner, if the business is owned by an association or partnership; or

(c) An officer or some other person specifically authorized to sign the application, if the business is owned by a corporation.

4. If the application is signed pursuant to paragraph (c) of subsection 3, written evidence of the signer's authority must be attached to the application.

5. For the purposes of this chapter, a person shall be deemed to conduct a business in this state if a business for which the person is responsible:

(a) Is incorporated pursuant to chapter 78 or 78A of NRS;

(b) Has an office or other base of operations in this state; or

(c) Pays wages or other remuneration to a natural person who performs in this state any of the duties for which he is paid.

6. A person who takes part in a trade show or convention held in this state for a purpose related to the conduct of a business is not required to obtain a business license specifically for that event.

(Added to NRS by 1991, 2450; A 1993, 2422; 1999, 3113)

NRS 364A.135 Revocation or suspension of business license for failure to comply with statutes or regulations.

1. If a holder of a license under this chapter fails to comply with a provision of this chapter or a regulation of the department adopted under this chapter, the department may revoke or suspend his license. Before so doing, the department must hold a hearing after 10 days' written notice to the licensee. The notice must specify the time and place of the hearing and require him to show cause why his license should not be revoked.

2. If the license is suspended or revoked, the department shall give written notice of the action to the holder.

3. The notices required by this section may be served personally or by mail in the manner provided in NRS 360.350 for the service of a notice of the determination of a deficiency.

4. The department shall not issue a new license to the former holder of a revoked license unless it is satisfied that he will

comply with the provisions of this chapter and the regulations of the department adopted pursuant thereto.

(Added to NRS by 1993, 2069)

NRS 364A.140 Imposition, payment and amount of tax; filing and contents of return.

1. A tax is hereby imposed upon the privilege of conducting business in this state. The tax for each calendar quarter is due on the last day of the quarter and must be paid on or before the last day of the month immediately following the quarter on the basis of the total number of equivalent full-time employees employed by the business in the quarter.

2. The total number of equivalent full-time employees employed by the business in the quarter must be calculated pursuant to NRS 364A.150.

3. Except as otherwise provided in NRS 364A.152 and 364A.170, the amount of tax due per quarter for a business is $25 for each equivalent full-time employee employed by the business in the quarter.

4. Each business shall file a return on a form prescribed by the department with each remittance of the tax. If the payment due is greater than $1,000, the payment must be made by direct deposit at a bank or credit union in which the state has an account, unless the department waives this requirement pursuant to regulations adopted by the commission. The return must include a statement of the number of equivalent full-time employees employed by the business in the preceding quarter and any other information the department determines is necessary.

5. The commission shall adopt regulations concerning the payment of the tax imposed pursuant to this section by direct deposit.

(Added to NRS by 1991, 2451; A 1993, 2070, 2423; 1999, 1489)

NRS 364A.150 Calculation of total number of equivalent full-time employees; exclusion of hours of certain employees with lower incomes who received free child care from business.

1. The total number of equivalent full-time employees employed by a business in a quarter must be calculated by dividing the total number of hours all employees have worked during the quarter by 468.

2. To determine the total number of hours all employees have worked during the quarter, the business must add the total number of hours worked by full-time employees based in this state during the

quarter to the total number of hours worked by part-time employees based in this state during the quarter and to the total number of hours worked in this state by employees described in subsection 6. A "full-time employee" is a person who is employed to work at least 36 hours per week. All other employees are part-time employees. An occasional reduction in the number of hours actually worked in any week by a particular employee, as the result of sickness, vacation or other compensated absence, does not affect his status for the purposes of this section if his regular hours of work are 36 or more per week. All hours for which a part-time employee is paid must be included.

3. Except as otherwise provided in subsection 7, the total number of hours worked by full-time employees of a business during the quarter may be calculated by:

(a) Determining from the records of the business the number of hours each full-time employee has worked during the quarter up to a maximum of 468 hours per quarter and totaling the results; or

(b) Multiplying 7.2 hours by the number of days each full-time employee was employed by the business up to a maximum of 65 days per quarter and totaling the results.

4. Except as otherwise provided in subsection 7, the total number of hours worked by part-time employees of a business during the quarter must be calculated by determining from the records of the business the number of hours each part-time employee has worked during the quarter and totaling the results.

5. The total number of hours all employees have worked during the quarter must be calculated excluding the hours worked by a sole proprietor or one natural person in any unincorporated business, who shall be deemed the owner of the business rather than an employee.

6. To determine the total number of hours all employees have worked during the quarter, in the case of a business which employs a natural person at a base or business location outside Nevada, but directs that person to perform at least some of his duties in Nevada, the calculation must include the total number of hours actually worked by that person in Nevada during the quarter. To calculate the number of hours worked in Nevada, the formula in paragraph (b) of subsection 3 must be used for full-time employees, and the formula in subsection 4 must be used for part-time employees.

7. Except as otherwise provided in subsection 8, if a business employs in a calendar quarter a person whose monthly income for that calendar quarter is 150 percent or less of the federally designated

level signifying poverty, the business may exclude the total number of hours which the employee worked during that calendar quarter in calculating the total number of hours worked by employees of the business during the quarter if the business provided to the employee for the whole calendar quarter:

(a) Free child care for the children of the employee at an on-site child care facility; or

(b) One or more vouchers for use by the employee to pay the total cost of child care for the calendar quarter at a licensed child care facility that is within a reasonable distance from the business.

8. The number of hours excluded pursuant to subsection 7 must not reduce the total tax liability of the business by more than 50 percent.

9. As used in this section, the term "on-site child care facility" has the meaning ascribed to it in NRS 432A.0275.

(Added to NRS by 1991, 2453; A 1993, 2424; 1997, 3320)

NRS 364A.151 Exclusion of hours from calculation for employment of pupil as part of program that combines work and study.

If a business employs in a calendar quarter a pupil as part of a program supervised by a school district which combines work and study, the business may exclude the total number of hours worked by the pupil in that quarter, and an equal number of hours worked by one full-time employee or one part-time employee in that quarter, in calculating the total number of hours worked by all employees pursuant to NRS 364A.150.

(Added to NRS by 1995, 411)

NRS 364A.152 Responsibility of operator of facility for trade shows or conventions to pay tax on behalf of participants who do not have business license; exception.

1. Except as otherwise provided in subsection 2, a person or governmental entity that operates a facility at which one or more trade shows or conventions, or both, are held, is responsible for the payment of the taxes imposed by this chapter on behalf of the persons who do not have a business license issued pursuant to this chapter but who take part in the trade show or convention for a purpose related to the conduct of a business.

2. An organization that is created for religious, charitable or educational purposes is not responsible for the payment of taxes on behalf of other persons pursuant to subsection 1 if:

(a) It holds a current certificate of organization or is currently qualified by the secretary of state to do business in this state;

(b) The trade show or convention is the first or second such event held at a facility operated by the organization during the calendar year;

(c) No more than two trade shows, conventions, or both, during that year will be held at a facility operated by the organization; and

(d) The organization notifies the department in writing, not less than 30 days before the date the trade show or convention begins, that it is not responsible for the payment of the taxes.

3. The taxes due pursuant to subsection 1 must be calculated, reported and paid separately from any taxes otherwise due from the operator of the facility pursuant to this chapter.

4. The operator of the facility shall pay:

(a) An amount equal to the product of the total number of businesses taking part in the trade show or the convention multiplied by the number of days on which the trade show or convention is held, multiplied in turn by $1.25 for each trade show or convention that is held in the facility; or

(b) An annual fee of $5,000 to the department on or before July 1 for the fiscal year beginning on that day.

5. If the operator of a facility at which a trade show or convention is held has not paid the fee provided in paragraph (b) of subsection 4, he shall file a return on a form prescribed by the department and remit the tax pursuant to paragraph (a) of subsection 4 for each quarter in which a trade show or convention is held.

6. The commission shall adopt such regulations as it deems necessary to carry out the provisions of this section.

(Added to NRS by 1993, 2421; A 1995, 2196)

NRS 364A.1525 Requirements to qualify as organization created for religious, charitable or educational purposes.

1. For the purposes of this chapter, an organization is created for religious, charitable or educational purposes if it complies with the provisions of this section.

2. An organization is created for religious purposes if:

(a) It complies with the requirements set forth in subsection 5; and

(b) The sole or primary purpose of the organization is the operation of a church, synagogue or other place of religious worship at which nonprofit religious services and activities are regularly conducted. Such an organization includes, without limitation, an integrated auxiliary or affiliate of the organization, men's, women's or youth groups established by the organization, a school or mission society operated by the organization, an organization of local units of a church and a convention or association of churches.

3. An organization is created for charitable purposes if:

(a) It complies with the requirements set forth in subsection 5;

(b) The sole or primary purpose of the organization is to:

(1) Advance a public purpose, donate or render gratuitously or at a reduced rate a substantial portion of its services to the persons who are the subjects of its charitable services, and benefit a substantial and indefinite class of persons who are the legitimate subjects of charity; or

(2) Provide services that are otherwise required to be provided by a local government, this state or the Federal Government; and

(c) The organization is operating in this state.

4. An organization is created for educational purposes if:

(a) It complies with the requirements set forth in subsection 5; and

(b) The sole or primary purpose of the organization is to:

(1) Provide athletic, cultural or social activities for children;

(2) Provide displays or performances of the visual or performing arts to members of the general public;

(3) Provide instruction and disseminate information on subjects beneficial to the community; or

(4) Operate a school, college or university located in this state that conducts regular classes and provides courses of study required for accreditation or licensing by the state board of education or the commission of post-secondary education, or for membership in the Northwest Association of Schools and Colleges.

5. In addition to the requirements set forth in subsection 2, 3 or 4, an organization is created for religious, charitable or educational purposes if:

(a) No part of the net earnings of any such organization inures to the benefit of a private shareholder, individual or entity;

(b) The business of the organization is not conducted for profit;

(c) No substantial part of the business of the organization is devoted to the advocacy of any political principle or the defeat or passage of any state or federal legislation;

(d) The organization does not participate or intervene in any political campaign on behalf of or in opposition to any candidate for public office; and

(e) Any property sold to the organization for which an exemption is claimed is used by the organization in this state in furtherance of the religious, charitable or educational purposes of the organization.

(Added to NRS by 1995, 2195)

NRS 364A.153 Responsibility of certain agencies to collect tax from out-of-state businesses engaged in creating or producing motion pictures in Nevada. Repealed. (See chapter 580, Statutes of Nevada 1999, at page 3120.)

NRS 364A.160 Exemption for natural person with no employees during calendar quarter. A natural person who does not employ any employees during a calendar quarter is exempt from the provisions of this chapter for that calendar quarter.

(Added to NRS by 1991, 2450)

NRS 364A.170 Partial abatement of tax on new or expanded business.

1. A business that qualifies pursuant to the provisions of NRS 360.750 is entitled to an exemption of:

(a) Eighty percent of the amount of tax otherwise due pursuant to NRS 364A.140 during the first 4 quarters of its operation;

(b) Sixty percent of the amount of tax otherwise due pursuant to NRS 364A.140 during the second 4 quarters of its operation;

(c) Forty percent of the amount of tax otherwise due pursuant to NRS 364A.140 during the third 4 quarters of its operation; and

(d) Twenty percent of the amount of tax otherwise due pursuant to NRS 364A.140 during the fourth 4 quarters of its operation.

2. If a partial abatement from the taxes otherwise due pursuant to NRS 364A.140 is approved by the commission on economic development pursuant to NRS 360.750, the partial abatement must be administered and carried out in the manner set forth in NRS 360.750.

(Added to NRS by 1991, 2450; A 1993, 1180; 1999, 1747)

NRS 364A.175 Exemption for activities conducted pursuant to certain contracts executed before July 1, 1991.

1. To the extent allowed in subsection 2, there is exempted from the taxes imposed by this chapter the activity or activities conducted by a business pursuant to a written contract for the construction of an

improvement to real property which was executed before July 1, 1991, or for which a binding bid was submitted before that date if the bid was afterward accepted, if under the terms of the contract or bid the contract price or bid amount cannot be adjusted to reflect the imposition of the tax imposed by this chapter.

2. The number of hours in a quarter during which an employee actually worked exclusively on a job under a contract which is exempt pursuant to subsection 1 must be excluded in any calculations for that employee made pursuant to the formulas for determining the total number of hours of all employees pursuant to subsections 3 and 4 of NRS 364A.150. If the number of hours an employee worked in each week of the quarter, excluding the exempt hours and including any hours of compensated leave, does not exceed 36 hours per week, the employee's total hours for the quarter must be calculated pursuant to subsection 4 of NRS 364A.150. In all other cases the hours must be calculated pursuant to subsection 3 of NRS 364A.150. If the business does not maintain records which allow the hours worked on separate contracts to be segregated, all hours worked by any employee who works on jobs under both exempt and nonexempt contracts must be included in the calculations made pursuant to NRS 364A.150.

(Added to NRS by 1993, 1367; A 1993, 2425)

NRS 364A.180 Extension of time for payment; payment of interest during period of extension. Upon written application made before the date on which payment must be made, for good cause the department may extend by 30 days the time within which a business is required to pay the tax imposed by this chapter. If the tax is paid during the period of extension, no penalty or late charge may be imposed for failure to pay at the time required, but the business shall pay interest at the rate most recently established pursuant to NRS 99.040 for each month, or fraction of a month, from the last day of the month following the date on which the amount would have been due without the extension until the date of payment, unless otherwise provided in NRS 360.232 or 360.320.

(Added to NRS by 1991, 2454; A 1993, 2071; 1999, 2492)

NRS 364A.190 Payment of penalty or interest not required under certain circumstances. Notwithstanding any other provision of this Title, in any action by the department for the payment of taxes due pursuant to NRS 364A.140, a person is not required to pay any penalty or interest for taxes due for the four quarters before the quarter in which the action is filed if the person responsible for the business had not received any correspondence from the department concerning the tax and was otherwise unaware of the liability.

(Added to NRS by 1991, 2454)

NRS 364A.230 Remedies of state are cumulative. The remedies of the state provided for in this chapter are cumulative, and no action taken by the department or the attorney general constitutes an election by the state to pursue any remedy to the exclusion of any other remedy for which provision is made in this chapter.

(Added to NRS by 1991, 2459)

OVERPAYMENTS AND REFUNDS

NRS 364A.240 Certification of excess amount collected; credit and refund. If the department determines that any tax, penalty or interest has been paid more than once or has been erroneously or illegally collected or computed, the department shall set forth that fact in the records of the department and certify to the state board of examiners the amount collected in excess of the amount legally due and the business or person from which it was collected or by whom paid. If approved by the state board of examiners, the excess amount collected or paid must be credited on any amounts then due from the person or business under this chapter, and the balance refunded to the person or business, or its successors, administrators or executors.

(Added to NRS by 1991, 2457)

NRS 364A.250 Limitations on claims for refund or credit; form and contents of claim; failure to file claim constitutes waiver; service of notice of rejection of claim.

1. Except as otherwise provided in NRS 360.235 and 360.395:

(a) No refund may be allowed unless a claim for it is filed with the department within 3 years after the last day of the month following the close of the period for which the overpayment was made.

(b) No credit may be allowed after the expiration of the period specified for filing claims for refund unless a claim for credit is filed with the department within that period.

2. Each claim must be in writing and must state the specific grounds upon which the claim is founded.

3. Failure to file a claim within the time prescribed in this chapter constitutes a waiver of any demand against the state on account of overpayment.

4. Within 30 days after rejecting any claim in whole or in part, the department shall serve notice of its action on the claimant in the manner prescribed for service of notice of a deficiency determination.

(Added to NRS by 1991, 2457; A 1995, 1064)

NRS 364A.260 Interest on overpayments; disallowance of interest.

1. Except as otherwise provided in NRS 360.320, interest must be paid upon any overpayment of any amount of the fee or tax imposed by this chapter at the rate of one-half of 1 percent per month, or fraction thereof, from the last day of the calendar month following the period for which the overpayment was made. No refund or credit may be made of any interest imposed upon the person or business making the overpayment with respect to the amount being refunded or credited.

2. The interest must be paid:

(a) In the case of a refund, to the last day of the calendar month following the date upon which the person making the overpayment, if he has not already filed a claim, is notified by the department that a claim may be filed or the date upon which the claim is certified to the state board of examiners, whichever is earlier.

(b) In the case of a credit, to the same date as that to which interest is computed on the fee or tax or amount against which the credit is applied.

3. If the department determines that any overpayment has been made intentionally or by reason of carelessness, it shall not allow any interest on it.

(Added to NRS by 1991, 2458; A 1999, 2492)

NRS 364A.270 Injunction or other process to prevent collection of tax prohibited; filing of claim condition precedent to maintaining action for refund.

1. No injunction, writ of mandate or other legal or equitable process may issue in any suit, action or proceeding in any court against this state or against any officer of the state to prevent or enjoin the collection under this chapter of the tax imposed by this chapter or any amount of tax, penalty or interest required to be collected.

2. No suit or proceeding may be maintained in any court for the recovery of any amount alleged to have been erroneously or illegally determined or collected unless a claim for refund or credit has been filed.

(Added to NRS by 1991, 2458)

NRS 364A.280 Action for refund: Time to sue; venue of action; waiver.

1. Within 90 days after a final decision upon a claim filed pursuant to this chapter is rendered by the Nevada tax commission, the claimant may bring an action against the department on the grounds set forth in the claim in a court of competent jurisdiction in Carson City, the county of this state where the claimant resides or maintains his principal place of business or a county in which any relevant proceedings were conducted by the department, for the recovery of the whole or any part of the amount with respect to which the claim has been disallowed.

2. Failure to bring an action within the time specified constitutes a waiver of any demand against the state on account of alleged overpayments.

(Added to NRS by 1991, 2458; A 1999, 2493)

NRS 364A.290 Right of appeal on failure of department to mail notice of action on claim; allocation of judgment for claimant.

1. If the department fails to mail notice of action on a claim within 6 months after the claim is filed, the claimant may consider the claim disallowed and file an appeal with the Nevada tax commission within the 30 days after the last day of the 6-month period. If the claimant is aggrieved by the decision of the commission rendered on appeal, he may, within 90 days after the decision is rendered, bring an action against the department on the grounds set forth in the claim for the recovery of the whole or any part of the amount claimed as an overpayment.

2. If judgment is rendered for the plaintiff, the amount of the judgment must first be credited towards any fee or tax due from the plaintiff.

3. The balance of the judgment must be refunded to the plaintiff.

(Added to NRS by 1991, 2458; A 1999, 2493)

NRS 364A.300 Allowance of interest in judgment for amount illegally collected. In any judgment, interest must be allowed at the rate of 6 percent per annum upon the amount found to have been illegally collected from the date of payment of the amount to the date of allowance of credit on account of the judgment, or to a date preceding the date of the refund warrant by not more than 30 days. The date must be determined by the department.

(Added to NRS by 1991, 2458)

NRS 364A.310 Standing to recover. A judgment may not be rendered in favor of the plaintiff in any action brought against the department to recover any amount paid when the action is brought by or in the name of an assignee of the business paying the amount or by any person other than the person or business which paid the amount.

(Added to NRS by 1991, 2459)

NRS 364A.320 Action for recovery of erroneous refund: Jurisdiction; venue; prosecution by attorney general.

1. The department may recover a refund or any part thereof which is erroneously made and any credit or part thereof which is erroneously allowed in an action brought in a court of competent jurisdiction in Carson City or Clark County in the name of the State of Nevada.

2. The action must be tried in Carson City or Clark County unless the court with the consent of the attorney general orders a change of place of trial.

3. The attorney general shall prosecute the action, and the provisions of NRS, the Nevada Rules of Civil Procedure and the Nevada Rules of Appellate Procedure relating to service of summons, pleadings, proofs, trials and appeals are applicable to the proceedings.

(Added to NRS by 1991, 2459)

NRS 364A.330 Cancellation of illegal determination: Procedure; limitation.

1. If any amount in excess of $25 has been illegally determined, either by the person filing the return or by the department, the department shall certify this fact to the state board of examiners, and the latter shall authorize the cancellation of the amount upon the records of the department.

2. If an amount not exceeding $25 has been illegally determined, either by the person or business filing a return or by the department, the department without certifying this fact to the state board of examiners, shall authorize the cancellation of the amount upon the records of the department.

(Added to NRS by 1991, 2459)

MISCELLANEOUS PROVISIONS

NRS 364A.340 Proof of subcontractor's compliance with provisions of chapter. A person who:

1. Is required to be licensed pursuant to chapter 624 of NRS; and

2. Contracts with a subcontractor who is required to be licensed pursuant to that chapter and to have a business license and pay the tax imposed by this chapter,

shall require proof that the subcontractor has a business license and has paid the tax imposed by this chapter before commencing payments to the subcontractor. For the purposes of this section, a subcontractor proves that he has a business license and has paid the tax imposed by this chapter by presenting a receipt for or other evidence that he made the last quarterly payment required pursuant to this chapter.

(Added to NRS by 1991, 2456)

NRS 364A.350 Penalty for false or fraudulent returns, statements or records.

1. A person shall not:

(a) Make, cause to be made or permit to be made any false or fraudulent return or declaration or false statement in any return or declaration, with intent to defraud the state or to evade payment of the tax or any part of the tax imposed by this chapter.

(b) Make, cause to be made or permit to be made any false entry in books, records or accounts with intent to defraud the state or to evade the payment of the tax or any part of the tax imposed by this chapter.

(c) Keep, cause to be kept or permit to be kept more than one set of books, records or accounts with intent to defraud the state or to evade the payment of the tax or any part of the tax imposed by this chapter.

2. Any person who violates the provisions of subsection 1 is guilty of a gross misdemeanor.

(Added to NRS by 1991, 2454)

NRS CHAPTER 602, DOING BUSINESS UNDER ASSUMED OR FICTITIOUS NAME

NRS 602.010 Filing of certificate with county clerk.

1. Every person doing business in this state under an assumed or fictitious name which does not show the real name of each person who owns an interest in the business, must file with the county clerk of each county in which the business is being conducted, a certificate containing the information required by NRS 602.020.

2. A person intending to conduct a business under an assumed or fictitious name may, before initiating the conduct of the business, file a certificate with the county

clerk of each county in which the business is intended to be conducted.

[Part 1:156:1923; NCL § 4450]— (NRS A 1969, 67; 1973, 545; 1993, 1022)

NRS 602.015 Filing by corporations doing business in state on July 1, 1969. Any corporation conducting, carrying on or transacting business in this state under an assumed or fictitious name or designation on July 1, 1969, shall within 30 days after July 1, 1969, file the certificate required by NRS 602.010.

(Added to NRS by 1969, 68)

NRS 602.017 Adoption of fictitious name including "Corporation," "Corp.," "Incorporated" or "Inc."

1. No person may adopt any fictitious name which includes "Corporation," "Corp.," "Incorporated," or "Inc." in its title, unless that person is a corporation organized or qualified to do business pursuant to the laws of this state.

2. No county clerk may accept for filing a certificate which violates any provision of this chapter.

(Added to NRS by 1981, 240)

NRS 602.020 Contents and requirements of certificate.

1. The certificate must state the assumed or fictitious name under which the business is being conducted or is intended to be conducted, and if conducted by:

(a) A natural person, his full name and street address, either residence or business;

(b) An artificial person required to make annual filings with the secretary of state to retain its good standing, its name as it appears in the records of the secretary of state;

(c) A general partnership, the full name and street address, either residence or business, of each partner who is a natural person, and if one or more of the partners is an artificial person described in subsection (b), the information required by subsection (b) for each such partner; or

(d) A trust, the full name and street address, either residence or business, of each trustee of the trust.

2. The certificate must be signed:

(a) In the case of a natural person, by him;

(b) In the case of an artificial person required to make annual filings with the secretary of state to retain its good standing, by a person required to sign the annual filing;

(c) In the case of a general partnership, by each of the partners who is a natural person,

and if one or more of the partners is an artificial person described in subsection (b), by an officer of the corporation or an authorized representative of the artificial person; or

(d) In the case of a trust, by each of the trustees.

[Part 1:156:1923; NCL § 4450] + [2:156:1923; NCL § 4451]—(NRS A 1969, 67; 1993, 1022)

NRS 602.030 Time for filing certificate. The certificate must be filed no later than 1 month after the commencement of business under an assumed or fictitious name.

[Part 3:156:1923; NCL § 4452]— (NRS A 1969, 67; 1973, 545; 1993, 1023)

NRS 602.040 Filing of new certificate. On every change in the partners of a general partnership or trustee of a trust doing business under an assumed or fictitious name, a new certificate containing the information required by NRS 602.020 must be filed with the county clerk within 1 month after such change.

[4:156:1923; NCL § 4453]— (NRS A 1973, 545; 1993, 1023)

NRS 602.050 Index of fictitious names: Maintenance by county clerk; contents. Every county clerk shall keep, in alphabetical order, in a book or other suitable index provided for that purpose:

1. A register of all the names of the corporations, businesses, or fanciful or fictitious designations, as shown in the certificates.

2. Unless it is a corporation, the name of each person shown to be interested in or a partner in such a business.

[5:156:1923; A 1955, 16]—(NRS A 1969, 67; 1977, 468; 1981, 1795; 1991, 1323)

NRS 602.055 Certificate of termination.

1. Any person who has filed a certificate may, upon the termination of the business or his ownership in it, file with the county clerk where the certificate is on file a certificate of termination stating that the person who filed the certificate has terminated the business being conducted under the assumed or fictitious name or his ownership in it and the date of the termination.

2. The certificate of termination must be signed in the same manner as required by NRS 602.020, except that it is sufficient if signed in the case of a general partnership by

only one partner or in the case of a trust by only one trustee.

3. Upon the filing of a certificate of termination, the county clerk shall note the termination in the book or other suitable index required by NRS 602.050.

(Added to NRS by 1993, 1021)

NRS 602.060 Certified copies of certificate and register entries prima facie evidence. A copy of the certificate so filed and copies of the entries in the county clerk's register, when duly certified by the county clerk as true and correct, shall be prima facie evidence of the facts stated therein and admissible in evidence in all courts of this state.

[6:156:1923; NCL § 4455]

NRS 602.070 Commencement of action barred when certificate not filed. No action may be commenced or maintained by any person, mentioned in NRS 602.010, or by an assignee of such a person, upon or on account of any contract made or transaction had under the assumed or fictitious name, or upon or on account

of any cause of action arising or growing out of the business conducted under that name, unless before the commencement of the action the certificate required by NRS 602.010 has been filed.

[7:156:1923; A 1925, 44; NCL § 4456]—(NRS A 1969, 68; 1973, 545; 1993, 1023)

NRS 602.080 Applicability of chapter to certain partnerships.

1. Partnerships which were engaged in business before March 20, 1923, and which had complied with the provisions of chapter 40, Statutes of Nevada 1887, are not required to comply with the provisions of this chapter except as to subsequent changes in membership of the partnerships.

2. Limited partnerships formed and foreign limited partnerships registered pursuant to chapter 88 of NRS are not required to comply with the provisions of this chapter.

[10:156:1923; NCL § 4459]— (NRS A 1969, 68; 1973, 546; 1987, 376)

NRS 602.090 Penalty. A person doing business in this state without complying with the requirements of this chapter or having falsely filed a certificate of termination, is guilty of a misdemeanor.

[8:156:1923; NCL § 4457]— (NRS A 1969, 68; 1993, 1023)

APPENDIX J: NEVADA SECRETARY OF STATE FEES AND SERVICES SCHEDULES

DEAN HELLER
Secretary of State

101 North Carson Street, Suite 3
Carson City, Nevada 89701-4786
Phone: (775) 684 5708

FEE SCHEDULE
(Effective 10/1/95)

INITIAL FILING FEE FOR PROFIT CORPORATIONS:
(Fee based on the value of the total number of authorized shares stated in the Articles of Incorporation)

$25,000 or less..	$125.00
$25,001 and not over $75,000..	$175.00
$75,001 and not over $200,000..	$225.00
$200,001 and not over $500,000..	$325.00
$500,001 and not over $1,000,000...	$425.00
For the first $1,000,000...	$425.00
For each additional $500,000...	$225.00
Maximum fee...	$25,000.00

For the purpose of computing the filing fee, the value (capital) represented by the total number of shares authorized in the Articles of Incorporation is determined by computing the:

    (a) total authorized shares multiplied by their par value or;
    (b) total authorized shares without par value multiplied by $1.00 or;
    (c) the sum of (a) and (b) above if both par and no par shares.

Filing fees are calculated on a minimum par value of one-tenth of a cent (.001), regardless if the stated par value is less.

INITIAL FILING FEE FOR NON PROFIT CORPORATIONS WITHOUT STOCK: $25.00

INITIAL FILING FEE FOR LIMITED LIABILITY COMPANIES: $125.00

INITIAL FILING FEE FOR LIMITED PARTNERSHIPS: $125.00

INITIAL FILING FEE FOR LIMITED LIABILITY PARTNERSHIPS: $125.00

MISCELLANEOUS FOR PROFIT FEES:			
Certificate of Amendment, minimum fee	$75.00	Certification of documents – per certification	$10.00
Certificate pursuant to NRS 78.209, minimum fee	$75.00	Preclearance of any document	$100.00
Certificate pursuant to NRS 78.1955	$75.00	Miscellaneous filings	$20.00
Restated Articles , minimum fee	$75.00		
Certificate of Correction, minimum fee	$75.00		
Mergers/Articles of Exchange	$125.00	**MISCELLANEOUS NON PROFIT FEES:**	
Notice of Cancellation	$30.00	Non profit – Certificate of Amendment/Correction	$25.00
Certificate/Articles of Dissolution	$30.00	Non profit – List of Officers and Directors	$15.00
Notice of Withdrawal	$30.00	Non profit – Late fee on Annual List	$ 5.00
List of Officers, Directors and Resident Agent	$85.00	Non profit – Certificate of Dissolution	$25.00
Late fee on List	$15.00	Non profit – Reinstatement	$25.00
Change of Resident Agent/address/records office	$15.00		
Resignation of Resident Agent	$20.00	All other fees, unless otherwise denoted by statute, are the	
Reinstatement	$50.00	same as those for profit business entities.	
Name reservation	$20.00		

NOTICE: _Filings not accompanied by adequate fees for services requested will be returned unfiled._

State of Nevada
Secretary of State
101 North Carson Street, Suite 3
Carson City, Nevada 89701-4786

Phone: (775) 684 5708

COPIES AND CERTIFICATION SERVICES FEE SCHEDULE

The following is a list of copies and certification services and the associated fees. Fees are per document unless otherwise noted.

SERVICE REQUESTED:

Copies..	$1.00 per page
Certification of Document..	$10.00
Certificates:	
Certificate of Existence (evidence of good standing – short form).............	$15.00
Certificate of Existence (listing amendments – long form).....................	$20.00
Certificate Evidencing Name Change....................................	$15.00
Certificate of Fact of Merger...	$20.00
Certificate of Default..	$20.00
Certificate of Revocation..	$20.00
Certificate of Dissolution...	$20.00
Certificate of Withdrawal..	$20.00
Certificate of Cancellation..	$20.00
Certificate of Non-Existence..	$20.00
Miscellaneous Certificates..	$20.00
Apostille (Hague Treaty Nations)/Certification (Non-Hague Treaty Nations)...	$20.00
Exemplification...	$20.00

EXPEDITE SERVICE:

Expedite service is available for copies, certificate and certification services. Fees for expedite service are in addition to the fees as listed above.

24 Hour Expedite Service: Order may be picked up or mailed out within 24-hours.

Copies:	
1 to 10 pages..	$25.00
11 to 100 pages..	$50.00
100 or more pages..	$75.00

Certificates (per entity name):	
1 to 10 certificates..	$25.00
11 to 20 certificates...	$50.00
21 to 30 certificates...	$75.00
31 or more certificates...	$100.00

4-Hour Expedite Service: Order may be picked up or mailed within 4-hours.

CERTIFICATES ONLY (per entity name):	
1 to 10 certificates..	$50.00
11 or more certificates...	$100.00

BASIC INSTRUCTIONS:

1. All orders may be received in writing with fees enclosed at the above address. Telephone orders with payment by VISA or Mastercard may be called into our Customer Service Department at (775)684-5708. Trust account and credit card customers may fax *expedite orders only* to (775)684-5645. Trust account orders must be received on company letterhead.

2. Other than orders specified as a pick-up, all orders are mailed out via first-class mail, unless a prepaid envelope, express mail number or Federal Express number is provided.

3. We *do not* fax orders back to customers. Each order will be returned to one address only.

Nevada Secretary of State Form COPIES1999.01
Revised on: 02/12/99

State of Nevada
Secretary of State
101 North Carson Street, Suite 3
Carson City, Nevada 89701-4786

Phone: (775) 684 5708

SPECIAL SERVICES
24-HOUR
EXPEDITE SERVICE

IMPORTANT: To ensure expedited service, please mark "Expedite" in a conspicuous place at top of the service request. Please indicate method of delivery.

EXPEDITE SERVICE:

The Secretary of State offers a 24-hour expedite service on most filings processed by this office. If you choose to utilize the 24-hour expedite service, please enclose with your filing an additional $50.00 per filing and/or order. Please note that this expedite fee is in addition to the standard filing fee charged on each filing and/or order.

EXPEDITE FEES:

The expedite fee for most services provided by the Secretary of State of State is $50.00 per filing. There are, however, several services that have different expedite fees. The main filings and the associated expedite fees are as follows:

Articles of Incorporation	$50.00
Articles of Organization, Limited Liability Companies	$50.00
Articles of Organization, Limited Liability Partnerships	$50.00
Certificate of Limited Partnership	$50.00
Foreign Qualifications	$50.00
Amendments and Mergers	$50.00
Reinstatement	$50.00
Preclearance of any document	$50.00
Apostilles	$25.00
Certificate of Good Standing	$25.00
Annual Lists and late lists	$25.00
Name Reservation	$10.00
Resident Agent Changes	$10.00
Resident Agent Resignation	$10.00

For information regarding the expedite fee for services not listed above, please call this office at (775)684-5708.

TIME CONSTRAINTS:

Each filing submitted receives same day filing date and may be picked up within 24 hours. Filings to be mailed will be mailed out no later than the next business day following receipt.

Expedite period begins when filing or service request is received in this office in fileable form.

The Secretary of State reserves the right to extend the expedite period in times of extreme volume, staff shortages, or equipment malfuction. These extensions are few and will rarely extend more than a few hours.

DEAN HELLER
Secretary of State

200 North Carson Street,
Carson City, Nevada 89701-4201
Phone: (775) 684 5708

UNIFORM COMMERCIAL CODE FILINGS FEE SCHEDULE

The following is a list of Uniform Commercial Code services and the associated fees. Fees are per document unless otherwise noted.

SERVICE REQUESTED:

UCC-1 Financing Statement or National Form	$15.00
UCC-2 Any changes to an existing filing including continuation, release, assignment, amendment, termination, etc.	$15.00
UCC-3 Information requested or Federal Tax Lien Search (one per form)......................	$15.00
(Use only one debtor name, spouse. D.B.A. or tradename per form)	
One Page Security Agreement..	$20.00
Federal Tax Lien Filing, Federal Tax Lien Release Filings, Corrections on Federal Tax Liens or Federal Tax Lien Re-Fillings (one per form)	$20.00
National Form UCC-2 Change Form or UCC-3 Search Form...............................	$20.00

NOTE: If you choose not to use UCC filing forms approved by the Secretary of State Dean Heller or fail to submit all copies of the forms, the fee for UCC-1, UCC 2, and UCC-3 is $20.00

ADDITIONAL FEES FOR UCC-1 AND UCC-2 FILINGS:

Attachments (per page)..	$1.00
Additional pages to Security Agreement (per page).................................	$1.00
Additional debtor name, spouse, D.B.A., tradenames, etc. (each)	$1.00
Copies (per page)...	$1.00

SECURED PARTY SEARCHES:

Debtor or Secured Party Search (using Nevada form).................................	$15.00
Debtor or Secured Party Search (using non-Nevada form)	$20.00

Access charges by the Nevada Department of Information Services. Please call the UCC Division at (775)684-5708 for further information.

24 Hour Expedite Service: *Order may be picked up or mailed out within 24-hours.*

For an extra charge, 24 hour expedite service (excluding mail time) is available for any UCC filing.

Expedite fee for UCC-1, UCC-2, UCC-3..	$25.00
Expedite fee for 1-10 Copies	$25.00
Expedite fee for 11-99 Copies..	$50.00
Expedite fee for 100 or more Copies..	$75.00

1. Other than orders specified as a pick-up, all orders are mailed out via first-class mail, unless a prepaid envelope, express mail number or Federal Express number is provided.

2. We *do not* fax orders back to customers.

APPENDIX K: TEMPLATE ARTICLES OF INCORPORATION

ARTICLES OF INCORPORATION OF

ABC CORPORATION

FIRST. The name of the corporation is: ABC CORPORATION

SECOND. The resident agent for this corporation shall be:

The address of said agent, and the principal or statutory address of this corporation in the State of Nevada, shall be _____, located in _____ County, State of Nevada. This corporation may maintain an office, or offices, in such other place or places within or without the State of Nevada as may be from time to time designated by the Board of Directors, or by the bylaws of said corporation, and that this corporation may conduct all corporation business of every kind and nature, including the holding of all meetings of directors and stockholders, outside the State of Nevada as well as within the State of Nevada.

THIRD. The objects for which this corporation is formed are as follows: to engage in any lawful activity.

FOURTH. That the total number of voting common stock authorized that may be issued by the corporation is TWENTY FIVE THOUSAND (25,000) shares of stock with NO par value, and no other class of stock shall be authorized. Said shares may be issued by the corporation from time to time for such considerations as may be fixed from time to time by the Board of Directors.

FIFTH. The governing board of this corporation shall be known as directors, and the number of directors may from time to time be increased or decreased in such manner as shall be provided by the bylaws of this corporation, providing that the number of directors shall not be reduced to less than one (1). The name and post office address of the first Board of Directors shall be one (1) in number and listed as follows:

Name: _____

Address: _____

_____

SIXTH. The capital stock, after the amount of the subscription price, or par value, has been paid in, shall not be subject to assessment to pay the debts of the corporation.

SEVENTH. The name and post office address of the Incorporator signing the Articles of Incorporation is as follows:

Name: _____

Address: _____

EIGHTH. The corporation is to have perpetual existence.

NINTH. No director or officer of the corporation shall be personally liable to the corporation or any of its stockholders for damages for breach of fiduciary duty as a director or officer or for any act or omission of any such director or officer; however, the foregoing provision shall not eliminate or limit the liability of a director or officer for (a) acts or omissions which involve intentional misconduct, fraud or a knowing violation of law; or (b) the payment of dividends in violation of Section 78.300 of the Nevada Revised Statutes. Any repeal or modification of this Article by the stockholders of the corporation shall be prospective only and shall not adversely affect any limitation on the personal liability of a director or officer of the corporation for acts or omissions prior to such repeal or modification.

TENTH. This corporation reserves the right to amend, alter, change or repeal any provision contained in the Articles of Incorporation, in the manner now or hereafter prescribed by statute, or by the Articles of Incorporation, and all rights conferred upon stockholders herein are granted subject to this reservation.

I, THE UNDERSIGNED, being the Incorporator hereinbefore named for the purpose of forming a corporation pursuant to the General Corporation Laws of the State of Nevada, do make and file these Articles of Incorporation, hereby declaring and certifying that the facts herein stated are true, and accordingly have hereunto set my hand this _____.

_____

Incorporator Signature

_____

Incorporator Name Print

STATE OF   )
) SS:
COUNTY OF   )

On this _____, 19____ in _____, _____ County, State of _____, before me, the undersigned, a Notary Public in and for the aforementioned city, county and state, personally appeared _____, known to me, or proven to be to my satisfaction the person whose name is subscribed to the foregoing document and acknowledged to me that he/she executed the same.

_____

Notary Public

APPENDIX L: SAMPLE BYLAWS

BY-LAWS

OF

ABC CORPORATION

A Nevada Corporation

1. SHAREHOLDER'S MEETINGS

1.1. **TIME.** An annual meeting for the election of directors and for the transaction of any other proper business and any special meeting shall be held on the date and at the time as the Board of Directors shall from time to time fix.

1.2. **PLACE.** Annual meetings and special meetings shall be held at such place, within or without the State of Nevada, as the Directors may, from time to time, fix. Whenever the directors shall fail to fix such place, the meetings shall be held at the principal executive office of the corporation.

1.3. **CALL.** Annual meetings may be called by the Directors, by the Chairman of the Board, if any, Vice Chairman of the Board, if any, the President, if any, the Secretary, or by any officer instructed by the Directors to call the meeting. Special meetings may be called in like manner and by the holders of shares entitled to cast not less than ten percent (10%) of the votes at the meeting being called.

1.4. **NOTICE.** Written notice stating the place, day and hour of each meeting, and, in the case of a special meeting, the general nature of the business to be transacted or, in the case of an Annual Meeting, those matters which the Board of Directors, at the time of mailing of the notice, intends to present for action by the shareholders, shall be given not less than ten days (or not less than any such other minimum period of days as may be prescribed by the Nevada Revised Statutes) or more than sixty days (or more than any such maximum period of days as may be prescribed by the Nevada Revised Statutes) before the date of the meeting, by mail, personally, or by other means of written communication, charges prepaid by or at the direction of the Directors, the President, if any, the Secretary or the officer or persons calling the meeting, addressed to each shareholder at his address appearing on the books of the corporation or given by him to the corporation for the purpose of notice, or, if no such address appears or is given, at the place where the principal executive office of the corporation is located or by publication at least once in a newspaper of general circulation in the county in which the said principal executive office is located. Such notice shall be deemed to be delivered when deposited in the United States mail with first class postage therein prepaid, or sent by other means of written communication addressed to the shareholder at his address as it appears on the stock transfer books of the corporation. The notice of any meeting at which directors are to be elected shall include the names of nominees intended at the time of notice to be presented by management for election. At an annual meeting of shareholders, any matter relating to the affairs of the corporation, whether or not stated in the notice of the meeting, may be brought up for action except matters which the Nevada Revised Statutes requires to be stated in the notice of the meeting. The notice of any annual or special meeting shall also include, or be accompanied by, any additional statements, information, or documents prescribed by the Nevada Revised Statutes. When a meeting is adjourned to another time or place, notice of the adjourned meeting need not be given if the time and place thereof are announced at the meeting at which the adjournment is taken; provided that, if after the adjournment a new record date is fixed for the adjourned meeting, a notice of the adjourned meeting shall be given to each shareholder. At the adjourned meeting, the corporation may transact any business which might have been transacted at the original meeting.

1.5. **CONSENT.** The transaction of any meeting, however called and noticed, and wherever held, shall be as valid as though had at a meeting duly held after regular call and notice, if a quorum is present and if, either before or after the meeting, each of the shareholders or his proxy signs a written waiver of notice or a consent to the holding of the meeting or an approval of the minutes thereof. All such waivers, consents and approvals shall be filed with the corporate records or made a part of the minutes of the meeting. Attendance of a person at a meeting constitutes a waiver of notice of such meeting, except when the person objects, at the beginning of the meeting, to the transaction of any business because the meeting is not lawfully called or convened and except that attendance at a meeting shall not constitute a waiver of any right to object to the consideration of matters required by the Nevada Revised Statutes to be included in the notice if such objection is expressly made at the meeting. Except as otherwise provided in theNevada Revised Statutes, neither the business to be transacted at nor the purpose of any regular or special meeting need be specified in any written waiver of notice.

1.6. CONDUCT OF MEETING. Meetings of the shareholders shall be presided over by one of the following officers in the order of seniority and if present and acting: the Chairman of the Board, if any, the Vice-Chairman of the Board, if any, the President, if any, a Vice President, or, if none of the foregoing is in office and present and acting, by a chairman to be chosen by the shareholders. The Secretary of the corporation, or in his absence, an Assistant Secretary, shall act as secretary of every meeting, but, if neither the Secretary nor an Assistant Secretary is present, the Chairman of the meeting shall appoint a secretary of the meeting.

1.7. PROXY REPRESENTATION. Every shareholder may authorize another person or persons to act as his proxy at a meeting or by written action. No proxy shall be valid after the expiration of eleven months from the date of its execution unless otherwise provided in the proxy. Every proxy shall be revocable at the pleasure of the person executing it prior to the vote or written action pursuant thereto, except as otherwise provided by the General Corporation Law. As used herein, a "proxy" shall be deemed to mean a written authorization signed by a shareholder or a shareholder's attorney in fact giving another person or persons power to vote or consent in writing with respect to the shares of such shareholder, and "Signed" as used herein shall be deemed to mean the placing of such shareholder's name on the proxy, whether by manual signature, typewriting, telegraphic transmission or otherwise by such shareholder or such shareholder's attorney in fact. Where applicable, the form of any proxy shall comply with the provisions of Nevada Revised Statutes.

1.8. INSPECTORS - APPOINTMENT. In advance of any meeting, the Board of Directors may appoint inspectors of election to act at the meeting and any adjournment thereof. If inspectors of election are not so appointed, or, if any persons so appointed fail to appear or refuse to act, the Chairman of any meeting of shareholders may, and on the request of any shareholder or a shareholder's proxy shall, appointment inspectors of election, or persons to replace any of those who so fail or refuse, at the meeting. The number of inspectors shall be either one or three. If appointed at a meeting on the request of one or more shareholders or proxies, the majority of shares represented shall determine whether one or three inspectors are to be appointed.

    1.8.1. The inspectors of election shall determine the number of shares outstanding and the voting power of each, the shares represented at the meeting the existence of a quorum, the authenticity, validity, and effect of proxies, receive votes, ballots, if any, or consents, hear and determine all challenges and questions in any way arising in connection with the right to vote, count and tabulate all votes or consents, determine when the polls shall close, determine the result, and do such acts as may be proper to conduct the election or vote with fairness to all shareholders. If there are three inspectors of election, the decision, act, or certificate of a majority shall be effective in all respects as the decisions, act, or certificate of all.

1.9. SUBSIDIARY CORPORATIONS. Shares of this corporation owned by a subsidiary shall not be entitled to vote on any matter. A subsidiary for these purposes is defined as a corporation, the shares of which possessing more than twenty five percent (25%) of the total combined voting power of all classes of shares entitled to vote, are owned directly or indirectly through one or more subsidiaries.

1.10. QUORUM; VOTE; WRITTEN CONSENT. At all meetings of the stockholders, each stockholder shall be entitled to one vote for each share of stock in his own name on the books of the corporation, whether represented in person or by proxy. The holders of a majority of the voting shares shall constitute a quorum at a meeting of shareholders for the transaction of any business. The shareholders present at a duly called or held meeting at which a quorum is present may continue to do business until adjournment notwithstanding the withdrawal of enough shareholders to leave less than a quorum if any action taken, other than adjournment, is approved by at least a majority of the shares required to constitute a quorum. In the absence of a quorum, any meeting of shareholders may be adjourned from time to time by the vote of a majority of the shares represented thereat, but no other business may be transacted except as hereinbefore provided.

1.10.1.   In the election of directors, a plurality of the votes cast shall elect. No shareholder shall be entitled to exercise the right of cumulative voting at a meeting for the election of directors unless the candidate's name or the candidates' names have been placed in nomination prior to the voting and the shareholder has given notice at the meeting prior to the voting of the shareholder's intention to cumulate the shareholder's votes. If any one shareholder has given such notice, all shareholders may cumulate their votes for such candidates in nomination.

1.10.2.   Except as otherwise provided by the General Corporation Law, the Articles of Incorporation or these By-Laws, any action required or permitted to be taken at a meeting at which a quorum is present shall be authorized by the affirmative vote of a majority of the shares represented at the meeting.

1.10.3.   Except in the election of directors by written consent in lieu of a meeting, and except as may otherwise be provided by the Nevada Revised Statutes, the Articles of Incorporation or these By-Laws, any action which may be taken at any annual or special meeting may be taken without a meeting and without prior notice, if a consent in writing, setting forth the action so taken, shall be signed by holders of shares having not less than the minimum number of votes that would be necessary to authorize or take such action at a meeting at which all shares entitled to vote thereon were present and voted. Directors may not be elected by written consent except by unanimous written consent of all share entitled to vote for the election of directors. Notice of any shareholder approval pursuant to Nevada Revised Statutes (NRS) without a meeting by less than unanimous written consent shall be given at least ten days before the consummation of the action authorized by such approval, and prompt notice shall be given of the taking of any other corporate action approved by shareholders without a meeting by less than unanimous written consent to those shareholders entitled to vote who have not consented in writing.

1.11. BALLOT. Elections of directors at a meeting need not be by ballot unless a shareholder demands election by ballot at the election and before the voting begins. In all other matters, voting need not be by ballot.

1.12. SHAREHOLDERS' AGREEMENTS. Notwithstanding the above provisions, in the event this corporation elects to become a close corporation, an agreement between two or more shareholders thereof, if in writing and signed by the parties thereof, may provide that in exercising any voting rights the shares held by them shall be voted as provided therein or in NRS, and may otherwise modify these provisions as to shareholders' meetings and actions.

2. BOARD OF DIRECTORS

2.1. FUNCTIONS. The business and affairs of the corporation shall be managed and all corporate powers shall be exercised by or under the direction of its Board of Directors. The Board of Directors may delegate the management of the day-to-day operation of the business of the corporation to a management company or other person, provided that the business and affairs of the corporation shall be managed and all corporate powers shall be exercised under the ultimate direction of the Board of Directors. The Board of Directors shall have authority to fix the compensation of directors for services in any lawful capacity.

2.1.1.   Each director shall exercise such powers and otherwise perform such duties in good faith, in the manner such director believes to be in the best interests of the corporation, and with care, including reasonable inquiry, using ordinary prudence, as a person in a like position would use under similar circumstances.

2.2. EXCEPTION FOR CLOSE CORPORATION. Notwithstanding the provisions of Section 1, in the event that this corporation shall elect to become a close corporation as defined in NRS, its shareholders may enter into a Shareholders' Agreement as provided in NRS. Said Agreement may provide for the exercise of corporate powers and the management of the business and affairs of this corporation by the shareholders, provided however such agreement shall, to the extent and so long as the discretion or the powers of the Board in its management of corporate affairs is controlled by such agreement, impose upon each shareholder who is a party thereof, liability for managerial acts performed or omitted by such person pursuant thereto otherwise imposed upon Directors as provided in NRS.

2.3. QUALIFICATION AND NUMBER. A director need not be a shareholder of the corporation, a citizen of the United States, or a resident of the State of Nevada. The authorized number of directors constituting the Board of Directors until further changed shall be [NUMBER OF DIRECTORS]. Thereafter, the authorized number of directors constituting the Board shall be at least three (3) provided that, whenever the corporation shall have only two shareholder, the number of directors may be at least two, and whenever the corporation shall have only one shareholder, the number of directors may be at least one. Subject to the foregoing provisions, the number of directors may be changed from time to time by an amendment of these By-Laws adopted by the shareholders. Any such amendment reducing the number of directors to fewer than five cannot be adopted if the votes cast against its adoption at a meeting or the shares not consenting in writing in the case of action by written consent are equal to more than sixteen and two-third percent of the outstanding shares. No decrease in the authorized number of directors shall have the effect of shortening the term of any incumbent director.

2.4. ELECTION AND TERM. The initial Board of Directors shall consist of the persons elected at the meeting of the incorporator, all of whom shall hold office until the first annual meeting of shareholders and until their successors have been elected and qualified, or until their earlier resignation or removal from office. Thereafter, directors who are elected to replace any or all of the members of the initial Board of Directors or who are elected at an annual meeting of shareholders, and directors who are elected in the interim to fill vacancies, shall hold office until the next annual meeting of shareholders and until their successors have been elected and qualified, or until their earlier resignation, removal from office, or death. In the interim between annual meetings of shareholders or of special meetings of shareholders called for the election of directors, any vacancies in the Board of Directors, including vacancies resulting from an increase in the authorized number of directors which have not been filled by the shareholders, including any other vacancies which the General Corporation Law authorizes directors to fill, and including vacancies resulting from the removal of directors which are not filled at the meeting of shareholders at which any such removal has been effected, if the Articles of Incorporation or a By-Law adopted by the shareholders so provides, may be filled by the vote of a majority of the directors then in office of the sole remaining director, although less than a quorum exists. Any director may resign effective upon giving written notice to the Chairman of the Board, if any, the President, the Secretary or the Board of Directors, unless the notice specifies a later time for the effectiveness of such resignation. If the resignation is effective at a future time, a successor may be elected to the office when the resignation becomes effective.

2.4.1. The shareholders may elect a director at any time to fill any vacancy which the directors are entitled to fill, but which they have not filled. Any such election by written consent shall require the consent of a majority of the shares.

2.5. INDEMNIFICATION OF DIRECTORS, OFFICERS, EMPLOYEES AND AGENTS. The corporation may indemnify any Director, Officer, agent or employee as to those liabilities and on those terms and conditions as are specified in NRS. In any event, the corporation shall have the right to purchase and maintain insurance on behalf of any such persons whether or not the corporation would have the power to indemnify such person against the liability insured against.

2.6. MEETINGS.

2.6.1. TIME. Meetings shall be held at such time as the Board shall fix, except that the first meeting of a newly elected Board shall be held as soon after its election as the directors may conveniently assemble.

2.6.2. PLACE. Meetings may be held at any place, within or without the State of Nevada, which has been designated in any notice of the meeting, or, if not stated in said notice, or, if there is no notice given, at the place designated by resolution of the Board of Directors.

2.6.3. CALL. Meetings may be called by the Chairman of the Board, if any and acting, by the Vice Chairman of the Board, if any, by the President, if any, by any Vice President or Secretary, or by any two directors.

2.6.4. ORDER OF BUSINESS. At all meetings of stockholders and directors the following shall be the order of business so far as is practicable:

2.6.4.1. Calling the roll

2.6.4.2. Reading, correcting, and approving of the minutes of the previous meeting R

2.6.4.3. Reports of officers

2.6.4.4. Reports of committees

2.6.4.5. Unfinished business

2.6.4.6. New business

2.6.4.7. Election of Directors (for stockholders)

2.6.4.8.　　　　Election of Officers (for directors)

2.6.4.9.　　　　Miscellaneous business

2.6.5.　　　NOTICE AND WAIVER THEREOF. No notice shall be required for regular meetings for which the time and place has been fixed by the Board of Directors. Special meetings shall be held upon at least four days notice by mail or upon at least forty-eight hours notice delivered personally or by telephone or telegraph. Notice of a meeting need not be given to any director who signs a waiver of notice, whether before or after the meeting, or who attends the meeting without protesting, prior thereto or at its commencement, the lack of notice to such director. A notice or waiver of notice need not specify the purpose of any regular or special meeting of the Board of Directors.

2.7. SOLE DIRECTOR PROVIDED BY ARTICLES OF INCORPORATION. In the event only one Director is required by the By-Laws or Articles of Incorporation, then any reference herein to notices, waivers, consents, meetings or other actions by a majority or quorum of the directors shall be deemed to refer to such notice, waiver, etc., by such sole director, who shall have all the rights and duties and shall be entitled to exercise all of the powers and shall assume all the responsibilities otherwise herein described as given to a Board of Directors.

2.8. QUORUM AND ACTION. A majority of the authorized number of directors shall constitute a quorum except when a vacancy or vacancies prevents such majority, whereupon a majority of the directors in office shall constitute a quorum, provided such majority shall constitute at least either one-third of the authorized number of directors or at least two directors, whichever is larger, or unless the authorized number of directors is only one. A majority of the directors present, whether or not a quorum is present, may adjourn any meeting to another time and place. If the meeting is adjourned for more than twenty-four hours, notice of any adjournment to another time or place shall be given prior to the time of the adjourned meeting to the directors, if any, who were not present at the time of the adjournment. Except as the Articles of Incorporation, these By-Laws and the General Corporation Law may otherwise provide, the act or decision done or made by a majority of the directors present at a meeting duly held at which a quorum is present shall be the act of the Board of Directors. Members of the Board of Directors may participate in a meeting through use of conference telephone or similar communications equipment, so long as all members participating in such meeting can hear one another, and participation by such use shall be deemed to constitute presence in person at any such meeting.

2.8.1.　　　A meeting at which a quorum is initially present may continue to transact business notwithstanding the withdrawal of directors, provided that any action which may be taken is approved by at least a majority of the required quorum for such meeting.

2.9. CHAIRMAN OF THE MEETING. The Chairman of the Board, if any and if present and acting, the Vice Chairman of the Board, if any and if present and acting, shall preside at all meetings. Otherwise, the President, if any and present and acting, or any director chosen by the Board, shall preside.

2.10. REMOVAL OF DIRECTORS. The entire Board of Directors or any individual director may be removed from office without cause by approval of the holders of at least a majority of the shares provided, that unless the entire Board is removed, an individual director shall not be removed when the votes cast against such removal, or not consenting in writing to such removal, would be sufficient to elect such director if voted cumulatively at an election of directors at which the same total number of votes were cast, or, if such action is taken by written consent, in lieu of a meeting, all shares entitled to vote were voted, and the entire number of directors authorized at the time of the director's most recent election were then being elected. If any or all directors are so removed, new directors may be elected at the same meeting or by such written consent. The Board of Directors may declare vacant the office of any director who has been declared of unsound mind by an order of court or convicted of a felony.

2.11. COMMITTEES. The Board of Directors, by resolution adopted by a majority of the authorized number of directors, may designate one or more committees, each consisting of two or more directors to serve at the pleasure of the Board of Directors. The Board of Directors may designate one or more directors as alternate members of any such committee, who may replace any absent member at any meeting of such committee. Any such committee, to the extent provided in the resolution of the Board of Directors, shall have all the authority of the Board of Directors except such authority as may not be delegated by the provisions of the General Corporation Law.

2.12. INFORMAL ACTION. The transactions of any meeting of the Board of Directors, however called and noticed or wherever held, shall be as valid as though had at a meeting duly held after regular call and notice, if a quorum is present and if, either before or after the meeting, each of the directors not present signs a written waiver of notice, a consent to holding the meeting, or an approval of the minutes thereof. All such waivers, consents, or approvals shall be filed with the corporate records or made a part of the minutes of the meeting.

2.13. WRITTEN ACTION. Any action required or permitted to be taken may be taken without a meeting if all of the members of the Board of Directors shall individually or collectively consent in writing to such action. Any such written consent or consents shall be filed with the minutes of the proceedings of the Board. Such action by written consent shall have the same force and effect as a unanimous vote of such directors.

3. OFFICERS

3.1. OFFICERS. The officers of the corporation shall be a Chairman of the Board, or a President, or both, a Secretary and a Chief Financial Officer. The corporation may also have, at the discretion of the Board of Directors, one or more Vice Presidents, one or more Assistant Secretaries and such other officers as may be appointed in accordance with the provisions of Section 3 of this Article. One person may hold two or more offices.

3.2. ELECTION. The officers of the corporation, except such officers as may be appointed in accordance with the provisions of Section 3 or Section 5 of this Article shall be chosen annually by the Board of Directors, and each shall hold his office until he shall resign or shall be removed or otherwise disqualified to serve, or his successor shall be elected and qualified.

3.3. SUBORDINATE OFFICERS, ETC. The Board of Directors may appoint such other officers as the business of the corporation may require, each of whom shall hold office for such period, have such authority and perform such duties as are provided in the By-Laws or as the Board of Directors may from time to time determine.

3.4. REMOVAL AND RESIGNATION. Any officer may be removed, either with or without cause, by a majority of the directors at the time in office, at any regular or special meeting of the Board, or, except in case of an officer chosen by the Board of Directors, by any officer upon whom such power of removal may be conferred by the Board of Directors.

3.4.1. Any Officer may resign at any time by giving written notice to the Board of Directors, or to the President, or to the Secretary of the corporation. Any such resignation shall take effect at the date of the receipt of such notice or at any later time specified therein; and, unless otherwise specified therein, the acceptance of such resignation shall not be necessary to make it effective.

3.5. VACANCIES. A vacancy in any office because of death, resignation, removal, disqualification or any other cause shall be filled in the manner prescribed in the By-Laws for regular appointments to such office.

3.5.1. In case the entire board of directors shall die or resign, any stockholder may call a special meeting in the same manner that the president may call such meetings, and directors for the unexpired term may be elected at such special meeting in the manner provided for their election at annual meetings.

3.6. CHAIRMAN OF THE BOARD. The Chairman of the Board, if there shall be such an officer, shall, if present, preside at all meetings of the Board of Directors, and exercise and perform such other powers and duties as may be from time to time assigned to him by the Board of Directors or prescribed by the By-Laws.

3.7. PRESIDENT. Subject to such supervisory powers, if any, as may be given by the Board of Directors to the Chairman of the Board, if there be such an officer, the President shall be the Chief Executive Officer of the corporation and shall, subject to the control of the Board of Directors, have general supervision, direction and control of the business and officers of the corporation. He shall preside at all meetings of the shareholders and in the absence of the Chairman of the Board, or if there be none, at all meetings of the Board of Directors. He shall be ex officio a member of all the standing committees, including the Executive Committee, if any, and shall have the general powers and duties of management usually vested in the office of President of a corporation, and shall have such other powers and duties as may be prescribed by the Board of Directors of the By-Laws.

3.8. VICE PRESIDENT. In the absence or disability of the President, the Vice Presidents, in order of their rank as fixed by the Board of Directors, or if not ranked, the Vice President designated by the Board of Directors, shall perform all the duties of the President, and when so acting shall have all the powers of, and be subject to, all the restrictions upon, the President. The Vice Presidents shall have such other powers and perform such other duties as from time to time may be prescribed for them respectively by the Board of Directors or the By-Laws.

3.9. SECRETARY. The Secretary shall keep, or cause to be kept, a book of minutes at the principal office or such other place as the Board of Directors may order, of all meetings of Directors and Shareholders, with the time and place of holding, whether regular or special, and if special, how authorized, the notice thereof given, the names of those present at Directors' meetings, the number of shares present or represented at Shareholders' meetings and the proceedings thereof.

3.9.1. The Secretary shall keep, or cause to be kept, at the principal office or at the office of the corporation's transfer agent, a share register, or duplicate share register, showing the names of the shareholders and their addresses; the number and classes of shares held by each; the number and date of certificates issued for the same; and the number and date of cancellation of every certificate surrendered for cancellation.

3.9.2. The Secretary shall give, or cause to be given, notice of all the meetings of the shareholders and of the Board of Directors required by the By-Laws or by law to be given, and he shall keep the seal of the corporation in safe custody, and shall have such other powers and perform such other duties as may be prescribed by the Board of Directors or by the By-Laws.

3.10. CHIEF FINANCIAL OFFICER. This officer shall keep and maintain, or cause to be kept and maintained in accordance with generally accepted accounting principles, adequate and correct accounts of the properties and business transactions of the corporation, including accounts of its assets, liabilities, receipts, disbursements, gains, losses, capital, earnings (or surplus) and shares. The books of account shall at all reasonable times be open to inspection by any Director.

3.10.1. This officer shall deposit all moneys and other valuables in the name and to the credit of the corporation with such depositaries as may be designated by the Board of Directors. He shall disburse the funds of the corporation as may be ordered by the Board of Directors, shall render to the President and Directors, whenever they request it, an account of all of his transactions and of the financial condition of the corporation, and shall have such other powers and perform such other duties as may be prescribed by the Board of Directors or the By-Laws.

3.11. RESIDENT AGENT. The resident agent shall be in charge of the corporation's registered or principal office in the state of Nevada, upon whom process against the corporation may be served and shall perform all duties as required of him by statute.

4. CERTIFICATES AND TRANSFERS OF SHARES

4.1. CERTIFICATES FOR SHARES. Each certificate for shares of the corporation shall set forth therein the name of the record holder of the shares represented thereby, the number of shares and the class or series of shares owned by said holder, the par value, if any, of the shares represented thereby, and such other statements, as applicable, prescribed by relevant Sections of the General Corporation Law of the State of Nevada (the "Nevada Revised Statutes") and such other statements, as applicable, which may be prescribed by the Corporate Securities Law of the State of Nevada and any other applicable provision of the law. Each such certificate issued shall be signed in the name of the corporation by the Chairman of the Board of Directors, if any, or the Vice Chairman of the Board of Directors, if any, the President, if any, or a Vice President, if any, and by the Chief Financial Officer or an Assistant Treasurer or the Secretary or an Assistant Secretary. Any or all of the signatures on a certificate for shares may be a facsimile. In case any officer, transfer agent or registrar who has signed or whose facsimile signature has been placed upon a certificate for shares shall have ceased to be such officer, transfer agent or registrar before such certificate is issued, it may be issued by the corporation with the same effect as if such person were an officer, transfer agent or registrar at the date of issue.

4.1.1. In the event that the corporation shall issue the whole or any part of its shares as partly paid and subject to call for the remainder of the consideration to be paid therefor, any such certificate for shares shall set forth thereon the statements prescribed by the General Corporation Law.

4.2. LOST OR DESTROYED CERTIFICATES FOR SHARES. The corporation may issue a new certificate for shares or for any other security in the place of any other certificate theretofore issued by it, which is alleged to have been lost, stolen or destroyed. As a condition to such issuance, the corporation may require any such owner of the allegedly lost, stolen or destroyed certificate or any such owner's legal representative to give the corporation a bond, or other adequate security, sufficient to indemnify it against any claim that may be made against it, including any expense or liability, on account of the alleged loss, theft or destruction of any such certificate or the issuance of such new certificate.

4.3. SHARE TRANSFERS. Upon compliance with any provisions of the General Corporation Law and/or the Corporate Securities Law of 1968 which may restrict the transferability of shares, transfers of shares of the corporation shall be made only on the record of shareholders of the corporation by the registered holder thereof, or by his attorney thereunto authorized by power of attorney duly executed and filed with the Secretary of the corporation or with a transfer agent or a registrar, if any, and on surrender of the certificate or certificates for such shares properly endorsed and the payment of all taxes, if any, due thereon.

4.4. RECORD DATE FOR SHAREHOLDERS. In order that the corporation may determine the shareholders entitled to notice of any meeting or to vote or be entitled to receive payment of any dividend or other distribution or allotment of any rights or entitled to exercise any rights in respect of any other lawful action, the Board of Directors may fix, in advance a record date, which shall not be more than sixty days or fewer than ten days prior to the date of such meeting or more than sixty days prior to any other action.

4.4.1.   If the Board of Directors shall not have fixed a record date as aforesaid, the record date for determining shareholders entitled to notice of or to vote at a meeting of shareholders shall be at the close of business on the business day next preceding the day on which notice is given, or, if notice is waived, at the close of business on the business day next preceding the day on which the meeting is held; the record date for determining shareholders entitled to give consent to corporate action in writing without a meeting, when no prior action by the Board of Directors has been taken, shall be the day on which the first written consent is given; and the record date for determining shareholders for any other purpose shall be at the close of business on the day on which the Board of Directors adopts the resolution relating thereto, or the sixtieth day prior to the day of such other action, whichever is later.

4.4.2.   A determination of shareholders of record entitled to notice of or to vote at a meeting of shareholder shall apply to any adjournment of the meeting unless the Board of Directors fixes a new record date for the adjourned meeting, but the Board of Directors shall fix a new record date if the meeting is adjourned for more than forty-five days from the date set for the original meeting.

4.4.3.   Except as may be otherwise provided by the General Corporation Law, shareholders on the record date shall be entitled to notice and to vote or to receive any dividend, distribution or allotment of rights or to exercise the rights, as the case may be, notwithstanding any transfer of any shares on the books of the corporation after the record date.

4.5. REPRESENTATION OF SHARES IN OTHER CORPORATIONS. Shares of other corporations standing in the name of this corporation may be voted or represented and all incidents thereto may be exercised on behalf of the corporation by the Chairman of the Board, the President or any Vice President or any other person authorized by resolution of the Board of Directors.

4.6. MEANING OF CERTAIN TERMS. As used in these By-Laws in respect of the right to notice of a meeting of shareholders or a waiver thereof or to participate or vote thereat or to assent or consent or dissent in writing in lieu of a meeting, as the case may be, the term "share" or "shares" or "shareholder" or "shareholders" refers to an outstanding share or shares and to a holder or holders of record or outstanding shares when the corporation is authorized to issue only one class of shares, and said reference is also intended to include any outstanding share or shares and any holder or holders of record of outstanding shares of any class upon which or upon whom the Articles of Incorporation confer such rights where there are two or more classes or series of shares or upon which or upon whom the General Corporation Law confers such rights notwithstanding that the Articles of Incorporation may provide for more than one class or series of shares, one or more of which are limited or denied such rights thereunder.

5. CORPORATE CONTRACTS AND INSTRUMENTS-HOW EXECUTED

5.1. The Board of Directors, except as in the By-Laws otherwise provided, may authorize any officer or officers, agent or agents, to enter into any contract or execute any instrument in the name of and on behalf of the corporation. Such authority may be general or confined to specific instances. Unless so authorized by the Board of Directors, no officer, agent or employee shall have any power or authority to bind the corporation by any contract or agreement, or to pledge its credit, or to render it liable for any purposes or any amount, except as provided in the NRS.

6. CONTROL OVER BY-LAWS

6.1. After the initial By-Laws of the corporation shall have been adopted by the incorporator or incorporators of the corporation, the By-Laws may be amended or repealed or new By-Laws may be adopted by the shareholders entitled to exercise a majority of the voting power or by the Board of Directors; provided, however, that the Board of Directors shall have no control over any By-Law which fixes or changes the authorized number of directors of the corporation; provided, further, than any control over the By-Laws herein vested in the Board of Directors shall be subject to the authority of the aforesaid shareholders to amend or repeal the By-Laws or to adopt new By-Laws; and provided further that any By-Law amendment or new By-Law which changes the minimum number of directors to fewer than five shall require authorization by the greater proportion of voting power of the shareholders as hereinbefore set forth.

7. BOOKS AND RECORDS - STATUTORY AGENT

7.1. RECORDS: STORAGE AND INSPECTION. The corporation shall keep at its principal executive office in the State of Nevada, or, if its principal executive office is not in the State of Nevada, the original or a copy of the By-Laws as amended to date, which shall be open to inspection by the shareholders at all reasonable times during office hours. If the principal executive office of the corporation is outside the State of Nevada, and, if the corporation has no principal business office in the State of Nevada, it shall upon request of any shareholder furnish a copy of the By-Laws as amended to date.

7.1.1.　　The corporation shall keep adequate and correct books and records of account and shall keep minutes of the proceedings of its shareholders, Board of Directors and committees, if any, of the Board of Directors. The corporation shall keep at its principal executive office, or at the office of its transfer agent or registrar, a record of its shareholders, giving the names and addresses of all shareholders and the number and class of shares held by each. Such minutes shall be in written form. Such other books and records shall be kept either in written form or in any other form capable of being converted into written form.

7.2. RECORD OF PAYMENTS. All checks, drafts, or other orders for payment of money, notes or other evidences of indebtedness, issued in the name of or payable to the corporation, shall be signed or endorsed by such person or persons and in such manner as shall be determined from time to time by resolution of the Board of Directors.

7.3. AGENT FOR SERVICE. The name of the agent for service of process within the State of Nevada is [AGENT FOR SERVICE OF PROCESS].

8. CERTIFICATE OF ADOPTION OF BY-LAWS

ADOPTION BY INCORPORATOR(S) OR FIRST DIRECTOR(S).

The undersigned person(s) appointed in the Articles of Incorporation to act as the Incorporator(s) or First Director(s) of the above-named corporation hereby adopt the same as the By-Laws of said corporation.

Executed on [DATE OF FIRST MEETING]

[INCORPORATOR/INITIAL DIRECTOR]

THIS IS TO CERTIFY:

That I am the duly-elected, qualified and acting Secretary of the above-named corporation; that the foregoing By-Laws were adopted as the By-Laws of said corporation on the date set forth above by the person(s) appointed in the Articles of Incorporation to act as the Incorporator(s) or First Director(s) of said corporation.

IN WITNESS WHEREOF, I have hereunto set my hand and affixed the corporate seal on [DATE OF FIRST MEETING].

[NAME OF SECRETARY], Secretary

[SEAL]

CERTIFICATE BY SECRETARY OF ADOPTION BY SHAREHOLDERS' VOTE.

THIS IS TO CERTIFY:

That I am the duly-elected, qualified and acting Secretary of the above named corporation and that the above and foregoing Code of By-Laws was submitted to the shareholders at their first meeting and held on the date set forth in the By-Laws and recorded in the minutes thereof, was ratified by the vote of shareholders entitled to exercise the majority of the voting power of said corporation.

IN WITNESS WHEREOF, I have hereunto set my hand on [DATE OF FIRST MEETING].

[NAME OF SECRETARY], Secretary

APPENDIX M: INITIAL LISTING OF OFFICERS, DIRECTORS AND RESIDENT AGENT

DEAN HELLER
Secretary of State

101 North Carson Street, Suite 3
Carson City, Nevada 89701-4786
(775) 684 5708

IMPORTANT: READ ALL INSTRUCTIONS CAREFULLY BEFORE COMPLETING FORM.

FILING DEADLINE: Pursuant to NRS 78.150 Initial List of Officers, Directors and Resident Agent form *MUST* be filed on or before the first day of the second month following filing date. Example: If corporation filed on October 15, 1999 list must be filed by December 1, 1999.

TYPE or PRINT the following information on the Initial List of Officers, Directors and Resident Agent Form:

1. The *FILE NUMBER* of the corporation.

2. The *NAME* of the corporation *EXACTLY* as it appears in the Articles of Incorporation.

3. The *DATE* of incorporation.

4. The *STATE, TERRITORY or COUNTRY* where the corporation is organized should be entered on the third line after the letter A and before the word CORPORATION.

5. The *FILING PERIOD* is the month and year of incorporation TO the month and year 12 months from that date. Example: if the incorporation date was 1/12/99 the filing period would be 1/1999 to 1/2000.

6. The names and addresses of the *RESIDENT AGENT, PRESIDENT, SECRETARY, TREASURER and DIRECTORS* should be entered in the boxes provided on the form.

7. The *SIGNATURE of an OFFICER*, including his/her title and date signed MUST be included in the areas provided at the bottom of the form.

8. Form and applicable *FEES and PENALTIES* must be returned to the Secretary of State.

ADDITIONAL FORMS may be obtained through our document-on-demand service at 800-583-9486, on our website at http://sos.state.nv.us or by calling 775-684-5708.

FILE STAMPED COPIES: If you wish to have the page 2 certificate file stamped and returned, enclose a *self-addressed stamped envelope.*

CERTIFIED COPIES: You *must* send in the number of copies you would like certified and returned to you in addition to the original list to be filed. A filing fee of $10.00 for each certification is required. Copies received without the required fee will be returned uncertified. The Secretary of State keeps the original filing.

EXPEDITE FEE: Filing may be expedited for an additional $25.00 fee.

NOTE: The Las Vegas Satellite Office will only accept *expedited* filings. Regular filings must be sent to the Carson City address.

Filing may be submitted at the office of the Secretary of State or by mail at the following addresses:

Secretary of State	**Secretary of State-Satellite Office**
Status Division	**Commercial Recordings Division**
101 N. Carson Street, Suite 3	**555 E. Washington Avenue, Suite 2900**
Carson City, NV 89701-4786	**Las Vegas, NV 89101**
775-684-5708 Fax 775-684-5725	**702-486-2880 Fax 702-486-2888**

(PROFIT) INITIAL LIST OF OFFICERS, DIRECTORS AND RESIDENT AGENT OF

FILE NUMBER

_____
(Name of Corporation)

_____
(Incorporation Date)

A _____ CORPORATION
(State of Incorporation)

FOR THE FILING PERIOD _____ TO _____

The corporation's duly appointed resident agent in the State of Nevada
upon whom process can be served is:

Office Use Only

Important: Read instructions before completing and returning this form.

1. Print or type names and addresses, either residence or business, for all officers and directors. **A president, secretary, treasurer and at least one director** must be named.
2. Have an officer sign the form. *FORM WILL BE RETURNED IF UNSIGNED.*
3. Return the completed form with the $85.00 filing fee. A $15.00 penalty must be added for failure to file this form by the 1st day of the 2nd month following incorporation date.
4. Make your check payable to the Secretary of State. Your cancelled check will constitute a certificate to transact business per NRS 78.155. If you need a receipt, return page 2 certificate and **ENCLOSE A SELF ADDRESSED STAMPED ENVELOPE.** To receive a certified copy, enclose a copy of this completed form, an additional $10.00 and appropriate instructions.
5. Return the completed form to: Secretary of State, 101 North Carson Street, Suite 3, Carson City, NV 89701-4786, (775) 684-5708.

FILING FEE: $85.00   LATE PENALTY: $15.00
THIS FORM MUST BE FILED BY THE 1ST DAY OF THE 2ND MONTH FOLLOWING INCORPORATION DATE

NAME	TITLE(S) **PRESIDENT**

PO BOX	STREET ADDDRESS	CITY	ST	ZIP

NAME	TITLE(S) **SECRETARY**

PO BOX	STREET ADDDRESS	CITY	ST	ZIP

NAME	TITLE(S) **TREASURER**

PO BOX	STREET ADDDRESS	CITY	ST	ZIP

NAME	TITLE(S) **DIRECTOR**

PO BOX	STREET ADDDRESS	CITY	ST	ZIP

NAME	TITLE(S) **DIRECTOR**

PO BOX	STREET ADDDRESS	CITY	ST	ZIP

NAME	TITLE(S) **DIRECTOR**

PO BOX	STREET ADDDRESS	CITY	ST	ZIP

I hereby certify this initial list.

X Signature of officer

Title(s)

Date

Nevada Secretary of State Form INITIAL LIST-PROFIT1999.0
Revised on: 01/11/0

APPENDIX N: QUALIFICATION TO DO BUSINESS IN NEVADA FORMS AND INSTRUCTIONS

DEAN HELLER
Secretary of State

101 North Carson Street, Suite 3
Carson City, Nevada 89701-4786
(775) 684 5708

Instructions For Qualification To Do Business In Nevada
(PURSUANT TO NRS 80)

<u>IMPORTANT: READ ALL INSTRUCTIONS CAREFULLY BEFORE COMPLETING FORM.</u>

Before commencing or doing any business in this state (see exceptions in NRS 80.015), every corporation (for profit or nonprofit) organized pursuant to the laws of another state, territory, the District of Columbia, a dependency of the United States or a foreign country, must file in the office of the secretary of state:

1. A certificate of corporate existence issued not more than 90 days before the date of filing in Nevada by an authorized officer of the jurisdiction of its incorporation.

2. A certificate of acceptance of appointment executed by its resident agent which must be a natural person residing in this state or another corporation which has a registered office located in this state. The statement must set forth a street address in this state for the service of process, and may have a separate mailing address such as a post office box, which may be different from the street address. The street address of the resident agent is the registered office of the corporation in this state. The resident agent's signature is not required to be notarized.

3. An acknowledged statement executed by an *officer* of the corporation setting forth the general purposes of the corporation and the total authorized stock, the number and par value of shares having par value and the number of shares having no par value. If the application is for a nonprofit, nonstock corporation, indicate that fact in section 5 on the application.

The attached form may be used to comply with requirements 2 and 3 as indicated above.

<u>A file stamped copy of the document most recently filed by the corporation in its home jurisdiction verifying the total authorized stock must be attached. If the application is for a nonprofit, nonstock corporation, provide official verification.</u>

4. Please use the modified name resolution form <u>only</u> if the name of your corporation is not available for use in Nevada. The resolution form must be notarized.

IMPORTANT

<u>INITIAL LIST OF OFFICERS:</u> Pursuant to NRS 80.110, each corporation qualified under the laws of this state shall, on or before the first day of the second month after the filing of its articles of incorporation, and annually thereafter, file its list of officers, directors and resident agent. The fee is $85.00 per year, $15.00 for nonprofit corporations. Forms will be mailed to you upon the qualification of your corporation and annually thereafter to the corporation's resident agent.

<u>COPIES:</u> You <u>must</u> send in the number of copies you would like certified and returned to you in addition to the original form to be filed. A filing fee of $10.00 for each certification is required. Copies received without the required fee shall be returned uncertified. NRS 78.105 requires that a corporation receive at least one certified copy to be kept in the office of the resident agent. The Secretary of State keeps the original filing.

<u>FILING FEE:</u> Filing fee is based on the number of shares authorized. Please see the attached fee schedule. The filing fee for a nonprofit corporation is $25.00. Filing may be expedited for an additional $50.00 expedite fee.

<u>NRS 80.190:</u> This requires each foreign corporation doing business in this state to publish a statement, not later than March in each year, of its last calendar year's business in two issues of a newspaper published in this state. If the corporation keeps its records on the basis of a fiscal year other than the calendar, the statement shall be published not later than the end of the third month following the close of each fiscal year. *The Secretary of State does not publish or file these statements.*

<u>RESIDENT AGENT:</u> If you are in need of a resident agent in the state of Nevada, please contact this office or visit our web site at *http://www.sos.state.nv.us* for a list of individuals or companies who have registered with the Secretary of State.

Filing may be submitted at the office of the Secretary of State or by mail at the following addresses:

<table>
<tr><td align="center">Secretary of State
New Filings Division
101 N. Carson Street, Suite 3
Carson City, NV 89701-4786
775-684-5708 Fax 775-684-5725</td><td align="center">Secretary of State-Satellite Office
Commercial Recordings Division
555 E. Washington Avenue, 2nd Floor
Las Vegas, NV 89101
702-486-2880 Fax 702-486-2888</td></tr>
</table>

DEAN HELLER
Secretary of State

101 North Carson Street, Suite 3
Carson City, Nevada 89701-4786
(775) 684 5708

<table>
<tr><td colspan="2" style="text-align:center">QUALIFICATION TO
DO BUSINESS IN
NEVADA
(PURSUANT TO NRS 80)</td><td>Office Use Only:</td></tr>
</table>

Important: Read attached instructions before completing form.

Name of Corporation (*must be the same as shown on the certificate of existence*)	
State of Incorporation	
Name and Title of Officer Making the Statement:	Name Title
Resident Agent Name and Street Address: (*must be a Nevada address where process may be served*)	Name , **NEVADA** _____ Street Address City Zip Code
Shares: (*No. of shares corporation authorized to issue. Please attach documentation*)	Total authorized stock: _____ (a) Number of shares with par value: _____ (b) Par value of each share: _____ (c) Number of shares without par value: _____
Purpose:	The purpose of this Corporation shall be:
Signature of Officer Making Statement: (*Signature must be notarized*)	Name Signature
Notary:	This instrument was acknowledged before me on _____,_____ by _____ Name of person As _____ Title of Officer Of _____ (Name of party on behalf of whom instrument executed) _____ Notary Public Signature (affix notary stamp or seal)
Certificate of Acceptance of Appointment of Resident Agent:	I, _____ hereby accept appointment as Resident Agent for the above named corporation. _____ Signature of Resident Agent Date

This form must be accompanied by appropriate fees. See attached fee schedule.

Nevada Secretary of State Form FORQUAL1999.01
Revised on: 02/16/99

APPENDIX O: NEVADA LIMITED LIABILITY COMPANY ARTICLES OF ORGANIZATION FORMS AND INSTRUCTIONS

DEAN HELLER
Secretary of State

101 North Carson Street, Suite 3
Carson City, Nevada 89701-4786
(775) 684 5708

IMPORTANT: READ ALL INSTRUCTIONS CAREFULLY BEFORE COMPLETING FORM.

1. *Name of the Limited-Liability Company.* The name must contain the words Limited-Liability Company, Limited Company or Limited or the abbreviations L.L.C., LLC or LC . The word "company" may also be abbreviated. The name must be distinguishable from the name of a limited-liability company, limited partnership, limited liability partnership, or corporation already on file in this office. A name may be reserved, if available, for 90 days by submitting a written request with a $20.00 filing fee to the office of the Secretary of State. For details you may call (775) 684-5708 or write to the Secretary of State, 101 North Carson Street, Suite 3, Carson City, NV, 89701-4786.

2. *Resident Agent.* Persons wishing to file articles of organization in the State of Nevada must designate a person as a resident agent who resides or is located in this state. Every resident agent must have a street address in the state of Nevada for the service of process, and may have a separate mailing address such as a post office box, which may be different from the street address

3. *Dissolution Date.* State the latest date upon which the company is to dissolve. This provision is optional.

4. Limited-liability companies may be managed by one or more manager(s) or one or more members. Please state whether the company is managed by members or managers. If the company is to be managed by one or more managers, the name and post office or street address, either resident or business, of each manager must be set forth. If the company is to be managed by the members, the name and post office or street address, either residence or business, of each member must be set forth.

5. On a separate 8 ½" x 11" sheet, state any other provisions which the members elect to set out in the articles of organization for the regulation of the internal affairs of the company, including any provisions which under NRS Chapter 86 are required or permitted to be set out in the operating agreement of the company.

6. One or more persons may organize a limited-liability company. Indicate the names and addresses of the organizers executing the articles. Remember that organizer's signatures must be acknowledged.

7. Resident agent must complete and sign certificate of acceptance at bottom of form or attach a separate signed certificate of acceptance.

IMPORTANT

COPIES: Pursuant to NRS 86.561 you *must* send in the number of copies you would like certified and returned to you in addition to the original articles to be filed. A filing fee of $10.00 for each certification is required. NRS 86.241 requires that a corporation have at least one certified copy to be kept in the office of the resident agent. The Secretary of State keeps the original filing.

FILING FEE: $125.00 Filing is required. Filing may be expedited for an additional $50.00 expedite fee.

Filing may be submitted at the office of the Secretary of State or by mail at the following addresses:

Secretary of State **New Filings Division** 101 N. Carson Street, Suite 3 Carson City, NV 89701-4786 775-684-5708 Fax 775-684-5725	**Secretary of State-Satellite Office** **Commercial Recordings Division** 555 E. Washington Avenue, 2nd Floor Las Vegas, NV 89101 702-486-2880 Fax 702-486-2888

DEAN HELLER
Secretary of State

101 North Carson Street, Suite 3
Carson City, Nevada 89701-4786
(775) 684 5708

Limited Liability Company
Articles of Organization
(PURSUANT TO NRS 86)

Office Use Only:

Important: Read attached instructions before completing form.

1. Name of Limited Liability Company:

2. Resident Agent Name and Street Address:
(must be a Nevada address where process may be served)

Name

_____, **NEVADA** _____
Street Address   City   Zip Code

3. Dissolution Date:
(OPTIONAL—See Instructions)

Latest date upon which the company is to dissolve (if existence is not perpetual): _____

4. Management:
(Check one)

Company shall be managed by _____ Manager(s) **OR** _____ Members

Names Addresses, of Manager(s) or Members:
(Attach additional pages as necessary)

Name   Name

Street Address   Street Address

City, State, Zip   City, State, Zip

5. Other Matters:
(See instructions)

Number of additional pages attached: _____

6. Names, Addresses and Signatures of Organizer(s):
(Signatures must be notarized)
Attach additional pages if there are more than 2 organizers.

Name   Name

Street Address   Street Address

City, State, Zip   City, State, Zip

Signature   Signature

Notary:

This instrument was acknowledged before me on   This instrument was acknowledged before me on

_____,_____ by   _____,_____ by

_____   _____
        Name of person   Name of person
As organizer   As organizer

of _____   of _____
(Name of party on behalf of whom instrument executed) (Name of party on behalf of whom instrument executed)

_____   _____
    Notary Public Signature   Notary Public Signature

(affix notary stamp or seal)   (affix notary stamp or seal)

7. Certificate of Acceptance of Appointment of Resident Agent:

I, _____hereby accept appointment as Resident Agent for the above
named limited liability company.

_____   _____
Signature of Resident Agent   Date

This form must be accompanied by appropriate fees. See attached fee schedule.

Nevada Secretary of State Form CORPART1999.01
Revised on: 02/16/99

APPENDIX P: NEVADA BUSINESS TRUST ORGANIZATION FORMS AND INSTRUCTIONS

DEAN HELLER
Secretary of State

101 North Carson Street,
Suite 3
Carson City, Nevada
89701-4786
(775) 684 5708

Instructions for
Certificate of Business Trust

IMPORTANT: READ ALL INSTRUCTIONS CAREFULLY BEFORE COMPLETING FORM.

1.   *Name of Business Trust.*   The name of a business trust formed pursuant to the provisions of Title 7 of NRS must contain the words "Business Trust" or the abbreviation "B.T." or "BT." The name must be distinguishable from the names of corporations, limited liability companies, limited partnerships or limited liability partnerships on file in the office of the Secretary of State. A name may be reserved, if available, for 90 days by submitting a written request with a $20.00 filing fee.

2.   *Resident Agent.* Persons forming a business trust in the State of Nevada must designate a person as a resident agent who resides or is located in this state. Every resident agent must have a street address in this state for the service of process.

3.   *Resident Agent Mailing Address.* A resident agent may have a separate mailing address if different from the street address.

4.   State the name and post office box or street address, either residence or business of at least one trustee. Use an additional 8 ½ x 11 white sheet if more than 1 trustee will be listed.

5.   This section is optional and is required only if the trust is to engage in insurance or banking. Pre-approval from the State Insurance Commissioner or the State Financial Institutions Division is necessary if either of these purposes is stated.

6.   Additional information that is part of the certificate may be stated on a separate 8 ½ x 11 white sheet. This is an optional provision. If the additional information is contradictory to information on the form, the entire filing will be returned for correction.

7.   Names and addresses of the persons forming the business trust are required. Each person forming the business trust must sign the certificate. An additional 8 ½ x 11 white sheet will be necessary if more than 2 persons are forming the business trust.

8.   Resident agent must complete and sign the certificate of acceptance at bottom of the form or attach a separate signed certificate of acceptance.

IMPORTANT

COPIES: The number of copies to be certified and returned to those forming the business trust <u>must</u> be sent in addition to the original article to be filed. A fee of $10.00 for each certification is required. Copies received without the required fee shall be returned uncertified. Nevada law requires that a business trust receive at least one certified copy to be kept in the office of the resident agent. The Secretary of State keeps the original filing.

FILING FEE: Filing fee for a certificate of business trust is $125.00. Certificates received without the appropriate fees will be returned unfiled. Filing may be expedited for an additional $50.00 expedite fee.

Filing may be submitted at the office of the Secretary of State or by mail at the following addresses:

<table>
<tr>
<td align="center">

Secretary of State
New Filings Division
101 N. Carson Street, Suite 3
Carson City, NV 89701-4786
775-684-5708 Fax 775-684-5725

</td>
<td align="center">

Secretary of State-Satellite Office
Commercial Recordings Division
555 E. Washington Avenue, 2nd Floor
Las Vegas, NV 89101
702-486-2880 Fax 702-486-2888

</td>
</tr>
</table>

Nevada Secretary of State Form CORPINST1999.01
Revised on: 07/09/99

DEAN HELLER
Secretary of State

101 North Carson Street, Suite
Carson City, Nevada 89701-
(775) 684 5708

Office Use Only:

Certificate of Business Trust

Important: Read attached instructions before completing form.

Name of Business Trust: *(must include the words business trust, B.T. or BT.*	
Resident Agent Name and Street Address: *(must be a Nevada address where process may be served)*	Name **NEVADA** _____ Street Address
Resident Agent Mailing Address: *(if different from address above)*	Name _____ , _____ _____ Mailing Address
Names, Addresses, of Trustees: *(must include the name and p.o. box or street address, either residence or business of at least one trustee) Attach additional pages if than 1 to be listed.*	Name _____ , _____ _____ Address
Purpose: *(Optional See Instructions)*	
Other Matters: *(See instructions)*	Number of additional pages attached: _____
Names, Addresses and Signatures of Each Person Forming Business Trust: *(must be signed by each person forming business Attach additional pages if there are more than 2.*	Name Name Address City, State, Zip Address Signature Signature
Certificate of Acceptance of Appointment of Resident Agent:	I, _____ hereby accept appointment as Resi for the above named business trust. Signature of Resident Agent

This form must be accompanied by appropriate fees. See attached fee schedule.

Nevada Secretary of State Form CORPART1989.01
Revised on: 07/09/99

APPENDIX Q: APPLICATION AND INSTRUCTIONS FOR IRS FORM SS-4, EMPLOYER IDENTIFICATION NUMBER

Form **SS-4**

(Rev. February 1998)

Department of the Treasury
Internal Revenue Service

Application for Employer Identification Number

(For use by employers, corporations, partnerships, trusts, estates, churches, government agencies, certain individuals, and others. See instructions.)

▶ **Keep a copy for your records.**

EIN

OMB No. 1545-0003

Please type or print clearly.

1 Name of applicant (legal name) (see instructions)

2 Trade name of business (if different from name on line 1)

3 Executor, trustee, "care of" name

4a Mailing address (street address) (room, apt., or suite no.)

5a Business address (if different from address on lines 4a and 4b)

4b City, state, and ZIP code

5b City, state, and ZIP code

6 County and state where principal business is located

7 Name of principal officer, general partner, grantor, owner, or trustor—SSN or ITIN may be required (see instructions) ▶

8a Type of entity (Check only one box.) (see instructions)

Caution: *If applicant is a limited liability company, see the instructions for line 8a.*

- ☐ Sole proprietor (SSN) _____
- ☐ Partnership
- ☐ REMIC
- ☐ State/local government
- ☐ Church or church-controlled organization
- ☐ Other nonprofit organization (specify) ▶ _____
- ☐ Other (specify) ▶
- ☐ Personal service corp.
- ☐ National Guard
- ☐ Farmers' cooperative
- ☐ Estate (SSN of decedent) _____
- ☐ Plan administrator (SSN) _____
- ☐ Other corporation (specify) ▶ _____
- ☐ Trust
- ☐ Federal government/military

(enter GEN if applicable) _____

8b If a corporation, name the state or foreign country (if applicable) where incorporated

State

Foreign country

9 Reason for applying (Check only one box.) (see instructions)
- ☐ Started new business (specify type) ▶_____
- ☐ Hired employees (Check the box and see line 12.)
- ☐ Created a pension plan (specify type) ▶
- ☐ Banking purpose (specify purpose) ▶ _____
- ☐ Changed type of organization (specify new type) ▶ _____
- ☐ Purchased going business
- ☐ Created a trust (specify type) ▶ _____
- ☐ Other (specify) ▶

10 Date business started or acquired (month, day, year) (see instructions)

11 Closing month of accounting year (see instructions)

12 First date wages or annuities were paid or will be paid (month, day, year). **Note:** *If applicant is a withholding agent, enter date income will first be paid to nonresident alien. (month, day, year)* . . . . ▶

13 Highest number of employees expected in the next 12 months. **Note:** *If the applicant does not expect to have any employees during the period, enter -0-. (see instructions)* . . . . ▶

Nonagricultural	Agricultural	Household

14 Principal activity (see instructions) ▶

15 Is the principal business activity manufacturing? . . . . ☐ Yes ☐ No
If "Yes," principal product and raw material used ▶

16 To whom are most of the products or services sold? Please check one box. ☐ Business (wholesale)
☐ Public (retail) ☐ Other (specify) ▶ ☐ N/A

17a Has the applicant ever applied for an employer identification number for this or any other business? . . . . ☐ Yes ☐ No
Note: *If "Yes," please complete lines 17b and 17c.*

17b If you checked "Yes" on line 17a, give applicant's legal name and trade name shown on prior application, if different from line 1 or 2 above.
Legal name ▶ Trade name ▶

17c Approximate date when and city and state where the application was filed. Enter previous employer identification number if known.

Approximate date when filed (mo., day, year)	City and state where filed	Previous EIN

Under penalties of perjury, I declare that I have examined this application, and to the best of my knowledge and belief, it is true, correct, and complete.

Business telephone number (include area code)

Fax telephone number (include area code)

Name and title (Please type or print clearly.) ▶

Signature ▶

Date ▶

Note: *Do not write below this line. For official use only.*

Please leave blank ▶

Geo.	Ind.	Class	Size	Reason for applying

For Paperwork Reduction Act Notice, see page 4.

Cat. No. 16055N

Form **SS-4** (Rev. 2-98)

General Instructions

Section references are to the Internal Revenue Code unless otherwise noted.

Purpose of Form

Use Form SS-4 to apply for an employer identification number (EIN). An EIN is a nine-digit number (for example, 12-3456789) assigned to sole proprietors, corporations, partnerships, estates, trusts, and other entities for filing and reporting purposes. The information you provide on this form will establish your filing and reporting requirements.

Who Must File

You must file this form if you have not obtained an EIN before and:

• You pay wages to one or more employees including household employees.

• You are required to have an EIN to use on any return, statement, or other document, even if you are not an employer.

• You are a withholding agent required to withhold taxes on income, other than wages, paid to a nonresident alien (individual, corporation, partnership, etc.). A withholding agent may be an agent, broker, fiduciary, manager, tenant, or spouse, and is required to file Form 1042, Annual Withholding Tax Return for U.S. Source Income of Foreign Persons.

• You file Schedule C, Profit or Loss From Business, or Schedule F, Profit or Loss From Farming, of Form 1040, U.S. Individual Income Tax Return, and have a Keogh plan or are required to file excise, employment, information, or alcohol, tobacco, or firearms returns.

The following must use EINs even if they do not have any employees:

• State and local agencies who serve as tax reporting agents for public assistance recipients, under Rev. Proc. 80-4, 1980-1 C.B. 581, should obtain a separate EIN for this reporting. See Household employer on page 3.

• Trusts, except the following:

1. Certain grantor-owned revocable trusts. (See the Instructions for Form 1041.)

2. Individual Retirement Arrangement (IRA) trusts, unless the trust has to file Form 990-T, Exempt Organization Business Income Tax Return. (See the Instructions for Form 990-T.)

3. Certain trusts that are considered household employers can use the trust EIN to report and pay the social security and Medicare taxes, Federal unemployment tax (FUTA) and withheld Federal income tax. A separate EIN is not necessary.

• Estates

• Partnerships

• REMICs (real estate mortgage investment conduits) (See the Instructions for Form 1066, U.S. Real Estate Mortgage Investment Conduit Income Tax Return.)

• Corporations

• Nonprofit organizations (churches, clubs, etc.)

• Farmers' cooperatives

• Plan administrators (A plan administrator is the person or group of persons specified as the administrator by the instrument under which the plan is operated.)

When To Apply for a New EIN

New Business.—If you become the new owner of an existing business, **do not** use the EIN of the former owner. IF YOU ALREADY HAVE AN EIN, USE THAT NUMBER. If you do not have an EIN, apply for one on this form. If you become the "owner" of a corporation by acquiring its stock, use the corporation's EIN. Changes in Organization or Ownership.—If you already have an EIN, you may need to get a new one if either the organization or ownership of your business changes. If you incorporate a sole proprietorship or form a partnership, you must get a new EIN. However, do not apply for a new EIN if you change only the name of your business.

Note: *If you are electing to be an "S corporation," be sure you file Form 2553, Election by a Small Business Corporation.*

File Only One Form SS-4.—File only one Form SS-4, regardless of the number of businesses operated or trade names under which a business operates. However, each corporation in an affiliated group must file a separate application.

EIN Applied For, But Not Received.—If you do not have an EIN by the time a return is due, write "Applied for" and the date you applied in the space shown for the number. Do not show your social security number as an EIN on returns.

If you do not have an EIN by the time a tax deposit is due, send your payment to the Internal Revenue Service Center for your filing area. (See Where To Apply below.) Make your check or money order payable to Internal Revenue Service and show your name (as shown on Form SS-4), address, type of tax, period covered, and date you applied for an EIN. Send an explanation with the deposit.

For more information about EINs, see Pub. 583, Starting a Business and Keeping Records, and Pub. 1635, Understanding Your EIN.

How To Apply

You can apply for an EIN either by mail or by fax. You can send the completed Form SS-4 directly to the service center to receive your EIN in the mail.

An IRS representative will use the information from the Form SS-4 to establish your account and assign you an EIN. Write the number you are given on the upper right-hand corner of the form, sign and date it.

Mail or FAX the signed SS-4 within 24 hours to the Tele-TIN Unit at the service center address for your state. The IRS representative will give you the FAX number. The FAX numbers are also listed in Pub. 1635.

Taxpayer representatives can receive their client's EIN by phone if they first send a facsimile (FAX) of a completed Form 2848,

Power of Attorney and Declaration of Representative, or Form 8821, Tax Information Authorization, to the Tele-TIN unit. The Form 2848 or Form 8821 will be used solely to release the EIN to the representative authorized on the form. Application by Mail.—Complete Form SS-4 at least 4 to 5 weeks before you will need an EIN. Sign and date the application and mail it to the service center address for your state. You will receive your EIN in the mail in approximately 4 weeks.

Where To Apply

The Tele-TIN phone number listed below will involve a long-distance charge to callers outside of the local calling area and can be used only to apply for an EIN. THE NUMBERS MAY CHANGE WITHOUT NOTICE. Use 1-800-829-1040 to verify a number or to ask about an *application by mail or other Federal tax matters.*

For obtaining an EIN number for a NEVADA corporation, contact the IRS at the following address:

INTERNAL REVENUE SERVICE
Attn: Entity Control
Mail Stop 6271-T
PO Box 9950
Ogden, UT 84409

Or, fax your completed Form SS-4 to the Internal Revenue Service at:

(801) 620-7115

If you are in immediate need of the EIN, you may request that the IRS advise you of the number by faxing a reply to you at your fax number. The IRS will then follow-up with notification by mail.

Specific Instructions

The instructions that follow are for those items that are not self-explanatory. Enter N/A (nonapplicable) on the lines that do not apply.

Line 1.—Enter the legal name of the entity applying for the EIN exactly as it appears on the social security card, charter, or other applicable legal document.

Individuals.—Enter the first name, middle initial, and last name. If you are a sole proprietor, enter your individual name, not your business name. Do not use abbreviations or nicknames.

Trusts.—Enter the name of the trust.

Estate of a decedent.—Enter the name of the estate.

Partnerships.—Enter the legal name of the partnership as it appears in the partnership agreement. Do not list the names of the partners on line 1. See the specific instructions for line 7.

Corporations.—Enter the corporate name as it appears in the corporation charter or other legal document creating it.

Plan administrators.—Enter the name of the plan administrator. A plan administrator who already has an EIN should use that number.

Line 2.—Enter the trade name of the business if different from the legal name. The trade name is the "doing business as" name.

Note: *Use the full legal name on line I on all tax returns filed for the entity. However, if you enter a trade name on line 2 and choose to use the trade name instead of the legal name, enter the trade name on all returns you file. To prevent processing delays and errors, **always** use either the legal name only or the trade name only on all tax returns.*

Line 3.—Trusts enter the name of the trustee. Estates enter the name of the executor, administrator, or other fiduciary. If the entity applying has a designated person to receive tax information, enter that person's name as the "care of" person. Print or type the first name, middle initial, and last name.

Line 7.—Enter the first name, middle initial, last name, and social security number (SSN) of a principal officer if the business is a corporation: of a general partner if a partnership: or of a grantor, owner, or trustor if a trust.

Line 8a.—Check the box that best describes the type of entity applying for the EIN. If not specifically mentioned. check the "Other" box and enter the type of entity. Do not enter N/A.

Sole proprietor.—C heck this box if you file Schedule C or F (Form 1040) and have a Keogh plan, or are required to file excise, employment, information, or alcohol, tobacco, or firearms returns. Enter your SSN in the space provided.

REMIC.—C heck this box if the entity has elected to be treated as a real estate mortgage investment conduit (REMIC). See the Instructions for Form 1068 for more information.

Other nonprofit organization.—C heck this box if the nonprofit organization is other than a church or church-controlled organization and specify the type of nonprofit organization (for example, an educational organization).

If the organization also seeks tax-exempt status, you must file either Package 1023 or Package 1024, Application for Recognition of Exemption. Get Pub. 557, Tax-Exempt Status for Your Organization, for more information.

Group exemption number (GEN).—If the organization is covered by a group exemption letter, enter the four-digit GEN. (Do not confuse the GEN with the nine-digit EIN.) If you do not know the GEN, contact the parent organization. Get Pub. 557 for more information about group exemption numbers.

Withholding agent.—If you are a withholding agent required to file Form 1042, check the "Other" box and enter "Withholding agent."

Personal service corporation—Check this box if the entity is a personal service corporation. An entity is a personal service corporation for a tax year only if:

• The principal activity of the entity during the testing period (prior tax year) for the tax year is the performance of personal services substantially by employee-owners, and

• The employee-owners own 10% of the fair market value of the outstanding stock in the entity on the last day of the testing period.

Personal services include performance of services in such fields as health, law, accounting, or consulting. For more information about personal service corporations, see the Instructions for Form 1120, U.S. Corporation Income Tax Return, and Pub. 542, Tax Information on Corporations.

Limited liability co.—See the definition of limited liability company in the Instructions for Form 1065. If you are classified as a partnership for Federal income tax purposes, mark the "Limited liability Co." checkbox. If you are classified as a corporation for Federal income tax purposes, mark the "Other corporation" checkbox and write "Limited liability Co." in the space provided.

Plan administrator.—If the plan administrator is an individual, enter the plan administrator's SSN in the space provided.

Other corporation.—This box is for any corporation other than a personal service corporation. If you check this box, enter the type of corporation (such as insurance company) in the space provided.

Household employer.—If you are an individual, check the "Other" box and enter "Household employer" and your SSN. If you are a state or local agency serving as a tax reporting agent for public assistance recipients who become household employers, check the "Other" box and enter "Household employer agent." If you are a trust that qualifies as a household employer, you do not need a separate EIN for reporting tax information relating to household employees; use the EIN of the trust.

Line 9.-Check only one box. Do not enter N/A.

Started new business.—C heck this box if you are starting a new business that requires an EIN. If you check this box, enter the type of business being started. Do not apply if you already have an EIN and are only adding another place of business.

Hired employees.—C heck this box if the existing business is requesting an EIN because it has hired or is hiring employees and is therefore required to file employment tax returns. Do not apply if you already have an EIN and are only hiring employees. For information on the applicable employment taxes for family members, see Circular E, Employer's Tax Guide (Publication 15).

Created a pension plan—Check this box if you have created a pension plan and need this number for reporting purposes. Also, enter the type of plan created.

Banking purpose.—C heck this box if you are requesting an EIN for banking purposes only, and enter the banking purpose (for example, a bowling league for depositing dues or an investment club for dividend and interest reporting).

Changed type of organization—Check

this box if the business is changing its type of organization, for example, if the business was a sole proprietorship and has been incorporated or has become a partnership. If you check this box, specify in the space provided the type of change made, for example. "from sole proprietorship to partnership."

Purchased going business.—C heck this box if you purchased an existing business. Do not use the former owner's EIN. Do not apply for a new EIN if you already have one. Use your own EIN.

*Created a trust.—*Check this box if you created a trust, and enter the type of trust created.

Note: *Do not file this form if you are the grantor/owner of certain revocable trusts. You must use your SSN for the trust. See the Instructions for Form 1047.*

Other (specify).—C heck this box if you are requesting an EIN for any reason other than those for which there are checkboxes, and enter the reason.

Line 10.—If you are starting a new business, enter the starting date of the business. If the business you acquired is already operating, enter the date you acquired the business. Trusts should enter the date the trust was legally created. Estates should enter the date of death of the decedent whose name appears on line 1 or the date when the estate was legally funded.

Line 11.—Enter the last month of your accounting year or tax year. An accounting or tax year is usually 12 consecutive months, either a calendar year or a fiscal year (including a period of 52 or 53 weeks). A calendar year is 12 consecutive months ending on December 31. A fiscal year is either 12 consecutive months ending on the last day of any month other than December or a 52-53 week year. For more information on accounting periods, see Pub. 538, Accounting Periods and Methods.

Individuals.—Your tax year generally will be a calendar year.

*Partnerships.—*Partnerships generally must adopt the tax year of either (a) the majority partners; (b) the principal partners; (c) the tax year that results in the least aggregate (total) deferral of income; or (d) some other tax year. (See the Instructions for Form 1065, U.S. Partnership Return of Income, for more information.)

*REMIC.—*REMICs must have a calendar year as their tax year.

*Personal service corporations.—*A personal service corporation generally must adopt a calendar year unless:

• It can establish a business purpose for having a different tax year, or

• It elects under section 444 to have a tax year other than a calendar year.

*Trusts.—*Generally, a trust must adopt a calendar year except for the following:

• Tax-exempt trusts.
• Charitable trusts, and
• Grantor-owned trusts.

Line 12.—If the business has or will have employees, enter the date on which the business began or will begin to pay wages. If the business does not plan to have employees, enter N/A.

Withholding agent.—Enter the date you began or will begin to pay income to a nonresident alien. This also applies to individuals who are required to file Form 1042 to report alimony paid to a nonresident alien.

Line 13.—For a definition of agricultural labor (farmworker), see Circular A, Agricultural Employer's Tax Guide (Publication 51).

Line 14.—Generally, enter the exact type of business being operated (for example. advertising agency, farm, food or beverage establishment, labor union, real estate agency, steam laundry, rental of coin-operated vending machine, or investment club). Also state if the business will involve the sale or distribution of alcoholic beverages.

Governmental.—Enter the type of organization (state, county, school district. municipality, etc.).

Nonprofit organization (other than governmental).—Enter whether organized for religious, educational, or humane purposes, and the principal activity (for example, religious organization—hospital, charitable).

Mining and quarrying.—Specify the process and the principal product (for example, mining bituminous coal, contract drilling for oil, or quarrying dimension stone).

Contract construction.—Specify whether general contracting or special trade contracting. Also, show the type of work normally performed (for example, general contractor for residential buildings or electrical subcontractor).

Food or beverage establishments.—Specify the type of establishment and state whether you employ workers who receive tips (for example, lounge—yes).

Trade.—Specify the type of sales and the principal line of goods sold (for example, wholesale dairy products. manufacturer's representative for mining machinery, or retail hardware).

Manufacturing.—Specify the type of establishment operated (for example, sawmill or vegetable cannery).

Signature block—The application must be signed by (a) the individual, if the applicant is an individual. (b) the president, vice president, or other principal officer, if the applicant is a corporation, (c) a responsible and duly authorized member or officer having knowledge of its affairs, if the applicant is a partnership or other unincorporated organization, or (d) the fiduciary, if the applicant is a trust or estate.

Some Useful Publications

You may get the following publications for additional information on the subjects covered on this form. To get these and other free forms and publications, call 1-800-TAX-FORM (1-800-829-3676). You should receive your order or notification of its status within 7 to 15 workdays of your call.

Use your computer.—If you subscribe to an on-line service, ask if IRS information is available and, if so, how to access it. You can also get information through IRIS, the Internal Revenue Information Services, on FedWorld. a government bulletin board. Tax forms, instructions, publications, and other IRS information, are available through IRIS.

IRIS is accessible directly by calling 703-321-8020. On the Internet, you can telnet to fedworld.gov. or, for file transfer protocol services, connect to ftp.fedworld.gov. If you are using the WorldWide Web, connect to http://www.ustreas.gov

FedWorld's help desk offers technical assistance on accessing IRIS (not tax help) during regular business hours at 703-487-4608. The IRIS menus offer information on available file formats and software needed to read and print files. You must print the forms to use them: the forms are not designed to be filled out on-screen.

Tax forms, instructions, and publications are also available on CD-ROM, including prior-year forms starting with the 1991 tax year. For ordering information and software requirements, contact the Government Printing Office's Superintendent of Documents (202-512-1800) or Federal Bulletin Board (202-512-1387).

Pub. 1635, Understanding Your EIN Pub. 15, Employer's Tax Guide Pub. 15-A, Employer's Supplemental Tax Guide

Pub. 538, Accounting Periods and Methods

Pub. 541, Tax Information on Partnerships Pub. 542, Tax Information on Corporations Pub. 557. Tax-Exempt Status for Your Organization

Pub. 583, Starting a Business and Keeping Records

Package 1023, Application for Recognition of Exemption

Package 1024, Application for Recognition of Exemption Under Section 501(a) or for Determination Under Section 120

Paperwork Reduction Act Notice

We ask for the information on this form to carry out the Internal Revenue laws of the United States. You are required to give us the information. We need it to ensure that you are complying with these laws and to allow us to figure and collect the right amount of tax.

The time needed to complete and file this form will vary depending on individual circumstances. The estimated average time is:

Recordkeeping 7 min.

Learning about the law or the form 18 min.

Preparing the form 45 min.

Copying, assembling, and sending the form to the IRS 20 min.

If you have comments concerning the accuracy of these time estimates or suggestions for making this form simpler, we would be happy to hear from you. You can write to the Tax Forms Committee, Western Area Distribution Center, Ranch Cordova, CA 95743-0001.

APPENDIX R: NEVADA FORMS AND INSTRUCTIONS FOR UCC-1 FINANCING STATEMENT

DEAN HELLER
Secretary of State

200 North Carson Street
Carson City, Nevada 89701-4201
(775) 684 5708

Instructions for Financing Statement N-UCC-1

IMPORTANT: READ ALL INSTRUCTIONS CAREFULLY BEFORE COMPLETING FORM.

1. PLEASE TYPE THIS FORM USING BLACK TYPEWRITER RIBBON.

2. IF THE SPACE PROVIDED FOR ANY ITEM IS INADEQUATE:

   a. Note "Contd." in the appropriate space(s).

   b. Continue the item(s) preceded by the Item number on an additional 8 ½" x 11" sheet.

   c. Head each additional sheet with the Debtor's name as it appears in Item No. 1 of this form.

3. NUMERICAL IDENTIFICATION: Social Security , Federal Tax, Transit/ABA Numbers and Zip Codes are to be included so statements may be more readily indexed and information rapidly retrieved through use of electronic data processing equipment.

   a. If the Debtor, Secured Party or Assignee is an individual, include Social Security Number in the appropriate space.

   b. If the Debtor, Secured Party or Assignee is other than an individual or a bank, include Federal Taxpayer Number in the appropriate space.

   c. If the Secured Party or Assignee is a bank, include Transit and/or ABA Number in the appropriate space.

4. Remove Secured Party and Debtor copies.

   Send IN DUPLICATE to the Filing Officer (i.e. Secretary of State or County Recorder) with the correct filing fee. The original will be retained by the Filing Officer. The remaining copy will be returned with the filing date and time stamped thereon. In Item number 10, indicate the name and mailing address of the person or firm to which the copy is to be returned. Please include a self-addressed stamped envelope.

5. FILING FEE: NEVADA STATE FORM or National Form.. $15.00

                 Any other state form.. $20.00

   For each page of attachment(s).. $1.00

   Each additional debtor(s) name, tradename, tradestyle, DBA $1.00
   (Spouse is an additional debtor)

   "PUBLIC UTILITY" filing: In accordance with NRS 105.010. Fees stated above are applicable to Public Utility filings.

   THE CORRECT FEE MUST BE RECEIVED BEFORE PROCESSING. THE CHECK SHOULD BE MADE PAYABLE TO THE APPROPRIATE FILING OFFICER (i.e. Secretary of State or County Recorder). A letter must accompany this form if you wish to charge applicable fees to your trust account. Please provide trust account number in the space provided in item 10.

6. SIGNATURES: Before mailing be sure the financing statement has been properly signed. If either item 7C or 7D is checked, only the signature of the Secured Party is required.

7. Secured Party must file a termination statement with the Secretary of State (UCC Division) within one month following termination of security interest or within 10 days following written demand by the Debtor. Failure to do so will result in liability of the Secured Party to the Debtor for $100.00 in addition to any loss resulting from such failure.

UNIFORM COMMERCIAL CODE – FINANCING STATEMENT – FORM N-UCC-1

This FINANCING STATEMENT is presented for filing pursuant to the Nevada Uniform Commercial Code

IMPORTANT: Read instructions before filling out form. This form must be accompanied by appropriate fees.

1. DEBTOR (ONE NAME ONLY)	1A. SOCIAL SECURITY OR FEDERAL TAX NO.	
☐ LEGAL BUSINESS NAME ☐ INDIVIDUAL (LAST NAME FIRST)		

1B. MAILING ADDRESS	1C. CITY, STATE	1D. ZIP CODE

1E. RESIDENCE ADDRESS	1F. CITY, STATE	1G. ZIP CODE

2. ADDITIONAL DEBTOR (IF ANY) (ONE NAME ONLY)	2A. SOCIAL SECURITY OR FEDERAL TAX NO.	
☐ LEGAL BUSINESS NAME ☐ INDIVIDUAL (LAST NAME FIRST)		

2B. MAILING ADDRESS	2C. CITY, STATE	2D. ZIP CODE

2E. RESIDENCE ADDRESS	2F. CITY, STATE	2G. ZIP CODE

3. ☐ ADDITIONAL DEBTOR(S) ON ATTACHED SHEET

4. SECURED PARTY	4A. SOCIAL SECURITY NO. FEDERAL TAX NO. OR BANK TRANSIT AND A.B.A. NO.
NAME	
MAILING ADDRESS	
CITY STATE ZIP CODE	

5. ASSIGNEE OF SECURED PARTY (IF ANY)	5A. SOCIAL SECURITY NO. FEDERAL TAX NO. OR BANK TRANSIT AND A.B.A. NO.
NAME	
MAILING ADDRESS	
CITY STATE ZIP CODE	

6. This FINANCING STATEMENT covers the following types or items of property (if crops or timber, include description of real property on which growing or to be growing and name of record owner of such real estate; if fixtures, include description of real property to which affixed or to be affixed and name of record owner of such real estate; if oil, gas or minerals, include description of real property from which to be extracted).

6A. _____
SIGNATURE OF RECORD OWNER

6B. _____
(TYPE) RECORD OWNER OF REAL PROPERTY

6C. _____
MAXIMUM AMOUNT OF INDEBTEDNESS TO
BE SECURED AT ANY ONE TIME (OPTIONAL)

7. Check if Applicable	A. ☐ Proceeds of collateral are also covered. NRS 104.9306	B. ☐ Products of collateral are also covered. NRS 104.9402	C. ☐ Proceeds of above described original collateral in which a security interest was perfected (Debtor's Signature Not Required). NRS 104.9402	D. ☐ Collateral was brought into this State subject to security interest in another jurisdiction (Debtor's Signature Not Required). NRS 104.9402

8. Check if Applicable	☐ DEBTOR IS A "PUBLIC UTILITY" IN ACCORDANCE WITH NRS 105.010

9.	11. This Space for Use of Filing Officer: (Date, Time, File Number and Filing Officer)
(Date_____)	
By _____	
SIGNATURE(S) OF DEBTOR(S) (TITLE)	
TYPE NAME(S)	
By_____	
SIGNATURE(S) OF SECURED PARTY(IES) (TITLE)	
TYPE NAME(S)	

10. Return Copy to:	
⌈ ⌉	Trust Account Number (If Applicable)
NAME ADDRESS CITY, STATE AND ZIP	
⌊ ⌋	_____

GLOSSARY

Accumulated Earnings. The accumulation of taxable earnings within a corporation. A corporation which has excess accumulated earnings can be assessed a separate tax by the IRS unless there is a justification for the buildup, such as to cover the company's repurchase liability. The purpose of this tax is to penalize those corporations which the IRS believes are limiting their dividend declaration in order to reduce the stockholders' declared income.

Amendment. The process of making changes in articles of incorporation or articles of organization that are filed by a state government. An amendment is necessary to formally change the name of the entity, or to change the capital stock structure.

Attorney's Opinion. A lawyer's written statement that a certain matter or particular action complies with applicable legal requirements and/or is duly authorized or binding.

Bearer Shares. Shares of capital stock that is issued payable to bearer. This type of stock is allowed under Nevada statutes for privately held corporations. Public corporations are prohibited from issuing bearer stock.

Blue Sky Laws. State laws protecting the public from deceptive securities transactions. Varying from state to state, such laws typically govern the registration of brokers and securities and contain anti-fraud provisions.

Bond. A certificate evidencing indebtedness. A legal contract sold by an issuer promising to pay the holder its face value plus amounts of interest at future dates.

Business Judgment Rule. A judicial doctrine which shields corporate officers and directors from personal liability for actions taken in good faith and with reasonable care.

Buy-Sell Agreement. An agreement between shareholders of a privately held corporation and the corporation itself, made to govern the operations of the corporation and to define how shares of stock will be transferred. In small corporations, such an agreement can be used to set estate tax value of stock, define what happens if a shareholder is disabled, restrict the transfer of stock to outsiders and the like. It can also protect the corporation against a disqualifying act and provide other mechanisms for maintaining, and ending S Corporation status.

Bylaws. A rule adopted by an organization chiefly for the government of its members and the regulation of its affairs.

C Corporation. A corporation that pays tax on its own income under the general rules of Subchapter C of the internal Revenue Code.

Calendar Year. An accounting period that ends each December 31, which is the period most S corporations must adopt as a permitted year.

Capital Gains Tax. The tax imposed on the capital gains of a taxpayer. The tax treatment of capital gains and losses depends on whether the gains and losses are long-term or short-term, and on whether the taxpayer is a corporation or not. The long-term and short-term capital gains of corporations are taxable at the same rates as their ordinary income. For non-corporations, the maximum tax rate on net long-term capital gains is lower than the top rate on ordinary income.

Capital Stock. The outstanding shares of a joint-stock company considered as an aggregate.

Carryback. For federal income tax purposes, the portion of a net operating loss deductible from net income of the prior three years. This amount is absorbed and the remainder carried forward to offset future years net income.

Carry Forward. To offset for tax purposes one period's loss against a subsequent period's net income. Losses which are unused may generally carry over to another year. Such tax benefits may enhance the value of a target to a buyer burdened with high taxes.

Close Corporation. A corporation whose stock is not publicly traded but held by a few persons (as those in management). The organizational structure of this type of corporation must comply with strict statutory requirements and limitations.

Closely Held Company. A company whose shares are held mostly by a small group of investors, management, founders, and/or their families.

Common Stock. All capital stock except for preferred stock.

Contribution to Capital. A contribution of cash or other property that a shareholder makes to a corporation that increases the corporation's paid-in capital but for which the shareholder does not receive stock. The contribution increases that shareholder's basis in stock.

Controlled Group. A group of corporations which are grouped together for one tax purpose or another. Control may be through parent-subsidiary relationships or common control, such as a brother-sister controlled group. Control means ownership of a certain percentage (generally, either at least 80%, or, less frequently, at least 50% of the total combined voting power of all classes of voting stock or of the total value of shares.

Corporation. A body formed and authorized by law to act as a single person although constituted by one or more persons and legally endowed with various rights and duties including the capacity of succession.

Disqualifying Act. An act by the corporation or shareholder that causes the corporation to cease to be an eligible corporation and that generally results in termination of S corporation status.

Double Taxation. Taxation by the federal government of corporate earnings once at the corporate level and again at the shareholder level upon distribution of dividends.

Fiscal Year. An accounting year that ends on a date other than December 31. C corporations may elect to use a fiscal year. S corporations may generally use a fiscal year only if it is a natural business year.

Fraudulent Conveyance. A contractual misrepresentation of the nature, quantity, or existence of transferred assets. Also, a term denoting potential risk for sellers and lenders.

Fringe Benefits. Employee benefits and perquisites, other than qualified retirement plans.

Limited Liability. Liability (as of a stockholder or shipowner) limited by statute or treaty.

Natural Business Year. A fiscal year that is permitted for an S corporation because the corporation can show that 25 percent of gross receipts have been realized in the last two months of such a year for the last three years.

Passive Income. Income to certain taxpayers (including S corporation shareholders) that is subject to the passive activity loss (PAL) rules because the taxpayer does not materially participate in the business activity producing the income. Generally includes receipts from royalties, rents, dividends, interest, annuities, and the sale and exchange of stock and securities.

Preemptive Rights. Giving a stockholder first option to purchase new stock in an amount proportionate to his existing holdings.

Preferred Stock. Stock guaranteed priority by a corporation's charter over common stock in the payment of dividends and usually in the distribution of assets.

Qualified Retirement Plan. A pension or profit sharing plan that qualifies under the Internal Revenue Code for deductible contributions by an employer that are not included in employee income until plan distributions are made.

S Corporation. A corporation that is eligible, and does elect to be taxed under Subchapter S of the Internal Revenue Code. Basically, shareholders pay tax on the corporation's income by reporting their pro rata shares of pass-through items on their own individual income tax returns.

S Corporation Termination. A cessation of S corporation status by operation of statute because the corporation either (1) fails to continue to meet the qualifications for S corporation status, or (2) has C corporation earnings and profits plus excess passive investment income for three consecutive years.

Shareholder's Basis in Loans. The measure of loans made directly by a shareholder to an S corporation, which can be used to provide additional basis for the deduction of losses after the shareholder's basis in stock is exhausted. It is calculated using the initial amount of the loan, adjusted to reflect S corporation pass-through items.

Shareholder's Basis in Stock. The measure of a shareholder's equity investment in a corporation, which is used to measure the gain or loss when the stock is sold.

Stock Certificate. An instrument evidencing ownership of one or more shares of the capital stock of a corporation.

Stock Option. A right granted by a corporation to officers or employees as a form of compensation that allows purchase of corporate stock at a fixed price at a specified time with reimbursement derived from the difference between purchase and market prices.

Stock Split. A division of corporate stock by the issuance to existing shareholders of a specified number of new shares with a corresponding lowering of par value for each outstanding share.

Voting Trust. A trust that is formed to vote shares of stock. Can be an eligible shareholder of an S corporation.

INDEX